While scholars of traditional imperial history see the formation of the larger British Atlantic world as a consequence of competing European powers' efforts at nation building, Atlantic historians see the transatlantic empire shaped more by the motives of a wide variety of subnational groups. Elizabeth Mancke and Carole Shammas have compiled a volume that reflects these different viewpoints concerning the transatlantic experience during Britain's rise to world dominance between the sixteenth and nineteenth centuries.

In the book's opening chapters, contributors consider the effect of transatlantic emigration, discussing European and African migration and slave trade; the enslavement of Native American peoples; and the ways individuals adapted their national and religious identities in a world of expanding cultural influences. The second section addresses the roles played by trade, religion, ethnicity, and class in linking the Atlantic borders, with essays examining how mariners circulated political and religious news along with trade goods; how British common law supplanted the diverse legal systems of the early colonies; and how Protestant leaders in the colonies challenged the theological assumptions of their European contemporaries. The chapters in the final section address the increasingly complicated legal relationships between the British sovereign and colonial charterholders; the simultaneous establishment of a British colonial government in East Florida and the Royal Gardens of Kew; the popularity of imperial landscape art in eighteenth-century Britain; and the ties Pennsylvania Quakers maintained with their British relations.

The Creation of the British Atlantic World provides insight into the competing forces that forged the Atlantic world as well as the reciprocal relationships between the growing British Empire and the individuals, groups, and subnations within that empire.

The Creation of the British Atlantic World

Anglo-America in the Transatlantic World

Jack P. Greene, General Editor

The Creation of the British Atlantic World

Edited by Elizabeth Mancke
and Carole Shammas

The Johns Hopkins University Press
Baltimore and London

© 2005 The Johns Hopkins University Press
All rights reserved. Published 2005
Printed in the United States of America on acid-free paper
9 8 7 6 5 4 3 2 1

The Johns Hopkins University Press
2715 North Charles Street
Baltimore, Maryland 21218-4363
www.press.jhu.edu

Library of Congress Cataloging-in-Publication Data

The creation of the British Atlantic world / edited by Elizabeth Mancke and
Carole Shammas.
    p. cm.—(Anglo-America in the transatlantic world)
    Includes bibliographical references and index.
    ISBN 0-8018-8039-4 (alk. paper)
    1. United States—History—Colonial period, ca. 1600–1775. 2.   Great
Britain—Colonies—America—History. I. Mancke, Elizabeth, 1954–
II. Shammas, Carole. III. Anglo-America in the trans-Atlantic world.
    E188.C89 2005
    973.2—dc22   2004015977

A catalog record of this book is available from the British Library.

Contents

10   Chartered Enterprises and the Evolution of the British
     Atlantic World   *Elizabeth Mancke*   237

11   Seeds of Empire: Florida, Kew, and the British Imperial
     Meridian in the 1760s   *Robert Olwell*   263

12   A Visual Empire: Seeing the British Atlantic World from a
     Global British Perspective   *John E. Crowley*   283

13   "Of the Old Stock": Quakerism and Transatlantic
     Genealogies in Colonial British America   *Karin Wulf*   304

     Notes   321
     List of Contributors   391
     Index   395

The Creation of the British Atlantic World

Introduction

Carole Shammas

> The idea of *Atlantic* history has always been at odds with the much older and more deeply entrenched conception of the past as, preeminently, the history of nation-states, a mainstay and the last vestige of the paradigm of power. The project to create or to uncover an Atlantic history called not just for considering events and developments in a broad transoceanic framework but, more importantly, for reconceiving the entire historical landscape in which they occurred, a landscape in which contemporary regional or cultural similarities, not ultimate membership in some as yet uncreated national state, would provide the principal criteria of organization.
>
> JACK P. GREENE, "BEYOND POWER"

Atlantic history is flourishing as never before. Yet the tension vis-à-vis other conceptual frameworks that Jack Greene mentioned nearly a decade ago persists. For example, the coeditor of a recent volume on the British Atlantic world and a strong proponent of an Atlantic perspective finds himself still having to confront the question, "is [early modern Atlantic history] not just a more acceptable way to study the history of the Spanish, Portuguese, French, British, and Dutch seaborne empires?"[1] This question attains even greater saliency when the project is not simply the Atlantic but the *British* Atlantic. Some deny that one Atlantic existed during most of the early modern period. Instead, it is argued, three Atlantic subregions existed: a North European Atlantic linking western European ports with the eastern North American seaboard and a few West Indies islands; a Spanish Atlantic, linking Seville to the Caribbean and the American mainland; and a Portuguese Atlantic, linking Lisbon to Brazil and West Africa. "Insofar as Atlantic history has been written, it has tended to be an Atlantic history compartmentalized into these three zones of European settlement, trade, and colonial rule," writes the distinguished historian of the Spanish Empire, J. H. Elliott. The overlap of Atlantic geography with nation and empire is notable. Obscuring the division between the Iberian and the British Atlantics raises problems similar to those identified in Fernand Braudel's path-breaking *The Mediterranean . . . in the Age of Philip II*, in which Ottoman Islam and Latin Christendom were thrown together too blithely for some readers to discern any unified Mediterranean culture. Still another shortcoming with the Atlantic paradigm is the increasing tendency over the early modern period for activities in the Atlantic, Pacific, and Indian oceans to merge, a situation that the framework of imperial history accommodates more handily than does Atlantic history.[2]

So, what does the Atlantic history approach offer, particularly if it is prefaced by the name of an empire or nation-state, that traditional imperial history does not? To its advocates, Atlantic history carries fewer presuppositions about cultural hierarchies and displays more openness to multidirectional effects. Much of early modern European imperial history has been consumed with one central issue in two parts: how did western Europeans with obscure global pasts rise to worldwide dominance in this period; and why did the British, specifically, come to be the premier imperial power by the mid-eighteenth century. In widely consulted surveys of overseas activities, such as J. H. Parry's classic *The Establishment of the European Hegemony, 1415–1715*, the actors are a synecdoche for their European country of origin, men propelled forward by a national imperative to defeat their rivals. Each western European country had its own trajectory, yet initiatives always originated on the eastern side of the Atlantic and crossed to the Americas. Ralph Davis makes two strong points in his preface to *The Rise of the Atlantic Economies*, which, despite its title, adheres more closely to the imperial approach than the Atlantic history paradigm: (1) "the main influences on European economic development arose within the countries of Europe themselves," and (2) Europe had no "special unity in its course of development." Transatlantic activities are best studied as a contest among western European nations in which the most enterprising wins.[3]

The alternative perspective, which generally prevails among those calling themselves Atlantic historians, is well described in the introduction to *Strangers within the Realm: Cultural Margins of the First British Empire*, published in 1991. Its editors, Bernard Bailyn and Philip D. Morgan, like Greene, write of a new way to view British imperial development in the Atlantic and by implication the imperial developments of other nations. They envision it as "the recruitment of a wide variety of peoples, their interaction, their conflicts, their partial absorption, and their creation of new cultures."[4] The authors of the individual chapters focused on the non-English ethnicities and races in the British Empire—the Irish, Scots, Indians, Africans, Dutch, Germans, Scotch-Irish—as well as groups outside the thirteen colonies, particularly in the West Indies and Canada. These groups are no longer confined to the receiving end of transatlantic culture, but rather helped define it. The approach is particularly well suited to the transatlantic experience of Africans.[5] Scholars who emphasize environmental and geographic forces or aspire to a natural history of the ocean also find this approach welcoming, although much less of this type of Atlantic history has been produced to date.[6]

New support for an Atlantic perspective has come from an unlikely source—scholars investigating the ideology and workings of the British Empire itself. They contend that the terminology associated with empire building is inappropriate for describing how contemporaries identified themselves and their intentions until at least some point in the eighteenth century. Even though the first volume of the *Oxford History of the British Empire* adheres to a more political view of expansion across the Atlantic, its editor, Nicholas Canny, admits in his introduction that the "study of the British Empire in the sixteenth and seventeenth centuries presents special difficulties because no empire, as the term subsequently came be understood, then existed, while the adjective 'British' meant little to most inhabitants of Britain and Ireland."[7] In subsequent chapters, several authors drive home that point by noting the difficulty the English had in justifying the legitimacy of their American settlements, the reluctance of the early Stuart governments to support overseas expansion, and the lack of references to an *empire* in America until well after the Restoration.[8]

In his recent monograph, Atlantic history proponent David Armitage has painstakingly traced the slow expansion of the term *British Empire* to include transatlantic settlements in its meaning. Not surprisingly, he finds that English writers during the sixteenth and most of the seventeenth century did not create an imperial ideology based on Protestantism or the exploits of their seadogs, much less expand the concept of expansion from an English activity to a British one. The crucial step toward conceptualizing a British empire was not taken before the Glorious Revolution, in his view, when the idea of an empire of trade was grouped with traditions of religious and civil liberty to identify a distinctive British community. People did not commonly refer to a British empire until the second quarter of the eighteenth century, decades after

4 The Creation of the British Atlantic World

the Act of Union joined the Scottish and English parliaments. Moreover, he finds, provincials—Irish unionists, American planters, and officials—took the lead in employing imperial terminology not residents of the English metropolis.[9] Another study, this one finding ethnic and national identity of questionable importance in "the early modern British world," further elucidates why theorizing about a transatlantic British empire was a nonevent for so long.[10] Examining how contemporaries in England, Scotland, Ireland, and the American colonies conceived of their ethnicity and national identity, Colin Kidd discovers an ever shifting mix of Celtic Briton, Gothic Saxon, and Norman elements, none of which were utilized for their racial content as much as their association with ancient constitutions, kingdoms, Biblical chronologies, and ecclesiastical polities. With national identity not dependent on either ethnic or civic territorial definitions as much as institutional histories and pedigrees, the only clear pedigree that led to "British Empire" in the seventeenth century was the Stuart dynasty, a particularly insecure foundation for the creation of a transatlantic imperial edifice. A third scholar of non-European English warfare in the period up to 1688 considers the whole empire business absurd. "Many colonial peripheries which have become retrospectively matters of obsessive interest to scholars," Bruce Lenman claims, "were of very little contemporary interest indeed to the core English population."[11] Basically, transatlantic settlements formed by colonists in America or by the East India Company in Asia, according to this view, were on their own.

The newer version of imperial history—known as "The New Imperial History"—considers such matters as empires within Europe, the impact of the "periphery" on the "core," the development of a seaborne citizenry, and the formation of a subaltern class fitting in well with the transnational and regional approaches found in the historical work on the Atlantic world.[12] Both aim at expanding the number of actors and depict the Atlantic from the fifteenth to the eighteenth century as a multinational zone in that migrants entered more often as part of a maritime exploit, trading company, plantation complex, or social, religious or ethnocultural group than as an instrument of a European nation-state strategy. The sea and the coastal cities of the Atlantic became places where males from different classes, races, and religions intermingled and sometimes fought. Enslaved Africans and Indians, white indentured servants, and ship crews made unreliable subjects of a European Crown as did sectaries disappointed with the religious orthodoxy of their homelands and merchant/planters preoccupied with finding the best price for crops destined for shipment to transatlantic consumers.[13] Control from the homeland authorities tended to be irregular and disruptive rather than unifying, and colonists often feared that attention from the metropolis would only mean interference in their trading arrangements or with their forms of government and religious practice.

One danger, of course, in painting Crown, court, and the metropolitan political nation as reluctant imperialists and colonials indifferent to king and country is that it can encourage a return to the "fit of absent mindedness" theory of global domination. Atlantic history has little time for or interest in examining the place of imperial politics in the shaping of the transatlantic experience. In *Strangers within the Realm,* only one contribution, an analysis of "who cared about America" in Britain, dealt much with the issue of imperial structure, and the answer to who cared reaffirmed that what existed in the Atlantic world was an empire of trade. Britons with the greatest continuing investment in the thirteen colonies had mercantile not political interests, and the governmental influence of these overseas traders waxed and waned, strong in the first two-thirds of the eighteenth century but at a low point right before the American Revolution.[14] British Atlantic history, as illustrated by a recent collection of essays, [15] tends toward nonpolitical causation, and when it does focus on politics it is the politics of the Revolution and slavery that mark dissolution of empire.

What keeps the traditional imperial approach alive and volumes like the new *Oxford History of the British Empire* continuing to issue from university presses is the presence of much documentary evidence concerning national competitiveness in the creation of the Atlantic world.[16] Those in and around the court and sailing the seas routinely attributed imperialist motives to their enemies and, proudly, to themselves.[17] As has been recently pointed out, the divergent paths taken by China and Western Europe in overseas expansion were not due to big gaps in living standards or technology but were heavily influenced by the objectives of ruling dynasties and the responses of the polity. The Qing rulers of the Chinese empire discouraged any migration unrelated to the shoring up of imperial boundaries and the protection of ancestral homelands in Manchuria. In Western Europe, the existence of culturally homogeneous yet autonomous states, it is theorized, led to heightened competition among them and a positive view of colonization after two kingdoms, Portugal and Castile, enjoyed substantial success in their transatlantic endeavors. Wars and rivalries within Europe spilled over into the Americas.[18]

Research on the persons involved in overseas colonization and trading companies in the sixteenth and seventeenth centuries supports the notion that, from the Elizabethan period on, at least one part of the English polity had a consistent strategy of not just Atlantic but overseas expansion to the West and the East. In the late sixteenth century, a powerful group comprising courtiers, City of London merchants, and West Country gentlemen formed a militant Protestant expansionist network that aimed for dominion beyond Ireland in the Atlantic and the capture of oceanic trade routes to East Asia. Membership in these two endeavors even overlapped, as leaders put together an alternative foreign policy featuring a much more aggressive stance in non-European areas of the globe than did the official policy of the Tudor and early Stuart monarchs.[19] Indeed, the Crown seldom reined in these adventurers because of the economic and political support they furnished and because any curtailing of their activities was equated with being soft on Catholicism and selling out to the more powerful Habsburg and Bourbon dynasties. In this period the eastern seaboard of North America was colonized and trading forts established in Asia and Africa, while Puritan politicians pressured the Crown to build a naval force that could secure and enhance these outposts and the new commercial initiatives they represented. Those in the new overseas trades disproportionately joined the ranks of the Puritan/Parliamentary cause, while English colonists, rather than celebrating the freedom that disorder provided, feared instead that a distracted metropolis might abandon them.[20]

One might argue that the alternative policy became the official policy with Cromwell's assumption of power during the Interregnum, when he launched the "Western Design" in the Caribbean, funded a state navy, and implemented navigation acts. The later Stuart kings, it is generally conceded, did not reverse these policies of Cromwell and used proprietary grants and trade monopolies to solve patronage problems.[21] Looking at the creation of the Atlantic world from this perspective revives the view that overseas expansion before the eighteenth century was more a deliberate strategy on the part of an influential segment of the English polity and very much connected to the nation-building enterprise, even if the theorizing about empire can not be compared to what occurred after the Glorious Revolution, the Act of Union, or the Seven Years' War.

These differences in viewpoints concerning the transatlantic experience are reflected in the contributions to this volume. The authors are less interested in a descriptive history of the Atlantic world and more concerned with exploring the transformation of peoples, institutions, and ideas as they circulate around and across the ocean.[22] The first chapters address the issue of what difference crossing the Atlantic made in the status and identities of groups and individuals. The second section asks what kept those bordering the Atlantic connected. If the Atlantic world is to be a useful concept, the elements that integrate it must be made explicit. The role of trade, religion, ethnicity, and class are palpable in these essays. Most of these authors trace the movements of people, institutions, and ideas from one region to another across the ocean with minimal reference to empire. What comes through, though, in the course of relating the history of these movements is the continual appearance of imperial representatives and policies. The issue of empire in the shaping of the transatlantic experience is raised directly in the final section.

Part One: Transatlantic Subjects

A masterful account of the national and subnational social groups that were pushed or pulled across the ocean and the encounters that produced hybrid communities during the early modern period opens this section. In their essay, James Horn and Philip D. Morgan provide an up-to-date analysis of both the European and African migrations to the Americas. As part of this rethinking of European expansion, they make two particularly noteworthy points. First, between 1500 and 1820, about 2.6 million Europeans emigrated across the Atlantic compared to 8.75 million Africans. In other words, out of every four transatlantic immigrants, only one was from Europe, while three came from Africa. Needless to say, much more attention has been lavished on that one in four, even though the African crossing might be more comprehensively documented. Among the most important current research projects in early modern history is the systematic analysis of slave ship manifests, revealing the size, the geographical origin, and the destinations involved in this forced emigration.[23] A second point of importance made by Horn and Morgan is that migration in Western Europe during this period was more to the east—nine emigrants out of ten—than to the west and into the Atlantic. In Africa, however, the transatlantic migration far outweighed the northeast migration over the Sahara. Also, Horn and Morgan stress the regional nature of migration from both continents. Inhabitants of the Americas were not a geographical cross-section of the homeland population, and the points of origin did not stay constant over time. Such patterns lay the groundwork for studying the push factors that provided the free, indentured, and enslaved populations of the colonies.

The next chapter directs our attention to the Native American population. Indian cultures played a critical role in the creation of the Atlantic world. They are a much ignored explanation for why most colonists for two centuries turned their backs on the interior of North America and gazed with telescopic intensity on the string of port cities across the Atlantic.[24] If one adopts an Indian perspective, it might well seem that nothing good came from the Atlantic. From the sixteenth century on, not only did it bring an endless stream of aggressive European settlers and enslaved Africans, but for many Indians the high seas must have been associated with their own captivity, whether they were being shipped out to labor in another colony or transported to England as a trophy. Joyce E. Chaplin thoughtfully reflects on the recent attention given this topic, comparing the treatment of Indian captivity with the history of African-American slavery and with the captivity narratives of English colonists. She argues that the significance of Indian captivity is often missed because so many more Africans entered bondage. While it is true that Indian slavery constituted a small percentage of all slavery in North America, in early years and in specific locales it played a devastating role in destroying communities already weakened by deaths from disease and warfare. Initiatives to end Indian slavery came earlier than those aimed at emancipation of African Americans, which raises new questions about the process involved in ending bound servitude. Similarly Chaplin suggests that the scholarly attention lavished on captivity narratives of colonists should be balanced with the accounts of Indian captivity rather than bringing in more far-fetched comparisons with Old World narratives of female bondage in epistolary novels.

The next two chapters, authored by Mark L. Thompson and David Barry Gaspar, respectively, are microhistories that remind us that, even if full-blown imperial visions did not fill the heads of Atlantic travelers, long before 1750 dynastic allegiances were not entirely irrelevant to the identities of those who crossed the Atlantic. Thompson relates the exploits of Captain Thomas Yong, an Englishman with Catholic sympathies, who in 1634 left London bound for the Delaware River with a commission from Charles I to explore and colonize the area. Once there, the prior claims of both Indian nations and the Dutch bothered Yong little. The former lost their rights to dominion after seeming to accept Yong's offer of defense, and the latter's failure to be in residence along the banks of the Delaware disqualified their claims. Yong's rationalizations for claiming the land for the English Crown owed much to the commission itself, which allowed him to take territory "not actually in the possession of any

Christian Prince" and to accept the allegiance of Indians who were "willing to submit themselves under our Obedience." Yong, his Catholicism perhaps a factor, justified his actions not so much ethnically, as an Englishman, but as a subject of the king. He was not the only one, however, for whom the king served as a synecdoche for a national group.[25]

A hundred years later, those operating under the king's commission had grown more wary of dismissing the claims of other "Christian Princes." David Barry Gaspar finds that in the eighteenth century, as the imperial system evolved, the recognition of a person's claim to be a subject of a European monarch brought more respect from British subjects. He considers the issue of national identity not from the individual but the British colonial government's perspective by examining the 1724 decision of Antiguan officials to repatriate a group of black Cape Verdeans who claimed to be subjects of the king of Portugal. Why, he asks, would slave-owning elites on the West Indian island recognize these Cape Verdeans' claims to Portuguese subjecthood when they so blatantly ignored the rights of those Africans imported to work in the sugar fields? Gaspar draws attention to the close alliance in this period between Britain and Portugal that proved exceedingly profitable for the former. Cape Verde, because of its strategic position between Africa and the Americas, played an important role in a slave trade more and more dominated by the British. It also seems, however, that the piracy which brought the Cape Verdeans into Antigua was no longer countenanced the way it had been a generation or so earlier, when the taking of an ocean trip left the allegiance of persons and property up for grabs. The age of Ralegh, Drake, and Sir Henry Morgan had ended.

The international context in which the Antiguan drama played out is of some importance here. Portugal and Britain had enjoyed a long diplomatic and commercial alliance in which English merchants and the cloth trade occupied a privileged position in the ports of Portugal and her colonies in exchange for protection against Spanish aggression. In the decade prior to 1724, English exports to Portugal had soared.[26] Robert Walpole, who had just begun his long career as "prime" minister, "wanted stability and prosperity at home; peace abroad . . . Further it was his intention to control the institutions of government more thoroughly than they had ever been controlled before."[27] The incident of the Cape Verdeans occurred during a diplomatic crisis in which Spain threatened to make agreements allowing Austria's cloth trade to gain a foothold in Iberia. Trouble with Portugal, a faithful purchaser of British cloth, was not what the government wanted at this point. The sensitivity of a colonial governor and assembly to the authority of the king of Portugal and the international policy concerns of the Walpole government seem related.

The last contribution in this section is by an historian of Africa, Ray A. Kea. He has pieced together the unusual history of the Catholic woman Marotta from the Popo Kingdom in the Bight of Benin, who, after being enslaved, surfaced in the records of the Danish-controlled island of St. Thomas in the Caribbean. There she ultimately gained freedom in the mid-eighteenth century and joined a Moravian congregation. The Moravian missionaries, during a short period in the 1730s, arrived in St. Thomas and baptized nearly half of the enslaved population. Planter rage threatened the continuance of the congregation and testimonials were gathered from some of those saved through Jesus Christ. Her story supports both the history of the Atlantic as a history of group migrations and a history of empires. Marotta, whose identity seemed to be much more bound up with liberation Christianity and her African homeland than with any European empire, nonetheless, found herself in the position of having to appeal for permission to worship to a faraway monarch in a land she had never seen.

Part Two: Transatlantic Connections

Chapters in Part Two focus on the processes involved in linking both sides of the Atlantic. As appears to have been the case with American Indian cultures on the eastern seaboard of North America, Western Europeans and Africans had for centuries turned their back on the Atlantic or had given it no more than myopic glances. The newfound ability to navigate the ocean made possible colonies, but it did not necessarily produce an Atlantic culture. What propelled the nonmigrant and the transplanted to keep in contact with one another and think of themselves as part of a common community? One scholar has recently argued that during the civil wars in England, Scotland, and Ireland and the Interregnum, English colonial governments exhibited not an enhanced disaffection from the empire but instead a "compulsion to remain connected." Instability in England during the civil war period did not produce an independent attitude on the part of colonists because they feared that their legitimacy depended on their connection with whomever or whatever held sovereignty in England.[28]

The most extensive investigation of transatlantic communication in the period following the Interregnum is Ian K. Steele's *The English Atlantic,*

1660–1740: An Exploration of Communication and Community and he finds government ties less than robust.[29] Steele looked carefully at the ways Britons on both sides of the Atlantic kept in touch. He discovered that commerce gave more structure to the communication networks than did politics, and that commercial communications grew at a faster rate than did political communications. Steele's findings reconfirm the longstanding view of a weak-willed imperial network prior to 1763, one that stood in marked contrast with those of the much more activist Spanish and French empires. Cromwellian Western Designs and the schemes of late-seventeenth-century Stuart militaristic governors appear as exceptions not the rule.[30] The Namierite model of patronage and deference politics was expanded to incorporate the eighteenth-century colonies in monographs done a generation ago and little new has appeared to alter the picture since.[31] The history of patronage connections becomes a history of disconnection between mother country and colonies, foreshadowing the American Revolution.

On the other hand, the notion of a British empire of trade holding the Atlantic together has enjoyed growing popularity in recent years as interest in material culture has grown. The emergence of the great trading companies, escalating demand for tropical goods, and the colonial importation of consumer durables are all part of the story.[32] The chapters in this section are not interested in challenging or affirming that the empire of goods provided more of a raison d'être for the transatlantic community than imperial structures as they are trying to understand how and in what ways people on both sides conversed and the role of those conversations both in the making of a transatlantic culture and in making it British.

April Lee Hatfield focuses on the go-between role of mariners in seventeenth-century English American ports and communities. Although ostensibly concerned with commercial communication, she finds they also circulated all kinds of information, including news of religion and politics. Her examination of local records, moreover, reveals an international conversation going on among the seafaring population. She makes the interesting point that the influence of mariners was greater in the seventeenth century than later because more colonial inhabitants lived near ports or waterways, mariners' port-stays were longer, and, of course, newspapers and other printed matter were very limited.

Historians consider the English common law to be one of the most important elements binding Anglo-Americans to Great Britain. William M. Offutt in his intriguing chapter finds that seventeenth-century English settlers drew on a diverse body of legal sources beyond those represented by the common law and that the legal systems of the various colonies differed from one another. Over time, the colonies grew more alike and the common law came to dominate. Other scholars have attributed this process to colonial commercialization, to social development requiring more complex institutional structures, or to a conscious effort by an anxious creole elite to improve their colonial culture through anglicization. Offutt, in contrast, views the encroachment of the common law as commencing in England for political reasons and spreading to all the colonies at approximately the same time, the era of the Glorious Revolution.

Given the religious motivations for migration among a substantial portion of the American colonial population, one might assume that sectarian ties played a big part in transatlantic communications. The connections of New England Puritans and of Pennsylvania Quakers have received the most attention in the historical literature.[33] The personal transatlantic connections of Puritans are usually seen as deteriorating rather quickly although the theological conversation continued over a longer period. Restoration distaste for the Interregnum and Puritan excesses made New Englanders appear as unattractive relics, and no single organizational structure reached across the ocean to encompass both British dissenters and New England sectaries. One of the most radical parts of the dissenter tradition, Quakers did develop, however, a well-organized international structure that kept connections strong, even if adherence to the principles of their sect weakened their influence within Pennsylvania. As Karin Wulf demonstrates at the end of this volume, international Quaker connections and a cultural attachment to Britain survived the American Revolution.

A rejuvenated Church of England, attracting followers within the dissenter strongholds of the northern colonies, is sometimes viewed as yet another institution that encouraged the anglicization of colonial society and thereby fostered transatlantic ties.[34] The chapters by Avihu Zakai and Wolfgang Splitter, however, indicate both the limitations of the anglicization theory and the peculiar form it took in some places.

While some New England clergy transformed themselves into latitudinarian and enlightened Anglicans, Zakai examines the considerable religious energy in New England that perpetuated the dissenter stance by critiquing metropolitan trends. His chapter concerns the response of Jonathan Edwards to British Enlightenment discourse, a subject first made famous by Perry Miller many decades ago. In Zakai's rendering, Edwards is involved in a transatlantic dialogue but the two-way conversation was primarily with Protestant theologians in Britain and Europe who were also disturbed by Enlightenment efforts to excise Christian beliefs from philosophy and history.

Wolfgang Splitter's informative chapter on the problems experienced by German Lutherans in expanding across the Atlantic provides some useful comparisons with the work on British religious groups and a surprising twist on the anglicization theme. By the mid-nineteenth century, thanks to increased Northern European migration, the Lutheran Church could boast more congregations than any other denomination. A century earlier, however, Lutheran membership growth was stagnant and Splitter provides some of the reasons why. The Lutheran Church occupied a niche similar to the Anglican. It was accustomed to being an established church with a tax base and a church hierarchy that controlled access to the ministry. Overseas, it largely confined itself to missionary efforts within the German community. Rather than being in competition with the Anglican Church, the Lutheran hierarchy encouraged cooperation with the Anglican charity school movement through its envoy to the Hanoverian Court in London. Lutheran pastors preferred allying with Anglican interests to joining forces with the more expansionist Moravians or itinerant preachers who established congregations in the colonies. From the picture Splitter provides, the Lutheran establishment actually facilitated the entrenchment of the British in America.

Part Three: Imperial Visions and Transatlantic Revisions

The presence of a British imperial system in the Atlantic becomes more difficult to avoid as one moves through the eighteenth century; its partial collapse after the American Revolution also raises questions about the means by which a transatlantic culture continued to exist. In the sixteenth century, England failed miserably in establishing colonies and ranked far behind the Portuguese and Dutch in maritime skills and trade. Only in piracy against the Spanish did the English excel. England's seventeenth-century troubles—the collapse of its principal export, woolen cloth, and its religious wars—however, proved beneficial for commerce and colonization as tropical goods, religious émigrés, and, at the end of the century, slaves filled the sea lanes of the Atlantic. A population owing allegiance to the English monarch spread along the American east coast, driving out the Dutch and reducing the claims of the Spanish. The 1707 Act of Union made the English Atlantic British as Scots became a major force in trade and planting. Wars and trade treaties in the first half of the eighteenth century transformed the British into the premier conveyor of people and goods from Europe and Africa over the Atlantic. At the end of the Seven Years' War, the British, having trounced France and its Indian allies, reigned supreme in the North Atlantic region, and the imperial structure in America seemed more secure than ever. A monumental reversal of fortune, however, soon followed. In a twenty-year period all the pillars came tumbling down, after what is usually viewed as an understandable but misguided attempt to tighten control over the empire and place it on a firmer financial footing. American colonists reacted angrily to the abridgement of their rights and ultimately took up arms in a revolution. The British Empire in the Atlantic shrank notably, thirteen colonies shed their British identity and fashioned a new republican vision, and the British regrouped, ultimately creating a new and different global empire in which ventures in the Indian Ocean and the Pacific eclipsed early Atlantic ventures.

The papers in this last section beg to differ with some of the elements in this particular telling of the story. Elizabeth Mancke takes a comprehensive two-century look at the legal relationship between the English and then British sovereign and those holding charters on such crucial matters as the power to grant land, decide the governance structure, and engage in military action and foreign policy. If one looks at the entire Atlantic empire, not just the thirteen colonies, and considers the situation of all those in the empire, including Indians, French Canadians, and slaves, both the view that the metropolis made a sudden shift toward more authoritarian control and against individual rights becomes more problematic.

Both Robert Olwell and John E. Crowley found an increased tendency in the last half of the eighteenth century for the metropolis to define and conceptualize the empire as a whole, melding together all parts, Atlantic and elsewhere. Conflicts with the thirteen colonies only seemed to speed on this process. Olwell juxtaposes the simultaneous developments of the Royal Gardens at Kew during the 1760s and the establishment of a British colonial government in East Florida. As we know from a recent book on the subject, the Crown intended Kew Gardens as a botanical showcase of global flora drawn primarily from the empire and categorized and named by British subjects.[35] The new governor of East Florida, Alexander Grant, who owed his position to the patronage of the royal favorite, Lord Bute, repaid the favor by sending back to Britain colonial seeds and plants for Kew Garden, a pet project of Bute. Florida, like its seeds, was marketed as an exotic product meriting its own "King's Botanist" in the person of John Bartram. The Atlantic world was becoming an "other" in a way that it had never been previously, yet that otherness was controlled, if not domesticated, through scientific methods.

Crowley, in a fascinating statistic, finds that four thousand books published in English before 1800 had the words colony or plantation in their titles, but only 124 had the term *British Empire* and 87 percent of those were printed in 1763 or later. He argues that a topographical preoccupation with empire accompanied this new linguistic turn. Landscape art, so popular in eighteenth-century Britain, soon was produced for all parts of the empire. Military officers, trained in landscape drawing for the purposes of waging war, often served as the artists. The mood of their imperial landscapes, however, was picturesque: beautiful and nonthreatening with little difference in atmosphere between the Atlantic, Indian, or Pacific arenas.

Appropriately ending this section, Karin Wulf examines how those of British ancestry in the United States related to Britain after the Revolution and the extent to which they perpetuated a transatlantic culture. She studies the way Deborah Norris Logan, the representative of a leading Pennsylvania Quaker family, rearranged her family's history in the early national period to fit a changing Atlantic world but also to establish firmly its British roots. This veneration for having been from Britain was not extinguished even during the period of intense American-British hostility. Genealogy became a new basis for maintaining transatlantic connections.

If the selections in this volume do not resolve the tension mentioned at the beginning of this introduction—the split between those who explain a transatlantic world as the consequence of competing European states striving for empire and those who see it launched through the serendipitous workings of a variety of subnational groups traversing the ocean for a variety of motives, especially economic and religious—they do provide some clues as to the relationship of one to the other. So many of the defining features of the Atlantic world—the preponderance of Africans in the transatlantic migration, the decline of the Indian population, the boom in tropical goods that kept a diverse maritime population employed, the popularity of evangelical Christianity—cannot be explained simply as the outgrowth of rivalries among European dynasties bent on nation building. Imperial officialdom seemed spread too thin over vast expanses with small budgets and nonexistent troops to foster and control transatlantic developments. Yet many chapters in this book contain episode after episode where imperial acts, whether directly or more often by proxy, affected the flow of events. The constant creation of chartered trading companies, the issuance of commissions to adventurers and grants to proprietors meant never a dull moment for those trying to make a fortune, a war, or a professional career. From early in the seventeenth century, Crown-sanctioned colonial courts relied upon the legal traditions of the metropolis to adjudicate among settlers, and when the Glorious Revolution proved to the winners the superiority of the common law, the legal traditions everywhere narrowed to conform more closely to metropolitan practice. What is perhaps most surprising is how diverse people and obscure places got tangled up with imperial institutions: a British captain's slaves unexpectedly freed by a West Indian governor fearful of disrupting Anglo-Portuguese relations; Newfoundland fishermen pleading for the establishment of a colonial government; a West Indian woman from Africa finding that the right to practice her evangelical Christian faith could best be secured by a petition to a Danish Queen; Lutheran clerics looking to the Anglican establishment for support. Only the American Indians of the eastern seaboard, who had their own authority structures in place, adopted as much as possible an avoidance strategy when it came to both the Atlantic and empire.

The empire being recognized in these chapters, however, is not the highly conceptualized empire of civil servants and colonial office reports, but a simpler form, essentially an authority that could protect subjects and adjudicate. High-definition imperial politics dominated the transatlantic experience in the last third of the eighteenth century, although not everywhere in the Atlantic. After the American Revolution, new means of forging transatlantic ties were fashioned by those segments of the U.S. population that had the closest links to the British polity before the Revolution. In subsequent years other segments would identify and seek connection with other nations and continents across the ocean. This legacy of empire is the one with which the Atlantic world is now most familiar.

Part I / Transatlantic Subjects

CHAPTER ONE

Settlers and Slaves

European and African Migrations to Early Modern British America

James Horn and Philip D. Morgan

Without minimizing the tragic consequences of the Middle Passage or blurring the fundamental distinction between free and coerced migrations, there is value to comparing white and black migrations to North America and the Caribbean. To aim at Atlantic history is to grapple with the complex forces that shaped migrant experience, no matter what the type, and it must encompass population movements from all parts of the Atlantic rim. The Atlantic was the first ocean to see intensive and continuing contact between the lands migrants left and those they came to inhabit. Over time, a variety of links, bonds, and connections drew the territories around the Atlantic more closely together. Europe, Africa, and the Americas became part of an increasingly cohesive and integrated world.

Common characteristics, as well as sharp contrasts, among the various migration streams become evident when they are studied as parts of a whole. By bringing together two largely separate literatures—European migration and the slave trade—it is be possible to gain a clearer view of the general influences that worked upon transatlantic migration, together with a more refined understanding of what set the two streams apart. To this end, the following essay will explore five themes. First, what was the magnitude and pace of migration, coerced and free, to early America? When did African outpace European migration and why? Although African migration was much greater in absolute terms than its European counterpart, was it also greater relative to the homeland population? Second, what was the character and social composition of the two migrations? Did, for example, women and children comprise a larger proportion of the coerced or free migration? What were the most important differences in the social composition of migrants from different regions? Third, to what degree did the shipboard conditions of each stream differ? What was the degree of mortality, the level of violence? Fourth, the regional specificity of migration is a crucial feature of early modern migration. Were there parallels in the types of regional links between source and migrant societies, no matter whether the focus is on Europe or Africa? Exploring regional influences leads inevitably to one final topic: the extent of the transfer and survival of particular social and cultural forms, which in turn raises large questions of ethnicity and identity. To what extent, if at all, did Europeans and Africans undergo a similar process of creolization?[1]

Magnitude and Pace of Migration

Between 1500 and 1820, 2.5 million European emigrants left for the New World. Prior to 1640 the vast majority were Spanish and Portuguese settlers, numbering about 400,000 in all, roughly seven times the sum total of British, French, and Dutch emigrants. Thereafter, British emigration dwarfed all other European flows. From 1640 to 1700, for example, 300,000 British migrants left for the New World, a total approaching twice that of all other European emigrants combined. Throughout the eighteenth and early nineteenth centuries the numbers of British emigrants always exceeded those of their European rivals (see Table 1.1).

Between 1500 and 1820, more than 8.5 million enslaved Africans made the Middle Passage to the Americas. Up to this time, this forced migration was the largest known intercontinental migration in world history. Before 1640, 90 percent of the roughly 800,000 Africans who left their homelands arrived in Portuguese ships. Thereafter, the British, who had been slow to transport slaves, emerged as the premier slave-trading nation. The British carried over 40 percent of the Africans forced to leave for the New World between 1640 and 1820. The number of Africans arriving in the Americas rose staggeringly—2.75 million between 1700 and 1760, over 4 million between 1760 and 1820. Africans outnumbered European emigrants to the New World 1.9 to 1 between 1640 and 1700, 3.4 to 1 between 1700 and 1760, and 4.9 to 1 between 1760 and 1820 (Table 1.1).

Table 1.1

European and African migration to the Americas, 1500–1820 (in thousands)

	Europeans	Africans	Ratio (Europeans/Africans)
1500–1580			
Spain	100	10	
Portugal	90	63	
Britain	0	1	
Total	190	74	2.6:1
1580–1640			
Spain	90	100	
Portugal	110	590	
Britain	50	4	
France	4	0	
Netherlands	2	20	
Total	256	714	1:2.8
1640–1700			
Spain	70	10	
Portugal	50	226	
Britain	303	371	
France	45	150	
Netherlands	13	160	
Total	481	917	1:1.9
1700–1760			
Spain	90	0	
Portugal	250	812	
Britain	289	1,286	
France	51	456	
Netherlands	5	221	
Germany	97	0	
Total	782	2,775	1:3.4

(continued on p. 22)

Table 1.1 *(continued)*

	Europeans	Africans	Ratio (Europeans/Africans)
1760–1820			
Spain	70	186	
Portugal	105	1,535	
Britain	615	1,590	
France	20	674	
Netherlands	5	137	
Germany	51	0	
Other	5	183	
Total	871	4,305	1:4.9
1500–1820			
Spain	420	306	
Portugal	605	3,226	
Britain	1,257	3,252	
France	120	1,280	
Netherlands	25	538	
Germany	148	0	
Other	5	183	
Total	2,580	8,785	1:3.4

Sources: David Eltis, *Rise of African Slavery* (Cambridge, U.K., 2000), Table 1.1, 9, 10; idem, "Atlantic History in Global Perspective," *Itinerario: A Journal of European Overseas Expansion* 23 (1999), 141–161; P. C. Emmer, "European Expansion and Migration: The European Colonial Past and Intercontinental Migration; An Overview," in Emmer and M. Morner, eds., *European Expansion and Migration: Essays on the European Intercontinental Migration from Africa, Asia, and Europe* (New York, 1992), 3; Auke Jacobs, *Los Movimientos Migratorios entre Castilla e Hispanoamerica durante el Reinado do Felipe III, 1598–1621* (Amsterdam, 1995), 122–125, 171; Victorino Magalhes Godinho, "Portuguese Emigration from the Fifteenth to the Twentieth Century: Constants and Changes," in Emmer and Morner, eds., *European Expansion and Migration,* 18–24; Stanley L. Engerman and Joao Cesar das Neves, "The Bricks of Empire, 1415–1999: 585 Years of Portuguese Emigration," *Journal of European History* 26 (1997), 471–510; Henry A. Gemery, "Emigration from the British Isles to the New World, 1630–1700: Inferences from Colonial Populations," *Research in Economic History* 5 (1980), 179–231; idem, "European Emigration to North America, 1700–1820: Numbers and Quasi-Numbers," *Perspectives in American History,* New Series, 1 (1984), 283–342; idem, "The White Population of the Colonial United States, 1607–1790," in Michael R. Haines and Richard H. Steckel, eds., *A Population History of North America* (New York, 2000), 143–190; Aaron S. Fogleman, "Migrations to the Thirteen British North American Colonies, 1700–1775: New Estimates," *Journal of Interdisciplinary History* 22 (1992), 691–709; idem, "From Slaves, Convicts, and Servants to Free Passengers: The Transformation of Immigration in the Era of the American Revolution," *Journal of American History* 85 (1998), 43–76; Stanley L. Engerman, "France, Britain, and the Economic Growth of Colonial North America," in John J. McCusker and Kenneth Morgan, eds., *The Early Modern Atlantic Economy* (Cambridge, U.K., 2000), 230–241.

Migration to British North America and the Caribbean reflected these general New World patterns. During the first phase of settlement of British America (to 1640), European emigrants outnumbered their African counterparts by over 30 to 1, a more marked imbalance than occurred during the founding periods of the Spanish and Portuguese western empires. In the 1630s alone, about 40,000 whites left their native shores for British America, whereas a much smaller number of Africans—no more than 5,000—were forced to join them. The following decade represented the high watermark of white migration when approximately 70,000 settlers arrived, but thereafter the gap between black and white migrants narrowed rapidly because British plantation owners increasingly tapped into the more elastic supply of African rather than European labor.[2] By the 1660s, the number of white emigrants was in gradual decline, falling to slightly below 50,000 during the decade, while African emigrants had risen to approximately the same level. By 1680—and this was to remain true for another century—more blacks than whites left their respective homelands for British America. In fact, from 1680 to 1780 the ratio was always more than 3 to 1. From 1600 to 1825 about 2,672,500 Africans, about twice as many as the number of Europeans, left their native lands for North America and the Caribbean. In sheer number of emigrants, British America was more black than white (Table 1.2).

Although black emigration was larger than white in absolute numbers, the rate of emigration as a proportion of homeland populations was similar. In the two centuries after 1580, England experienced a net migration of about 1.3 million, the majority going to Ireland and other parts of Europe rather than to the Americas. By premodern standards, the scale of emigration was enormous. It represented a quarter of England's population at the mid-point (1680) of the two centuries. Although annual migration in absolute terms would be higher in the nineteenth century, annual rates of emigration relative to the domestic population never exceeded those of the mid-seventeenth century, when they were between 2 and 3 per 1,000. This large outflow, however, did not denude the country of population, which nearly doubled in the period, rising from 3.6 to 7.0 million people. Similarly, when the slave trade was at its height between about 1750 and 1850 with approximately 8 million people forced to leave the subcontinent, this number represented perhaps a third to a quarter of the population of Western Africa at its midpoint. Annual rates of forced migration were generally between 2 and 3 per 1,000 although they could be higher

Table 1.2

European and African migration to British America, 1600–1825 (in thousands)

	Mainland		Caribbean		Total	
	Europeans	Africans	Europeans	Africans	Europeans	Africans
1601–25	6.0	0	0.1	0	6.1	0
1626–50	34.3	1.4	80.9	26.6	115.2	28.0
1651–75	69.8	0.9	64.6	94.2	134.4	95.1
1676–1700	67.0	9.8	32.9	182.5	99.9	192.3
1701–25	42.0	37.4	27.1	266.9	69.1	304.3
1726–50	108.8	96.8	28.7	342.2	137.5	439.0
1751–75	194.3	116.9	33.3	635.5	227.6	752.4
1776–1800	230.0	24.5	22.3	592.5	252.3	617.0
1801–25	300.0	73.3	30.0	171.1	330.0	244.4
1600–1825	1,052.2	361.0	319.9	2,311.5	1,372.1	2,672.5

Sources: EUROPEAN MIGRATION: Russell R. Menard, "Toward African Slavery in Barbados: The Origins of the West Indian Plantation Regime," in *Lois Green Carr: The Chesapeake and Beyond: A Celebration* (Crownsville, Md., 1992), 26; David Galenson, *White Servitude in Colonial America: An Economic Analysis* (Cambridge, U.K., 1981), 212–218; Henry A. Gemery, "Emigration from the British Isles to the New World, 1630–1700: Inferences from Colonial Populations," *Research in Economic History* 5 (1980), 179–231; idem, "European Emigration to North America, 1700–1820: Numbers and Quasi-Numbers," *Perspectives in American History,* New Series, 1 (1984), 283–342; Aaron S. Fogleman, "Migrations to the Thirteen British North American Colonies, 1700–1775: New Estimates," *Journal of Interdisciplinary History* 22 (1992), 691–709; idem, "From Slaves, Convicts, and Servants to Free Passengers: The Transformation of Immigration in the Era of the American Revolution," *Journal of American History* 85 (1998), 43–76; David Eltis, "Atlantic History in Global Perspective," *Itinerario: A Journal of European Overseas Expansion* 23 (1999), 141–161; E. A. Wrigley and R. S. Schofield, *Population History of England, 1541–1871: A Reconstruction* (Cambridge, Mass., 1981), 208–209; Henry A. Gemery, "The White Population of the Colonial United States, 1607–1790," in Michael R. Haines and Richard H. Steckel, eds., *A Population History of North America* (New York, 2000), 143–190; Stanley L. Engerman, "A Population History of the Caribbean," in Haines and Steckel, eds., *A Population History of North America,* 490–501; U.S. Bureau of the Census, *Historical Statistics of the United States* (Washington, D.C., 1961), 451. AFRICAN MIGRATION: Calculations kindly supplied by David Eltis based on David Eltis, Stephen D. Behrendt, David Richardson, and Herbert S. Klein, eds., *The Trans-Atlantic Slave Trade: A Database on CD-Rom* (Cambridge, U.K., 1999).

in different regions for brief periods of time. At the Bight of Benin in the early eighteenth century they seem to have been over 3 per 1,000 and at the Bight of Biafra in the late eighteenth century 4 per 1,000. And in specific places at particular times noticeable depopulation apparently occurred.[3]

But if transatlantic migration is considered as a part of overall migration, then European rates were probably greater than their African equivalents. Far more Europeans moved east than west. Within seventeenth- and eighteenth-century Europe for every transatlantic migrant about nine moved east. Africa had a northern and eastern migration in the form of a trans-Saharan slave trade together with, from the late eighteenth century, a traffic to India and newly developing Indian Ocean sugar islands. But these two African migration streams were always much smaller than transatlantic departures. As part of overall continental migration, Europe's migration was almost certainly much larger than Africa's.[4]

The pace of emigration varied considerably, relative to destinations in America. In the seventeenth century, half of the 356,000 Europeans and 96 per-cent of the 315,000 Africans who emigrated for British America went to the West Indies. Another third of the Europeans and the remainder of the Africans went to the Chesapeake. Only 1 in 10 Europeans and almost no Africans went to New England or the Middle Colonies. During the "long" eighteenth century (down to about 1825), the Caribbean still attracted the largest number of migrants—some 2 million Africans and 140,000 European immigrants and sojourners—whereas the mainland received about 1 million Europeans and 348,000 Africans.[5]

Migration waxed and waned in response to many factors. Throughout the period, trading companies and thousands of individual merchants (large and small), responding to fluctuations in supply and demand in regional markets, played the dominant role in recruiting, capturing, and transporting Europeans and Africans to America. Governments generally gave tacit approval to colo-nizing schemes and trading ventures that might increase revenues, and in some cases took the lead in devising policy and recruiting settlers (as in the case of the reorganization of French colonies under Louis XIV and Colbert), but for the most part they left the peopling of colonies and trade in servants and slaves to the mercantile community. Economic vicissitudes in Europe and perceived opportunities in America account for the movement of large numbers of inde-pendent settlers but, without question, the enormous and continuing demand for field laborers in the plantation colonies was the underlying cause of the mass migrations of poor whites and enforced transportation of blacks throughout the period.[6]

A common feature of both European and African streams, albeit more pervasive in the African case, was the role of war and social conflict. Civil war in England, campaigns against the Irish, and the wars against Scottish Jaco-bites led to the coerced migration of thousands of prisoners to British colonies. Religious persecution led 200,000 Huguenots to flee France in the late seventeenth century, several thousand of whom ended up in British America. Emigration from the Palatinate, Wurttemberg, Hesse, Nassau, and other "German" territories in 1708–9 was prompted in part by French armies overrunning much of the Rhineland during the War of Spanish Succession. The French returned during the wars of Polish Succession (1733–38) and Austrian Succession (1740–48) causing further hardships in the region. Puritans, Quakers, Baptists, Waldensians, Moravians, Schwenkfelders, Mennonites, Salzburg Protestants, and even Catholics sought sanctuary in the New World.

By comparison, perhaps two out of three African migrants became slaves through kidnapping or as prisoners of war. Wars waged by one African state against another were the primary mechanism for the acquisition of slaves. Some slaves were victims of religious wars or jihad, though religion was often a pretext for war, the principal purpose of war was to procure slaves in exchange for imported goods, including firearms. Guns were usually important trade goods in most African regions. Warfare in much of western Africa deviated from that in Europe mostly in terms of objectives: the aim was not just to defeat an enemy army or seize territory but rather to acquire people, war prisoners and noncombatants alike, both of whom were subject to enslavement.

International wars, of course, also shaped the timing of migration: in the short term by disrupting flows, but in the long term by facilitating them. Wars dislocated trading patterns, cut off markets, and forced up shipping costs. Even more important, armies competed for people likely to emigrate; they were population sumps, siphoning off the pool from which emigrants were drawn. As a result, job opportunities expanded at home for prospective emigrants. Thus, in periods of war, the supply of indentured servants dwindled, but rose with peace, as tens of thousands of servicemen were discharged in a saturated labor market. A sharp decline in the supply of servants, which helps explain the shift to slavery in the Chesapeake, owed much to the wars of King William III (1688–97) and of Queen Anne (1702–13). Much later, the American Revolutionary War disrupted the slave trade so effectively that Thomas Clarkson termed it a practical experiment in abolition, and it effectively ended the indentured servant and convict trades at least to North America. Long term, British successes in international wars brought more American territories into the empire. As new colonies came under British control, more migrants (particularly forced migrants in the case of Caribbean territories) were shipped to them.[7]

This comparison of the magnitude and pace of voluntary and coerced migrations to the New World suggests the centrality of the coerced migration stream. From the late seventeenth century onward, Africans increasingly dominated among migrants to the Americas. Europeans moved much more within Europe than to the Americas. Throughout the seventeenth century, for example, the Scots were proportionately more numerous emigrants than the English, but they left primarily for Ireland, Poland, and Scandinavia. Similarly, of the 46 million German-speaking adults who lived in central Europe throughout the eighteenth century, perhaps one-third of them became migrants at some time in their lives, but only a fraction (0.2%) came to North America. By contrast, Africa's migration stream was heavily oriented toward the Atlantic. By 1700 the Atlantic slave trade dwarfed the North African and Mediterranean trades, which remained fairly constant until after 1800 when they too began to rise, albeit much more modestly than the westward trade. Western Africa was pulled more firmly into the Atlantic orbit than large parts of Europe.[8]

Character of Migration

Between a half and three-quarters of Europeans arrived in the colonies under some form of labor contract as indentured servants, redemptioners, soldiers, felons, or political prisoners, and most of them (roughly 70 to 90%) were male. The largest group, indentured servants, contracted to serve between four and seven years in return for their passage, board and lodging, and various types of freedom dues on completion of service. In the seventeenth century, they were typically young (in their teens or early twenties), single, unskilled casual workers, or on the tramp. Although contemporary opinion was frequently critical—describing them variously as petty criminals, prostitutes, and vagrants—occupations of male servants who emigrated from Bristol and London across the period suggest a trend toward respectable, if modest, social origins. By the eve of the American Revolution, less than a fifth were described as laborers compared to 69 percent from artisanal and service backgrounds. According to Bernard Bailyn, there was no mass exodus of "destitute unskilled urban slum dwellers and uprooted peasants," from either England or Scotland on the eve of the Revolution; rather movement was characterized by "certain segments of the lower middle and working classes, artisans, and craftsmen with employable skills, for whom emigration would seem to have represented not so much a desperate escape as an opportunity to be reached for." Convicts, who made up about a quarter of British immigrants to mainland America between 1718 and 1775, by contrast, continued to be drawn mainly from unskilled or low-skilled classes.[9]

Free settlers, who arrived more or less unencumbered by indentures, came from an equally wide range of backgrounds as servants. A regular flow of merchants and petty traders made their way to the Chesapeake, Southern colonies, and West Indies to set up on their own or to represent established firms. Like servants, many were young, single males from the major European port towns serving colonial commerce. By contrast, large numbers of independent farmers, artisans, and tradesmen from provincial England, Scotland, and southwest Germany migrated to New England, the Maritime Provinces, New York, Pennsylvania, or North Carolina accompanied by their families, kin, and friends. Sex ratios were more balanced (around 60% male), and settlers were typically older compared to those going to the Southern colonies and islands. Crucially, possession of a skill and financial resources, together with the support of kin and friends in America, radically set apart migrants of this category from indentured servants and sojourners.[10]

African forced migration to the New World was predominantly male and adult, but comprised far more females and children than the indentured servant traffic. European traders certainly sought primarily men, and indeed they partly achieved their goal, for men constituted about a half of all Africans shipped across the Atlantic. Counting both men and boys, the slave trade was about two-thirds male. Nevertheless, African sellers ensured that European buyers had to purchase far more women and children than ideally they desired. The female share of slaves arriving in the New World during the seventeenth century seems to have exceeded the female share of free migrants, and by the early nineteenth century, the two were similar. Perhaps even more notable, a higher proportion of children left Africa for the Americas than left Europe. Consequently as David Eltis has noted, "forced migrants from Africa were much more demographically representative of the societies they left behind than were" European indentured servants. "Before 1800," he notes, "at least four-fifths of the females and over 90 percent of the children sailing to the Americas were not European," but rather African.[11]

Regional contrasts were striking in the age and sex of Africans leaving the coast. The proportion of males sailing from Upper Guinea (Senegambia to Windward Coast) was much larger (almost 75%) than elsewhere and the proportion of children smaller (just 6%). West-Central Africa by contrast had more children (over 20%) among the slaves leaving its shores than other African coastal regions. In the Bight of Biafra women were almost as numerous as men among slaves carried to the Americas. Indeed, in the second half of the seventeenth century, when the traffic from this region first became significant, females were consistently in the majority of those who sailed to the Americas—the only large region in Atlantic Africa, as well as any part of the Old World, for which this was the case. Outlining these regional variations is much easier than explaining them. The dominance of men and absence of children in the flow of captives out of Upper Guinea seems to be attributable to the large distances slave captives traveled before reaching the coast, thereby putting a premium on men, and this region's proximity to the trans-Saharan trade, which absorbed large numbers of females. On the other hand, the near equality of men and women leaving Niger Delta ports seems to be explained in part at least by a tendency to devalue women's labor in this region, thus making more women available to European ship captains. Domestic slavery in the Bight of Biafra was not predominantly female, as it was in other parts of Africa; women were less vital to agricultural production and thereby more expendable. Whatever the explanations, the age and sex of captives varied far more by African region than by the European nation buying the slaves. African-centered, and especially region-specific, explanations for these variations are therefore necessary.[12]

Little is known about the social status of African slaves brought to the Americas, but, because most slaves were the victims of warfare, they probably represented a fairly broad cross-section of their societies. Probably more blacks than whites had a military background, for many captives were soldiers and their auxiliaries; and early settlers in the New World sometimes made use of African slaves for their military prowess. A few prominent African merchants and nobles did make the Middle Passage, but they were the exceptions. Most African slaves who made the transatlantic passage were similar to the white indentured servants of the seventeenth century. They were young, mostly unskilled (that is, not tradespeople, for the most part, although they possessed agricultural skills), and of humble social origins.[13] But, overall, the African migration, primarily because of its age and sex composition, was more representative of its homeland population than was the case of the European migration.

Conditions of Migration

Mortality was always three or four times higher for slaves and crews of slavers than for free migrants and their crews. The slave trade on average recorded about 60 deaths per month per 1,000 people shipped. This rate was four times greater than that among German emigrants to Philadelphia in the eighteenth century and about five times higher than that among British convicts to Australia in the late eighteenth and early nineteenth centuries. The only group to approximate mortality rates on slavers was British convicts to North America in the early eighteenth century (56 deaths per month per 1,000 between 1719 and 1736), and their mortality levels soon improved significantly (dropping to 12 per month per 1,000 between 1768 and 1775). No recorded voyage in the north Atlantic appears to have generated the appalling conditions typical for a slave vessel and almost no ship carrying servants or convicts crowded its passengers on anything like the scale of slave ships, which generally included far more individuals per unit of space than did other vessels.[14]

Shipboard mortality in both European and African traffics varied greatly by port, suggesting the importance of the health of those going on board and the shore-based conditions of the ports from which they sailed. In Africa mortality varied markedly among ports even within the same region, which suggests that different slaving hinterlands—with varying distances from inland point of capture to the coast, different epidemiological zones to be traversed, and varying food supplies along the way—were critical in determining death rates on board ship. Along the Gold Coast, for example, the death rates on ships leaving Cape Coast Castle were 40 percent higher than those leaving Anomabu; in the Bight of Biafra mortality rates were 50 percent higher on ships leaving Old Calabar as opposed to Bonny. Old Calabar had the highest recorded rate (at 23 per 100 slaves shipped), which was four times higher than, say, Cabinda or Malembo in West-Central Africa.[15]

Appalling as mortality rates on slaving vessels were, deaths in the Middle Passage were always a small part of overall mortality in the process of enslavement. Far more slaves died either in Africa in being captured, marched to the coast, and detained in barracoons or in America through initial seasoning than on board ship. Estimates of losses in the Middle Passage alone range from about 2 to 20 percent of all deaths attributed to the slave trade, thus a small proportion of the overall mortality loss. The vast majority of slaves who left Africa made it alive across the Atlantic—about 85 percent of those shipped—compared to about 90 percent of servants. Measured this way the difference was not large. In addition, mortality rates in the slave trade, as in the other trades, generally declined over time. Death rates declined on French slave ships fairly consistently from the 1720s to the 1770s, and on British ships from the 1750s onward. In the 1790s, the death rate of slaves on British ships was 32 per month per 1,000, a rate that French vessels had reached in the 1770s (although French rates increased thereafter). Falling death rates were perhaps largely attributable to "gradual improvements in empirical knowledge related to disease prevention." By the later stages of the British slave trade, about 95 percent of slaves shipped were arriving in the Americas—not much different from the proportions of free migrants.[16]

On a much lesser scale overall, higher than normal death rates in pre-embarkation and post-disembarkation also characterized European migration. Grouping servants together before a voyage increased their chances of infection. Convicts were particularly prone to "gaol fever," as they waited months—sometimes half a year—before boarding a ship; perhaps one in ten inmates of Newgate, a veritable "tomb of the living," died annually, never making it to their transports. On the other side of the Atlantic, the seasoning period took a heavy toll of Europeans, in some cases, even more lethally than for Africans. In the Caribbean, white servants died at faster rates than African slaves. Certainly, British army recruits died at a staggering rate in the Caribbean, compared to their African counterparts. In the islands, death rates of Europeans typically ran 100 per 1,000, often much higher during yellow fever epidemics, while for newly-arrived Africans 40 per 1,000 were common. In the Chesapeake, the transition from white servants to black slaves has been explained by the seasonality of diseases, with whites getting sick more often than blacks at peak agricultural times and with the spread of virulent forms of malaria and hookworm, which again affected whites more than blacks.[17]

A distinguishing feature of slave voyages was their level of violence, both manifest and latent, a feature largely absent from ships transporting free or bound migrants. About 20 percent of Middle Passage costs involved precautions against revolt. On average a slaving vessel carried thirty crew members—twice the number of comparably sized merchant ships—primarily for deterrence. To the same end, slaving vessels divided their slaves via barricades and platforms, routinely shackled the men, and fairly bristled with firearms, swivel guns, and cannon. Slaving vessels were the most heavily armed and crewed ships for a reason: about one in ten experienced an insurrection. The forces of repression usually won out, for almost all of the ships affected by resistance still managed to reach the Americas with a large proportion of their original captives. The average number of slaves killed in insurrections was twenty-five, about 8 percent of a typical complement. During the Middle Passage, fifteen times as many slaves died from disease as lost their lives in revolt. Overall, then, the loss of slaves through insurrections represented a fairly modest cost to slave traders. Nevertheless, had enslaved Africans been less rebellious, many more people would have been shipped across the Atlantic. If the costs of shipping had been lower, encouraging greater demand for a cheaper labor force, more slaves would have been subjected to the voyage. Because insurrection was a constant source of concern for owners of ships and their crews, slaves by their actions and threats of action helped reduce the numbers of Africans forced into slavery.[18]

Shipboard violence was rarely a feature of ships carrying European migrants. Convict ships were the one major exception. "Much like African slaves," Roger Ekirch observes, "convicts found themselves chained below deck in damp quarters with little light or fresh air." If, as one shipper claimed, convict voyages required somewhat more sailors than say a servant voyage, crew size rose only from about twelve to fifteen, half the size of a typical slave ship crew. Some convicts escaped before their ships left sight of land; others mounted insurrections at sea. Twelve uprisings are known to have occurred, making convict ships almost four times less likely to experience revolts than slave vessels.[19]

In short, the circumstances of migration were far worse for slaves than for all other transatlantic passengers. Europeans generally encountered fewer new diseases en route to their port of embarkation, at the transshipment point, or on the voyage than did Africans. Furthermore, nonslave voyages were much less crowded than their slave counterparts. Finally, voluntary migrants faced less violence and, in turn, mutinied less often than coerced migrants. Many Europeans experienced a harrowing transatlantic crossing, but the experience of most Africans was far more traumatic.

Regional Migrations

Regionalism is a key characteristic of early modern migration. Most migrants leaving England for America in the seventeenth century came from London, the Southeast, East Anglia, and the West Country. The eighteenth century, by contrast, saw large-scale movements from northern England, Ulster, southern Ireland, the western districts of the Scottish Borders and Low-lands, the Highlands, and Hebrides. French migrants came chiefly from north-ern and western provinces of Brittany, Normandy, Aunis, and the Atlantic port towns of Rouen, Saint-Malo, Nantes, La Rochelle, and Bordeaux. Atlantic France, west of a line from Rouen to Toulouse, was the seedbed of migrants, whereas the inland provinces of the eastern part of the country, apart from Paris and the Île de France, experienced much lower levels of emigration. Dur-ing the sixteenth and first half of the seventeenth centuries, the origins of Span-ish emigrants were heavily skewed toward the southwest. Andalusia alone contributed between a third and a half of all migrants. During the peak period of outflow, in the 1560s and 1570s, half of those who left were from just thirty-nine communities. In the late seventeenth and eighteenth centuries, the char-acter of Spanish emigrants changed dramatically, with far higher numbers of people moving from the poorer provinces of the north coast, the east, and from the Balearic and Canary Islands. German emigration embraced a wide variety of regions in the Protestant areas of the Palatinate, Nassau, Hesse, Baden-Durlach, and Wurttemberg, as well as from the Swiss cantons of Basel, Berne, and Zurich.[20]

Most settlers who went to British America in the seventeenth century were of English and Welsh origin: some 300,000 compared to between 20,000 and 40,000 Irish, 7,000 Scots, and a few thousand French Protestants, Dutch, Danes, and Swedes. During the following century a strikingly different pattern emerged. Emigration from England and Wales fell dramatically: fewer than 80,000 arrived in 1780 compared to approximately 115,000 Irish and 75,000 Scots. Even before the enormous influx of Irish migrants after the Revolution, 70 percent of all British settlers who arrived in mainland colonies between 1700 and 1780 were from Ireland and Scotland. Whereas during the seventeenth cen-tury settlement of North American coastal regions and the islands had been carried out largely by the English, in the eighteenth century the great expan-sion of European settlement into the backcountry was undertaken principally by Ulster and Catholic Irish, Scottish settlers, and tens of thousands of German and Swiss migrants who arrived in increasing numbers after 1730. Migrants from southern Ireland (amounting to about 45,000), as well as much larger numbers of Protestants from Ulster, were major contributors to the flow of settlers who made their way to the Middle and Southern colonies down to 1780. Emigration from the Scottish Highlands, of small proportions before midcentury, grew rapidly after the end of the Seven Years' War and may have totaled 15,000–20,000 between 1760 and 1775. On the eve of the American Revolution, approaching a fifth of all British emigrants were from the Highlands and islands off Scotland, second only to London as a source of migrants. Scots flooded into the backcountry, from Georgia to upper New York, and played a leading role in the expansion of British settlement in Canada and the Maritime Provinces. As America became the favored destination of tens of thousands of Irish and Scots so the character of European transatlantic migration was transformed.[21]

After the Revolution, the pace of European immigration surged once more. Irish settlers to the United States, Newfoundland, and New Brunswick (chiefly from Ulster) may well have numbered about 250,000 between 1780 and 1819, compared to some 150,000 English, Welsh, and Scots, 50,000 Germans, and 12,000 French. Approximately 10,000 Highlanders made their way to Nova Scotia, Cape Breton, Prince Edward Island, and to eastern Upper Canada, where they joined about 40,000 exiles from the United States, together with thousands of free blacks and Indians, who moved to lands administered under the British Loyalist assistance scheme. Approaching half a million Europeans moved to the United States and British North America, in 1780–1820, foreshadowing the massive tide of immigration after 1840.[22]

West-Central Africa sent more slaves to the New World than any other African region and did so throughout the whole history of the trade, except for a half-century from 1675 to 1725. Other regions were pulled into the slave trade orbit one after another, and, in most cases, experienced high levels of outmigration for about a century or more. The Bight of Benin became a major exporter of people after about 1675 (indeed, the leading exporting region for the next fifty years), the Gold Coast after 1700, the Bight of Biafra after 1725, and Senegambia, the Windward Coast, and Sierra Leone after 1750. These last three regions were exceptional for not maintaining a high volume of slave exports for a century or more and were minor suppliers of slaves to the New World. Thus, the impact of migration tended to be felt in a lockstep sequence, with different regions bearing the brunt of outmigration at different times. The decline of the slave trade also occurred in a regional sequence: on the Windward Coast after 1780, the Gold Coast after 1808, and the Bight of Benin and West-Central Africa not till about 1860. Only in West-Central Africa, with its huge catchment area and constantly expanding slaving frontier, was the outflow consistently large.[23]

The British trade mirrored most of these general regional developments but deviated in some important ways. Perhaps the most notable difference was the importance of the Bight of Biafra to the British slave trade. As early as the 1660s the British acquired more slaves in the Bight of Biafra than all other regions combined. Overall, this African region supplied at least as many slaves to British Empire traders as the next two most important regions—West-Central Africa and the Gold Coast—combined. The British took proportionately fewer slaves from the Bight of Benin than most other national carriers. At various times, other African regions became important suppliers. During the 1760s and 1770s, for example, Sierra Leone became the second most important source of British slaves. The reasons why the British centered their activities in the Bight of Biafra are not fully known, but faster than usual loading rates played an important role.[24]

In both Africa and Europe, movement to the Americas should be located within much broader domestic and external migratory patterns. Transatlantic migration was part of a larger expansion movement, which saw Europeans and, to a lesser degree, Africans move east as well as west. Of the million or so migrants from the British Isles in the seventeenth century, as many moved to Europe as went to America. Approximately 30,000 Huguenots settled in Switzerland and a similar number in Central Europe after the Revocation of the Edict of Nantes in 1685. German-speaking immigrants to America represented only a fifth of the total movement out of the Holy Roman Empire and Helvetic Confederation. The great majority, numbering hundreds of thousands, moved to Hungary, Prussia, Poland, and Russia. Throughout the period, tens of thousands moved each year in seasonal occupations or trekked from one part of Europe to another in search of work. Without a doubt, the scale of involuntary movement within Africa was greater than in Europe: it occurred in response to marked rainfall variations, periodic famines, local political oppression, and the urge to establish new kinship groupings. Spectacular mass migrations linked to catastrophes and ecological displacements should not overshadow, in Igor Kopytoff's words, "innumerable movements to local frontiers." The most sparsely populated continent in the world, Africa was a place where people constantly left settlements and moved beyond the edge of their villages, usually into a no-man's land between established polities, into local frontier zones. Furthermore, African farmers could secure a livelihood only by mobile and extensive exploitation of the land through shifting cultivation and pastoralism. Migrations were therefore frequent in sub-Saharan Africa.

Although not involuntary migrants, English indentured servants who took ship from London were merely a small fraction of the large numbers of young and unemployed workers who flooded into the metropolis, a tiny proportion of the huge volume of lower-class movement within the country and between the various countries of the British Isles, a movement that had elements of serious constraint as well as freedom.[25]

Ports in both Europe and Africa drew on hinterlands of varying sizes. London attracted migrants from all over England and beyond. In the seventeenth and eighteenth centuries, the city and its rapidly growing suburbs absorbed between 5,000 and 10,000 migrants annually, a small proportion of whom took ship for the colonies. Provincial cities and towns such as Bristol, Liverpool, Glasgow, or Londonderry drew on more restricted hinterlands, usually less than 100 kilometers from the port. The migration fields of French Atlantic ports such as Rouen, La Rochelle, and Bordeaux were also typically smaller than that of London, but greater in extent to British outports at about 200 kilometers. In the eighteenth century the average march to the coast ranged from about 100 kilometers in the Bight of Biafra to well over 600 kilometers in West-Central Africa, with Sierra Leone, the Windward Coast, Bight of Benin, Gold Coast, and Senegambia falling in the middle and in ascending order.[26]

The distribution of Africans and Europeans in the New World was no random, unsystematic business; rather, it was patterned and specialized. In the same way that vessels carrying European servants, convicts, and free migrants carried most of their human cargoes from a single port in Europe, slaves left in similar fashion from Africa. London dominated the English servant trade throughout the period, followed at different times by Bristol, Liverpool, and the Scottish outports. Rotterdam—and, to a lesser extent, Amsterdam, Hamburg, and London—dominated the trade in German migrants, while La Rochelle was the major port of departure for French engagés sailing to St. Christopher, San Domingue, and French Canada; Nantes and St. Malo to Canada and Guadeloupe; and Bordeaux to the Antilles and mainland colonies in the eighteenth century. The concentration of African departures from just a few ports is notable. Two-thirds of African slaves shipped from known points left from just over twenty ports in Africa. In general, the slave trade of any African region was heavily centered at one or two places. Whydah on the Slave Coast (Bight of Benin) probably supplied more than a million slaves to Atlantic destinations, likely making it the single most important shipping point for slaves in sub-Saharan Africa; Cabinda, Benguela, and Luanda were the primary ports of West-Central Africa, and all three ranked in the top five embarkation points for slaves; about 80 percent of all slaves from the Bight of Biafra left from just two outlets, Bonny and Calabar; and three-quarters of Africans departing the Gold Coast went from either Cape Coast Castle or Anomabu.[27]

Ships leaving on a slave voyage would normally trade in only one African region, though occasionally at several locations in that region. Only about one in ten slave vessels traded at two or more ports; and only one in twenty traded across regional boundaries. One reason that most slavers headed for specified destinations is that Africans in different coastal regions had distinct preferences for merchandise. Europeans had to select different goods for different markets. Thus, most cowries went to Bight of Benin ports; manillas (or wristlets) would sell only in the Bight of Biafra; cloths appropriate for one section of the coast would be unpopular in another. In addition, European captains would return time and again to the same African region to trade with familiar African merchants. Many Liverpool captains traded for slaves only at Old Calabar in the Bight of Biafra; one Dutch captain sailed nine times from Amsterdam to the Gold Coast. Patterns of trade, once established, were routinely maintained. Knowledge hard won, such as learning the best time to arrive at a specific locale to minimize delays, the optimum size of vessel for a particular market, the availability of local food supplies, the best time to leave an African region for a particular American destination, and so on, tended to keep trade in familiar channels.[28]

Most transatlantic ships disembarked their migrants at a single port in the Americas. European immigrants formed their first impressions of New World society as they picked their way through the busy streets of Philadelphia, Charleston, New York, Boston, Bridgetown, and Kingston. Over 70 percent of 111,000 Germans who arrived in America between 1683 and 1775 landed in Philadelphia, while large numbers of Irish immigrants before the Revolution landed in the Philadelphia and Delaware Valley ports, New York, and Baltimore. The majority of immigrants to Virginia and Maryland, servants and convicts, were sold on shipboard as merchants plied the region's principal rivers. Over 95 percent of slave ships landed all their slaves at one place. An intra-America trade existed, but it was aimed primarily at mainland Spanish America. Most slaves arriving in the Dutch Caribbean, for example, soon ended up on the Spanish Main; and about a fifth of Africans arriving in Jamaica were transshipped to other Spanish Caribbean islands or the mainland. But, for the most part, Africans landed in one territory would remain in it: the notion, for example, that many slaves entering North America had first spent time in the Caribbean is a myth. Only about 5 percent of slaves imported into North America came via the Caribbean; the vast majority came direct from Africa. In any particular American territory, one or two ports generally garnered most arrivals. Over a third of all French slave vessels sailed into just one port, Cap Français in northern Saint Domingue. "In 1790, the peak year of the French slave trade," notes David Geggus, "French ships landed at least 40,000 Africans in Saint Domingue," about a half of them in Cap Français, "a record for any American port to that date." Almost nine out of ten Africans entered Jamaica through Kingston.[29]

The destinations of free and coerced migrants, which, at least in the beginning, were largely the same, diverged over time. Wherever staple crops were produced, the demand for labor was highest; the magnets for all types of migrants, especially in the earliest years, were plantations. Migrants, coerced and free, gravitated to the most highly productive rural areas. Most of the British migrants in the seventeenth century went to the Caribbean, and this region was also the primary destination for Africans. Sugar plantations garnered (literally, consumed, might be a better way of expressing it) a staggering 90 percent of the Africans brought across the Atlantic. But by the end of the seventeenth century, life expectancy in mainland plantation areas had improved significantly over that of the islands, and migrants with a choice tended to head for the healthier zones, either the non-plantation temperate latitudes of North America or the most northerly of the mainland plantation areas. Thus, in the eighteenth century, a marked differential occurred in the destinations of most Europeans and Africans, with the former moving to the temperate parts of North America and the latter to the southern parts and more especially the Caribbean.

Ethnicity and Identity

To what degree were migrants able to transfer their homeland cultures? To what extent were they forced to transform those cultures? What role did ethnicity play in constructing their lives in the New World? Free white settlers, unlike slaves and servants, had much greater opportunities to determine where and with whom they wanted to settle, and many chose to reside with people they deemed of similar background and outlook. Separatists and radical Pietists set out from Europe with the intention of creating communities in America that assuaged their spiritual needs and reflected their social values. Puritans who went to the West Indies, Chesapeake, and New England during the seventeenth century, and German sectaries such as Mennonites, Moravians, Amish, Dunkers, Schwenkfelders, and Waldensians who moved into the backcountry of the Middle and Southern colonies in the eighteenth century frequently migrated in groups and established themselves in distinct settlements. Aside from particular religious or ethnic groups, which were always a tiny minority of the total immigrant flow, German and British settlers did not necessarily set out to create ethnic enclaves in the colonies, but the timing of their arrival coinciding with official and private schemes to populate the frontier with Protestant settlers induced the great majority to move to abundant, fertile lands of the interior where white society evolved as a complex mosaic of European cultures— German, Scotch-Irish, English, Scots, Irish, and French—and where local communities took on distinctive ethnic characteristics of dominant groups.[30]

Slaves never had the luxury to decide with whom to live, but the nonrandom, specialized character of the slave trade often meant that many Africans arrived in a particular New World setting alongside Africans from the same coastal region. Particularly early in the history of many slave societies, one or two African regions supplied most slaves. Thus, in the third quarter of the seventeenth century, for example, three-quarters of the Africans who landed in Barbados came from just two regions: the Bight of Biafra (supplying 48%) and the Bight of Benin (28%). A similar pattern was evident in Jamaica. In the first quarter of the eighteenth century, four-fifths of the island's Africans came from just two regions: the Gold Coast (46%) and the Bight of Benin (34%). As a final example, in the early eighteenth century, just one region, the Bight of Biafra, supplied about 60 percent of Africans to the York Naval District in Virginia, which received more of the colony's Africans than the other four naval districts combined. Africans from the same coastal region, then, often predominated in specific American locales, particularly early in time. A basis for shared communication existed.[31]

Yet, even though many Europeans and Africans arriving in the Americas shared a distinctive local, perhaps ethnic identity, the conception of homogeneous peoples being swept up on one side of the ocean and set down en masse on the other is problematic. Ethnic mixing and the reconstitution of identity started well before the migrants ever set foot on a ship. Even ports in Britain or France that recruited migrants from restricted geographical areas led to the mingling of people from different backgrounds and diverse localities. The high proportion of British and French emigrants from urban backgrounds, for example, suggests that immediate links with local society had been severed before migrants embarked for the mainland and Caribbean. Perhaps no European migration was as diverse as the German-speaking one. The origins of the vast majority of settlers lay within a territorial range stretching from Switzerland to the Middle Rhine, but smaller contingents came from virtually every other region of central Europe. Thousands of migrants left the Neckar Valley and towns west of the Rhine below the Mosel during the middle decades of the century. In the Palatinate, as in the Kraichgau, many towns included numerous Swiss families who had moved into the area a generation or two earlier, some of whom eventually made their way to Pennsylvania in the tide of German migration.[32]

The diversity of immigrants' backgrounds and the high levels of mobility that characterized European society, particularly along the northwestern Atlantic seaboard, D. W. Meinig argues, eroded the sharp edges of regional and (in some cases) national identities. "The Midlands laborer who had spent a decade in London before emigration," he claims, "was already an Englishman in a larger sense; the Glaswegian agent bound for the Potomac who had done a tour of duty in the West Indies was already in some degrees a British American; the man who in his youth had left a Tipperary cottage for the docks of Kinsale . . . was no longer an Irish peasant." Huguenot, Walloon, and Flemish artisans who had lived in England for several years were at least partly anglicized by the time they arrived in the colonies. Particular customs, traditions, dialects, and religious practices continued to exert a powerful influence on people at the local and regional level and remained vital elements of individual and group identity, but such identities were not immutable. Mobility and sustained contact with other peoples and cultures led to the evolution of new identities that frequently coexisted alongside older ones. Settlers took on multiple identities that embraced both inherited Old World traditions and the development of new forms of cultural expression in America.[33]

African Atlantic ports were no more the home communities of slaves than European ports were of servants. Because many African slaves came in tortuous and convoluted ways from the interior to the coast, whatever ethnic identity they originally had was undoubtedly in flux. Identities were no doubt reshaped as slaves moved to the coast, a process often taking months, occasionally years, and as they awaited shipment in the barracoons and in the holds of ships as loading proceeded. Africans employed pidgin and even creole languages on the coast as they tried to communicate with one another. Many slaves became identified by their port of embarkation—Calabars, Cormantees, Pawpas or Popos, and so on. But such identifications masked diversity. To take one example, the identities of so-called Calabars shifted over time. In the first half of the seventeenth century, the ascription encompassed primarily Ijo-speakers, the peoples forced into the trade when Elem Kalabari (later known as New Calabar) was the Bight of Biafra's major port. Later in the century, Bonny and most particularly Old Calabar, located on the Cross River, some 150 kilometers from Elem Kalabari, became the region's primary ports and drew primarily on Efik-speaking peoples, at least in the latter half of the seventeenth century. The common term *Calabar* thereby disguises a radical transformation in the languages spoken by, and even more the identities of, slaves shipped to the Americas. Most Africans went to America either in the company of strangers or with fellow victims of the trade with whom they had only recently become acquainted.[34]

Although local identities were strong in both Europe and Africa, the scale of linguistic and cultural diversity, as well as political decentralization, was far greater in Africa than Europe. Most Africans owed primary allegiance to a small kinship-based unit, a village, or district, not a large political entity. As Karen Fog Olwig notes of Danish West Indian slaves, they "did not seem to identify strongly with nations, so when asked the name of his nation, a slave often responded 'the name of the place where he lived in Guinea.'" To be sure, precolonial state formation shaped group identities in places—the growth of Asante on the Gold Coast and Dahomey on the Slave Coast instilled a degree of unity in those who were incorporated into them—but these tended to be the exceptions. Most other parts of Africa experienced no large-scale political centralization in precolonial times. Furthermore, linguistic and cultural diversity was much greater in Africa than Europe. The Bight of Biafra region, for example, was home to at least four major languages—Yoruba, Igbo, Edo, and Ijo—and their respective dialects, together with many other minor languages, including Efik, which was spoken by many who came to the New World as slaves. To point to the predominance of the Bight of Biafra as a region of origin for a particular New World locale's slave population is therefore not to say that slaves from that region shared an ethnic identity or mutually intelligible language. The proportion of Igbo speakers among slaves entering the Chesapeake, for example, was about a quarter.[35]

Because the development of the nation-state was much more advanced in early modern Europe than Africa, cultural and ethnic heterogeneity in the

Americas could lead, as Ned Landsman has argued for the Scots of central New Jersey, to a strengthening of national identity. The encounter with different cultures in the New World, he suggests, "helped to unify settlers from diverse and seemingly unconnected regional backgrounds under a common national banner," and created "ethnic identities that seemed more Scottish, or more German, or even more English, than their European counterparts." Protestant settlers from Ulster, who might have been of English, Scottish, or Irish ancestry, became commonly known in America as "Irish" or "Scotch-Irish." Immigrants from the Palatinate, Wurttemberg, Hesse-Darmstadt, Nassau-Dillenburg, and dozens of tiny principalities who poured into London in the late spring and summer of 1709 were lumped together simply as "poor Palatines" by the English and the tag stuck when a contingent moved to New York the following year. Subsequently, Swiss and German-speaking migrants were uniformly dubbed "Dutch" or "Palatines."[36]

New identities emerged in the Americas out of disparate African elements, but they did not follow any straightforward national form. Thus, for example, many Africans from the Bight of Biafra who had never heard the name Ibo in their own lands and identified themselves instead by their villages or districts came to accept—at least to some degree—the term abroad. This was ethnogenesis, rather than a strengthening of national identity. Similarly, the Bambara in Louisiana certainly included the ethnic group of that name, generally non-Muslim, comprising the dominant people of the new kingdoms of Segu and Kaarta in eighteenth-century Senegambia, but the term came to include any slave soldier serving in Senegal, many Malinke-speaking peoples, and even all people from east of the Senegal and Gambia Rivers—thereby combining both Bambara and non-Bambara victims of Bambara raiders. Finally, in Cuba, descendants of Yoruba-speakers and some of their neighbors became "Lucumi." "Just as Apulians, Sicilians, and Calabians all became Italians in the United States," George Brandon analogizes, "Oyos, Egbas, Ijebus, and Ijeshus all became Lucumis in Cuba." While Lucumi culture had a Yoruba focus, it incorporated traits from far afield. People sold by the Yoruba became Lucumi; people of Allada and the Ibo were integrated into the so-called Lucumi nation. Some Lucumi words and phrases are not Yoruba in origin, and seem to be Ewe or Fon in derivation. In the New World, invented, reconstituted identities became more wide-ranging than had been true in the homelands.[37]

One reason for this development was the continuing influx of peoples from ever more diverse places in Africa and Europe. As noted, one or two African coastal regions often dominated the early history of a New World slave society, but over time more mixing occurred. By the last quarter of the eighteenth century in Barbados, for example, the two leading African regions supplied only just over half of the island's Africans, and the dominant supplier was now West-Central Africa (at 37%), a region that provided no slaves to the island a century earlier. Similarly, in late eighteenth-century Jamaica, the Bight of Biafra (at 41%) was the leading supplier of Africans, a region that had supplied only a sixth of the island's slaves a century earlier. By the 1730s in York Naval District, Virginia, the Bight of Biafra, though still the primary supplier, was providing less than half of the incoming Africans; West-Central Africa, Senegambia, the Windward Coast, and the Gold Coast provided the rest. Moreover, other naval districts in Virginia received Africans from a much wider range of regions than did York. Increasing heterogeneity is the dominant feature of African migration into most North American and Caribbean regions.[38]

The movement of people from Africa and Europe to the New World and from one part of America to another was closely connected. British Atlantic colonies were not isolated fragments cut off from another. From the beginning, whether or not settlers opted to stay in one place or move elsewhere depended on economic cycles and changing perceptions of opportunity. Thousands of planters and their slaves moved from the West Indies to the mainland, large numbers of Chesapeake settlers eventually ended up in the Carolinas, Pennsylvania, Kentucky, and Tennessee. After 1720, hundreds of thousands of settlers poured into the backcountry, pushing across the Susquehanna River into the rich lands of the Cumberland Valley, south along the Great Wagon Road to the Shenandoah Valley, the Carolinas, and Georgia, and beyond the Appalachians to the vast expanse of the Ohio River basin. Tens of thousands of exiles, black and white, fled from the thirteen colonies to other parts of the Atlantic rim during the American Revolution, while tens of thousands more trekked further into the American interior once the war was over, anticipating the major westward impulse of the nineteenth century. All along the expanding frontier, Irish, German, Swiss, French, Highland Scots, English, and Welsh settlers, together with enslaved African, African Americans, and local Indian tribes, evolved as distinctive societies, where ethnic diversity and cultural borrowing were taken for granted. Colonial societies were always more pluralistic than their metropolitan counterparts. Both whites and blacks in the New World had to absorb a wider range of people than the populations they left behind in the Old World.

Just as ethnic identities were fluid and permeable, so social and cultural development for any group in North America and the Caribbean involved borrowing, adaptation, modification, and invention. Slaves were the most ruthless *bricoleurs*, picking and choosing from a variety of cultural strains, precisely because of the diversity of their origins, the New World experience of being thrown together, and the denial of resources to recreate institutions, languages, and family structures known in their homelands. Their plasticity was of an extreme kind, because they had been subjected to an extreme horror. Nevertheless, the same process of jettisoning what was no longer applicable, adapting what seemed relevant to the new situation, and borrowing from others occurred to Europeans, albeit to a much less marked degree. Both Europeans and Africans of course borrowed from each other and from Native Americans. Both developed significant creole populations within their midst, which entailed yet further transformations. The extent of cultural fusion, syncretism, and blendings in which all newcomers engaged—whether in language, architectural styles, religious exoticism, and so much more—perhaps best summed up in the term, creolization, is the story of all peoples in North America and the Caribbean, to greater or lesser degrees.

CHAPTER TWO

Enslavement of Indians in Early America

Captivity without the Narrative

Joyce E. Chaplin

Most discussions of slavery in British America have focused on African-American slavery, although several thousand native Americans suffered the same fate. Why has the Indian experience received comparatively little attention? It is largely because the number of enslaved Indians—thousands as opposed to the millions of enslaved Africans—has not appeared to merit significant attention and because the Indian slave trade has been mostly understood as a frontier phenomenon, geographically peripheral to the colonies. Yet there are three reasons why this historical problem should be recognized as constitutive of rather than marginal to American history: Indian slavery had tremendous cultural consequences for both British and Indian peoples; its existence questions the way we have read captivity narratives and identified an "American" literature; and it reveals significant debates over the political status of Indians, then and now. If American history is marked by the tension between slavery and freedom, ignoring the Indian experiences of these statuses leaves an enormous gap in the story. This essay will survey the secondary literature, along with selected primary sources, in order to argue that inclusion of Indian slavery in the larger narrative of British Atlantic history would significantly change the nature of that narrative according to the three points stated above.

First, recent scholarship on seventeenth-century New England and the eighteenth-century Lower South has shown that enslavement of Indians served important colonial political and economic functions, indicating that these factors should be examined in other regions. The proportion of Indian people forcibly removed from their societies was in many cases dramatically high, especially after epidemics and warfare reduced the size of Indian nations; the absolute numbers of captives may seem low, but expressed as percentages of surviving groups, they were devastating and provided significant opportunity for settlers to subordinate the survivors. This fact had implications for the overall definitions of natives. The idea of "Indian" still implicitly identifies a person physically and culturally separate from colonial or later U.S. authority. Indian *slaves* were, however, subordinate and proximate to British settlers. Indeed, the U.S. definition of Indians as separate and remote was a result of the colonial enslavement that had made the Indians seem so by alienating them from their native populations and language groups, by sending them as far away as Europe or the West Indies, or by categorizing them as "blacks." Further, the definition of Indians as peoples who lay far within the continent of North America was a result of post-revolutionary rejection of Indian slavery and willed ignorance about the Indians who had lived, or were still living, near and subordinate to white authority. If Indian slavery was an Atlantic development that reduced natives to commodities in order to serve colonial ends, the continentalist idea of Indians as distant inhabitants of a yet-unconquered land was a paradoxical result of that earlier, Atlantic, experience.

Second, recent examination of the genre of the captivity narrative has given copious attention to the experience of English people whom Indians enslaved, a tiny group compared to those Indians enslaved by the English. Because enslaved Native Americans did not write sustained narratives that criticized their oppressors (unlike English or African captives), it has been easier for scholars to generate historiographies on enslaved English and Africans than on Indians. Enslaved Indians are therefore "without" a narrative in two senses: they *lack* the critical body of written testimony that has drawn attention to white captives and black slaves, and (in the early modern sense of the word "without") they are *outside* of several important narratives that have structured colonial American history and delineated status in the greater Atlantic world. We need to reexamine Indians' early writing to detect a distinctive commentary on their own captivity within English culture. Indian slavery is therefore significant as a way to reassess literary expression during English colonization; knowledge of that slavery helps us reclassify our ideas of *English, American,* and *Atlantic* as labels for cultural formation and reformation. The new Atlantic history has been competing with older ideas of a continental American history; looking more carefully at Indians, rather than creole settlers, might help us determine what is Atlantic, and what American, in British America.

Third, English enslavement of Indians, and then the later British and U.S. rejections of that practice, raised intriguing questions about Indians' civil status in the British Empire and the United States. To be a subject under British law carried with it a sense of subordination; colonists realized that enslaved Indians under their authority might be subjects of England or Britain. By the middle of the eighteenth century, most colonial and British authorities agreed that subordinate Indians were subjects, but that the subordination—especially enslavement—which had brought them to this condition ought somehow to be ameliorated. Thus the gradual eighteenth-century movement to reject Indian slavery, as colonial legal cases generated decisions that defined Indians' default status as free. As Indians were released from bondage, the new republic that emerged during and after the American Revolution made parallel decisions to deny Indians status as citizens; the freedom that most Indians gained was a precondition to their exclusion from the states. Residual Indian populations within the areas of white settlement were defined into invisibility, often by being recategorized as "black," both in cases of still-enslaved individuals whom whites classified as more African than Indian and in cases of free Indians whose identity was merged with that of free blacks. These trends demonstrate how the fates of enslaved Indians and Africans were connected and that the manner in which the first group had been freed might have established a blueprint for the latter's emancipation without civil equality.

Indian slavery accordingly reveals important assumptions about assignment of roles within the English-speaking Atlantic world. For this reason, I will look at a broad range of conditions of bondage—including instances where Indians were kidnapped and exhibited in England, were taken as hostages, or were forced to adapt to colonial norms—in order to assess the precise meanings of their exploitation. Most of my evidence comes from the existing, and expanding, secondary literature on Indian slavery and its related problems; what I want to do is point out that these excellent studies of an important

problem have so far failed to have the impact they deserve and to urge scholars to think in ways that would allow study of Indian slavery that greater
impact.[1]

Indian Slaves and European Colonial Strategies

European enslavement of Indians did not begin with the English, but with
the Spanish. Christopher Columbus had been eager to seize the peoples of the
Caribbean, as proof of his contact with the Indies, as subjects for conversion to
Christianity, and as property and labor. The *encomienda* system routinized the
enslavement of Indians for laborers on agricultural estates and in mines. Later
criticism, especially by the Crown and by members of the Dominican order
(particularly Francisco de Vitoria), fueled the argument over the status of Indians and the duties of Christians toward them. That argument culminated with
the famous debate between Bartolomé de Las Casas and Juan Ginés de
Sepúlveda in 1550. As part of his defense of Indians, Las Casas portrayed them
as innocent and delicate, too frail for the burdens and tortures their masters
were heaping upon them. Eventually, the Spanish monarchy regarded Indians
as rational beings who were capable of conversion, as true subjects with access
to the Spanish legal order, and as persons not routinely to be enslaved. Meanwhile, Spanish and Portuguese use of sub-Saharan Africans as slaves, and entry
into a slave trade with Africa, meant that enslaved Africans were conversely represented as foreigners who were fit for hard and degrading work, antitheses of
the delicate Indians who had a political relationship to the Crown. (Las Casas
later repented his recommendation of Africans as slaves.) Spain's New Laws of
1542 formally proscribed Indian slavery except in instances when Indians
resisted missionaries and Spanish authorities. Meanwhile, an African slave
trade accelerated. Other Catholic nations, including the Portuguese and
French, would permit Indian slavery, as would Protestants like the English.
Although Spanish Florida (and later Spanish Louisiana) prohibited most forms
of Indian slavery, the other colonizing powers in North America did not.[2]

The English fostered Indian slavery despite their loud recitations about the
Black Legend, that is, the denunciation of Spanish cruelty (including enslavement of the Indians) that Las Casas had begun but which the English appropriated as part of their colonizing propaganda. Their rhetoric conferred moral
superiority on the English, but in the end the English followed Columbus's
model rather than Las Casas's.[3]

The literature on Indian slavery in the English colonies, however slim, gives the basic outlines of the problem. In 1913, Almon Wheeler Lauber provided what is still the best overview with his *Indian Slavery in Colonial Times within the Present Limits of the United States*. (If anything, Lauber's calculations of the numbers of Indians enslaved are too low.) During King Philip's War, for instance, New Englanders took at least 400 Indians as war captives and kept or sold them as slaves to the West Indies; at this point, Indian slaves greatly outnumbered the handful of enslaved Africans in New England. In Carolina in 1708, there were 1,400 Indian slaves, 4,080 whites, and 4,100 blacks. In 1726, Louisiana had 229 Indian slaves in a population of 1,952 free heads of household, 276 workers and servants, and 1,540 black slaves; subsequently, and as in Carolina, numbers of black slaves rose while those of Indian slaves fell. But English slaving against Indians continued in the South, with South Carolina and Virginia making serial wars against the Apalachee, Tuscarora, Yamassee, Chickasaw, and Choctaw.[4]

In terms of legal structures that regulated enslavement of non-Europeans, Indian slavery was in some ways more significant than African-American slavery. On the continent (in contrast to the Caribbean), statutory recognition of slavery more closely followed the pattern of English enslavement of Indians than of Africans, occurring first in New England (Massachusetts, 1641; Connecticut, 1650) and then in the Chesapeake (Virginia, 1661; Maryland, 1663). Some colonies, including Connecticut and Pennsylvania, but especially New Jersey and Maryland, nevertheless had very few Indian slaves despite proximity to native populations. Other colonies later proscribed certain kinds of Indian slavery, especially imports from other colonies, which were banned from Rhode Island in 1676 and from New York in 1679. New York was especially keen to prohibit imports of slaves from Spanish Central America and even returned such slaves to Spanish territories. These bans did not necessarily end Indian slavery. In South Kingston, Rhode Island, for instance, there were 935 whites in 1730, along with 333 blacks and 223 Indian slaves. Until the Revolutionary War, advertisements for runaway Indian slaves appeared in the *Boston News-Letter*.[5]

Since Lauber, no one has attempted a comparable, updated view of Indian slavery throughout the British colonies. Barbara Olexer has done a narrative overview that lacks analysis or assessment of sources; Yasuhide Kawashima and Peter H. Wood have briefly surveyed Indian servitude in, respectively, the northeast and southeast of North America. More recent work has looked at specific regions, colonies, or Indian groups. The Lower South has attracted the most attention because South Carolina was most involved in slave raiding and trading, with activities that peaked during the Yamassee War of 1715–17. Alan Gallay has given a fresh look at the dimensions of the Indian slave trade in the Lower South, estimating that, from 1670 to 1715, between 24,000 and 51,000 Indians were sold, mostly abroad. Hilary Beckles has established West Indian demand for slaves from the continent. Examinations of slavery in the lower Mississippi Valley and Ohio Valley have likewise pointed out the presence and cultural significance of enslaved Indians in these regions; African slaves were more common in the former place, but among the *habitants* of the Ohio Valley in the 1730s, Indian slaves outnumbered African slaves. And as mentioned above, labor-hungry English colonists took Indians from Spanish territory in Central America.[6]

More recently, scholars have emphasized the implications of Indian slavery for regions outside the colonial Lower South. Indian slavery had a disastrous impact in New England, where the English combined enslavement with war as a deliberate strategy to break the power of Indian groups and to clear land for colonial settlement. New attention to the Chesapeake, building on Edmund Morgan's careful analysis of the multiple origins of slavery in Virginia, has pointed out that colonists there were quick to take Indians as slaves and to sell them to the West Indies. Scholars who want to see the full range of these local studies can consult Russell M. Magnaghi's extremely useful bibliography on *Indian Slavery, Labor, Evangelization and Captivity in the Americas* (1998). This compendium includes material on all new world regions as well as white captivity narratives and has bracingly forthright annotations for each entry.[7]

Together, these studies show the extent of Indian slavery, both in terms of the territory it covered and the peoples it involved: all regions of British America and all colonies had Indian slaves and a broad array of peoples were enslaved, from former allies of the English (such as Tuscarora), to individuals who were taken from powerful Indian nations (including the Creek), to members of smaller and more vulnerable groups (such as the Patuxet or Guale). The English enslaved Indians in every part of North America they settled, or where they wanted to stake a claim, as in territories within or bordering Spanish Florida and French Louisiana, and they carried away captive peoples to exhibit in Britain itself. The Indian slave trade connected the continent to the West Indies, drawing together distant and disparate colonists while it violently redistributed Indian peoples over all colonial regions. Indeed, English use of the generic term *Indian* to describe radically different persons was perhaps a verbal manifestation of willingness to regard America's natives as easily uprooted and transplanted.

It is above all significant that the English took American natives captive long before they brought African captives to America and even as they recited the horrors of the Black Legend. The first native captives appear in the records in 1502, evidently being some men that an English ship's crew had brought from "the new found isle" in the west. The next recorded victims were Inuit, one man whom Frobisher took in 1576 and then three more people in 1577. Other captives were taken at Roanoke and in New England, including the Roanok men Manteo and Wanchese, the Abenaki man Skidwarres, the Wampanoag man Epenow, and—best known—the Patuxet man Squanto. By 1610, Neal Salisbury has concluded, English slave-raiding along the North American coast "had become routine." In Shakespeare's day, public exhibition of live Indians and of preserved Indian corpses had already become a byword for English curiosity about the exotic. The search for native captives in America therefore preceded any systematic English trade in African slaves.[8]

Further, it preceded English use of, perhaps even knowledge of, any Indian slaveholding and slave trading. Though much of the scholarship on English enslavement of Indians begins with these pre-Columbian practices, it seems unlikely that English propensity to regard Indians as moveable property (rather than as subjects of political and legal systems worth the respect of Europeans) could not have existed without such practices. The English plucked Indians and Inuit from North America long before they comprehended the dimensions of native populations or their laws or trading systems. The size of the English trade in native slaves might have been smaller in the absence of Indian slaveholding, but the trade needed no indigenous spark to start it.[9]

Enslavement filled English demands for labor or profits, but it was also a strategic maneuver to establish English authority. Select individuals, for instance, were proffered or taken as hostages, as when Englishmen at Jamestown seized the female leader of the Paspahegh (and her children) in 1610. Massachusetts sentenced Indians to slavery for certain crimes, a punishment not applied to white criminals and evidently meant to impress Indians with the might of colonial law. In other cases, groups designated as dangerous or obstructive were subjected to war and enslavement, a fate that befell the Pequot and Wampanoag in New England, whose wartime survivors (of the 1630s and 1670s, respectively) were considered lawful slaves, many of whom were sold to the West Indies. During Bacon's Rebellion, Nathaniel Bacon held up the prospect of taking Indians as slaves as an incentive for his supporters; he meant any Indians, whether allied to Virginia or not. In more conventional terms, the English considered enslaveable the Lower South's Yamassee, Tuscarora, and Apalachee because they were on the wrong side of conflict.[10]

This was above all a demonstration of English colonial power: designated tribes or nations were reduced in numbers by deliberately genocidal military tactics and then the survivors treated as slaves. These intentions were clearly stated in Tom Law's poem *The Rebels Reward* (1724), which described the 1720s conflict between New Englanders and the Abenaki who denied British authority over them. English troops killed the Indians, razed their villages, and took away plunder:

> They brought away a Squaw
> and likewise Children three
> Which only were preserved
> our Bond Slaves for to be.[11]

If some Indians were considered as property, other natives were held against their will by English people or were coerced into remaining with the English, enduring captivity of another sort. Early cases of kidnapped Indians and Inuit taken to England set this pattern. Powhatan's daughter Pocahontas is the most famous example of this captivity as state of limbo. When betrayed by other Indians and handed over to the English at Jamestown, and after her father declined to ransom her, Pocahontas converted to Christianity and married an Englishman. While legal marriage to an English person would not be common for even anglicized Indians, others shared Pocahontas's ambiguous fate. Consider the case of an Indian wife of an English trader in eighteenth-century South Carolina. Her husband's will set her free (and gave her two other Indian slaves as her property) but stipulated that their mestizo children should be raised by white friends; the woman, though manumitted, was alienated from her people and her children alienated from her. As with these children, some individuals were removed to be educated, either in schools or in colonial households; removal trained Indians not to be Indians. One Massachusett man, Caleb Cheeshautemauk, even graduated from Harvard College in 1665.[12]

Others who had been taken from their peoples found their way to English settlements, maintaining a nominal freedom despite their literal and cultural orphanhood. This was what happened to Squanto, who returned from slavery in England and Spain to discover he was the last surviving Patuxet and opted for friendship with the Pilgrims at Plymouth. In the early eighteenth century, the Towasa man Lamhatty, who had been enslaved by Creeks and then traded to the Shawnee, eventually traveled to Virginia where he was a servant of Colonel John Walker. Initially, "noe body" could be found who "understands his language" but then some of "his Country folks" were located. Lamhatty then provided information to Walker and Robert Beverley about his homeland on Florida's Gulf Coast, the basis of a 1708 English map of the area. Eventually he "became verry melancholly" in his captivity, "often fasting & crying Several days together," and then suddenly Lamhatty "went away & was never more heard of."[13]

Two other types of captivity existed: among Indian groups that remained within English settlements and under colonial law and among groups that survived near the settlements and tried to maintain independence from colonial law. Especially in New England, scattered Indian neighborhoods and even towns survived through the colonial period, subordinate to—yet separate from—the surrounding English settlements, and therefore termed *Settlement Indians*. The Virginia Pamunkey, Massachusetts Mashpee, and Carolina Catawba are examples of the latter experience, in which small, surviving Indian nations carefully kept themselves Indian rather than accept full anglicization and submit to English control. Arguments have been made for a similar cultural survival among "Praying Indians," those Christian Indians who lived in Praying Towns in Massachusetts and Plymouth. While these communities were small, their heroic effort to maintain some degree of freedom from the English makes them important as examples of the complex ways in which Indians had to monitor threats to their liberty and cultural autonomy. They were partial hostages or captives to English plans for expanded settlement.[14]

The regionally focused studies that look at Indian slavery have begun to give a more precise sense of the dimensions of the Anglo-Indian slave trade and to indicate its contribution to economic development. Any estimate of the capital accumulation represented by Indian slaves sold to the West Indies would shed essential light on the development of commercial economies in the colonies. Work being done at the University of Kansas is attempting to measure the level of capital improvement that Indian labor created in early America. Even a rough estimate would be invaluable, indicating which places, problems, and industries warrant further attention. At the moment, the tendency is still to assume that Indian slavery played a larger part in the southern colonies than in northern ones. But this may have more to do with the development of regional historiographies than with historical reality. We tend to think of New Englanders, in relation to Indians, as captives; we think of Southerners, in relation to Indians, as slave traders. In part, this reflects differences between Indians in the northeast versus those of the southeast: the former region had a smaller Indian population and (outside Iroquoia) less powerful confederations. There would indeed have been fewer Indians for New Englanders to enslave and an Indian population that keenly wanted white war captives to avenge their dead and supplement their dwindling populations. Southern regions meanwhile had larger and more powerful populations, hence the perception that there were that many more Indian people for colonists to enslave.

But these different views of northern and southern colonies were products of contemporary colonial sources. New England puritans wanted to represent themselves as a people much tested by the Lord; their captivity among Indians was partial proof of their place in the cosmic scheme of things. Southern settlers, meanwhile, wanted to present themselves as successful entrepreneurs who made profits from the resources they found in America, including Indian labor. Historians have followed their subjects' leads; hence Alan Gallay has emphasized the economic significance of Indian trading to members of Georgia's Bryan family, and John Demos has stressed the spiritual significance of Indian captivity to members of the Williams family. But we must acknowledge the converse situations, the better to understand the economic importance of Indian slaves to New England's Winthrops and the cultural importance of Indian slavery to Georgia's McIntoshes.[15]

Indian and African Enslavement

Captive and enslaved Indians were thus spread throughout the colonies and their very ubiquity says much about longstanding English assumptions about their own cultural superiority and imperial destiny. Yet several important problems in colonial (and U.S.) history have not taken Indian slavery into account and several misapprehensions about slavery and Indians persist. Indian slavery is still seen as incidental: it was an option that the English supposedly took up only reluctantly, one that they never chose above enslavement of Africans, and one that built upon or exploited existing forms of Indian slavery, requiring little English effort to instigate. It is as if scholarly explanations of Indian slavery have stumbled over the Spanish decision *not* to enslave Indians (and to import African slaves) and have assumed that this must have set a precedent for subsequent European colonization of the Americas. Again, English repetition of the Black Legend has done much to occlude our view of the past by excluding Indian slavery from the received versions of early American history and of the history of slavery.

Much of the general history of slavery is still understood to mean the history of enslavement of Africans and African Americans. So, for example, the year 1619 is the usual mark of the beginning of slavery in anglophone America, because it is the first date by which we know that servants of African descent were living in Virginia. Likewise, slavery is assumed to end between 1865 and 1877 with the defeat of the Confederate States of America and with Reconstruction, disregarding the eradication of Indian slavery that occurred before. The important moments for the definition and dissolution of slavery remain tied to the fates of enslaved Africans.

Even within this specialized focus, however, there are two different patterns set by Winthrop D. Jordan and David Brion Davis. Jordan has tended to discount the significance of Indian slavery to the broader history of slavery, while Davis has seen it as an important foundation for the exploitation of peoples of African descent. Subsequent scholars have followed either Davis or Jordan. Jordan's *White over Black* has, for example, emphasized English tendencies to think better of Indians than of Africans, and Jordan has concluded that Indian slavery "never became an important institution in the colonies." George Fredrickson has agreed that Indians were mostly not "integrated into the European economy as a source of labor." John Elliott, echoing Fredrickson and others who consider Indian slavery as unimportant in Anglo-America, draws a sharp contrast between Spanish and British America. He sees the Spanish as more willing to mix (however forcibly) with Indians, while the English kept natives as far away as possible. The dates within the title of Peter Kolchin's *American Slavery, 1619–1877* indicate the equation between black slavery and slavery *tout court*, and Kolchin has stressed that Indian slavery "never reached very substantial proportions." Robin Blackburn and Ira Berlin have simply assumed this point; Blackburn's recent overview of new world slavery has discussed Indian slavery only in the Iberian cases, and Berlin has only pointed out that Indian slaves were gradually swallowed up in the larger African-American slave population in North America, disregarding the implications of this shift in proportions among racially defined populations. David Eltis's African focus

on *The Rise of African Slavery in the Americas* left him only a little room to discuss enslavement of Indians. Betty Wood is therefore unusual in her careful and
illuminating attention to the interconnected histories of Indian and African
enslavement.[16]

Scholars studying slavery in particular regions have more successfully con-
nected the experiences of Indians and Africans. Foundational work by Peter
Wood and Edmund Morgan, and the recent studies of Daniel Usner, Philip
Morgan, and Alan Gallay, have assessed Indian and African enslavement in
South Carolina, Virginia, and Louisiana. Each place had Indian slaves and
English people whose attitudes about slavery were very much informed by
their experience with Indians as well as Africans. These works follow Davis's
insistence that African slavery built on and never truly diverged from the
modes by which Europeans (including the English) enslaved Indians.[17]

Indian slavery is still easily dismissed because of the often repeated notion
that the English thought Indians made bad workers. Arguments for English
preference for African slaves have stressed four factors: body (belief that Indians were weak and sickly), culture (Indians were haughty and disinclined to
perform demeaning work for others), security (fear that Indians from nearby
tribes could more easily escape than enslaved Africans and then avenge themselves through warfare), and demography (Indians were never a very substantial labor pool, especially once their numbers began to dwindle from epidemics
and war). Lauber laid out these reasons in 1913 and, by and large, historians
have followed rather than questioned him. Again, David Brion Davis proves the
exception, warning that the "medical" explanation is especially overstated; it
certainly provided no detectable curb on English pursuit of Indian captives.[18]

The cultural explanation itself suffers from a logical flaw. Statements that
Indians were unsuited to slavery sit awkwardly with contentions that Indians
themselves practiced slavery and expected submission from those war captives
designated as potential adoptees. Both positions (Indians made poor slaves;
Indians were the ones who fueled the native slave trade) appear in dismissals
of Indian slavery, as if together they constituted proof of the practice's
marginality to the English rather than contradicting each other. William Bartram displayed the longevity of this contradiction when in the 1790s he stated
that Indians were wild people who "make war against, kill, and destroy their
own species" but that their own slaves were "the tamest, the most abject creatures that we can possibly imagine: mild, peaceable, and tractable." Again stating without resolving the paradox, Bartram said "the free Indians, on the

contrary, are bold, active, and clamorous. [Masters and slaves] differ as widely from each other as the bull from the ox." In fact, English opinions on the suitability of enslaved Indians for work were by no means unanimously low; Caribbean assessments may have been different. In 1652, Barbados resident Richard Ligon said that Indians were "very active . . . and apt to learne any thing, sooner then the *Negroes*," though they were "craftier" and less reliable.[19]

Nor did the English dismiss Indians as constitutionally unfit for hard work. Instead, the English assumed that Indians (like Africans) inherited remarkable bodily strength, especially resistance to pain and fatigue. Discussions of male warriors' prowess in battle and their fortitude when tortured contributed to this conclusion; a parallel argument asserted that Indian women were inured to hard agricultural work and experienced little or no pain in childbirth. Africans had similar characteristics, the English maintained, as well as good resistance to disease, something that Indians lacked. But this Indian weakness, while encouraging colonists to imagine that the native population would dwindle and recede, was not part of a sustained argument that Indians made bad workers. Indeed, the belief that Indian women gave birth remarkably easily, with little pain, and that they could return to work shortly thereafter, resembled similar thinking about African women. Far from thinking that Indians were unfit for slavery, there may have been an idea that it improved them. Thomas Jefferson, even as he criticized Indian slavery, suggested that Indian women produced more children in captivity: "the Indian women so enslaved produced and raised as numerous families as either the whites or blacks among whom they lived." These assessments make clear that colonists thought Indians' bodily fortitude and fecundity made them worth enslaving.[20]

Finally, the argument that the small numbers of Indian slaves make the phenomenon marginal gets us nowhere. True, the numbers of Indian slaves were smaller than those of African slaves. But the absolute figures tell us little about the impact of slavery on native communities; slaves as percentages of Indian populations would give a better sense of what was at stake. For example, North Carolinians sold slightly over 400 Tuscarora into bondage during the Tuscarora War (1711–13), a number which was over half of the estimated Indian population outside colonized areas in North Carolina. The 5,500 slaves that white South Carolinians extracted before 1752 represented slightly over 5 percent of the larger southeast's entire Indian population—the percentage would of course have increased over the course of the century, as native population declined. When the French took approximately 450 slaves out of the Natchez nation between 1729 and 1731, that enslaved group (most of whom were sold in St. Domingue) outnumbered the survivors who sought refuge with the Chickasaw. In short, slavery, like war and epidemics, drastically diminished native population and even (in cases of smaller Indian language groups) assisted extinction. Historians who wish to argue that Indian slavery was not very significant should consider carefully: not significant for whom?[21]

Narratives of Captivity

It is especially unjust that Indian slavery is dismissed because of its "small" numbers when an even smaller group, white captives of Indians, have had so much scholarly attention lavished upon them. That white captivity explained something primal about the colonial experience has long been an assumption of those who study early American history and literature. The first scholars of the captivity narrative singled it out as a peculiarly American genre and sometimes gave it a generative role in the formation of an American literature; it seemed to describe a uniquely American fate and revealingly positioned white American culture on a frontier between Europeans and Indians. The genesis of American culture and identity seemed to have resulted from violent contact with Indians, and the captivity narrative became evidence for American exceptionalism.[22]

In the past decade, however, scholars have questioned the American-ness of the captivity narrative, pointing out that it was an Old World genre transplanted to the Western Hemisphere. At least since the Crusades, European Christians had experienced enslavement by Muslims in the Near East and North Africa. Redeemed captives who testified that they had not turned infidel constructed the foundation for all later captivity literature, which burgeoned in the late Middle Ages and the early modern period, as Europeans faced new conflicts with non-Christians. The Hebrew Bible, especially accounts of the Babylonian captivity of the ancient Jews, shaped Catholic and later Protestant comprehension of having to live subject to idolaters and pagans. The captivity narrative thus had both old-world and transatlantic significances for European migrants who found themselves subordinated to alien peoples and wished to record their fate as part of a cosmic plan in which God severely tried his chosen people.[23]

Recent scholarship on English and American literatures has likewise emphasized a larger, Atlantic context for the captivity narrative. Scholars of

Samuel Richardson's novel, *Pamela* (1740), have noted its similarity to captivity narratives, especially Mary Rowlandson's germinal *Sovereignty and Goodness of God* (1682); both narratives have female protagonists held by godless male kidnappers and their female accomplices, and both women uphold their Christian faith during bondage. In this way, English and American literature were linked rather than divided by the Atlantic and they converged as much as they diverged. No longer is the captivity narrative a peculiarly American genre indicative of an exceptional white creole identity.[24]

In similar fashion, scholars have placed black slave narratives in the larger captivity genre. One of the most widely read Indian captivity narratives was in fact the account of a free black man, John Marrant, who lived among the Cherokee in the late eighteenth century. Slave narratives proper, that is, written testimony that escaped or former slaves gave of their experience in bondage, greatly resembled Christian captivity narratives. Freed slaves, such as Olaudah Equiano and Harriet Jacobs, drew on the scriptural format of bondage among the infidel to make sense of their trials; they were especially powerful in denouncing their white masters and mistresses as godless infidels, Christians in name only.[25]

These developments in the fields of English and American literature deepen our comprehension of the transatlantic past—a past that remarkably connects the disparate experiences of captives among Turks, Iroquois, or Alabama planters—but they draw our attention away from Indians and from their experience of the Anglo-Indian frontier, which were also important parts of the post-Columbian experience. This atlanticization (or globalization) of the captivity narrative has perhaps gone too far. We should not return to the old view of American exceptionalism; nor should "Atlantic" become a grab-bag in which we deposit all manner of texts. We should distinguish between cases of literary convergence and mere parallels. Those who have labored to locate the island on which William Shakespeare set *The Tempest* have warned us to be careful to understand that the island is *in* the Mediterranean but also gestures *toward* the Caribbean; those gestures define very specific convergences between old and new worlds. The Rowlandson–Richardson case is unlikely to have even this limited convergence. It is more likely a parallel between American and English genres rather than convergence: no one has demonstrated that Richardson read Rowlandson and then snatched up a pen to create *Pamela*, merely that the two stories were similar and perhaps resonated similarly to the same audience.[26]

A better case for convergence between old and new worlds appeared in a different strain of fiction, one that emphasized Indian slavery. These were English stories about the Caribbean, the most famous example being Daniel Defoe's *Robinson Crusoe* (1719). The historical Alexander Selkirk, the unfortunate Scot whose ordeal loosely inspired *Robinson Crusoe*, had lived alone on a Pacific Ocean island; on his Atlantic island, Crusoe captures and enslaves Friday, a native of a neighboring island off South America. How did Defoe imagine Friday into being?

Enslavement of Caribbean natives had been a trope of European literature about America since the 1500s and remained a surprisingly distinctive element of English stories about the Caribbean. Crusoe's popularity was rivaled by that of the story of Inkle and Yarico, an Englishman and his Caribbean Indian mistress, whom he betrays and sells into slavery, pausing only to raise her price when he learns that she is carrying their child. Richard Ligon first told the story in 1657 and it went through over sixty versions in eight European languages before 1808. It was treated in poems and an opera; at the height of its popularity, Goethe considered doing his own version and Mary Wollstonecraft included one in a literary anthology. We have been told again and again that Rowlandson's and other captivity narratives were bestsellers, but they clearly had competition. As the creation of Yarico and Friday show, the English (and Europeans generally) were at least as fascinated by enslaved Indians as they were by white captives of Indians.[27]

Scholars of early America continue, however, to regard the white captivity narrative as the Ur-text of American "identity." Peter Mancall and Jill Lepore have recently used this label to describe accounts dating from King Philip's War in the 1670s; David Waldstreicher has applied the term to the experience of prisoners of war during the American Revolution. But these statements of American-ness show the maturation rather than the genesis of the captivity narrative in America—the genre had probably entered its baroque period, in which metaphor and embellishment were proliferating accretions upon the basic storyline.[28]

If there was anything "American" about captivity, it was the Indians' experience of being held, against their will, within colonial English culture. They, much more than English captives of Indians, had to formulate a new means of expression, one that indeed was a metalogue of their newly atlanticized condition: writing in English exemplified the experience of captivity among the English. Ethnohistorians have recognized that colonists' education of Indians was mostly done by force and that educated Indians used their bitter gain to critique their educators. Interestingly, Indians referred to the acquisition of literacy as a form of captivity. Virginia's Governor Alexander Spotswood wrote in 1711 that Indians feared that children sent to the College of William and Mary would be enslaved. Eleazar Wheelock related that Indian parents wanted him to treat their children (whom he taught) with the kindness "according to which they are wont to treat their Captives." Samson Occom wrote that his education resulted from entrapment by the determined Jonathan Barber. Indian children "used to take Care to keep out of [Barber's] way," but "he used to Catch me Sometimes and make me Say over my Letters."[29]

Furthermore, converted or anglicized Indians who became literate were sometimes in a condition that resembled captivity. Praying Indians on the islands of Martha's Vineyard and Chappaquidick were physically cut off, both from other Indians and from settlement populations. Even their patrons recognized their geographic and cultural specificity; one of the missionaries called them "*Island-Indians*" as opposed to "the Multitudes of *Indians* then on the *Main* [land]." Jill Lepore has pointed out that literate Indians were dangerously subject to attacks both from English and from non-anglicized Indians; they were truly alienated. Their plight should adjust our sense of what narratives by ostensibly free (because not legally enslaved) Indians may have been saying.[30]

Categorization of captivity narratives therefore needs to be reworked—the English creole place within it demoted and Indian narratives re-assessed as possible descriptions of captivity. Reading Samson Occom alongside examples of white captives like Mary Rowlandson and Mary Jemison would, for instance, be highly useful. Jemison, an English girl who grew up among the Iroquois and thought of herself as Iroquois, wrote an account of her life that has been classified as a captivity narrative. But in contrast to Rowlandson, Jemison did not think of herself as a captive; and in contrast to Samson Occom, she did not use the themes of trial by God and isolation from one's native culture that typified the classic captivity narrative.[31]

Reexamination of Indian writings, such as those of Occom, as an important type of captivity narrative would force us to make some more intelligent decisions in the ongoing discussion about old-world versus new-world voices and genres, which has tended to consider only the comparison between metropolitan and creole whites. The comparison sharpens if we included early examples of Indian writing that reveal Indian regret at being held hostage in their native lands and that use slavishness as a strategy of resistance. Consider one of the

Mashpee Indian petitions, this from 1752 (translated from Massachusett), that their land rights be respected: "Oh! Our honorable gentlemen and kind gentlemen in Boston . . . Oh!, Oh!, gentlemen, hear us now, Oh! ye, us poor Indians." Ability to write and deploy European cultural idioms also permitted Indians to record their sufferings as versions of the spiritual trials recounted in white captivity narratives. Thus another Massachusett speaker wrote in the margin of an Algonquian Bible, "I am not able to defend myself from the happenings in the world."[32] Discourse on freedom and slavery is at the foundation of imperial and American literatures; to include Indian captivity in this phenomenon would enrich our understanding of it.

Enslavement and Hybridity

Even as we cast a stronger light on early Indian writing in order to explain a genuine American captivity within a broader range of *Atlantic* experiences, we should also reexamine the extent to which Indian slavery made colonists' experiences *American,* that is, different from that which existed across the Atlantic. Understanding the extent and penetration of Indian slavery—and therefore of Indian people—into colonial settlements makes those settlements look less European and more hybrid. This is a possibility that historians have been slow to recognize, instead seeing colonial societies as variations on those back in the Old World. Most discussions of hybridity see it as a condition that explains something about post-Columbian Indian societies, which seemed to adopt captives, objects, and customs from outsiders at faster rates than did colonial societies. This is suspiciously lopsided, however, and comprehending how Indians (and their possessions and ideas) were forcibly included in colonial settlements may give us a more accurate view of things.[33]

It is likewise striking that colonial historiography has assumed that whites and Indians were separated culturally and physically in a way we no longer assume to be the case for whites and Africans or African Americans. The most recent monographs on enslaved Indians have made the experience seem remote from English settlements, either on the frontiers of these places or in regions settled by other European groups. But the situation that James F. Brooks has described for the southwest in *Captives and Cousins* (2002), where slavery mingled populations on every possible social level, might have existed in areas of British America. We recognize that black slavery's exploitation involved intimate contact and violation. Recent scholarship that has explored sexual relations between blacks and whites, and the resulting interpenetration of white and black families, has underscored the connections between peoples of African and European descent in the United States. What we have not yet examined is how this forced intimacy might also describe contact between enslaved Indians and whites. If Indian slaves were scattered through all the colonies, Indians were not geographically isolated from white settlements.[34]

Closer analysis of Indian slavery therefore sheds light on the nature and extent of "racial" mixture or mestizoism in early America. Recognition that the colonies had mestizo or métis populations has been much better realized in works on the Lower South, New France, and the lower Mississippi Valley— indeed, all recent work on the latter region has stressed the eventual mixture of Indians, Africans, and Europeans. Peter Wood has detected the use of the Spanish term *mustee* (a person of Indian-African ancestry) in eighteenth-century South Carolina. Further, sexual unions between black and Indian slaves, and a tendency (in English, Spanish, and French colonial law) to connect African ancestry with subordinate status, meant that mustee peoples were eventually submerged, either within the white population or in the populations of slaves and free blacks, depending on local and personal circumstances. This does not mean that such features were unknown outside the Lower South and Louisiana; mixture of Indians and Africans occurred even in New England.[35]

This mixing allowed whites increasingly to classify people of composite ancestry as not truly Indian. That is, people who came under the classifications of mestizo, métis, or mustee would lack the default free identity associated with whites and would eventually be denied the few benefits of Indian, that is tribal, identity. The latter dilemma would, by the nineteenth century, confront mestizo peoples in the United States and métis in Canada. Moreover, persons with mixed Indian and African parentage would, over time, be classified as black. The term mustee was less often used to identify Indian ancestry; instead, anyone with African ancestry was denominated as black and often as enslaved. In this manner, Indian slaves and Indian slavery become invisible (to whites) because by the eighteenth century they were subsumed under the labels that described the larger and therefore more visible population of black slaves. More attention to this process of erasure, including Indian reactions to it, is necessary, not least to discredit the continuing assumption that people of mixed ancestry cannot be Indian.[36]

Cultural mixture is as important a phenomenon as mestizoism, but we do not know much about the impact Indian slaves had on colonial cultures. Did their status differ markedly to that of free Indian servants? What tasks did they perform in which regions? Did slaves or hostages instruct colonists in how to raise corn or tobacco, or did free Indians accomplish this? Did Indian slaves perform much of the labor in the southern forest industries? What did it mean to have an Indian slave in a colonial household? How about several Indian slaves? This last question has received attention only when Indian slaves seemed to make trouble, hence the work on Tituba in Salem, Massachusetts, where the 1692 witchcraft controversy shoved her into the spotlight. But in many other instances, and in quieter ways, Indians must have influenced households and individuals. Stephen Longfellow (great-great-grandfather of the poet who wrote *Hiawatha* and *Evangeline*) was by 1727 a fellow member in the Byfield, Massachusetts, church with his Indian slave. Longfellow's experience may have been surprisingly common. In 1774 in Rhode Island, 35.5 percent of that colony's Indians lived (as slaves and servants) in white households. Because of Indian slavery, the little commonwealths, peaceable kingdoms, and plantation households of early America contained and were affected by Indians.[37]

Slaves, Subjects, and Citizens

If the practice of Indian slavery has received little attention, English debate about this enslavement has had even less. Most of the literature on English perceptions of the justice of colonial Indian policies focuses on the seventeenth century and sees a logical continuation from Spanish debates of the sixteenth century; Roger Williams's writings on Indian land rights are counterparts to the Las Casas–Sepulveda debates several generations earlier in New Spain. But a second and possibly more important phase of debate began in the late seventeenth century and continued through the eighteenth, forming a little-recognized precedent for subsequent criticism of the Atlantic slave trade and, eventually, black slavery.[38]

Roger Williams had been unusual in his concern, midway through the seventeenth century, over English treatment of Indians. By the 1670s and 1680s, however, more and more powerful figures wondered whether Indians benefited from English colonization in the New World. The strongest criticisms came from New England missionaries, whose current place in the literature classifies them as imperialists, determined to destroy Indian religion and custom in order to reduce natives to Christian civility. This negative view is not inaccurate, yet some evangelizers had more complex views of Indians and their cultures. John Eliot deplored colonists' abuse of his Praying Indians, as many New England colonists refused to distinguish between types of Indians. Further, English supporters of the missionary effort saw good reason to permit Indians a degree of cultural continuity. Robert Boyle (president of the evangelizing New England Company that financed missionaries like Eliot) requested that Indian converts *not* be dissuaded from using their native languages lest they lose the ability to nudge other Indians toward Christianity.[39]

Criticism of violence toward Indians within British territories increased. During the 1660s, the Commissioners of the United Colonies in New England, an alliance among the northernmost colonies, kept asking the New England Company for matériel to use against nonallied Indians; Boyle declined by reminding the commissioners that the company must "abate all charge that is not Essentiall to the being of this good worke" of evangelization. Like Boyle, John Locke had strikingly pacific attitudes toward Indian religions and disapproved the use of force in order to convert them: "Not even *Americans,* subjected unto a Christian Prince, are to be punished either in Body or Goods, for not imbracing our Faith and Worship." As secretary to Anthony Ashley Cooper, Locke was involved in the Carolina proprietors' attempts to regulate the Indian trade in Carolina and to prevent Indian slavery. None of this is to say that Boyle and Locke had fully tolerant and respectful views of Indians; Locke's argument that civil people were justified in taking lands in which human labor had not been mixed was an important moment in defining English superiority over Indians. But if there had once been a long list of accepted abuses of Indians, some items were being struck from the list.[40]

These humanitarian efforts toward Indians eventually criticized slavery. The proselytizing Associates of Dr. Bray, for instance, were important in envisioning American colonies that did not rely on slavery; Georgia was an experiment in part inspired by the Associates. The Georgia Trustees' challenge to black slavery is well known, but they accompanied it with a ban on Indian slave trading which, as earlier in Carolina, proved ineffective. Other legal challenges to enslavement of Indians were more successful and showed a creeping suspicion that Indians' status as free peoples should be recognized. The earliest bans of Indian slavery (on imports to Rhode Island and New York, discussed above) were primarily concerned with security; during the 1670s Indian wars in New England and Virginia, legislators in Rhode Island and New York did not want defeated and angry people to be sent to their colonies. But the laws had no implication for the Indians already held as slaves.[41]

A stronger attack on Indian slavery occurred in Virginia. A 1691 act that declared legal any act of trade with any Indian could later be construed to mean that Indians were free persons capable of independent actions. A similar act restated the point in 1705. And in 1777 the House of Burgesses declared that any Indians brought into Virginia since the 1705 act were not slaves; this free status extended to their descendants. Court cases from 1792 and 1793 widened the implications of earlier legislation to declare all Indians free, a point the Supreme Court of Virginia made again in 1806 and 1808. In South Carolina, a 1740 act clarifying the categories of persons who could be held as slaves excepted "free Indians in amity with this government," a clause that came to mean that the burden of proof for enslaved status for an Indian was on the claimant, not on the Indian. Therefore, in both South Carolina and Virginia, Indians were assumed to be free unless proved otherwise; over time, the burden of proof became too great to be legally maintained. In New York and Rhode Island, prohibitions on imports of Indian slaves and growing disinclination to use law to protect slaveholders chipped away at Indian slavery. Other colonies did not take action; aside from Virginia, South Carolina, Rhode Island, and New York, "none of the colonies ever declared Indian slavery illegal."[42]

Yet the erosion of Indian slavery should inform scholars' discussions of the American Revolution's "contagion of liberty" and the northern colonies'/states' "first emancipation" of black slaves. Knowing that revolutionary Virginia and South Carolina—the first divided over slavery and the latter deeply committed to it—had already questioned the enslavement of Indians should make scholars approach revolutionary-era debates about freedom and bondage with new insights. That New York was dismantling Indian slavery but Massachusetts did not should likewise make us think more carefully about the "first" emancipation in these and other northern states. Yet the key work on the first emancipation ignores Indians altogether, and recent studies of individual states' actions in relation to slaves during and after the Revolution have privileged the narrative about enslaved Africans.[43]

Attacks on Indian slavery were accompanied by questions about Indians' political status. Colonial and metropolitan laws described Indians in a variety of ways, ranging from enemy or neutral aliens, aliens under Crown protection, denizens or residents of the colonies, or subjects. Even within each of these categories, distinctions abounded. Naturalization effected by the Crown was less definitive than that done by Parliament; naturalization performed in the colonies was not always recognized in the metropole, as colonial Jews would discover.[44] Multiple legal or political statuses were thus available to Indians. All were initially aliens, as far as colonizers were concerned. Subject status was the least likely category for Indians at the start of English colonization but became a serious possibility over time.

Often, discussions of Indians as subjects occurred when Indians became subordinate to the English. The earliest use of the term for Indians that I have found is from 1615, when Virginia's governor declared that the tributary and geographically displaced Chickahominy were "King IAMES his subjects." Circa 1669, Robert Boyle pointedly wrote the Commissioners of the United Colonies in New England that "the Collony in which those [Praying] Indians are is as equally bound to protect them as others thay being now his majesties subjects." New York's governors claimed sovereignty over the Iroquois Confederacy (without Iroquois knowledge, let alone consent) during the 1680s in order to draw the Iroquois away from the French and subject their diplomatic decisions to approval in Albany. In contrast to these cases, Connecticut passed a unique 1695 act that granted naturalization to the Mohegan man Abimelech, who gained "the privilege and protection of his Majesties lawes this Colony alowes his subjects here." This was done probably to settle a dispute over land and the deliberateness of this act for one person reveals its extraordinary nature.[45]

Only slowly would assertions that Indians were subjects become something that British authorities considered active legal claims rather than mere rhetoric or regional strategy, and it was rare to find Indians who were enthusiastic about their new status. Still, the same logic that had encouraged New York authorities to claim British sovereignty over the Five Nations would also lead them (in a less self-interested way) to declare Indians from Central America subjects of Spain and to try to repatriate them, as they would have done for any foreign prince's subjects.

The end of the Seven Years' War (which itself had raised questions about loyalties of Indians toward Britain or France) was an important context for the strengthening of British claims that Indians within the borders of the empire were something other than aliens, perhaps even denizens or subjects. The Proclamation of 1763, which drew its famous line between British settlements and Indian territories, was one such statement of sovereignty. Indeed, the Canadian historiography (and Canadian law relating to First Nations peoples) has interpreted the Proclamation of 1763 as creating a distinct relationship of native allegiance to the crown that protected First Nations' property rights and self-government. The U.S. historiography has only recently considered this possibility, with studies by Richard White and Eric Hinderaker both examining the 1760s as a key moment for intensified British claims of sovereignty over Indians in the Ohio Valley.[46]

The movement toward subject status for Indians had implications for all forms of slavery. As Christopher Brown has recently pointed out, definition of black slaves as subjects was a key step in the reform process that eroded first the Atlantic slave trade and then British slavery itself. The earlier Indian experience would strengthen the case for this progression. Indeed, when Granville Sharp claimed the status of subject for black slaves in 1767, he also asserted it for all inhabitants of the Crown's domain, including Indians. The statuses of the two peoples were being compared and sometimes confused. Retellings of the Inkle and Yarico story had, over the course of the eighteenth century, made Yarico African rather than Indian, thus blurring the fates of the two peoples. The story in fact had its "greatest currency" during the debate over the African slave trade; abolition of the trade led to decline of the story, the last English version of which appeared in 1808. The tale continued in the Caribbean itself, however, where the evils of slave trafficking were not so easily forgotten.[47]

The line from Indian emancipation to black emancipation was nevertheless a wandering one. Indeed, the new emphasis that Indians were free people and potential citizens was sometimes used to reinforce the inferior statuses of others. In 1784, the anonymous *Cursory Remarks on Men and Measures in Georgia* attacked Jewish claims to citizenship in that state by referring to the superior status of Indians. The pamphlet cited a recent court case in which an Anglo-Creek man had sued a Jewish merchant in Savannah. The lawsuit failed, but the pamphlet's author emphasized that Jews had less right to equal status under the law than did Indians, who were after all free. Indians' liberty meant they would "rise above the Jew" and "the Negro" or "African Slave" and be on a par with the free mulattos and mestizos who had been naturalized by the Georgia Assembly. Even if Indians were not "citizens," they should have the "rights of free aliens," a conclusion that revealed white propensity to think of Indians as outsiders.[48]

Indian Enslavement and Historical Narratives

The extent to which attacks on Indian slavery made a difference to the lives of Indians in the early republic is still unknown. More scholarship on court cases in the states from the 1780s onward would be necessary before we can draw any conclusions. Some white commentators seemed to think that the institution was fading away; others pretended it had never existed. Thomas Jefferson blamed "the Spaniards" for starting Indian slavery, but admitted that the "inhuman practice" had prevailed in Virginia, too. William Bartram was less forthcoming. Traveling through the southeast, Bartram described Indian and European slaves among Indians, omitting any discussion of the considerable English enslavement of Indians in that region. Bartram slipped only once; he described a man whose mother was "a Chactaw slave" and whose father was Anglo-Creek, although Bartram then related fears that he himself might fall into "cruel captivity" among the Choctaw, returning to his dominant point that it was Indians, not Euro-Americans, who practiced slavery.[49]

Unwillingness to discuss the enslaved status of many Indians was accompanied by reluctance to redefine them as fellow citizens. Realization that Indians might be described as American citizens (as they had been described as British subjects) haunted political decisions in the early republic. Article IX of the Articles of Confederation declared that the United States had power over Indian affairs so long as the Indians in question were "not members of the states." The status of Indians "not taxed" by the states, as denoted in Article I, Section 2, of the Constitution, was the more lasting example of indecision: an uneasy and negative admission that some Indians, free and taxed, might be enumerated in the states and within the federal union. Gradual accumulation of state laws that banned enslavement of Indians likewise moved toward the logic of equal rights.[50]

Yet the eventual expulsion of the largest Indian populations from the southern states showed the dramatic alteration of this logic: Indians were neither citizens nor the property of citizens. Pequot William Apess passionately disputed consignment of Indians to these marginal and exploited statuses. In 1835, protesting Massachusetts' discriminatory taxation of the Mashpee yet refusal to regard them as true citizens of the state, Apess was bitterly sarcastic: "Heigh-ho! It is a fine thing to be an Indian. One might almost as well be a slave." Inserted for rhetorical effect, particularly as debate over the peculiar institution escalated in the 1830s, Apess's statement also reveals awareness among natives that their historical statuses had never been fully divorced from the chattel slavery that was now legally restricted to persons of African descent in the southern states.[51]

For Indians, an inchoate idea of subject status may have pointed toward freedom, but freedom did not lead to real citizenship let alone equality. That this Indian story of enslavement and freedom was played out before the similar story within the historical narrative of black slavery deserves more exploration; black slavery's ending in 1865 was prefigured in the earlier ending of Indian slavery. Indian slavery's earlier demise, like its earlier beginnings, must be worked into the larger interpretation of the American past in order to demonstrate the tremendous human cost of British colonization in the Atlantic world. Indian slavery has long been without a coherent narrative, yet the narrative of American history is incomplete without the story of Indian slavery.

CHAPTER THREE

"The Predicament of Ubi"

Locating Authority and National Identity
in the Seventeenth-Century English Atlantic

Mark L. Thompson

By 1634, the year Londoner Thomas Yong set sail for the Delaware River, England's empire in the northwestern Atlantic had already begun to take shape. Small English settlements, few older than a decade, dotted the eastern edges of the North American continent and the Caribbean Sea. These young colonies in the West Indies, the Chesapeake, and New England marked the outer rim of England's emerging overseas empire. They also defined a new frontier for Englishmen's aspirations to authority and power.

These American spaces were no *res nullius*,[1] not least because numerous indigenous peoples already inhabited them. Many of these sites had long functioned as nodes in maritime trading networks linked to various states in western Europe. As a consequence, men like Captain Yong, who sought to explore and colonize the Delaware River, soon discovered that manifesting and embedding English political authority in these spaces often required complex negotiations with—or concerted violence against—representatives of indigenous polities and agents of European states.

Yet if encounters with indigenous inhabitants and Europeans posed their own special problems for English colonizers, reproducing authority was no simple task even in domestic colonial spaces. English colonists routinely reinterpreted or subverted metropolitan discourses of authority to suit their own purposes. They had good reason to do so, given that traditional guarantees to liberty and law were often ambiguously located in the new political spaces of the colonies. Perhaps more importantly, the colonists' distant locations facilitated efforts to circumvent or resist metropolitan directives.[2]

The creation of an English Atlantic empire was thus an inherently contested process, both among English subjects and in relation to foreigners. Although the grounds for contest varied greatly, certain key questions arose nearly everywhere. The political dimension of colonization raised the practical but theoretically vexing question of how to locate and rank divergent sources of authority in these newly defined spaces. This question posed a difficult political and constitutional problem for Europeans, who conventionally associated political authority, law, and legal/political traditions with fixed and discrete sets of actors, institutions, and spaces in their native metropoli. Indigenous Americans lacked experience with the text-centered legal cultures of the European arrivals, but they were no less keen observers of political authority and power. They too sought to illuminate the contours of these relationships when they negotiated with Europeans.

Thomas Yong, whose writings are the subject of this chapter, intended his correspondence to describe his observations and to serve certain instrumental purposes, not to establish himself as a significant or novel political thinker. Yet his correspondence implicitly addressed many of the political and constitutional questions raised by his own, and other, imperial endeavors. The solution to these problems was not the vaunted "Ancient Constitution" or the common law, at least in their more conventional and liberal senses. Yong repeatedly referred to himself as bound by law and English custom, but he relied upon a different form of legal authority that was more applicable to his circumstances as an explorer and a colonizer at the periphery of the realm. In Yong's writings, legal and political authority resided most visibly in the Crown, and allegiance and subjection featured as the primary modes of political affiliation. This allegiance to the king gave Yong authority to act in a "lawfull" capacity outside the realm and at its remote, contested borders. Although liberty and the common law may have been at the heart of early modern Englishmen's national and imperial identities, in Yong's imperial imagination expressions of allegiance to the Crown legitimated actions that appeals to rights and liberties could not. Such appeals to English liberty were better suited to established societies than to contested Atlantic spaces governed (if at all) by an inchoate, sovereign-centered law of nations.[3]

Fashioning himself as a dependent of the Crown allowed Yong to represent and create authority outside of specific institutional settings and in a variety of legal and political spaces. This authority rested on allegiance, which joined subject and sovereign in an ideal yet no less real political body that extended across space and through time. As Sir Edward Coke wrote in his opinion on Calvin's Case (1607),

> ligeance, and faith and truth, which are her members and parts, are qualities of the mind and soul of man, and cannot be circumscribed within the predicament of *ubi* [i.e., location] . . . [L]igeance of the subject was of as great an extent and latitude, as the royal power and protection of the King and *converso* . . . Now seeing power and protection draweth ligeance, it followeth, that seeing the Kings power, command and protection, extendeth out of England, that ligeance cannot be local, or confined within the bounds thereof.[4]

In keeping with the legal and political theory of allegiance, this pattern held true across the four settings that Yong described in his correspondence: in negotiations with officials in England; in politicking among English planters in Virginia; in encounters with Indians in the Delaware River; and in disputes with Dutch traders visiting their "South River."

Such a ubiquitous political language had to be adaptable if it were to be useful. Yong's writings show that it was. Yong elaborated a rhetorical dependence on the Crown in each encounter he described, but the character of his dependence—and the extent of his authority—changed from one space to the next. In some spaces he represented an unalloyed dependence, such as when he was addressing the king and his officials; in other locations, such as in Virginia, he joined a language of subjection with a patriotic language of service to king and country. His representations of himself as an authoritative figure also changed according to his location. In fact, the more distant his position from England and the Crown—the putative fountainhead of his own authority—the more authoritative he represented himself to be.

Yong calibrated his representation of his own authority to the jurisdictional statuses of the spaces he entered, each of which he treated implicitly as a discrete territory subject to possession and governance. Although such territories had natural characteristics significant in early modern scientific and geographic discourses (which were themselves intertwined with legal and political discourses), Yong was concerned with identifying who owned and controlled the space, and, consequently, who had power and authority over the agents within that space.[5] As an Englishman culturally attuned to legal thinking, Yong realized instinctively that the jurisdictional status of a space shaped the statuses of the agents within it.[6] These statuses were hardly static, however. Spaces and identities were both subject to contest, and disputes over one nearly always involved disputes over the other.

The contested linkage between space and identity was not merely a matter of legal constructions. In maritime and colonial encounters Europeans consistently depicted themselves and others as members of "nations," collectivities defined vaguely and often inconsistently by a political, linguistic, or territorial affiliation, among many other possible characteristics. Yong's writings show that discussions of authority and allegiance in such settings easily shifted into discussions of "nations" and ethnic or national peoples, as occurred when Yong confronted trespassing "Hollanders of Hudson River" and complained that "the Dutch" had injured the king of England and his subjects. Locating authority in the Atlantic world thus often meant locating oneself and others in a nation. In such spaces national identity combined identifications with authority and nation: a construct we might call "national subjecthood." For a "national subject" such as Yong, to be English was to be both a subject of the king of England and a member of the English people. Such a view of self also entailed viewing others as belonging to similar ethnopolitical categories.[7]

Yong's writings about his voyage to North America in 1634–35 show how a single figure could improvise practical solutions to the theoretical problems posed by the extension of political authority into different kinds of Atlantic spaces. His accounts of negotiating authority in several distinct spaces— metropolitan, domestic colonial, indigenous, and contested colonial—also demonstrate how acts of political and national identification varied according to spatial contexts. Finally, subsequent ideological manipulations of his voyage's historical memory suggest how voyages such as Yong's might have shaped political thought and practice in the English Atlantic more generally.

Domestic Metropolitan Space: England

Evidence regarding Thomas Yong's background is regrettably scarce. Born in 1579 in the Cornhill parish of London, Yong was at least of the "better sort"; his captain's commission referred to him as a "Gentleman," and the honorific

"Mr." invariably preceded his name in records, as it did the name of his father, Gregory Yong, a "Grocer" originally from Yorkshire. By 1634, the fifty-five-year-old captain apparently had achieved "some affluence and position," though his plans for a voyage to North America suggest that he aspired to more than comfortable wealth.[8] Yong's affiliation with English Catholicism seems at once to have aided and hindered these aspirations. Although no direct evidence confirms that Yong himself was an active Catholic, his numerous connections to prominent English Catholics and his concerns about the application of the oath of allegiance to himself and his officers suggest strongly that he or certain members of his party belonged to that faith.[9]

Yong's concerns about the oath of allegiance appear repeatedly in the correspondence and records preceding the voyage. These documents from Yong's time in England show him elaborating his dependence as a subject of Charles I while seeking authorization for his voyage. The dependence he articulated was not merely rhetorical, for Yong required from the king a special commission authorizing a variety of discretionary powers. Once granted, these powers and privileges had the potential to make Yong a very powerful figure. Yet, to obtain them, he required the direct intervention of the king and his agents. Yong's dependence on royal favor may have been all the more acute as a consequence of the legal handicaps his countrymen placed on him or his associates for being Catholics. Yong could not rely on the common law for justice; in fact, he seemed to have required the king's aid in circumventing important English laws that discriminated against Catholics.

Details of Yong's plans for a voyage to North America first appeared in an undated petition addressed to Charles I that was probably written before April 1634.[10] In this petition, Yong requested letters that would release him completely from the jurisdiction, and the interference, of any and all of the king's officers in England and America. Wary of being stopped or delayed by overzealous agents of the Crown, Yong asked that the king declare that he was "well satisfied of the fidelitie, allegiance, loyall proceeding and great devotion of Mr. Yong to His Majesties Service," and that he had employed Yong on a mission "private to himselff." Yong thus sought to use the influence of the king as a means to circumvent lower officials' jurisdictional prerogatives.[11]

Yong's insistence on freedom of action appears related to his Catholic connections. In planning his expedition, Yong requested that the king free "Mr. Alexander Baker, who is under command in regard of some questions which occurred long ago, concerning conscience." Yong hoped that Baker, who was "now at libertie upon bonds," could join the mission as the ship's cosmographer.[12] One possible explanation for Mr. Baker's predicament "concerning conscience" is that he was a Catholic in bad stead with local officialdom. He may have refused to swear the oaths of supremacy and allegiance that had become so important in testing the loyalty of English Catholics in the first decades of the seventeenth century.[13] If Baker, Yong, or other voyage participants were Catholics, then Yong had good reason to fear the application of these oaths in Virginia. The colony's officials strictly applied the oaths of allegiance and supremacy mandated in the 1609 charter, and just a year before Yong's arrival the colony's assembly had renewed legislation requiring the commander of the fort at Point Comfort to administer to all visitors "the oathes of supremacy and allegiance, which yf any shall refuse to take that then he comit him or them to imprisonment."[14]

In a subsequent letter to the king's secretary of state, Sir Francis Windebanke, dated April 1634, Yong asked the secretary to speak to the king's "searcher" at Gravesend. Yong wanted Windebanke to "signifie to him in His Majesties' name that Mr. Yong, his nephew Mr. Evelin, Mr. Baker his Cosmographer, and Mr. Scott his Phisition, have already given satisfaction to his Majestie, in swearing their allegiance, and that, therefore, they are not more to be questioned in that point."[15] This passage suggests that Yong's earlier request for the king to testify to Yong's allegiance may have been more than a rhetorical gesture. Rather, Yong may have hoped to free his officers and himself from pointed queries about their faith. Connections to such prominent Catholics as Lord Baltimore, Sir Tobie Matthew, and Sir Edmund Plowden may have helped Yong obtain support for his voyage, but they seemed also to create peculiar difficulties that required special intervention from royal officials.

Yong also wanted to avoid unnecessary interference because he had a secret mission. He intended not only to explore and colonize the Delaware Valley, but also to discover whether the river led to a northwest passage to the Pacific Ocean.[16] If English officials were free to charge him duties, to question his allegiance, or to reveal his grander purpose, then the voyage and its fantastic design might have risked failure. Although most other European exploring "nations" had long given up on finding a northwest passage in this part of North America, Yong's mission would have been invaluable to the English Crown if his geographical theories had proved to be correct. Much was at stake, for if Yong or another Englishman did not discover this invaluable throughway, then Dutch or other European explorers and merchants might seize it for themselves.

This agenda made the effort to free Baker all the more important because Yong had already received his commission from the king. The king had granted the commission to "our trustie and welbeloved Subject *Thomas Young of London* Gentleman" on September 23, 1633, but subsequent difficulties in preparing for the voyage apparently had delayed it until the next spring. The commission contained all the provisions Yong had mentioned in his correspondence with Crown officials, such as freedoms of movement and trade. It also contained a number of additional powers of extraordinary scope, including powers to make war and peace, to kill enemy prisoners, to seize trespassing ships, and to set up forts, factories, and mines in areas he discovered in North America. He also possessed important political powers as a colonizer, including the authority to bring inhabitants of those "discovered" regions into the king's allegiance and to place settlers in those locations under the allegiance of the king. The commission testified as well that Yong had powers to act "in as absolute manner as any Generall of any Army of ours."[17] According to his new commission, "Captain" Yong would have the authority of a "General" once he left the realm.

The royal origins of the authority and powers that the king had delegated to Yong figured prominently in the commission. The document even represented the king's subjectivity by directly addressing its readers in his voice and persona. It acknowledged that Charles was "graciously pleased to accept to the endeavours of the said *Thomas Young*" and was willing to aid Yong's efforts "with our Power and Royal Authority, of our especial grace, certain knowledge and meer motion."[18] Through such language, the commission offered tangible evidence of a mystical and expansive royal authority embedded in and embodied in Thomas Yong. Yong remained a dependent of the king, but outside of the realm of England he now possessed impressive authority.

Domestic Colonial Space: Virginia

When Yong and his party left England in May 1634, they intended to go directly to the Delaware River, but storms during the seven-week Atlantic crossing damaged their ship. Stopping in Virginia gave him time to make repairs and to "meet dayly with severall of the best & most understanding sort of the Inhabitants of this place." Over the course of ten to twelve days, Yong used these contacts to inform himself as best he could of "the State of this country," particularly its political affairs.[19] His account of the wranglings of

Virginia's political elite reveals yet another iteration of Yong's persona as a patriotic English subject shaped by the characteristics of a jurisdictional space.

When Yong was in England, his efforts to obtain his commission reflected his dependence on the king's pleasure, even as he asked for extraordinary intervention from the Crown and its agents. In Virginia Yong continued to depict himself as a loyal dependent, but there he sought to turn his authorization to political ends. Lacking express authority to intervene in Virginia's political affairs or in its relations with Maryland, Yong instead exercised his innate capacity to make moral judgments. As an outsider he could not express his own civic virtue in this space, but his lengthy letter to prominent Catholic courtier Sir Tobie Matthew allowed him to reveal the dangers posed by disloyal subjects in Virginia. Yong framed himself as a counselor to the prince, as someone who spoke as a civic observer rather than as a civic actor.[20]

Employing the vocabulary of a moral and political critique, Yong denounced the prominent Virginian planters who opposed the colony's governor, Sir John Harvey, and who protested the founding of Maryland as an infringement of their corporate privileges. Yong had no official authority or power to discipline the corrupt and sinful opponents of Harvey and Lord Baltimore, but he claimed an implicit authority, even a duty, to report his judgments to metropolitan authorities who did have powers to act. Bound by his allegiance to the Crown, Yong sought to wield power in Virginia in a reflexive, telegraphic manner via a link to the ultimate source of authority and power in the metropolis. Although Matthew, Yong's correspondent, was not a royal official, Yong specifically asked that he circulate the letter among officials in the metropolis, including "my Lord Treasurer or my Lord Cottington or Mr. Secretary Windebanke."[21] By shaping the judgments of royal officials, he hoped to manipulate their actions upon agents in the colonies.

Yong's portrayal of Virginia's governor, Sir John Harvey, reveals his ideals of the virtuous official and the proper relation between government, people, and king. Harvey was "a gentleman in good faith . . . of a noble mynde and worthy heart" who scrupulously obeyed the king's orders. He had carefully observed the king's command to aid the Marylanders, despite suffering as a consequence the "extreame hatred & malice from all the rest of the country." He was "a great reformer of the abuses in the Government, especially in point of justice, which, at his first entrance, was full of corruption & partiality, the richest & most powerfull oppressing & swallowing up the poorer, though now much amended by his care & zeale to justice."[22] In Harvey, justice, honest government, and the advancement of the common good stood in opposition to the "corruption" of the wealthy and powerful. His was no government in the name of the local elite; he sought to protect the liberties of the weak and to promote the good of all.[23]

Virginia's council, by contrast, were "factious & turbulent spirits" who used their "strength & power" to stymie the governor. The council was "for the most part united in a kind of faction against the Governor." They opposed "every proposition of his, however beneficial to the country, choosing rather to deprive themselves of the good, that might arise to themselves thereby, than that he should be the author of such a benefitt to the country." Yong deemed only two members of the council "indifferent," or disinterested. One was "Captain Purfree a souldier and a man of an open heart honest & free, hating for ought I can see all kinds of dissimulation & basenesse." The other was "an honest playne man but of small capacity & lesse power."[24] One embodied martial virtue, the other the simple moral virtue of a freeman.

Yong identified Captain Samuel Mathews as "the head & cheefe supporte" of the council-as-faction.[25] This "ancient planter" was "a man of bold spirit, turbulent & strong in the faction of the more refractory sort of the country." In contrast to the virtuous and obedient Harvey, Mathews was "a great opposer & interpreter of all letters & commands that come from the King & state of England." He was "apt also to possesse & preoccupate the judgments of the rest of his fellow councellors that letters from the King & from the Lords [were] surreptitiously gotten," Yong claimed. According to Yong's informants, Mathews even argued that "the obedience to them may & ought to be suspended" until they had inquired into and received confirmation of commands from England. Claiming that "the Lords are not sufficiently instructed in the necessities" of government in Virginia, Mathews pretended that "every kind of disobedience" was actually beneficial to the state. The actions of Mathews and his associates in the council approached outright treason. "I have bene informed," Yong said, "that some of the Councellors have bene bold enough, in a presumptuous manner, to say, to such as told them, that perhaps their disobedience might cause them to be sent for into England, That if the King would have them, he must come himself and fetch them." Unlike Yong, who put "duty both to God & his Ma[jes]tie" above all, these men sought to turn government to their own private ends and against law, justice, and legitimate authority.[26]

Yong proposed royal and metropolitan remedies for the colony's ills. He suggested that an "order taken in England" was the only way to counteract the dangerous Virginians. The agent of royal authority, Virginia's governor, could only implement such an order, however, if he were given "some strong & powerful addition to his present authority by some new power from England." Even the disobedient councilors recognized that disciplinary power could only originate in England when they boasted they would answer for their disobedience only if the king himself came to get them.[27]

In Yong's assessment, opposition to the governor—the king's representative—was destroying, rather than protecting, liberty; subverting, rather than preserving, law and justice. Instead of acting in proper obedient, loyal, dependent fashion, these men were acting according to their own corrupted judgments. Their "uncristianlike" behavior even threatened the future existence of the colony. Virginia's overmighty councilors had lost both their Christian virtue and their civic virtue by subverting royal authority. Yong lacked authority in Virginia to take action against these "factious & turbulent spirits," but through writing he sought to mobilize royal authority on behalf of Harvey and the besieged Marylanders.[28] In Yong's words, he was bound "by duty both to God & his Ma[jes]tie . . . not to passe over so foule practises and undutiful proceedings toward his Ma[jes]tie and his Ministers in these parts, in silence, without a relation of the truth thereof."[29] By relating the truth to his superiors, Yong thus sought to restore the moral and political order in the colony, an order based (as Coke wrote) on the "ligeance of the subject" and the "royal power and protection of the King."

Indigenous Space: The River of the Indian Nations

Misfortune at sea had brought Yong to Virginia, but his primary destination remained the Delaware River Valley, where he sought to plant a lasting, profitable settlement. In time he hoped to transform an uncivilized indigenous space into an ordered and commodifiable colonial space attached to the national and dynastic space of his native England. Such a transformation involved not only the labor of explorers, settlers, and administrators, but also the rhetorical work of men like Yong. In order to make colonization possible, Yong needed to redefine both the nature of the space and the nature of the individuals within it. He had to inscribe the space into existing geographic and proprietary discourses and at the same time define the peoples who occupied and traversed this space as subjects who belonged to nations.

Yong sought to accomplish these tasks by depicting the Delaware Valley as a territory that could be owned and governed legitimately by his sovereign

and no other Christian prince. While representing himself and other Europeans as agents of nations with sovereign lords or kings, Yong depicted the
valley's indigenous inhabitants as nations governed by comparable kings.
Through such transformative language, the indigenous inhabitants' "kings"
became legitimate rulers who could transfer land and sovereignty to an
English master.

Yet Yong's labeling of the indigenous inhabitants of the Americas as "Indians" complicated any application of European political categories to them. For
while the indigenous inhabitants of the region clearly lived in hierarchical
political societies, they did not have the visible institutions that tied even the
most distant provincial jurisdictions in Europe's imperial states to their
metropolitan centers.[30] The opaqueness of political institutions in the indigenous space encouraged a colonizing agent such as Yong to employ his political
vocabulary in novel, and often distorting, ways. We see, for example, a distinct
change in the way Yong represented himself in encounters with indigenous
peoples along the Delaware. In England and Virginia, Yong framed his identity
as a political agent in ways appropriate to these domestic political spaces; he
drew from languages of dependent authority, patriotism, and civic critique
because he was dealing with fellow subjects and countrymen. Along the
Delaware River, however, the indigenous audience knew nothing of Yong's status or his political culture except what they had observed of him and other
Europeans. Indigenous space thus required and enabled Yong to adopt different modes of self-presentation.

Yong responded to this representational challenge by magnifying his own
individual authority to act. He depicted his relations with Indians along the
Delaware River as taking place on an individual level between fellow powerful
men. Although Yong claimed the territory in the name of his king, he did so in
a grand fashion that glorified himself. Along the Delaware River, Yong had discovered an ideal place to become a powerful and authoritative figure. Yet Yong's
identification as a national subject also shaped this persona, for Yong portrayed
his individual greatness as an expression of his membership in a greater collec-
tivity: England. In encounters with Indians, his small ship-bound party
became representatives of English people and English authority in general. In
parallel fashion, the indigenous people along the river became nations and
miniature polities who could become dependents of English authority.

Yong departed for the Delaware Bay on July 20, 1634, after making repairs
in Virginia. When he and his men entered the bay five days later, they tried

contacting Indians along the shore, but failed; each time Indians saw his ship, they ran away. Finally, two days later, an Indian at the river's edge beckoned for Yong and his men to disembark. Through his interpreter, Yong inquired about the bay's extent and the current state of affairs along the river. The Indian informed him that "the people of that River were at warre with a certaine Nation called the Minquaos, who had killed many of them, destroyed their corne, and burned their houses." The Indian's account of another ship's visit led Yong to conclude that "Hollanders . . . had bene there trading for furrs." In exchange for "some trifles, as knives and beades and a hatchett," Yong obtained valuable intelligence that enabled him to begin constructing a mental map of the river's native inhabitants and its European contestants—the "nations" with whom Yong would have to negotiate in order to claim the river.[31]

Proceeding upriver, Yong met another Indian, who sold him a "store of Eeles" in exchange for a knife and a hatchet. As Yong "was discoursing with him concerning the River"—yet again seeking valuable geographical and political information from an indigenous source—the Indian suddenly "fell into a great passion of feare and trembling." Yong inquired "what the matter was, and comforted him, and bad him feare nothing," offering a kind of sentimental paternal protection. The fearful Indian pointed to a canoe approaching the ship, "in which, he said, were some of the Minquaos and that they were enimies to him, and to his Nation, and had already killed many of them, and that they would kill him also, if they saw him, and therefore he desired me to hide him from them." Yong honored the request before engaging the new arrivals who had so terrified the "trembling" Indian. This patriarchal role was new to Yong, who had depicted himself as a deferential subordinate in England and as a peer to the prominent men of Virginia. Among unfamiliar Indians in the Delaware Valley, however, he could act on his own authority and be a powerful figure in his own right.[32]

Yong's unnamed interpreter (who had almost certainly been mediating between Yong and the first Indian) "understood but only some few words" of the Minquaos' language. Instead, Yong's party was "forced for the most part to gather their meanings by signes the best wee could." By these signs "They told us, they were Minquaos, and that one of them was a king, (for soe all the Indians call them, who are most eminent among themselves, and they are in nature of Captaynes or Governors of the rest, and have power of life and death, of warre and peace, over their subjects, Some have 1000, some 500, some more, some lesse)."[33] Yong thus depicted Indian society and politics as organized along vertical lines of authority, thereby creating a monarchical vision of politics in the Indian communities along the Delaware River.

But for Yong, not all kings were equal. Indian kings were more like "Captaynes or Governors"—men like Yong himself. The distinction, however appropriate, served the ideological purposes of Yong and his sovereign. By qualifying the status of Indian leaders, Yong supported the arguments of his king, a *real* king, who two years prior to Yong's voyage had denied that "the Indians were *possessores bonae fidei* of those countries, so as to be able to dispose of them either by sale or donation, their residences being unsettled and uncertain, and only being in common."[34] Yong's authoritative persona was in large part the product of such doctrines; at no point did he worry that indigenous authorities might have jurisdiction over *him*.

After exchanging gifts, these "Minquaos" departed. Yong then dropped off the non-Minquao (Delaware) Indian and sailed further upriver, where he met another king along with forty to sixty Indians, presumably his "subjects." This king told Yong he "was welcome into the Countrey, and that he came to see me with desire to make peace with me, in regard he understood by an Indian that I was a good man, and that I had preserved him from the Minquaos, who would otherwise have slayne him." After inquiring about trade, the king gave Yong two otter skins and some corn. The king said he had nothing better to offer because Minquaos had "harrowed his countrey, and carried much beaver from him and his subjects, and that the rest they had trucked away to the Hollanders, who had lately bene there." Yong interpreted the gift-giving as a direct interaction with the Indian king, who, as the sovereign of his people or "his subjects," welcomed Yong into "his countrey," a country that was his jurisdiction to govern as its king.[35]

Yong imagined native political authority as mirroring that in his own country. Yong told the Indian king that he had been "sent thither by a great king in Europe, namely the king of England." Just as the Indian king possessed authority over the Delaware River/Valley (or a part of it), so did Yong's king possess authority over England in Europe. Yong explained further that he had come "to discover that Countrey and to make peace with them, if they desired to imbrace it." If they accepted this offer of peace, he would "defend them from their enimies." Yong wrote that the Indian king was "very joyfull to hear this" and asked Yong to stay a few days in order to meet with another king (the local king's father-in-law) and "another king also who was his neighbour, and the proprietor of that part of the River, wherein I then rode." Here again Yong spoke explicitly in terms that linked political authority, territorial authority, and land as property, with an Indian king as "proprietor."[36]

Despite the parallels Yong drew between Indian and European political authority, he seemed to presume that indigenous peoples would readily submit themselves to a European king who had a lawful claim to the territory. Alternatively, he may have expected they could be easily displaced, for after agreeing to stay for two more days to wait for the other kings to arrive, Yong offhandedly declared that "In the meane time, I tooke pos[s]ession of the countrey, for his Ma[jes]tie and there set up his Ma[jes]ties armes upon a tree, which was performed with solemnities usuall in that kind." The Indians' acceptance of peace and the offer of defense had accompanied Yong's taking formal possession of "the countrey" for the King of England, notwithstanding Yong's earlier mention of an Indian "proprietor" of the river. Whether the peace was meant to authorize Yong's act of possession is unclear. Ultimately, the two actions seem to have been distinct. Nevertheless, the Indians' willing submission added a surface layer of consent to an a priori claim to the territory, perhaps in ideological distinction to the practices of Spanish colonizers.[37]

Yong's relation does not spell out whether formal English possession required the Indians' invitation or welcome, but his commission, drafted 3,500 miles away in England, offers a clear guide to the intended meanings of Yong's actions along the Delaware. He had explored a river not possessed by "any Christian Prince, Country or State," entered into "Friendship and Alliance with the Princes, Governours and People" of the Delaware Valley, taken possession of "such Countries, Lands and Territories," and erected the king's "Banners"—or what Yong called "his Ma[jes]ties armes"—upon a tree. He seemed not to have formally initiated any of the Indians into the English monarch's "Faith and Allegiance," but something approaching such an action would come later.[38]

After Yong "tooke pos[s]ession of the countrey," these Indians along the river asked Yong to protect them against their enemies, the Minquaos. Yong replied that he would first pursue peace with the Minquaos, but if they refused, then he and soldiers under his command would join these Indians in war against them. Yong thereby sought to set up himself and the English as mediators and perhaps as overlords for both groups. He even offered to "invade the Minquaos within their own countrey, upon this condition, that they [the river Indians] shall renounce all trade or alliance with all other persons, save only his Ma[jes]ties Ministers and subjects, and that they shall be wholy dependant on him [the king of England]." The Indians were "very joyfull" when they heard this offer, "accepted the conditions[,] and soe wee made a solemne peace," Yong wrote. After they departed, "it was spread all over the river, that I had made peace with them, and that I was a just man, and would defend them against their enimies the Minquaos."[39]

By Yong's reckoning he had brokered a relationship of formal political dependence between these local kings of the river and the king of England. In exchange for English protection, the Indians had renounced any connections to the unnamed Dutch, and perhaps even to the distant Spanish or French. Yong wrote as though his offer of military protection distinguished him from European agents such as the Dutch, who had traded with the Indians but had not made permanent settlements. The Indians may not have become true English subjects, but they apparently had become something akin to feudal dependents of the Crown. This dependence was channeled through Yong, however, whose own status had been elevated rhetorically in the process. By Yong's own account, his new reputation among the Indians as "a just man" who would protect them from the Minquaos had transformed him into a virtuous and powerful king-like figure, a patriarch capable of protecting a whole people through his own person.

After several days' wait, the Minquaos never arrived, so Yong decided to leave. Disappointed by Yong's departure, one king sent his brother along with Yong, perhaps as a guide, but more likely as a symbol or guarantee of their new alliance. After spending one night entertaining the two kings and some of their men, Yong met with the rest of the Indians and gave each king presents. In Yong's retelling, the meeting was a convocation of peoples:

> First the ancient king, and afterward the yonger, called together all their people, and made to them a long oration to this purpose. That wee were a good people. That wee were just. That wee were ready to defend the oppressed from the crueltie of their neighbours. That wee were loving people, as a testimony whereof they shewed me the presents I had given them. That wee had brought thither such things as they stood in need of, for which wee desired only Beaver and Otter skinnes, whereof they had to spare.

The kings then commanded their peoples "to trade lovingly and freely with our people, that they should be carefull that no injuries were either privately or publikely done to them." Yong and his men were the moral equivalents of Virginia's Governor Harvey: "just," "loving," "good" protectors. The proper sign of gratitude, it seemed, was to trade with them.[40]

Only in this last meeting, when the Indian kings had spoken of the virtues of Yong's (English) people, did Yong depict authority as though it were expressed and constituted collectively as a civic act rather than as a deferential act between king and subject. Yong's account shows clearly that the chiefs were seeking their peoples' approval of the newcomers and a communal event was necessary to obtain this consent. In the rhetorical linkage of peoples and systems of authority, the episode depicts nation formation at its most basic level. Yong and his men had become representatives of the English, "a good people." In turn, the Indian kings and their subjects had become a people capable of forging an alliance with the English.

But even this communal, national moment reflected back on Yong. The kings told their people that Yong's party of Englishmen were to be treated as "friends and Brothers, and that for me in particular they should honor and esteeme of me as a Brother of their kings, and that they should be carefull to carrie themselves dutifully towards mee, with a great deale more complement, then I expresse."[41] By depicting the Delaware River and Valley as a territory owned and governed by indigenous kings and inhabited by their subjects, Yong elevated himself through the Indian kings' speeches nearly to the status of one himself.[42] As an authorized English subject in an indigenous American space, Yong was able to manifest extraordinary power and authority, at least in his own account.

Contested Colonial Space: The Charles River or the South River?

Yong's royal commission signified his authority to "take possession of all such Countries, Lands and Territories, as are yet undiscovered or not actually in the possession of any Christian Prince, Country or State." In his meetings with the Indians of the Delaware River (which he had renamed the "Charles River" in honor of his monarch), Yong acted as though the river and its surrounding lands met these criteria. Yet the Delaware River, New Netherland's "South River," had been the object of Dutch exploration and trade since the mid-1610s. From 1624 to 1626 it was the site of one of New Netherland's first settlements, and from 1631 to 1632 it had been the site of a short-lived Dutch whaling colony on land purchased from local Indians. Whether these actions had established "possession" was of course a matter for debate. When men on armed vessels conducted such debates, however, the threat of violent force offered a powerful alternative to reasoned legal discourse. Both methods of dispute resolution were characteristic of much of the Delaware's seventeenth-century history.[43]

Whereas spatial and jurisdictional language was usually implicit or improvised in early indigenous-European encounters, it was elaborately constructed in intra-European encounters. Unlike most early seventeenth-century North American Indians, who had only a limited ability to negotiate Europeans' legal rhetoric, Europeans active in the Atlantic world were very capable of offering rhetorical challenges in the language of law and jurisdiction. In such contested colonial spaces, as we shall see, authorized agents strongly identified themselves according to their national subjecthood—that is, according to their joint statuses as subjects and members of a people. Although these agents projected foremost their status as authorized representatives of their sovereigns, they also employed an ethnic mode of identification as members of European nations.

In the Chesapeake, Yong had discovered that local Indians played important intermediary roles in the disputes between colonists in Virginia and Maryland. Indians along the Delaware River apparently had a similar influence on relations between English and Dutch visitors to their lands, for Yong claimed they passed along news of his presence on the Delaware to New Netherland's officials soon after his arrival. That, at least, is how Yong interpreted the appearance of a vessel bearing "Hollanders of Hudson River" about a month after he had entered the bay. When these visitors anchored near Yong's ship, Yong sent some of his men to find out who they were and from where they had come. He also ordered that they bring the master of the vessel to him. Soon afterward the ship's master and its merchant arrived in their own boat.[44]

Once the two Hollanders boarded the English vessel, Yong immediately challenged their right to enter a "Country" that he had (re)claimed for his king only days before.[45] Ignoring the history of Dutch involvement in the river, Yong asked the traders why they had come and whether they had a commission from the English king. When they said that they came to trade with a commission from "the Governor of new Netherlands," Yong responded that he "knew no such Governor, nor no such place as new Netherlands." Yong then informed them that "this Country did belong to the crowne of England, as well by ancient discovery as likewise by possession lawfully taken, and that his Ma[jes]tie was now pleased to make more ample discovery of this River, and of other places also, where he would erect Collonies, and that I was therefore sent hither with a Royall Commission under the great Seale to take possession heereof."[46] Yong's professed ignorance of New Netherland's existence was pure dissimulation. Only a year earlier the Dutch navigator and patroon David Pieterszoon de Vries had met with Virginia's Governor Harvey, described the Dutch settlement at New Netherland, and discussed his explorations in the Delaware River.[47] Yong surely had received news of the Dutch navigator's visit. But, as we have seen, the terms of his commission required that the territories he claimed for the Crown have no inhabitants who were subjects of other Christian princes or states. Yong sought to hammer the past into a useful tool for his present purposes.

Yong intended his queries and assertions to be interpreted as veiled threats, and the Dutch traders recognized them as such. "I perceaved by their countenance that this newes strooke them could [cold] at heart, and after a little pawse they answered me, that they had traded in this River heeretofore." Enjoying this masterful performance, or at least its theatrical relation, Yong criticized the Dutch for pretending that they had authority to trade or settle in the territories of the English king. Yet he depicted the dispute as a diplomatic one that could be resolved with diplomatic politeness; "good manners" obliged "the Dutch" to cease their usurpation of the English king's rightful possessions. The two Hollanders responded by asking to see Yong's commission, which he gladly showed them. "After they had read it, and considered well thereof, apprehending the power I had, if they should trade without licence, to make them prize, they desired me to give them a Copie thereof." Highlighting his own relationship to the English Crown, Yong refused their request, saying "it was not the custome of England for his Ma[jes]ties Ministers to give Copies of their Commissions."[48] This recitation of his faithful stewardship of his commission showed Yong to be at once a deferential English subject and a powerful agent of English royal authority.

Yong told his Dutch visitors that he would decide their fate once his lieutenant returned from an exploratory foray. The lieutenant, Yong's nephew Robert Evelin, returned the next day, and Yong "sent for the Hollanders to dine" with him. This time Yong invited more guests than the shipmaster and the chief merchant, who had attended him previously. He spent the day "making them wellcome" and putting a gentlemanly face on their dispute. In an after-dinner toast, the Dutch shipmaster and merchant finally acknowledged Yong's authority: "Heere Governor of the South River, (for soe they call this) I drinke to you and indeed confesse your Commission is much better than ours, how say you Copeman (who is the head marchant) said he is it not. To whome the Copeman answered yes indeede, I have not seene a larger Commission."[49] Politic sociability, suitably doused with liquor, thus preempted the violence that political patriotism might have demanded. Yong had demonstrated his authority not merely by conspicuously displaying his commission—the King's personal seal affixed prominently to it—but also by representing himself as an authoritative person. In this case, an authority created through performance and bolstered by visible power obviated the necessity to use that power; the Netherlanders had openly and freely expressed their consent to Yong's authority, just as the Indians had consented to the authority of Yong and his English king.

Although the day's conviviality had elicited the desired public admission of his authority, Yong waited until the next day to inform the Dutch traders of his decision. He announced that because they were "subjects to so ancient allies of my Prince, and . . . neighbours heere, and . . . had carried themselves Civilly," he had treated them "with all Curtesy . . . [he] might lawfully use." But after showing them his commission Yong said he could allow them to stay only two days longer. Nevertheless, these traders had performed admirably in Yong's seaborne court masque, so the English captain granted them the token gift of providing themselves "of whatever they should need"—perhaps a euphemism for trade with the local Indians—without suffering harassment from Yong and his men.[50]

Within two days, the Dutch ship weighed anchor and began to sail downriver. Yong dispatched his lieutenant, Evelin, in a smaller craft to accompany them. Notwithstanding their acknowledgment of his authority, Yong wanted "to watch them least they should doe me ill offices with the Indians, in their way homewards."[51] Yong probably knew from his own experiences that outward signs of obeisance could mask connivance or dissembling; even if his authority was natural and real, submission might not be. Under the eye of Yong's deputy, the Dutch traders departed without incident. As they traveled downriver the traders and Yong's lieutenant occasionally went aboard each others' vessels "after the manner of the Sea." Their discussions revealed the artifice that lay behind their acknowledgment of Yong's authority. The Dutch merchant told Evelin that "if they [the Dutch] had bene in possession at my arrivall they would not have removed, for all my Commission."[52]

At the close of his letter to Windebanke, Yong briefly recounted a later encounter with "the Hollanders," which probably occurred in October 1634. This time "the Governor of the Dutch plantation" sent them "with a Commission to plant and trade" along the river, thus countering claims based on

English authority with an equivalent Dutch authority. After "much discourse to and fro," these Hollanders "publikely declared, that if the king of England please to owne this River, they will obey, and they humbly desire that he will declare to them their limitts in these parts of America, which they will also observe." Once again, the Dutch disputants in Yong's account had deferred readily to his authority. If this incident actually transpired as Yong described it, then these spokesmen for "the Dutch plantation" almost certainly had over-stepped their authority. Yong again may have exaggerated others' authority in order to highlight his own.[53]

As in Virginia and among the Indians of the Delaware, Yong described his spatial location in territorial, jurisdictional terms. He and his Dutch disputants together constructed a national vision of different peoples with their own politics, and they framed their statuses in relation to this space. Bearing his grand commission from the Crown, Yong was certain of his own privileged and empowered status in the Delaware. The traders from New Netherland, by contrast, he reduced to objects of his authority without legitimate authority of their own. Although Yong used his dependent relationship to the king to aggrandize himself in dealings with the Indians and the Dutch alike, he emphasized this linkage to a much greater degree when dealing with these fellow Europeans in the Delaware. Because they shared this language of authority, Yong could wield his commission to create impressive authority in this contested colonial space. Of course, the size of Yong's ship, crew, and guns might have been the deciding factor in these negotiations along the Delaware, but in the logic of Yong's retelling the issue was really about deference to English royal authority.

Conclusion

Yong never found a northwest passage, despite his confident assertion that he would find "that mediteranean Sea, which the Indian relateth to be four days journey beyond the Mountains," whose rivers he knew "discharge[d] themselves both into the north and South Seas."[54] Nor was he able to establish a permanent colony along the Delaware under his king's allegiance. If Yong placed English settlers along the Delaware—and we do not know conclusively whether he did—then they did not remain there for long. Within a year of Yong's voyage, Dutch traders transported a group of English settlers from the Delaware to Manhattan so they could be returned to Virginia.[55] Although many efforts to claim the river for the English Crown followed Yong's adventure, none succeeded until thirty years later, when a royal naval force invaded New Netherland and made it the English colonial province of New York.

Yong's effort succeeded in one respect: the narrative of his voyage to the Delaware became one more piece of evidence to support the English Crown's claims to the river and the territory that surrounded it. In a proclamation that likely dates from 1642, Charles I confidently asserted that the Delaware fell under his jurisdiction, notwithstanding its current state of illegal occupation by "diverse aliens both Sweads and Duch and alsoe some of our Native English Subiects comminge from our Province of new England." Charles demonstrated the antiquity of his claim by tracing his "actuall and reall possession" back to the time of his "Progenitor, Kinge Henry the 7th," who had given a grant to "one Gobott [Cabot] of Bristoll . . . who had actuall possession and homage of the said indian captaines." A recitation of other claims followed, each confirming that Charles's royal predecessors had "taken possession and homage of the said Indians there." This chain of historical precedents extended even to the immediate past, in which Charles himself had authorized the voyage of "one captaine Younge."[56]

Several interrelated concepts animated Charles's proclamation. These same political and legal concepts—authority, allegiance, jurisdiction, and national difference—animated the writings of "captaine Younge," or Thomas Yong, the latter-day representative of Charles's authority in the Delaware. In both men's writings, these concepts powerfully transformed their rhetorical subjects. Merchants, navigators, and governors became agents who embodied the will and authority of monarchs, kingdoms, and peoples; indigenous "captaines" turned into proprietors and princes of native nations; unauthorized Dutch, Swedish, and English occupants of the space became transgressing subjects and trespassing aliens; indigenous homelands and hunting lands converted into territories of a Christian monarch. Both men likewise sought to depict English royal authority crossing, encompassing, and colonizing space.

In articulating this vision and adding a further piece of evidence to support the English Crown's claims to the Delaware, Yong had succeeded. He performed vital rhetorical work by representing himself as taking possession of the territory, negotiating the subjection of the river's indigenous peoples, and obtaining the deference of the Dutch. His narrative affirmed not only that the Delaware was a space the English Crown could and did possess, but also that the territory's inhabitants were dependent peoples whom the Crown could legitimately dispossess of their lands.

Yong's representation of himself as a dependent of the English Crown was essential to this rhetorical task of transforming the Delaware into English territory. Just as necessary were Yong's assertions of ethnic or national difference, categorical constructions that allowed Yong and others to speak of peoples as objects and representatives of authority. When Yong referred to "a certaine Nation called the Minquaos," "the Hollanders" of "the Dutch plantation," and the Indian king's description of Yong and his men as "a good people," he was using an ethnicized national language that linked explicit ideas of subjecthood to implicit ideas of peoplehood and national difference. At these moments of categorical slippage, we begin to see how discrete types of identity could combine to form a more general practice of national identification. Early modern national identities may have been more "regnal" than "ethnic,"[57] but in the messy social practice of contested colonial spaces, ethnic boundaries easily became associated with regnal loyalties. This was not an exclusively European practice; Indians identified European settlers by their national origin and encouraged Europeans to view them as belonging to different nations.

Yet as intertwined as political and ethnic identities in contested spaces could be, social actors in the Atlantic world remained capable of performing many other roles, discourses, and modes of identity—religious and cosmopolitan ones prime among them—that offered alternative ways of framing encounters. Not all encounters resulted in conflict, and even in contested spaces there was room for common ground. Throughout Yong's writings, we see possibilities of transcending or displacing allegiances and national affiliations. Yong's strong Catholic connections in England show how awkwardly religious affiliation could stand in relation to national orthodoxies. In Virginia, the "factious & turbulent spirits" in the council certainly had staked out a space resistant to assertions of royal authority. Along the Delaware, Yong turned paternal relations with Indians and Dutch traders into political relations, but many other merchants and colonists lacking Yong's fervent royal allegiance would act otherwise. For such actors, the personal could be constructed separately from the political. Yong was different. For him, or the loyal persona he constructed, allegiance was everything: "I shall acknowledge myself infinitely bound to his Majesty and whether he favour me . . . or no, I will yet be sure to serve him, and love him, and venture my life for him, and for the honour of my Country, with the same alacrity; and will by God's grace, both live and die an honest man."[58]

CHAPTER FOUR

"Subjects to the King of Portugal"

Captivity and Repatriation in the Atlantic Slave Trade
(Antigua, 1724)

David Barry Gaspar

By the early 1700s the Atlantic slave trade, through which the forced migration of Africans to the Americas as slave labor was organized, had been in existence for about two hundred years. Already, the trade had long been "at the heart of a wide net of commerce and production that touched every shore of the Atlantic basin" giving rise to an integrated multinational community. This community, best described perhaps as an extensive plantation complex, operated predominantly as "an economic and political order" centered on "slave plantations in the New World tropics" including the Caribbean islands. Though the complex was "divided into competing national spheres, each under the separate rule of a European power, the patterns of society and economy had much in common." The slave trade was so central to the Atlantic plantation complex in its role for recruiting labor that changes related to the trade in one sector of the complex as a whole or within a European national sphere could affect its other sectors. In those days of slow, long-distance, oceanic communication, buyers and sellers of slaves on the eastern and western shores of the Atlantic basin tried to be as well informed as possible about trends that might affect their interests in this most vital and lucrative branch of commerce. In the

Caribbean sugar colonies, planters and dealers in slaves tended to be concerned not only about maintaining a steady flow of African slave labor at reasonable prices to their shores but also about conditions, particularly on the African coast, that might impede trade.[1]

It was therefore at least partly because of the great dependence of the British Caribbean sugar island of Antigua on slave traders from Britain for supplies of slaves, and on the stability of trading relations on the African coast, that the slave-owning legislators of that island reached the uncommon decision in 1724 to support the repatriation of several blacks who were taken from the Cape Verde Islands, just off the western coast of Africa. Evidently, a shrewd understanding of Antigua's place within the Atlantic plantation complex, in the context of British trading interests and European imperial competition within the Atlantic basin, shaped the decision to repatriate the Cape Verdeans. That decision and the set of circumstances that gave rise to it can be discussed with a local Caribbean focus on Antigua, but it may be more illuminating to use an Atlantic approach because different regions of the basin are involved. In giving an Atlantic context to the circumstances surrounding the captivity and repatriation of the Cape Verdeans, the goal of this chapter is to "tease meaning from documents by relating them to the surrounding world of significance, passing from text to context."[2] What light do the events of 1724 throw on the slave trade and on the wider world of the Atlantic basin that was shaped by this trade?

The Evidence of an Atlantic Incident

On November 12, 1724, Governor John Hart of the British Leeward Islands in the Caribbean arrived at the island of Antigua aboard British man-of-war *Hector* under the command of Captain Humphrey Orme. On the night of Hart's arrival a remarkable incident occurred: "two Negroe Men swam a Quarter of a Mile, tho chained by the leggs to each other; from on board the Sloop two Brothers, Peter Roure Master; to the Hector then at Anchor in the Harbour of St. Johns," Antigua's main port, "and informed Capt. Orme they were Subjects to the King of Portugal, and inhabitants of the Cape Verde Islands, and were clandestinely taken away by the said Roure, with intention to sell them as slaves in the West Indies." The two black Cape Verdeans also told Captain Orme that twenty-five of their countrymen, "free Negroes," were being held on the sloop *Two Brothers* "under the same circumstances." It is not clear what language the Cape Verdeans used to communicate with Orme, but as natives of a

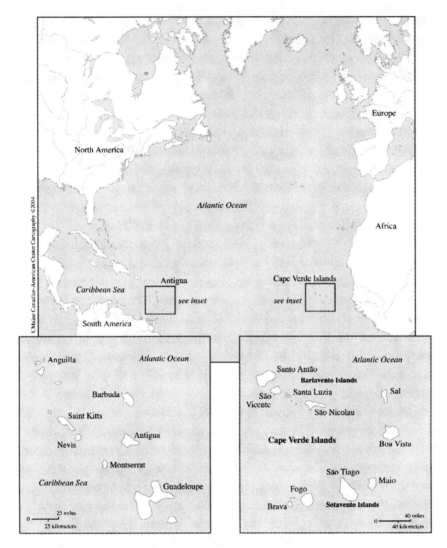

Fig. 4.1. The North Atlantic World

group of islands that British ships frequently touched at on their Atlantic voyages, sometimes to purchase slaves, it is possible that they may have known enough English to convey their message. Indeed, Captain Roure of the sloop *Two Brothers* had originally intended to do some of that kind of trading when he went to those islands. He arrived at Antigua on November 9, 1724, not long before Governor Hart. When Captain Orme heard the tale of the two captives who swam to his ship, he responded promptly. Orme did not explain why he pursued a particular line of action, but it can be inferred that he believed there were sufficient grounds to hold Roure accountable. Orme quickly sent one of his officers aboard the sloop and seized her pending an inquiry. He then brought the matter to the attention of Governor Hart, who took the necessary steps for recording depositions about the allegations against Roure.[3] Depositions of two of the sloop's crew, John Jones and Richard Condrick, were taken on November 14, 1724, two days after the governor was back in port, while those of two others, William Snary and Mathew Peterson, were taken on the following day, along with that of Francisco Delgaudo, one of the two Cape Verdeans who swam over to the *Hector*.[4] These depositions contain several valuable details about the circumstances that resulted in a formal inquiry.

The seaman John Jones, who was about twenty-three years of age, testified that he joined the crew of the *Two Brothers* around February 1724 at the port of Bristol, England, with the understanding that the sloop was bound for the Gambia River in Upper Guinea on the west coast of Africa and then on to the West Indies, in particular to the British sugar colony of St. Christopher (or St. Kitts), one of the Leeward Islands.[5] Jones agreed to a wage of twenty-six shillings sterling a month for the voyage, which originally did not involve Antigua as a destination. When the *Two Brothers* left Bristol in March 1724, however, Captain Roure did not head directly for the African coast. He first sailed west across the Celtic Sea to Kinsale, Ireland, where he took on provisions, such as beef, pork, cheese, and butter, some of which could be sold along the route of the voyage as opportunities arose. From Kinsale the sloop headed south for the Portuguese province of Madeira to take on corn, according to seaman Jones, but here British trading vessels usually also purchased wine.[6] From Madeira the sloop continued south and called at "the Island of Salt," or Sal, in the Cape Verde Islands to load that valuable commodity of the Atlantic for which the island had been named.[7] Captain Roure then took the sloop west to the island of São Nicolau ("St. Nicholas") in the group of small islands where he "took one Negro on Board as a Passenger to go for England" at this person's request. For this traveler the trip to England would take many weeks following a far from direct route. From São Nicolau, Roure then sailed south to the island of São Tiago ("St. Iago"), where the bishop of the Cape Verde Islands came aboard as a passenger. From São Tiago Roure took the sloop due east to the island of Maio ("May") and then back to the island of Fogo, and from there further west to the island of Brava ("Bravo"). Roure next sailed some distance north to the island of Santo Antão ("St. Antonio"), and then back to São Nicolau. The sloop's back and forth movement among the islands appears to be consistent with a search for profitable trading opportunities, particularly for slaves that could be sold later in the Caribbean. So far, however, Roure had not been able to purchase any slaves.

At the island of São Nicolau, seaman Jones testified, Roure "took in several Negroes that are now on board the said sloop *Two Brothers* in order to go a Turtling to the Island of Salt [Sal]" not far to the east. The bishop of Cape Verde was still aboard, but was put ashore at Boa Vista just south of Sal. Roure then turned north for Sal, where he left the blacks whom he had hired to catch turtles. He then returned to Boa Vista, picked up the bishop, and proceeded south to São Tiago where the bishop disembarked. From São Tiago, Roure sailed to nearby Maio island where three "Negro Women and a Young Negro Child" embarked. After this he returned to Sal where he had left the hired blacks to catch turtles. Here, he remained for about eight or nine days, according to seaman Jones, "and then took all the Negroes on Board being in number Twenty Five, and proceeded to Sea" bound for St. Christopher on the other side of the Atlantic Ocean. Jones added that during the first night when the *Two Brothers* was making its way westward across the ocean, taking full advantage of the northeast trade winds, Captain Roure, "having Two Pistolls Stuck by his Sides and a Sword in his hand," ordered his crew to shackle all of the blacks and take them below "in the hole." Jones testified that Roure's overall intimidating manner made it abundantly clear to the crew that they had no choice in the matter. If they did not follow Roure's commands, he would most certainly have "shot or stuck them." They followed the captain's orders. Jones stated finally that the hapless captives aboard the sloop had agreed with Roure "to be put on Shore, some at the Island of St. Nicholas, and some at Bonavista," before they had ever embarked on the *Two Brothers*.

The depositions of seamen William Snary, Richard Condrick, and Mathew Peterson generally corroborated that of John Jones, except for other interesting details that throw some light on the maritime worlds of the Atlantic basin of the 1720s. William Snary was about thirty years old when he, like John Jones, shipped aboard the *Two Brothers* at Bristol.[8] Snary's wage, like Jones's, was fixed at twenty-six shillings sterling a month for a voyage directly from Bristol to the Gambia River, and from there to the British Leeward Islands. When the *Two Brothers* left Bristol the following month and headed first for Kinsale, Ireland; it stayed there more than three weeks, according to Snary, "and took in some

Provisions and about Twenty Casks of Brandy." The sloop then left for Madeira "in Company with the Henrietta Sloop whereof one Baker was Master." At Madeira the *Two Brothers* stayed for about one week. Captain Roure loaded aboard a cask of wine and some corn, and then moved on south to the Cape Verde archipelago. Snary pointed out that the bishop of these islands actually hired the sloop over a three-month period to take him from island to island, and finally to the island of São Tiago where he lived. According to the seaman, the two black women, a girl, and a child who boarded the sloop at Maio were promised passage across to Boa Vista. When Roure returned to Sal to pick up the blacks who were catching turtles, he took all of them aboard and "the Turtle they had got and Salted up" and put out to sea for the West Indies. Snary concluded with the information that the *Two Brothers* was bound for St. Christopher in the Caribbean, and that Roure intended to head next for the neighboring island of St. Eustatius, a busy Dutch trading center where he expected to sell all of the blacks he had aboard, none of whom he had purchased legitimately.

Roure most likely believed that it would be easy to sell his human cargo to the enterprising merchants of St. Eustatius who were not likely to ask questions about its origins. In an official report of 1724 prepared for the Board of Trade in London, Governor Hart described St. Eustatius as "a barren spot of about Five English Miles in length, belonging to the Dutch West India Company (where they have a Factory) who annually send theither from Two to Three Thousand Negroes, the Greatest part of which are disposed off to the French of Martinique and Guardeloupe." The inhabitants of the British Leeward Islands that Hart administered also traded there "for Negroes and other Merchandize which they pay for in Sugars or ready money, the Dutch Factors refusing Bills of Exchange. And these sugars are clandestinely sent there in the Night, to the Dimunition of His Majesty's Revenue and the British Navigation."[9] It may be surmised therefore that Captain Roure had probably all along intended to do business at St. Eustatius rather than at any of the British Leeward Islands, even though he had been signing on a crew for a trip from Bristol to St. Christopher, by way of the Gambia River.

When seaman Richard Condrick, according to his deposition, signed on to sail with the *Two Brothers* he was about twenty-four years of age.[10] He joined the evidently still shorthanded sloop early in May 1724 at Madeira, also at a wage of twenty-six shillings sterling a month, for a voyage from Madeira to the Gambia River and then to the British Leeward Islands. From Madeira the sloop went directly to the Cape Verde Islands. On the matter of the seizure of the blacks who had been catching turtles for Captain Roure on the island of Sal, Condrick pointed out that, in following Roure's orders to secure the Cape Verdeans, the crew members were all armed with pistols and cutlasses. Condrick believed that the islanders were taken away "contrary to their Inclinations" or kidnapped. He also added that Roure landed "Two or three Anchors of Brandy" at the island of São Nicolau, and that he heard seaman John Jones and others among the crew say that Roure purchased the brandy at Kinsale, Ireland, before Condrick joined the crew at Madeira.

In his deposition, seaman Mathew Peterson, who was about twenty-two years of age, said that he joined the crew of the *Two Brothers* at Kinsale in March 1724 and agreed with Roure for a voyage to the Gambia River, then to the Leeward Islands, and then back to Britain, at the same wage as for seamen Jones, Snary, and Condrick.[11] Petersen made it clear that when Roure, after reaching the Cape Verde Islands, took aboard the two black women, a girl, and a child at Maio as passengers bound for Boa Vista, he did not take them there but proceeded directly to Sal, and from there set sail for the Caribbean. The passengers who boarded the sloop at Maio were therefore among the blacks that Roure ordered the crew to shackle. But most of the captives were the men who had trustingly agreed to catch turtles for Roure. One of them, Francis Delgaudo, deposed that he was "a Christian Negro and a Subject of the King of Portugal," an identity that would become quite important to the investigation about Captain Roure's dealings in capturing several other Cape Verdeans.[12] Delgaudo was about thirty years of age. He testified that he and his comrades, "who are all Christians except one," were hired by Roure to catch turtles. Instead of paying them for their work (at the rate of four pieces of eight a month each) and returning them to their home islands, Roure put them in chains "forcing them to these parts contrary to their inclinations." Unable to write, Delgaudo attached his mark to his deposition; seamen Jones, Snary, Condrick, and Peterson signed their depositions. With five depositions in hand, including Delgaudo's, Governor Hart was persuaded that there was strong enough evidence to proceed against Roure and he issued a warrant for his arrest.[13]

Roure, aware that the proceedings thus far implicated him in some highly questionable acts that might be construed as piracy, went into hiding. In tiny Antigua of only 108 square miles, he could not be found, though allegedly "very diligent search was made for him." Roure and the people who must have helped him to drop out of sight most likely had a good understanding of the proceedings involved in matters such as the one in which he had become embroiled. It was to Roure's advantage to remain at least temporarily inaccessible. From his hiding place Roure sent a letter to Governor Hart presenting his side of the story and explaining why he was in hiding. "I am concealing myself," Roure wrote, "not because I am conscious of any guilt that were truth known, can affect my life, but for the difficulty of making my innocence appear and to avoid the reproach which allwaies attends an Arraignment, and especially for so horrid a crime as Piracy." In this letter and in a subsequent formal petition to the governor, Roure explained that he had foolishly entered into some shady dealings with Father Deogue, a priest in the Cape Verde Islands, who agreed to sell him several blacks, who were clearly saleable as slaves, at a very reasonable price. Unable to pass up a good deal—for after all a prime purpose of his voyage from Bristol was to pick up some slaves—Roure bought the blacks from Deogue although the priest told him that "some management must be used to bring them on board." By the 1720s the captains of slave trading ships had been purchasing slaves at the Cape Verde Islands in small numbers for years. The "management" Roure used to take away the blacks that Deogue offered was to pretend to hire them to catch turtles, evidently not an unusual practice. In the Caribbean and elsewhere turtles were very valuable for their meat, eggs, shells, and for their supposedly useful medicinal properties.[14] Roure ended up seizing both the Cape Verdean turtle-catchers and the turtles they caught, a very profitable haul altogether.

Also aboard Roure's sloop at the Cape Verde Islands at that time were seven other islanders who ended up sharing the same fate of captivity as the rest. Roure explained that two of these blacks agreed voluntarily to remain with him wherever he might go. The other five were passengers aboard the sloop "which I was under a necessity of taking on board, because refusing them a Passage from one Island to another would have been inconsistent with my declared intention of going from Island to Island to purchase Slaves and returning them on shore on the Island they designed to would have endangered the escape of the rest from me." Roure insisted that he never intended to sell any of these blacks. He said he intended to send them back home at the first opportunity. He also pointed out that neither his crew nor the blacks he brought to Antigua could have known about his private dealings with the Portuguese priest, Deogue, at the Cape Verde Islands.

Roure's disclosures threw new light on the matter, very different indeed from what had come out in the depositions already taken. Roure added that he could prove that "I have hitherto had the reputation of a fair Trader, that I am not in indigent circumstances, and that my Father is worth £8000. It is then improbable & allmost impossible to suppose that for the value of 26 Negroes, I should commit a fact which I know to be heinous and would not only destroy my Character, but my Life." The sloop's captain pleaded that although he could not fully justify how he had acquired the Cape Verdean captives, he was not guilty of piracy committed knowingly. As further proof of this, he mentioned that soon after he arrived at Antigua, Captain Turnell agreed to buy the blacks at £25 (island currency) each in bills of exchange, which he would have accepted if he had acquired them through deliberate and premeditated piracy. Finally, Roure, throwing himself at the mercy of the whole legal system that threatened to hold him accountable for committing piracy, asked the governor for his protection "that I may not for a mistaken ignorance remain under the Apprehensions of a prosecution." When the governor later wrote to the Board of Trade in December 1724, sending along several documents related to the case, he did not mention Roure's letter but referred only to his formal petition that was very similar to the letter.[15]

The Antiguan Resolution

A close reading of Roure's letter and formal petition to Governor Hart reveals that his primary concern was to find a way to deal with possible charges of piracy. It may be argued also that it was the specter of piracy that haunted many areas of the Atlantic basin during the 1720s that first drew the attention of both Captain Orme of the warship *Hector* and of Governor Hart to the case involving Roure and the Cape Verdeans. A 1720 report from the island of Nevis in the Leeward Islands drew attention to the maritime predation practiced by the pirates of the *Royal Rover*, who had "committed a great many depredations upon the coast of Guinea." These pirates had taken a Portuguese vessel off the coast of Brazil, and they were the same predators who "were formerly in a ship they called the King James which they sunk and betook themselves to this," the *Royal Rover*. Governor Walter Hamilton of the Leeward Islands, who wrote the report, described this vessel as "a ship of force capable of mounting 30 guns and had once near 200 men (and as far as I can learn) was in the service of His Imperial Majesty when she was taken but she is now much out of order for which reason I suppose they quitted her" for another vessel, "a Rhode Island sloop, which they took and fitted out for their use," giving the Portuguese vessel they had captured to the captain of the sloop. The pirates extracted from the Portuguese vessel "a vast booty, most in *moidores,* not valuing the rest of the cargo (which consisted of sugar, tobacco, and Brazil plank)." Hamilton paid much attention to the menace of piracy whose effects reached directly into the islands' government. Later in 1720 he observed that "these seas are again infested with pirates of considerable force." Some of them had recently, "openly and in the daytime burnt and destroyed our vessels in the Road of Basseterre" in the island of St. Christopher "and had the audaciousness to insult H. M. Fort." In exasperation Hamilton described the pirates as "these vermine," "these villains," and felt that "nothing but force will subdue them," because offers of pardon evidently were not working.[16]

When John Hart, formerly governor of Maryland, took over the reins of government of the Leeward Islands in 1721, piracy continued unabated. After a tour of inspection of the Virgin Islands within his jurisdiction around the middle of 1724, Hart wrote that "Altho' I cou'd gett no possitive proof that the inhabitants of these Virgin Islands (especially at Tartola and Spanish Town) aid and assist the pirates, who frequently come amongst them; Yet there is a strong presumption, that they hold correspondence with them, and furnish them with provisions, which I shall endeavour to prevent for the future."[17] Evidently then, a heightened awareness of the prevalence of piracy that touched the shores of the Leeward Islands, as well as other regions of the Atlantic basin to the detriment of British interest, initially drove Hart to investigate the suspicious voyage of Captain Roure that brought him to Antigua.

Based on the information in the case before him against Roure, Governor Hart was disposed to send the Cape Verdeans back home to their islands. Of course, it was their word against Roure's regarding what had happened, but nonetheless, the case carried some significant implications beyond those of piracy, particularly in regard to Anglo-Portuguese relations. Hart sought the advice of his council members and the attorney general about repatriating the Cape Verdeans and about how to proceed against the sloop *Two Brothers* and Roure. Meanwhile, Captain Orme of the warship *Hector* offered his help in repatriating the islanders. Orme proposed to take them aboard his ship to Barbados and then on to England, en route to their respective islands. The Antigua council supported this plan as the "most ready way" to proceed, referring to the Cape Verdeans as "the Portuguese." The council recommended that Orme be supplied with provisions for the trip, and that Governor Hart, who had taken a personal interest in the case, be reimbursed for expenses incurred in maintaining the Cape Verdeans. The Antigua assembly, however, disagreed. The assembly suggested that the legislature should pass a special act to sell the sloop *Two Brothers* and much of its "Cargo and Apparell," such as masts, sails, anchor, and other equipment, in order to pay for the passage of the blacks who must be repatriated by a more direct route, "for We Apprehend if they should be sent to Barbados they will be sent back again hither."[18]

In regard to what direct action might be taken against the *Two Brothers*, the Antigua attorney general submitted a legal opinion that it was doubtful that seizing the blacks on land was piracy; and even if piracy was proved, Roure himself could not be found and tried as captain of the sloop and therefore the principal perpetrator or miscreant. Nothing could be done against Roure judicially "unless he was personally present." Roure most probably understood this, and that would partly explain why he went into hiding, although the other reasons that he gave for such behavior were strong and persuasive enough. But were the Cape Verdeans seized on land strictly speaking? Such fine points of law and procedure were often involved in cases of suspected piracy during the 1720s. The sloop's crew, who had simply followed the captain's orders, it may also be argued, were certainly not as culpable as Roure, if they were at all culpable.[19] Some crew members of captured pirate ships often escaped punishment by claiming that they were forced by the captain and others to turn pirate. From his hiding place at this juncture in the case Roure sent a formal petition through some of his influential friends at Antigua to Governor Hart covering some of the same ground as in his earlier letter and stressing that he was sorry for what he had done in "depriving Freemen of their liberty." Here, Roure was admitting to a lesser charge than piracy and implying also that he might be given an opportunity to make amends.

In his petition Roure introduced at least two new themes or issues: "he offered to give sufficient security to transport the Portuguese to their own Country, provided he might have his pardon."[20] Attached to the petition was a testimonial in support of Roure signed by twenty-six Antigua merchants and other influential residents, who certified that "we personally know or are acquainted with the character of Peter Roure, Master of the Sloop Two Brothers, and that he has alwaies had the reputation of an honest man and a fair Dealer, And we firmly believe that (far from being a Pirate) he would not knowingly be guilty of, on the contrary would detest, any acts he thought Piratical."[21] These two documents, the petition and the testimonial, Governor Hart showed to his council, who then advised that Roure should be pardoned "on condition he entered into Security of a thousand Pounds immediately to send back the said Negroes, and produce a certificate in six Months time of their being delivered at the Cape de Verde Islands." Following the advice of the council and of the attorney general, Hart granted the pardon. The council had originally wanted Roure to post security of £2,000, but this was reduced.[22] It may be argued that in proposing that he would arrange for the safe repatriation of the Cape Verdeans by the most direct route, Roure had his own interest primarily in mind, because once the Cape Verdeans arrived home it would be possible for the authorities there to determine how many of them were genuinely free persons, as they claimed, and which among them had belonged to the Portuguese priest with whom Roure had dealt. Besides making a gesture to undo the injustice the Cape Verdeans experienced, Roure felt that by providing full security for their repatriation, he could also be of service to Governor Hart for "a full and Speedy reparation to the Nation of Portugall." At the same time his action would "give an instance of National Justice that will ever prevent an Application, to the great honour" of Britain and the governor's reputation.[23]

Here, Roure had crafted a clever solution to his predicament, and one he thought would benefit everyone concerned. It certainly made the job of the Antigua governor and the legislature easier in a case for which the evidence of piracy was not firm enough. By tying together the interests of Portugal, Britain, the governor, Antigua, the Cape Verdean blacks, the owners of the sloop and her cargo, and his own, Roure provided an extraordinarily inclusive Atlantic framework for the case in which he was involved, perhaps with secret legal advice from some of his friends. Such an Atlantic contextualization of the case could not have escaped Governor Hart and everyone else in Antigua who was connected with it in some way or who heard about it. Indeed, the Cape Verdean captives themselves initially provided an Atlantic framework when they were driven to claim themselves "Subjects to the King of Portugal." For both Hart and Roure, however, repatriation of the Cape Verdeans was the most critically important element in a much more complex course of action to resolve a difficult situation that possessed Atlantic ramifications. Accordingly, Hart saw to it that the Cape Verdeans were sent home not aboard Roure's sloop but aboard another one, the *Mary,* under Captain George Roach, who was hired for that particular purpose[24]—a decision that would have helped persuade the authorities of the Cape Verde Islands that their counterparts at Antigua were acting in good faith. Before they left Antigua, the Cape Verdeans were given ample provisions for their return voyage, and they were paid the wages that they should have received from Roure for catching and salting turtles at the Cape Verde Islands. It is not clear who actually paid out these wages.[25]

Why was Captain Roure pardoned? It was not unusual for colonial governors to issue pardons in cases of piracy under extenuating circumstances, and it must be remembered too that the charge of piracy against Roure rested on evidence that might be taken as largely circumstantial. In his commission from the Crown as governor of the Leeward Islands, Hart was authorized "to pardon all Piracys Robberies and Offences at Sea, that are or shall be Committed by any Persons who shall Come within his government." Accordingly, Hart, exercising his authority, issued Roure's pardon, a document that was most carefully prepared and that presented a clear summary of the case for the ultimate benefit of not just Roure but everyone concerned. The charge against Roure as outlined in his pardon was that according to "sundry affidavits" he was believed to have been principally involved "with takeing Severall Negros from some or one of the Cape De Verde Islands under the Dominion of the King of Portugall to the Number of about twenty six and that the same Negroes or Most of them are free Subjects of the said King of Portugall, with whom we are in perfect Amity." The document then traced what was reported to have happened at the Cape Verde Islands, which resulted in Roure's seizure of the Cape Verdeans, whom he took to Antigua aboard his sloop "with Intent to sell them for Slaves." But several details of the case made it doubtful that actual piracy had occurred, including Roure's claim that, as far as he knew, he purchased at least some of the Cape Verdeans, those he hired to catch turtles, from a priest. Also, his crew might be inclined to believe he forced them to commit "so foul a Crime" as piracy because they were not aware of the purchase. The pardon also revealed that Roure had found "three able and Sufficient" residents of Antigua to post bond "with Sufficient penalty" to transport the Cape Verdeans "in three Months time" back to their homes, when it could be determined who was free and who was not, "By which means full Satisfaction will be made to the Justice and Laws of Nations and to the said Negroes in their private Capacitys." Ultimately, the strength of the case against Roure turned on the quality of the evidence that was "so very Doubtfull" that a pardon was justified. Even in the construction of Roure's pardon the Antigua authorities paid some attention to the importance of preserving the good relations that existed between Britain and Portugal.[26] While this concern was only briefly mentioned in the pardon, the Antigua authorities kept it foremost in mind in resolving the situation that Roure had precipitated, and they addressed it more directly in another important document connected with the case.

International Appeasement

Governor Hart also took another step, or what amounted to a precaution, to buttress the justice of his decision to repatriate the Cape Verdeans, all of them. He prepared an "Instrument of Writing" for the benefit primarily of the Portuguese authorities at the Cape Verde Islands and elsewhere that explained the unfortunate actions of Captain Roure and the measures that were taken to deal with them at Antigua. This document, like Roure's pardon, throws much light on the issues with which the official mind of the Antigua governor and his legislative and legal advisers grappled in 1724.[27]

Hart explained to authorities in London that he prepared the "Instrument of Writing" under the seal of the Leeward Islands for a very specific purpose and sent it to the authorities of the Cape Verde Islands by the sloop captain who brought back the captured natives of those islands. The purpose was so that "all Governors and other officers belonging to His Majesty of Portugal on the Cape de Verde Islands, might know, how much such an Action, as this of Roure's was abhorr'd by Me; And to the Intent that no Reprizals might be made . . . on the Vessell which I sent back with the said Negroes to the said Islands." Hart hoped that the Portuguese authorities would accept his gesture and the course of action he took against Roure "as a Reparation for the Injustice and Violence offerd to the Subjects of the King of Portugal," and understand also that "no such wicked Attempts will be countenanced in any of the British Governments, which might be of very ill consequence, if tolerated, to our Trade in those parts, so many of our Ships touching at the Cape de Verde Islands for Water and trading thither for salt, who might, tho innocent, find the Resentments of the Portugueze inhabitants there, being most of them Negroes."

Hart's "Instrument of Writing" to the Portuguese authorities contained more details about the case against Roure than the report he sent to the Board of Trade. In the first document, for example, Hart recorded that after he was informed about the violence the Cape Verdean captives endured from Roure and his crew, he "caused the said Negroes to be freed from their Irons, directed proper provision to be made for their Subsistence, and ordered their Cloaths and all that had been taken from them" be returned. Beyond providing such information about details relevant to the crime Roure allegedly committed, Hart was concerned with fully explaining why he dealt with the charges in a manner that did not lead to a trial, and indeed precluded one, but to which the Antigua authorities nevertheless directed proper attention. Perhaps the most pertinent reason was his desire to deal expeditiously and effectively with a situation that ultimately may not have amounted to piracy, strictly speaking, but which nonetheless involved some delicate issues. Under the circumstances, repatriation of the Cape Verdeans took priority over other matters. It did not take Hart long to form this opinion and act upon it.

Why did he favor speedy repatriation? Hart wrote that it was imperative that he should do all in his power to preserve not only the "perfect Amity and Mutual Friendship" that existed between Britain and Portugal, but also the "good correspondence and Commerce between the Subjects of both Nations." Hart was also motivated to favor repatriation "out of an abhorrence of all wrongs and Injustice and as much as in me lyes to preserve Inviolable the Laws of Nations," and so that "Speedy Reparation may be made to the said Negroes, or as many of them, as on their Return shall appear to be injured." Sending the Cape Verdeans back home could help preserve good relations between Britain and Portugal and all that such relations entailed, but it was also true that, as Roure himself pointed out, the transactions at the Cape Verde Islands that led to Roure's predicament could be investigated. If the authorities at those islands found that Roure had a lawful right to any of the black islanders, Hart stated quite plainly, then they should be returned to Antigua by the same sloop that had taken them home, for the benefit of the owners of the sloop *Two Brothers* and its cargo.

Repatriation, the Rules of Enslavement, and Atlantic Politics

It is not clear what happened in the end, but the whole incident about Captain Peter Roure and the sloop *Two Brothers* at the Cape Verde Islands and at Antigua definitely opens a window into several aspects of Atlantic relations or realities, and the links between zones of provenance (supply) and zones of reception (demand) across the Atlantic Ocean in regard to the slave trade during the 1720s. Accordingly, at least five features of the Atlantic world of the early eighteenth century deserve attention in their capacity to illuminate the case of Captain Roure and the wrongful seizure of the Cape Verdeans: piracy; understandings about lawful and unlawful forms of trading in slaves; the recourse of the Cape Verdeans to claims of identity as Portuguese subjects; Anglo-Portuguese relations; and awareness or concern among Caribbean slaveowners about relations among nations in the Atlantic basin and conditions of trade, particularly the slave trade on the African side of the ocean.

It has already been argued that the phenomenon of rampant maritime predation in the Atlantic during the early 1720s cast the incident involving the sloop
Two Brothers in a particularly negative light. That Roure escaped prosecution for
piracy is related, however, to some of the conflicting details of the case. More
importantly, it is also related to the relevance of the case to existing Atlantic relations and Britain's interest within those relations. Had Roure in fact kidnapped
or "panyared"[28] the Cape Verdean blacks and taken them by force to Antigua to
sell them into slavery? Roure's answer was that he had purchased most of them,
and extenuating circumstances explained why his shackling them could not be
perceived as piracy, because shackling was a normal precaution all slave dealers
were forced to take when crossing the Atlantic Ocean to the Caribbean with
slaves. The difficulty of proving that piracy had occurred persuaded both Roure
and Governor Hart to favor repatriation of the Cape Verdeans, though they had
different reasons. Repatriation therefore emerged as a very important feature of
this whole affair of "depriving Freemen of their liberty," and it strongly indicates
the interpretive appropriateness and value of an Atlantic contextualization that
transcends narrower and more regionally confined analysis.

That the Cape Verdean blacks were meant to be definitely repatriated con-
tributes much to an Atlantic reading of the voyage of the sloop *Two Brothers*.
The vast majority of Africans and people of African descent, free or slave, who
were taken to the Americas by force lived and died there. The Atlantic slave
trade involved overwhelmingly one-way traffic to the Americas. Any case of
repatriation of the victims of this forced migration is not only surprising but
also assumes significance as a striking aberration that should be investigated.
Only a few cases have so far come to light for the British slave trade and the
Anglo-American world from the seventeenth to the early eighteenth century.

The first case involved the voyage of the vessel *Rainbow* from Boston, Massachusetts, to the west coast of Africa in 1645.[29] Captained by James Smith, the
Rainbow was scheduled to call at the Cape Verde Islands, the West African
coast, Barbados, and then back to Boston. Instead of going to the Cape Verde
Islands, however, Smith took the vessel to Madeira for wine and then on to the
African coast where the crew of the vessel, led by the mate, kidnapped some
natives who were enticed aboard. They may also have captured other natives
when they attacked some villages. Eventually, the *Rainbow* made its way back
to Boston with two African captives aboard, whose presence "raised serious
questions for Massachusetts officials," who found that Smith and his crew had
"stolne" the Africans in contravention of the law of the colony and had done

so on a Sabbath. The Massachusetts "Code of Fundamentals, or Body of Liberties" of 1641 restricted slave trading; it ruled that among the Puritans "There shall never be any bond slaverie, villinage or Captivitie . . . unles it be lawfull Captives taken in just warres and such strangers as willingly selle themselves or are sold to us." The General Court of the colony determined that the law had certainly been broken; it prosecuted Smith and his mate and resolved that the Africans should be repatriated. The court then went further. It proposed a law in 1646 to "sufficiently deterr all others . . . in such vile and most odious courses" as "the haynos and crying sinn of man stealing." Also, the Africans were to be sent home "by the first opportunity (at the charge of the country for present)" with a document that recorded the court's determination not to condone such criminal behavior. The case would probably not have been pursued had the Africans been purchased instead of taken by force.

A similar principle, bearing perhaps no relation by then to religion and morality, as for the Puritans, influenced perceptions of so-called lawful and unlawful practice in the British slave trade by the early eighteenth century. In 1724 Governor Hart of Antigua authorized the repatriation of the captured Cape Verdeans for several reasons, one of them being that there was some doubt that the islanders were lawfully acquired through purchase. Another relevant case occurred in 1729, again in Antigua.[30] This one involved the kidnapping of some free African traders at Cape Appolonia on the Gold Coast in Lower Guinea. The Antigua legislature ruled on that occasion that the traders who were "illegally and forcibly brought away" by the captain of the sloop *Catherine* should be repatriated. The case of the sloop *Two Brothers* of 1724 must have served as a useful precedent for the ruling of 1729, although such a connection was not stated officially.

Another interesting case of repatriation comes from seventeenth-century Barbados. In 1693 the legislature of that sugar colony issued an order "for Lieutenant Powell to send back to Madeira a negro and a Portuguese whom he had taken from that Island, paying their passage and restoring to them any money that he has taken from them." In 1722, at St. Christopher in the Leeward Islands, yet another case of wrongful enslavement of free men, if not their repatriation, came to light. Two "Indians," Juan Hyacinthe and Augustino Hosea, came before the governor and council of the colony to plead for their freedom "they being free born Subjects of the Kingdom of Spain." Juan and Augustino alleged that they were "forced away from the Dutch colony of Carracoe [Curaçao]," where they lived as free men and were sold into slavery at St. Christopher. The governor and council believed their story, "but as their Remedy is at Law, And they being Paupers," the solicitor general was assigned to present their case in formal proceedings. It is not clear how the case was resolved, but the governor and council evidently took it seriously enough and were disposed toward setting the two men free.[31]

The three cases of unlawful acquisition of slaves that involved the British Leeward Islands in 1722, 1724, and 1729 occurred at a time when there was reportedly a marked increase on earlier importation trends of African slaves, but it remained true that these islands generally needed more slaves than were actually delivered.[32] In spite of the great demand for slaves, the island legislatures appear to have upheld principles that concerned the legitimate acquisition of slaves for sale. That is to say, in colonies heavily dependent on imported slave labor, and where access to freedom by such enslaved persons was not encouraged, the legislatures still did not condone unlawful enslavement of free persons through direct involvement by British slave traders. They much preferred that the slaves be lawfully purchased elsewhere before they were transported for sale in the islands. By this process British subjects were not expected to deprive people of their freedom deliberately, but they were justified in trading for slaves with others, such as the collaborative African traders on the coast who had presumably already acquired captives for sale. Reverend William Smith who lived for several years in Nevis, one of the Leeward Islands, and who left that island during the early 1720s, observed that "Now and then, these poor Creatures are, by private Traders, stole away out of their own Countries, to the eternal scandal of us Christians; But the usual method of coming by them is, to purchase them."[33] The reference here to Europeans as Christians was only meant to differentiate them from Africans, as was common at that time, and not to draw attention to any strong religious scruples. British ideas about the legitimacy of purchasing slaves rather than acquiring them by any other means would appear to be in line with justification of a recognized business transaction. Slaves, in other words, were to be acquired by fair not foul means.

Nevertheless, the approach of the Leeward Islands' legislatures to what they understood to be unlawful or unallowable enslavement of free persons gives rise, of course, to at least two pertinent considerations. First, the legislatures could only become involved in cases that actually came to their attention, and evidently few cases did. Second, there was much opportunity for shady dealings in the trade for slaves. Even free black traders themselves might become ensnared in the nets cast to capture slaves.

The case of the Cape Verdeans taken to Antigua in 1724 provides evidence that opportunity for the capture and enslavement of free persons of African descent was not confined to coastal West African regions. For such people the growing demand for slaves during the early eighteenth century made freedom quite precarious. As a result the Cape Verdeans came close to being sold into slavery in Antigua. One is left to wonder what recourse would have been left to them if they had claimed they were free men and Portuguese subjects after they were already sold in the colony. They evidently obtained the intervention of Governor Hart at a strategic moment: before their sale there. Would the governor then have done enough to simply set them free? Apparently not. Hart believed that the complicated details of the case, and the questions and interests involved, required a more elaborate and comprehensive resolution, the centerpiece of which was repatriation of the Cape Verdeans. Simply to free them at Antigua was a local solution. To repatriate them also was much more. It was an Atlantic solution crafted primarily to preserve and promote British hegemonic interests in the Atlantic basin and elsewhere within the Portuguese seaborne empire. That solution, indeed, was suggested implicitly from the very beginning when the two Cape Verdeans slipped over the side of the sloop *Two Brothers,* swam across to the man-of-war under Captain Orme, and, in explaining their plight, announced that they were "Subjects to the King of Portugal."

A similar case connected with the identity of captive Portuguese subjects was under investigation in Barbados in early 1724, when the meaning of such a claim made in such particular circumstances was articulated quite explicitly.[34] Four "Portugueze mulatos," who were seized by pirates at the Cape Verde Islands, were later transferred to a trading vessel and sold at the island of Saint Lucia in the Caribbean. The resident of Barbados who bought them took them with him back to Barbados. The four men managed to contact the governor of Barbados seeking their freedom. They claimed that "they were freemen, Christians, and subjects of the King of Portugal, and could not be sold as slaves." That indeed was exactly what the Cape Verdeans at Antigua meant to convey when they too claimed Portuguese identity, although precisely how they communicated their message is uncertain. Only an official English interpretation of their complaint or appeal has survived.

The Cape Verdeans, in declaring their identity as Portuguese subjects, expected to be understood. They were drawing upon a common understanding, tantamount to a convention among Europeans within the Atlantic trading community, that free subjects of European rulers could not be reduced to slavery, a condition at that time reserved for other people who could not claim that privilege. That understanding had emerged and was nurtured by the increasing intensity and regional reach of the Atlantic slave trade, which, at the same time, increased opportunity for its subversion. Captain Orme understood what the Cape Verdeans meant; so too did Governor Hart and the Antigua legislature. Even Captain Roure was forced to admit that he understood, and therefore he must accept some responsibility for the plight of the Cape Verdeans. Caught in a tangle of misfortune, these islanders certainly understood what they should do to recover their freedom and drew attention to their Portuguese identity as "Subjects to the King of Portugal," although they obviously carried multiple identities. But, under the circumstances, only one was likely to work with the European-connected authorities in the Caribbean. By the eighteenth century, the Luso-African communities of the Cape Verde Islands and the West African coast from Senegal to Sierra Leone identified themselves as Portuguese based upon "a priori characteristics, primarily skin color," having been "drawn increasingly into a European discourse on identity" that was shaped by expanding involvement with Africa, primarily through the slave trade and slavery. By defining themselves as Portuguese, or more precisely as Portuguese subjects, partly to escape the clutches of enslavement as happened to millions of Africans from the continent, the Cape Verdeans at Antigua in 1724 were also identifying themselves "by reference to what they were not": they "could not be sold as slaves."[35]

Governor Hart and the Antigua legislature finally agreed to repatriate the captured Cape Verdeans primarily in the interest of preserving Anglo-Portuguese relations, which, during the second decade of the eighteenth century, were extremely advantageous to Britain particularly in economic terms. Not only did British vessels regularly stop for water, food, salt, slaves, and repairs at the Cape Verde Islands, located strategically at the "crossroads of the Atlantic, where wind and current brought together the ships of Europe, Africa, the West Indies, and North and South America"; Britain also enjoyed thriving commercial relations with Portugal through which access to valuable goods originating in Brazil was also acquired. Such relations were facilitated to no small degree by the existence of a sizeable British merchant community in Lisbon.

Commercial treaties between London and Lisbon, signed during the seventeenth century, had been advantageous to both countries, but it was a similar agreement, signed in 1702 as part of an alliance brokered by John Methuen between England and Portugal before the start of the War of the Spanish Succession (1702–13), that opened the way for British domination of commercial relations with Portugal during the first half of the eighteenth century. One contemporary observed in 1730 that British trade in Lisbon "is the most considerable of all; many people think it is as much as all the other Nations put together." British trade (visible and invisible) became so important within the operation of the economy of Portugal that, according to Braudel, the term *commercial colonization* aptly describes the dominant role of that trade. "Anglo-Portuguese trade reached a peak" during the 1720s. At that time textiles made up 80 percent of British exports to Portugal, and among other minor exports were codfish, corn, and some products from British colonies in the Americas. The British also benefited greatly from Portuguese exports, chief of which was wine; but bullion was important too. Between 1700 and 1760 Britain consistently "achieved a surplus in her visible trade with Portugal," and also earned "considerable sums" from "invisible" trades, "principally the employment of a large and growing capital by English merchants in the credit granted to textile purchases in Portugal, the sale of Newfoundland cod by West of England fishermen, the use of English ships in Portugal's colonial and foreign commerce, and the English merchants' varied interests as principals in other branches of Portuguese trade and economic life." By the 1720s, certainly, the growth of British trade with Portugal and its dependencies was made possible by the expansion of that market for British goods.[36]

Understanding, therefore, the importance of good relations with Portugal in at least preserving and enhancing the development of the British Atlantic economy, Governor Hart and the legislature of Antigua wisely organized the repatriation of the wrongfully captured Cape Verdeans in 1724. In doing so they also acted to promote the interests of the Leeward Islands and Britain's other colonies in the Americas in regard to their trade with Portugal's provinces and colonies in the western Atlantic for wine, slaves, and other products. According to a report from the Leeward Islands in 1724, the islanders traded "to Madeira for wines, for which the greatest part is paid in bills of exchange to London, or exchanged for negroes and provissions."[37] Any disruption of Britain's favorable relations with Portugal might be quite damaging to the trade and general well-being of the Leeward Islands which not only benefited greatly from trade with the Portuguese islands but also depended heavily on the importation of various goods, including food, from Britain carried in ships that touched regularly at these islands on their way to the Caribbean.

The case of the capture and repatriation of the Cape Verde blacks in 1724, to be best understood, must be approached from the vantage point of its Atlantic ramifications, in much the same way as the principal parties in the case variously must have done. In the end Governor Hart of the Leeward Islands agreed to send the Cape Verdeans back home primarily in the interest of Britain's Atlantic empire, which depended on good relations with the Portuguese, particularly at these islands. The voyage and route of the sloop *Two Brothers* attests to the value of the islands to British Atlantic interests. But Captain Roure's transactions there were also only part of a much longer chain of events related to a voyage that connected western and eastern boundaries of the Atlantic Oceans as parts of an integrated Atlantic world where European national spheres overlapped.

Perhaps the most revealing aspect of the voyage of the sloop *Two Brothers* is the claim of immunity from enslavement made by the Cape Verdeans that Captain Roure captured. These islanders understood sufficiently the wider Atlantic implications of their predicament, of being unlawfully, as Portuguese subjects, captured in one part of the Atlantic basin and intended for sale in another thousands of miles away from home. They were aware that there were enslaved blacks in the Cape Verde Islands and that slave traders often came there from various nations to purchase them or to acquire other goods or services. In this frontier environment of international commerce and slavery, they were conscious of the important differences between free and slave status, the value of slaves to European traders, and the difficulties that free blacks faced trying to elude the grasp of such traders. Free blacks at these islands learned how to evade these men, particularly by claiming an identity connected to their status as subjects of the Portuguese crown. Whether they were originally free men or not, the two Cape Verdeans who made their dramatic escape from the sloop *Two Brothers* challenged the lawfulness of their capture by Roure and appealed to the Antigua authorities' understanding of the unwritten international rules or protocols under which persons might be enslaved. Asserting that they were free subjects of the king of Portugal, they implied that they had right on their side, and, thus empowered, interpreted their and their comrades' capture as a matter that challenged Portuguese authority at the Cape Verde Islands and elsewhere. The Cape Verdeans projected an argument of Atlantic significance that the Antigua authorities had no difficulty understanding, particularly where their own interests and those of the British Atlantic community intersected.

CHAPTER FIVE

From Catholicism to Moravian Pietism

The World of Marotta/Magdalena,
a Woman of Popo and St. Thomas

Ray A. Kea

> Outside the walls of your birthplace, you have the right to choose the
> name that is attractive to you.
>
> YORUBA PROVERB

Marotta/Magdalena was a West African/Caribbean woman of the late seventeenth and early eighteenth centuries, an engaging figure who was multilingual
and literate in two and possibly three languages. By all accounts she was a
devout and pious woman, dutiful and conscientious in her religious obser-
vances. Her life story belongs to the history of West Africa, where she carried
the name Marotta, and to the history of the African Diaspora, from which she
took the name Magdalena. In short, her story in the context of the West African
and Caribbean societies in which she lived offers an important African perspective on the making of the Atlantic world.[1]

Marotta was probably born in the mid or late 1650s in Great Popo, the trading and political center of the Popo Kingdom, located in the western section of
the Bight of Benin, a densely populated, commercial and urban landscape.[2] At
the time, Great Popo and the other ports in the western Bight had small Christian congregations, as did certain other coastal towns in Lower and Upper
Guinea, and Marotta grew up in a Catholic community.[3] Her father was Roman
Catholic and taught her the basic tenets of the faith. As a child, she learned to
read and write her own language (Aja-Ayizo) and perhaps Portuguese as well.

Her family's household, the community of Christians, and her hometown represented the different levels of social and political interaction and forms of social, cultural, and material capital within which she developed.[4]

Sometime in the 1690s, she was sold into slavery during a time of civil wars, mercenaries and warlords, and military conquests by armies of musketeers on the western Bight. She was transported to the Danish colony of St. Thomas in the West Indies, a forced displacement from a slave exporting, urban complex to a slave importing, rural colonial production complex.[5] Marotta's new home belonged to what is sometimes called the "extended" or "greater Caribbean," a coastal and littoral region stretching from Virginia to the eastern part of Brazil.[6] In the early 1730s her owner manumitted her on account of her advanced age, by then over seventy years. By this time she was literate in Dutch Creole, the lingua franca in the Danish Caribbean islands, as well as her own language, Aja-Ayizo. In 1736 she joined the Moravian Brethren, known variously as *Unitas Fratrum* (United Brethren), *evangelisches Brüder* (Evangelical Brethren), Moravians, Herrnhuters, and Hussites. Prior to her conversion to Moravian Pietism, she informed the Moravian missionaries about her life as a Christian in Popo. To commemorate the occasion, she took the name Magdalena in honor of the Danish-Norwegian Queen Sophia Magdalene. The former Popo citizen-subject became one of the acknowledged leaders of the Moravian Church on St. Thomas and a church elder in 1739, and, as someone literate in Aja-Ayizo and Dutch Creole, she was able to address Danish authorities on behalf of the Moravian community of St. Thomas. The letters and petitions she wrote or co-wrote were concerned with the plight and welfare of converted slaves and freed persons on St. Thomas. She died in 1745.

The Popo Kingdom and the Bight of Benin

Marotta/Magdelana's life as a dedicated and "crusading" Moravian Pietist was grounded in the political and cultural milieu of Great Popo, where she lived the first three decades of her life. Popo and Ardra belonged to what Magdalena, in her 1739 petition to the Danish-Norwegian queen, called *ad ga Tome*, that is, "Aja country," which in her translation to Dutch Creole she simply called "Africa." The Popo Kingdom, where she was a subject, owed tribute to the Kingdom of Ardra (or Allada), the dominant polity on the western stretch of the Bight of Benin.[7] Ardra had higher levels of political and economic activity than did Popo. With its tributary dependencies, it formed a cultural-political system that can be designated Greater Ardra. The Benin Kingdom, an imperial city-state formation on the eastern section of the Bight, exercised suzerainty over Greater Ardra until the 1670s. Benin was an area of high population density where economic, political, and ideological power were highly concentrated, leading to a high level of economic and intellectual production.[8] The ruling dynasties and political and merchant classes of the Ardra and Popo Kingdoms were actively involved in the expanding Atlantic trade. In the 1670s Great Ardra, the capital, exported an annual average of three thousand enslaved Africans from its ports to the Americas. Marotta herself was caught up in this contested process of forced migration.

Marotta's life in Popo necessarily included a cultural and symbolic universe which generated the conceptual and affective vocabularies that allowed her to comprehend and to organize her relationship to social reality.[9] She would have known three metaphysical systems—*Vodun, Ifa,* and Catholicism—the first two of which had their historical and social roots in the urban regimes on the Slave Coast and their hinterlands. *Vodun* was a hegemonic formation, a meta-language, in much of Lower Guinea. It was a metaphysical site of representational practices and of modes of signification about the worlds of the living, the dead, and the cosmos. *Ifa,* or *Fa,* was a complex of meta-languages associated with divination discourses and practices and was equally widespread. As a dominant cultural, theological, and symbolic order, it, along with Vodun, constituted a universe of signs and an economy of signification. As urban vocabularies, Ifa and Vodun organized communities of discourse and textual/speech communities. The communities were internally variable, and hence heteroglossic ("dialogic"), and contributed to the domestication and contextualization of events, actions and relationships, and the urgencies and ruptures of everyday life. That is, they provided a theoretical understanding of and perspective on the making of the societal order, an important consideration as West Africa became integrated into the Atlantic world.[10]

In the second half of the sixteenth century, Catholicism became part of the Ardra and Popo religious pantheon as a specific ritual process and textual practice, an utterance with a new point of view on the world. In contrast to Ifa and Vodun, which imaginarily united society by constructing a normative order and a social cohesiveness across and against class and status, Catholicism formed an enclave realm of ritual, was not an active proselytizing enterprise, and became the faith of a dedicated few, among them Marotta's family. What we know of Marotta's Catholic background comes from what she told Moravian missionaries. A Moravian missionary's diary entry, dated October 29, 1744, relates that Magdalena was baptized *(getauft)* in her childhood *(Kindheit)* by a Spanish priest *(Spanischen Domine)*.[11] The diary does not give the date of the baptism nor does it identify the Spanish priest, however, a probable identification is possible. A well-known Spanish mission, comprising twelve Capuchins, visited the Ardra and Popo kingdoms in 1660 and 1661, and one of them likely baptized Marotta.

Presently, nothing is known about her father or mother, apart from what Marotta told Moravian missionaries in 1736. She related that her father taught her the tenets of the Catholic faith. He was evidently a practicing and literate Christian, and either he or another teacher taught her to read and write her mother tongue, Aja-Ayizo, and possibly Portuguese. Some other social traits can be suggested. He was a free person of some social standing, a property owner, and, in all likelihood, a former student at the São Tomé seminary. Marotta's family probably enjoyed a level of consumption unavailable to the average urban commoner. According to the Moravian missionary Spannenberg, Marotta "used to make a yearly offering of a lamb or goat to God in order to placate the divinity and ensure her own well-being," probably a practice adapted from her family's tradition in Great Popo. A recent study details the growth of the livestock industry in the Bight of Benin, particularly in seventeenth-century Ardra. The study notes that Ardra commoners did not consume meat produced by the expanding industry, because they could not afford the expense. Marotta's family, on the other hand, appears to have been able to afford, at least once a year, not to consume a lamb or a sheep but to turn the animal into a religious offering.[12]

Interpreters and translators in seventeenth-century Greater Ardra were associated with Christianity, because they were the people who most often knew Portuguese. Marotta's father likely earned his income as a royal interpreter of Portuguese at the Great Popo royal court, the royal court of Great Ardra, or as an interpreter to a prominent, high-ranking officeholder in one or another of the political capitals. As a tributary subject of the Ardra ruler he would have been obliged to serve in that ruler's court, at least occasionally. Until the late 1670s the slave trade of the Popo Kingdom had to be conducted at Great Ardra. Jean Barbot, the French Huguenot trader, reported that when Popo was under Ardra suzerainty, the Ardra ruler "obliged the inhabitants [of Popo] to bring their slaves to Ardres [Great Ardra], in order to exact duties on them."[13] Marotta's father could have served as a translator in such commercial transactions when they involved European merchants.

There are no histories of the institution of interpreting/translating in the Bight of Benin ports, and thus we know little about the lives of individual interpreters/translators or about interpreters/translators as discursive communities. We do know that in the seventeenth century there were among the Ardra kings' subjects a small number of Portuguese-speaking interpreters and, among them, a smaller number of professed Christians. One can assume that the Popo royal court had Portuguese-speaking interpreters, as well. Portuguese trade at Great Popo dates from about 1553 and shortly afterwards in Ardra. Persons trained in the Portuguese language and converts to Christianity soon appeared in the two kingdoms. They would have been the sons or other male relatives of high status families. Some of them would have received an education at the São Tomé seminary, where they would have learned Portuguese and the tenets of Catholicism.[14]

São Tomé was an important base for Portuguese and Vatican inspired missionary projects. By 1494, African priests were trained in Lisbon and sent to the island, presumably to convert enslaved laborers and to conduct missionary activities in the Bight and beyond. In 1534 the diocese of São Tomé was founded and served as a central locus for the evangelizing activities of various Catholic orders (Augustinian, Franciscan, Jesuit, and Capuchin), which soon developed their own historical dynamic and institutionalized expressivities.[15] Great Popo probably developed its own small community of Catholics. One early seventeenth-century writer reported that long-standing contact with the traders and priests of São Tomé caused the people of Lower Guinea to speak a type of Portuguese that came to be known as the *lengua de São Tomé*.[16] In the mid seventeenth century, an unspecified number of political notables associated with the Ardra royal court and government knew São Tomé Portuguese. One of the Spanish Capuchins who visited Ardra in 1660 noted that "Captain Carta," one of the highest-ranking officers of state (*den principaelsten adel*, according to a mid-seventeenth-century Dutch commercial guide), spoke Portuguese and also understood Spanish.[17] In 1670 a French emissary on a trading mission to Ardra noted in his journal that King Tezifon, his eldest son, and most of the officials in the Ardra government spoke Portuguese, that is, the "language of São Tomé."[18] Presumably, some, if not all, of them could read and write the language. Tezifon is said to have been educated in the São Tomé seminary and instructed in Christianity, but was not baptized.[19] Presumably, Marotta's father belonged to the Catholic community of Great Popo and Great Ardra and may have received his education at the São Tomé seminary or in Great Ardra.

The coming of the Capuchin Order of Saint Francis mission to Ardra arose out of an initiative from Toxonu (Toshonu), the Ardra sovereign (d. ca. 1661).[20] Toxonu's principal motives were to revive Ardra's slave trade with Europeans and to heed the requests of subjects from São Tomé for Catholic priests.[21] In 1657 Bans (or Vans), a Portuguese-speaking ambassador from the king, arrived in Cartagena in New Spain *(Cartagena de las Indias)*. He requested the establishment of regular commercial relations with Great Ardra and the sending of Christian missionaries. Reportedly, the king himself was willing to accept baptism. Don Pedro Zapata, the Spanish governor, provided them with an interpreter-catechist, who knew Spanish and Aja-Ayizo.[22] The embassy then continued to the Spanish royal court at Madrid, where Philip IV responded enthusiastically to the embassy's mission, particularly to its request for missionaries.[23]

Twelve Capuchins from Castile volunteered to serve in the mission to Ardra. One of the priests, José de Naxara, assisted by the ambassador, now baptized and renamed Philip Zapata, and an interpreter, Antonio, translated the short catechism containing common prayers, the creed, and brief descriptions of Catholic doctrine from Spanish into the language of Ardra. Printed in Madrid in 1658 under the title *Doctrina Christiana*, Thornton argues that the catechism was the work of the interpreter-catechist who joined the embassy in Cartagena. He suggests that "the interpreter-catechist's conceptions of Christianity may well have been themselves the product of the Allada Christian community, transported across the Atlantic when the interpreter was enslaved, and then enlarged and ultimately printed overseas. In any case, the catechism returned to Africa with the Capuchin missionaries."[24] They arrived at the port of Jakin in January 1660 and were met by a senior administrator ("Capitan Zupi"), a number of high-ranking officials *(capitaines y fidalgos)*, and a "huge crowd of Blacks" *(de grande muchedumbre de negros)*, that is, the attendants, servants, slaves, and clients of the officials. One of the Ardra king's interpreters, a black Christian named Mateo López from São Tomé, served the mission as its official interpreter.[25] The missionaries were lodged in a wing of one of the royal palaces.[26] There were already communities of Christians in Greater Ardra, but these were not the objects of the missionaries' efforts.[27] Their purpose was to create a congregational space that would encompass the entire Ardra Kingdom.

The Capuchins apparently hoped the dynastic prestige and political clout of the Ardra monarch would enable them to succeed, but in the end the king failed to cooperate. The historian Robin Law reports that "the Spanish Capuchin mission achieved nothing whatever." In spite of his earlier commitment to become a Christian, Toxonu, the Ardra sovereign, refused baptism and instruction in the Christian faith, and he denied the missionaries' request to be allowed to preach to the people in the capital. The priests found it increasingly difficult even to secure audiences with him, and the king eventually relegated them to the port of Offra. The ambassador, Bans or Philip Zapata, and the royal Christian interpreters, including Mateo López, were unwilling to defy the king in order to help them. Appeals to Ardra officials were unsuccessful and attempts to preach to people in the streets of Offra were met with physical assault. Four of the missionaries embarked on a Dutch ship and arrived in Spain in 1661. The remaining three went to the Popo Kingdom, but they had no success there in gaining new converts. After a few months stay, they sailed to the Americas on a Dutch ship.[28]

The failure of the Capuchin mission rests on the fact that it gained no new adherents or converts. One can surmise that Marotta's father had his young daughter baptized by one of the three Capuchins who visited Great Popo in 1661. Her baptism indicates that the missionaries interacted with the Great Popo Christians, ministering to their needs in different ways. But this was not the purpose of their mission. Their assigned task was to expand the faith and find new converts. Still, the notion of failure has to be seen as relative. The local Catholics would have received copies of the *Doctrina Christiana*. In all likelihood Marotta knew about it even if she had not studied it. Certainly, the Christians of Greater Ardra carried a memory of the Capuchin mission. In the 1690s at the port of Whydah there were two or three elderly men who clearly remembered the mission, and in Ardra itself Old and New Testaments and copies of the *Doctrina Christiana* were still in circulation.[29]

John Thornton argues that the "Portuguese settlements in West Africa . . . practiced a syncretic form of Christianity," but the Catholic Church was willing to accept it.[30] I would propose that the Greater Ardra Christian communities developed in the course of the sixteenth and seventeenth centuries their own hermeneutic and theological traditions. One might postulate that the presumed "syncretic" character of Greater Ardra Christianity derives from the fact that Ardra cosmology helped to determine, in ways not yet understood, its formal and material properties. In any case, one should understand that the historical relationship between different communities of discourse, textuality, and praxis—Ifa, Vodun, and Catholicism—was probably continuous. While they were obviously different in fundamental ways, they shared a central tension between their foundational concepts (ideality) and the immediate facts of social existence in Greater Ardra. In the midst of destabilizing and violent changes in the Bight of Benin in the later seventeenth century, Christian and non-Christian congregations alike would have faced uncertainty, moral dilemmas of one sort or another, and personal crises.[31]

In the West Indies Magdalena's understanding of the Christian Holy Trinity was expressed in a language that depended on an Ardra cosmology and Aja-Ayizo concepts: *Pao*, God the Father, *Mau*, the Son, and *Ce*, the Holy Spirit. The theological language *(lengua Arda)* of the *Doctrina Christiana* drew upon the same cosmology and, with one exception, the same conceptual source for its categories of the Holy Trinity, but the categorical terms are different: *Vodu*, God the Father, *Lisa* (meaning "Christ"), the Son, and *Espiritu Santo*, the Holy Spirit. *(Doctrina Christiana* is translated *Pranvi elisà.)* The Ardra Christian congregation utilized both theological vocabularies, though in the present state of knowledge it is not possible to explain precisely what these significant differences in religious language meant.

The catechism may represent a chronologically older interpretative tradition in the religious thought and practices of the Ardra-Popo Christians. In the catechism an Aja-Ayizo word for Holy Spirit was not used. To express it the translator borrowed a Spanish term. Scholars have maintained that the catechism reflects a seventeenth-century Ardra cosmology in which the godhead was composed of two elements, Vodu and Lisa, and that these two conceptual categories were borrowed by Ardra and Popo Catholics.[32] If, as Thornton suggests, an Ardra interpreter-catechist who had been transported to Cartagena as a slave produced the catechism, then the language of the catechism would have been in use among Ardra-Popo Christians during the first half of the seventeenth century. The language of the *Doctrina Christiana* and the language of Magdalena's two petitions would appear to represent two different hermeneutical traditions in the Ardra-Popo Christian community.

Does the vocabulary in Magdalena's petitions express new appropriations of the Greater Ardra "syncretic" Christian tradition? That is to say, a reflective and self-conscious Catholic community of hermeneuts borrowed new conceptual terminology from Vodun (and perhaps Ifa) cosmological thought and applied it to their own Christian expression. They thereby created a culture of piety that was distinctively different from an earlier tradition of piety and worship. In contrast to the *Doctrina Christiana*, "Holy Spirit" had a translated Aja-Ayizo equivalent—Ce or Se. Who or what was *Pao*? Is it related to *Da*? In eighteenth-century Ardra and Dahomey cosmologies the godhead is triadic. *Da* is described as the controller of life, the sustaining power of the universe, and the force of life and motion. *Mawu* is described as the creator of all the gods and goddesses (deities of the earth, the sea, and the sky). In two petitions, written in the Aja-Ayizo language, Magdelana referred to *Vo dú maú (vodun mawu)*, which in her translation into Dutch Creole, she translated as *die Heere Jesus*, "the Lord Jesus."[33] Se represented the human spirit, the source of thought, foresight, and reason. It was the inner force or energy that guided a person's destiny. It was an individual's conscience.[34]

Can we make additional inferences about the thought and activity of Greater Ardra Catholicism? The two theological vocabularies could represent two contending hermeneutical traditions in the same Christian community and not an earlier and a later phase of a single tradition. If Magdalena's words are in any way representative, it can be said that the Ardra-Popo Christians formed a self-reflective congregation of hermeneuts. In the present state of knowledge it is not possible to explain precisely what the vocabulary changes mean. One can postulate that they represent new interpretations in the religious conceptions of the Catholic congregation, or they could represent two distinct but overlapping theological traditions in the same community. Only further research can resolve some of the issues raised here.

St. Thomas, Marotta, and the Moravian Brethren

Three main islands made up the Danish Virgin Islands in the Caribbean: St. Thomas (1672), the largest island, St. John (1675), and St. Croix (1733). They formed a sugar producing periphery to an importing Danish core centered on Copenhagen. The islands consisted of three spatial elements: the "wilderness" (a space of marronage), the plantation sector (a space of production), and the harbor-town sector (a space of trade and administration). Two hierarchically ranked, racialized worker status groups were employed in the plantation and harbor sectors: *bussal* slaves and *creole* slaves. The "wilderness" represented their site of resistance.[35]

Marotta arrived on St. Thomas when the island's economy was rapidly growing. In November 1685 a treaty between the Danish West Indies and

Guinea Company and the Brandenburgh African Company allowed the Brandenburgh Company to sell slaves on St. Thomas. From 1690 to 1698, thirty-two
Brandenburgh slave ships, each with approximately five hundred or more
enslaved Africans on board, sailed to St. Thomas, one of the most important
slave marketing centers in the West Indies. In fact, Dutch interlopers supplied
far greater numbers of slaves for the St. Thomas market than did the Danish
Company.[36] Marotta was likely transported aboard a ship owned by the Brandenburgh Company, which was particularly active at Slave Coast ports in the
1690s. As the Danish historian Georg Nørregaard noted, the raison d'être for
Danish slave traffic was "the supply of coerced labor it secured for the islands
of St. Thomas, St. John, and St. Croix."[37] During her years of enslavement,
Marotta lived and worked on the estate of the Danish planter Johannes Lorentz
Carsten, owner of the largest plantation on St. Thomas and of more than 150
slaves. In the early 1730s when she was quite advanced in years, Carsten manumitted her.[38]

Around this time, the Evangelical Moravian Brotherhood commenced
activities on St. Thomas. Whereas the policy of the established Danish
Lutheran Church opposed the conversion of slaves to Christianity, the Moravians launched a missionary drive on the island among the slaves and freed
blacks. The Brotherhood *(Evangelische Moravische Broedergemeente)*, founded
in 1722 by Count Nikolaus Ludwig von Zinzendorf (d. 1760) in Herrnhut, Sax-
ony, was an outgrowth of the seventeenth-century Pietist movement in the
German Lutheran Church. Pietism, with its emphasis on "Christocentric
piety," dominated the Brotherhood's missions. The redeeming properties of
divine grace were made universally available to humanity by means of the
physical and spiritual sacrifice of Jesus Christ. An act of faith was superior to
an act of reason. Humanity was naturally depraved and prone to sin; and "heathen people" had to be brought to salvation. Zinzendorf's dream was to create
an ecumenical and evangelical church with the divine task of converting "sav-
ages, slaves, and other heathens." The peregrinations of his sect signaled the
beginning of the modern Protestant missionary movement.[39]

The Moravians were not abolitionists and were not opposed to slavery and
the Atlantic slave trade. The particular doctrinal practices of Unitas Fratrum
included the following: (1) the cultivation of devout study and private meetings; (2) the recognition of Christian priesthood among all of the faithful by
giving the laity a share in church government; (3) insistence upon the necessity of vital personal piety; (4) kindly persuasion in dealing with heretics and

unbelievers instead of bitterness; (5) rhetoric banished from the pulpit and replaced by sincerity in speech; (6) emphasis on doctrine and the doctrine of general priesthood; and (7) emphasis on practical Christianity.

In the Danish Caribbean context, Moravian Pietism functioned as a disciplinary and disciplining institution and a cultural formation that organized a dominant ideology, Christian evangelism, into a power and a praxis. As a structuring authority, it imposed its own "model" of self and identity. It was an arbiter of private not social morality. The morality of the plantation regime was not at issue; rather the Moravians' basic obligation was to convert "heathen" slaves. Domination was not imposed from just one point, from "outside," but internally in the "heathen" slaves' subjectivities.[40] The Moravian enterprise cannot be treated as an epiphenomenon or as a reflection of some more fundamental substratum. It needs to be understood as a real social force existing in its own right as an autonomous "level" of social practice with its own determinations and effects. What is the nature of man and where does it come from? Moravian theology affirmed the existence of a true individual self that was predisposed to sin and that needed to be saved by the demands of moral commandments, rituals, and faith. It formed a unitary and regulatory discourse. It defined, regulated, and colonized, and thereby "hegemonized" particular relationships and practices. Pietism's "archive" and its politics of representation could not validate "heathen" African discursive and cultural formations—beliefs, values, rituals, ceremonies, and the like—it could only configure them as absences and negations.[41] Marotta the Catholic was a different matter.

African cultural and ideological differences were constructed as "heathenism," "nonreason," "spiritual blindness," and "sinfulness," according to the imperatives and the classificatory schemes of the "great internments" described by Foucault. The evangelizing Moravian missionaries, according to one historical interpretation, helped to eradicate the African beliefs held by enslaved workers in the Danish Caribbean.[42] The Moravian faith can be interpreted as one of the religious forms of modernity. There is no doubt that the Moravian missionary regime, with its ritual practices, discourses, and lines of articulation and intensity, produced truth effects that defined, by rules of inclusion and exclusion, the concrete acts and discourses among the proselytes.

The initiative for bringing the Herrnhuters to St. Thomas lay with Anton Ulrich ("Anthon Ulerich"), who was born a slave on St. Thomas in about 1715. In 1729, his master Count Laurvig (or Larwig), a plantation owner, one of the

directors of the Danish West Indies and Guinea Company, a royal court official, and a leading advocate of Pietism, took him to Copenhagen. There he
served the Count as *Kammer-Moor* (chamber Moor, i.e., valet) and regularly
visited the Danish court. In 1731, von Zinzendorf was in Copenhagen to attend
the coronation of King Christian VI. He brought three Moravians with him to
the royal court, including the carpenter David Nitschmann. Ulrich met
Nitschmann and von Zinzendorf while in attendance at court. Nitschmann
spoke to Ulrich about Christ the Savior, and later recorded their conversation.

> The witness [i.e., Ulrich] opened his heart and told the story of how he had sat
> at the beach of St. Thomas and sighed for a revelation from above, and how he
> asked God to send him a light about the doctrine which was talked about by the
> Christians. He then described in glowing colors the pitiable exterior and interior
> conditions prevailing among the African slaves there, naming especially his sis-
> ter Anna and his brother Abraham, and said that these shared with him the desire
> to get to know God without having the leisure for it because of slavery: That
> Anna frequently prayed to God that He might send her somebody to teach them
> the way to Salvation. If that happened they would be converted to Christianity
> and many Africans with them.[43]

Von Zinzendorf took Ulrich to Herrnhut, where the former Kammer-Moor
addressed the Moravian Congregation. Ulrich described not only how the
slaves suffered under an unbelievably oppressive slavery but also how they
lived "in heathen blindness and a horribly sinful state, simply because they
knew nothing about God or Christ." He emphasized that the adversities in the
slaves' conditions of existence made it impossible for them to achieve the good
life and confirmed that it would, indeed, be difficult to spread Christianity
among them: their conditions of work left them little time to learn about it
and their owners would oppose their conversion.[44] The religious culture of
Lutheranism, as alibi for the slave owners, had to be transformed into a religious culture, such as Moravian Pietism, which showed ways to overcome the
brutality and oppression of the slave owners.[45]

Ulrich's inspirational talk stirred the congregation to send missionaries to
the Caribbean, which can be described, in historical terms, as a colonized space
at the anguished and profitable margins of the "West." Two evangelical brethren,
Johann Dober and Tobias Leopold, felt that they were called by God to travel to
St. Thomas to save the enslaved "heathens." To prove their commitment and
determination, they were willing to let themselves be sold as slaves. They arrived

on St. Thomas in 1732 and began to proselytize on the Grande Princesse plantation, an estate owned by the Danish West Indies and Guinea Company. Their first converts were Anna and Johann Abraham, Anton Ulrich's siblings.[46]

The missionary project of the Moravian Brethren enjoyed the support of the directors of the Danish West Indies and Guinea Company.[47] Like Count Laurvig, Count Karl von Plessen was a company director, a plantation owner, a royal court official, and a Pietist. Both men were strong supporters of von Zinzendorf and staunch advocates of Moravian missionary work, which they viewed as one facet of their colonization project. In 1733, for example, von Plessen issued a "Memoria" detailing how St. Croix could be transformed into a sugar-producing colony. He envisioned the creation of 800 sugar cane plantations on the island for 1,600 Whites *(Weise)* and a labor force of 30,000 to 40,000 Blacks or slaves *(Negres oder Sclaven)* to work the land. In addition, there was to be a special settlement *(Ansiedlung)* for the Moravian Brethren *(Märische Brüder)*, and their charge was to Christianize the Blacks. Under these conditions, as guests of Count von Plessen, the Brethren were not prepared to oppose or challenge slavery.[48]

In 1734 eighteen Moravians, both men and women, arrived on St. Thomas as missionary-settlers and began preaching among the slaves and baptizing those among them who accepted the Word. The leader of the missionaries, Friedrich Martin, joined them two years later and extended the proselytizing throughout St. Thomas and on St. Croix.[49] From the beginning of the Moravians' missionary activities on St. Thomas, their biggest supporter was Johannes Lorentz Carsten, on whose plantation Marotta lived. Born in the West Indies, he was the wealthiest planter on St. Thomas. The first slave baptisms occurred on his estate. He owned the house where the missionaries held their first meetings, and he helped them to buy a plantation together with nine slaves. The missionaries renamed the plantation "Bethel" and called their plantation mission station "New Herrnhut."[50] Two of his own slaves, Domingo Gezu ("Mingo Gesu"), Marotta's son and a plantation supervisor *(Unteraufseher)*, and Andreas, became Friedrich Martin's first local male assistants. In short, Carsten did all that he could to promote the Brotherhood's project, even though his activities led other plantation owners to accuse him of desiring the emancipation of all slaves who became members of the Moravian Church. Carsten vigorously denied the charge. He published a strongly worded piece in which he made it clear that at no time did he ever advocate that any slaves who were baptized became legally free *(dass die Negers wenn sie getauff worden, von ihrem Sclaven-Stand frey seyn solten).* By 1739 he was living in Amsterdam, having sold his plantation to the Evangelical Brethren.[51]

Anton Ulrich was right when he stated that most plantation owners would oppose all attempts to evangelize among the slaves. They and the governor vehemently opposed the missionizing efforts of the Herrnhuters and tried in every way possible to put an end to their activities on the island. The more slaves that joined the Moravians the greater the planters' physical opposition and vitriol became. They argued three points: Satan created the Blacks; conversion practically eliminated the distinction between "white" Christians and "black" heathens; and conversion would lead to a slave rebellion like the one that had occurred on the island of St. John in 1734. The reaction of the slave owners to the agency of the enslaved draws attention to the constructedness and instability of the plantation order. Relations of power were organized around planters' constructions of race, class, culture, and gender.[52] Within the plantation system's economy of power and symbolic order, the planters were interpolated as inherently superior subjects, and as natural masters they could, with seeming impunity, physically assault their workers, whom the signifying discourses constructed as racialized inferiors and subhuman. The slaves' appropriation of Pietism destabilized the plantation owners' notion of Blacks. The dominant modes of inscription could not view the converts in their "leisure and humanity," hence the pitiless resolve to stop Moravian evangelism.

The planters and the Lutheran pastor demanded that the governor put an end to all forms of proselytizing on the grounds that the Herrnhuters were not properly ordained to carry out missionary work or properly trained to teach Christianity to "heathens." The new faith defied established authority, infused the slaves with ideas of liberation, and was a nursery of revolt. The new converts were attacked and beaten, books were burned, and church services were disrupted. Friedrich Martin, his wife, and his closest associates were arrested. Martin was sentenced to "lifelong penal servitude" and his wife "was to be sold into slavery and excommunicated from the [Lutheran] church." When von Zinzendorf arrived on St. Thomas, he discovered that all of the missionaries were living under terrible conditions in the local prison.[53]

The count's presence changed the situation. As a confidante and relative of the Danish royal family, he carried much political weight. Von Zinzendorf and the Moravians had the unconditional support of the Danish-Norwegian king. Backed by royal approbation and the encouragement of the directors of the Danish West Indies and Guinea Company, von Zinzendorf came out in strong support of the converted slaves and the Moravian missionaries. With the royal family backing the Evangelical Brethren, the Danish governor was in no position to continue his opposition. In a letter dated February 1739 he stipulated the twelve conditions that the missionaries had to accept in order for them to be officially allowed to live and work on St. Thomas and the other islands.[54]

In a letter, written in Dutch Creole and addressed to the St. Thomas congregation, von Zinzendorf spelled out in detail the obligations and duties of the church members to God, Bas Martin, and the King of Denmark. He proudly announced that the "Cross of Jesus Christ" was known in fifty-one of St. Thomas' plantations and more than a hundred believers from several different plantations were attending Martin's school.[55] Schooling in the faith, he explained, released believers from the slavery of Satan *(slaverey van Duivel)* and brought them to the freedom *(vryheid)* of Christ. But there were some believers who were misguided and held wrong ideas *(valsche gedachten)* about what they were to do in the world: they thought that they did not have to work and that they were free persons. But Martin correctly taught them that they must work and the little time they had to themselves could be spent in learning. They must trust their owners, obey their overseers, and perform their work piously and quickly. Everyone must remain in the place that God had ordained for him or her. There was no question of acquiring a legal free status as a result of baptism. There are no indications in the sources that any members of the St. Thomas congregation openly grumbled about or challenged von Zinzendorf's words.[56] On his return to Europe in 1739 the count composed a hymn *(Welch ein Heer, zu Gottes Ehr')* to celebrate the successful work of the Moravian Brethren in the Danish Caribbean colonies.[57]

Moravian Pietism and Marotta

The Moravian Church on St. Thomas constituted a new normative horizon and the basis for collective solidarity for slaves and freed persons alike. The Pietist Magdalena and her fellow converts were striving for psychic security and personal happiness, effected by sublimating anxiety and despair into a quest for and love of community.[58]

Moravian practice required believers to compose a *Lebenslauf,* that is, a detailed autobiographical inventory of one's "heathen" life and "sins,"[59] an obligation that reinforced the power of the church over believers. It provided a form of relief for the psychological consequences of a Christian notion of the self that was grounded elsewhere. The statement of a group of anonymous enslaved Africans *(bussaler)* is instructive: "We have come here from far away, across the ocean from Guinea. We have neither father nor mother, therefore we wish to learn about our Father in heaven, so that we shall not be unhappy."[60] The enslaved believers filled the abstract notion of church with a positive cultural content. This self-aware religiosity of the proselytes is readily apparent in their letters, or documents of human bondage.

In 1736 the missionaries made their first contact with Marotta, whom they described as "an old Guinea woman of the Papaa nation." Throughout St. Thomas she enjoyed a wide reputation as a deeply devout and pious person. One might suggest that she possessed a certain moral wisdom. Spannenberg recorded a conversation with her:

> She fears God and acts righteously. Before she eats anything at all in the morning, she falls on her knees, lowers her face to the earth, and prays. Before she goes to sleep, she does the same thing, manifesting a great and extraordinary respect before God. She said that she had learned these practices from her parents and that others in her land served the Lord in a similar manner . . . She could not understand why the Whites showed such little respect before God and seemed only to be paying Him compliments. She said that until someone showed her a better way, she would persist in her practices in order that God might not become angry with her . . . she had never yet heard the gospel of Jesus Christ . . . She then told us how she made her offerings. When she gets new fruit, whatever kind it might be, she eats none of it, until she has taken some and burned it. Then she falls down on her knees and thanks God from her heart for having given her life and health to enjoy and fruit to plant. Only then does she consume the fruit . . . She had some vague notions concerning the trinity, from which one could clearly conclude that Christian missionaries must have visited her fatherland. She said that there was only one God, the Father, who is called *Pao*. His Son *Masu* is the only door, through which it is possible to come to the Father. And then there is also the [Holy] Spirit called *Ce*. She had been taught all this by her father in Guinea. But she was quite unfamiliar with the idea that the Son of God had become man and that He saved and redeemed mankind through His death. She used to make a yearly offering of a lamb or a goat to God in order to placate the divinity and ensure her own well-being. At first she could not grasp why such offerings were now neither necessary nor valid, as the result of the Son of God having given Himself as a sacrifice for all of us. After she had been advised by the

brethren to pray to God for the grace which would enable her to believe these things, she beat her breast with joy and gave testimony that: "In here, I am now certain that what you have said is true." From that time on, she no longer made her customary sacrifices. Rather she prepared a lamb on the high feast days and invited several Blacks as guests. They then joined together in prayer, which they wished to offer up to God in place of fine-smelling smoke offering.[61]

Marotta's account of her Christian faith was an ontological affirmation of being. She was conscious of her own biography. As an *ermeneus* she must be seen as a subject of knowledge and of belief. Her faith was an articulation of an identity that was not in search of spiritual salvation or beatific happiness, at least as these attributes were understood by the Moravian Brethren. Her Catholic theology, taught to her by her father, allowed her to interpret the missionaries' Pietism. In Moravian eyes, she possessed only "vague notions" concerning the Trinity, and, hence, her beliefs were not congruent with the Christological theology of the missionaries. She was not redeemed through the sacrifice of Christ. For Marotta serving the "only one God," "His Son," and "the [Holy] Spirit" through prayer and offerings was a sign of authenticity and autonomy. In 1736 she joined the Moravian Church. In December the following year she was baptized. The event was commemorated with a name change: Marotta became Magdalena. She chose the name of the reigning Danish-Norwegian queen, Sophie Magdalene.[62] Henceforth, she was known as Elder Magdalena, a position she held until 1741, when the frailties of age and ill health forced her to resign from her leadership position.

By 1738 the Congregation numbered 650 male and females, including slaves and freed persons. According to the church's organizational practice, it was divided into small groups. Oldendorp explains:

Such groups were composed of five, six, or ten persons, who came together once a week under the tutelage of a missionary or his aide in order to discuss their inner growth in the knowledge of Jesus Christ, to exchange confidences about their individual problems, to encourage one another, and to ask forgiveness for one another. These groups were organized by sex. Martin himself looked after the two groups of baptized persons. The remaining groups were led by [assistants]. Even aged Magdalena, who was unable to move around much owing to her weakness, took it upon herself to further the growth in Christ of those Blacks living nearby her with whom she associated. She assisted others as well, and her efforts were blessed with success.[63]

The growing number of Pietists among the slave population necessitated the appointment of "church workers." In 1739, Petrus "was consecrated as Elder of all the brethren, and Magdalena . . . was installed as elder of all the sisters in a ceremony involving blessings and the laying on of hands. She was to be called venerated evangelical elder."[64] The converted slaves and freed persons were in the process of creating a community imagined from within the precepts of Moravian Pietism. But, it was a community formed according to specific gender relations, institutional rules, and doctrinal principles, all under the plantation's industrial character. With the founding of their own church organization, the converts institutionalized certain expressions of cultural and social autonomy, expressions defined in part by the converts' loyalties and responsibilities toward their Pietist beliefs and their own church.

In February 1739 von Zinzendorf agreed to carry two petitions to the king on behalf of the missionaries and proselytes. One, addressed to the king of Denmark, was written by four men and three women "in the name of 650 black pupils *[swarte scholieren]* of Jesus Christ," all of whom had been baptized by the missionary leader Friederich Martin. One of the women was Magdalena, who wrote the second petition in the name of the congregation of 250 women.[65] The determined attempts of enslaved and freed Pietists to write their own texts underline the extent to which the planters had suppressed their powers of speech, their image-making capabilities, and their self-representation.[66] In their appeal to the Danish monarch, the two petitions functioned as sites of cultural explanation as well as affirmation. The petitions inscribe what the converts had to say about their own cultural and public space, a space composed of an opening—an opportunity to worship Lord Jesus—and a closing—a cessation of the slave owners' violent actions against their desire to found a church. On the one hand, the petitions can be viewed as functioning within a discursive context that embodied the hegemonic relations and authority structures of a plantation society. On the other hand, they can be seen as part of the symbolic pact constituting the history of the Caribbean working class and the history of the demands of capital accumulation in the kingdom of Denmark. We might say that the Moravian converts drew their own portraits in their struggles in the island's history and space of production.

Magdalena's petition, written in Dutch Creole and Aja-Ayizo, provides access to the self-representations of Magdalena and through her words the women's congregation, as well as their conscious self-reflections on being in the world of plantation society. It identifies the logos of the world that gives meaning to a person's life and ensures the ontological status of the world, "Lord Mau" in Popo and "Lord Jesus" in the "land of the Whites." It is also the expression of a refusal. In their efforts to redefine themselves, Magdalena and the women converts gave vent to an unwillingness to conform to the planters' intimidating dictates. The multiple Atlantic locations expressed in the petition—Popo ("Lord Mau/Mawu"), St. Thomas (*Bas* Martin), and Copenhagen ("Great Queen")—defined locations of meaning and an economy of signification for St. Thomas's Moravians. Magdalena reworked these positions into a personal statement that tells us how she made sense of her social milieu, with its fissures and contradictions, and how she organized reality in her mind and expressed it in her behavior.

Magadalena was a signatory to several letters written in February 1739. They included a letter addressed to the islands' governor and two letters addressed to the Danish king. In the letter to the governor, signed by Friedrich Martin and Magdalena *(Magdalenen)* and several *knegten en maagden van Jesus Christus* ("male and female servants of Jesus Christ"), a lengthy explanation concerning the Moravian religious mission is presented. They served God and his church and they worked for the Danish king.[67] In another letter, signed by Magdalena *(Madlena)* and five other persons who had been baptized by Martin, the converts describe the brutal treatment inflicted on them by the plantation owners. They also spelled out their desire to learn more about "the Lord" and asked the king to support their church and to encourage their efforts to learn more about Jesus.

By 1740 nearly one half of the enslaved population and an unknown number of freed persons on St. Thomas had been baptized. Maroonage and insurrections ostensibly belonged to the past. The new dispensation introduced a new project. The contained space of the Moravian congregation existed within the hegemonic structure of the Danish colonial plantation system. The organizers of this system, the absolutist monarchial regime—the Danish West Indies and Guinea Company, the Copenhagen commercial patriciate, and the nobility—shared a "general interest" with an enslaved working class. The general interest was the achievement of spiritual salvation and moral certitude through the sacrifice and grace of Jesus Christ.[68] If the maroons of St. Thomas were liminal figures and their communities were anti-structures within the framework of the plantation system, Magdalena and her co-religionists were not liminal, but integral.

Moravian Pietism inscribed believers in subject positions that sustained the power-knowledge relation. It rested on specifiable institutional supports—church, congregation, school, and the Herrnhut plantation—which operated in a social space different from that occupied by the slave owners' political and racializing ideologies. The specificity of the slaves' adherence to Pietism can be regarded as a particular space that might be variably filled with different kinds of practice at different times, and not simply as a set of practices related to each other in certain necessary and unchanging ways. This is to propose that the "community of imagination" to which Magdalena and the other converts belonged is not an essentialist identification. The Pietist values of the Christian congregation were capable of varied expressions, including petitions, marronage, open insurrection, and religious revivalism. The congregation's church-building project within the plantation regime's *Lebenswelt* carried an economy of belief that was more complex and more contradictory and ambivalent than one might presume. From the historian's perspective, it belonged to a counterculture of modernity.

Magdalena and her fellow communicants organized in order to represent their own corporate institution and their own public space, albeit one contained within a dominant metropolitan cultural and ideological field. One can surmise that the converts were actively engaged in defining a Christian religious culture for themselves. Within the structure of the methods of production and class relations, the converts were seeking to transcend their estrangement by gaining a new enunciatory position. But it must be remembered, too, that the appropriation of Herrnhuter Christianity meant the appropriation of a particular religious form of modernity.[69] It was both an acculturating force and an interpolating agent, the converted subalterns' unequal dialogue with capital (accumulation) and the appropriation of surplus value, as it were.

Marotta and the other converts recoded their estrangement, the reification of their labor, as Moravian Pietism. As enslaved agents of social production, they strove for civil agency within the St. Thomas plantation society. To become agents of the civil they had to be affirmed in the religious. Her appropriation of Moravian Pietism reflects, to some extent, her vision of how plantation social life could be, at some level, reconstituted and symbolically refurbished. She committed herself, therefore, to a particular network of support, namely, the Moravian Church, its leadership, and its doctrines. One of the effects of this commitment among the community of slaves and freed persons was the establishment of a church as a public institution. Conversion to a new and apparently influential public cult organization can be interpreted as the community's embodiment of imaginary ("utopic") possibilities and an ideological ("spiritual") rejection of the civil demands of the St. Thomas plantation system. Moravian Pietism allowed Marotta, the former Popo citizen, to overcome some of the tension between the existing and the visionary. In her subjective economy of desire and hope—that space of internal representations—Marotta chose Moravian Pietism.[70]

A Transatlantic Christian Identity

Marotta/Magdalena was a Christian on both sides of the Atlantic. In her Popo homeland she belonged to one of the Greater Ardra Catholic congregations. On the island of St. Thomas, where she lived as both a slave and a freed woman, she converted to Moravian Pietism. Her understandings of Catholicism and Pietism, with its Christological focus, were expressed in a language that was grounded in an Ardra cosmology (Ifa and Vodun) and the appropriation of Aja-Ayizo concepts. As suggested above, Christians of seventeenth-century Greater Ardra seem to have had two identifiable hermeneutical traditions, as shown in the comparison of the Aja-Ayizo language text of the *Doctrina Christiana* and that of Magdalena's 1739 petition. The comparison reveals important differences in basic religious terminology. Since the religious terminology of both traditions was drawn from the conceptual vocabulary of Vodun, the implication is that in the course of the seventeenth century the intellectual relationship between Greater Ardra Catholics and Vodun thought changed. At different times the Christian congregation borrowed categories and concepts from Vodun cosmology for their own hermeneutical purposes. The catechist-interpreter who composed the *Doctrina Christiana* represents the earlier tradition, and Magdalena's petition represents the later one. Her petition identifies her as a living embodiment of an "African" and a "Caribbean" Christianity.

The petition reveals her understanding of Moravian Pietism, in its Christocentric form, as well as her determination to assist the converts' and missionaries' efforts to found a church on St. Thomas. Catholics in Greater Ardra did not face persecution because of their beliefs. Subjects, of whatever religious persuasion, were allowed to practice their faith without interference. Religious pluralism was the norm, in part because religious belief and practice were associated with gender, occupations, and/or social statuses. Marotta's willingness to write an appeal to the Danish-Norwegian queen, requesting protection from the violence of the St. Thomas slave owners, reflects her own view of the appropriate role of a ruler toward his/her subjects. In Popo she was a citizen in an established political order where her right to worship as a Christian was not an issue. As a subject of the Danish royal family she expected the same kind of protection from violence and the right to worship that the Catholic communities in Popo and Greater Ardra enjoyed. Her petitions and letters demonstrate her determination to create a new Pietist congregation of slaves and freed persons in the Danish West Indies.

APPENDIX: MAGDALENA'S PETITION TO THE
DANISH-NORWEGIAN QUEEN SOPHIA MAGDALENE

Great Queen! At the time when I lived in Poppo, in Africa *[ad ga Tome]*, I served the Lord Mau *[bruhu mau]*. Now I have come into the land of the Whites *[voltomé]*, and they will not allow me to serve the Lord Jesus. Previously, I did not have any reason to serve Him, but now I do. I am very sad in my heart that the Black women on St. Thomas are not allowed to serve the Lord Jesus. The Whites do not want to obey Him. Let them do as they wish. But when the poor black brethren and sisters want to serve the Lord Jesus, they are looked upon as maroons. If the Queen *[Neacanda]* thinks it fitting, please pray to the Lord Jesus for us and let her intercede with the King to allow Baas Martin to preach the Lord's word, so that we can come to know the Lord and so that he can baptize us Blacks in the name of the Father, the Son, and the Holy Spirit. May the Lord save you and bless you, along with your son and daughter and your whole family. I will pray to the Lord Jesus for you. In the name of over 250 black women, who love Lord Jesus, written by Marotta, now Madlena of Poppo in Africa.[71]

Part II / Transatlantic Connections

CHAPTER SIX

Mariners, Merchants, and Colonists in Seventeenth-Century English America

April Lee Hatfield

A crowd of Virginians, its members ranging from seamen to gentlemen, was on board Richard Ingle's ship the *Reformation* in Accomack County, Virginia, to witness "a great dispute" between Ingle and the brothers Francis and Argoll Yardley in the summer of 1643. The argument started when "young" Francis, supporting Charles I, and Ingle, supporting Parliament, began to discuss the English Civil War. Their discussion turned into an argument and the argument deteriorated into name-calling. As tension rose, Ingle rushed into the cabin of the ship, where a group of Virginians was talking, grabbed a pole ax and a sword and stormed back on deck. Argoll Yardley, a justice of the peace, accused Ingle of intending to use the weapons against Francis and announced that he was arresting Ingle "in his Majesties name." Ingle, answering that if Yardley had arrested him in the name of the King and Parliament he would have obeyed, drew out his sword and ran it at Argoll Yardley's chest, "as if hee would have peirced his body but touched him not." Argoll Yardley immediately fled to shore.[1] Then Ingle, "in a dominereing way florished his sworde and Comaunded all the Virginians saying gett you all out of my shipp." He weighed anchor before all were able to get off, however, and sailed to Maryland with eighteen or twenty men "that did belong unto Accomack" still on board. The day after they arrived in Maryland, many "Planters and others in Maryland" were on board the ship, and Ingle (in the presence of the Virginians) bragged to the Marylanders about his actions in Accomack.[2]

The use of ships as congregation points is clear in this case in which Ingle took twenty Virginia planters (which included only those who were unable to get off the ship before it weighed anchor) up the Chesapeake to interact with the Marylanders. Not only did methods of trade require such congregation on ships, but they encouraged ships to serve as social centers and places of information exchange. As such, they also became locations for political action. When the Accomack–Northampton County clerk recorded these events, the justices showed no surprise at the number of colonists, including at least one member of their own court, on board. This case, in the records because of the politically explosive events that occurred, illustrates the numbers of "planters and others" who could be found on board many ships, conversing about commercial transactions but also about events in England and other colonies. This story illustrates just one possible setting of interaction for seventeenth-century mariners and colonial residents. They also met on docks and in storehouses, public houses, courthouses, private homes, and agricultural fields. During those meetings, ships' merchants, masters, and common seamen shared information with less mobile colonists about places they had been. Maritime networks not only linked individual English colonies with one another and with England but also connected residents of England's colonies to an international Atlantic world, with especially strong connections among Dutch and English mariners and colonists. The information mariners shared always expanded the worlds of the colonists who heard it and reinforced their place in the Atlantic world.

While we have learned a great deal in recent years about the place of mariners in the eighteenth-century Atlantic world, we know much less about their role in the seventeenth century, and much of what we do know for the eighteenth century concentrates on northern port cities or, even more specifically, on northern port cities during the Revolution.[3] While available sources probably do not allow us to learn as much about seventeenth-century mariners as their eighteenth-century counterparts, their central role in the formation and functioning of the Atlantic world makes such an exploration vital if we are to understand what it meant to its residents. Indeed, the pervasiveness of transatlantic and intercolonial maritime ties to seventeenth-century colonial societies and their importance to colonial survival suggest that such connections were more crucial to the lives of individual colonists in the seventeenth century than in the eighteenth.

Through an analysis of the interaction between seventeenth-century settlers and mariners, this chapter makes the point that such contacts broadened the worlds of settlers and thereby provided an Atlantic context within which we need to understand individual colonies and the worldviews of those who lived in them. Mariners, who provided the most numerous and frequent links to distant parts of the Atlantic world, became enmeshed in local societies in a number of ways. Most visibly, mariner-settler contacts in colonial courts demonstrate the economic, political, and social significance of the connections that maritime networks provided between colonial outposts and the metropole. Colonial courts were critical for protecting the enormous personal and financial investments people made when they became participants in the Atlantic world. Colonies required commerce for their survival and that commerce required legal protection. Maritime cases forced the adoption of uniform practices among dispersed colonial courts and encouraged the integration of each colony into a wider Atlantic world.

The chapter will also explore other spaces that provided opportunities for mariner-settler contacts. The time required for lading and repairing ships and awaiting favorable weather often forced long stays in particular locales, facilitating the formation of economic and personal relationships between mariners and colonists. During ships' lading periods, taverns and the ships themselves became centers of social interaction and information exchanges between mariners and residents. In labor-poor colonial communities, sailors easily participated in local economies, particularly through activities relating to preparation of their ships' cargoes. Such social interactions allowed colonists to use maritime networks to garner information from other parts of the Atlantic world and to maintain a sense of connection to residents of other colonies and Europe and thereby blunt feelings of isolation.

Finally, the chapter will outline regional trade and settlement patterns that affected the nature of mariner-settler interactions and therefore the nature of each society's relationships to the Atlantic world. Patterns of commercial exchange shaped the maritime networks within which other kinds of connections were forged and information exchanged. Ships and mariners came to each colony from various parts of Europe, the Americas, and Africa. Each new colony depended on England and on those colonies already established and all colonies continued to depend on transatlantic and (to varying degrees) inter-colonial ties through the seventeenth century.

Sites of Mariner-Resident Interactions

The economic viability of colonial societies required courts that could deal with the unpredictability and dispersed nature of transatlantic and intercolonial business. Beginning in the fourteenth century, English admiralty law developed in response to the specific needs of traders. Following continental European maritime law, which grew out of Roman civil law with adaptations developed by continental merchants, English admiralty law was separate from English civil law. It provided for quick trials that would not interfere with voyages and procedures that were recognized by foreign as well as English mariners.[4]

Before the establishment of colonial vice-admiralty courts at the end of the seventeenth century, traders' needs for legal action throughout their voyages legitimized the power of colonial and county courts throughout the Atlantic world. Mariners' use of those courts was a key means of bringing seamen and colonists into contact. Because business was international, courts' jurisdictions had to include foreign as well as domestic mariners. Courts in English colonies heard cases involving Dutch mariners, and New Netherland courts dealt with English cases, apparently with the full expectation among mariners that these courts' decisions were binding, even if they included injunctions, such as future wage payment, that would only be met after a ship left a particular colony.

Colonial assemblies included traders and merchants who were acutely aware of mariners' need for access to courts. In 1641, the Massachusetts common liberties provided that "everie man whether Inhabitant or Forreiner, Free or not Free shall have libertie to come to any publick Court, Counsell, or Townmeeting; and either by speech or writing, to move any lawfull, seasonable, or material question." Massachusetts elaborated this law in 1672 to provide that all strangers would "have Liberty to Sue one another in any Courts of this Colony ... and that any Inhabitant may be sued by any Strangers who are on Immediate Imploy by Navigation, Marriner or Merchant, in any of our Courts." Recognizing the importance of the sea to its residents, in 1672 the Massachusetts General Court explicitly extended its authority over Massachusetts colonists to the ocean, ruling that any resident who committed heresy at sea (except those in waters under the jurisdiction of another commonwealth) was to be imprisoned in Boston and fined or whipped. A series of Massachusetts maritime laws about the decision-making rights of various part-owners in ships applied not only to those residing in New England, but also to nonresidents whose ships were in New England when problems arose. Because part-owners often lived in different places, this was necessary, otherwise differences between owners "may be a great obstruction of Trade."[5]

Local courts' jurisdiction over the affairs of intercolonial merchants and mariners highlighted those traders' residence within an Atlantic community. The use of colony and county courts by mobile merchants and mariners in turn expanded the world view of court members and anyone present in court on a day an intercolonial case was heard. Sending letters of attorney for collection of debts incurred through trade was the most prevalent intercolonial use of courts. In March 1655, Edmund Scarborough submitted a petition to the Northampton County, Virginia, court relating to debts owed by his trading partner Major Edward Gibbons of Massachusetts. Basing its decision partly on the testimony of mariners, the court ruled that a judgement against Gibbons' estate would stand.[6] The New Englander had to abide by the decision of a Virginia court, in part because, as a trader, his property was dispersed and therefore available for seizure by more courts than the one where he resided. Other routine transactions required mariners to use courts other than those where they resided. In March 1680, Boston mariner John Clarke and Boston merchant Jarvis Ballard were both in Virginia when Clark sold his two-and-a-half story house on Boston's Back Street to Ballard. Two of the Virginia witnesses traveled to Massachusetts and swore to the Suffolk County court that the sale had occurred.[7]

New Amsterdam courts heard cases between crews and masters of English vessels, and were particularly likely to act on seamen's behalf if the ships were foreign.[8] A New Netherland court, for example, had the master of the Barbadian ketch *Contentment* commit to paying his seamen several months' wages if they would return with him to Barbados.[9] In 1658 New Amsterdam officials arrested the English master of a ship sailing from Virginia to New England because two crew members complained he owed them back pay. The court refused to allow the master to continue to New England until he put up security, although he asserted that the seamen were deserters and that he was on official business for Governor Samuel Mathews of Virginia.[10]

A disagreement between London merchants and a Salem, Massachusetts, shipowner and master provides an especially good illustration of the way in which both intercolonial and transatlantic trade depended on its participants' acceptance of local courts' decisions throughout the Atlantic world. The case, from the 1650s, involved a Boston ship and events in the Caribbean, the Chesapeake, New England, and England. The disputants' use of courts illustrates that traders' reliance on county and colonial courts and their obedience to their decisions reinforced the ties that linked different parts of the English colonial world.

In September 1654 in London, the English merchants William Selby and Joseph Huffey agreed to rent the ketch *Hopewell* of Boston for an American voyage. Salem, Massachusetts, merchant William Chichester was part owner and master of the *Hopewell*. He agreed to take Huffey and Selby and their goods from England to Ireland, from there to Virginia or Maryland, and then back to England or Holland. They followed the most common route from the British Isles to the American mainland colonies, stopping in the Caribbean to provision the ship and perhaps to trade. While in Antigua, Chichester (the master) had repairs done on the ship and bought food and other necessities, borrowing the equivalent of 28,000 pounds of tobacco from the merchants Huffey and Selby to pay for them. The Antigua court recorded Chichester's promise to repay Huffey and Selby in Virginia tobacco within thirty days after arriving in the Chesapeake. William Selby decided to stay in Antigua and used the Antigua court to make his partner Joseph Huffey his attorney to trade in the Chesapeake, receive the debt due from Chichester, and send the ketch to England or Holland.[11]

Three months later Huffey and Chichester were in Virginia, where Huffey sued Chichester in the Lower Norfolk County court for the tobacco Chichester had borrowed in Antigua. Huffey presented the Antigua bills as evidence to the Lower Norfolk court. In a second case, the shipmaster Chichester sued Huffey for £1,300 past due rent from a voyage they had taken the previous year, when Huffey had rented the *Hopewell* for six to ten months to sail from Boston to Barbados, where he would trade New England goods for Caribbean merchandise to take to Virginia, trade that merchandise for tobacco to take to England or Holland and exchange for European goods to bring back to Boston. Chichester complained that not only had Huffey not paid for his use of the vessel but had forced him to take several other voyages, keeping the *Hopewell* out of its owners' hands for almost a year after the agreed date of return.[12]

The court called several of the *Hopewell*'s crew to testify. Likely many of these Boston-based ship's crewmembers were New Englanders. They described events in Antigua and in England, making it clear that ordinary seamen, in addition to captains and masters, were privy to events and communications that masters and captains reported at each stop. The mariners dealt with courts in Antigua, Lower Norfolk, and Dartmouth, England. Their experiences and testimony in courts throughout the English Atlantic world and their cooperation with the Lower Norfolk court suggests that they thought of this Virginia county court (which was made up of men deeply involved in either intercolonial or transatlantic trade) as part of their world and competent to deal with complex intercolonial and transatlantic issues.[13]

The men involved in the cases were not Virginians, but they needed their problems solved in Virginia. The outcome is not recorded, but the significance of the cases is in their routineness. Because courts heard similar cases involving events in other colonies, they heightened the perception of the colonial world as bound together, legitimizing those aspects of colonial court jurisdiction involving trade. These cases also tied mariners to multiple colonies and connected local magistrates and others at court to an intercolonial maritime world.

Rumors spread along trade routes, and mariners used courts to try to keep their reputations intact. One night in 1664 Timothy Blades and a Mr. Morgan began to argue while the two were on board a sloop in the Potomac River. The argument turned into a fight, and during the struggle both fell overboard. Timothy Blades was rescued, Morgan drowned. Virginia authorities charged Blades with murder, but the Westmoreland County court acquitted him on November 1, 1664. Blades, to protect himself against damaging intercolonial maritime gossip, had a copy of the acquittal transcribed into the Suffolk County, Massachusetts, record book the following June.[14]

Even in cases where sailors themselves were not using courts, their mobility required others to use intercolonial networks to resolve legal issues. In 1661 in New Haven Colony, Mary Andrews requested a divorce from her mariner husband, William Andrews, Jr., on the grounds that he had married another woman. He had also been absent from Mary and New Haven for eight or nine years. Thomas Kimberly, Sr., told the court that his son had written him from Virginia telling him that he had been in Bristol, where he had heard that William Andrews was married in Ireland and that he wrote to him that his wife was alive in New England. Another witness, Richard Miles, Jr., told the court that "being in Barbados in September" 1660, he had seen William Andrews and learned from Andrews's shipmaster that Andrews was married to a Cornish woman living in Ireland.[15] Not only did William Andrews's position as a mariner provide him with the mobility needed to get into such a predicament, but the similar mobility of other mariners and merchants and their sociability in various locations ensured that that information would eventually reach New Haven and his first wife.

Courtrooms were among several locations in which settlers and mariners interacted. They also socialized in taverns, homes, on ships, and in fields. Trade routes were less rigidly set and more at the mercy of currents and winds in the seventeenth century than the eighteenth.[16] That inefficiency made seamen's lives both unpredictable and flexible. They might spend more time in particular ports than expected, or have opportunities to desert (or legally leave one ship) and join other crews, more often during the seventeenth century than would be true later. In 1633 when English captain John Stone needed a pilot to help him in New Netherland, he asked Dutch merchant David Peterson De Vries, whose ship was on the way out of New Netherland, "for the sake of our acquaintance, whether I would furnish him a man to pilot him in." De Vries asked his crew for volunteers, and "when one offered to make a long voyage" the seaman transferred ships.[17] This sort of flexibility emphasized the international character of the Atlantic world and the diverse knowledge that mariners brought to the colonies they visited. Mariners, who regarded the north Atlantic rim as their preserve, broadened the worlds of colonial residents by their lengthy seventeenth-century stays in American colonies.

Sometimes merchants' opportunities for socializing in other colonies worried colonial courts. In 1657, the New Haven Colony court fined William East £5 for drunkenness and warned him to stay sober or risk whipping. East's drunkenness was a problem not only at home, but when he traveled to other colonies. Witness Richard Baldwin said that he had heard from the Dutch by a trustworthy man, that East's "cariage ther was exceeding gross, that Vergenia men and sea-men would scoff at him and reproach religion for his sake, saying, This is one of yor church members, but some answered, No, but he is not, for he is cast out for such courses."[18] Mariners' and merchants' travels were one of the principal means of spreading news and impressions about other colonies, well beyond the economic transfers that were the purpose of their trips.

Throughout the seventeenth century the long stays of ships in all colonies obliged many seamen to look for local lodging rather than staying onboard the ship for months at a time. In the spring of 1655, Mrs. Godfrey told the Lower Norfolk, Virginia, court that the surgeon John Rise owed her husband for several days diet for himself and "divers seamen" and for washing, storage of his goods, and lodging.[19] Sailors sometimes preferred layovers to continuing their journeys. In the winter of 1631–32, merchant and ship owner Henry Fleet had difficulty convincing his crew to travel from Virginia to New England, "all of them resolving not to stir until the spring." The master and his mate, however, had both agreed to deliver Virginia corn to New England and ultimately, "with threats and fair persuasions," Fleet and the master prevailed.[20]

When mariners congregated in public houses, they interacted with colonial residents, discussing far more than the business of their trade. In 1642, Andrew Jacob told the Accomack County, Virginia, court that he had met indentured servant Robert Warder, who had previously been a stranger to him, at the house of Anthony Hodgkins. Hodgkins operated a licensed ordinary in his house, making it a congregating point for colonists and mariners alike. Jacob witnessed a conversation in which the gunner of Wattlington's ship reminded London merchant Samuel Chaundler that he had, in an earlier trip to Virginia, promised to free Warder from his servitude for £6. The gunner had brought the money to buy Warder's freedom but Chaundler had sold three years of Warder's time to another master and so could not keep his promise.[21] "The gunner of Wattlington's ship" probably was not a county resident, or Jacob and the court clerk would have known his name, but he was a key player in this case and was socializing at the ordinary with Virginians when the events transpired and had become friendly enough with Warder to put up the money for his freedom, indicating the potential significance of mariner-settler socializing in congregating places such as Hodgkins's ordinary.

Ships in port became centers of social interaction for residents of all colonies, but their importance was enhanced in the Chesapeake, where dispersed trade and settlement patterns made it less likely that a public house would be accessible. In part this practice of congregating on ships grew out of Chesapeake trade itself, which required a great deal of contact among many individuals. Much of the business of ships in seventeenth-century Virginia and Maryland was piecemeal, with settlers buying in small quantities and individual mariners, as well as masters and merchants, doing much of the selling (in terms of sales made, if not in terms of volume sold). To facilitate these various trades residents had to board ships or mariners had to disembark.[22]

In all regions, merchants sailing with their ships, or shipmasters who acted in their stead, were entertained while in port by wealthy merchants, planters, and members of colonial governments, including governors who were always interested in whatever information mariners might bring with them. Shipmasters were often part-owners in the ships they sailed or relatives of the owners, and were generally of higher social status than most of the seamen they commanded.[23] Such elite mariners, if from England, were likely to have families, homes, and perhaps local offices in the Thames-side parishes of Stepney, Whitechapel, or Rotherhithe.[24] While their concentration in dockside communities put all London mariners at the center of long-distance information networks, ship captains and masters also possessed access to political and economic connections throughout London. Dutch mariners came from Amsterdam, Rotterdam, and Middleburg, and, for colonists, they personalized access to Europe.

Dutch merchant David Peterson De Vries (a merchant of very high status) spent time with governors throughout English and Dutch colonies and also described other ship captains, such as John Stone, who were guests of and well acquainted with governors and merchants in individual colonies. His descriptions of his travels in the colonies reveal a clear expectation among colonial elites that the arrival of ship captains provided welcome opportunity to socialize and receive news. When De Vries spent the winter of 1642–43 in Virginia, Governor William Berkeley asked him for his company as he was "in need of society." De Vries spent several four- to five-day visits with Berkeley over the winter and was grateful "for the friendship which had been shown me by him throughout the winter." However, De Vries could not pass all his time with Berkeley because he had promised to help a Dutch trader who had never been to the Chesapeake before. The two Dutch traders and the ships' crew spent several months going "daily from one plantation to the other, until the ships were ready, and had their cargoes of tobacco," as Virginia trading required, thereby sharing their knowledge and experiences with more Virginians than Berkeley.[25] Like De Vries, many of those merchants and captains were Dutch rather than English. In 1652 Barbados Governor Daniel Searle reported that most ships trading at the island were Dutch.[26] The Navigation Acts shifted some of that trade to New Englanders, but continued Dutch presence through the late seventeenth century attests to the international character of the Atlantic world that English American colonists inhabited.[27]

Some shipmasters had strong permanent ties to specific colonies, cultivating social relations that served economic purposes in a world where business transactions were often aided by personal acquaintance. In an investigation of forty-nine shipmasters doing business in Barbados in the 1640s and 1650s, Larry Gragg found evidence that ten of them were also colonial landowners, though that number is probably low.[28] As landowners, shipmasters had neighbors and local involvements further ensuring they shared their Atlantic experiences with residents. While common seamen were less likely than elites to bring specific desired price information or letters, they nevertheless lived at the hub of information exchange in each place they traveled and carried news and impressions between those people they contacted while in port.[29]

Colonists sometimes learned information about events in Europe from other colonies, because communication was faster that way than from England directly. Until Carolina developed exports for European markets, much of its communication with England had to come by way of other colonies. On June 27, 1670, for example, Joseph West wrote from Albemarle Point to Proprietor Anthony Ashley Cooper, explaining that he had sent an account of their proceedings in Carolina in his last letter (of May 28), which he had sent by way of Virginia.[30] On January 1, 1662, a New Englander wrote that the mariner Mr. Wats had recently come from Virginia with the information that there was "a general discontent among the seamen [in England] against the King." Wats had learned the information from ship captain Higginson, who had recently come from London to Virginia, and also by speaking "with many other seamen, as well Bristol men as Londoners, who were formerly for the K: but are now discontent[ed] with him, & wish for another Cromwell."[31] Seamen not only offered reports of events in England but colored them with their own opinions. Usually, they were the first and sometimes only source of information about events elsewhere.

Mariners and colonists cultivated friendships with one another for economic and social reasons and sometimes maintained those relationships for years. On De Vries's way out of the Chesapeake in the spring of 1643, he spent the night with Newport News merchant and councilor Captain Samuel Matthews, whom he described as a "good friend" met on an earlier visit to the region. Such relationships were not limited to the wealthy. On his way back from Matthews's house to the ship, De Vries ran into a resident ship carpenter, who "bid me welcome, and was glad that he had me in his house, as I had, some years ago, on board of my ship, well treated him, and he hoped to treat me well now."[32] These and other encounters with people he had met before in his trading, and his references to interactions shipboard and on land, suggest a relatively intense level of interaction between residents and mariners.

Regional Variations in Mariner-Settler Interaction

Mariner-resident interactions in English America varied depending on the settlement and economic patterns of different colonies. The English Caribbean islands, except Jamaica, were small enough that the majority of residents lived close to port. Almost all free Barbadians had reason and ability to spent time in Bridgetown and thereby come into direct contact with mariners. Seamen and residents, both free and enslaved, worked together on wharves preparing and moving cargoes. During the seventeenth century, it commonly took several months to load sugar cargoes, providing ample time for interaction between mariners and Barbadian residents, particularly in Bridgetown. Most ships from Europe destined for the North American mainland followed the prevailing winds south along the European coast, west to the Caribbean, and north to the mainland. Many stopped in the Caribbean for several weeks before continuing on, providing additional opportunities for residents and mariners to exchange news and impressions from throughout the Atlantic world.[33] Mariners took advantage of a Caribbean scarcity of seamen to desert their ships and rehire themselves to other ships at higher wages.[34] The frequency of these desertions suggests busy maritime communities that allowed mariners to disappear into towns to escape the notice of their shipmasters, despite the small size of the islands and port towns. Such temporary disappearances would have been less likely if close interactions between mariners and residents had not been routine.

All classes of colonists winnowed useful information from conversations with mariners. We know from the work of David Barry Gaspar (in this volume) and Julius Scott that by the eighteenth century slaves' participation in maritime communication extended beyond ports and allowed many slaves to learn of events in other parts of the Atlantic world. These communication networks became more visible during the Haitian Revolution, but the ease of information exchange about that event indicates that such networks were well established beforehand.[35] The welcome that prominent colonial residents extended to ship captains as house guests allowed planters to learn recent market information. Ship captains, in turn, garnered knowledge of the Caribbean world to pass on to those mainland colonists who produced goods for the islands.

Barbadian legislation in 1652 sought to prevent seamen from accumulating debts in port and thereby delaying departures of laded ships, testimony to "the great freqenting of Taverns and Ale-houses" by mariners and the likelihood that a "master of a family within the Iland" would "entertain such Seamen into their Houses."[36] Socializing between residents and mariners was acceptable so long as it did not interfere with trade. A 1668 law banned inland tippling houses that legislators accused of being located expressly "to trade and deal with Servants and Negroes for stolen Goods." That legislation, however, made explicitly clear that licensed "persons dwelling in any [of] the Sea-port-towns, or Bays within the Island" were not the intended targets, another acknowledgment that public houses provided a necessary arena for information exchange between residents of the island and mariners that the island's commerce required.[37]

The Chesapeake had, perhaps, the most unusual sailor-resident interactions. The Chesapeake's expansive network of navigable waterways provided colonists access to direct shipping. In 1688 John Clayton wrote of Virginia that "the great number of Rivers and the thinness of the Inhabitants distract and disperse a Trade ... Ships in general gather each their Loading up and down an hundred Miles distant; for they must carry all sort of Truck that trade thither, having one Commodity to pass off another." Clayton, like his contemporaries and historians since, blamed the lack of towns in the Chesapeake on the number of rivers and their estuaries that allowed colonists to isolate themselves in dispersed settlements. Port towns were unnecessary. Though many praised towns as efficient and safe in theory, colonists were unwilling to give up their direct maritime access and take their goods to other shipping points.[38]

The practice of sailing into the navigable rivers and estuaries to numerous trading points maximized the opportunities for colonists and mariners to interact, and so the Chesapeake's unusual geography encouraged contact between sailors and settlers.[39] As in the Caribbean, ships and their crews often stayed in Virginia and Maryland for months to collect cargo or to wait for favorable weather or during war for other ships to form a convoy. Transatlantic shipping in the seventeenth-century Chesapeake was seasonal, with ships arriving in the late fall or early winter and leaving in the spring. This pattern changed dramatically at the end of the century, when ships began arriving in the spring and departing in the summer.[40] During the 1670s, English merchants estimated that their traders in Virginia might need as long as 210 days to load a ship with 300 hogsheads of tobacco.[41] During the months that ships remained in the Chesapeake, captains commonly stayed with wealthy colonists; seamen stayed on the ship or with colonists, and taverns and ships became centers of social interaction and information exchange. In 1699, a ship's captain received explicit instructions that if he could not return to Philadelphia before winter weather, he was to head for the Chesapeake or Bermuda to sell his cargo and "unship the crew" for the winter.[42] Presumably, they would be on their own to find lodging among Chesapeake or Bermuda colonists until spring, when the ship would sail again.

Chronic labor shortages in the seventeenth-century Chesapeake meant that sailors easily became enmeshed in the local economy while their ships were waiting to collect ladings. Though most of their work was trade related and involved preparing settlers' cargoes for shipment, nevertheless it firmly linked many to the region. While local shallops collected tobacco from particular neighborhoods to transfer to ships, generally this collection did not occur until the ships arrived, and their crews could help load and man the shallops. Ships trading in intercolonial goods found even less prior cargo consolidation than did those trading in tobacco. As a rule, they purchased livestock directly from farmers, who slaughtered and processed meat on the spot, with crew members watching or helping. The pervasive maritime culture in Virginia made merchant-planters and even mariner-planters common. Local courts often postponed cases involving free colonists at all economic levels if one of the participants had business that had taken him out of the country. The headright system allowed mariners to acquire land, and they could avoid the control of local merchants by marketing their products directly.

Colonial leaders tried several times to concentrate trade in a few locales both as a safety measure and to facilitate the collection of taxes but never succeeded in doing so during the seventeenth century.[43] Only after 1700, with the development first of Norfolk and later of other port towns and cities, did the highly localized orientation of trade begin to change. In 1705 Francis Mackemie described changes in Chesapeake marketing that came with the development of Chesapeake port towns: "Norfolk Town at Elizabeth River . . . carry on a small Trade with the whole Bay . . . You may frequently buy at the three beginnings of Towns, at Williamsburg, Hampton & Norfolk, many things which strangers have no opportunity of having elsewhere at any rate; and at more modest Prices than are expected at Private Plantations." His observation also captures the highly personal nature of Chesapeake trade which made commerce more difficult for "strangers" than for those with acquaintances.[44]

Local patterns of Chesapeake participation in the Atlantic trades varied. Virginia's western peninsulas and Maryland's Western Shore grew high-quality tobacco prized in European markets. Colonists on the Eastern Shore and in Virginia's Southside counties (south of the James River) grew low-grade tobacco, and colonists often found trade in naval stores (pitch, tar, and pipe staves), Indian corn, grain, livestock, and salted meats more profitable. In the tobacco dependent regions of Virginia and Maryland, mariners connected settlers largely to Europe. In contrast, regions that produced goods for intercolonial trade tied Chesapeake settlers into networks that afforded them multiple contacts to other colonies as well as to Europe.[45]

New Netherland/New York and New England shared a pattern that would become the more familiar model of the eighteenth century: the loci of both transatlantic and intercolonial trade were urban. Residents in towns that grew up around natural ports were thoroughly enmeshed in the Atlantic world through their contact with mariners, merchants, and other travelers. Settlers in their hinterlands, by contrast, were much less exposed to such contacts. Early in these colonies' development, much of the European population lived near ports. By the end of the century, however, major port towns like Boston and New York contained only 5–10 percent of their colonies' populations.[46] As a result, intercolonial and transatlantic mariners' interactions with residents were more geographically specific than in the Chesapeake and therefore did not extend so thoroughly into the ranks of those producing agricultural goods. Merchants established storehouses and developed much more efficient procedures for trade than did their counterparts in the Chesapeake. This relative efficiency meant that even though ships often had extended stays and crew members hired out their labor, their interactions with residents were significantly concentrated.

The prevalence of seamen in ports and their further concentration in taverns and inns posed problems of social order in New Amsterdam in ways that they did not in the Chesapeake. The Dutch West India Company responded to social disruptions by attempting to restrict the activities of seamen in New Netherland. It passed laws in 1638 stipulating that "no person belonging to any ship, yacht or sloop shall be at liberty to remain on shore at night . . . but . . . shall return on board by sundown" and that "no person shall be allowed to lodge at night or after sundown any of the Company's servants who are detained on the ships or sloops."[47] The company punished seamen more rigorously than residents for breaking these laws. The courts in New Amsterdam seem to have been more lenient than the West India Company, and by midcentury the laws against seamen staying on shore at night were either being ignored or had been repealed.[48]

The Dutch West India Company also tried to prevent seamen from engaging in petty trade, a common means of interaction (sometimes free of customs duties) between seamen and residents in New Netherland as in other colonies. In New Netherland's early years the company outlawed such trading. As was the case with time on shore, New Amsterdam courts allowed more leeway than the West India Company desired, and crew members at mid-century traded small amounts without prosecution, though in 1659 the company instructed Governor Peter Stuyvesant to abolish the practice again. In response to labor shortages in New Netherland, company officers could require seamen do manual labor on land or sea. Often they worked on public building projects, such as repairing Fort New Amsterdam, with other crew members, and hence had limited contact with residents, especially compared to seamen working onshore in the Chesapeake.[49]

If the maritime laws of New Netherland had indeed been enforced, residents and common seaman in New Amsterdam would have interacted relatively little. But clearly more socializing occurred than the laws suggest. Dutch merchant De Vries's time with the colony's governors suggests that merchants were as welcome in New Netherland as elsewhere. While in New Amsterdam in 1642 he spent time daily with Commander Willem Kieft "generally dining with him when I went to the fort." As well, some officials encouraged such socializing. They permitted Dutch, French, and English taverns to operate in New Amsterdam. Kieft proudly told De Vries that he had "a fine inn, built of stone, in order to accommodate the English who daily passed with their vessels from New England to Virginia, from whom he suffered great annoyance, and who might now lodge in the tavern."[50] Kieft had found it a burdensome expectation that he, as governor, should entertain visiting shipmasters; establishing an inn was a great improvement. Stuyvesant, less sanguine about the presence of such inns and taverns, exaggerated their number when he complained "that nearly the just fourth of the city of New Amsterdam consists of brandy shops, tobacco or beer houses," indicating that more opportunities existed for mariner-settler interactions than the West India Company would have preferred.[51]

Extended port stays in seventeenth-century New Netherland allowed for the formation of close economic and social relationships.[52] Indications of these stays are found in court decisions protecting sailors from unemployment while their ships were in port. In 1662 the Court of Burgomasters and Schepens ordered a master to rehire an English seaman and pay him "until the bark is again afloat." That the case went to court at all suggests that the ship was in port for some time, that the English mariner was familiar enough with New Amsterdam to bring suit, and that he knew nonresident mariners as well as residents could bring suit. Maritime cases in New Amsterdam were often settled by arbitration, and the court attempted to choose arbitrators who included at least one countryman of any foreign seaman involved.[53] At least some seamen spent enough time in New Amsterdam to form personal relationships. In 1647 Abraham Willemsen, a seaman from Holland, married a New Netherland woman. The Supreme Court of New Netherland allowed him to stop working for the West India Company and to settle in New Amsterdam as a carpenter.[54] Evidence of close personal relationships between mariners and residents indicates significant socialization between seamen and those New Netherlanders who lived in New Amsterdam, despite legislation restricting it.

New England's trade was also concentrated in port towns. A 1683 Massachusetts law stipulated that Boston and Salem were to be the colony's only legal ports of entry for goods enumerated by the Navigation Acts.[55] Similar laws to establish ports of entry for Virginia were ignored, but in New England they were perhaps more enforceable because they reinforced prevailing practice rather than attempting to counteract it as in Virginia. New England ports not only shipped agricultural surpluses for intercolonial trade but also acted as entrepôts for transatlantic trade, which required storehouses and coordination of trade. As a result, colonists had less financial incentive to break the laws restricting trade to port towns.

Massachusetts did not have laws restricting the movement of seamen like New Netherland did, perhaps in part because the large population of mariners who lived in Boston or Salem when they were not at sea, and who had family and property there, legitimized the visible presence of all mariners. Maritime laws in Massachusetts had more in common with those of Barbados, where the legal intent was the smooth functioning of commerce not the control of seamen. Laws addressing seamen's behavior tried to limit the financial liability of mariners rather than restrict them to their ships. A 1660 law attempted to control seamen's "immoderate Drinking and other vain expences in Ordinaries." The lawmakers worried that because seamen were "oftentimes arrested for debts so made when the ships are ready to set sayle," their frequenting of ordinaries threatened to cause "damage to the Masters and Owners of the vessels" by impeding the ships' departures. The law therefore stipulated that no one selling alcoholic beverages could "arrest, attack or Recover by Law any Debt, or debts so made by any Sayler or Saylers" unless the master or owner of his ship allowed it in writing.[56]

Massachusetts legislation encouraged maritime commerce and indicated that assembly members saw public houses as a crucial part of that commercial activity. Businesses licensed for common entertainment, for example, were required to erect "some inoffensive Sign, obvious, for direction of Strangers."[57]

Despite regulations to prevent innkeepers from entertaining permanent residents at night or on lecture days, all licensed persons were allowed to entertain land travelers "or sea-faring men" at night when they were on shore "for their necessary refreshment" and "so there be no disorder among them." As well, on lecture days any "strangers, lodgers, or other persons . . . may continue in such houses of common entertainment during meale times, or upon lawfull busines, what time their occasions shall require."[58] The Massachusetts government attempted to limit residents' frequenting of taverns, but the law's explicit exceptions for anyone whose "occasions . . . require[d]" their presence at public houses to conduct "lawfull busines" could include residents doing business with traveling merchants or shipmasters. These qualifications allowed residents to spend evenings or lecture days in taverns and suggest the General Court's recognition that public houses served as important places of business transaction.[59]

During the 1670s, partly in response to King Philip's War and the presence of refugees in Boston, the colonial government tried to restrict tavern use.[60] The government ordered county courts not to license more public houses than absolutely necessary, and licensed houses were to provide "for the refreshing and Enterteinment of Travailers and Strangers only."[61] The following decade the General Court found that the number of people licensed to retail wine and liquor outdoors in Boston was "not sufficient for the accomodation of the Inhabitants and Trade of the Town, by reason whereof sundry Inconveniencies do accrew." It ordered that the Suffolk County court license five or six more public houses in the town.[62]

The only prohibition to shipboard social interactions between residents and seamen in Massachusetts was intended to prevent "corrupt persons, both such as come from forraine parts, as also some others here inhabiting or residing," from spending too much time with "the young people of this Country." Anyone who caused "children, servants, apprentices, schollers belonging to the Colledg, or any Latine schoole" to spend their time "in his or their company, ship or other vessel, shop or house, whether Ordinary, Tavern, victualing house, cellar or other place" was to pay a forty shilling fine.[63] The preamble suggests that this sort of interaction was frequent, and the lawmakers were only attempting to control children and servants, not prevent socializing or business among free adults. Their grouping of ships and shipmasters with tavern and ordinary keepers reveals the prominent place of the maritime world among Boston's social locations. Another law from 1668, which allowed mariners to entertain on board ship with the master's permission, also suggests an attempt to help facilitate commerce rather than control socializing.[64]

New England also developed as an American center for shipbuilding and repair, activities that complemented its role as an entrepôt. Ship repairs extended port stays, sometimes for crews from various parts of Europe and colonial America. Marcus Rediker argues that by the eighteenth century Boston was popular among mariners, who thought it "a good town for 'frolicking,' not least because of its 'well rigged' young women." Long port stays, "while their captains, plagued by Boston's lack of an agricultural staple, searched high and low for a full cargo" and perhaps had ship repairs done as well, provided the seamen ample opportunity to judge Boston's social merits.[65] As in Barbados, busy ports provided mariners with desertion opportunities, as indicated by laws against it.[66] Economically, all Bostonians were firmly part of the Atlantic world, and their conversations with mariners in port pulled them firmly into its social and cultural networks. The impression given by seventeenth-century Massachusetts laws is that the colony valued trade and in its pursuit gave merchants and mariners leeway in their social and economic activities.

The overlap of transatlantic and intercolonial trade patterns sometimes encouraged the formation of complicated relationships among mariners and merchants throughout the Atlantic world. In April 1643, in Virginia, the New England mariner Phillip White, the Virginia ordinary keeper Anthony Hodgkins, and the Rhode Island seaman George Roome bound themselves to the Virginia Quaker merchant Thomas Bushrod to pay by the end of the following December 1,200 pounds of pork to Manhattan tailor Richard Clecke and 1,000 pounds of pork to Manhattan merchant Isaac Allerton.[67] That a New Englander, a Virginian, and a Rhode Islander made themselves partners to transport pork from Virginia to New Netherland provides a striking illustration of the degree to which intercolonial trade fostered the development of economic and social webs among colonies.

A 1639 voyage illustrates the complicated nature of intercolonial trade involving multiple English colonies and Dutch New Netherland. That summer, Barniby Brian took tobacco on consignment from Virginia's Eastern Shore to New England. He returned to Virginia without the tobacco or anything to show for it, and his clients took him to court. Their suit showed that Brian stayed in New England longer than necessary, went on to Manhattan, and spent all the profits drinking and socializing in both places. He was gone for months, though his seamen testified that he could have returned in ten days with bills of exchange; collecting a return cargo would have taken longer. While in New England, Brian spent his time in the Boston ordinary and sometimes at the Noddles Island house of Massachusetts merchant Samuel Maverick. With little reason to return to his Virginia creditors, Brian planned a Caribbean voyage and recruited seamen in Boston but apparently never went. Brian had received liquor and fish in exchange for the tobacco, but drank and shared the liquor at Noddles Island and gave away the fish in Manhattan. He took six of the seamen recruited for the Caribbean voyage to New Amsterdam and allowed them to spend forty days on the boat at the charge of the Virginians who funded the voyage.[68]

Brian's voyage indicates both the social networks of the maritime world and the complicated and often flexible trading practices, including successive voyages to several colonies before returning to one's home port. Although Brian's socializing, in this case, was the voyage's downfall, it was generally a necessary part of any trading venture and mariners of all social levels expected their time in port to provide them with time to socialize.

Implications and Conclusions

As seventeenth-century colonial societies developed, mariners were integral to facilitating transatlantic and intercolonial communication. They, thereby, were key to creating an Atlantic world that would possess real meaning for its inhabitants. Beyond the exchange of goods that was of course their primary function, mariners' interaction with settlers worked against colonial isolation by providing colonists with information about other places and a sense of residence in an Atlantic world that extended beyond their own colony's borders.

The nature, intensity, and diffusion of mariner-settler interactions varied regionally, but all colonies' courts provided important spaces within which mariners and colonists interacted. Courts also functioned through their intercolonial decisions to create ties linking colonies more closely to one another. The need of mariners and merchants to use courts in a variety of locations meant they had to adjudicate cases extending beyond their normal jurisdiction and had to respect one another's decisions. These requirements and the practice of carrying decisions (verbally or in writing) from one colony to another created official and legal ties between colonies, adding to the economic networks that mariners created and the more informal social transatlantic and intercolonial links that their travels facilitated.

Although we currently know more about how information exchange networks worked during the eighteenth century than the seventeenth, they may in fact have been more important to larger percentages of colonial residents during the seventeenth century. Greater proportions of seventeenth-century colonists lived where they would have unmediated contact with mariners. In the seventeenth century, mariners often offered colonists their only source of intercolonial and transatlantic news, whereas by the early eighteenth century, newspapers provided many colonists with alternative sources of information. As well, the time that mariners spent in all colonial ports was longer during the seventeenth century than the eighteenth, when experience in trade routes and efficiencies of scale decreased port times and therefore mariner-resident interaction times.[69] So although the volume and value of goods traded in the Atlantic increased as time passed, the actual degree to which average residents experienced colonial societies as maritime societies decreased.[70]

In the seventeenth century, shipping and mariners were familiar to almost all Chesapeake residents and to all urban and many rural residents elsewhere. The local activities of sailors, ship captains, and merchants in English colonies made it possible for economic exchange networks to shape and create an Atlantic world that could then assume social, cultural, and legal, as well as economic, significance. Mariners thus created networks that facilitated the flow of information between colonies as well as between Europe and America, thereby placing seventeenth-century colonial residents firmly within a maritime Atlantic world.

CHAPTER SEVEN

The Atlantic Rules

The Legalistic Turn in Colonial British America

William M. Offutt

> Among the many settler societies established by Europeans, first in America beginning in the sixteenth century and then in other sections of the globe starting in the nineteenth century, law functioned as the principal instrument of cultural transplantation. Intending to create offshoots of the Old World in the New, the large number of emigrants to the colonies insisted upon taking their law with them and making it the primary foundation for the new societies they sought to establish . . . For English people migrating overseas to establish new communities of settlement, the capacity to enjoy—to possess—the English system of law and liberty was thus crucial to their ability to maintain their identity as English people and to continue to think of themselves and to be thought of by those who remained in England as English.
>
> JACK P. GREENE, "EMPIRE AND IDENTITY FROM THE
> GLORIOUS REVOLUTION TO THE AMERICAN REVOLUTION"

From the beginning of English colonization in North America, settlers imported the social and cultural capital associated with "their law" in order to create and improve their new societies. However, to write of "the English system of law and liberty" in the singular (as Greene has above) masks the plural nature of English laws and English legal systems in the 1600s. The multiple sources of law that colonists would use to construct their legal identity included the knowledge of settlers—some of whom had legal training, and most of whom had legal experiences—and memories of law in action in the Old World. Forms, books, letters, manuals, documents, and a range of "institutions, practices, devices and learned behaviors" were needed for "making physical spaces productive and social and cultural spaces agreeable."[1] These importations of social and cultural capital—what I will call *legal capital*—did not end once the "primary foundation for the new societies" was laid but rather continued throughout the colonial era. Yet colonial historians have not consistently plotted the flows of legal capital during the early modern British Empire and thus have obscured (to continue the metaphor) the mergers and acquisitions, the borrowings and the dividends involved in colonial law.

The legal inheritances from which settlers in different colonies drew to create their own identities were incredibly complex, and the common law was but one of perhaps fifteen brands of law and courts that governed the affairs of an average Englishman in 1600.[2] England's legal culture provided an enormous range of possibilities for the colonial "legal imagination" to draw upon. *Legal imagination* is defined as the ability of both the leaders and the population to construct a world of legal meaning out of the events, actions, and subjects of social life.[3] Thus, legal imagination mentally translates the social facts of everyday life into legal categories and projects solutions through the use of legal resources (e.g., courts) that either existed or could be developed. The parameters of any society's legal imagination—the range of situations that can be considered subject to law and the range of solutions conceivable within the law—vary. From their founding, British North American colonies included both a high level of general legal awareness among the average population and a number of legal "literates"[4] who could draw on the legal capital transferred around the Atlantic to produce an expansive colonial legal imagination. As colonists with their varied levels of legal knowledge struggled to establish their own identities expressed through law, they made choices among multiple legal traditions and theories that held profound significance for the future of their new societies.

This chapter argues that the colonial legal imaginations, nourished by transatlantic flows of legal capital from multiple sources, produced intellectually impressive and socially successful results in the early years of English North American colonies. Thus, in their first years, colonial governments erected unified courts (instead of the multiple courts with multiple laws of England), in which they tried to accommodate, prioritize, and integrate multiple legal inheritances into a coherent system. This intellectual accomplishment should not be seen as a primitive reaction to the disorienting experiences of the first years of settlement. Rather, it should be seen as the creation of particularly active and sophisticated legal imaginations that expressed themselves in a discourse created in each colony between the legally literate and the citizenry. In most colonies, the legal system so constructed paid social dividends throughout the seventeenth century. This chapter further argues that by the late 1600s the multiple sources of legal capital that had originally nourished colonial legal imaginations were slowly dying. The common law—conveyed through treatises, form books, legal training, and imperial oversight of statutes—became virtually the only form of legal capital still flowing across the Atlantic. Consequently, the common law established its transatlantic dominance over colonial legal systems and thus over colonial legal imaginations. This takeover was the legalistic turn in colonial life, the changes in legal practice and court usage, which made English common law the standard, the changes that predated widespread commercialization and replication of English patterns of social life.

The Atlantic Rules, Phase I: The Laws of England to 1680s

On the eve of English colonization in North America, the English legal imagination drew from a rich and diverse legal legacy. Not including statute law passed by Parliament, the average Englishman might have encountered law in common law courts (King's Bench, Common Pleas), equity courts (Chancery), ecclesiastical courts, admiralty courts, prerogative courts (e.g., Star Chamber), borough courts, manor courts of leet and baron, law merchant courts, as well as local courts of the village, hundred, or county.[5] In addition, England in the early 1600s saw many different advocates of far-reaching reforms: some wanted to reshape the common law; some wished to adopt Biblical law or import civil law from the Continent. Each of these positions possessed a substantial following.[6] Thus, the jurisdiction and authority of each of these law systems was not fixed but rather became part of a rich debate that saw advocates involved in what today might be called marketing and positioning campaigns for their versions of law. Richard Ross, for example, has explored how common lawyers (as part of common law courts' intense competition for business) used memory in legal debates in late Elizabethan and early Stuart England, a period when published lawbooks were just beginning to acquire authority as the singular repository of law. If common law was unwritten law and based in the custom, use, and practice of the people, then lawyers were to be remembrancers, investigators, assessors, and brokers of the law, "specialists in weaving immemorial lineages out of the threads of legal records and in tearing them apart." Texts were teachers, reminders, and prompts, designed to help lawyers assemble commonplace books organized under topical headings that involved a cycling between text and memory.[7]

With law being plural, unregulated, and flexible, significant campaigns favoring alternative law systems emerged in the early 1600s, in part as a defense against jurisdictional incursions by common law courts. Champions of the Court of Requests and ecclesiastical courts fulminated against common law writs of prohibition that took their caseload away, while "civilians" (students of continental civil law systems) wrote particularly in favor of the Court of Admiralty. Insurance, charters, bills of exchange, even contract law in international trading were governed in Admiralty by the law merchant and not the common law, and the civilians saw Admiralty as more responsive to merchant needs for resolving disputes than the fictions of common law.[8] Law reformers' calls for rationalization and codification, particularly in criminal matters, found an influential advocate in Francis Bacon, who brought proposals both to Parliament and to the general public in the 1610s and 1620s. The generation of law reformers who wrote an enormous volume of pamphlets and tracts during the English Revolution built on this foundation. Neither the rejection nor ultimate repeal of much of the law reform agenda in Restoration-era England diminished the significance of this aspect of the plurality of legal discourse; reform proposals were (and are) integral to both the rule of law and the legal imagination.[9]

The intellectual abilities of common lawyers did not necessarily offer them advantages over the advocates of alternative laws. Complaints about "the impoverished nature of English legal education and scholarship" followed English lawyers who predominantly learned their craft through apprenticeship. The division in English law practice between the "upper branch"—barristers, distinguished by legal learning at the Inns of Court—and "lower branch" practitioners of law—solicitors—was neither linguistically nor operationally clear regarding who got to appear in which court and which proceedings in 1600. Another group of lawyers practiced civil law in ecclesiastical and admiralty courts; yet another group worked primarily in Chancery. Legal practice was thus "fluid and transitional," and no one group could claim a secure professional monopoly over the English legal imagination.[10] Of even more importance was the fact that legal practitioners who chose to cross the Atlantic need not have trained at the Inns of Court or even be tied to the common law in order to exercise their legal abilities. Because more than one brand of law transferred to the colonies, no single type of lawyers could monopolize legal practice and control legal thought.

The diversity of law that influenced the colonial enterprise appeared first in the charters granted to companies and proprietors. Starting with a patent of 1578 to Sir Humphrey Gilbert, clauses governing legislative power granted to colonists required the laws passed be as near as conveniently "agreeable to the lawes and policies of England," or be "not contrarie to the lawes of this our realm of England," or "be not repugnant to the laws of England," or, in combination, be "consonant to reason, and bee not repugnant or contrarie, but as neare as conveniently may bee agreeable to the Lawes, Statutes and rights of this our Kingdome of England."[11] Historians have tended to interpret the term *Lawes* as if it meant separate statutes or rules in a unitary system of common law, which is an anachronism. In the context of the plurality of legal discourses and practices in the England of the late 1500s and early 1600s, *Lawes* most probably meant brands of law, types of legal reasoning, an expansive but not infinite range of legal sources. Thus, on departure from England, the hurdle colonial law would have to clear to comply with the charter was not very high; the legal imagination of settlers would be free to choose from among all the brands of English law for inspiration and yet still be in conformity with their charter.

Although most if not all adult transatlantic migrants would have carried some ideas regarding law and laws with them, the bulk of the legal capital taken to the New World in the 1600s was imported by those whom Mary Bilder described in her study of colonial Rhode Island as "legal literates." In abandoning the anachronistic attempt to categorize colonial legal talent in the seventeenth-century in terms of professionals versus amateurs, and adopting an analysis of the spectrum of skills displayed by participants in the legal system, she has reshaped the interpretation of colonial legal participation. Literacy by itself was required to initiate legal actions, but legal literacy required knowledge of laws and legal process in order to draft the appropriate documents. Rhode Island explicitly allowed "attorneys" to plead cases for others, and these men's skills were also used in a variety of legal jobs such as court and town clerk, treasurer, colony assistant, and even Governor. Some of the legal literates trained in England, others learned in Rhode Island through observation and participation in litigation. Regardless of their background or abilities, legal literates formed "a legal community comfortable with the creative interpretation of the laws of England." These men bought and borrowed English lawbooks (e.g., "how-to" practice manuals, commentaries, and non–common law texts), copied records and documents, traveled and discussed legal issues, and used English laws under the Rhode Island "not contrary and repugnant" charter clause as the starting point for colonial law. The 1647 Code, which appears to have actually been written by legal literates in the 1660s as a revision and codification of Rhode Island's laws, merged English law with their own charter understandings and legal interpretations.[12]

All colonies at or soon after their founding had a significant number of resident legal literates who could utilize the written forms of common law as well as merge disparate strands of English laws into new colonial forms. Justice in Virginia under the first and second company charters did not rely on common law but rather drew on conciliar justice precedents from the frontier regions of the kingdom and on English notions of prerogative or military justice. Such ideas of swift and summary justice merged with common law and other English law systems as legal literates in the 1620s and 1630s founded the county courts controlled by local magistrates. By the 1640s, copies of Dalton's *Countrey Justice,* a guide for justices of the peace, and Swinburne's *Briefe Treatise of Testaments and Last Wills,* a handbook for those in England who had to deal with church courts, circulated in Virginia, and the General Assembly was licensing "attorneys" and regulating their fees. "How-to" manuals enabled these legal literates to utilize appropriate legal terms and forms in a unified and telescoped court system that reflected a considered transatlantic judgment on the laws of England.[13]

By 1660, legal literacy (but not a formal legal profession) and the rule of law (but not the rule of common law alone) permeated Virginia. Virginia's justices of the peace could individually dispense summary justice in small cases and handle some probate matters, and, when sitting *en banc,* could act on matters that in England were distributed to common law, ecclesiastical, equity, and admiralty courts, plus administer local government. Legal literates in late seventeenth-century Virginia included those lay justices, other lay officers in the legal system (e.g., clerk, sheriff, burgess), and many legal practitioners who combined planting, trading, and lawyering. One sample found forty-one attorneys who appeared before eight county courts between 1660 and 1700; a 1699 list found only two "barristers" (i.e., legally trained lawyers) out of thirty-one legal practitioners.[14] Virginia's Chesapeake neighbor, Maryland, saw a similar blossoming of legal literacy as lay justices of the peace presided over a county court system similar to Virginia's in its vast jurisdiction, as individuals who learned to plead for themselves began to appear in court for others, and as those practitioners began to be regulated by courts by the 1660s.[15]

In early Massachusetts, historians have long identified the use of non–common law sources, from Julius Goebel's examination of local law and custom in

Plymouth, through David Grayson Allen's look at local land law practices transferred to Massachusetts Bay, to John Frederick Martin's findings of the use of corporation law to divide the land and govern New England towns.[16] The legal knowledge of some Massachusetts residents, such as John Winthrop's training at the Inns of Court and serving as a justice of the peace before emigration, has been noted, but the overall significance of the legal capital provided by a large number of men familiar with multiple legalities has been underestimated. By the late 1630s, there were a half-dozen legal practitioners providing legal services for a fee in Massachusetts. Thomas Lechford, trained at an Inn of Court, drafted over 650 legal documents in three years of practice in the colony. Others who did not practice nonetheless had studied law; some colonists possessed Dalton's justice of the peace manual or abridgements of English statutes; and most of the original magistrates had had legal experience in England. Even Maine had legal practitioners in the 1640s, and one, Thomas Gorges, wrote to England to have his lawbooks shipped to him.[17]

The high level of legal literacy produced an extremely complex and well-thought-out debate on Massachusetts's laws in the 1640s. Legal literates mediated the legal capital that flowed into the colony, and that legal capital included the laws of God and the pamphlets of law reformers as well as concepts from the Continent (civil law, natural law) and from the disorganized world of English laws (local customs, justice of the peace/magistracy powers). Codification itself, by topic headings arranged alphabetically in the manner of Dalton, represented a success for the law reform agenda, and much of the substantive content comprehensively merged law reform ideals with multiple legal strands.[18] To take one example from the Massachusetts Code of 1648, the provision for appeal from inferior to superior courts involving the possibility for a full rehearing of a case on the merits did not have its roots in common law. Rather, appeal's origins lay in canon law, civil law, corporation law, and equity as well as in religious and political discourse. Appeals in this sense had begun in Massachusetts practice in the 1630s, and the codification of the procedure under its own title in 1648 reflected a transnational, transatlantic integration of legal capital. "The culture of appeal was the result of sophisticated understandings of an English and Western European tradition of civil and ecclesiastical law."[19] The outcome was an encouragement of litigation (with forms and arguments drafted by a wide variety of legal literates) that served the function of integrating a contentious and increasingly diverse population, while the church and community lost influence.[20]

One other source of legal capital existed for the colonial legal imagination to draw upon, and that was other colonies. There is evidence that Winthrop and others in Massachusetts possessed copies of Virginia's laws and that they, though reluctant to take anything as a model that came from a non-Puritan colony, may have modeled their appeal provisions on Virginia's corporate law version of appeal.[21] That colonial legal literates read such material does not mean that they copied the examples blindly. The 1648 Massachusetts Code had influence over other New England colonies (Connecticut in 1650, New Haven in 1655, New Hampshire in 1679). Following the conquest of New Netherland in 1664, Governor Nicholls was instructed to study New England's codes in preparation for drafting new laws for New York. The Duke of York's laws, promulgated in 1665, illustrated both the mimetic and creative impulses of legal literates; fifty-five of the seventy-six subject headings in the Duke's laws matched those in the 1648 Code. While some provisions were transferred nearly verbatim (e.g., barratry, forgery, fornication), most saw substantial revisions and amendments, especially in areas of decedents and real property.

Subsequently, the legal literates who drafted laws for West New Jersey and Pennsylvania examined, of necessity, the Duke's laws in force in those jurisdictions prior to the Quaker takeover (1676 in West New Jersey and 1681 in Pennsylvania). From that starting point, Penn and other founders made enormous alterations to meet the particular legal needs of Quakers and to implement desires for law reform. Yet Pennsylvania also reached back to Massachusetts for models of some provisions not included in the initial transmission of legal rules from New York.[22] In another sector of the British Atlantic, the 1661 slave code of Barbados was borrowed by Jamaica, South Carolina, and Antigua in the late 1600s and may have been partially adopted by Virginia.[23] When combined with the impact of continuing immigration (including royal officials), with merchants' increased shipping and expanded networks of credit and debt, and with the fact than many average individuals were still connected to legal concerns in the old country (e.g., land holdings, inheritances, transmittal of funds),[24] legal capital now flowed in multiple directions and from multiple sources around the British Atlantic.

Perhaps the most effective transatlantic transfer of non-common law legal capital occurred in the Delaware Valley during the 1670s and 1680s. Quakers responsible for founding the colonies of West New Jersey, Pennsylvania, and Delaware had become, by necessity, extremely legally literate in manipulating legal forms in their struggles against various prosecutions in England.[25]

Quakers also had become quite cognizant of the law reform literature of 1640–60, and had participated in the pamphlet debates over law reform. Edward Billing, Quaker law reform pamphleteer of 1659, and William Penn, whose own acquittal in 1670 set a precedent for jurors not being prosecutable for their verdicts, drafted in England *The West New Jersey Concessions* of 1676. Penn, prior to his own departure in 1682, authored many drafts of his *Frame of Government* with *Laws Agreed upon in England,* which then formed the basis for *The Great Law,* a code adopted by the first Pennsylvania Assembly (which included Delaware) in 1683. These transatlantic flows of legal capital embodied much of the law reform agenda in terms of procedure as well as substance and integrated into a unitary legal system principles of local law, common law, equity, ecclesiastical law, admiralty, and innovations (such as affirmations instead of oaths) designed to address particular legal concerns of Quakers.[26]

Legal literates, including court clerks with drafting talent like Phineas Pemberton, Inns of Court trained attorney David Lloyd, practitioners who rode a circuit through multiple county courts, and German legal scholars such as Daniel Pastorius, all participated in court alongside individuals who pled their own cases under the simplified law reform code.[27] Lawbooks and tracts from a variety of brands of law arrived early in the Delaware Valley, including writings on the law merchant and maritime law, on the laws of Jamaica, on courts leet, on equity and common law, on law reform (by Penn and others), as well as how-to manuals and form books. Pastorius drew on his own European learning, his own library of English lawbooks and manuals, the library of other legal literates in Pennsylvania, and even precedents from New York to draft a treatise on legal practice for use in Pennsylvania that included hundreds of pages of forms and precedents designed to make the law easily accessible to all.[28] The legal imagination of the Delaware Valley thus drew upon multiple sources of transatlantic legal capital to create a sophisticated merger of legal forms, procedures, and substance.

These products of the colonial legal imagination in the Chesapeake, in New England, and in the Delaware Valley created a social context of legal participation far different from that seen in England. The clientele for these courts was far broader than the clientele served by common law courts. These Atlantic rules—multiple brands of law carried from England, merged into a single law, and adjudicated in a unitary court system—produced different legal systems that legitimated themselves by drawing wide strata of colonial residents into the legal system. English legal systems had always relied on broad participation of laypeople to make the system work, but the welter of jurisdictions, the different subject matters in each jurisdiction, and the threshold costs of complexity, time, and money required for bringing some issues before a court had meant that the social profile of participation varied among courts. For example, ecclesiastical courts that dealt with marriages, divorces, violations of sexual and other moral norms, orphans, and probate served a far different and socially more diverse clientele than did admiralty courts or even Courts of Common Pleas operating under common law for dispute resolution. In the colonies, however, magistrates and county courts encompassed all of these subjects and all of these clienteles, and more, drawing previously dispersed participants into one forum at one time.

The best illustration of the social significance of the Atlantic rules appears in the many recent examinations of women's participation in colonial legal systems during the 1600s. Cornelia Dayton's study of Connecticut's seventeenth-century legal system concluded that "women found fewer barriers to coming to court over civil matters than they would confront in courtrooms hewing rigidly to common law procedures."[29] Though the law reforms enacted in New Haven and carried over into Connecticut after 1665 did not specifically call for improving women's status, the result was a higher level of women's involvement in legal matters, including administration of estates and suing on debts, and a higher level of women's voices and needs being taken seriously on a wide range of issues, including defamation, morals offenses, divorce, and rape. In other New England settings, common law strictures and remedies were not the limits, as women's speech drew intense legal interest and defamation suits sought to compel defendants, a high percentage of them women, to tender apologies—an ecclesiastical remedy—for a variety of offensive verbiage that disrupted the community.[30] In the Chesapeake, women's voices achieved a certain parity with men's, as gossip and sexual accusations resulted in up to half of the civil slander caseload involving women, and the remedies sought were far more inventive than mere common law damages. The sexual double-standard also seemed lessened, as couples and not just unmarried women with bastards were prosecuted for premarital sexual sin.[31] When combined with the widespread appearance of women in testamentary proceedings as administrators and executors in the 1600s, a picture of greater legal inclusion emerges.

The breadth of issues dealt with by colonial court systems encouraged participation breadth. Essex County, Massachusetts, was able to utilize common law, equity, and innovative interpretations to resolve land disputes and title uncertainties; residents and nonresidents, merchants, creditors and debtors, ethnic insiders and outsiders all turned to the courts.[32] The law reforms in the first years of British settlement of the Delaware Valley involved an extremely high percentage of the newly arrived settlers, as well as already resident Swedes, Quakers and non-Quakers, farmers, artisans, merchants, and servants, in legal proceedings.[33] At the local level in Virginia, county courts merged a variety of English legal precedents, encouraged and received widespread local participation at court day, and produced a level of stability and order comparable to English local society. Although they were hardly voluntary participants, in Virginia even slaves accused of crimes were brought to the regular court system for trial until 1692.[34] To the extent that colonial legal systems, lacking in traditional methods and powers for compelling assent, relied on voluntary usage and participation by the local population in order to achieve legitimacy and authority, the merger of English laws would concentrate the imagination of the populace onto a single legal forum. In that forum, many colonies required that the laws of the colony be read at each session, and Massachusetts even required parents to read the capital laws of their colony to their children (no doubt a soothing bedtime reading).[35] This practice deviated from the English legal fiction that ignorance of the law was no excuse and reflected the shakiness of the newly constituted legal authority. Given the diversity of legal sources impinging on the collective legal imagination, colonial magistrates could not presume their populace had knowledge of the laws but rather had to teach the populace about the laws regularly.

Prior to the 1680s, the colonial legal imagination had used a variety of imported legal capital to erect sophisticated legal systems. The legal literates of these colonies, who were primarily responsible for this merger of laws, were not operating in an intellectual vacuum or responding merely to local conditions. Rather, they took the variety of rules imported across and around the Atlantic and created functioning, integrative legal systems. The law was not simplified because of experience in the New World, but rather the law remained quite complex in its mixed, inherited form now operating in unified courts. The choice of forum was simplified, but the plurality of laws was still very much inherited, very much English.

The Atlantic Rules, Part II: The Legalistic Turn after 1680

By the time of the Glorious Revolution, the pluralism of legal systems in England had been reduced. At the end of the seventeenth century, the common law had clearly become privileged as the one law that served as the standard. Ecclesiastical courts lost their jurisdiction over sexual offenses to the common law courts during the English Revolution and did not regain it in the Restoration. Prerogative courts were destroyed. Civilian law theorists, particularly those writing for the law merchant, had lost all influence and retreated to academic irrelevancy by 1700. The common law courts triumphed over admiralty for merchants' causes by recognizing the customs of merchants as questions of fact to be determined under the appropriate common law action, thus avoiding any doctrinal changes that would have incorporated the law merchant. Law reformers were vanquished by the common lawyers, and law reformers' influence in England declined dramatically. Although Chancery and Admiralty continued to exist, common law essentially became unchallenged and unchallengeable, "illogical but workable."[36]

Thus the flow of legal capital to British America from other than common law sources began to dry up. Immigrants arriving from England looked to the common law for their analysis of colonial law, and by that standard, colonial courts were found badly wanting. William Fitzhugh, born in England and trained in the law there, arrived in Virginia in 1674 and immediately began to complain about the lack of common law adherence in the courts. For Fitzhugh, "understanding of the common law was 'the only guide, & which is only to be learn'd out of antient Authors,'" and Fitzhugh set about to correct that deficiency by advocating study in England and adherence to English common law precedent. In 1697, barrister Edward Chilton wrote to complain that Virginia's courts had merged "Chancery, King's Bench, Common Pleas, Admiralty, and Spirituality" into one court where "the Sense of the Law [singular] was mistaken, and the Form and Method of Proceeding was often very irregular." Chilton blamed this sorry state on the lack of legal education among the creole Virginians. Framed in the terms used for this chapter, Chilton argued that the stock of legal capital imported by the original settlers who had been educated in England had been depleted, and English educated lawyers, relying on books and proper pleading, needed to import common law to remake Virginia's legal imagination.[37] Virginia's unregulated bar and unlearned gentry serving as justices of the peace did not have the intellectual resources to withstand such a challenge.

In colony after colony, the same pattern emerged by the end of the seventeenth century: common law became the only source of legal capital. In New York, the process was starkest, for the legal pluralism involved a non-English population that had used Dutch civil law prior to the 1664 conquest. The Duke of York's laws included more legal pluralism than merely utilizing models from New England and multiple English laws—there was recognition of Dutch law for existing contracts, land titles, and practices of inheritance, and juries decided only those cases concerning English settlers. Yet over time, English legal literates using English legal forms supplanted Dutch notaries whose drafting skills had been essential to the functioning of the civil law system. By the 1680s, a new charter and set of laws attempted to restructure law enforcement for the whole colony through counties (not through towns as under the Dutch) and imposed an English land system in the name of English liberties defended by the common law. By 1691, in the aftermath of Leisler's Rebellion, the jurisdictions of the courts were set explicitly in terms of common law, and the town courts, a legacy of the Dutch period, gave way to courts run by justices of the peace. During the 1690s and the early 1700s, a "thoroughgoing metamorphosis of practice" attributable to new lawyers arriving in the colony occurred. They achieved a higher level of legal certainty at the price of ossification due to common law.[38]

In New England, the Dominion of New England under Governor Edmund Andros launched an aggressive attack on deviation from the common law. New England towns were not legal corporations, were not accepted by the common law, and therefore had no legal authority to grant, divide, or hold land, a legal conclusion that rendered virtually all land titles worthless. Equity powers were taken from county courts (where they had been exercised but never formally authorized by legislation) and given to a new court of chancery. In county courts, common law forms with fictitious parties began to appear, and dismissal of cases for technical flaws in pleading increased dramatically. Jury pools were drawn according to English property qualifications for service. Although Andros and the Dominion were overthrown in early 1689, Massachusetts's 1691 charter required conformity with the common law, and subsequent legislation limited the county courts to hearing civil cases triable at common law, with only limited equity powers. The rhetoric of law became more formal, complex, and specialized in late seventeenth-century Massachusetts. By the early eighteenth century, records of individual justices of the peace show their performance was tightly controlled in accordance with English common law practice.[39]

In late-seventeenth-century Connecticut, court practices on a wide variety of issues became constrained by common law rules. All suits for trespass were filed as common law actions. Defamation actions for being a "bad neighbor" were dismissed because such vague charges did not fall within common law categories of actionable words. The decline of defamation suits was a stark example of the narrowing of the legal imagination. During the twenty years after Andros and the Dominion's downfall, there was a shift to orderly pleading, technical common law pleading, in land and debt cases. In prosecutions for fornication, Connecticut male defendants began using lawyers who successfully invoked common law protections against conviction if the only evidence was the woman's word. At the same time, in rape cases, Connecticut was importing the English common law's suspicion of women's charges, a position that was backed up by readings from imported English law treatises.[40] In Connecticut, as in Massachusetts, the importation of legal capital from but one source—the English common law—came to dominate the legal imagination in the 1690s and beyond.

Even the Delaware Valley's legal imagination, which had diverse flows of legal capital in the 1670s and 1680s, soon registered signs of a common law takeover in the 1690s and early 1700s. Evidence of common law pleading, presumably taken from formbooks, appears from the very beginning of the court records alongside simpler language reflecting law reform notions. By the 1690s, a majority of plaintiffs were clearly using common law forms or Latin in their pleadings, and simple pleadings in plain language disappeared by the first decade of the 1700s. Defendants flooded the dockets with pleas previously not seen in the Delaware Valley—oyer, imparlance, and special imparlance—which were used primarily to delay and thus to undermine law reform's ability to deliver swift and cheap dispute resolution. By 1701, the Pennsylvania legislature was passing acts instructing justices (somewhat schizophrenically) to conform to the methods and practices of the common law while also implementing law reform goals of "brevity, plainness and verity in all declarations and pleas, and avoiding all fictions and color in pleadings." By 1707, David Lloyd would be fighting a losing battle to keep the common law action of ejectment, which had a declaration riddled with fictions to try land titles, out of Pennsylvania legal practice.[41] The legal literates of the Delaware Valley, the last significant importers of multiple forms of legal capital into British North America, could not resist the common law's takeover of their colonies' legal imaginations.

Who were the agents of this takeover, the transmitters and advocates of common law capital? Imperial officials were one source. Although governors like Berkeley and Andros may have desired more common law conformity, it was only with the establishment of the Board of Trade in 1696, and its subsequent reviews of colonial legislation for the purpose of disallowance by King-in-Council, that common law standards became rigorously enforced. In Joseph Smith's analysis, the question of "repugnancy to the laws of England" became a "mere matching" analysis in the area of colonial judicial procedure. For the Board, "the ancient tradition that the accepted common law ways of proceeding constituted 'due process' colored the official attitude, for certain disallowances cannot otherwise be explained."[42] The Board matched a wide range of colonial legal practices against the common law and found them wanting: the use of affirmations instead of oaths; colonial methods of service of process, attachment, proof, and execution of judgments; and a variety of criminal penalties. In terms of colonial court structure, the Board of Trade's policy was first to freeze in place the existing court system and not allow further legislative innovation. Second, if possible, the Board's goal was to separate out chancery, probate, and admiralty matters through governors' prerogative powers to establish courts. It is hardly surprising that the highest percentage of disallowed colonial legislation and the longest battles over courts occurred in Pennsylvania, where the non-common law sources of legal imagination were strongest.[43]

The improvements in quantity and quality of shipping and communications around the English Atlantic in the late seventeenth and early eighteenth centuries helped make imperial supervision more effective, and also made transmission of legal capital easier and cheaper. In Virginia, wealthy families began to encourage sons to go to England and return home with an Inns of Court education; early eighteenth-century Virginia also attracted the migration of common law trained Englishmen and Scots who become practicing attorneys in Williamsburg.[44] Legal literature entering Virginia in the luggage of the arriviste legal literates or as imports for a growing local market was enormous by comparison with that of the seventeenth century. The personal law libraries of Virginians became dominated by common law case reports, common law treatises, and practical aids: manuals, collections of forms, and guides for common law pleading and conveyancing were by far the most popular category of common law publishing. A survey of law treatises published and imported in the 1700s throughout the colonies shows case reports, statutory compilations, practice manuals, abridgements, dictionaries, and formularies dominant in colonists' law collections. Chancery, ecclesiastical, continental/civil law, and admiralty works were far rarer (although law merchant works still appeared, with merchant practices now considered facts to be proven in common law actions). Furthermore, by 1711 colonial publishers had begun producing justice of the peace manuals developed from English books that incorporated and transmitted common law information for the American county courts.[45] By 1700, the text had triumphed in English legal practice over memory and custom as *the* source authority of the law, and the vast majority of law texts available to colonial practitioners confined the legal imagination to common law channels.

The professionalization of colonial legal literates, that is, the creation of a group whose primary source of income stemmed from legal practice, occurred in all these colonies around 1700. This professionalization did not mean the imposition of education requirements for admission to practice; college education and Inns of Court training remained rare, as most practitioners learned by local reading and apprenticeship. Furthermore, the status and reputation of lawyers did not particularly improve, as public opinion continued to view such practitioners suspiciously, as pettifoggers, and many colonies imposed licensing and fee restrictions in this period.[46] What professionalization did signify was that there was now a regular and lucrative demand for technically correct legal drafting and pleading that was beyond the talents of most of the law-using public. In South Carolina, a group of attorneys operated as gatekeepers for all civil litigation in the colony; in order to get on the docket, a litigant had to hire one of these attorneys to do the drafting and pleading. In Maryland, planters, clerks, and merchants who practiced law part-time were replaced by circuit-riding attorneys who monopolized the cases appearing in various county courts between 1690 and 1710. In Massachusetts, professionals appeared in Boston in the generation following the 1691 charter, and more lawyers (although still part-time) appeared in the other parts of the province to plead with greater technicality and precision, including in Maine.[47] All colonies registered this rise in the number of professional legal practitioners at roughly the same time as the dominance of common law over the older Atlantic rules asserted itself. It seems likely that these practitioners were both a cause of the common law's takeover and the prime beneficiaries of the consequent demand for technical precision as prerequisite for effective use of the law.

This legalistic turn among practitioners occurred *prior to* the eighteenth-century colonial litigation explosion that focused on debt and commercial transactions. Furthermore, these practitioners' use of Atlantic rules preceded other expressions of social replication (or anglicization) noted in depictions of mid-eighteenth-century colonial life. Changes in the colonial legal profession have long been noted as signs of anglicization, but changes in the substantive law were at work as well. Law was thus a leading and not a trailing indicator of this phenomenon. The most prominent example of changes in Atlantic rules preceding changes in colonial practices involves the adoption of new forms and procedures for the exchange of commercial paper.

Bills of exchange worked by having the drawer of the bill (A), who had positive credit with B (the drawee), order B to pay a third party C a sum of money that A owed to C. Negotiability of bills of exchange, often drawn on London drawees, meant a bill would often be endorsed multiple times (e.g., C would endorse the bill to D when C owed D money; D could then endorse the bill to E, and so on) before being presented by the last holder for payment by B. Thus, bills of exchange that passed as money served as crucial credit instruments in the functioning of transatlantic trade. A recent study of New York merchants found that they accepted and negotiated bills of exchange obtained in the West Indies, Amsterdam, southern Europe, Newfoundland, Philadelphia, and the Carolinas, while Boston merchants regularly sought out good bills on London drawn in the Chesapeake. As communication improved and intercolonial posts expanded, bills became "a postman's commodity."[48] In the specie-poor colonial economies, good bills of exchange drawn on London were the next best thing to cash. But confidence in commercial paper depended not merely on the reputation and willing execution of the provisions but also on a common set of Atlantic rules regarding acceptance, protest, transfer requirements, and negotiability.

In the 1500s there had been doubts and confusion in the common law about the enforceability of commercial documents that were not sealed: bills of exchange but also bills of lading, contracts of insurance, the assignment/endorsement of debts, and bearer notes. Much of the advocacy for the admiralty courts to enforce the law merchant reflected traders' uncertainty regarding the outcome of their cases in the common law courts. By the beginning of the 1700s, all such doubts had been resolved as commercial practices were fitted into the categories of common law or ratified by statute. The transfer of bills of exchange by endorsement—free negotiability—was established for the most part by English legal decisions of 1693 and 1696. A 1704 act of Parliament made promissory notes assignable. A 1697 statute outlawed the penal bond, the favorite method for enforcing arbitration among merchants; the following year, however, Parliament passed a law to allow the direct enforcement of arbitration awards in common law courts.[49] These elements of the legal infrastructure for commerce emerged within the common law because of the needs of English and Atlantic merchants; they were available for colonists to adopt if and when a colonial economy had need for them.

This clarification of the law of bills and notes closely preceded the litigation explosion that started around 1710. Studies of Massachusetts, Connecticut, New York, New Jersey, and Virginia caseloads showed a surge in litigation rates; most cases involved a debt or contract dispute. The number of debt actions in Hartford County, Connecticut, went from 35 in 1700, to 87 in 1710, to 653 in 1730. Book debt, based on account books, dominated the earlier caseload, because written instruments (bills, bonds, and notes) were involved in only 17 percent of the 1700 debt cases. By 1730, however, written instruments were present in 80 percent of the much larger caseload. This shift from book debt to standardized written instruments reflected the increased number of significant transactions, the increased legal certainty desired by the parties (and now clearly offered by the common law to written instruments), and the benefits of assignability. In New Haven, the debt caseload quadrupled between the first decade of the 1700s and the 1720s, and quadrupled again by the 1740s. By 1740, most of this litigation was on notes and bonds under the more complex and "orderly" pleading requirements begun in the 1690s and now vigorously enforced. This increased use of written instruments occurred in the same time period in New York, where jury trials became increasingly rare in debt cases during the early 1700s; in such cases, the written instrument had left nothing for a jury to decide. In the first half of the eighteenth century, the litigation rate (number of cases per hundred residents) doubled in both New York City and rural Dutchess County, with 85 to 90 percent of the cases being debt related.[50] The Atlantic rules for economic transactions, rules that had only recently been clarified, increasingly permeated the colonial economy.

It seems ironic and almost counterintuitive that at the same time law was becoming more complex, more expensive, and more requiring of specialized legal assistance, the litigation rate rose dramatically. Although there is little analysis of the socioeconomic character of litigation in either England or the colonies in the eighteenth century, logic suggests that since costs increased, the social composition of the law-using public must have changed between the seventeenth and the eighteenth century and become more skewed toward those most able to afford litigation. Those engaged in economic transactions that involved amounts significant enough to warrant embodying in a written

instrument were those who could afford to hire the attorneys to draft the documents and prosecute or defend any default. Thus, in civil litigation, the colonial legal imagination increasingly resembled the English legal imagination. An
average person who sought to invoke legal processes and courts now faced
more formidable cost and information barriers than in the seventeenth century. After the legalistic turn, a process described by Cornelia Dayton as
"mutual exclusion," such threshold costs limited the general public's legal
imagination, discouraged the poor from bringing suits, and encouraged them
to develop strategies to avoid being sued.[51]

There is much evidence about women's changing place in the colonial legal
imagination during this turn. Women in Connecticut became increasingly
marginal participants in an eighteenth-century economy increasingly dominated by bills and notes; Dayton found their participation rate essentially cut
in half in this litigated economy.[52] In New Netherland's courts, Dutch women
had appeared regularly in debt cases as independent traders or as widows
inheriting under mutual wills. Under English common law practices, the number of female traders dropped precipitously, mutual wills nearly disappeared,
and women's appearances in debt cases in New York courts dwindled in the
late-seventeenth- to mid-eighteenth-century period.[53] In Virginia after 1680,
de facto legal privileges granted to wives to function as feme soles in the economy disappeared as common law principles of coverture became more literally
and strictly applied.[54] Because of the legalistic turn, women's presence in most
common court business—debt and contract—declined, and thus the court
participation profile in the colonies paralleled that of the gender-stratified
English common law courts.

In other aspects of colonial legal practice, the legalistic turn acted to mute
women where once they had been heard. While previously sufficient, after 1728
in Massachusetts an unmarried women's oath of paternity regarding her bastard
child was not accepted as proof unless it conformed to the common law requirements that the accusation be made during childbirth. In late seventeenth-century Virginia, evidence from women that was hearsay or based on "common
fame" became less effective in obtaining convictions for consensual sexual
offenses as justices of the peace adhered more strictly to common law. Common
law formalities extended to punishment in those cases that resulted in convictions; ecclesiastical penalties were out, secular punishments, such as fines, were
in. In colonial Connecticut, prosecutions of men for consensual sexual offenses
that formerly resulted in a confession of guilt now led to the defendants asking

for trials, using lawyers in their defenses, and invoking common law evidence standards that required corroboration of the woman's accusation beyond her mere word. In both Virginia and Connecticut, rape and sexual violence convictions became virtually impossible to obtain after 1700, as the English legal practice of suspicion of women's charges became incorporated into colonial practice. When combined with the decline in defamation cases (where women had often appeared), women's presence in court shrank still further.[55]

The legalistic turn did not wholly consume the colonial legal imagination, but rather limited its scope in three critical and intertwined areas: control over legal processes, economic transactions, and gender roles. Experimentation and deviation from the common law could still be found in other topics. One significant area where Atlantic rules did not develop into conformity was land law. While in England, land was the law's favorite, a unique species of property and the soul of the common law, in British America, land was just another commodity reconceptualized in diverse rules. Each colony struggled with methods of distributing land, registering ownership, and resolving border and possession disputes; in no colony did English rules prevail. In two articles, John Hart has proven not only that colonial legislatures passed a wide variety of innovative laws controlling or directing the use of land, but also that many of those laws neither conformed to English law and tradition nor were they struck down by Privy Council review.[56] In fact, until the Revolution, land law remained particularly ambiguous, and the legal imagination of settlers more active, the closer one got to the periphery of settlement.[57] The Privy Council treated other legal topics as predominantly "local" in nature, such as slavery, inheritance, and marriage; common law rules in these areas were either nonexistent or intermingled with ecclesiastical precepts. These were the backwaters that the Atlantic legal tide did not swamp, where the colonial legal imagination could still play with multiple legal sources. But they were the exceptions in the overall turn toward common law legalism.

Conclusion: Greene's Synthesis Refined

The synthesis of colonial development presented by Jack Greene's *Pursuits of Happiness* in 1988 can now be clarified and certain turning points more definitively established thanks to the work done recently in colonial legal history.[58] The initial stage of colonial development Greene described as social simplification characterized by the dominance of local experience over metropolitan inheritance in a period of unsettledness and disorientation. Yet the laws and legal practices that emerged in the colonies established in the 1600s reflected complex legal inheritances rather than simplification and adaptation in response to small populations and confusing experiences. Of the social capital that was transplanted to colonial British America in the early years of settlement, the legal capital component clearly fixed a palpable limit to social disorientation. Although the legal systems created were different from the English, the fusing of diverse legal inheritances by colonial legal literates working within populations that possessed expansive legal imaginations actually represented a triumph of metropolitan legal thought and a touchstone for settlers' identity as English.

Greene's model then traced colonial societies through stages of social elaboration and social replication, with the duration of each stage and the timing of the shift from one stage to another varying from region to region. Overall, however, these stages moved colonial societies away from relying on their experience and toward the adoption of metropolitan modes of behavior. However, the timing of the shift in colonial legal systems toward a legalistic mode of operation, which required a heightened mimicry of the metropolis' common law requirements, did not vary from region to region. Rather, that shift appears to have begun in all colonies at roughly the same time (the mid-1680s to mid-1690s). A concatenation of events converged on all colonies during this period: increased imperial supervision; victory of the common law with a concomitant decline in alternate legal discourses; clarification of critical rules essential to the operation of transatlantic trade; and the replacement of the original legal literates with new legal practitioners trained only in common law and utilizing the increasingly dominant common law texts. Replication of what laws applied, of how law was to be practiced, and of whose problems the law would consider and whose issues were to be ignored, had been accomplished by 1710 in the bulk of colonial court dockets, both civil and criminal. In so doing, the colonial legal imagination, both of legal literates and of the population as a whole, became confined almost entirely to the common law.

This restriction of the legal imagination to the common law occurred before the large-scale replication by colonists of English society patterns of behavior and consumption, before the substantial anglicization of the legal profession described so influentially by John Murrin, before the changeover to commercial paper in most intracolonial dealings, and before the litigation explosion of 1710–30. The legalistic turn in the Atlantic rules seems to have formed the necessary legal infrastructure for these other elements of replication. Indeed, without the clarified rules for commercial paper's enforceability at law anywhere on the British Atlantic rim, it is hard to envision trade growing at the rate it did in the 1700s.

As the legal accomplishments of the founding generations submitted to the discipline of the common law, there remained little room for creativity in a colonial legal imagination so confined to that single source of legal capital. However, this reframed and newly channeled discourse would shift away from issues of everyday law to focus on constitutional issues. Colonists used common law reasoning in the 1700s to argue for an imperial constitution, separate and distinct from constitutional rules in the British Isles, which protected their liberty under the law.[59] Unlike the early years of colonization, where legal literates fused many inheritances into one legal system, now a single legal system—the common law—spun forth multiple constitutional understandings with which legal literates on both sides of the Atlantic had to contend. The legalistic turn thus provided, many years later, an intellectual foundation for the destruction of the first British Empire and its Atlantic rules.

CHAPTER EIGHT

Jonathan Edwards, the Enlightenment, and the Formation of Protestant Tradition in America

Avihu Zakai

Much has been written on the adaptability and replication of English norms of thought and behavior in colonial societies and the strong mimetic impulse found among colonial elites, as well as on the anglicization of colonial America and the rise of Anglo-American commercialism and consumer society.[1] Less attention, however, has been given to colonial *opposition* to intellectual developments and ideological transformations taking place in the centers of learning and scholarship in Europe during the eighteenth century. Yet voices of resistance to and rejection of British and European modes of thought had been raised in colonial British America prior to the era of the American Revolution, 1763–89, and these reveal the complexities involved in the development of the transatlantic intellectual world. In this chapter I want to focus on the dialectic implied in the ideological and intellectual negotiation and exchange between periphery and center by showing, first, that not only adaptation and replication but also opposition to European intellectual traditions played an important part in the creation of the Atlantic world; and second, how the rejection of certain European strains of thought influenced the formation of Protestant culture in America.

In what follows I shall explore the complex process of intellectual exchange through an examination of Jonathan Edwards's response to the Enlightenment fashioning of new modes of thought. I will to do so, more specifically, by focusing on Edwards's reaction to the emergence of new theories of ethics and morals and the shaping of new modes of historical thought in Britain and Europe during the eighteenth century. Given that Edwards's life of the mind reveals a lifelong involvement with contemporary European modes of thought, analysis of his reaction to Enlightenment theories of ethics and history may provide a good illustration of the process of ideological communication across the Atlantic. Indeed, many themes in Edwards's philosophical and theological enterprise provide evidence of the crucial transatlantic connection.[2] But Edward's work in the fields of ethics and history express more than anything else the complex process of transatlantic intellectual exchange. Edwards's philosophical and theological enterprise may be best understood, I will argue, within this broad intellectual context of early modern history. Edwards's works were primarily directed at and read mostly by Protestant theologians all over Europe—in England, Scotland, Wales, Germany, Switzerland, and Eastern Europe[3]—and very rarely if at all by any philosophers of note during the Age of Reason. His reaction against the emergence of new concepts of ethics and history played a key role in the creation of transatlantic evangelical culture and left an indelible mark on Protestant culture in America.

Edwards, the Enlightenment, and Protestant Evangelical Awakening

Much of Edwards's philosophical and theological work can be characterized as a struggle to rescue traditional Christian faith and belief from the menace of the new scientific exposition of the nature of reality and from Enlightenment theories of ethics and history. His philosophical theology was a reaction, in part, to new modes of thought that were gradually bringing about the exclusion of religious thinking and belief from history, from the physical world, and from the realm of morals.[4] Thus, in his "Scientific and Philosophical Writings,"[5] or his works on natural philosophy, Edwards reacted against the accompanying metaphysical and theological principles that implied a growing detachment of God from his creation and contributed to the disenchantment of the world. The same purpose characterized his philosophical and theological endeavor in the fields of ethics and history. In his "Ethical Writings"[6]

Edwards argued against the new theories in ethics and morals that rejected the traditional view that morality is based on the will of God and maintained rather that morality depends on human nature, or that virtue should be considered natural to human beings and hence that morals come naturally to man. Similarly, Edwards developed his philosophy of history in response to the Enlightenment narratives of history that rejected the Christian view of time and thus posed a threat to the traditional theological teleology of history.

Edwards was no stranger to the European republic of letters and was among those best qualified in colonial British America to criticize its ideas and values. From an early age, he passionately immersed himself in the theological and philosophical debates taking place in England and Europe. With the modernization of the Yale curriculum during 1717–18,[7] Edwards first encountered the new and revolutionary ideas of the scientific revolution and the early Enlightenment. For the rest of his life, dialogue with these early modern intellectual movements was part of his philosophical and theological enterprise. During the early eighteenth century strong negative reactions to the scientific revolution and the Enlightenment were expressed in many religious circles. This is not hard to understand given that the premises of these two intellectual movements seriously undermined the traditional Christian conception of the personal God who operates through history and concerns himself indefatigably with the affairs of intelligent creatures upon the earth. Evidently, the impersonal God of mechanical philosophy and the deists, the Lord of the physical world and the cosmic lawgiver, was radically different from the living God of the Bible whom Christians had worshipped for many centuries—God the Savior and Redeemer, the triune God of special as well as of general providence, Jesus the personal Savior, and the Holy Spirit, the mediating power between God and human beings. In medieval theology, "God had no purpose; he was the ultimate object of purpose" in a universe structured according to a grand theological teleology of order whose harmony reflects and symbolizes God's redemptive presence. In contrast, mechanical philosophy and deism held that "the cosmic order of masses in motion is itself the final good. Man exists to know and applaud it; God exists to tend and preserve it."[8]

Many Protestant revival movements of the early eighteenth century embraced the tremendous task of redefining the relationship between God and the world, of formulating a whole new set of religious convictions and persuasions that would express God's direct and immediate involvement in creation, and, consequently, of constructing new modes of religious faith and experience that would exhibit the living God's redemptive and saving presence within believers' lives.[9] Since "the search for the essence of true religion, as an objective 'presence of things outside myself' appeared to have bankrupted itself" in view of the flourishing of the scientific revolution and the Enlightenment, Protestant revival movements developed a new "theology of the heart" which emphasized rather "the illumination of the Holy Spirit in the individual heart."[10] Theirs was the attempt to combat mechanical philosophy and the Enlightenment, which placed divine redemptive activity mainly in the physical world of nature. Hence, "religious experience" was "the name Protestants gave to that which survived the attacks of the Enlightenment."[11] Evangelists therefore elevated the heart as the locus of God's redemptive activity and conceived the drama of salvation and redemption as taking place ultimately within the inner spiritual sphere of the soul through the immediate presence and vivid influence of the Holy Spirit. The soul, and not the external world of nature, is again the proper and main domain expressing divine redemptive activity within the world, and the heart is the sacred dwelling place within which the Holy Spirit directly operates and affects and transforms the human existential condition by its divine influence. To a large extent, then, the revolt against the predominant rational culture of the scientific revolution and the Enlightenment constituted an ideological and theological context for the emergence of Protestant evangelical movements during the first half of the eighteenth century.

Against the scientific and Enlightenment interpretation of the relationship between God and the world, Protestant evangelical movements attempted to construct an alternative culture of time and space. The evangelists formulated a new type of spirituality based on "experimental religion," that is, experienced religion, and developed the "theology of the heart," which stressed the Holy Spirit's direct influence on the soul and its ability to transform the human condition. So, according to John Wesley (1703–91), the Holy Spirit brings about a New Birth allowing a human being to feel "the love of God shed abroad in his heart." The essence of the New Birth is a profound existential change "wrought in the whole soul by the almighty Spirit of God," whereby human beings are "created anew in Christ Jesus."[12] By stressing to the utmost the "sense of the heart" as the locus of all religious life and experience, the evangelists declared the New Birth dependent on the experience of conversion. Instead of the mechanical God of nature of mechanistic philosophy, evangelists proclaimed with great enthusiasm that the revelation of God is manifested not only in the structure and harmony of the external, physical world of nature but, most important, in the inner sphere of the soul or the heart. It demanded, as with John Wesley, "the joy of surrender to Christ."[13] Likewise, for Jonathan Edwards, religion "consists in holy affections" or "the inner working of the Spirit" in the believer's heart;[14] hence it was essentially a kind of private experience evident in "the sense of the heart" and "religious affections" that are produced by the dwelling of the Holy Spirit in the depths of the soul.[15] Thus, against "the British Moral philosophers' movement toward a secularized understanding of the affections grounded in an innate "moral sense," Edwards grounded what he deemed to be specifically religious, that is, God-given "gracious" affections, in a new "spiritual sense."[16] Like other evangelists of his time, Edwards emphasized the personal, unmediated experience of New Birth and claimed that the regenerative process of "conversion by grace" is "immediate" and dependent upon God's Word and Spirit.[17]

Edwards was a leader in this Protestant evangelical awakening. During the revivals of the 1730s and 1740s, he not only rapidly emerged as a leader in New England but his various writings pertaining to the revivals were soon printed in Europe, and found an enthusiastic reception among Protestant theologians there. An English edition of his *A Faithful Narrative of the Surprising Work of God* (1737) appeared in London in 1737 and was soon reprinted in Edinburgh in 1737 and 1738. Its influence was felt also in the Welsh revival. A Scottish edition of *The Distinguishing Marks of the Work of the Spirit of God* (1741) appeared in 1743, and the sermon *Sinners in the Hands of an Angry God,* delivered on July 1741, was circulated in Glasgow in 1742. A Scottish edition of this sermon was published in 1745.[18] In England, Wesley eagerly read *The Faithful Narrative* in October 1738, and this work, as well as other writings, such as *Distinguishing Marks* and *A Treatise Concerning Religious Affections* (1746), exercised an enormous influence on the English Methodist movement, the "Wesleyan Revival."[19] Likewise, Edwards's *The Nature of True Virtue* (written in 1755, published in 1765) was regarded by orthodox Christians in England who opposed Enlightenment theories of morals and strove to emphasize the superiority of Christian ethics as "the most elaborate, acute, and rational account of this interesting subject."[20] Two of Edwards's works appeared in German in this period: *A Faithful Narrative* (1738) and *The Life of David Brainerd* (1749). Apparently, "the relevance of Edwards's kingdom of God was more sharply perceived in Eastern Europe than in his own congregation."[21] Edwards's interpretation of salvation history, where revival constituted the heart of divine activity in the order of time, was developed after the "Little Revival" (1734–35) and appeared in his series of sermons on the *History of the Work of Redemption* (preached 1739, published in 1774). It too greatly influenced transatlantic evangelicalism: "Assessments of the significance of the revivals subsequent to the Great Awakening would ensconce in American and British evangelical culture Edwards's vision of the pivotal role of revivals in God's grand scheme for mankind."[22]

Edwards's republic of letters, therefore, was related above all to the transatlantic Protestant evangelical world, where his works were in great demand and made a great impact. Thus, although he lived on the periphery of the eighteenth-century British Empire, Edwards's thought and actions were an integral part of the Atlantic world. The Great Awakening, in which he enlisted all his power and zeal, was inextricable, as he always maintained, from the long series of revivals and awakenings in the Old and the New Worlds, constituting an important dimension of the transatlantic evangelical movement. Edwards was, of course, fully aware of the international dimension and his role in it. Writing in 1745 to a friend in Scotland, he declared that the "Church of God, in all parts of the world, is but one; the distant members are closely united in one glorious head."[23]

Viewed in this ideological and theological context, Edwards's thought shows clearly that the development of an American culture during the eighteenth century did not depend on a simple and linear transference of ideas from the core culture in Britain nor on an easy accommodation of them in America; it was not, as Perry Miller puts it, simply a "movement of European culture into the vacant wilderness of America."[24] Rather, in some matters, the rejection of certain well-established European intellectual traditions helped the formation of a well-defined Protestant cultural space in America. Edwards's opposition to the Enlightenment concept of ethics and history is evidence not only of the growing readiness of people in the colonies to distance themselves from cherished European intellectual traditions but also of their growing confidence in their ability to forge new foundations for an American culture and identity, a process that climaxed during the era of the American Revolution, when Americans rejected British authority. Yet its origins can be traced many years before the struggle for independence. When well before 1763 Edwards was convincing colonists to criticize certain modes of thought predominant in the British intellectual world and not to accept them automatically, the center had already begun to lose some of its power and attraction over the periphery. "We have our books, and our learning from" England, wrote Edwards, "and are upon many accounts exceedingly liable to be corrupted by them. This country is but a member of the body of which they are the head, and when the head is so sick, the members it is to be feared, will not long be in health."[25] Together with social, political, and economic changes in British America during the eighteenth century, a significant ideological process was also under way, whereby ideas coming out of the center in the Old World were met with strong opposition in the colonial periphery.

By denouncing modes of thought and belief that had developed at the heart of the British Empire, Edwards asserted that the center was no longer a model to be emulated: "England, the principal kingdom of the Reformation," he observed, is overcome by "licentiousness in principles and opinions" such as "Arianism and Socinianism and Arminianism and deism." Nowhere in the world is there "so great apostasy of those that had been brought up under the light of the gospel to infidelity, never such a casting off the Christian religion and all revealed religion."[26] Indeed, much of Edwards's intellectual development can be characterized, in his own words, as a struggle "against most of the prevailing errors of the present day," which tended to "the utter subverting of the gospel of Christ."[27] This did not apply exclusively to religious thought and experience, for Edwards also fought against the British "School of Moral Sense," as well as against the new modes of historical thought, and it was in these spheres especially that he greatly influenced the creation of the transatlantic evangelical movement and the formation of Protestant culture in America.

Indeed, this New England divine and philosopher was "the most powerful enemy" of the "rational English Enlightenment."[28] His brilliance as a theologian and philosopher endowed Edwards's negative response to the new theories of ethics and philosophy of history with an enormous influence on, for example, the first and second Great Awakening. More specifically, his attack on the British school of "moral sense" was incorporated, adopted, and diffused by the New Divinity School and in fact was its hallmark during the eighteenth and nineteenth centuries: "The advocacy" of Edwards's "theory of moral agency was undoubtedly the most important mark of the New Divinity,"[29] and Edwards's followers, such as Joseph Bellamy (1719–90), Samuel Hopkins (1721–1803), and Jonathan Edwards, Jr. (1745–1801), "sought to defend Calvinism from rationalist attack and to focus it upon experience of grace as the definitive religious event."[30] More specifically, the "innovations of the New Divinity reveal Edwards's most creative and important contributions to New England theology." In their continuation of Edwards's "intellectual efforts to balance piety and moralism,"[31] the New Divinity men were his most important direct heirs, and part of the "most sustained, systematic, and creative intellectual tradition produced in this country—the New England theology."[32]

Likewise, Edwards's reaction to the new modes of historical thought, which were bringing about the secularization of the Christian theological teleology of history by according human beings a decisive role in shaping the course of history, led him to develop a singular evangelical historiography according to which revivals and awakenings, being the direct manifestation of the effusion of the Spirit of God, constitute the heart of the historical process. By placing revival at the center of salvation history, Edwards conditioned many generations of Protestants in America to see religious awakening as the essence of sacred, providential history. The publication of the *History of the Work of Redemption* in the 1770s, which is the best exposition of Edwards's philosophy of history, "helped to fuel the transference of religious convictions into the political realm," a transference that was important during the American Revolution and later crucial to the "revival of interest in eschatology" and the millennium "that occurred in the 1790s."[33] This book went through a "process of canonization during the Second Great Awakening, 1800–30, and added to [Edwards's] stature as the preeminent authority on revivalism." During the Second Great Awakening the work "proved to be popular both with lay readers and revivalistic preachers." Edwards's philosophy of history thus helped to create the revival tradition in America. "Indeed, the *History of the Work of Redemption* served to 'universalize' the revivals of the Second Great Awakening, situating them in a cosmic scheme of redemption and exciting interest in such evangelical causes as missionary work at home and abroad."[34]

Edwards and the Enlightenment Debate on Moral Philosophy

Edwards's long involvement with the issue of ethics and morals should be understood in the wider ideological context of early modern history and the "Enlightenment project," or its "new science of morals." The first half of the eighteenth century witnessed a growing and continuous attempt on the part of moderate, or rational, Enlightenment British thinkers to establish new concepts of moral theory.[35] Chief among them is the theory of a "moral sense," the *sensus communis* of classical thought. In claiming that the moral sense is the faculty by which we distinguish between moral right and wrong, the theory formulates a distinctive conception of moral judgement. The emerging theories of morals stood in contrast to traditional Christian teaching. Enlightenment writers, such as the Scottish philosopher Francis Hutcheson (1694–1746) and the Scottish philosopher and historian David Hume (1711–76), argued that it is possible to have knowledge of good and evil without, and prior to, knowledge of God. The main assumption behind this conception of ethics was the belief that human beings can know from within themselves, without reliance on traditional sources of religious authority, what God intends and expects of them as moral creatures. Edwards owned and read many works by Enlightenment moral theorists,[36] including Hutcheson's *An Inquiry into the Original of Our Ideas of Beauty and Virtue* (1725) and *An Essay on the Nature and Conduct of the Passions and Affections with Illustration on the Moral Sense* (1728)[37] and Hume's *An Enquiry Concerning Human Understanding* (1748), *A Treatise on Human Nature* (1739), and *An Enquiry Concerning the Principles of Morals* (1751). In these works he could see that the new theories of morals were leading to the detachment of the moral system from God. Accordingly, in his "Ethical Writings," such as *Charity and Its Fruits* (1738), *Concerning the End for which God Created the World* (1755), *The Nature of True Virtue* (1755), as well as in *Original Sin* (1758), Edwards directed a strong attack against the Enlightenment view of ethics and morals, claiming it was "evident that true virtue must chiefly consist in love to God,"[38] or that "all true *virtue*" is based on "love of Being, and the qualities and acts which arise from it."[39]

The moral sense theory arose within a larger intellectual development in the early modern period. John Locke's *Essay Concerning Human Understanding* (1689), led to a new theory of knowledge, which rejected external authority as the guarantor of truths. The scientific revolution paved the way for the belief that speculations about the will of God were no longer prerequisites for doing physics. Likewise, the moralizing tendency in British thought of the eighteenth century can be attributed in part to the gradual decay of theology and the reduced authority of religious sanctions. With the increasing insufficiency of theological ethics, where sanctions were the chief interest, moral philosophers attempted to find a substitute for religion as the basis of society and human conduct, thus emancipating ethics from the theological tradition of their time.

The term "moral sense" was first suggested by Anthony Ashley Cooper, third Earl of Shaftesbury, in *An Inquiry Concerning Virtue* (1699), and in *Characteristics of Men, Manners, Opinions, Times* (1711). In these works he appeals to psychological experience as a foundation for morals. He thus attributes to a moral sense our ability "*to be capable of* Virtue, and *to have a Sense of* Right *and* Wrong,"[40] or to distinguish between good and evil, virtue and vice, claiming that this sense, along with our common affection for virtue, accounts for the possibility of morality. In contrast to Thomas Hobbes, who offers a radically egoistic view of human nature, Shaftesbury argues that we have social impulses that are expressed in our sense of benevolence, beauty, and justice, and these are not reducible to self-interest. It was his conviction that "morality must be deduced from the nature of man as it is," and that "the human system or constitution is a complex compound of natural affection and a self-conscious faculty of reason and reflection, in which moral judgment and action have their origin."[41] Shaftesbury thus developed a system of nonintellectualist ethics based on the contention that there is "a form of moral appreciation and judgement that is affectional and sensory in its nature rather than intellectual."[42]

It was Francis Hutcheson, Shaftesbury's principal follower and a professor of moral theology at Glasgow, who first constructed an explicit theory of a moral sense, or a new moral philosophy in his *Inquiry into the Original of Our Ideas of Beauty and Virtue* (1725). Hutcheson's primary aim was to refute the egoistic interpretation of ethics, recently revived by Bernard Mandeville in *The Fable of the Bees; Or Private Vices, Public Benefits* (1705–29), where Shaftesbury's claim concerning the innate goodness of human beings is rejected. In defending the ancient view of man as an essentially social being, Hutcheson attacked "the notorious self-love theorists old and new, Epicurus, Hobbes, and Mandeville."[43] He first fits the moral sense into Locke's theory of knowledge, maintaining that it accounts for our knowledge of moral right and wrong as Lockean reflexive perception. Second, to refute Mandeville's interpretation of ethics as cynical egoism, Hutcheson claims that human beings have disinterested motives, namely, they can act for the sake of the good of others and not merely for their own self advantage, since "no love to rational Agents can proceed from Self Interest, every action must be disinterested, as far as it flows from Love to rational Agents."[44] This disinterested motive, which he terms "Benevolence, or Love"—the quality of being concerned about others for their own sake—constitutes "the universal Foundation" of the "Moral Sense."[45] Here lies the innate, God-given "moral sense" in human beings. Being divinely implanted at all times and places, this sense is universal and constitutes the natural (that is, God-given) goodness of mankind. The "Author of Nature," he thus declares, "has given us a Moral Sense, to direct our Actions, and to give us still nobler Pleasure."[46] Accordingly, the "frame of our nature" endows us with moral sense "by which we perceive virtue or vice, in ourselves or others,"[47] and this sense is the source of moral obligation. Hutcheson asserted the existence of several "internal" senses, among them honor, sympathy, morality, and beauty, but discussed only the latter two at length.

The same endeavor to ground morality exclusively in the benevolence of human nature appears also in David Hume's moral philosophy. For him, as with Hutcheson, morality is an entirely human affair based on human nature and not on a divine will. Yet there are considerable differences between them. The English and Scottish moralists who belonged to the Shaftesburian tradition believed that although morality may be deduced from human nature, it is God who constituted that nature and hence the moral faculty is a divine implementation. Hutcheson's moral sense depended on the existence of a superior being. While Hume agreed that "Mr. Hutcheson has taught us, by the most convincing arguments, that morality is nothing in the abstract nature of things, but is entirely relative to the sentiment of mental taste of each particular being,"[48] he himself "was the only eighteenth-century moralist" who argued for "an experimental theory of morals based solely on experience and observation of human behavior, society, and history, divorced from any attempt at religious explanation."[49] Believing that ethics and religion were separate subjects of inquiry, he attempted to provide an analysis of moral principles without connection to religion. Thus, while Hume saw himself as Hutcheson's follower in the ethics of sentiment, he did not adhere to Hutcheson's belief that moral sense depended on the existence of a superior being, or God. Instead, he defined "virtue as personal merit, or what is useful and agreeable to ourselves and to others."[50] Despite these differences, Hume, like Hutcheson, emphasized that the source of morals is feeling, not reason.

This Enlightenment debate on moral philosophy, especially its theory of innate moral sense, contained serious implications for Christian ethics. When Hutcheson expressed his views in public, the Presbytery of Glasgow condemned him for expressing dangerous ideas opposed to Christian teaching, namely, that the standard of moral goodness is the promotion of the happiness of others, and, most important, that a knowledge of good and evil does not depend on a knowledge of God. From the point of view of traditional Christian ethics, therefore, Hutcheson denied first that "post-lapsarian is inherently sinful and that all apparent morality can be reduced to a more or less complicated function of this sinfulness." Second, he denied that "man's moral institutions can be understood to arise from the prescriptions of an avenging God, whom his creatures follow in terror and hope."[51] Instead, his philosophy was based on a deep confidence in human nature. A still more serious challenge to orthodox Christianity was the absence of any theological foundations in Hume's moral philosophy, his refusal to search outside human nature for the origins of moral principles, and his tendency to follow the ancient classical moralists. "Hume made explicit his hostility to Christian ethics and allied himself with the classical moralists, especially Cicero."[52]

Hutcheson and Hume's theories of moral sense thus gradually freed ethics from its traditional subservience to theology: "The *emancipation of ethics* at the beginnings of the modern age went hand in hand with optimism, progress, and undeniable advancement of life. The loss of religious tradition may be painful—yet the moral foundations were still preserved."[53] But not for Edwards. Arguing against the secular moralists, or sentimentalists, he said that moral sense is "merely a variety of natural conscience," and thus cannot be the source of ethics and morals. In fact, much of what was claimed for the moral sense "was reducible to self-love . . . rather than virtue." Hence, "one cannot attribute to the natural man the pure inclinations of heart that constitute true virtue."[54] The source of true virtue is necessarily founded, as we are about to see, upon "spiritual and divine sense."[55]

Edwards would not accept a theory of morals or virtue based exclusively on human nature and therefore independent of God, who exercises "absolute and universal dominion" over the created order. The Deity determines that "the whole universe, including all creatures animate and inanimate, in all its actings, proceedings, revolutions, and entire series of events, should proceed from a regard and with a view to God, as the supreme and last end of all."[56] In reaction to the school of "moral sense," Edwards's purpose was "to reconstruct for religious authority a moral role that was not already expropriated by the new moral philosophy."[57] In his "Scientific Writings,"[58] composed during the early 1720s, Edwards had denounced the detachment of the order of grace from the order of nature, striving rather for the reenchantment of the world in the hope of demonstrating the infinite power of God's absolute sovereignty in both the "order of nature" and the "order of time."[59] In the realm of ethics he had argued that the will of God is the sole source of morality and virtue. Against Hutcheson and others, Edwards assessed moral matters by their "worth in the sight of God" and claimed that without "love to God there can be no true honor,"[60] or, conversely, that "nothing is of the nature of true virtue, in which God is not the *first* and the *last*."[61]

Edwards devoted much time and energy to the refutation of the moral sense theory. After the "Little Revival" of 1734–35, he preached a series of sermons in 1738, posthumously published in 1852 under the title *Charity and Its Fruits; Or, Christian Love as Manifested in Heart and Life.* Well acquainted with Hutcheson's writings,[62] he attempted to present in these sermons "a finely woven systematic treatise on the Christian moral life."[63] Accordingly, against the Enlightenment's concept of moral theory, he asserted that from "love to God springs love to man;" hence without "love to God there can be no true honor," or virtue.[64] In opposition to the attempts by Enlightenment writers to base ethics and morals on secular and naturalistic foundations, Edwards declared that the gracious affections stand above and beyond the natural affections of which all are capable, and true virtue stands above and beyond the disinterested benevolence that marks the ultimate achievement of natural man.

In his own day Edwards's theological standing rested significantly on his *Freedom of the Will* (1754), which is both a defense of Calvinism and an assertion of God's absolute sovereignty. In this work he attacks the Arminians' and deists' "grand article concerning *the freedom of the will requisite to moral agency*," the belief that absolute self-determination of will is necessary for human liberty and moral virtue. If the Arminian view is correct, he believed, God's providential and redemptive economy is contingent on the unpredictable actions of moral agents. God is not really almighty because the doctrine of free-will places human actions and their results beyond his control. Such a condition contradicts the doctrine of divine foreknowledge and the premise that God, as absolute governor of the universe, orders events according to his sovereign wisdom and will. Edwards argues that since "every event" in the physical as well as the moral world "must be ordered by God," the "liberty of moral agents does not consist in self-determining power." In this work he wished to demonstrate that "God's moral government over mankind, his treating them as moral agents . . . is not inconsistent with a determining disposal of all events." Human beings must do as they will, in accordance with their fallen nature, and they have liberty only in the sense that nothing prevents them from doing what they will in accordance with their nature. Because "nothing in the state or acts of the will of man is contingent" but "every event of this kind is necessary," God's foreknowledge eliminates the possibility of contingency in the world, for contingency is the antithesis of God's unlimited prescience. Given that "the power of volition" belongs only to "the man or the soul," there is no such thing as "freedom of the will." That freedom is incompatible with the individual's necessary willing of what he or she can will in accordance with a nature of self already determined.[65] In the end, Edwards saw the whole spectrum of moral endeavor solely in terms of his notion of the visible saints, whose character was "already determined."

The same effort to assert God's absolute sovereignty characterizes *Original Sin* (1758). This work played a part in the larger debates between the Enlightenment belief in the innate goodness of human beings and the emphasis placed by the Reformation on human depravity. Against the Enlightenment notion of human beings as fundamentally rational and benevolent, Edwards provided "a *general defense* of that great important doctrine"—of original sin. This doctrine proclaims both the depravity of the human heart and the imputation of Adam's first sin to his posterity: all Adam's posterity are "exposed, and justly so, to the sorrow of this life, to temporal death, and eternal ruin, unless saved by grace." The corruption of humankind, however, cannot be accounted for by considering the sin of each individual separately. It is essential to the human condition based on "the *arbitrary* constitution of the Creator" in creation.[66]

In *The Nature of True Virtue* (1755), Edwards responded more directly to the contemporary "controversies and variety of opinions" about "the nature of true virtue." His goal was to define the disposition that distinguished the godly, claiming that true "virtue most essentially consists in benevolence to Being in general." True virtue is a kind of beauty. In moral beings, virtuous beauty pertains to a disposition of heart and exercise of will, namely "that consent, propensity and union of heart to Being in general," or God, "which is immediately exercised in good will." True virtue in creatures, therefore, appears in the degree to which one's love coincides with God's love of his creation and agrees with the end that he intended for it. A true system of morals and ethics becomes inseparable from religion because the former is grounded on the latter; religion is the true foundation and only source of all virtue. And given that "true virtue must chiefly consist in love to God, the Being of beings," continues Edwards, "he that has true virtue, consisting in benevolence to Being in general [or God], and in that complacence in virtue, or moral beauty, and benevolence to virtuous being, must necessarily have a supreme love to God, both of benevolence and complacence." Against Hutcheson and Hume's disunion of morals and religion, Edwards claimed that virtue is by necessity grounded on God since the Deity "is the head of the universal system of existence."[67] For him regeneration was inextricable from true virtue and vice versa. No wonder orthodox Christians in England, who strove to emphasize the superiority of Christian ethics, considered Edwards's *The Nature of True Virtue* as "the most elaborate, acute, and rational account of this interesting subject."[68]

Clearly, Edwards was fully aware of the grave implications of the Enlightenment theories of ethics and morals for Christian faith and belief. He found great fault with "some writers on morality" who indeed "don't wholly exclude a regard to the *Deity* out of their schemes of morality, but yet mention it so slightly." He suspected, with reason, that these moral philosophers "esteem" God "less important" in the realm of morals and rather "insist on benevolence to the *created system* in such a manner as would naturally lead one to suppose they look upon that as by far the most important and essential thing in their scheme." He himself claimed that if "true virtue consists partly in a respect to God, then doubtless it consists *chiefly* in it," for the Deity should be "the supreme object of our benevolence." Hence, "unless we will be atheists, we must allow that true virtue does primarily and most essentially consist in a supreme love to God." Those who oppose this assertion deny that "God maintains a moral kingdom in the world." Morality, then, cannot be separated from God: "a virtuous love in *created* beings, *one to another,* is dependent on, and derived from love to *God.*" Moreover, the foundation of morality can not be separated from the theological teleology of order inherent in the universe: "they are good moral agents whose temper of mind or propensity of heart is agreeable to the *end* for which God made moral agents." And since the "last end for which God has made moral agents must be the last end for which God has made all things: it being evident that the moral world is the end of the rest of the world; the inanimate and unintelligent world being made for the rational and moral world."[69]

Edwards was almost alone in the eighteenth century in rejecting the ideas of the universal moral sense and the essential goodness of the common man, or "the psychological optimism of the Shaftesbury-Hutcheson gospel of the innate goodness of man," which only "the two great wars of the twentieth century and the Holocaust have been able to shake into ruins."[70] In the English Enlightenment of the eighteenth century, Edwards's views, strongly opposed to the then dominant philosophy of Locke and Hume, in fact illustrate the expiring power of Calvinism. But in terms of the formation of American culture, this New England divine's attack on the school of "moral sense" helped to create a well-defined American Protestant culture. Timothy Dwight, president of Yale College, called Edwards "that moral Newton, and that second Paul," and Lyman Beecher declared that in his youth "I had read Edwards's Sermons.

There's nothing comes within a thousand miles of them now."[71] More specifically, Edwards's "theory of moral agency was undoubtedly the most important
mark of the New Divinity."[72] Striving to ground religion exclusively in the
experience of saving grace and to define that experience as the ultimate religious event, New England theologians closely followed Edwards in his defense
of Calvinism against rationalist attacks by Enlightenment writers. Chief among
them was Joseph Bellamy, who, like Edwards, strove to see "connection between
regeneration and moral virtue." In the attempt to refute "the Enlightenment's
attack on orthodoxy," Hutchesonian "ethics, rationalist morality, and natural
religion turn up at every corner of Bellamy's arguments," where he denounces
them, among others, as "epicurean and atheistical."[73]

At the end of the eighteenth century, over a hundred ministers in New England were preaching Edwards's version of Calvinism; "by 1790 self-proclaimed
New Divinity pastors controlled New England churches in and west of the
Connecticut River Valley . . . and were scattered throughout Vermont and
Maine and even New York and New Jersey." Jonathan Edwards, Jr., was not far
from the truth when he said in 1787 that "a majority of the ministers [in Con-
necticut] mean to embrace the system of my father and Dr. Bellamy."[74] Later
on, during the nineteenth century, the legacy of the New Divinity continued to
be spread by New England ministers, among others by Lyman Beecher
(1775–1863), the father of Harriet Beecher Stow and leader of the New England
Second Great Awakening.[75]

Edwards's theology of morals and ethics and later his followers' great
emphasis on the traditional values of Christian faith and belief did not hin-
der the rise of the spirit of capitalism in America. On the contrary, the theology of the New Divinity greatly facilitated the growth of the capitalist
economy. One of the main reasons was that "Edwards and his followers para-
doxically equated self-interest with human depravity and identified self-interest as the source of most beneficial social, political, and economic behavior."
Given that virtue involves self-love, such a view indeed endorses self-interest.
"Thus, the New Divinity of Edwards and his followers taught New Englanders
(and perhaps their evangelical heirs to the present) that they needed both capitalism and salvation."[76]

Edwards's influence on Protestant America was not confined to the eighteenth and nineteenth centuries. His views about the corruption of human
nature, and concomitantly about God as the true foundation of virtue and
morals, were revived during the twentieth century by H. Richard Niebuhr, the

influential theologian of the New Orthodoxy. In his quest to understand contingent existence as the manifestation of divine glory as sheer grace, and in order to proclaim *soli Deo gloria,* Niebuhr "found Jonathan Edwards, more than any other precursor, to be his mentor."[77] Against the Progressive Era scholars and critics such as Charles Beard and Vernon L. Parrington, who argued during the first decades of the twentieth century that Edwards "demeaned man in order to glorify God," Niebuhr claimed that Edwards's pessimistic view of human beings had been confirmed in view of the "extent to which human brutality can go, of the fury that can be unleashed when the human animal is attacked," and the "shuddering of man's inhumanity to man" during the horrors of the twentieth century.[78] Modern history rather confirms Edwards's historical prognosis: "Edwards' intense awareness of the precariousness of life's poise, of the utter insecurity of men and of mankind which are at every moment as ready to plunge into the abyss of disintegration, barbarism, crime and the war of all against all, as to advance toward harmony and integration."[79]

Edwards and the Enlightenment Narratives of History

The same drive to uphold traditional religion informs Edwards's contribution to historical thought. His philosophy of history arose, in part, in opposition to intellectual developments in the early modern European period, and specifically to new modes of historical thought that led increasingly to the exclusion of theistic considerations from the realm of history.[80] His *History of the Work of Redemption,* a series of thirty sermons preached at Northampton in 1739, was composed within a specific context that witnessed the gradual exclusion of religious thought and belief from history, from the physical world, and from morals. Edwards's redemptive mode of historical thought, the view that the course of history is based exclusively on God's redemptive activity, may be seen, in part, as a response to Enlightenment narratives that rejected the Christian sense of time and vision of history. Against increasing de-Christianization and de-divination of the historical process, Edwards sought the reenthronement of God as the sole author and lord of history.

The "Enlightenment project" posed grave implications for traditional Christian thought and belief, especially in the realm of time and history. The Enlightenment "was one of the greatest of all revolutions"; it was "the revolution of man's autonomous potentialities over against heteronomous powers which were no longer convincing."[81] This is clear in the new attitude toward history and the growing importance attached to human autonomy and freedom in determining its course and progress. The Enlightenment mind "refuses to recognize an absolutely supernatural or an absolutely super-historical sphere," and attempts to free historical thought "from the bonds of scripture dogmatically interpreted and the orthodoxy of the preceding centuries."[82] Instead of ordering the structure of history on the dimension of "sacred time,"[83] or the operation of divine providence, Enlightenment historical narratives were based on secular, "historical time."[84] Hume, Voltaire, Bolingbroke, and Gibbon, to name only a few among the Enlightenment historians, attempted to "liberate history writing from its subservience to theology" and to free it from the theological view that conceived "the course of human history as the realization of a divine plan."[85] Instead of seeing the historical process as contingent on a metaphysical reality beyond and above it, Enlightenment historians attached the highest importance to human beings' actions and deeds. This process of "de-divination of the world" meant that traditional Christian symbols were "no longer revelatory of the immersion of the finite world in the transcendent."[86] No longer considered as the narrative of a God-given providential plan or as revealing the teleological scheme of time, the historical realm was more and more defined as a space of time intended for the realization of the possibilities and abilities inherent in the nature of human beings. "For the men of the Enlightenment the idea of world-history was particularly congenial. It fitted in with their notion of progress, their view of mankind, advancing steadily from primitive barbarism to reason and virtue and civilization."[87] In place of the religious vision of history as the drama, or tragedy, of human salvation and redemption, which would be realized only *beyond* history, historical thought during the Enlightenment developed the concept of "progress," or the notion of an immanent human advance based on the belief that utopian visions regarding human freedom and happiness could be fulfilled *within* history. *Historia Humana,*[88] or the annals of human history, gradually replaced salvation history in the European mind.

For traditional religious thought and belief, such a transformation regarding the historical realm carried profound consequences. "In much the same way that the world became the object of scientific inquiry in the sixteenth and seventeenth centuries through a process of desacralisation, so too, religious practices" were "demystified by the imposition of *natural laws.* As the physical world ceased to be a theater in which the drama of creation was constantly redirected by divine intervention, human expressions of religious faith came increasingly to be seen as outcomes of natural processes rather than the work of God or of Satan and his legions."[89] Once considered the sole source and locus for human life, experience, and expectations, religious thought and belief were being pushed out of nature and history. The "history of religion since the seventeenth century can be seen as the driving-back of faith from history, from the physical world, and from the realm of morals." Thus, "religion, withdrawing from its claim to give objective truth about the nature of reality in all its aspects, ends by seeking to stimulate certain sorts of inner feeling in those who care for that sort of thing."[90] Having based their historical narratives on the "secular, historical" time-dimension, in contrast to Christian "sacred time," the time-dimension of grace, Enlightenment historians refused to assign divine agency an exclusive role in determining the passing of time. They thus arrived at the de-Christianization of history.

Edwards owned and read many works by Enlightenment historians,[91] among them Pierre Bayle's *Historical and Critical Dictionary* (1702), Samuel Pufendorf's *An Introduction to the History of the Principal Kingdoms and States of Europe* (1702), Henry St. John, Lord Bolingbroke's *Remarks on the History of England* (1731), and *Letters on the Study and Use of History* (1752), and David Hume's *Essays Moral, Political and Literary* (1742), which included "Of the Study of History." In these works he discovered, to his great dismay, that the divine agency was no longer considered intrinsic to history. Rather, these writers found religion a great obstacle to the development of human institutions, the advance of civil society, and the fostering of reason and freedom, which became the hallmark of the "Enlightenment project." "The 'Enlightenment narrative'" was "both a historiography of state and a historiography of society;"[92] its proponents were skeptical of the "chronology of Christian universal history." Instead they aimed "to modify or transform their readers' sense of national self-awareness through the writing of narrative history."[93]

Acquaintance with the various Enlightenment historical narratives enabled Edwards to assess their threat to the Christian theory of history. For example, in the *Historical and Critical Dictionary,* Pierre Bayle, the French philosopher who was also a pioneer of disinterested, critical history, "carries out the 'Copernican Revolution' in the realm of historical science." Instead of assuming that all historical facts are based on the authority of the Bible, and that the validity of the Scriptures in turn rests on that of the Church, whose authority rests on tradition, Bayle "no longer bases history on some dogmatically given objective content which he finds in the Bible or in the doctrine of the Church." His influential

Dictionary was not a mere treasure of knowledge but directly challenged traditional religious historical interpretation. "His sharp and unsparing analytical mind freed history once and for all from the bonds of creed and placed it on an independent footing."[94] This is evident, for example, in the entry on "David," where Bayle declares: "It is perfectly permissible for a private person like myself to judge facts contained in Scripture when they are not expressly qualified by the Holy Ghost."[95]

Likewise, Edwards owned Samuel Pufendorf's *An Introduction to the History of the Principal Kingdoms and States of Europe,* where the German historian and the founder of modern natural law praises the value of universal history—that is, of Europe—for the political education of the ruling elite. He emphasizes the need "to understand modern history," or the history of the modern "nations" of Europe, as well as their various forms of government.[96] The uses of studying history are thus primarily political and social and much less theological and religious. The same can be said about David Hume, who in his essay "Of the Study of History," claims that history's main use is to reveal the progress of "human society" from "its infancy . . . towards arts and sciences" and to present "all human race, from the beginning of time" in order to improve human "knowledge" and "wisdom."[97] *Historia Humana,* the annals of human institutions, laws, manners, nations, and so on, in contrast to the sacred, became the enterprise of the Enlightenment. Thus Hume wrote that the chief use of "history" is "to discover the constant and universal principles of human nature, by showing men in all varieties of circumstances and situations," enabling us to "become acquainted with the regular spring of human action and behaviour."[98]

The writing of civil history about civil government and society, instead of the sacred history of God's providence and the annals of the church, was the focus of the Enlightenment historical narrative. This can be seen, for example, in *Remarks on the History of England* by Henry St. John, first Viscount Bolingbroke. In this work, published in weekly installments in 1730–31, Bolingbroke deals almost exclusively with human institutions, or "the spirit which created and has constantly preserved or retrieved, the original freedom of the British and Saxon constitutions."[99] Further, in Ephraim Chambers's *Cyclopaedia; or an Universal Dictionary of Arts and Sciences* (1728), another book Edwards owned, the English forerunner of the French *Encyclopédie* makes the distinction between "*History*" in general and "*Sacred history.*" The first deals with the "*history of nature*" as well as "the *history of actions* . . . either of a single person, a nation, or several persons and nations," and the second "lays before us the mysteries and ceremonies of religion, visions or appearances of the Deity, etc. miracles, and other supernatural things, whereof God alone is the author." Chambers adds a third category, "*Civil history*," which deals with "peoples, states, republics, communities, cities, etc."[100] This division clearly displays the growing erosion in the Christian narrative of history.

More serious, though, for traditional religious thought and belief were the Enlightenment historians' denunciations of the Christian interpretation, or the theological teleology, of history. Hume argued, for example, that religion "has contributed to render CHRISTENDOM the scene of religious wars and divisions. Religions," and this includes Christianity, "arise in ages totally ignorant and barbarous" and "consist mostly of traditional tales and fictions." Such negative views do not refer only to the past. On the contrary, in "modern times, parties of religion are more furious and enraged than the most cruel factions that ever arose from interest and ambition."[101] Such unfavorable characterizations obviously left no room for accepting the traditional Christian interpretation of history. Instead, Enlightenment historians emphasized its destructive role in terms of the growth of civil society in Europe and the development of European civilization, in general.

Also grave for the traditional Christian narrative of history was the threat to the authority of the Bible itself as a historical source and its inability to portray adequately the "history" of the "first ages." This was the major assault levied by Lord Bolingbroke on sacred, ecclesiastical history in *Letters on the Study and Use of History.* The "historical part" of the "Old Testament," wrote Bolingbroke, "must be reputed insufficient" to the study of history "by every candid and impartial man" since the Jews had been "slaves to the Egyptians, Assyrians, Medes, and Persians." Not only is the Bible an insufficient and unreliable source, but "history has been purposely and systematically falsified in all ages" by church historians. Moreover, "ecclesiastical authority has led the way in this corruption" of history "in all ages." In the pagan world, for example, how "monstrous were the absurdities that the priesthood imposed on the ignorance and superstition of mankind." Since "the foundations of Judaism and Christianity" were not built on truth but on "voluntary and involuntary errors," it is no wonder that "numberless fables have been invented [by ecclesiastical historians] to raise, to embellish, and to support" faith. Instead of providing historical truths, the Christian interpretation of history has led to the "abuse of history": "Deliberate, systematical lying has been practiced and encouraged

from age to age" by church historians, "and among all the pious frauds that
have been employed to maintain a reverence and zeal for their religion in the
minds of men, this abuse of history has been the principal and most successful." Sadly, noted Bolingbroke, this "lying spirit has gone from ecclesiastical to
other historians."[102]

Edwards was fully aware of these modes of European historical thought.
Continually acquiring books from England, and always closely following intellectual developments in Europe, he was by no means a novice in the thinking
of Enlightenment historians. Reacting against Enlightenment historical narrative, Edwards asked: "Shall we prize a history that gives us a clear account of
some great earthly prince or mighty warrior, as of Alexander the Great or Julius
Caesar; or the duke of Marlborough, and shall we not prize the history that
God has given us of the glorious kingdom of his son, Jesus Christ, the prince
and savior of the world."[103] In attempting to understand the nature and meaning of divine agency in the order of history, Edwards concluded that revivals,
being "special seasons of mercy"[104] or grace, constitute a unique dimension of
sacred time, or epochs of time, *kairos,* in history. Through the effusion of the
Spirit, God orders major and decisive turning points in salvation history in
terms of fulfilled or realized time. These constitute the main stages in sacred
providential history, and only through these can history, its goal and destiny,
be properly understood. Paul Tillich made a distinction between *chronos*—
"quantitative time," or "clock time, time which is measured"—and *kairos*—
"the qualitative time of the occasion, the right time," such as "the right time for
the coming of Christ"—and made special use of it in his philosophy of history.[105] *Kairos* is a special time or epoch in salvation history in which the eternal judges and transforms the temporal.[106] Before Tillich, however, Edwards
had already proposed this concept and made it the cornerstone of his philosophy of history. His historical narrative deals primarily with the "rise and continued progress of the dispensation of grace towards fallen mankind,"[107] or the
outpouring of the Spirit of God as "dispensations of providence," and, correspondingly, with its immediate historical manifestations in the form of decisive periods, or epochs, of awakenings as they appear in "special seasons of
mercy"[108] throughout history.

The fullest and most systematic exposition of this philosophy of salvation
history is found in the thirty sermons on the *History of the Work of Redemption*
(1739). Instead of conceiving history as the direct result of human action, and
as a manifestation of immanent human progress, as Enlightenment historians

believed, Edwards constructed it exclusively from the perspective of God and the manifestations of his redemptive activity in creation. In such a theological and teleological context, history is designed by divine providence as a special dimension of time meant solely for the accomplishment of God's plan of redemption, and therefore it should be understood only from the perspective of its maker and author. History is a grand sacred span of time destined from eternity for God's self-glorification—the display of the Deity's excellence in creation—as evidenced in His work of redemption; hence human beings' existence, as well as their history, are totally dependent on God. In his theological teleology of history, therefore, Edwards's main goal was to define "God's end in making and governing the world,"[109] to decipher God's "great design" in the order of time, and to understand the Deity's ultimate aim in the "affairs of redemption."[110] He attempted to assert God's redemptive activity and to show the power of the "wheels of providence,"[111] or "the chariots of his salvation,"[112] in history, continually demonstrating the "design that God is pursuing, and [the] scheme that he is carrying on, in the various changes and revolutions that from age to age happen in the world."[113] Given that the "work of redemption" constitutes the "great end and drift of all God's works,"[114] he attempted to explain it as part of the fabric of the entire creation, claiming it constituted the essential dynamism behind the grand teleology of sacred order inherent in the structure of the universe: "The work of redemption may be looked upon as the great end and drift of all Gods works & dispensations from the beginning & even the end of the work of creation it self."[115] The "affairs of redemption," he came to think, dealt with the cause and destiny, nature and meaning, of the creation as a whole.

Edwards argued that the outpouring of the Spirit of God, as manifested in the form of revivals and awakenings, was the ultimate mark of the divine agency in history. Throughout history, God's "work of redemption" determines the existential condition of human beings and their life. "God advances his work of redemption" most of all "through successive effusions of his Spirit."[116] Hence, the *History of the Work of Redemption* deals primarily with the "first rise and continued progress of the dispensation of grace towards fallen mankind;"[117] it is based on the effusion of the Spirit in the form of "dispensations of providence," manifested in periods of revivals, or "special seasons of mercy."[118] In sum, "from the fall of man to this day wherein we live the Work of Redemption in its effects has mainly been carried on by remarkable pourings out of the Spirit of God . . . [and] the way in which the greatest things have been done toward carrying on this work has always been by remarkable pourings out of the Spirit at special seasons of mercy."[119] History therefore is the grand "theater" of God, because His transcendent ends determine the drama of human history upon the earth. Yet history is not merely the "theater of God's judgments," for God continuously and progressively exhibits in history, through His word and work, the divine plan of redemption for fallen humanity.

For Edwards, earthly, mundane events are intelligible only by reference to the cosmic battle between Christ and Satan. Such an evangelical theodicy points beyond law and history to the eschatological moment, the judgment of individuals according to their standing in the order of grace, or their relationship to Christ. The heart of history, then, are revivals, whereby the Spirit of God constantly advances the work of redemption. These awakenings are the sole and exclusive domain of God's will and hence outside the reach of human agency. Edwards "made the phenomenon of the revival the key element in the drama of redemption. He conceived of revivals as the engine that drives redemption history."[120]

The premises of such a philosophy of history constituted the main source of Edwards's apocalyptic and eschatological interpretation of the Great Awakening in 1740–43 and of his defense of this New England revival. On the basis of the redemptive mode of historical thought, he proclaimed the magnitude and significance of this event in the overall course and progress of salvation history, becoming its most ardent champion in New England and the British world as a whole. If Edwards was the leader of that moment of *kairos*, which inaugurated the revival tradition in America, not the least reason for this was his assigning it a vital role within providential history. The revival demanded its own historian, a person who could expound its meaning in the broadest sense and provide it with the fullest historical justification in addition to the theological one. This figure was found in Edwards. His interpretation of the revival placed it in the wider context of salvation history, thus infusing this specific New England historical moment with a glorious meaning in sacred history. By showing the continuity between this provincial event and similar awakenings in the Old World, Edwards made the Great Awakening an inseparable part of the universal history of God's work of redemption.

Without a knowledge of Edwards's historical thought, it would be difficult to understand some of his most important works pertaining to the Great Awakening, among them *Sinners in the Hands of an Angry God* (1741), *The Distinguishing Marks of a Work of the Spirit of God* (1741), and *Some Thoughts Concerning the Revival* (1742). The Great Awakening was not to be judged as a mere provincial event leading only to the conversion of some fallen American colonists. On the contrary, together with other revivals taking place at that time in the Protestant world, as in Scotland and Germany, it illuminated the general scheme of God's historical work of redemption. On the basis of this theological teleology of history Edwards interpreted the New England revival as an integral part of the general Protestant evangelical awakening in the early eighteenth century, claiming it heralded "the commencement of that last and greatest outpouring of the Spirit of God, that is to be in the latter ages of the world."[121] Believing that the power of the Spirit is universal and thus not related to any particularistic center, he saw in the Great Awakening clear proof of that "glorious work of God, so often foretold in Scripture, which in the progress and issue of it, shall renew the *world of mankind*" (emphasis added).[122] Accordingly, from the Deity's point of view, which it was Edwards's aim to expound, history is a grand theater in which God reveals his redemptive plan, and revivals, such as the Great Awakening, illustrate the historical necessity, or indeed inevitability, of the progress of God's historical scheme of redemption.

This philosophy of salvation exercised enormous influence in New England and Protestant America in general. Edwards, "who saw tantalizing signs of the approaching millennium in the Great Awakening," is considered "the putative father of American postmillennialism," or the belief that the coming of Jesus would occur only after the millennium.[123] During the early nineteenth century, one evangelist described Edwards's *History of the Work of Redemption* as "the most popular manual of Calvinist theology," partly because in his philosophy of history Edwards offered "an original contribution to evangelical historiography." For antebellum evangelists Edwards's philosophy of salvation history provided the main source for understanding history as a "grand narrative propelled by a divine 'design and covenant of redemption.'" He emerged "as an authority not only on personal piety and individual conversion, but also on the 'morphology' of revivals and their millennial significance." As "the father of the great colonial revival," or the Great Awakening of the 1740s, "Edwards had laid the groundwork for the Second Great Awakening."[124]

Edward's influence, according to one nineteenth-century evangelical, is evident in the fact that he persuaded "a generation that feared more than they knew about revivals of their utility and benefit."[125] Likewise, H. Richard Niebuhr argues that Edwards's philosophy of history influenced nineteenth-century evangelists' understanding of "the coming of the kingdom," leading them to believe that "the divine sovereignty was the fruition not only of divine goodness but of human badness in conflict with that unconquerable goodness."[126] Further, his theology of history, emphasizing that "effort to progress toward the coming of the kingdom by self-discipline," led not only to "the recognition of divine sovereignty" within the realm of history but "ushered in . . . a new awareness of the coming kingdom." Through his and others' efforts during the Awakening, "the coming of the kingdom" became "the dominant idea" in American Protestantism.[127] Niebuhr sees Edwards's theme of "God's redemption of the world as at once the core of the Christian movement in America and the central meaning and significance of the culture."[128] In this context, the effect of Edwards's philosophy of salvation history "was to legitimate and foster popular expressions" of Protestant religious thought and experience, which encompassed "the Shakers as they developed Ann Lee's visions, Joseph Smith, Jr., and the Latter-day Saints, John Humphrey Noys and his Perfectionists . . . and even the remarkable Mary Baker Eddy."[129]

The theme of the formation of American culture and identity—or of "Becoming America," as in the title of a recent study[130]—runs through the historiography of early America. As the term suggests, to be an American means to be significantly different from others. The formation of an American identity was not only the outcome of impersonal social, political, and economic conditions but also, and most significantly, of conscious convictions and persuasions developed by the colonists, through which they defined their self and place in time and space, in some cases in deliberate opposition to dominant ideas that characterized British and European thought during the eighteenth century. In this context, Edwards contributed much to forging the ideological foundations of a distinct Protestant culture in America.

As Edwards's thought shows, and his legacy in America reveals, the formation of the Atlantic world and the creation of an American culture was a very complex process. The great influence he exerted on American history throws light on the dialectic relationship between periphery and center and on the fact that the formation of the American self was based to a large extent on the rejection of certain British and European modes of thought. Well before the American Revolution, Edwards was among the first to raise serious objections against modes of thought coming to America from the center in Britain. Periphery, it might be noted, has its own advantages in terms of acquiring fame and prominence. In England, Edwards might count as only one among the many Protestant evangelists in the first half of the eighteenth century who attempted to revitalize religious life and experience within a well-defined religious culture and tradition; in America, on the other hand, due to his brilliance as a theologian and philosopher and in the absence of a centralized religious establishment, he was able to inaugurate an American Protestant tradition. Yet, as I have attempted to show, the creation of such a religious tradition was not unrelated to the wider intellectual context of the early modern era. On the contrary, it was essentially a reaction to the Enlightenment "new science" of ethics and history. Edwards's genius enabled him to forge, out of his criticism of the "Enlightenment project," a novel tradition most adapted to the American mind. Its powerful influence on and its afterlife in American culture and history have not diminished over time; its manifestations are still evident in many spheres of American life and thought at the turn of the third millennium.

CHAPTER NINE

Order, Ordination, Subordination

German Lutheran Missionaries in Eighteenth-Century Pennsylvania

Wolfgang Splitter

In November 1742, Heinrich Melchior Mühlenberg (1711–87) arrived in Philadelphia as a Lutheran minister under the sponsorship of the Francke Foundations, located in Halle, Prussia, whose diverse interests ranged from charity and schooling, to printing and brewing, to medicine and mission work. Mühlenberg's posting to Pennsylvania originated in the concern of Friedrich Michael Ziegenhagen (1694–1776), the Lutheran chaplain in the Hanoverian court in London, that the United Brethren, commonly known as the Moravians, under the leadership of Count Nikolaus Ludwig von Zinzendorf (1700–60), were winning the battle for control of Lutheran parishes in North America. While Ziegenhagen could convince Gotthilf August Francke (1696–1769), the director of the foundations, of the urgency to send a Lutheran pastor to Pennsylvania, he had less success persuading any colonial parish to give Mühlenberg a formal call and to pay for his keep. As the Lutheran church councilors at Philadelphia, New Hanover, and Providence told the court preacher in 1739, they had not issued "such a call for a pastor as you have wished us to send [because] . . . no one is willing to subscribe to the support of a clergyman . . . until we first see what kind of a man we are to get, and know that he is worthy of confidence."[1]

The careers of Mühlenberg and his fellow Halle evangelists in Pennsylvania reflect the transatlantic struggle among Pietist Lutherans, as well as the many difficulties of ministering to independent-minded colonists in a foreign environment. This essay centers on the Halle pastors' attempts to introduce "order" into their congregations in response to the challenges of their rivals, the unfamiliar individual freedoms in America, the religious heterogeneity of the colony, and the absence of state support. It argues that the Francke Foundations' mission in Pennsylvania was reactive, defensive, monoethnic, and intraconfessional. It was *reactive* in that the Hallensians answered calls from colonial parishes and did not offer their services on their own initiative. It was *defensive* as a result of their emphasis on strengthening the faith of Christians instead of proselytizing pagans. It was *monoethnic* in regard to their focus on German-speakers and their neglect of blacks and Indians.[2] It was *intraconfessional* inasmuch as the missionaries rarely attended to Protestants other than Lutherans. Instead of being pioneers of Christianization, Mühlenberg and his colleagues became conservative innovators in ecclesiastic organization.[3]

In Quest of the Conductor's Baton: Halle's Struggle for Spiritual Supremacy

On his landing in Philadelphia in the fall of 1742, no one was waiting for Mühlenberg. His patrons had kept silent lest the Moravians had time to sway the Lutherans against the pastor from Halle.[4] Received by a Lutheran-turned Moravian, the divine learned that "most" Lutherans in town "had gone over to Count Zinzendorf." Others "had accepted an old preacher named Johann Valentin Kraft" (1680?–1752?), who had "pretty well made himself the master," so that "his countrymen in Germantown, Philadelphia, New Hanover and Providence adhere[d] to him."[5] Some New Hanover Lutherans "had hired a man as preacher whose profession was that of a quacksalver."[6] Whereas this vagrant, on hearing that Mühlenberg "had been sent by the Court Preacher, . . . adopted a wholly submissive attitude toward" him, Zinzendorf and Kraft defied his claims. Presiding over self-styled consistories, each of them had appointed elders and deacons.[7] The count, who posed as "inspector of all Lutheran churches in Pennsylvania," had "installed pastors in several places." Kraft, who likewise "wanted to be inspector and superintendent," planned to entrust two minor parishes to Mühlenberg's care while reserving the important Philadelphia charge for himself.[8] He even "consulted with the deacon's wife as to how" his new colleague "could best take a wife—whether" he "should take a girl from the city or the country."[9]

Mühlenberg considered Director Francke and Court Preacher Ziegenhagen the only superiors to whom he was accountable. Thus submission to orders from Kraft or Zinzendorf was unacceptable to him. Mühlenberg was confident of prevailing over his rivals, as his credentials included certificates of matriculation and graduation from Göttingen University, a document of ordination from the Lutheran consistory at Leipzig, two letters from Ziegenhagen specifying the conditions of his mission, and, possibly, Francke's draft of his 1741 call.[10] By all accounts, however, he was not in possession of an autograph in which the three congregations accepted him as parson on the terms set by Ziegenhagen. His testimonials, while impressive to some Lutherans, failed to persuade most that they should prefer him over Zinzendorf, whose followers were numerous in Philadelphia, or over Kraft, who enjoyed "considerable respect"[11] with his Hessian countrymen. Some New Hanoverians "had . . . been taken in" by obscure preachers "so often" as to suspect him, too, of having fabricated his credentials.[12] Church councilors doubted whether his call was "genuine."[13] Parishioners watched for any sign revealing his doctrinal stance. Kraft therefore advised him to "be of good cheer and merry, or else they might regard" him "as a Pietist. Several people said that" he "was secretly a Moravian."[14]

Anxious to resolve the confusion, Mühlenberg first sought arbitration by an impartial jury, only to discover that "[a]ccording to local laws no religious question can be decided by the authorities . . . If an upright pastor and servant of God wanted to bring a religious question or complaint before the magistrate, he would be laughed to scorn and turned away."[15] The charter Charles II granted to William Penn in 1681 guaranteed the right to free practice of religion in Pennsylvania, which an act of Parliament subsequently confirmed.[16] A royal decree of 1728 limited the jurisdiction of English bishops in the colonies to the Anglican Church.[17] In case of quarrels in Lutheran parishes, Mühlenberg reported, the Anglican bishop of London "cannot be judge, and the civil authority also has no power to judge in religious and ecclesiastical matters because the laws do not cover that."[18] In view of his call lacking legal protection, the Hallensian therefore devised a strategy to augment his standing step-by-step.

At Christmas 1742, Mühlenberg summoned the elders and deacons from New Hanover and Providence, whom his testimonials had meanwhile swayed in his favor, and asked them to sign a document he himself had composed in broken English. Therein they acknowledged him "as a lawfull called, ordained, and by our Supplications Sent and represent Minister, by the Reverend Frederick Michael Ziegenhagen." They "promise[d] to furnish" him "with all Necessaries what is required for his living in the lawfull Vocation" and vowed to "turn away from Such a Sort of Preachers, which are . . . creeping into Houses and Congregations without Vocation."[19] Now that the Lutherans in New Hanover and Providence had formally accepted him, Mühlenberg directed his attention to Philadelphia, where Kraft and Zinzendorf continued to wield much influence. To oust Kraft, he brought in the authority of the Swedish Lutheran Church, which was one of the oldest ecclesiastic bodies in America and had long ministered to colonial Germans. Mühlenberg asked Peter Tranberg, pastor in New Jersey from 1726 to 1741, to assemble the German Lutheran elders and deacons in the Swedish church in Philadelphia.[20] Kraft stayed away, but Zinzendorf "sent his spy to find out what was going to happen." Tranberg read Mühlenberg's credentials to the audience and told them "that among the Swedes they would not accept anyone as a pastor unless he had a lawful call and a certificate of ordination." After this exhortation, the councilors attending pointed out "that they had not accepted Mr. Kraft as their pastor, nor had they extended him a call because he was unable to present any testimonials from Germany."[21] Two days later, "the deacons and elders, some of whom Mr. Krafft had created, came to" Mühlenberg "and also subscribed the acceptance."[22] Those signatures rounded off Mühlenberg's victory over Kraft, and on New Year's Day 1743 he finally prevailed over Zinzendorf, too, when the count left for New York to return to Europe.

Variations on the German Theme: Institutionalization and Constitutionalization

A few weeks after his arrival, Mühlenberg had thus legitimated his calls as the parson in Philadelphia, New Hanover, and Providence. But despite Zinzendorf's departure, the Moravian challenge remained strong, Kraft continued to be active in Lancaster County, and other itinerants offered their ministrations in neighboring places. To prevent these competitors from intruding in his parishes, Mühlenberg had the congregants pledge in writing that they "will not

Suffer to be administered the holy Baptism and the Lord's Supper . . . by Such a Minister which is not lawfull called, neither Sent or ordained."[23] Yet unlike rules in Germany, provincial legislation did not distinguish "lawfully" from "unlawfully" installed clergy. Whenever Hallensians filed a lawsuit against an uneducated braggart posing as a regular pastor, legal officials dismissed their cases by arguing that "we do not know who among you has the greatest claim and best recommendation for a call!"[24] In Pennsylvania, the only qualification that candidates for the ministry had to meet was "irreproachable" conduct.[25] Hence, when Mühlenberg presented his many credentials to the governor to contrast favorably with preachers of dubious backgrounds, he merely earned some customary compliments seasoned with satirical remarks.[26] As Mühlenberg concluded after nine years of service in America, "Wanting to receive help from civil authority does not work out well in this country, for civil authority has nothing to do with churches and religious affairs."[27]

Mühlenberg believed that to stabilize the Franke mission in Pennsylvania, the parishes needed church statutes and a provincial Lutheran organization. "If more pastors come into the country who are working for the same purpose, church order will have to be regularized," he wrote to Halle. "As soon as there are a few more of us we propose to hold a synod to legitimize ourselves as Lutherans and to expose those who give themselves out to be Lutherans and are not."[28] Mühlenberg's ambitions moved closer toward realization after Pastor Peter Brunnholz (d. 1757), joined by Catechists Johann Nicolaus Kurz (1720–94) and Johann Samuel Schaum (1721–78), arrived from Halle in 1745 and Pastor Johann Helfrich Handschuh (1714–64) followed in 1748. By that time the Francke missionary outreach had expanded to ten parishes. Hallensians served in Germantown, Lancaster, New Hanover, Philadelphia, and Providence, while the two catechists performed some ministerial duties in Earltown, Lancaster, Tulpehocken, York, and Raritan, New Jersey.

In 1745 Francke proposed "to arrange for certain meetings or conferences" in which the clerics would "come together in prayer and also consider all necessary matters."[29] Mühlenberg did not need to be persuaded of the importance of such gatherings, as they would give the Halle mission an "official" veneer. In August 1748, five German divines, a Swedish provost, and some thirty delegates from ten Pennsylvania parishes assembled in Philadelphia for the first Lutheran "conference or synod."[30] In his opening address, Mühlenberg pointed out that this convention was "only a trial and test" that aimed "to create good order."[31] Three ecclesiastic bodies developed out of this conference: a pastoral college (ministerium), an association of parishes (united congregations), and an annual meeting (convention).[32] These boards, whose duties were not defined until 1781, did not correspond to institutions in the provincial churches in Germany, because neither the government nor the clergy in Pennsylvania had any coercive power in religious affairs owing to the separation of church and state and voluntary church membership.[33]

From the outset, the Pennsylvania ministerium was dominated by the Halle missionaries, largely a consequence of Mühlenberg's policy of exclusion. Many Lutheran clerics were not invited to the 1748 conference: ordained pastor Johann Conrad Andreä (1703?–54) and self-styled preacher Johann Philipp Streiter (d. 1756) were refused on the grounds of the former's disrepute and the latter's want of formal training; Johann Valentin Kraft, Johann Caspar Stöver (1707–79), and Tobias Wagner (1702–69) owed their rejection to Mühlenberg's strong dislike of each of them.[34] As chairman of the ministerium, Mühlenberg cited five reasons why "we can have no fellowship and close brotherhood" with these and "other so-called preachers." First, "they decry us as Pietists," a blame associated with the Hallensians' reputation as bookish and seclusive evangelicals. Second, "they have not been sent hither, have neither an inner nor an external call," thereby indiscriminately lumping all freelancers together.[35] This criterion the college would wave if it suited them, as they did in 1754 when they invited a newly arrived cleric to join them after being dismissed from his Württemberg parish.[36] Third, the pastors barred from the convention "are not willing to observe the same Church Order that we do," a reference to the solo effort of liturgical standardization the Hallensians made in their congregations in 1748.[37] Fourth, he suspected the absentees to "care for nothing but their bread." Fifth, the itinerants were "under no Consistorium" and gave "no account of their official doings."[38] Two years later, the ministerium would open its meetings to freelancers and even adopt most of them as members.[39]

The Hallensians clearly tailored the criteria for excluding divines from the pastoral board to their strategic goal of transforming this body into a consistory and of turning the convention into a synod in order to set the foundation for a colonial Lutheran church under their leadership. In the ministerium, their majority guaranteed that no preacher would be accepted without their approval. In the convention (which Handschuh and Kurz called "synod" as early as 1748),[40] the practice of granting parish delegates advisory status protected the clergy from being overruled by the laity. Not until 1792 were lay representatives put on a par with pastors.[41] In dealings with individual congregations, the Hallesian missionaries asserted their authority over the laity. When the Lancaster Lutherans protested the substitution of Handschuh for Kurz as the pastor to be installed, they warned the vestry "that if even one of them were troublesome and dissatisfied with our counsel and arrangement, they would get neither one of the men with our consent and we would turn to the other vacant congregations and withdraw our aid entirely." Yielding to this blunt extortion, in the end "all agreed and asked for Pastor Handshue." When Mühlenberg and Brunnholz were appointed as parsons in Philadelphia and Germantown in 1745, they themselves "drew up a call in English . . . and entered" their "names on behalf of the congregations."[42] His early troubles with unwanted rivals taught Mühlenberg to take the initiative.[43] By stipulating their terms of service, the pastors ostensibly reduced the laity's part to that of passive bystanders.

The shortage of regular preachers and the unconditional pledges of loyalty they exacted from some parishes encouraged the Hallensians to place their parishes under the tutelage of their patrons abroad. Joined by representatives from Philadelphia and New Providence, in 1753 they acknowledged Francke and Ziegenhagen, "apart from God," as "the only superintendents, rulers, directors, and guardians" of their congregations, on whom they conferred the "right and authority" to supply them with "honest, orderly, and faithful Evangelical teachers" and to decree "ordinances" and "discipline for all time," lest "vagabonds or uncalled, self-styled preachers . . . penetrate our church and cause disorder and quarrel."[44] By the early 1750s, Mühlenberg was also scheming on setting up the German Lutheran Church as a European-American institution. To that end he drafted congregational rules that would have subordinated the parishes of the Hallensians to Francke and Ziegenhagen, who, however, refused to ratify the statutes and assume the superintendency of the colonial Lutherans.[45] The investiture of a German Lutheran bishopric for America would have entailed incalculable risks for the Francke Foundations, whose mission work was based on voluntary charity and whose finances were increasingly strained. Moreover, it could have brought the two members of the Society for the Promotion of Christian Knowledge into conflict with political and church leaders in Britain. Thwarted in Halle, Mühlenberg turned to the Stuttgart consistory and to Johann Philipp Fresenius (1705–61), senior of the Frankfurt ministerium, as further patrons, a move which would have pleased immigrants from Swabia and Hesse who resented the Hallensians' predominance among the Lutheran clergy.[46]

Attuning to the Pennsylvania Theme: Negotiated Authority and Backstage Maneuvers

For lack of support from Europe, Mühlenberg sought to align Lutheran parishes to the Anglican model practiced in Pennsylvania. The first Lutheran ordinance to do so, his 1755 statute for the Germantown congregation appointed two politicians as trustees: former Anglican priests William Smith (1727–1803), provost of the College of Philadelphia, and Richard Peters (1704?–76), provincial secretary. In exchange for defraying one-third of the construction costs (and reducing the Lutherans' dependence on German donors), it allowed the Anglicans to use the newly built Lutheran church. It no longer named Francke and Ziegenhagen as supreme ecclesiastic authorities and reserved one seat on the board of trustees for the ministerium instead. By virtue of its 1755 charter, the college protected the rights and liberties of the Germantown Lutherans.

Mühlenberg's engagement of Smith and Peters in his project of restructuring the parish in Germantown was part of a larger deal between the Hallensians and the proprietary party. In this anti-Quaker platform under Anglican generalship the missionaries found their natural ally who shared their distaste for the German sectarians, if for political reasons. In 1754 Mühlenberg intimated his interest in Smith's scheme to open English charity schools for German children.[47] Though they were perfectly aware of the schools' political aim to neutralize Pennsylvania's large German element by Anglicizing German youth and driving their parents away from the ruling Quaker party, he and his associates ignored Francke's admonition that, "as regards political purposes, we rightly do not interfere with them."[48] On the contrary: readily serving as teachers, they disseminated proprietary views and put students against "such Vagabonds . . . who pretend to be Preachers but are inordinate, vicious persons, . . . corrupt the Morals of People and make great disturbances."[49] Mühlenberg, whose plans for a Lutheran press Francke had foiled, even cajoled proprietary leaders into publishing a German weekly. Under Handschuh's editorship the short-lived *Philadelphische Zeitung* tried to combat Christoph Sauer's (1693–1758) *Pen[n]sylvanische Berichte,* a pro-Quaker journal with a strictly anti-Halle stance.[50] Francke found it "somewhat dubious" that Handschuh "as a preacher" had "to engage in writing calendars and newspapers."[51]

Since the 1750s the missionaries had been aware of the benefits of having congregations incorporated by the proprietor.[52] Aside from manifesting the

Penns' confidence in the loyalty and respectability of a denomination, this act secured a parish the exclusive use and ownership of its church properties. To ensure their hold on the largest Lutheran congregation in America, the Hallensians therefore put incorporation of St. Michael's Church in Philadelphia on their agenda after the Quaker-led legislature appealed to the king to replace the proprietary system with royal government in 1764. Although Mühlenberg declined "to interfere in such critical, political affairs" and "begged" the St. Michael's vestry not "to become involved in the dangerous controversy between our provincial assembly and the proprietors," he himself rushed to the support of the anti-Quaker alliance. At Smith's request he "translate[d] a few lines of English," which was in fact antiroyal literature to be spread among the Germans.[53] Around the province he harangued Lutherans against any change of rule and procured signatures for a counterpetition to London.[54]

On the eve of the 1764 election Mühlenberg "[h]ad an uncommon amount of running to and fro." In a last-minute canvass he was busy rallying parishioners behind the proprietary party and its German candidate Heinrich Keppele (1716–97), "the ruling elder" of St. Michael's.[55] Finding his home "besieged with visitors," Mühlenberg did not miss out on this opportunity to mobilize them for the ticket. On polling day he joined Lutherans who "unanimously decided that it would be a good thing if several German citizens were elected to the Assembly." He agreed with them "because we German citizens are not bastards but His Majesty's loyal subjects and naturalized children," with "the right and liberty to have one or more German citizens in the Assembly and learn through them what is going on."[56] Proprietor Thomas Penn (1702–75) thanked the cleric for his services in defeating the Quaker plan to alter the form of government, which unmistakable proof of his political involvement Mühlenberg concealed from his patrons.[57]

By fall 1765, the Quakers recovered enough to have their nervous opponents eagerly court the Germans—for Mühlenberg, the unique chance to apply to the proprietors for incorporation of St. Michael's Church. A few days before the vote, he received "an exceptionally handsome charter with the great provincial seal and marvellous privileges."[58] "This has been done by the finger of God!" he rejoiced, knowing that the proprietors had *their* fingers in the pie. As Governor John Penn (1729–95) confessed, his family had granted the charter to the Lutherans "with a view to engage these people to vote against the Quaker faction."[59] Calling upon his "old friend[s]" Smith and Peters as "intermediaries," Mühlenberg had given the latter "a description of the state of our so-called United Congregations" to take along on his trip to London in 1764.[60] Mühlenberg's cryptic remark that he had "not hesitate[d] to declare the truth, come what may," suggests that he intended his intimate account to get the proprietors in the mood for chartering St. Michael's.[61]

This act of incorporation symbolized "the final farewell to the model of the European mother church."[62] Now this German Lutheran parish was organized fully in accordance with provincial law. Documenting the Penns' trust in the ability of the Hallensians to control their flocks and manage their affairs on their own, the charter was a big gain in prestige that bolstered the clerics' self-confidence. The fact that Mühlenberg accomplished this project he had long been "working on day and night," without seeking advice from Francke and Ziegenhagen, reveals how far their mutual estrangement had progressed.[63] Whereas he kept silent about incorporation toward his superiors, he reported on it to Friedrich Wilhelm Pasche (1728–92), lecturer at St. James' Chapel in London and Ziegenhagen's future successor.[64] No earlier than 1773 did the *Halle Reports* publish the text of the charter and an excerpt from Mühlenberg's letter to Pasche.[65]

Francke and Ziegenhagen watched the missionaries' endeavors to increase their authority with mixed feelings. Created in 1750, the post of "superintendent" of the "united congregations" was "not recognized by the authorities in Halle, who in all their correspondence say not a word concerning it, since it seemed to be an infringement upon the European superintendency of the Pennsylvania churches."[66] Also, when the ministerium elected a "president" in 1760, Francke suppressed this news in the *Halle Reports*.[67] Despite his refusal of the leadership of the colonial Lutherans Francke expected to be consulted prior to weighty actions of the board, which now wielded powers like a German consistory. In 1748, for example, it obliged Kurz "to undertake nothing important . . . without communicating with the 'College of Pastors,' and receiving their opinion, and acquiescing in their advice."[68] "The Tenor of ye Synod extendeth so far, that ye Majority of Votes, may translocate a Minister from one Congregation to an other, if they find it suitable, or may suspend yea even discharge a Minister," Mühlenberg told Peters in 1764.[69]

A Conservatory for Conservatives: Recruiting Young Lutheran Clergy

By 1760, the ministerium had seized control of most Lutheran parishes in Pennsylvania. While its members shouldered ever more responsibilities, their rejection of qualified freelancers greatly impaired the formation of a provincial church.[70] Realizing that their restrictive policy impeded the improvement of spiritual care, they eased the requirements for admission. From 1750 to 1769, ten persons joined without having completed academic studies of Lutheran theology, three to five of whom had not matriculated in theology before starting as irregulars or coming in contact with the ministerium.[71] Still, the body ordained five or six of these men.[72] One of the novices, Nicolaus Hornell, was an escaped prisoner who never vindicated himself of murder charges; Paul Daniel Bryzelius had been ordained by the Moravians; and a Johann Samuel Schwerdtfeger had "willfully had himself ordained by a couple of men like himself."[73] The college nevertheless accepted all ordinations as valid. Wondering that "so many [pastors] submit[ted] to the united ministerium," Francke warned Mühlenberg not to be too liberal of receiving "individuals who previously were not known."[74]

Whereas German-born Halle missionaries were ordained at an average age of 26.6 years, American-born pastors in the ministerium were 20.4 years old at ordination.[75] Ordained at the age of sixteen, Pennsylvania-born Gotthilf Mühlenberg (1753–1815) became the youngest member, while his older brother Friedrich (1750–1801), aged twenty, was just average. On their return after seven years of studies at Halle, Johann Georg Knapp (1705–71) of the Francke Foundations raised doubts about the maturity of their personalities and their proficiency in theology. "One has not yet observed true earnestness with both of them but rather gathered from their company and the like that their character is still lax," the director judged in 1770. He did not hold "any one of them to be competent in the office of preacher, as a beginning of a real change of their hearts" could "not be noticed with them, even granting the lack of sufficient knowledge."[76] Defying Halle's assessment, the pastoral college ordained the two brothers five months later.[77]

The gradual lowering by the ministerium of professional standards for admission is also evident from the share of university-educated German theologians. Their ratio dropped from 100 percent in 1748 to 93 percent in 1754, to 80 percent in 1760, and to 63 percent in 1769, before going up slightly to 65 percent in 1773.[78] On the eve of the Revolution, one in every three members was self-taught or a semi-autodidact. At some point, they went through ordination. The board condoned the practice of allowing not yet ordained members to act as ministers: former law student Johann Andreas Friderici (b. 1712?), for example, never graduated in theology but served as a parson.[79] For the Hallensians, to whom learned pastors were a main distinction that separated the Lutheran church from non-ecclesiastic Protestant groups, such concessions to pressing need were hard to make.

Three reasons effected a de-academization of the Pennsylvania German Lutheran clergy. First, the missionaries placed adherence to Pietist Lutheranism above formal qualification so that non-Pietist pastors like Johann Siegfried Gerock (1724–88), Bernhard Michael Hausihl (1727–99), or Tobias Wagner were outsiders in the ministerium. Second, the average ratio of parishes per pastor, while disadvantageous in 1748 (8:1), grew more disproportionate until 1776 (10:1) even after another six Hallensians arrived by 1770.[80] The shortage of professionals induced the college to admit nonacademics, too. Similar to the apprentice system in the trades, senior ministers tutored young hopefuls in theology and the classical languages and supervised their services as school-masters and auxiliary preachers before proposing them for examination and ordination.[81] Third, the benefit of sending German-born pastors "into a wholly unfamiliar climate," where they had to "undergo a metamorphosis," gave rise to question. "The parishes," Mühlenberg noted in 1766, "are seldom suited to them, and so are they to the parishes and their miserable condi-tions."[82] "It is difficult for the theologues who come from Europe to get a prac-tical understanding of the distinction between the *ecclesia plantata* [i.e., the church planted in Europe] and the *ecclesia plantanda* [i.e., the church to be planted in America]."[83]

Only a Lutheran seminary for American-born youth could produce divines who were acquainted with colonial life. "The intention is good," Francke com-mended Mühlenberg's plan for such an academy. Yet doubting its viability, he insisted that the students "be continuously kept in subordination to the preachers" and "their augmenting the number of itinerant, godless preachers be avoided . . . In view of the freedom there, it" would be "hard permanently to ensure such subordination," he predicted.[84] With his opposition, Francke reacted to dismal portrayals of Pennsylvania as a "free, unbridled country," where "one may be very easily seduced into carnal indulgence and dissolute habits."[85] Due to "unlimited, so-called freedom of conscience," he read in pas-toral reports, "Satan, who deceives the whole world, has his fully stocked fair and almost every possible type of sectarian mode" in the province.[86] He heard of "many sad examples . . . of disobedient children" who "boast of their free-dom from their parents."[87] In the colony "a father has no control over his son after he is twenty-one years old," Mühlenberg moaned. "Children here know

... this law generally before they learn the fourth commandment."[88] Given these somber accounts, Francke's successor Gottlieb Anastasius Freylinghausen (1719–85) felt no incentive to pay more than lip service to the Lutheran seminary that Johann Christoph Kunze (1744–1807) operated in Philadelphia from 1773 to 1776 to train young Americans for the ministry.[89]

Revolution in Rehearsal: Fermentation and Politicization

Overt manifestations of self-assurance, individualism, and anti-authoritarian spirit in Pennsylvania did not blend with the credo of the Hallensians, who taught that "God is a God of order, and in His congregations everything must be done orderly."[90] "Order" required laymen to honor the clergy's eminent role in German society by submitting to the authority that flowed from the pastoral office. After the adoption of the 1530 Augsburg Confession, divines formed a distinct estate in Germany.[91] In Lutheran territories the sovereigns acted as bishops, exercising the privilege to present a candidate for a vacant position *(ius patronatus)* and to invest him with that office *(ius episcopale)*. This personal union of head of state and church obliged the pastor to be loyal to his ruler, who in turn empowered him to exact spiritual and worldly obedience from the subjects. A fixed salary paid from church taxes made the minister independent of his parish.

In Pennsylvania the situation of divines was different. Deferential appellations, which in Europe instilled the laity with respect for clerics, carried little weight in "a free country where the peasant has as much a right to give commands as the inspector."[92] Devoid of governmental support, ministers entirely relied on the congregants for their income and therefore were subject to people's scrutiny even more than in Germany. When Johann Friedrich Handschuh got married in 1750, elders in Lancaster "took offense at" his bride's "humble birth and low orgin," which, they feared, "would later reflect upon the pastor, too, and weaken his authority." As they argued, "Since he was a public person and such a marriage was a matter of great consequence ... he should have consulted the council first."[93] Social control deeply encroached upon a preacher's privacy. "In your external conduct," Mühlenberg advised Catechist Schaum, "be thoughtful and circumspect, in every relation ... inasmuch as you have persons gazing upon you from all sides." To avoid gossip and ridicule, he admonished his young colleague to "beware of land speculation, secret marriage engagement, the purchase of horses, watches, and of exchanging of any kind."[94]

While laymen closely watched their parsons, lest moral lapses or unorthodox teachings escape their vigilance, the Hallensians combated what they regarded as sinful licentiousness. Because in "this free land" of Pennsylvania they had "no other weapons against the vices than prayer, exhortation and exclusion from the Lord's Supper," they tightened the requirements for communion.[95] In Lancaster, for example, Handschuh barred a "prostitute" from the sacrament, who had shown due remorse over "her former sinful life with hand and mouth to lead a quiet, chaste and Godfearing life through God's grace henceforth" by publicly notifying her "from the pulpit of the silencing of her name" on the list of communicants.[96] "Each one who intends to commune must come to the parsonage or schoolhouse and register with the pastor," Mühlenberg explained his own regulations for administering the Lord's Supper. "Whatever one learns from each congregation member in conversation or from circumstances is entered in the form of notes alongside the name" to gain "an understanding of inner and outer conditions and . . . an insight into relationships in the estate of marriage, between neighbors, parents, children and friends."[97]

In 1749 Handschuh made a pioneering attempt to regulate church discipline and augment pastoral authority by defining the rules for membership and admittance to communion in Trinity Church at Lancaster. He called on "everyone strictly and firmly [to] abide by our good and Christian church discipline, so that one keeps an eye on the other and duly reports to the pastor what may be of importance."[98] In his 1762 ordinance for St. Michael's Church in Philadelphia, Mühlenberg empowered the parson to reject at his own "conscientious liberty" those persons from communion and sponsorship "who evidently, or according to irrefutable testimony," were "found guilty of gross sins and violations of the saving doctrine of our Lord Jesus Christ."[99] A friend of his, Swedish provost Carolus Magnus von Wrangel (1727–86), even "made a table in which he wrote the names of parents, children and servants, and noted their excellencies and their defects, so that in looking over it he had the condition of the whole congregation before his eyes."[100] In 1772, Justus Heinrich Christian Helmuth (1745–1825) tightened the reins of order in Lancaster after people had given "great offense" by communing without having him screen their moral condition first. By recording the names of nearly thirteen hundred "souls wishing to be admitted to the Lord's Supper" he kept track of how often individuals communed and who did not.[101]

Halle-style order and discipline evoked resistance from parishioners who rejected control of their private lives. At weddings preachers reproved "unruly" guests "in vain" for "tippling, racing, dancing, jumping, and the like."[102] At funerals they "often" observed "considerable disorder" caused by individuals who, attending "on account of the drinks" only, "scandalize[d] respectable people."[103] Because provincial law prohibited merriments on Sundays, parishioners "reveled all the more frivolously on the days after holidays," giving in to "tippling, fiddling, dancing and engaging in all the other abominations that go with them." The misdemeanor of "grown and half-grown boys" who, by "stripping naked on the banks and bathing in the river," caused "great offense on Sundays during divine service" completed the picture of "Sodom and Gomorrah," where "the best and most devout parents" had "their troubles trying to guard their children against the poisonous, pestilential plague" of "freedom and frivolity." "It is impossible to force people in this country," Mühlenberg remarked on the clergy's powerlessness; "often the more one tries to stop this sort of thing, the worse it becomes."[104] At Lancaster, Pastor Helmuth had a hard time keeping his register, as congregants, being "very cautious of having their names recorded," were "quick to say: This is a bond, this is a stamp act, this is Moravian-style."[105]

Such lamentations about moral laxity notwithstanding, the most serious challenge to a provincial Lutheran church under Hallensian leadership arose from an idea "even well-meaning Lutherans" cherished, "namely that one should insist on imaginary Pennsylvania freedom and not give . . . preachers too much room."[106] Asserting their rights as parishioners, "boozers and loafers" in New Hanover were "accustomed to say: Since we have to hire a preacher with our own money let us rather have a jolly one, for Mühl[en]berg is too strict for us."[107] In the same vein, one "so-called Lutheran . . . preferring to remain free by himself," strictly insisted "that in Pennsylvania neither the devil nor a parson could tell him what to do."[108] In Philadelphia, the Lutherans would only tolerate a pastor if he was "a talented, humble, friendly man" and did "not dominate the people," for "the Americans" did "not want to suffer" any domination at all.[109]

In such "free air and an unfenced country" where there was "no governing authority" in the parishes, and elders and deacons were "of no account," regulating church life aroused much controversy.[110] "For several years we have already discussed a church constitution," Mühlenberg told his superiors in 1752, "but we do not yet know how to strike a true balance so that pastors do not dominate congregations and congregations also do not dominate pastors."[111] In the 1750s "disgruntled individuals" in Germantown saw "their old rights and liberties" violated by "the sovereign rule of the elders and pastors," especially by Handschuh, whose church statute forbade the parishioners to accept freelance preachers and obliged them and their offspring to recognize the missionaries as their "rightfully called and sent" parsons and Francke and Ziegenhagen as their "legitimate superiors and benefactors."[112] In a manifesto the anti-Halle faction refused "to have anything to do with the present so-called United Preachers [i.e., the ministerium]."[113]

Elsewhere, malcontents mobilized more opposition to Halle clergy while Sauer's paper impressed on readers to retain the same scope of "freedom which the province enjoys [at large], and not let themselves be encumbered with" divines who did "not please them." On no condition should they relinquish their "liberty to dismiss" a parson "in case he misbehaves in his teaching, life, and conduct, or gets unfit for preaching."[114] Encouraged by such articles, Lutherans in the Raritan Valley demanded preachers from Germany, "but no Hallensians," whom they denounced as "pietists, Herrnhuters, rogues, swindlers, thieves who steal from the offerings."[115] At Reading, Pennsylvania, some people "hoped to free themselves of the Halle pietists at once" by joining the followers of Pastor Andreä in Germantown.[116] In Philadelphia, a dispute arose over a provision Mühlenberg wanted to have inserted in his renewed call after Brunnholz had died in 1757. This provision, which secured him a fixed salary and confirmed him as a minister sent from Halle and London at the request of the St. Michael's parish, met with suspicion from Heinrich Keppele. As this elder objected, it "did not suit a free people in the American air, where they like to exercise *jus episcopale* and *patronatus* at the same time."[117] Lingering on for years, the deep dissension over the rights and duties of clergy, vestry, and laity and over the relationship to the European patrons brought this largest Lutheran congregation in America to the verge of destruction.[118]

In the decade before the Revolution, Lutherans all across Pennsylvania challenged the jurisdiction of the ministerium, arguing that "this is a free country, where neither Pope nor Council, neither Synod nor Coetus has any authority over us."[119] Slogans of this tenor acquired a political undertone in the wake of the Stamp Act crisis. In 1769, a strife over Halle's Johann Andreas Krug (1732–96) divided Holy Trinity Church in Reading. "[O]pposed to church discipline," the anti-Krug party was said to hold "that the pastor was appointed to preach on Sunday, but not trouble himself about their habits and ways of living."[120] Revolving around conflicting views clerics and congregants held on moral and religious standards, the contention centered on rules Krug had drawn up to tie his charge to the ministerium. Dissidents accused him and Mühlenberg of introducing "tithes" to support the parson, of "laying an intolerable yoke upon them and their children," and of "abducting them . . . into slavery." They objected to Krug's contacts with Court Chaplain Ziegenhagen, "compared the new church ordinance to the stamp act," and "composed manifestoes of freedom against it."[121] The 1772 revised regulation, which ended the bitter feud, "reserve[d] to the congregation the right to choose and call the pastor and schoolmaster, and also to dismiss them," in case it found a teacher's "life and conversation" no longer "irreproachable."[122] Devoid of any moral qualifications for membership (unlike the St. Michael's ordinance),[123] the Reading statute vaguely obliged all parishioners "to live uprightly" and honor the Augsburg Confession. The laity defiantly stressed their "will and determination" to "seek such teachers . . . who are of good report and good testimony of those who are without." "To support" their "common freedom and free will, it" was their "earnest request and petition to all men . . . be they rulers or subjects, that they by no means profane" the church, the parsonage, and the schoolhouse.[124] Ordinary Lutherans thus judged a "teacher's" observance of apostolic regulations and his "profanation" of their church properties according to their own standards.

By the early 1770s, imperial politics had added enough fuel to the ongoing fermentation in German Lutheran congregations to make the Stamp Act the handy cue that gave the disputes between clergy and laity a political thrust. People now drew parallels between the relations they maintained to the ministerium and the European patrons on the one hand and the relations the colonists entertained to the mother country on the other. To them, London was the capital of British subjugation of the king's subjects in America as well as the seat of Ziegenhagen, who, by way of secret correspondence with Francke and the missionaries, was pulling the strings and high-handedly interfering with matters that exclusively concerned the Pennsylvania Lutherans.

The Fanfare of Revolution: Loyalties and Liabilities

The politicization of the German Lutherans coincided with a period of transition in the Francke evangelizing work. In 1771 Gottlieb Anastasius Freylinghausen became director of the Foundations after the death of Gotthilf August Francke in 1769 and the brief tenure of Johann Georg Knapp. In 1776 Halle's Friedrich Wilhelm Pasche succeeded Court Chaplain Friedrich Michael

Ziegenhagen in London. Meanwhile, a new generation of Halle missionaries mounted Pennsylvania pulpits. Immigrating between 1764 and 1770, this young guard included Johann Ludwig Voigt (1731–1800), Johann Andreas Krug (1732–96), Christoph Emanuel Schultze (1740–1809), Johann Christoph Kunze (1744–1807), Justus Heinrich Christian Helmuth (1745–1825), and Johann Friedrich Schmidt (1746–1812). Among these preachers may also be counted Mühlenberg's American-born sons Johann Peter Gabriel (1746–1807), Friedrich Augustus Conrad (1750–1801), and Gotthilf Heinrich Ernst (1753–1815), who were all sent to Halle, and Jakob Göring (1755–1807), a native of York County, whom Helmuth prepared for the ministry.

These reinforcements might have ensured the prospering of the Francke mission had not the Revolution radically changed the political landscape. Few Hallensians agonized over the predicament of siding with the rebels or the loyalists. Tentatively vacillating and watching the tide of battle, most of them came to the conclusion that "the young people are right in fighting for their God-given native liberties," as all of them had been in America long enough to imbibe some rights of man views and to value liberty as a divine gift.[125] Circulating among them shortly after its publication in 1776, Thomas Paine's *Common Sense* even persuaded old Mühlenberg to reconcile Rom. 13:1–4—"the infallible rule for Christians" to discern legitimate from illegitimate authority—with the revolutionary zeitgeist.[126] "Be subject to that government which has power to protect *and which is willing with God's help to defend, in so far as this is possible, the rights and liberties granted by God and man*"; he adapted St. Paul's epistle to popular social contract philosophy by incorporating the idea of mutual obligations imposed on both ruler and ruled.[127]

Behind their carefully structured facade of unpolitical preachers who pretended "not [to] understand *Corpus politicum*" the clerics awoke to the impossibility of "keep[ing] themselves undisturbed by political matters" as the Pennsylvania Test Acts forced them out of hiding and marital bonds brought them in immediate proximity to political figures.[128] Also, the longtime close relations between German and "English Lutherans," Mühlenberg's favorite term for the Anglicans, caught the attention of Presbyterian revolutionary leaders.[129] They were suspicious of the ease with which the Anglicans, whom they accused of forcing dissenters under a "yoke of spiritual bondage and jurisdiction," and the Lutherans interacted, preaching and officiating in each other's churches.[130] Lutheran pastor Peter Mühlenberg had been ordained as an Anglican priest in 1772, and his father owed many thanks to "old friend"

William Smith "for his two benefactions toward me and our German brethren in the faith":[131] for protecting the Germantown Lutheran parish under the charter of the College of Philadelphia and interceding with the Penn family for incorporation of St. Michael's Church.

Years before, Mühlenberg offered much praise for the Presbyterian clergy, who "have established seminaries in various places, educate their own ministers, keep strict discipline, and tolerate no ministers except those who have good moral character and the ability to speak."[132] But after the legislature closed down the College of Philadelphia in 1779 and voided its charter of 1755 on charges that under Smith's headship it had forfeited the privileges by abandoning its nondenominational character, he heavily resented "the Presbyterian politico-Christiani" then in power.[133] Their assault on that presumed Tory stronghold was a threat to the German Lutherans, for it deprived the Germantown parish of the rights and liberties Mühlenberg had negotiated with Smith in 1755 and raised the question of whether the St. Michael's charter of 1765 would be left untouched. Before long, some vestrymen-turned-politicians who adhered to the Presbyterian-led Constitutionalist party started to press for renewal of incorporation of St. Michael's.[134] Intent on curtailing pastoral powers in favor of lay rights, they insisted that interim rector Kunze had acted "wholly at variance with our republican form of government" by postponing the 1778 election to the church council because of the ongoing war.[135] They cited the fact that Mühlenberg, on being "told on all sides that the English . . . officers have singled me out for revenge," had retired to Providence in 1776 but remained rector, as another breach of the charter.[136] People's annoyance with Mühlenberg's continued absence culminated in a "revolution," which ended with Kunze's installation as rector in 1779.[137] Under the 1780 act of incorporation, Constitutionalist Friedrich Kuhl (1728–1813) became "president" of the combined congregation of St. Michael's and Zion. Besides borrowing this title from the 1776 Pennsylvania constitution, the new charter adopted its egalitarian spirit by abolishing the clerics' privilege of being ex officio head of the parish.[138]

Going on Public Stage: Minister-Professors and Pastor-Politicians

Kunze's advancement to rector marked the ascent of a new "generation of evangelical minister-professors" who "adroitly combined themes of republican politics, common-sense moral reasoning, and scientific Baconianism to provide 'the first new nation' with a sophisticated Christian rationale for social order, political stability, and intellectual self-confidence."[139] Parish pastors Kunze, Helmuth, Schmidt, and Gotthilf Mühlenberg also pursued serious studies and joined learned associations. Helmuth was active in Philadelphia's Uranian Academy, which named him trustee in 1787. He and Kunze, who later wrote tracts on celestial phenomena, shared an interest in the universe with Schmidt, a distinguished mathematician who furnished German almanacs with astronomical calculations. In 1784 Kunze and Helmuth, out of "love of science," supported the construction of "a large and elegant Air Balloon."[140] His research of botany and mineralogy earned Mühlenberg membership in scientific societies. In the 1780s the American Philosophical Society received the three men into its ranks.[141] Whereas the British colonies had been "profoundly *private* societies" in which "the right of an individual in ordinary times *not* to venture beyond his private space into the public realm was yet another powerful symbol of the liberty . . . of free men," the American republic, those "minister-professors" sensed, was a body politic in which the enjoyment of freedom and property obliged them to accept responsibility for the general weal by promoting higher education and institutional charity for the marginalized.[142]

The war with Britain was far from over when Kunze, who had long since endeavored to recapture Halle's spirit of erudition by establishing a Lutheran seminary, and Helmuth began to revive the idea of a replication of the Francke Foundations within the newly emerging University of Pennsylvania.[143] At the center of their ambitious plan was education of young German males who, like Helmuth himself, came from poor families. As the two ecclesiastics envisioned, gifted German boys who had finished elementary parish school would be trained in religion and the arts and sciences at a *Gymnasium*-style Latin school or academy to become pastors or teachers. After graduation, they would go to the university. Kunze's appointment as professor in a classics department in 1780 cleared the way for the project. The subjects Kunze and Helmuth taught reflected August Hermann Francke's (1663–1727) pedagogical concept of integrating theoretical studies and practical skills. Courses in German grammar, Latin, the Greek Testament, history, geography, and vocal music focused on edification, whereas classes in English reading, writing, bookkeeping, and mathematics prepared the students for managing parishes and schools.[144] In late 1781, Helmuth could report to Halle that "our schools, especially the German-Latin School[,] bloom."[145] On Kunze's call to the New York Lutherans in 1784, he took over the professorship.

As Anthony G. Roeber has noted, "Helmuth never regarded this initiative for educating a talented meritocracy to be divorced from his broader social vision."[146] Kunze shared this vision. "In a country that is lacking academic professions and in which merely trade and commerce are profitable businesses, we must start to make poor people scholars," Kunze urged the German Society of Pennsylvania to sponsor college education.[147] Because the society's charter limited relief to *immigrant* suffering, Helmuth founded the "Society for the Relief of the Needy Poor" in 1785 to support *indigenous* German-Americans. Though pastoral students, clerics, teachers, and *their* widows were the only ones eligible for aid from the organization, the inclusion of females was a novelty that deviated from Philadelphia poor relief patterns, which excluded traditional alms recipients—such as widows, single mothers, and single women—by "a new emphasis on training and encouragement of able-bodied males."[148] But this shift in the objective of charity, which had occurred in the 1760s, did not square with Helmuth's "Halle-inspired conviction that relief of physical needs and education in a proper religious context for the working poor had to proceed hand in hand." In pursuit of his goal to make evangelical charity a public concern, Helmuth, who "was no stranger to making and investing money and no more embarrassed by riches than were his mentors in Halle," became a busy fundraiser and venturous investor.[149]

In all their charitable efforts Helmuth and Kunze never lost sight of their aim to prepare German-Americans for the Lutheran ministry. Yet the sluggish response of Pennsylvania's rural Germans required a new approach to educating sons of poor families who could not afford tuition. Thus Helmuth, who had earlier trained Jakob Göring, intensified the private tutoring of young hopefuls. In the 1780s and 1790s, he and Schmidt, who succeeded Kunze in Philadelphia in 1786, had some twenty students of Lutheran theology and related subjects under their instruction. Critics could interpret the introduction of this tutorial system as tacit admission of failure of Helmuth's high-flown academic plans. Rather than raise educational standards, this system was likely to lower them as fewer and fewer university-trained teachers were available.[150] What induced Helmuth, Kunze, and Schmidt to push the training of German-American clergy was not just the shortage of divines but also the weakness of people's attachments to Lutheran confessional symbols caused by the mounting influence of liberal Deism and Calvinist-tinged evangelicalism. "You may have gathered from the communication from Halle how busy the pigs are churning up the garden in Germany," Helmuth, in 1784, put the ministerium on alert against heresy flourishing in Europe. "The Satanist . . . is nurtured and revered" and "unfortunately the Antichrist rises among us, too . . . Where shall we get preachers?" he asked in a call to his colleagues to encourage parents to have their boys trained for the ministry. "From Germany? Perhaps a secret Arian, Socinian, or Deist, for out there it is teeming with all this vermin. No, God forbid! None from Germany."[151] Incidentally, that same year Mühlenberg charged Pastor Johann Wilhelm Kurz (1732–99) with making a tenet of heathen Parseeism an article of his Lutheran faith.[152]

Helmuth's rejection of clerics from Germany expressed utter mistrust of Halle University and the Francke Foundations, where anticonfessional principles and enlightenment ideas had made headway. Revealingly, the ministerial ordinance of 1781 ruled that "those who are sent by . . . the Orphans' Home at Halle, or by any Evangelical Consistory . . . in Europe" were "to be deemed unworthy of reception only if objections made to their reception be declared weighty and well-founded by a majority of the votes."[153] The fact that the statute provided for the *possibility* of a Hallensian being found "unworthy" of admission testifies to strong reservations toward the Foundations—even if the 1784 convention applied to Halle for "at least two new" pastors—so that in 1786 Johann Friedrich Weinland (1744–1807) arrived as the last missionary.[154] How deeply differing views of religion now separated the Hallensians from their parent institution is apparent from a letter Kunze wrote in 1804. Denial of the divinity of Christ was precisely what "men are at present doing boldly in Germany through pulpit, life, and pen—and who eat the bread of the Church," he did not except Halle from his verdict. "God preserve us, my dear brethren, in this sad time, from apostles coming from there!"[155] While Kunze and other critics stayed in contact with Halle long after the death of Mühlenberg in 1787, their bonds were no more of that intimate nature that had characterized the early pioneers' filial relationship to the "Fathers" in Europe.

In their endeavor to bring up a vanguard of educated American-born clergy, Helmuth and Schmidt soon faced sobering reality. German youth "now have so much English pride, that none wishes to be a German preacher," they stated in 1789; "the number of students has shrunk from 600 to 300, because they cannot learn in the German school what they need. They go to the English schools, forget their German, and become strangers to the church."[156] Alienated from their ancestors' ethnoreligious tradition, the new generation of German-Americans would raise their children "after the English fashion and in the English language," Helmuth believed.[157] To him, Schmidt, and Göring, maintaining the supremacy of German in Lutheran parishes was vital to preserving the confessional identity of the laity whose intercourse with English-speakers and reading of English literature exposed them to non-Lutheran concepts, such as Deism's rationalist repudiation of the Triune God and of Jesus Christ as the Savior, the Quaker doctrine of the "Inner Light," the Baptists' rejection of child baptism, or the Methodists' evangelical enthusiasm.[158] Against this background, the preachers' insistence on the German language was a reaction to the religious and socioeconomic transformation they witnessed in the Pennsylvania republic.[159]

In 1789 Helmuth founded a literary society dedicated to the memory of Johann Lorenz von Mosheim (1694–1755), the preeminent Protestant church historian of eighteenth-century Germany. He intended this Philadelphia society "to be the capstone of his efforts to provide a systematic educational program from elementary school to adulthood in which German culture and language could be directed under the auspices of Halle-inspired Lutheran teachers and pastors."[160] An aura of secretiveness surrounded this adult circle, whose foundation Helmuth withheld from his patrons and whose internal discussions—in German only—were not revealed to outsiders. By spurring religious discourse and preparing appropriate literature for German-speaking children, the von Mosheim Society entered into rivalry with the German Society of Pennsylvania of 1764 and with Anglicizing forces rallying round Friedrich Mühlenberg, who rejected German schools and expected German to yield to English soon.[161] For Helmuth, who predicted that Philadelphia "within a few years will look more like a German town than an English one," pastor-turned politicians like Friedrich Mühlenberg and his Anglican brother Peter personified the assimilated German-American preacher who deserted Lutheran tradition.[162] "I am afraid we already have too many politicians in the" ministerium "and too few true divines," and he feared the board to be drawn into the battle between Christian educators and Deist politicians over the nature of American republicanism and its relationship to the French Revolution.[163]

But Helmuth was not without political ambition himself. Whereas he barred the pro-Antifederalist German Republican Club from using the Lutheran schoolhouse in Philadelphia and forbade his parishioners to pray for Thomas Jefferson in the 1800 presidential election, he approved of a memorial service for Benjamin Franklin in Zion Church in 1790, issued an appeal to the German participants of Fries's Rebellion in 1799, condemning their conspiracy against the Federalist government (which uprising met with sympathy from the Republican Club and the German Society), and published *Lamentations over the Death of General Washington* in 1800.[164] His partisanship made Helmuth an easy target in the Federalist-Antifederalist conflict and pitted him and Schmidt, as well as the less affluent immigrants in the von Mosheim Society, against acculturated, well-to-do members of the Republican Club, several of whom served on the St. Michael's and Zion vestry. Germans led by Peter Mühlenberg not only challenged the pastors on theological grounds but "assaulted the charity and education mission Helmuth and his supporters had labored to bring to life. The traditionalists were, rightly, identified as loyal Federalists and bitter opponents of the French Revolution and the Jeffersonians who sympathized with it."[165]

Albeit nothing indicates that Helmuth's enormous investments in real estate and shipping companies were the result of dubious deals to finance his philanthropic projects, the riches he amassed invited Republicans to defame him as an "aristocrat." Besides, he operated as a private banker for his son Henry, who aspired to a career in the Federalist party. Becoming entangled in pastoral duties, public charity, political interests, and private obligations, Helmuth overreached himself. In 1804 his efforts to tie classical education and Pietist Lutheran doctrine to the German language suffered another setback, when German-Americans led by Peter Mühlenberg seceded from the Philadelphia congregation and established the bilingual St. John's Lutheran Church in 1806. The ensuing exodus of American-born Lutherans to English-speaking denominations deprived the "*German* Evangelical Lutheran Congregations in Pennsylvania and the Adjacent States" of politically important, socially influential, and economically successful individuals.[166]

Once the Lutheran mainstream in the Chesapeake colonies, Halle Pietism declined to a Lutheran sect, as the mass loss of coreligionists was not compensated for by converts from other ethnoreligious groups. Whereas the Moravians operated on a broad ethnic basis encompassing European settlers, African slaves, and native Americans, the Francke mission's intraconfessional concept proved a big hindrance. When Kunze proposed to turn evangelizing efforts toward the Indians in 1789, the time for such campaigns was long over.[167] While the language question divided German- and American-born Hallensians, the Francke Foundations moved to the verge of declension in the wake of the French Revolution. In 1806 they were closed in the dissolution of the Holy Roman Empire. Six years later, Helmuth found himself the last surviving Halle missionary: a lonely visionary of Lutheran philanthropy, whose great schemes had been thwarted by his inability to create a timely synthesis of Old World traditions and New World innovations.

Following Discordant Scores: Halle Conservatism versus Pennsylvania Libertarianism

The Halle clergy's failure to maintain the spiritual leadership of the German Lutherans in the infant Pennsylvania republic was a consequence of their professional ethos. Deeply rooted in Lutheran tradition, they advocated *order, ordination,* and *subordination* as preconditions for moral betterment effected by the pure propagation of the Gospel and the true recognition of the will of God. Implementing *order* through tight regulations of parish life, the divines clung to a Pietist confessionalism that precluded cooperation with colleagues who embraced a different brand of Lutheranism. This confessionalism made them opponents to religious pluralism, which they supposed to be the cause of indifferentism spreading in America. The Hallensians' attempts to tie their parishes to themselves, to their parent institution, and to their superiors conflicted with Pennsylvania libertarianism and voluntaryism. Their insistence on *ordination* as a prerequisite for a legitimate ministry revealed them as champions of a medieval concept of society that elevated clerics to a distinct estate with legal privileges, such as payment from state taxes or enforcement of pastoral acts in court. This concept collided with provincial law, which denied ecclesiastics a special status and reduced them to employees hired by their congregations. As a result of the separation of state and church and of the lack of legal protection of the ministry, lay preachers with little or no academic education performed the same functions in the colony that university-trained theologians discharged in Germany. With their demand for *subordination* the evangelists recurred to yet another European pattern, ascribing a dual role to parsons as heads of their parishes and deputies of their prince-bishops who exercised coercive power over their flocks. This authoritarianism, however, ran counter to the Pennsylvania spirit of individualism and egalitarianism, which imbued many German Lutherans, like most colonials, with reluctance to take orders from officials whose competence they suspected to extend beyond their control.

The strategic problem the Francke missionaries confronted was the question of which model the Lutheran Church in Pennsylvania was to adopt: the German or the American one. Initially, they strove to cast it in the German mold only to find out that such a replication of the established churches in

Europe was incompatible with circumstances in the colony. After their patrons in Halle and London refused the leadership of *ecclesia plantanda,* they abandoned the Old World design for an all-American solution. Incorporation of parishes, the adaptation of church ordinances and charters to republican ideas of democratic self-rule, the development of the ministerium into the governing body of the Lutheran community, and involvement in public affairs such as charity, schooling, or academia testified to the pastors' resolve to organize their church fully in line with Pennsylvania law. But while doing so, they neglected the fact that the Americanization of the statutory and institutional infrastructure of the Lutheran Church entailed an Americanization of its doctrinal superstructure, putting them into the quandary of how to make compromises without compromising their basic convictions. Trying to stem the tide of deism, sectarianism, and enthusiasm, after the Revolution they came to the bitter realization that Halle, too, had meantime succumbed to the overwhelming impact of rationalism and the Enlightenment on intellectual life. Left to their own devices in a battle on two fronts, the evangelists lost ground to a new guard of American-born clergy when declaring German Lutherans' ethnic awareness to be a touchstone of their faithfulness to authentic Lutheranism. Countless Americans of German descent reacted to this linkage of nationality and confessionalism by leaving the church of their ancestors, as it forced them to split their identities along ethnoreligious and sociopolitical lines and seemed intent on obstructing their full integration into their English-dominated homeland.

Part III / Imperial Visions and Transatlantic Revisions

CHAPTER TEN

Chartered Enterprises and the Evolution of the British Atlantic World

Elizabeth Mancke

In the late sixteenth and seventeenth centuries, royally chartered enterprises established the basis of the British Atlantic world from Davis Strait in the Arctic to the tropical climes of the Caribbean and West Africa. The history of these chartered enterprises and the history of the post-1763 colonial resistance to new imperial policies have long provided the narrative bookends for the early modern British Empire. In 1774 Thomas Jefferson justified "the united complaints of his Majesty's subjects in America," through a reference to the founding of the colonies: "America was conquered, and her settlements made, and firmly established, at the expence of individuals, and not of the British public." British Americans insisted that the parliamentary legislation following the Seven Years' War was unprecedented, and that between the founding of colonies under royal charters in the seventeenth century and their revolt in the late eighteenth century was a long period of limited metropolitan, and particularly parliamentary, involvement in the British American colonies.[1]

Both colonial American historians and British imperial historians have generally accepted, whether explicitly or implicitly, this juxtaposing of a founding narrative of chartered enterprises to a concluding narrative of colonial

rebellion. In the founding narrative, the Crown granted to companies and proprietors a wide range of rights and privileges. Companies could tax members
for company expenses and govern their officials and employees residing outside the realm. Both companies and proprietors could defend themselves from
attack and implicitly could negotiate with foreign powers, such as princes in
Asia or Indian leaders in North America. Charters for enterprises in the Americas included the right to occupy, if not claim, land. Some charters, particularly
to proprietors, included the right to establish governments. Many of these
rights and privileges became customary practices and were integral to
colonists' understandings of their constitutions, which, in the concluding narrative, were violated by the Ministry and Parliament and then compounded by
the king who did the stop the usurpations.[2]

Historians have treated the events between the 1763 Treaty of Paris and the
British recognition of American independence in the 1783 Peace of Paris as creating a precipitous fault in the development of the British Empire, a gulf
between the histories of the so-called First and Second Empires that gives them
distinct, if not unbridgeable, interpretive landscapes.[3] This essay reassesses the
1763–83 divide by taking a fresh look at chartered enterprises, not as a narrative
of the founding of the British Atlantic world but as a narrative of its growth, as
a study of the long political processes of imperial evolution. This approach has
two objectives. One, the demise of chartered enterprises as vehicles of colonial
and commercial expansion happened gradually and often mirrored the rise in
the influence of the metropolitan government. An analysis of their gradual
demise allows us to qualify 1763 as the critical date for the growth of metropolitan influence. Two, chartered enterprises were not exclusive to the thirteen
colonies that rebelled but operated throughout the British Empire. After 1783,
two of them, the East India Company (EIC) and the Hudson's Bay Company
(HBC), administered most of the empire's territory. Thus a broad examination
of chartered enterprises offers a bridge between the commercial and colonial
empires and between the early modern and modern empires.

The Logic of Chartered Enterprises

In the late sixteenth and seventeenth centuries, chartered enterprises were
attractive for both the Crown and investors. Poor by Spanish and French standards, dependent on Parliament to vote new taxes, and preoccupied with volatile
European politics, Elizabeth I and then the Stuart kings willingly chartered

groups of adventurers who wanted to undertake the expense and the possible rewards of enterprise in the extra-European world.[4] Chartered ventures offered English monarchs wide latitude for challenging the Iberians' overseas claims. Private adventurers organized and funded a diverse range of colonial and commercial enterprises throughout the Atlantic basin, more than the Crown alone could have done. The Crown could diplomatically defend ventures on the margins of Iberian control, such as Newfoundland, Virginia, New England, or the Leeward Islands and Barbados. Ventures that threatened to destabilize foreign relations, such as the Amazon Company that operated too close to Iberian interests, could have their charters revoked and the actions of company leaders discredited, a kind of diplomatic deniability that would have been difficult had ventures been funded directly by the Crown. Indeed, many early seventeenth-century charters included a clause reassuring "all Christian kings, princes and states" that if anyone shall "do any act of unjust and lawful hostility," that appropriate action would be taken, including if necessary putting the grantee "out of our allegiance and protection."[5]

While chartered enterprises let the Crown avoid many of the financial and foreign policy risks of overseas expansion, it could not ignore the long-term consequences of the ventures undertaken. Outright failures, such as voyages to find the Northwest Passage, had little immediate impact, but successes, whether marginal or enviable, created conditions that governing bodies in England could not ignore. In responding to the changes wrought by chartered enterprises, the Crown, Privy Council, and Parliament began to articulate their roles in the emerging empire. The metropolitan government's evolving response to the activities of chartered concerns—what it sanctioned, what it proscribed, which enterprises it took over, and which it let die—depended on the government's prerogatives and responsibilities, on its role in affairs beyond the realm, on whom it believed within its sphere of protection, if not sovereignty, and whom outside.

The configuration of those prerogatives and responsibilities and their distribution among the Crown, Privy Council, and Parliament shifted markedly in the early modern era. In the sixteenth and seventeenth centuries, the chartering of companies and proprietorships was the prerogative of the person, as much as the office, of the monarch.[6] By the end of the seventeenth century, grants for colonial ventures had largely ceased. The chartering of companies for commerce continued through the creation of the South Sea Company in 1711, but after the South Sea Bubble, parliamentary legislation in 1720 severely restricted the chartering of further commercial corporations, legislation that was extended to the colonies in 1741. By the early eighteenth century, the chartering and re-chartering of corporations, such as the United East India Company in 1709, had become Parliament's prerogative with royal approval. Parliament, in conjunction with the Privy Council, had also assumed considerable powers of oversight and regulation of overseas commerce, though less of colonization.[7]

All chartered enterprises, by the very nature of their creation, were incomplete sociopolitical entities and parts of a larger system. The uncertainties and risks of expansion into the extra-European world, the conditions that made chartered ventures attractive, also made their forms and functions highly plastic and hence their relationships to the larger system that engendered them uncertain and contested. Three conditions stemming from chartered enterprises triggered the intervention of the metropolitan government: the redefinition of Crown lands overseas; the Crown's prerogative over the civil governance of subjects; and relations with foreigners, and later non-British members of the Empire. These issues were neither exclusive to chartered enterprises nor fleeting. Rather they reflected the resumption of prerogative powers that had been delegated to chartered enterprises, the direct extension of them overseas, and the emergence of an imperial state structure that was constitutionally distinct from both the state within Britain and the colonial constitutions that had emerged over the seventeenth and eighteenth centuries.

Crown Land in the Extra-European World

A primary objective of the early English chartered enterprises (ca. 1560–1650) was to challenge the Iberians' hegemonic claims to the extra-European world with the establishment of English settlements overseas. In the sixteenth century, the English and French had insisted that Spain and Portugal's overseas claims be attended with the settlement of natural-born subjects. A monarch could not simply claim vast tracts of land by virtue of a papal bull, treaty, or royal fiat.[8] Petitioners for the Newfoundland Company recognized that principle when they noted that their venture to plant settlements on the island would create an English claim before another "forraine Prince or State" could do so. English knowledge of Newfoundland based on reports by fishermen allowed James I to assert in the 1610 Newfoundland Company charter that he could grant the land "without doing wrong to any other prince or state," because it was "so vacant" that "they cannot justly pretend any sovereignty or right thereto." Knowledge of European activities in other parts of the Americas was sketchier, which charters reflected. The 1606 Virginia Company charter stipulated that the grantees could establish settlements on lands "which are not now actually possessed by any Christian prince or people."[9]

Despite the importance of claiming land in the Americas, the English charters from the seventeenth century generally included only three references to land. First, charters stated the Crown's right to grant the land. If there was no known European claimant, charters generally stipulated land "not now actually possessed by any Christian prince or people," language used as late as the 1670 charter to the Hudson's Bay Company. If appropriate, charters referenced earlier grants. The Massachusetts Bay Company charter (1629) noted that the petitioners had received a grant of land from the Council of New England. The Maryland charter to Lord Baltimore noted that the granted land lay below 40° north latitude, the southern boundary of the Council of New England and within Virginia, the ungranted portions of which reverted to the Crown in 1624 when the King's Bench revoked the Virginia Company charter.[10]

Second, charters identified, in broad and frequently untenable terms, the area in which grantees had the right to plant colonies and engage in commerce. With the 1606 Virginia Company charter and the 1610 Newfoundland Company charter, James I divided eastern North America from 34° to 52° north latitude into three zones in which three groups of joint-stock shareholders had the English rights to attempt settlements. The London branch of the Virginia Company could settle between 34° and 41° north latitude, while the Plymouth branch (later reorganized as the Council of New England) could settle between 37° and 45°. The Newfoundland Company could establish settlements between 46° and 52° north latitude.[11] The reliance on lines of latitude reflected both a lack of knowledge of American geography and a disregard of indigenous organizations of the landscape. The 1624 grant of Nova Scotia was the first to use the physical landscape alone to define the limits of the grant, as did the Hudson's Bay Company charter in 1670.[12] Other charters after Virginia and Newfoundland's used combinations of lines of latitude and major features of the physical landscape to bound land. The frequent use of the "Western Sea" as the western boundary of many colonies—including Massachusetts, Connecticut, New York, Virginia, North Carolina, South Carolina, and Georgia—subsequently created disputes between colonies and the metropolitan government and later among states in the new United States.[13]

Third, charters stated broadly the feudal terms under which land was held, even though in practice those terms had little impact. Land in Virginia, New-foundland, Massachusetts, Connecticut, Rhode Island, and Rupert's Land was granted "as of our manor of East-Greenwich, in the county of Kent, in free and common soccage only, and not in capite." Cecilius Calvert, Lord Baltimore could "exercise, use and enjoy" his grant of Maryland "as amply as any bishop of Durham, within the bishoprick or county palatine of Durham." William Penn held Pennsylvania "as of our Castle of Windsor, in our county of Berks, in free and common soccage, by fealty only, or for services, and not *in capite,* or by Knight's service."[14] Besides stating the right of the Crown to grant the land, the extent of the grant, and a brief mention of the feudal terms of the grant, charters seldom included other references to terms of land ownership, and thus left many issues ambiguous and contentious. The problem originated in both a predictable English ignorance of what to expect when establishing overseas settlements in unknown lands and in a shifting political world within England.

One recurring ambiguity in landholding that encapsulated center and periphery relations was the definition of Crown lands. The problems arising from this definitional ambiguity ranged from questions of sovereignty, to the granting of land, to claims to natural resources on the land, such as timber and coal. By the time of the granting of the Restoration charters of the Royal African Company (1663) and the Hudson's Bay Company (1670), clauses were included "saving always the faith Allegiance and Sovereigne Dominion" over the land to the king. That principle was not assumed to be universal. In 1757, the attorney-general and solicitor-general in Britain rendered a legal opinion on whether the Crown had sovereignty over EIC territories in Asia. They deter-mined it had sovereignty over the land, but ownership of it depended on the means of acquisition.[15] While legal opinion generally recognized Crown sovereignty over extra-European territory held by its subjects, specific details concerning ownership and jurisdictional administration of Crown lands were not so easily resolved.

Crown claims to ownership of extra-European lands, rather than just a right to grant them and have sovereignty over subjects in them, first emerged with the revocation of the Virginia Company charter in 1624. The Privy Council promised that the existing property rights of colonists would be honored, while the undivided land reverted to Crown ownership.[16] The royal jurisdic-tion that could grant land in Virginia, however, remained undetermined. The colony's new royal government continued to grant land using the system instituted under company rule. The Stuart kings, meanwhile, asserted their prerogative to treat Crown lands in Virginia, and elsewhere in the Americas, as private preserves to grant to clients as they wished and increasingly under proprietary, rather than company, charters.

In 1632, George Calvert, Lord Baltimore petitioned Charles I for a proprietary grant of land in Virginia where he could establish a colony for Catholics. Before the patent for Maryland received the great seal, three drafts were abandoned after people with persisting interests in the defunct Virginia Company protested the granting of a proprietary colony to Baltimore using Virginia lands. These protests indicate the sensibility, however self-serving, that the Crown should only grant land in the colony through the royal colonial government.[17]

After 1649, the exiled Charles II used lands in North America to support men who remained loyal to him. He granted the Northern Neck of Virginia between the Rappahannock and Potomac rivers to royalist supporters. The government of Virginia had already patented some of that land to colonists, and it continued to patent land in the area through the 1650s. After the Restoration, the grantees with their patents directly from the king pressed their claims in Virginia, joined in 1673 by Lord Arlington and Thomas Culpepper, to whom Charles II had granted rights in the southern portion of Virginia, even though some of those lands had been patented to colonists in freehold tenure. The government of Virginia sent agents to England to negotiate a resolution to the jurisdictional confusion and resulting conflicts over land. They proposed a new charter for the colony that would include a clause in which the king would give up his personal right to grant land in the colony. That draft charter never received the great seal, and in 1676, in the wake of Bacon's Rebellion, Charles II issued a new "charter" for Virginia that articulated the Crown's prerogative more than colonists' rights and privileges.[18]

The success of colonial settlements increased the tendency of the Stuart kings to distribute North American land as they wished, particularly after the Restoration, and often against the advice of royal ministers who wished to see greater conformity among the colonies and to eliminate corporate and proprietary charters and the jurisdictional conflicts that were associated with them. During his reign, Charles II granted corporate company charters for the Royal African Company (1663) and the Hudson's Bay Company (1670), corporate colonial charters to Connecticut (1662) and Rhode Island (1663), and proprietary charters for Carolina (1663), New York (1664), the Bahamas (1670), and

Pennsylvania (1681).[19] One of the differences between the company and proprietary charters was the ownership of ungranted land, which under proprietary charters was inheritable and transferable because it had been granted to
named individuals. Ownership of the ungranted land that companies controlled was far murkier and more contested, whether in Virginia, Newfoundland, Massachusetts, Rupert's Land, or Bengal, because ownership was less
easily attached to individuals. In some of those places, the emergence of
ungranted lands as Crown lands—first in the person of the monarch and then
in the state—can be identified.

One of the Privy Council's many concerns with the Massachusetts Bay
Company's charter was the legality of common landholding in the colony, and
in New England more generally. Colonial governments in New England had
customarily granted land to groups of settlers who divided it among themselves. These groups became the basis of towns and congregations and the
undivided land was held in the name of the town. The "ownership" of common
land by towns—in conjunction with the hiring of ministers, the building of
meeting houses, and the funding of schools—invested them with corporate
functions. Under English law, though, they could not be corporations because
one corporation, in this case the Massachusetts Bay Company, could not create another corporation (e.g., a town). Only the Crown, Parliament, or royal
governments in some colonies could create corporations. Thus towns could
not legally own or control land, because towns did not exist as legal entities.[20]

After the revocation of the Massachusetts charter in 1684 and the creation
of the Dominion of New England, Governor Edmund Andros refused to
acknowledge the customary corporate practices of towns, and in some
instances he declared town commons to be wild and vacant lands, therefore
Crown lands, and granted them to others in his capacity as royal governor. In
anticipation of this problem, the colonies of Plymouth and Connecticut in 1682
and 1685, respectively, gave patents for the common lands to named groups of
proprietors. In 1698, Massachusetts did the same, but only after the upheavals
of the Andros regime.[21]

The 1691 charter of Massachusetts, which made it a royal colony with a royally appointed governor, instituted a major change in the definition of Crown
lands in North America. It reserved all trees twenty-four inches in diameter or
larger for masts for the royal navy. In 1705 Parliament passed "An Act for the
Encouraging of Importation of Naval Stores" that is most commonly seen as an
addition to the Navigation Acts. But it is also important for the way it redefined

property rights by giving the Crown preeminent claims to "Pitch, Pine, or Tar Trees" twelve inches or less in diameter from New Jersey through Maine. Further legislation in 1711 expanded the 1705 act to include all trees over twenty-four inches in diameter in British North America; when the French ceded Nova Scotia to the British in 1713, the terms of the Massachusetts charter and the 1705 and 1711 acts were interpreted to extend to this newest colony.[22] Together the charter and the legislation mark a shift from American lands and their resources being treated by British monarchs as a vast reserve of patronage to be distributed to clients to being defined in terms of state needs, in this case naval needs. For nearly a century, New England timbermen and governments challenged this redefinition of Crown lands and their resources: timbermen violated the law; colonial governments exploited technicalities in the legislation; Parliament responded with legislation to close the loopholes; governors protested a lack of money to survey land for naval stores; and the Board of Trade used the protection of naval stores to block royal approval of land grants in eastern Maine.[23]

In the mid eighteenth century, colonial governments and the metropolitan government became entangled in jurisdictional controversies over the administrative control of the trans-Appalachian West. Here the issue concerned colonies' western boundaries, which remained undefined after the revocation of charters. The growing British and French interest in the Ohio Country in the 1740s prompted colonial assemblies to resuscitate claims to the trans-Appalachian West, most notably Virginia's, based on the long-defunct Virginia Company charter. If it was British Crown land, there was still the question of which jurisdiction of the Crown had administrative control of it. For most colonists, it was one or more of the now royal colonies, based on the transfer of ungranted lands to the Crown and the colonial governments' administration of those lands, though some were not adverse to petitioning the Crown for a grant if it suited their purposes, as shareholders in the Ohio Company did in the 1740s and 1750s.[24]

After the Seven Years' War and France's cession of the trans-Appalachian West, tensions over the jurisdictional control of western lands intensified. Pontiac's uprising, beginning in 1763, precipitated the Royal Proclamation of 1763 that gave native peoples the first right of occupation west of the crest of the Appalachian Mountains. Natives could not extinguish their claims except through an agent of the Crown, and in 1754 the Board of Trade appointed two Indian superintendents, one each for the north and the south. They were to report directly to the Board of Trade rather than to any particular colonial government, and had the power to negotiate with native peoples in the west. By making the crest of the Appalachian Mountains the western limit of white settlement, the Proclamation effectively created western boundaries for many colonies, which colonists protested and violated. The western boundary of settlement was subsequently adjusted with the Treaty of Fort Stanwix in 1768, which some native nations, particularly the Shawnees, protested. The 1774 extension of Quebec's boundaries to include the Ohio Country, at the expense of the claims of Virginia, Massachusetts, Connecticut, and New York, further exacerbated tensions over the conflicting interpretations of jurisdictional authority over Crown lands in North America and the residual rights from the seventeenth-century charters.[25]

Both colonists and metropolitan officials would probably have agreed that the monarch no longer had personal discretion over Crown lands, and hence Crown lands were "state" lands. For most British North American colonists, the appropriate jurisdiction to administer those "state" lands was a colonial government. Along the seaboard, that had generally been the practice, and it can be argued that a number of colonial "quasi-states" had emerged over the seventeenth and eighteenth centuries, each of which claimed the right to grant "Crown" lands within their boundaries, however imprecise those boundaries might be. At the same time, the Crown had increasingly expanded the functional meaning of its prerogative over those lands, including a right to establish institutions that superseded colonial governments, particularly on matters that included more than one colony, such as naval stores, western lands, and Indian policy. Those new institutions helped to give form to an "imperial state," but its authority and jurisdiction remained contested in part because of lingering ambiguities from the seventeenth-century charters.

The East India Company's transformation from a commercial concern to a territorial power in the 1760s precipitated a similar constitutional dilemma over who had property rights to the new territorial acquisitions in Asia: the EIC or the Crown. The EIC charter of 1698, the basis of the 1709 charter, reserved to the Crown in perpetuity the "sovereign right, power and dominion" over EIC "forts, places, and plantations." The 1757 legal opinion that had confirmed Crown sovereignty—i.e., ultimate jurisdiction—had not clarified ultimate ownership. Lands acquired through EIC arrangements with Asians, such as Madras and Calcutta, were company possessions; acquisitions by conquest were the Crown's. Had territorial ownership alone been the question, the resolution might have been straightforward, but it arose during the dispute over the Crown's right—and by extension the British Treasury's right—to any of the *diwana*, or Bengali taxes, derived from the land, estimated in 1765 to be £1,600,000 annually. Legal opinion divided on whether the right to the territorial revenues derived from a grant from the Mughal emperor, and was therefore EIC property, or had been a spoil of war, and was therefore Crown property. Company supporters noted that the EIC "acknowledged the Emperor as *de jure* sovereign in Bengal." Could the British Crown be sovereign, as well? Supporters of the Crown's claim pointed to the royal navy's critical role in preserving the Company's interest, thereby emphasizing conquest. In 1773, a parliamentary resolution declared the EIC-conquered territories to be Crown land, though not until 1813 was it confirmed with legislation.[26]

In the case of the Hudson's Bay Company, the metropolitan government distinguished between company-owned and company-administered land. Rupert's Land, the territory drained by rivers flowing into Hudson Bay, was company-owned land by virtue of the 1670 charter from Charles II. The HBC also administered the arctic drainage basins and the Oregon Country: the former were Crown lands; the latter were jointly occupied by the British and Americans until 1846. Only when British settlers became a significant concern in these lands did Britain create colonies. Vancouver Island became a colony in 1849, with a governor appointed by the Colonial Office but otherwise under HBC administration for ten years. The 1858 Fraser River gold rush prompted the establishment of a second colony of British Columbia in that year. In 1866 parliamentary legislation merged the two colonies and in 1871 British Columbia joined the Dominion of Canada as a province. In Rupert's Land was the Red River colony at the intersection of the Red and Assiniboine rivers. Originally founded in the 1810s, its intended settlers were Scots. They, however, choose other British North American locations, and the Red River settlement became dominated by HBC retirees, their families, and independent Métis and was governed by the HBC. After the official creation of the Dominion of Canada in 1867, negotiations were begun among the HBC, Canada, and the British government to transfer Rupert's Land to the new dominion. Significantly, the British government had the Hudson's Bay Company transfer title to Rupert's Land back to the Crown, which then transferred it to the Canadians for £300,000, with the proceeds going to the HBC. Rupert's Land and the arctic drainage basins were organized as the Northwest Territories and became Crown land to be administered by the Dominion of

Canada. After a rebellion by the Métis, the Red River colony became the province of Manitoba in 1870. Jurisdictional problems soon surfaced as native peoples pressed their land claims and then new provinces asserted a right to administer Crown land within their boundaries, a right which the older provinces had.[27]

By the end of the seventeenth century, Crown land in the British Empire had effectively become "state" land, and British monarchs no longer asserted a right to treat them as royal preserves that they could distribute independently. That development reflects, in part, a shift in the function of the monarch in the empire. The Privy Council, usually working through the Board of Trade, attempted to retain jurisdiction over some overseas Crown lands, rather than letting colonial governments exercise jurisdiction. That ministerial claim of jurisdiction, often backed with parliamentary legislation, such as the 1705 and 1711 Naval Stores Acts, indicates the emergence of an imperial state bureaucracy with powers crafted for proactive regulation, rather than just oversight, of British affairs in the extra-European world, and which were distinct from powers operational within Britain itself. The jurisdictional controversies were never conclusively resolved and refractions of them continue down to the present in countries that were at one time British territories.

The Provision of Civil Governance

The Crown's first direct involvement in extra-European governance was in the Chesapeake, where, after near failure and great loss of life, the Virginia Company succeeded in establishing an English settlement and began tobacco cultivation. The Crown first intervened during the 1619 leadership struggles that resulted in Sir Edwin Sandys' faction unseating Thomas Smith as treasurer of the Virginia Company. Underlying the struggle were deepening financial and management crises, and which the 1622 Powhatan attack on the English settlements and the killing of 317 colonists only compounded. A coalition of shareholders, led by Robert Warwick and Thomas Smith, asked James I for an inquiry, which subsequently documented serious mismanagement and abuse of the king's subjects and recommended a new charter that would make the colony's government royally appointed and the company's government in London subject to royal approval. When shareholders refused to relinquish the old charter, the King's Bench issued a quo warranto to begin proceedings to determine whether managerial shortcomings constituted a violation of the charter.

The evidence graphically detailed inadequate supplies, rampant scurvy, and widespread death; on May 24, 1624 the court revoked the charter.[28]

After the revocation, James I considered issuing a new company charter. With the king's death the next year, Charles I ordered that the government of Virginia remain perpetually under royal control and that it was "not to be comyted to anie Companie or Corporation, to whom it maie be proper to trust Matters of Trade and Commerce." Charles I's order did not constitute a policy of royal governance of colonies. In the 1620s the Privy Council reviewed the Bermuda Company, formerly part of the Virginia Company, but better conditions in Bermuda effectively protected the rights of shareholders, and company government continued there until the revocation of the charter in 1684.[29]

The Crown and its ministers had no policy that defined an appropriate colonial government, nor a policy that defined the most elemental aspects of the metropolitan government's relationship to overseas dependencies. In 1624 James I told Parliament to stay out of the problems of the Virginia Company, that the Privy Council was handling the affair, and that no good could come from parliamentary interference, a position reiterated by Charles I. Under royal control, Virginia was to be governed by two appointed councils, one in England and one in Virginia. The former was never appointed and metropolitan oversight of the colony continued temporarily under the six-member Mandeville Commission, which had been appointed to establish a new government for the colony after the revocation of the charter. As members of the Privy Council, the commission business concerning Virginia became accepted as ministerial responsibility. Pursuant to the wishes of Charles I, and following his father's lead, the Virginia House of Burgesses, originally convened as promised in the Virginia Company's internal charter of 1618 to reform the governance of the colony, continued as part of the colony's customary government.[30]

If the Crown's ministers could not define how a colonial government should be constituted, it could identify when a company government had breached acceptable standards. No colony was more egregiously at odds with the metropolitan government than Massachusetts. The Puritan shareholders of the Massachusetts Bay Company had asked for and received a charter of incorporation from Charles I in 1629. While little distinguished that charter from others, the Puritans intended to use the company not for commerce but to establish a colony in Massachusetts that could distance and buffer them from the king, his ministers, and officials of the Anglican Church. A charter of incorporation, which John Winthrop physically carried to Massachusetts in

1630, provided the Puritans the best protection their domestic adversaries had to offer.[31]

Almost immediately upon learning that the Massachusetts Bay Company had moved its entire government and the charter to New England, the king and his ministers wanted the latter back. The King's Bench revoked the charter in 1637, but the court determined that it needed the physical document to make the revocation legal, which meant sending orders to Boston to have the charter returned. Winthrop procrastinated, and when Charles I was forced to convene Parliament in 1640, his political problems and a House of Commons sympathetic to the Bay Colony effectively nullified the orders to return the charter and bought the colony another four decades. After the Restoration, tighter control of England's overseas claims became an objective of Charles II's reign. Parliament passed the Navigation Acts, the king formed a succession of councils and committees to oversee foreign trade and plantation, the Privy Council reactivated the right of legal appeals to the Crown for subjects outside the realm of England, and the Privy Council made plans to revoke the charters of all the outstanding company and proprietary colonies and to establish royal governments.[32]

The Restoration Privy Council tried numerous stratagems to justify intervening in the Bay Colony and revoking its charter. It sent a commission to investigate the colony in 1664, ordered Massachusetts to send agents to report to the king, and established New Hampshire as a royal colony in 1679. Then in the 1680s, the attorney-general began proceedings to revoke the charter on the grounds that the colony had pretensions of being "a body Politic." The absence of an official Massachusetts Bay Company presence in London meant that the quo warranto writ to appear in court expired before it could be served. The court then served a writ of scire facias on the company's agent in London, which gave Bay Colony officials until Michelmas to respond to the court's charges. They chose not to plead the case, the court voided the charter, and New Englanders protested vehemently that it had been done illegally.[33]

The revocation of the Virginia and Massachusetts charters reflected an assertion by the Crown that it had a preeminent claim to provide civil governance for its subjects residing overseas. The proprietary charters, such as those for Maryland, Carolina, New York, and Pennsylvania, were granted to elite men, in most instances members of the aristocracy, and included the right to create governments for colonies and appoint necessary officials. The Privy Council increasingly advised against such charters, for example, opposing grants to Robert Barclay and the Earl of Doncaster. While it could not always persuade a monarch to desist from granting one, it could include stipulations that limited the autonomy of proprietors. The 1681 charter to William Penn for Pennsylvania, the last private grant, included clauses to remedy known problems. It guaranteed colonists the right of legal appeal to the Privy Council (a right the Massachusetts government prohibited its colonists), made explicit the Crown's prerogative to void laws that were "inconsistent with the sovereignty or lawful prerogative of us," and required Penn to keep "an attorney or agent . . . in or near our city of London."[34]

Maintaining control over civil governance was not just an excuse by the Privy Council to investigate the Massachusetts Bay Colony. Robert Mason claimed to be a proprietor of much of New Hampshire based on the grants that his grandfather, John Mason, had received from the Council of New England. Mason's claims challenged the claims of Massachusetts, and in the 1670s he asked the Lords of Trade to adjudicate the controversy and allow him to create a proprietary colony from his holdings. The men reviewing the case determined that John Mason's grant from the Council of New England was only for the land and that the right of government remained with the Crown; in 1679 New Hampshire was organized as a royal colony.[35]

Royal prerogative over civil governance was not exclusive to colonies. In the eighteenth century, the metropolitan government became concerned about matters of civil governance in Newfoundland, India, and the North American fur trade country, all parts of the "commercial" rather than "colonial" empire. The provision of courts for British subjects became the institutional cornerstone for the later establishment of colonial governments in all three places. In India and the North American fur trade country, the decision of the metropolitan government to provide mechanisms for judicial remedy impinged on the affairs of the East India Company and the Hudson's Bay Company, demonstrating that in some contexts these two joint-stock companies bore similarities to chartered ventures associated with colonization.

In the seventeenth century, the metropolitan government decided not to establish Newfoundland as a colony, defined as an overseas dependency with a resident English government. Britain provided limited governance of the fishery through the seasonal appointment of a naval commodore, who had the power to hear civil cases. A growing number of permanent settlers on the island, however, created a need for year-round and not just seasonal access to judicial remedy for disputes. In the fall of 1723, fifty-one wintering merchants and planters in St. John's met and decided to elect magistrates to serve for the winter to try civil and criminal cases. They signed a contract that justified their actions on the basis of John Locke's *Essay Concerning the True Origin, Extent, and End of Civil Government.* When the Board of Trade learned of this "body politic," it was not won over by the sophistication of the rationale, but it did recognize the need for year-round magistrates. By the end of the 1720s, the naval commodores had authority to appoint magistrates before sailing for England for the winter. Not for another century, however, would the British government appoint a year-round governor (1823) and authorize the calling of an assembly (1832).[36]

Calcutta, founded by the East India Company around 1690, had a Mayor's Court that tried civil and criminal cases involving company employees in Bengal. Parliament attempted to bring this court into greater conformity with judicial practices in Britain with the EIC's 1753 charter, followed by more specialized legislation in 1770. Neither act remedied the court's deficiencies. The EIC's near bankruptcy in 1772 precipitated an extensive parliamentary inquiry, and the resulting 1773 Regulating Act defined the establishment and responsibilities of a "Supreme Court of Judicature" with four royally appointed justices who would hold court at Fort William in Calcutta.[37] This court had the "full power and authority" to try cases "against any of his Majesty's subjects for any crimes, misdemeanors, or oppressions, committed or to be committed," and "any suits or actions whatsoever, against any of his Majesty's subjects in Bengal, Bahar, and Orissa." The "rules, ordinances, and regulations" made by the EIC's General Governor and Council for "the good order and civil government" of settlements in Asia were subject to the approval of the Supreme Court.[38] In the Regulating Act and subsequent legislation, Parliament distinguished between company government, civil government for ethnically British subjects in India, and government for natives of India.

In the North American fur trade country, the provision of British courts first came with the Quebec Act in 1774, which allowed for the continuation of French civil law in Quebec and extended the colony's boundaries south to the Ohio River and west to the Mississippi River. By enlarging Quebec to include the formerly French *pays d'en haut,* the British government could provide courts for people of European descent, predominantly French Canadians. After the 1783 Peace of Paris and the British cession of the Ohio Country to the Americans, the provisions of the Quebec Act applied north of the Great Lakes, until 1791, when the Constitutional Act provided for the division of Quebec into

Lower and Upper Canada. French civil law continued in Lower Canada, while English civil law applied in Upper Canada.[39]

Competition among the Montréal-based fur traders became so aggressive and volatile that Parliament passed the Canada Jurisdiction Act in 1803. It extended the jurisdiction of the courts of both Lower and Upper Canada into the fur trade territories not covered by the Hudson's Bay Company charter, in particular the Mackenzie River drainage basin. In 1804 the British government negotiated a merger of the various Montréal fur trading firms into the largest of them, the North West Company, which only intensified the rivalry of the Montréal traders with the HBC traders. When commercial competition exploded into armed conflict in 1816, the British government intervened again and convened talks between the two companies, which resulted in their merger in 1821 and a renewed charter for the Hudson's Bay Company that confirmed its rights to Rupert's Land.[40] Parliament also passed "An Act for Regulating the Fur Trade and establishing a Criminal and Civil Jurisdiction within certain parts of North America," that extended the 1803 legislation to include Rupert's Land and put the Mackenzie Basin and the Oregon Country under the exclusive British use of the merged companies. Significantly, both the 1803 and 1821 acts excluded civil cases concerning land, which had to be tried in courts in Britain rather than in either of the Canadas. Courts in those colonies, however, could try criminal and civil cases involving contracts or personal property.[41]

The above cases ranging over a two-century period from the revocation of the Virginia Company charter (1624) to the extension of the jurisdiction of the Upper and Lower Canadian courts to include cases originating in the fur trade country (1821) share the principle that civil governance of British subjects, regardless of their location in the world, originated with and remained tied to the Crown. To the extent that a chartered company failed to protect the welfare of subjects (the Virginia Company), or exceeded its right to act as a "body politic" (the Massachusetts Bay Company), or a group of merchants presumed to create a "body politic" (Newfoundland), or a critical mass of subjects overseas necessitated the creation of a "body politic" (the East India Company), or that fur traders needed access to courts, the metropolitan government intervened. That basic principle, whether applied to natural-born British subjects or conquered French-Canadians, changed little over two centuries.

What changed markedly, however, was the application of the principle and the institutionalized expression of sovereignty, which shifted from the person of the Crown, to the office of the Crown, and then to the Crown-in-Parliament.

In the 1620s, James I and Charles I were personally involved in the revocation of the Virginia Company charter and the royalization of that colony. By the 1680s, the Privy Council, in the name of the office of the Crown, initiated the revocation of the Massachusetts and Bermuda charters, as well as reviewed other company and proprietary charters, and advised Charles II against granting William Penn a proprietary charter to Pennsylvania. By the 1720s, the Board of Trade, a subcommittee of the Privy Council, made the decision to have naval commodores appoint year-round magistrates in Newfoundland. By the 1770s, the provision of courts in Bengal and the North America fur trade country came through parliamentary legislation. The locus of sovereignty for creating these institutions of civil governance overseas no longer lay in the person of the monarch but rather in the Crown-in-Parliament.

The curtailment of charters that delegated rights and privileges to subjects living and working in the extra-European world extended beyond the charters associated with overseas expansion. The Board of Trade, in response to the perceived republican excesses of New England towns, which after 1691 could be legally incorporated, proscribed the establishment of municipal governments in newly acquired colonies. The policy first affected Nova Scotia in the early eighteenth century, but subsequently was extended to all of post-1783 British North America. In 1774, in an attempt to restrain rebellious New Englanders, Parliament passed the Massachusetts Government Act, which included a provision to remove most of the corporate rights of the colony's towns. Before the 1830s, Saint John, New Brunswick, was the only urban center in British North America (what became Canada) that had a municipal charter. All other urban centers, including Halifax, Quebec, Montreal, Kingston, and York (later Toronto), were governed through the county courts with their royally appointed magistrates.[42] The principle that civil governance originated with the Crown became entrenched in post-1783 British ideology in the empire and continues to have currency in countries such as Canada that remain constitutional monarchies. In the United States, independence and rejection of a monarchical system of government made the source of civil government a contested principle, though strongly biased towards "the people."

Relations with Foreigners

During the Privy Council's review of the charters of company and proprietary colonies in the 1680s, it ordered the proprietors of the Bahamas to meet with it and explain why Robert Clarke, their governor in the islands, was issuing letters of marque to privateers. Licensing privateers, Clarke explained in an earlier letter, was "justiciable by the lawes of Nature and Nations and this more especially since it is grounded on lawful authority given by the Sovereign." The Bahamas, lying on the northeastern edge of the sea route out of the Caribbean to Europe, harbored pirates and privateers who preyed on Spanish ships. Clarke justified privateering as necessary for the colony's defense, but in one letter of marque he authorized offensive attacks on Spanish holdings far from the Bahamas. Clarke's encouragement of privateering contravened and jeopardized the 1667 and 1670 treaties of Madrid, which established peace between the English and Spanish. In the estimation of the Privy Council, Clarke exceeded the gubernatorial powers implied in the charter "given by the Sovereign." The Bahamian proprietors, once confronted by the Privy Council, quickly distanced themselves from Clarke and agreed to the issuing of orders for his arrest and to the principle that the charter "right to make peace and war" applied to Caribs only. The charter was not revoked at that time and the Bahamas remained a proprietary colony until 1718. Nevertheless, a sharp distinction was made between foreign relations with Europeans and non-Europeans, with the former shifted toward the Crown and the metropolitan government.[43]

No charter was ever revoked for the infringement of the Crown's prerogative over foreign relations, though charters were revoked under Spanish pressure, as happened with the Amazon Company.[44] But as the case of the Bahamas suggests, and which other cases substantiate, a marked shift occurred during the seventeenth century in the kinds of relations with foreigners the Crown was willing to delegate to chartered enterprises. Distinctions among types of relations with foreigners in the extra-European world, particularly between Europeans and non-Europeans, sharpened.[45] As the empire expanded over the eighteenth century, an increasing number of non-British peoples were incorporated into it, which changed their status from foreigners to either friendly aliens under the protection of the Crown or subjects.

Early English overseas expansion was confrontational by the very nature of the international configurations of power. One advantage of chartered enterprises for the Crown was that they allowed English monarchs to challenge the Spanish and Portuguese while retaining a degree of deniability that direct royal funding would have precluded. The competitive nature of expansion and contact, if not conflict, with foreigners made the right of defense a constant in charters, and which also included the right to ship "armour weapons ordnances munitions powder [and] shot," to organize defense against attacks, and "exercise martial law in cases of rebellion or mutiny." Through the first half of the seventeenth century, many charters included a clause addressed to "all Christian kings, princes and states" stating "that if any person or persons" associated with a colony or commercial enterprise "shall do any act of unjust and unlawful hostility," that procedures were available to remedy the situation, including, if necessary, putting offenders "out of our allegiance and protection." Further distinctions were made between those "Christian kings, princes, and states" in amity with England and those at war.[46]

While rights to transport armaments and ordnance overseas and to organize military units for self-defense remained constants in charters, after the Restoration charters began to distinguish between military conflicts with Europeans and non-Europeans. Charles II gave the Hudson's Bay Company the right to "make peace or Warre with any Prince or People whatsoever that are not Christians in any places where the said Company shall have any Plantacions Fortes or Factoryes." Similarly, the 1672 charter of the Royal African Company gave it the "full power to make and declare peace and war with any of the heathen nations that are or shall be natives of any countries within the said territories in the said parts of Africa as there shall be occasion." The 1683 East India Company charter contained a similar clause. William Penn's charter explicitly stated that war-making against any Europeans was not allowed, although the remoteness of the country and proximity to "so many barbarous nations" as well as "pirates and robbers," necessitated rights of self-defense.[47]

In the mid seventeenth century, the Iberians began to acknowledge English, French, and Dutch claims in the extra-European world. In 1641, the Dutch negotiated a treaty with the Portuguese, which included Portuguese acknowledgement of Dutch overseas claims in return for Dutch acknowledgement of the Portuguese repatriation of their crown after sixty years of Spanish control. A similar Luso-English treaty followed the next year. Spain first acknowledged non-Iberian claims in the 1648 Treaty of Munster, when it recognized both Dutch independence and overseas claims. It served as the model for Spanish recognition of English claims in the 1667 Treaty of Madrid, particularly the 1655 English conquest of Jamaica. One of the elements of the Iberian recognition of non-Iberian claims was an understanding that England, France, and the Netherlands would start to eliminate the use of privatized force overseas, particularly the licensing of privateers.[48] The language of the Restoration charters and the Privy Council's threat to revoke the charter for the Bahamas on foreign policy grounds reflect the reorientation of foreign affairs in the seventeenth-century Atlantic world.

The Iberian recognition of English overseas claims created international obligations to curtail the military discretion of colonies and companies in the Atlantic basin if directed against Europeans, but which was never fully achieved before the American Revolution. French challenges to the Hudson's Bay Company between 1670 and 1715 obliged the company to engage in offensive action. Governor William Phips of Massachusetts organized a New England force to take Acadia from the French during the Nine Years' War (1689–97). Board of Trade injunctions to colonial governors failed to keep them from issuing letters of marque for privateering until Parliament passed "An Act for the More Effectual Suppression of Piracy" (1700), which allowed for the transportation to England of persons charged with piracy in the colonies. During the War of the Austrian Succession (1740–48), New England governments organized a military force made up of colonial men to take Louisbourg from the French. Virginian military challenges to the French in the Ohio Country accelerated the tensions that contributed to the Seven Years' War (1756–63).[49]

The metropolitan government's ability to control the use of military force by colonies and companies against Europeans was hampered by the rights and privileges that colonists believed they had based on custom, many derived from charters. As well, the metropolitan government needed colonists to fight in the wars of the long eighteenth century (1689–1815), each of which had significant overseas theaters. The subordination of colonial and commercial military units to the command of the British army and navy was most successful in colonies conquered in the eighteenth century, such as Nova Scotia (conquered in 1710 and ceded in 1713) and Quebec (conquered in 1760 and ceded in 1763), or in the Caribbean colonies with their large populations of enslaved Africans and their small populations of whites. But in the older North American colonies, where militias were locally controlled, colonial units and British officers had quite different ideas about military command.[50]

Relations with non-British peoples in extra-European territories only slowly came under metropolitan control, and then only through discrete practices rather than through the uniform application of policy. Nevertheless, there are discernable patterns. The appointment of two Indian Superintendents for North America in 1754 was influenced to a great degree by the threat of war with France and the need for Indian military allies. Control of military force against native peoples and diplomatic negotiations with them were no longer the unquestioned rights of colonial governments. The Proclamation of 1763 and the Quebec Act of 1774, both of which recognized non-British systems of government, contravened the seventeenth-century charter obligations that colonial laws not be repugnant to English law. This principle of non-repugnancy, that previously had been nearly universal British practice overseas, had become determinable on a case-by-case basis in response to the growing numbers of non-British peoples in the empire. The Proclamation acknowledged the right of native self-government, except for the alienation of land. The Quebec Act allowed Catholics to hold public office, granted the Catholic Church the right to collect tithes, continued the seigneurial system of landholding, and established French, rather than English, civil law in the colony. Catholics in Grenada, which the French ceded to Britain in 1763, were given rights similar to those given to the Canadians.[51] The Proclamation of 1763 made the trans-Appalachian West a territory under the jurisdictional authority of the British imperial state, rather than the territory of colonies based on charters, which the extension of the boundaries of Quebec south to the Ohio River and west to the Mississippi River only confirmed.

The Proclamation of 1763 and the Quebec Act were not entirely parallel. In Quebec with its large French-Canadian population, the Crown claimed sovereignty over the territory and the prerogative to establish civil governance, the latter through royal proclamation and then parliamentary legislation. In the trans-Appalachian West, inhabited largely by native nations, the Proclamation created a new hybrid of domestic and foreign policy. By claiming sovereignty over the territory, both in terms of the ultimate ownership of the land and the ultimate jurisdictional authority, the Crown "domesticated" relations with native nations. But the Crown did not exercise its prerogative to establish civil governance over those nations, except insofar as it legitimated native rights of self-government, and thus continued to treat them as a kind of domestic alien. While the British had long recognized that native peoples governed themselves, they had not generally been treated as peoples under British jurisdiction. Without consulting native nations, the Proclamation of 1763 unilaterally brought them under the protection of the Crown, which was a significantly new development in British America, though it is not clear whether it made them subjects.[52] The restrained expression of Crown prerogative over the civil governance of native peoples contrasts sharply with its vigorous assertion of this prerogative when it involved European peoples. The separation of

Crown sovereignty over territory from civil governance was repeated in India, Rupert's Land, the Mackenzie Basin, and the Oregon Country, all imperial domains with predominantly non-European populations.

A number of developments contributed to the decisions to allow non-British forms of civil government in British territory, whether in Quebec, the trans-Appalachian West, or India. In some instances it was a practical question of money. In 1760, Jeffery Amherst, the general of the British army in North America, made the decision to eliminate unnecessary expenses, among which he included the annual distribution of gifts to native allies. That ill-considered decision fed native unease with the British and contributed to Pontiac's uprising in 1763. Gift-giving became financially prudent compared to the short-term costs of military defense and the long-term costs of coercion. Maintaining native self-governance became both a humane and fiscally sensible decision.[53] In Quebec, British officials found themselves choosing between conflicting principles. Governor James Murray decided to allow Catholics to practice law and serve on juries, even though these privileges violated the Test Act, because of the small number of Protestants and to maintain the English principle that the accused were entitled to a trial by their peers. A major shift in humanitarian sensibilities also contributed to a belief that it was coercive to oblige conquered peoples to change their customs of civil governance to English practices.[54]

Despite the similar impulses in the decisions by the British government to allow the continuation of French Canadian, French Grenadian, Native North American, and South Asian governmental practices, if not whole systems, the mechanisms and agents for acknowledging and implementing those decisions varied depending on whether groups were European. In territories or colonies with large European populations, such as Quebec and Grenada, the metropolitan government created civil governments with royally appointed officials. In the North American fur trade country and in India, the indigenous systems of government persisted, and in each place the Hudson's Bay Company and the East India Company, respectively, were agents for British administration. The civil governance of natural-born British subjects and non-British, but European, subjects, in contrast, had been claimed as Crown prerogative, increasingly expressed through the Crown-in-Parliament.

From the time of their initial chartering, companies and proprietors had engaged in diplomacy for trading purposes and for negotiating the use, if not transfer, of land to British subjects. But not until the second half of the eighteenth century did companies take on the role of intermediaries between the

British government and indigenous peoples who lived in lands claimed as part of the British Empire. The tacit delegation of this responsibility to the EIC and HBC, after more than a century of greater restrictions on chartered enterprises, suggests how slowly the British government assumed the mantle of imperial overlord vis-à-vis non-Europeans. Increasingly there emerged a distinction between the white settler colonies—which after 1783 included British North America, the Atlantic and Caribbean islands (notwithstanding their majority black populations), the Cape Colony, Australia, and New Zealand—and the other territories of the rest of the empire with their predominantly non-European inhabitants.

Conclusion

At the end of the seventeenth century, the near abandonment of chartered enterprises as vehicles for overseas expansion and the reviewing of existing company and proprietary charters for possible revocation had as much to do with the extension of prerogative powers into the extra-European world as with the utility of chartered enterprises. Indeed, the very success of many enterprises made the extension, rather than the delegation, of prerogative powers a real issue, particularly if the metropolitan government wished to counter and contain the centrifugal tendencies of expansion. The civil governance of subjects, the definition and administration of Crown lands, and foreign policy in the Atlantic world were of particular concern. The role of the Privy Council in making these decisions, including counseling the king to desist from granting more charters, reflects the shifting locus for the expression of prerogative powers in Britain, many of which became vested in the Crown-in-Parliament by the mid eighteenth century.

The survival of the Hudson's Bay Company and the East India Company and the embellishment of their powers in the post-1783 empire are apparent anomalies, particularly considering the scrutiny to which both companies were subjected in the mid eighteenth century.[55] Yet if we return to an observation made at the beginning of this essay about chartered enterprises assuming risks the Crown either could not or would not undertake, then the position of the HBC and EIC as new bastions of the empire makes more sense. In the late sixteenth and early seventeenth centuries, chartered enterprises bore the financial and foreign policy risks that expansion engendered. By the end of the seventeenth century, both of those risks had diminished, and in their place the risks associated with the success of ventures emerged, particularly the tendency of overseas subjects to arrogate too much power to themselves in matters concerning civil governance, control of Crown lands, and the exercise of foreign policy.

By the mid eighteenth century, the growth of empire, in particular the conquests of the Seven Years' War, necessitated decisions about how the governance of non-British peoples within the empire should be accommodated. Prior to then it had been a relatively minor concern. Many charters for the Americas only mentioned indigenous people as adversaries of colonization, against whom grantees were given rights of self-defense, or as candidates for religious conversion. The Rhode Island charter was distinctive in suggesting that an indigenous nation, specifically the Narragansett who were on good terms with the colony's leadership, be "given . . . encouragement, of their own accord, to subject themselves, their people and land, unto us."[56] Until the mid eighteenth century, native peoples were generally assumed either to be friendly aliens or enemy aliens, rather than some new form of subject. The Acadians in Nova Scotia were the first significant involuntary group of non-Protestant, non-British Europeans to be incorporated into British America, and their eventual deportation is testimony to the poverty of policy for governing non-British peoples brought under British sovereignty through conquest.[57]

By the conclusion of the Seven Years' War, the accommodation of non-British peoples into the empire had emerged as an unavoidable problem. Many were incorporated through conquest, such as the Canadians, Grenadians, and Bengalis. Others, particularly indigenous North Americans, were effectively incorporated through an extension of British claims in North America, particularly with the departure of the French as imperial competitors. The metropolitan government was faced with the quandary of forced assimilation, which had been disastrous and inhumane in the case of the Acadians, and destabilizing, expensive, and inhumane, in the case of the natives and Pontiac's uprising. Accommodation of non-British peoples also created risks for the metropolitan government, as reflected in debates in Parliament over the Regulating Act (1773) and the Quebec Act (1774) and reaction in the colonies to those acts and the earlier Proclamation of 1763. All those measures could be interpreted as violating the rights of colonists, elements of the British colonial constitutions, and the British constitution within Britain. Given these risks and limited precedents for governing non-Europeans in the extra-European world, the decision of the British government to leave some of the responsibility with the East India Company and the Hudson's Bay Company, each of which had over a century of experience with Asians and indigenous North Americans, respectively, is not surprising. Indeed, much of the late eighteenth-century debate over the consequences of the conquest of Bengal turned on whether and to what extent the British government should—or even could—assume the governance of territory in India.[58] British practices in Africa were similar. In 1750 Parliament revoked the Royal African Company's monopoly and chartered the Company of Merchants Trading to Africa, a regulated company to which all traders to Africa paid a fee for maintaining forts and intergovernmental relations in West Africa. One of the only post-1783 enterprises chartered for an overseas venture was the Sierra Leone Company, organized to repatriate freed slaves to Africa.[59] Only gradually did the metropolitan government assume direct responsibility for the civil governance of the non-Europeans, a process that extended into the second half of the nineteenth century.

The revocation of the seventeenth-century charters of the company and proprietary colonies reflects the extension of prerogative powers overseas, often through new and evolving institutions, such as the development of new definitions of Crown lands overseas. The accommodation of non-British peoples was also a new development that seemed to violate rights derived from charters and custom, as well as represented new expressions of prerogative power, whether through the Crown, as in the Proclamation of 1763, or through the Crown-in-Parliament, as in the Regulating Act and the Quebec Act. In these respects, there emerged a set of practices and institutions that deviated from both the constitution of the state within Britain and the constitutions of the colonies established in the seventeenth century, and thus indicate the emergence of an identifiable imperial state. Despite the seeming appearance of a strong and authoritarian imperial state at the end of the eighteenth century, the caution it exercised in extending prerogative powers over civil governance of all peoples within the empire indicates its unwillingness to test the limits of its authority if it could delay the acceptance of that new risk. For the metropolitan government, the political and constitutional accommodation of non-British practices within the British Empire—much of it initially through the administration of HBC or EIC—was intended to mitigate the risks involved with the incorporation of large numbers of non-British peoples into the empire. Many British Americans, however, interpreted those accommodations as creating political and constitutional threats, and chose independence rather than remain a member of that new British world.

CHAPTER ELEVEN

Seeds of Empire

Florida, Kew, and the British Imperial Meridian in the 1760s

Robert Olwell

On August 15, 1765, James Grant, the recently appointed royal governor of Britain's new colony of East Florida, wrote, "I am deeply engaged in the Botanical way, for the Duke of Cumberland and Lord Bute, having received very extensive commissions from both of them."[1] A few months later, Grant wrote to Bute directly, informing him apologetically that "it was too late last year when I arrived in this Province to think of making a collection of seeds for your Lordship, [as] we were rather in a helpless state in this infant colony at that time, [and] Botanists and proper people to assist them were wanting." Now, however, Grant assured Bute that "an assortment has been made this year consisting of fifty-seven articles, most of which have been put up . . . in three boxes directed for your Lordship . . . by the first vessel which sails for England." Grant promised Bute that soon, "with the assistance of Mr. [John] Bartram of Philadelphia, ["a botanist of reputation"] . . . I expect to send . . . a more considerable assortment of seeds."[2] In another letter, the governor expressed his wish that, "tho' I am a bad Botanist, [I hope] my zeal will make up for the want of skill."[3]

Since his arrival in St. Augustine the previous fall, Grant had found his work cut out for him. Britain had acquired Florida from Spain (in exchange for

Havana) in the treaty negotiations concluding the Seven Years' War in 1763. When the Spanish authorities departed from Florida the following year, they took virtually the entire population of the colony with them, including a small community of free Africans who had escaped slavery in the British colonies to the northward and the few hundred mission Indians who managed to survive two centuries of European diseases and a century of South Carolinians who, with their Indian allies, had sought to enslave them. The Spanish had even exhumed the bodies of deceased governors for reburial in Cuba.[4] Consequently, Grant was at first a governor without a colony, or at least without any colonial subjects. In a ritualized ceremony that must have seemed farcical, Grant was publicly proclaimed governor "with all due Solemnity" in the plaza of St. Augustine in October 1764 before a public that could not have consisted of more than the few dozen British settlers and speculators, who had already arrived in the colony seeking to buy property at bargain prices from the departing Spanish, the few red-coated soldiers who formed the garrison of the fort, and perhaps a few curious Indians.[5]

Florida in the mid-1760s was one of the farthest and loneliest outposts of the British Empire, and thus the three boxes that Grant shipped from St. Augustine to Lord Bute early in 1766 may seem an unlikely subject upon which to hang a study of the imperial imagination. After all, it might fairly be said, the journey of Grant's seeds from Florida to England comprised merely one of the many thousands of threads from which the early modern British Atlantic world was woven. But focusing attention upon the strange career of Grant's seeds allows us to transcend the historiographical boundaries that have often divided early modern British history. An older, more traditionally defined approach to a history of British Florida might include an account of Grant's gathering of botanical specimens but would ignore their fate once they departed St. Augustine. Similarly, historians of colonial America have studied American production, and more recently consumption, but seldom examine the other side of these transactions.[6] In the same vein, a history of British botany in the eighteenth century might describe how "exotic" seeds were planted and cultivated in British gardens and greenhouses but would devote little time to considering the process by which they were collected. Most likely, of course, neither early modern British nor colonial American history would mention Grant's seeds at all, for without examining both sides of their voyage, the strange journey they made would lack any context or significance.

The ultimate destination for Grant's seeds was the recently established "Exotic" garden at King George III's palace at Kew, the precursor of the famous Royal Botanical Garden that occupies the same site today. In a recent, pathbreaking book, Richard Drayton examined the role that the Royal Botanical Garden, and by extension botanical science, played in the creation and justification both of the British Empire and of "global" commerce, communication, and commodification. In studying the small confines of Kew, Drayton addresses a large issue: how "the knowledge of nature . . . transformed the boundaries of human power, and with it our attitudes to the universe and to ourselves."[7] In the 1760s, a period that Drayton treats only briefly, all of these ideas—long-distance capitalism, botanical science, and even the British Empire—were still in their formative stages. But just as Drayton argues that "in the story of a garden, we may explore the history of the world," a focus upon the cross-fertilization of a new garden and a new colony, and an examination of the larger world of ideas in which they were embedded, can illuminate the importance of the 1760s in the creation of a British imperial (and anti-imperial) imagination. By following the voyage of the seeds sent from St. Augustine at the edge of the British imperial world to Kew, at its very center, and by tracing the "imperial gaze" that looked from Kew back to Florida, we can begin to unite the "histories" that were being simultaneously cultivated on both sides of the Atlantic and demonstrate how, beneath the soil, their roots were very closely intertwined.

Over seventy-five years ago, Charles Andrews, one of the founders of colonial American history, argued that the famous Royal Proclamation of 1763, which barred colonial settlement west of the Appalachian crest and created the new colonies of Quebec and East and West Florida, revealed a new British plan to reorganize and govern the colonies according to an "imperialistic system of administration." Previously, suggested Andrews, under the "old colonial system," the British had viewed their American colonies as commercial outposts and had loosely governed them according to the economic-based theory of mercantilism. But in the course of the Seven Years' War, Andrews asserted, without "consciously or aggressively aiming at Empire," Britain nonetheless had acquired one in the Americas, Africa, and Asia. Consequently, Andrews argued, at the end of the conflict "a new issue, territorial imperialism, emerged to perplex the souls of British statesmen." For Andrews, the consequence of this change in Britain's conception of her colonies was both ironic and tragic.

Andrews described the spirit of "imperialism" that guided British colonial policy after 1763 as the "penalty of victory." In pursuit of its siren-call, British ministers would ultimately drive the American colonies to rebellion and destroy the first British Empire.[8]

Historians of the second British Empire also recognize the importance of 1763, a year which saw the acquisition of Senegal, Canada, and several Caribbean islands. But territorial gains in the Atlantic basin pale when compared to what was happening at the same time on the shores of the Indian Ocean. Military victories and diplomatic maneuvers during the Seven Years' War and after had made the East India Company into a major player in the politics of the subcontinent. The key year was 1765, not because of the Stamp Act crisis that disrupted British-American relations, but because of the East India Company's acquisition of the *diwani*, the authority to collect taxes in the Indian province of Bengal. This development immediately transformed the British relationship with India "from trader to sovereign" and, according to one historian, marked "the real beginning . . . of the British raj."[9]

Traditionally when students of "domestic" British history dealt with the 1760s, the pivotal year was 1760 and the crucial event was the accession of George III and the subsequent shake-up of domestic British politics.[10] While the American Revolution and its causes were naturally issues of great concern to the history of the United States, British historians (safe in the knowledge of a greater empire, or even later, of a non-imperial Britain to come) have tended to regard them as of little more than passing interest, a brief, if painful, bout of imperial indigestion that had no long-term ill-effects on the British body politic.[11] But the insularity of British domestic history has been challenged by emerging work on early modern state formation and the creation of national identities.[12]

In recent years, practitioners of the "new imperial history" have endeavored to look at all imperial relationships from the perspective of the colonized as well as the colonizer, and to consider all viewpoints, not just that of the metropolis, in defining the character and nature of the empire.[13] Here, too, events from the 1760s looms large, especially as these historians try to effect what one has called the "removal of the frontier between the domestic and external histories of Britain."[14] Recent studies of British society in the eighteenth century have begun to illuminate how important and pervasive a new sense of empire may have been in British culture in these years and the central role it may have played in the creation of the modern British state.[15] In the decade following the Seven Years' War, books that included the term "British Empire" in their titles became a commonplace as Britons eagerly sought information on the world they had won.[16] Scholars have begun to investigate how dreams (and nightmares) of empire deeply penetrated and profoundly shaped British society in this period. Kathleen Wilson, for example, notes that "the British empire permeated Georgian English culture at a number of levels, from literature and theater to philanthropy, fashion, gardening and politics."[17]

Rather than employing a telescope to outline the entire British-dominated world through the study of ministers and policies, the new imperial history instead scrutinizes the workings of the empire through a microscope and aims to see a world in microcosm, or, in the case of Kew and Florida, in a greenhouse and a jungle. The story of how two tropical "gardens"—one created under glass, and the other created, or at least defined, through the agents of the British Empire—were each products of the spirit of imperialism that was emergent in the 1760s, and were also powerfully influenced by the knowledge and image of each other, which suggests that Charles Andrews was right when he argued that something was altering the "souls" of Britons after 1763.

The Political Garden

As they crossed the Atlantic, Grant's seeds traveled from the margins of the British world to its very center. The seeds were eventually planted in the gardens and greenhouses at Kew palace, located on the banks of the Thames five miles southwest of London. Kew, along with the adjacent estate of Richmond, was the seat of George III's court from 1760 to 1778. The seeds gathered in the Florida swamps in late 1765 eventually bloomed at the feet of the king. Few men in the British world were more powerful or better connected than those who engaged Governor Grant to collect seeds. In the summer of 1765, the Duke of Cumberland, the king's uncle, was the commanding general of the army. From July until his death in October, he was the de facto head of the government, pulling the strings behind the ministry of Lord Rockingham. The Duke died before he received the seeds that Grant sent, but John Stuart, third Earl of Bute, was on hand to open the parcel.

Bute served as prime minister from May 1762 to April 1763, a period in which the Treaty of Paris was negotiated, ending the Seven Years' War, and through which Britain acquired Florida, Canada, and other new territories. Even after he resigned from office, Bute remained a central figure in the royal court. By acting as the personal advisor and "favourite" of George III, Bute bred resentment among both ministers and opposition. His Scottish ethnicity and his name (although he was not actually related to the Stuart "pretenders") led some to charge him with whispering "Scotch Politicks" (i.e., absolutist principles) in the young king's ear. In the 1760s, Bute became a lightning rod for political dissent and discontent. His influence with the king and the king's mother, with whom he was alleged to be having an affair, was thought to be so great that pamphlets and cartoons depicted Bute as a puppetmaster, directing the entire government "from behind the curtain."[18]

Bute helped brew the political storm that surrounded him. Soon after his coronation in October 1760, George III proclaimed himself a king "above party" and invited Tories to support his government. This gesture signaled the king's intent, acting with Bute's advice, to break with the Whig oligarchs, who had controlled the government for over forty years and who had limited the independence of the two previous Hanoverian monarchs. George III's ambition to "be king" and to keep his own counsel, soon caused conflict with William Pitt, the "great commoner" and prime minister who had led Britain to triumph in the Seven Years' War. Pitt's resignation in the fall of 1761 allowed George III to appoint Bute as prime minister, even though Bute had neither a political following nor a seat in the House of Commons. Determined to build a loyal base of "king's friends" in Parliament, Bute ruthlessly purged the government payroll of anyone who dared oppose him. By tying patronage solely to services rendered the prime minister, Bute challenged the old-boy network and reshuffled the political deck.[19] A mad scramble ensued over the next decade as men either struggled to retain or secure office under a succession of short-term prime ministers or joined in the rapidly evolving coalitions that soon coalesced to oppose the new regime.

As the arrival of Governor Grant's seeds indicates, other topics besides politics occupied the residents of Kew. The new king's coronation had other, less familiar consequences than the tremors it sent through the political world. In the words of a historian of science, "the accession of George III in 1760 had among its many effects the minor and rather freakish one of placing at the Nation's head ... a trio of enthusiastic botanists": the king, Lord Bute, and the king's mother, Princess Augusta.[20] From evidence in Grant's letters from Florida, we might add another botanical enthusiast, the king's uncle, the Duke of Cumberland. Moreover, Thomas Whately, assistant secretary of the treasury from 1763 until 1765, and best known to American historians for his ingenious invention of the concept of "virtual representation" in a pamphlet that he wrote in defense of the Stamp Act, was probably more famous in his own country for his writings on landscape gardening.[21]

The presence of so many "green thumbs" at King George's court reflects the surge of popular interest in plant collecting and in gardening among the leisure class throughout the empire—indeed throughout the European world—in the latter half of the eighteenth century. One explanation for the elite's sudden passion for botany was the popularization of the Linnaean method for ordering and classifying plants. Linnaeus's *Species Planterum,* published in 1753, introduced a binomial system of nomenclature that theoretically allowed all of creation to be categorized with two names, one for genus and one for species.[22] Moreover, those who discovered—that is, identified—new species, or even genera, would have the first claim to bestowing their new "scientific" name. Popular interest in the new science was furthered with the publication of Richard Pulteny's *General View of the Writing's of Linnaeus* in 1759.[23] Pulteny not only translated the Latin into English but he offered a simplified version of the Linnaean taxonomy that allowed an individual to classify a plant in its correct genus and species, or if the plant were yet "unknown" to name it and set it into its proper place in the kingdom of creation. Botany allowed ordinary people to take part in the Enlightenment project of discovery and of "ordering" the world.[24] In 1763, a contributor to the *Critical Review* wrote that "natural history, by a kind of national establishment [has become] ... the favorite study of the time."[25]

We might at first be inclined to separate the politics being practiced in Richmond palace from the activities in Kew garden: the first we might define as "work" (or politics) and the latter as "play" (or science). Certainly Bute viewed his time spent in the greenhouse and herbarium as an escape from the political cockpit. He and the royal family strolled through the gardens in their leisure hours. But Bute's botanical studies and his desire for seeds from Florida and other colonial outposts also served a political purpose. For both philosophical and patriotic reasons, Bute adamantly opposed the Linnaean system and championed his own alternative method. In part, Bute felt that the "sexual system" upon which the Linnaean classification was based was crude and artificial. He objected to the use of "barbarous Swedish names" for so many plant species. "In a few years," Bute complained, "The Linnaean Botany will be a good dictionary of Swedish." "I am surprised," he wrote, "to see all Europe suffer these impertinences." Over sixteen years, beginning in

1759, Bute spent the extraordinary sum of £12,000 of his personal fortune to publish his own "great botanical plan," a twenty-six-volume work entitled *The Vegetable System.*[26]

In the 1760s, a decade in which the very idea of a British Empire was being constructed, imperial politics and imperial science were closely intertwined. While George III and Bute conferred on how to organize the vast imperial territories that the nation had won in the Seven Years' War (including, of course, Florida), they were simultaneously playing with ideas of empire in the gardens and greenhouses at Kew. Bute, as prime minister and royal advisor, sought to bring order to the British political and imperial world; Bute, as botanist, undertook a similarly ambitious project to order the kingdom of nature.

Kew's entry into British politics began in the 1730s when Frederick, Prince of Wales and George III's father, first leased a modest country house and park adjacent to the royal palace at Richmond.[27] From the late 1730s through the next decade, political opponents of Walpole and the Whig oligarchy gravitated toward Prince Frederick, who, like all the Hanoverian heirs, was bitterly estranged from his father. These opposition politicians saw (or imagined) in Prince Frederick an alternative to what they perceived as the corrupt court of King George II. Many adherents of this faction described themselves as the party of the "Country" to indicate their position outside the royal court, off the royal payroll, and away from the influences of power.[28] Kew, as the Prince's country residence, posed a Tory-Country counterpoint to both the city and the Whig court of George II.

This opposition movement collapsed upon Frederick's sudden death in 1751, but Kew continued to be a site of political contention. His widow, Princess Augusta, continued to live at Kew with her young son, now the heir to the throne, and the king's political opponents began to return to Kew in the mid-1750s. Bute first appeared at Kew in the late 1740s as a member of this Tory-Country faction. With the death of Frederick, his influence at Kew rose dramatically, and by the mid-1750s, he was the chief political advisor to Princess Augusta, as she successfully endeavored to maintain her financial and political independence from her father-in-law. In 1755, Augusta appointed Bute as tutor to Prince George, then seventeen years old. Bute's sway over the immature and insecure prince was immense; before long Prince George was describing Bute as "my true friend" and assuring him that as "I am young and unexperienc'd, [I] shall exactly follow your advice, without which I shall inevitably sink."[29] George II, anxious to separate his grandson and successor from the influence of his political enemies, offered to finance an independent household for him. But the young prince, no doubt advised by Bute, continued to live with his mother at Kew until he came to the throne in 1760.

After George III was crowned, he took up his residence at Richmond, and for all practical purposes Richmond and Kew became one combined estate with two palaces: Richmond Palace, where the king lived, and the White House, or Kew Palace, his childhood home and the residence of his mother, Princess Augusta.[30] At the same time, of course, the meaning of Kew abruptly changed from the "Country" to the "Court." From 1760 until 1778, when he removed the royal court to Windsor, King George III spent the majority of his time there. Thus, in these crucial years, the grounds of Richmond-Kew were the very epicenter of the British state and nascent empire.

The seeds of Britain's imperial garden were sown in 1758 when John Hill, an Augustan prodigy (and prodigal) and an accomplished botanist, medical doctor, and playwright, published a short pamphlet entitled *An Idea of a Botanical Garden in England*. Under Bute's patronage, it was Hill who actually wrote *The Vegetable System*, and doubtless Bute encouraged, if he did not actually commission, the earlier work. In Hill's plan, the proposed garden would be divided into "the four great regions of the earth and destined for the reception separately of European, African, American, and Asiatic plants." Touring the garden, Hill wrote, "would be like visiting those great divisions of the earth in succession." Hill originally suggested that the garden be planted on the grounds of George II's palace at Kensington and proposed that "a weekly lecture might be given [to the public] on Saturdays," when the king was usually away.[31]

But it was at George III's palace at Kew, under Bute's guiding hand, that Hill's plan came to fruition. The process began in 1759, but was greatly accelerated after George III came to the throne the following year. Over the next decade, the grounds of Kew offered Bute and the young king a place to enact their budding imperial and botanical fantasies. As with Governor Grant in St. Augustine, Bute used his position to pester colonial officials for seeds and specimens for the planting beds at Kew. By 1767, Bute noted with pride that "the Exotick garden at Kew is by far the richest in Europe . . . getting plants and seeds from every part of the habitable world."[32]

While plants and seeds from the colonies took root in Kew's "Exotick garden," the entire estate was lavishly and expensively landscaped. William Chambers, a Scot and noted advocate of Chinoiserie, was given the commission. In

a 1757 book, Chambers argued against the prevailing classicism for more eclec-
tic and cosmopolitan styles and fashions. He noted that Roman Emperor
Hadrian, "at a time when the Grecian Architecture was in the highest esteem
among the Romans, had erected in his villa at Tivoli certain buildings after the
manner of the Egyptians and other nations."[33] Now on the grounds at Kew,
alongside a classical "temple of Victory" celebrating Britain's triumph in the
Seven Years' War, Chambers constructed more "exotic" buildings including a
"Moorish Temple," a "Turkish Mosque," and most famously a "Chinese
Pagoda." In a 1763 book about Kew that included engravings of many of the new
structures and vistas, Chambers described his achievement in heroic terms;
"what was once a desart is now an eden."[34]

Hill originally envisaged that the gardens at Kew would be open to the gen-
teel public one day each week with imperial pedagogy in mind. A guide that
eighteenth-century visitors could purchase from a shop outside the main gate
allows us to glimpse the message that the general public was supposed to take
from their visit to the gardens. The guide recommended that tours begin on
the lawn of the "White House" (or Kew Palace), the childhood home of George
III and the residence of Princess Augusta. Visitors were not allowed to enter the
house, but the pamphlet did provide a floor plan and descriptions and drawings of the principal rooms. The tour proceeded to the "Physic or Exotick Garden," which, visitors were told, included "all curious productions . . . collected
from every part of the Globe, without regard to Expence," so that "in a few
Years, this will be the amplest and best Collection of Plants in Europe." Visitors
continued through the flower garden, the aviary and menagerie (a prelude to
the royal zoo of the next century), and finally on to the landscaped grounds
and the exotic buildings. The most spectacular of these was the pagoda, 163 feet
high and "adorned with large Dragons." The strange plants, animals, and buildings presented in an orderly taxonomy and placed in the context of the civility
evident at Kew Palace (where all visits started) comprised an imperial museum
that exhibited not only the brave new world that Britain could claim and
aspired to order and rule, but also the nation's and the monarch's ability and
fitness to do so.[35]

Classifying a Colony

Promoters of British East Florida, many of whom met once a month at the
Shakespeare's Head tavern in London as "The East Florida Society," often

compared their pet colony to another mythic garden: Eden.[36] The first accounts of the colony listed an amazing cornucopia of crops that could be grown in Florida and testified to the healthfulness of its climate. One early published report claimed that "this country is blessed with a pure air and a prolific soil equal to any of our North American colonies."[37] As to why Spain had done so little with Florida in two centuries of possession, the answer lay in a crude, but popular stereotype: "the Spanish are too lazy."[38] Admitting we "know but very little of the country," one writer optimistically, if somewhat illogically, added that once Florida was "in the power of an active and industrious people ... it may possibly be found much better than we expected."[39]

More was at stake in Florida than merely the success or failure of a small colony. From the start, Florida also had a political meaning. The supporters of the government depicted Florida as a valuable acquisition that secured a peaceful and prosperous future. The author of one such laudatory account offered "thanks to the prudence of that wise administration which has given & secured such an Empire to Great Britain."[40] The government's political opponents, on the other hand, sought to use Florida as an issue to embarrass and ridicule the ministry. As soon as news of the terms of the peace treaty, including the trade of Cuba for Florida, were presented to Parliament, critics derided Florida as "a barren and uncultivated land, like Bagshot-Heath" or as "a barren inhospitable Desert."[41] Another opposition writer suggested speciously that Florida's extensive peat-bogs might furnish fuel to warm the bedchambers of West Indian planters during the severe Caribbean winters. Desperate for any and all good news about the colony, a pro-government editor printed the suggestion before the hoax was revealed.[42] That even the basic facts of Florida's landscape could be so hotly contested is evidence of how little was actually known of the colony at the time of its acquisition.

Like a rare plant, Florida had to be described and classified before its true character could be known. The same methods and taxonomies practiced at Kew could be used to "name" and impose order on far larger parts of the empire. The language of science and techniques of botany offered a way of narrating and describing the territories that Britain had acquired in the Seven Years' War. The case of Florida illustrates the close ties between science and imperialism. Not only were imperial officials, like Governor Grant, called on to serve the interests of science, but conversely scientists could put on the robes of empire. John Ellis, a noted botanist, was appointed London-based agent for the new colony of West Florida. In gratitude for this sinecure—a job that required little of his time and was, in effect, a scientific subsidy—Ellis promised the Board of Trade that "all the pay I demand from the Province is to be in rare plants and seeds for the Royal Garden at Kew."[43]

In fact, the roots of science and empire were so closely linked in this era as to be almost inseparable. In 1763, Archibald Menzies, assistant gardener at the Royal Botanic Garden in Edinburgh, yet another Bute project, published a brief essay in which he proposed that the new colony of British Florida be peopled with Greek settlers. In keeping with contemporary theories of the correlation between climates and cultures, Menzies suggested the "Greeks of the Levant," whom he described as a "frugal and industrious people, used to a hot climate, [and] familiar with the cultivation of exotic products," be transplanted to Florida.[44] The Greeks, Orthodox Christians who for colonization purposes could be considered "Protestants," would, it was supposed, readily exchange Turkish despotism for British liberty. For Britons infatuated with classicism, the prospect of becoming the patrons of the Greeks flattered notions of empire and national progress. "If this scheme was to succeed," one of the colony's promoters wrote Governor Grant, "you can guess how much it would raise the reputation of your government in becoming an asylum for Athenians, Spartans & the other fathers of civil and military perfection."[45]

The earliest firsthand account of Florida to reach a British public hungry for reliable news of the colony was published in 1766. Its author was Doctor William Stork, a physician and botanist, who visited St. Augustine briefly in 1765.[46] Stork's pamphlet employed the credibility of objective science to validate his celebratory description of the colony and "its future importance to trade and commerce." His book extolled Florida in practically Edenic terms. The reputed heat of the colony, for example, was "mitigated by a never failing sea-breeze." Stork described the colony as ideally suited for the profitable production of rice, cotton, silk, sugar, indigo, and wine. For British readers unfamiliar with the Native American word *swamp*, a type of land that Florida contained in abundance, Stork offered this definition: "a tract of land that is sound and good, but by lying low is covered with water."[47]

Stork's timely *Account of East Florida* whetted the appetite of a public eager for positive reports of Florida's economic potential, and its publication vastly increased interest in the colony. "Doctor Stork's Pamphlet has sett us all Florida mad," one new investor wrote Governor Grant in May 1766.[48] In June, another Florida "adventurer" acknowledged that "Stork's book has done a good deal" to encourage investment in the colony.[49] In promoting Florida, Stork was also promoting himself. In July, he sent a copy of the book to Grant in St. Augustine, boasting that "I have had the satisfaction to see this production of mine well received by the King, the ministers and the public in general, and may say without vanity [that] it is owing to this account . . . that . . . Florida is no longer looked upon as a barren useless heap of sand and a burden to the Nation. At my arrival in England prejudices ran so high against the . . . [colony] that it was actually proposed as a saving to the nation and a mortification to L[ord] Bute [that Florida be abandoned]."[50]

The rising interest in East Florida can be traced in the number of petitions for land grants in the colony that were received by the Privy Council. In 1764 and 1765, only twenty petitions for East Florida lands were submitted. In 1766, the year that Stork's book first appeared, seventy-one petitions were made. In the following year, the peak of the East Florida "bubble," this figure leaped to 122 petitions. By 1770, the Privy Council had received 199 petitions asking for almost three million acres of East Florida lands, over four times the number of petitions and fourteen times the amount of land as were received for other colonies (West Florida and Quebec) that had been organized by the Proclamation of 1763.[51]

As Grant's letter to Bute noted, an unlikely participant in this project of scientific imperialism was John Bartram, a Philadelphia Quaker and self-taught naturalist, one year older than the century. Interestingly, Bartram himself claimed that his science was innocent of any imperial ambitions. In a 1764 letter to Peter Collinson, an English friend, he wrote, "pray say no more about our great British empire . . . I make no difference who got it, if I could but travel safely in it."[52] Yet in 1765, Collinson's "repeated solicitations" moved King George to appoint Bartram to the newly created post of "King's Botanist to the Floridas" with a salary of £50 per year, Bartram declined neither the title nor the money.[53]

Bartram, accompanied by his son William, arrived in St. Augustine in November 1765. His commission as "Royal Botanist" charged him "to make observations on the soil, [and] the country . . . to gather specimens of plants, fossils, ores, etc."[54] In an early example of government-sponsored scientific exploration, three years before Cook's departure for the Pacific, Grant wrote that "I have given the Botanists a Boat, provisions, and hunters to attend them up the River St. Johns . . . they expect to make great discoveries and promised to go up the river as far as they possibly could go."[55] In 1766, an abridged and unauthorized version of Bartram's journal of the expedition was published in London, as part of the second edition of Stork's pamphlet.[56]

The seeds Bartram so carefully packaged in Florida eventually germinated in the greenhouses at Kew. In August 1766, Collinson wrote Bartram that "the Florida seeds and fossils came safe & were delivered to the king who is pleased with them." He also reported that the "Stuartia," a plant discovered by Mark Catesby in 1742 and named for Bute, "flowered for the first time in the Princess of Wales's garden at Kew which is the Paradise of our world where all plants are found that money or interest can procure."[57] A few years later, Bartram sent a cask containing lily pad roots and "two large Bull frogs," which he hoped would "be a great innocent curiosity for ye king."[58]

From the perspective of the colonial periphery, science offered a way to order and "classify" Florida for a metropolitan audience. Like an exotic plant, Florida was a new specimen to be added to the imperial collection, a new "paradise" whose plants, rivers, and projected towns could be named after wealthy and powerful Britons. In 1768, William Knox, East Florida's agent and the secretary to the Board of Trade, suggested to Grant that he name a town in the colony after Lord Hillsborough, the newly appointed secretary of state for the colonies. By doing so, Knox wrote, "you would both flatter his Lordship and engage his patronage not only to that town but to the province." "He is exceedingly fond of presents from America," the savvy agent also advised Grant; "any bird or animal that is curious or any of the products of the country would be a grateful offering."[59]

The Nature of Empire

Not all observers found the activities in Kew and Florida so pleasant or beguiling. Horace Walpole, for example, described Chamber's exotic constructions as "I dare say like the buildings of no country." Of "the great Pagoda," which reputedly cost £12,000 to construct, he noted derisively that it "sees neither London nor the Thames nor has one room in it."[60] Stork's Florida productions also attracted ridicule. Detractors asserted that a map Stork printed to accompany his book, "might as well serve for any part of Germany as for East Florida." Those who actually traveled to Florida soon discovered that Stork's "fable" contained "a good deal of the superlative" and also some calculated silences. Among other noted deficiencies, Stork's list of Florida fauna "omitted the insects of the country, particularly the muskito."[61]

Political motives engendered other objections to Kew and Florida. For Bute's enemies, his taste in architecture and his botanical ambitions were in perfect and perfidious harmony with his politics. To many of the government's opponents, the very idea that Britain had become an empire posed a threat to traditional "English" liberties and identities.[62] Those schooled in classical history quickly noted that Rome's attainment of empire closely preceded the death of the Roman Republic. Even while many Britons and British Americans celebrated the rise of the British Empire, others were already anticipating its fall, or at least were counting its costs. To these men, as Anthony Pagden notes, "the most unsettling danger posed by imperial expansion was the possibility that over reaching might finally result in the collapse of the metropolis's own political and moral culture."[63]

Before the 1760s, Britons had happily contrasted their "oceanic" empire, based on migration and trade, with the territorial empires of antiquity and of contemporary Spanish America, which were founded on conquest and tribute. But as Linda Colley notes, "the spoils of the Seven Years War made it far more difficult to sustain this flattering contrast . . . Now that Britain's empire no longer pivoted on commerce but was sustained by force of arms like earlier empires, what guarantee could there be that it would not in turn decay and destroy the mother country in the process?" Such worries, Colley concludes, "nagged at a whole generation of British intellectuals, most profitably Edward Gibbon who made the decision to chronicle the decline and fall of the Roman Empire just one year after the signing of the Treaty of Paris."[64]

In the same year, a more optimistic Briton saw Florida as the key to maintaining both Britain's new empire and traditional English liberties. In an anonymous pamphlet, written in 1763 but not published until nine years later, the author advocated that British Florida be made a colony in which "Negroes . . . are to be lifted up into an equality with Englishmen themselves." Accepting the common correlation between peoples and climates, which had also framed Menzies's "Greek Scheme," the writer thought it "Prudent to stock, in the farming dialect, the new acquisition of Florida with such a breed of men from whose industry we must reasonably expect the largest return." Africans, the author concluded, were best suited to settle Florida, yet the precarious position of the colony, threatened by Indians in the interior and Spaniards upon the coast, made it unlikely that individuals would hazard their valuable slave property there. Only free men, the writer argued, would render the colony secure by their willingness to defend it against attack. Thus, according to his plan, the government should purchase Africans via the slave trade and give them both land and freedom in Florida. Following the emerging logic of political economy (Adam

Smith was also at work upon *The Wealth of Nations* in these years) that saw free workers as more productive than bound, the author expected that these free black colonists would thrive and multiply. Ultimately, he wrote, the black "Englishmen" of Florida would, by virtue of their superior economic and biological productivity, displace slave laborers in the neighboring British colonies to the north and in the Caribbean. In a final utopian flourish, the pamphlet's author posited that this triumphant process might continue until the entire Western Hemisphere and even Africa itself were thus "colonized." The author grandly concluded by weaving together imperial ambition, economic desires, and anti-slavery hopes:

> wisely availing herself of both moral and physical causes, no longer weakened and disgraced by slavery or restrained by climate, but rising upon the sure foundations of equality and justice, might Great Britain, aggrandized and invigorated at home, stretch forth, with irresistible power, her sable arm through every region of the torrid zone, and (to complete the climax) the whole world become at last civilized, and an universal language be obtained by the same means as we should lift Great Britain into the seat of unenvied and unlimited dominion.
>
> Every other empire has weakened by extending; Britain alone has taken root at every step, and has constantly received back the strength and nourishment which it gave. It has not subdued but generated Nations.[65]

Britons commonly contrasted the blessings of the English constitution and English liberty with conditions in foreign nations. Most often, comparisons were made with arch-rival France, but the starkest contrast with the British way of life was more ably represented by references to the "Asiatic," "Turkish," or "Oriental" despotism of more distant and alien regions. Given such negative connotations, one historian notes, the attainment of empire in India "aroused anguished misgivings, often vented in attacks on the 'Nabobs,' who sullied Britain's name with their cruelty, as well as threatening to introduce tendencies to despotism and an influx of luxury."[66] Seen in this light, the new king's (or his Scottish advisor's) taste in architecture as expressed at Kew seemed ill-considered at the very least. Critics of the government were quick to see a troubling linkage between a king who "sports With Chinese gardens" and his suspected desire for "Chinese courts."[67] Similarly, a member of the House of Lords declared that "the riches of Asia have been poured in upon us . . . and have brought with them not only Asiatic Luxury, but I fear Asiatic principles of government."[68]

   The orientalizing effect of empire could also be seen in the horrific outcome of Menzies's proposal that Florida be colonized with Greeks. In 1767 Doctor Andrew Turnbull, with the assistance of a £2,000 government subsidy and the loan of a royal navy sloop, traveled to the Mediterranean and persuaded fifteen hundred "Greeks," the majority of whom were actually inhabitants of the British-controlled island of Minorca, to migrate to East Florida and establish the settlement of New Smyrna. In August 1768, after a long ocean voyage, the transplanted "Greeks" were set ashore at "Musquitto Inlet," forty miles south of St. Augustine. Whatever they may have been led to expect about their life in Florida, the settlers were not prepared for what they found. The site Turnbull had chosen for New Smyrna was an inhospitable sand bar overgrown with myrtle bushes and palmetto palms. On one side lay the sea, on the other, a trackless swamp. Everything, from the most basic shelter, to the gardens upon whose produce they would depend for food, to the indigo fields in which they were bound to labor, would have to be hacked from the dense jungle. Confronting the enormity of their situation, it seemed to many that they were being asked to dig their own graves. Within a few weeks of their arrival, frightened and desperate, they rose in revolt. Ultimately, British troops and a royal navy ship were needed to restore order at New Smyrna, after which two of the leaders of the "mutiny" were hanged. The remaining settlers were forcibly returned to their work. Just as they had feared, within one year half of them were dead. With little hope, the survivors struggled on wretchedly.[69] An eighteenth-century account of the episode noted bitterly that rather than remove the "Greeks" from Turkish despotism to British liberty, New Smyrna more closely resembled "a transplant[ed] Bashawship from the Levant."[70]

   Like Menzies and Stork, Turnbull, the "master" of new Smyrna, considered himself a botanist. Like them, as well as like Grant, Bute, and many others involved in East Florida's history, Turnbull was a Scot. The prominence of Scots in the offices of the new regime was bitterly noted in the English opposition press. The appointment of so many "foreigners" to positions of power and profit made the empire, and even the term *British* seem odious to many suspicious Englishmen. Just as Bute was accused of promoting his own countrymen into office in preference to Englishmen, and of planting "Scottish" political ideas into the mind of the young king, so was he also charged with despoiling the English landscape with alien building styles and encouraging exotic plants to take root in English soil. To the anti-imperialists, the nefarious proceedings at Kew came to symbolize and epitomize the corrupting foreign influences they saw at work in the government of George III. In one mock-heroic poem, the satirist cleverly inverted the message of the imperial garden and its political messages and pretension:

> Let Barbaric glories feast his eyes,
> August Pagodas round his palace rise,
> and finish'd Richmond open to his view,
> a work to wonder at, perhaps a Kew
>
> Nor rest we here, but, at our magic call,
> Monkies shall climb our trees, and lizards crawl;
> Huge dogs of Tibet bark in yonder grove,
> Here parrots prate, there cats make cruel love;
> in some fair land will we turn to grass
> (with the Queen's leave) her elephant and her ass . . .
>
> His royal mind when'er, from state withdrawn,
> he treads the velvet of his Richmond lawn;
> These shall prolong his Asiatic dream,
> Tho' Europe's balance trembles on its beam.

Ultimately, the author prophesied, "Our sons some slave of greatness may behold, cast in the genuine Asiatic mould."[71]

The pagoda at Kew was so well-known it became a symbolic shorthand for this anti-imperial and xenophobic strain of English political thought. In political cartoons of the period, the pagoda often appears in the background, without identification or comment, the artists apparently confident that their readers would not only recognize the building but also know what it was meant to represent.[72]

Bute's more determined critics were also suspicious of the botany being practiced at Kew. For the government's opponents, the "Exotic Garden" subverted the common view of the countryside as a nursery of the native English virtues of simplicity, independence, and self-reliance. Instead, the gardens at Kew were a seedbed for alien species brought from the far corners of the world for dissemination throughout the kingdom. Like all compelling conspiracy theories, all the pieces fit together. In his 1765 pamphlet, *Petition of an Englishman,* John Horne Tooke compared Bute to one of his rare plants: "they call you an upstart, and say you sprung up like a mushroom . . . [and] indeed it is true that you were reared in a HOT-BED." Later, Tooke facetiously advised place-hunting Scots to "Fly to Bute's Hot-House . . . there find the fost'ring Dung, and sheltering glass, that make Scotch cucumbers for melons pass."[73]

Perhaps the pinnacle (or nadir) of these attacks was reached in the first volume of the *Political Register*, an anti-government periodical published in 1767.[74] In this case, in a manner similar to the contemporaneous attacks on the French royal family, sexual deviance and immorality were added to the list of Bute's uncommon appetites in politics, plants, and building styles. On the frontispiece of the volume, a drawing depicts Bute as a centaur wearing plaid, of course, while behind him looms the pagoda. Around the image is the bizarre motto "The Centaur not Fabulous." The drawing is explained on the following page. "Of centaurs," the explanation began, "the most celebrated was Chiron. He was a great botanist and our bitter herb centaury takes its name from him. He thought all herbs bitter; because being very amorous, he could not find any amongst them, one that could abate the fever in his blood."[75] This reference was to the alleged sexual relationship between Bute and the king's mother, Princess Augusta, an allegation so infamous that it, like the pagoda, could be referenced in shorthand in political cartoons of the day. The same volume also offered readers a large foldout drawing entitled "A View of Lord Bute's Erections at Kew," the chief feature of which was a secret gate to allow Bute to go from his office to the house of the Princess undetected. Most brutally of all, among the "vulgar public" of Georgian London, the nickname for the pagoda at Kew was "Bute's Erection."[76]

Given the extraordinary venom and volume of the anti-Bute literature in the 1760s, perhaps we should not be surprised that attacks on Bute's role in negotiating the Treaty of Paris, including the exchange of Cuba for Florida, could segue easily to his efforts to redesign the grounds and buildings at Kew, to his "favourite studdy" of botany, or to his establishment of the royal botanical garden. But the contested meanings of Florida and Kew in the 1760s reveal more than merely the lengths to which Bute's critics and bad poetry could go. They also reveal a fierce contest about the idea of empire and national identity and whether it was English or British. If the creation of the gardens at Kew in the 1760s can be seen as evidence of how some Britons were interested in imagining, displaying, and ordering the world—and were simultaneously constructing a new role for Britain to play within it—the venomous and voluminous attacks upon Kew reveal how others saw the emergent ideas of empire and science as a threat to "traditional" English liberties and virtues. Likewise, the prospects and possibilities of Florida and other areas of the imperial enterprise drew similarly contested meanings and hopes. Some Britons eagerly read published accounts of Florida, sought information on or samples of rare tropical plants from there, and viewed the colony as an opportunity to acquire wealth and knowledge, as well as personal and national power. For others, however, the exotic garden at Kew, the "barren . . . Desert" of Florida, and the entire concept of empire were alien and dangerous things that were better left alone.

The strange career of Governor Grant's seeds and the conjoined histories of Florida and Kew allow us to view the eighteenth-century British Empire as a site of ideological and cultural construct and contest rather than a concrete political reality. The British Empire of the 1760s was created by and for ordinary people through consumption and print culture and was not merely a program determined by government elites behind closed doors. Ideas of empire were produced on the colonial peripheries of the Americas, Africa, and Asia and consumed in the British metropolis, as much as the reverse. To see the world in this way, as a story of individual action as well as a story of imperial structures, may be to turn Charles Andrews upon his head (or perhaps in his grave); but it also may be a way of returning him to the center of the historiographical debate. Indeed, upon review, Andrew's claim that after 1763 a spirit of "imperialism emerged to perplex the souls of British statesmen" might be, with its emphasis on sentiments and emotions ("souls") that is upon culture, be taken as a prophetic call for the return of imperial history. Most importantly, as Grant's three boxes of seeds traveled across the ocean and connected, literally as well as symbolically, the two shores of the British Atlantic, they carried the germ of the ideas and technologies that would soon transform the world.

CHAPTER TWELVE

A Visual Empire

Seeing the British Atlantic World from a Global British Perspective

John E. Crowley

In the second half of the eighteenth century, British visual culture created a global landscape of the homelands and the empire. Before the 1750s, people in Britain and the colonies showed little need to know how the colonies actually looked.[1] From the 1750s onward, a multitude of colonial scenes crucially reoriented British landscape art from the idealized to the topographic. Historians have neglected this development. Several books lavishly illustrate the history of the British Empire, but none of them considers the empire's being illustrated as a historical problem.[2] To most historians pictures provide useful supplementary detail, particularly to hold the attention of nonprofessional audiences, but they lack the explicit signification of verbal texts. This prejudice has survived the linguistic turn in the human sciences. Historians especially distrust visual images that claim to represent how scenes in the past really looked— their topography. This essay focuses on such images, not because they show reality photographically—that we shall never know—but because actors in the past conscientiously claimed that they had such reality and convinced others to see the world accordingly.

A topographic impulse in later eighteenth-century British landscape art aided understanding of a rapidly enlarging world of British experience—of the British Isles themselves, of new and potential imperial domains, and of cosmopolitan travel more broadly.[3] J. G. A. Pocock has long pleaded for a British history that not only went beyond the British Isles, the "Atlantic archipelago" in Pocock-speak, but also considered how Britain itself was a cultural construction whose physical domain varied over time depending on its inhabitants' self-identities and political interactions.[4] This view of British history, which bears so aptly on political culture, also applies to visual culture from 1750 to 1820. During that period, landscape art enabled people throughout British realms to convince themselves that they understood the appearance of distant and/or previously unfamiliar lands. This visual identification aided the conceptualization of a rapidly expanding colonial world and legitimized questionable imperial projects, including the assimilation of Canada's French-Catholic population, peace-keeping between First Nations and European settlers in the trans-Appalachian West, regulation of an indirect empire in the East Indies, protection of slave societies in the West Indies, and the penal transportation of free-born Britons to New South Wales. This essay surveys the representation of imperial landscapes previously unseen by Britons, or not seen carefully enough in Scotland, Canada, Polynesia, India, Australia, the Caribbean, and the United States.

Britons' Picturesque Landscapes: From the Idealized to the Topographical

For most of the early modern period, landscape art had low prestige in European culture. Artists measured their professional status by commissions for historical and portrait paintings. The most frequent exceptions, as in so many things in aristocratic Europe, were in the seventeenth-century Netherlands, where landscape art was one among many genres commissioned by commercial social groups. The other exceptions were in seventeenth-century Italy. Claude Lorrain, Salvator Rosa, and Gaspard Poussin painted idealized landscapes as settings for Roman historical and mythological scenes. Their works created the picturesque ideal for landscape painting in the first half of the eighteenth century. Picturesque initially meant looking like Poussin's, Lorrain's, and Rosa's pictures, as characterized by deep panoramas, irregular lighting, rugged landforms, and an atmosphere of cultural distance.[5] Aristocratic

Britons on the Grand Tour bought thousands of imitations, as reminders of landscapes and monuments they had seen. As John Locke explained in his *Thoughts Concerning Education*, pictures described unfamiliar places better than words: "When he [a young gentleman] can Write well, and quick, I think it may be convenient, not only to continue the exercise of his Hand in Writing, but also to improve the use of it farther in *Drawing*, a thing very useful to a Gentleman in several occasions; but especially if he travel, as that which helps a Man often to express, in a few Lines well put together, what a whole Sheet of Paper in Writing, would not be able to represent, and make intelligible."[6]

British professional artists considered a stay in Italy as essential for later commissions, which depended on familiarity with Italianate styles. Once back home, they made Britain look as much as possible like the Roman Compagna in the backgrounds to portraits, historical paintings, and the occasional landscape. Topographic pictures of the British landscape, ones that recognizably represented a specific geographic scene, were limited to "prospects" of public buildings, towns, and noble estates.[7]

Until the second quarter of the eighteenth century, British artists seldom did landscapes. Foreign artists working in metropolitan Britain produced most of the country's seventeenth- and early eighteenth-century landscapes. Dutch and Flemish artists painting in England in the seventeenth century inevitably brought some of their culture's rich *landschap* tradition with them. Anthony Van Dyck drew some watercolors of the English countryside, and his English portraits often have recognizable English scenes in their background, as do those of Peter Paul Rubens. Netherlandish artists, such as Wenceslaus Hollar and Alexander Kierinx, produced most of England's topographies in the mid-seventeenth century. When topographic prospects of aristocratic country houses became frequent after the Restoration, Dutch artists, notably Jan Siberechts and Leonard Knyff, usually painted them.[8] Knyff made the drawings for the extensive collection of country house prospects, *Britannia Illustrata* (1707). The commercial success of *Britannia Illustrata* encouraged a series of imitators over the next half century, under the title *Vitruvius Britannicus*. The popularity of the prospect also encouraged a few British artists in the 1730s and 1740s, notably George Lambert, to produce topographic landscapes of British agricultural scenes. These took a country house for granted rather than feature it, especially as English landscape gardening became a distinctive style. In the mid-1740s Thomas Smith and William Oram began publishing engravings that applied Italianate picturesque style to specific locales in Britain, notably in Yorkshire and Derbyshire. British landscapes found further representation as portrait artists, such as Arthur Devis, Edward Haytley, and Thomas Gainsborough, began to set conversation pieces in naturalistic countrysides conforming to the designs of William Kent and Capability Brown.[9] Gainsborough initially wanted to be a landscape painter and took Ruisdael as his inspiration. In 1748 he left London for a decade's painting in Suffolk, but he then moved to Bath where commissions were more forthcoming, even if mostly for portraits. He continued to paint landscapes, but they tended increasingly toward a classical style. He always dissociated himself from topographic painting. Similarly, most of his professional contemporaries painting landscapes, preeminently Richard Wilson, worked in a classically Italianate style, sometimes of British scenes, more often of Italian.[10]

Canaletto's celebrated stay in Britain from 1746 to 1755 narrowed the distinction between Italianate and topographic styles. His paintings and engravings of British scenes produced a shock of recognition among British viewers. They had been there and seen it themselves. The temptations posed by Canaletto's success compelled Joshua Reynolds to explain the subordination of landscape to history painting in the fourth of his *Discourses on Art*. Painting, he argued, was a "liberal art" when it involved intensive "mental labour" in producing and viewing works. The Roman school of art required such ennobling "exertion of mind": their paintings' "perfect form is produced by leaving out particularities, and retaining only general ideas." Shamelessly, the Venetian, Flemish, and Dutch schools "all profess to depart from the great purposes of painting, and catch at applause by inferior qualities." Reynolds readily conceded that the Venetians "accomplished perfectly the thing they attempted. But as mere elegance is their principal object, as they seem more willing to dazzle than to affect, it can be no injury to them to suppose that their practice is useful only to its proper end." Reynolds then mocked the Dutch for their visual interest in themselves: "The painters of the Dutch school have still more locality. With them a history-piece is properly a portrait of themselves; whether they describe the inside or outside of their houses, we have their own people engaged in their own peculiar occupations; working, or drinking, playing, or fighting. The circumstances that enter into a picture of this kind, are so far from being a general view of human life, that they exhibit all the minute particularities of a nation differing in several respects from the rest of mankind."[11] Reynolds's snobbish theories marked just how innovative a global British landscape would be. London was exotic, "ornamental" in Reynolds's language, for Canaletto;

Londoners themselves would have to go further afield to see pictures in the landscape.

Before long it would be fashionable to find landscapes in Britain itself that truly looked picturesque when observed with the appropriate sensitivity. Beginning in 1768, Reverend William Gilpin published a series of enormously popular guidebooks leading people to the exact spots where they could observe picturesque scenery in Britain: along the Wye River, in the hills of South Wales, and among the mountains and lakes of Cumberland and Westmoreland counties.[12] He urged that people travel with "a new object of pursuit, that of not barely examining the face of a country; but of examining it by the rules of picturesque beauty: that of not merely describing; but of adapting the descriptions of natural scenery to the principles of artificial landscape; and of opening the source of those pleasures, which are derived from the comparison." Topographic art became a respectable, even expectable, activity for British gentlemen and ladies in the second half of the eighteenth century, especially when they traveled to remote places. Refinement required drawing skills, among them the ability to represent landscape topographically.[13]

If British artists seldom represented the scenery and peoples of England, Ireland, Scotland, and Wales topographically before the middle of the eighteenth century, they had even less reason to do so for the colonies. Prior to the Seven Years' War, British public discourse referred infrequently to colonies overseas as part of an "empire" in the sense of a coherent set of territories governed from Great Britain. Coastal settlements of British subjects—commercial "plantations" and "colonies"—composed most of Britain's fixed interests overseas. Over four thousand publications in English before 1800 had the words "colony" or "plantation" (or their cognates) in their titles. Only 124 had the phrase "British empire," and only sixteen of them were published before 1763.[14] As Adam Smith reminded his readers at the conclusion of the *Wealth of Nations* (1776), Britain's empire "has hitherto existed in imagination only"; it had "been not an empire, but the project of an empire." Besides the Board of Trade, whose formal name was the Lords Commissioners of Trade and Plantations and whose primary focus remained on overseas commerce, there was no specialized bureaucracy for the colonies' administration. The Board's frustrating lack of direct power in the colonies made it a hothouse for imperial impulses. The paragon here was Lord Halifax, who as president of the Board (1748–61), lobbied unsuccessfully to have the Board directly rule the West Indies, with himself as a new secretary of state for the colonies. Instead the government continued to parcel out colonial administration as ad hoc subdivisions of more proximately metropolitan concerns of government: defense (the Admiralty), revenue and economic regulation (the Treasury), diplomacy (the Secretary of State for the Southern Department), and justice (the Privy Council). In times of war, the Royal Navy was critical to colonial defense, but such involvement was by definition transient, and few British regular troops served on permanent station overseas.[15]

Correspondingly, British artists lacked interest in representing how colonies in North America, the West Indies, or India, actually looked. Panoramic views of port cities were exceptions proving the rule that commerce, not territorial empire, mattered (Fig. 12.1). As Hugh Honour has lavishly shown in *The New Golden Land* and *The European Vision of America*, Europeans had a rich visual imagery of the Americas, but its authority did not depend on authenticity. Topographic scenes of American landscapes observed firsthand by artists such as John White in North Carolina in 1585, and Frans Post and Albert Eckhout in Brazil in the 1630s and 1640s, were very much exceptions to most early modern visual representations of worlds overseas, which drew effortlessly on imagination, allegory, and literary texts for their imagery.[16]

These exceptions show that European artistic traditions included topographic accuracy, which could have been directed at the colonies. It just was not

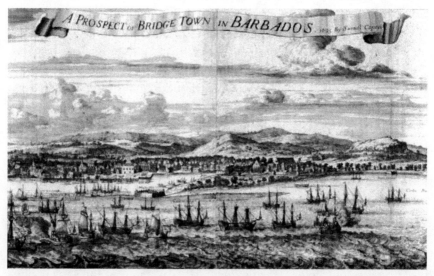

Fig. 12.1. Samuel Copen, *A Prospect of Bridge Town in Barbados* (London, 1695). Courtesy of the John Carter Brown Library at Brown University.

usual for most of the early modern period. The colonists themselves exerted no pressure for topographic representations; they had their portraits painted against stylized backgrounds of European landscapes.[17] But in the 1750s Britons began to develop a global landscape that visually linked colonial territories with metropolitan Britain. *Global* here means connected with each other over vast distances; *landscape* refers to the mental construction of a visually comprehended space. In the second half of the eighteenth century, landscape art increasingly integrated the Britain of the United Kingdom with the Britain of the empire in North America, the Caribbean, India, Australia, and strategic bases such as the Cape Colony. The formation of a global British landscape began as artists translated their first-hand images from the marchlands—watercolors, field etchings, and pencil-and-ink drawings—into paintings or engravings for wider consumption back in metropolitan Britain. The landscapes in question showed scenes of everyday experience, urban as well as rural, of human society as well as nature. Britons could visit the empire's realms imaginatively in landscape art, convinced that they would look that way if they went there themselves.

The Globalization of Britain's Atlantic World

This global perspective on the British Empire was new politically and economically, as well as visually. Before the Seven Years' War, British commercial and colonial interests in the Indian and Pacific Oceans were largely separate from those in the Atlantic. Beginning with that war these interests became global as activities in one oceanic sphere crucially affected the others. British strategy during the Seven Years' War called for attacks on Manila and Pondicherry as well as Quebec and Havana. Yet historiographic controversy about the relationship of British Atlantic and British Asian-Pacific interests has dealt with their relative importance and when that importance changed, rather than on their connections. P. J. Marshall has qualified Vincent T. Harlow's argument for a "shift to the East" with *The Founding of the Second British Empire, 1763–1793*, by observing that the West Indies remained the most important colonies for British trade until the early nineteenth century and that the economic importance of India to the British economy vastly exceeded that of China and the rest of the East.[18]

But such polarization in interpretation contradicts the intertwining of the empire's eastern and western parts. Most colonial American historians know that the Scottish historian William Robertson wrote a *History of America*, but how many know, or care if they do know, that he also wrote a history of India? American independence may have obstructed Robertson's plan to bring the story of Europe's American empires forward from the Spanish to the British, but it did not end his writing imperial history. In fact, at the conclusion of the Revolutionary War, with Edward Gibbon's encouragement, Robertson immediately began working on a *Historical Disquisition Concerning the Knowledge which the Ancients had of India; and of the Progress of Trade with that Country Prior to the Discovery of the Passage to It by the Cape of Good Hope* (1791). He concluded that the history of India should have entirely different implications for colonization from that of the Americas, and hoped "that if the account which I have given of the early and high civilization of India, and of the wonderful progress of its inhabitants in elegant arts and useful science, shall be received as just and well established, it may have some influence upon the behaviour of Europeans towards that people." Britons needed such influence because "in whatever quarter of the globe the people of Europe have acquired dominion, they have found the inhabitants not only in a state of society and improvement far inferior to their own, but different in their complexion, and in their habits of life." Precisely because such a reaction came so naturally to Europeans, Robertson cautioned against a repetition of the triumphalism to which they had succumbed so easily in dealing with the peoples of Africa and the Americas: "in the pride of their superiority, Europeans thought themselves entitled to reduce the natives of the former to slavery, and to exterminate those of the latter." He repudiated the tradition of European colonization in the Atlantic in order to urge a more enlightened, and thus humanitarian, imperialism in the East.[19]

Just as with Robertson's historiography, from the Seven Years' War on, British imperial officials increasingly moved back and forth between East and West, as can be illustrated by sketching a few careers. If any person's career exemplified the global expansion of Britain's empire out of the Atlantic world, it was Captain James Cook's. During the Seven Years' War, he took part in the attacks on Louisbourg and Quebec, and he made the crucial charts of the St. Lawrence for General James Wolfe's forces. After the war he surveyed and charted the south and west coasts of Newfoundland. British ships now regularly sailed through the Cabot Strait on their way to Quebec, and British fishing interests increasingly encroached on the western French Shore now that France's rights, sanctioned by the Treaty of Utrecht, had been renegotiated.

Cook's expertise, plus his status as a respected amateur astronomer, earned him command of the first British scientific expedition to the Pacific (co-sponsored by the Royal Society and the Admiralty) for observation from Tahiti of the solar transit of Venus in 1769. After the transit, he followed secret Admiralty orders and returned home westward at latitudes intended to find the Terra Australis. Along the way he charted New Zealand and surveyed two thousand miles of Australia's eastern coastline. The success of this voyage encouraged an even more ambitious expedition (1772–75) to explore the entire South Pacific for lands capable of colonization and/or peopled for commerce. None surfaced, however, besides the already discovered New Zealand and Australia. In July 1776, the Admiralty sent Cook on a third Pacific voyage, to look for the entrance to a northern oceanic passage between the Atlantic and the Pacific. Cook would be following up on the implications of the epic independent overland expedition (1770–72) from Hudson Bay to the Arctic Ocean by a Hudson's Bay Company ship's mate, Samuel Hearne. Hearne had determined the impossibility of a Northwest Passage through North America, but he appeared to have found an arctic but ice-free ocean linking the Atlantic and the Pacific.[20]

As Cook's career showed, the new global empire provided lots of horizontal mobility and second tries at success. Lord Cornwallis, for example, rather than ending his imperial career (which had begun with the foundation of the strategic base of Halifax, Nova Scotia, in 1749) with defeat at Yorktown, went on to global success. A few years later, as governor-general of India (1786–93), he codified British rule there and earned William Wilburforce's encomium for having "made the British name loved and revered" in India. Success in India led to his appointment as Viceroy of Ireland (1798–1801), where he crushed a French-sparked rebellion but then urged the parliamentary union of Great Britain and Ireland and also the civil emancipation of Roman Catholics.[21]

The Asian-Irish transfer of expertise, though in the other direction, also aided the career of a less well-known plenipotentiary of empire, Lord George Macartney. He had been chief secretary for Ireland (1769–72), governor of the Caribee Islands—Grenada, Tobago, and the Grenadines—(1775–79), and the first non-company governor of Madras (1780–86), before his gigantic, but unsuccessful, commercial embassy in 1792–93 to the Chinese imperial court. His last appointment was in 1796–98 as governor of Britain's new strategic colony at the Cape of Good Hope.[22]

The Cape Colony resulted directly from the Admiralty's pronounced interest since the 1780s in colonial development. Captain William Bligh, who had been sailing master on Cook's third voyage, had taken the *Bounty* to Tahiti in 1787 to gather breadfruit trees for transplantation to the West Indies as a new provisioning crop for the enslaved population. After his extraordinary trans-Pacific open-boat voyage to save his loyal crewmen, he went on the same mission again in 1792, this time successfully. He returned to the Pacific in 1805 as governor of New South Wales.[23]

The development of New South Wales illustrates on a continental scale how events in the British Atlantic world directly affected Britain's new global empire and vice versa. The Pacific colony also demonstrated the British government's new forthrightness in using naval and military authorities for colonial administration. The transportation of convicts changed from commerce with settler colonies to a strategy of imperial expansion based on military government and naval logistics. The chief alternative to Botany Bay as a penal colony was another of Cook's landings, Nootka Sound on Vancouver Island.[24]

In the generation after independence, the United States greatly expanded within North America, but the republic's interests also extended crucially from the Atlantic into the Pacific and Indian oceans. The first American ship to sail for China left deliberately on February 22, 1784, George Washington's birthday. In 1785 Elias Hasket Derby initiated a series of commercial voyages from the United States to non-Atlantic destinations by sending a ship to the Isle of France (present-day Mauritius) and then on to Canton. Soon thereafter he sent ships to the Philippines (Manila), Indonesia (Batavia), Myanmar (Rangoon), India (Calcutta and Bombay), and back to China and the Isle of France. These voyages made him the richest person in the United States.[25]

American trade to China depended critically on access to sea otter pelts from the Pacific Northwest. In anticipation of British claims to the Pacific Northwest based on Captain George Vancouver's exploratory voyage of 1792, Thomas Jefferson (aided by most of George Washington's cabinet) sponsored the American Philosophical Society's 1793 expedition by André Michaux "to find the shortest & most convenient route of communication between the U.S. & the Pacific ocean, within the temperate latitudes." Upon learning that France had sent Michaux as an agent to invade Spanish territories, Jefferson had him recalled, and the mission aborted. Jefferson expressed no further interest in a similar expedition until 1802, when he learned that Alexander Mackenzie, a North West Company agent, had crossed overland to the Pacific in the same year as the Michaux fiasco. Mackenzie's expedition entitled Britain to territorial claims from the Atlantic to the Pacific, but his disappointment in not finding a commercially viable route delayed publication of his journal until 1801. He had reached the Pacific by descending the Bella Coola River, but he now proposed that Britain capitalize on Cook's and Vancouver's discovery and explorations of the Columbia River. As soon as Jefferson read Mackenzie's journal, he immediately revived interest in a transcontinental expedition by the United States, to be led by Meriwether Lewis, to meet the British challenge.[26]

My favorite example of careers carrying Britons beyond the Atlantic world is James Macpherson, discoverer, translator, and forger of *Fingal* (1762), the great Scottish epic. He had discovered Ossian's work during expeditions to the Highlands and Hebrides in search of oral and scribal examples of traditional Gaelic poetry. In 1764, with the authenticity of *Fingal* under a cloud but having Lord Bute as his patron, Macpherson went to the new British colony of West Florida as secretary to Governor George Johnstone. After quarreling with his boss, Macpherson returned to London and wrote for the government; he refuted, for example, the Continental Congress's Declaration of Independence. In 1781, he became an agent for the Nawab of Arcot in his conflict with the East India Company, a job which gained him a fortune and enabled him to retire to his native Highlands and play the role of a traditional paternalistic laird.[27]

The precondition for these careers was the diplomatic outcome of the Seven Years' War, which had presented Great Britain with a global empire over non-British peoples. An empire of conquest now ruled Canada, Bengal, and the trans-Appalachian West of North America. In this context Sir William Blackstone, acting upon his self-imposed mandate for consistent codification, reversed nearly two centuries of constitutional development when including the old North American colonies in the same category:

> If an uninhabited country be discovered and planted by English subjects all the English laws are immediately there in force. For as the law is the birthright of every subject, so wherever they go they carry their laws with them. But in conquered or ceded countries, that have already laws of their own, the king may indeed alter and change those laws ... Our American plantations are principally of this latter sort, being obtained in the last century either by right of conquest and driving out the natives ... or by treaties. And therefore the common law of England as such has no allowances or authority there; they being no part of the mother country but distinct (though dependent) dominions.[28]

This empire's administration depended on professional standing armies stationed in the interior of North America, the Indian subcontinent, and before long, Australia. The regular army stationed increased numbers of troops in Ireland and in the Caribbean slave colonies, not to mention those sent to put down the rebellion in the thirteen colonies that became the United States. In the mid-1780s, the regular army had twelve infantry battalions in North America, eleven in the West Indies, nine on Gibraltar, twenty-one in Ireland, and nine in India.[29]

British military administration prevailed over these alien peoples; over the British subjects in the settler colonies along the Atlantic seaboard of North America it failed. That failure highlighted both the new authority assumed over territories overseas and the problems for British political culture with the application of military force to govern an empire. The cautionary example of Roman history warned about the dangers of despotism at home from excessive territorial expansion and the corrupting riches it brought home. (Edward Gibbon published the first volume of *The Decline and Fall of the Roman Empire* in 1776.)[30]

With the debacle of the American Revolution in mind, the British public needed assurance that imperial administrators' appreciation of local difference and respect for preconquest institutions would prevent costly counterinsurgency. The diplomatic success of the Indian superintendents in regulating trade and territorial disputes in the new British West between the Mississippi and the Appalachians had gone a long way toward keeping most of the peoples there loyal to Great Britain during the War of American Independence. The Quebec Act of 1774, with its withholding of representative government but its allowance for French civil law and toleration of the Roman Catholic Church, was a model for relativistic attitudes toward the needs among subject peoples for British institutions. In the 1770s and 1780s Parliament also declared its authority over the East India Company's rule in India. Parliament generally respected the company's long-standing relations with the Mughal Empire, but it had no reluctance in devising supervisory institutions and intervening directly to correct putative mismanagement and abuse of subject populations. Here, notoriously, Warren Hastings served as scapegoat to demonstrate the need for separation of commercial and political administration in India. The dreadful irony was that no one better appreciated than Hastings how Britain's assertion of sovereignty required expertise on India's indigenous cultures.[31] Rule in the new imperial territories depended on a new forthrightness with force, but the new empire's legitimacy at home depended on the political nation's confidence that government would get empire right this time.

Britain's Global Landscape

The representation of a benign imperial landscape compensated for the forthrightness of its conquest and the standing armies that remained. As Thomas Daniell explained in his account of *A Picturesque Voyage to India by Way of China* (1810), Britons' recent artistic interest in exotic landscapes marked their now benign interests abroad: "The passion for discovery, originally kindled by the thirst for gold, was exalted to a higher and nobler aim than commercial speculations . . . The shores of Asia have been invaded by a race of students with no rapacity but for lettered relics: by naturalists, whose cruelty extends not to one human inhabitant; by philosophers' extirpations of error, and the diffusion of truth. It remains for the artist to claim his part in these guiltless spoliations, and to transport to Europe the picturesque beauties of those favoured regions."[32] After midcentury, vast lands of global extent and diversity presented themselves for an imperial landscape. This landscape included the Scottish Highlands in the aftermath of the Stuart Rebellion as well as Canada and Bengal after 1763. In this more broadly defined British Empire from the 1750s on, British topographic and genre art became worldwide in scope. This new topographic art closely integrated imperial and artistic interests, Daniell's "guiltless spoliations."

Because firsthand observations had particular authority, army and naval officers played crucial early roles in this representation; their presence defined the empire of conquest. Many of them had training in landscape drawing in watercolor, ink, and pencil from the fraternal dynasty of Paul and Thomas Sandby at the Royal Military Academy at Woolwich. The nexus of training by the Sandbys, who wholeheartedly embraced the picturesque aesthetic of British landscape drawing, helped standardize the representation of the new British realms overseas. This standardization, in turn, made it easier for stay-at-homes to understand visual reports from remote realms.[33] Britain's visual empire began in one of its European marchlands, the Scottish Highlands, where the crucial figure in British topographic art, Paul Sandby, arrived in 1746 as a draftsman for the Board of Ordnance's survey of the region. The Board intended to improve geographic intelligence in case of subsequent rebellions. While there, Sandby learned to etch on the spot, and during his five-year stay he produced several series of Scottish prints, mostly of landscapes around Edinburgh and of rural genre subjects.[34] In Edinburgh, Sandby met another promising artist, Robert Adam, whose father had worked for the Board of Ordnance, designing the forts that had proved so ineffective in suppressing the rebellion of 1745. Sandby took Robert Adam and Adam's brother-in-law, John Clerk, on trips into the countryside to learn landscape drawing. Adam in turn introduced Sandby to Edinburgh society and likely patrons for his work.[35]

Both Adam and Clerk remained amateur painters, and they stimulated interest among Scots in firsthand renderings of their landscape. David Allan, the crucial artist for the development of Scottish genre painting, developed his career in this atmosphere, having trained in Italy during the 1770s. Paul Sandby had printed Allan's *Sketches of the Roman Carnival*, and Allan was keen to try Sandby's new aquatint process on Scottish subjects. He decided to illustrate Allan Ramsay's classic Scottish pastoral, *The Gentle Shepherd*, with a series of prints based on close observation of Highland society. Allan then claimed authority to pronounce on the poet's accurate portrayal of Scottish rural life: "I have studied the same characters on the same spot, and I find that he has drawn faithfully and with taste from Nature. This likewise, has been my model of imitation, and while I attempted in these sketches to express the idea of the poet, I have endeavoured to preserve the costume as nearly as possible by as exact delineation of such scenes and persons as he actually had in his eye."[36]

Nostalgia for a disappearing Celtic culture gripped South Britons as well. In 1771 Thomas Pennant, the noted zoologist, published the first extensively illustrated book of travels in Scotland, based on his tour around most of the coast in 1769. It contained twenty-nine illustrations, mostly of castles in dramatic settings, with a few waterfalls and lochs. The book's success encouraged Pennant to take another Scottish tour in 1772, this time beyond the Highlands to the Hebrides, and then to illustrate his published account with prints of genre scenes previously known only from verbal descriptions, such as the interiors of blackhouses. (His servant-artist, Moses Griffith, drew the scenes.) Samuel Johnson greatly admired Pennant's work, and pronounced him "the best traveller I ever read."[37]

Overseas, the visual creation of a global British landscape began in Canada. During the Seven Years' War officer-artists in the invading forces took their leisure by drawing scenes along the way of their campaigns. Richard Short, a purser on board one of the vessels in Wolfe's expedition to take Quebec, sketched a series of landscapes in Halifax and Quebec with both genre and imperial referents. In Halifax he sketched the Parade with troops drilling, but in the same scene he also included grocers selling vegetables out of their shop windows, making the town familiarly British. Noting that his drawings were "taken on the Spot, at the command of Vice Admiral Saunders," Short had them engraved and published in London and dedicated to Lord Halifax. Captain Hervey Smith, adjutant to General James Wolfe, sketched a French settlement on the Miramichi, so that it too combined the picturesque and the military: a detachment of British troops, with bayonets sharply silhouetted, descends on a hamlet set in a vast wooded valley (Fig. 12.2). Paul Sandby etched it for publication, first in 1760 as one of *Six Views of the Most Remarkable Places of the Gulf and River St. Lawrence* (dedicated to the Earl of Chatham), and in 1768 as part of the twenty-eight *Scenographia Americana*. (The six views were Quebec, Montmorency Falls, Île Percé, Gaspé Bay, the Miramichi River, and Cap Rouge.) Similarly, Thomas Davies, as a young Royal Artillery officer recently trained in landscape drawing at the Royal Military Academy, made drawings at Halifax and along the Saint John River during the British army's campaign against Louisbourg and destruction of Acadian settlements in 1757–58. About 1768 he published *Six Views of North American Waterfalls* (Niagara, three on the Casconchiagon or Little Seneca's River on Lake Ontario, the Passaic in New Jersey, and the Cohoes on the Mohawk River), dedicated to his former commander Sir Jeffrey Amherst. He returned to Canada in 1786, now a lieutenant colonel, and again made a series of watercolors, this time of scenery around Quebec. Over more than three decades he painted a wide variety of scenes and places in northeastern North America, in New York and New Jersey as well as Nova Scotia and Quebec, of settlements, indigenous inhabitants, and woods and waterfalls. Along with Davies, many British artists memorialized Niagara Falls decades before Americans began to make it their iconic landscape in the early nineteenth century.[38] As Davies's career suggests, the permanent presence of the British military in Canada guaranteed that its landscape would continue to be recorded for people back home. After the Treaty of Paris in 1763 gave Britain virtually all of eastern North America, the Admiralty directed Joseph Frederick Wallet DesBarres, a military engineer trained at the Royal Military College, to produce a thorough coastal survey of mainland North America to parallel Cook's survey of Newfoundland. The monumental *Atlantic Neptune* (1770–81) resulted. DesBarres accompanied the lavish charts with aquatinted engravings of invitingly picturesque scenery along the new imperial coastline. Exposure to new British landscapes made them irresistible to draw topographically. In Upper Canada, Elizabeth Simcoe, wife of General John Graves Simcoe, the colony's first lieutenant governor, immediately recognized the picturesque potential of the colony's lakesides and began to sketch and paint hundreds of its scenes, including Niagara Falls.[39]

Fig. 12.2. Paul Sandby after Hervey Smith, "A View of Miramichi, a French Settlement in the Gulf of St. Laurence, Destroyed by Brigadier Murray," in *Scenographia Americana* (London, 1768). Courtesy of the John Carter Brown Library at Brown University.

Topographic landscapes of Britain's new lands also served the public's education. As already mentioned, the Admiralty sponsored or cosponsored Britain's most important scientific explorations in the last third of the eighteenth century. These expeditions always included artists to provide visual landscapes along with more strictly scientific data. Captain Cook commanded the most celebrated British scientific voyages in this period, and the artists aboard his ships—William Hodges, Sydney Parkinson, and John Webber—brought home the most influential illustrations of British exploration throughout the Pacific. All of them drew and painted on the spot, in response to an imperative for descriptive accuracy attributable to Sir Joseph Banks and the Royal Society. Historians now celebrate Parkinson for his ethnographic figures and portraits of Polynesians, but his initial responsibilities on Cook's first voyage were to record flora and fauna. He began drawing humans only after the death of the expedition's designated topographic artist, Alexander Buchan.[40]

For Cook's second voyage the Admiralty named William Hodges as topographic artist, an inspired choice. (Banks would have sent the court painter

Johann Zoffany, but he withdrew the Royal Society's support from the expedition when he found the accommodations too small.) Hodges showed extraordinary openness to new visual and cultural experiences, which he painted out-of-doors in oils, a radical departure from the European studio tradition.[41] The huge popularity of the previous two voyages' illustrated accounts made the art of Cook's third voyage a project in its own right, not just a means to scientific ends. In commenting on the choice of John Webber as the voyage's artist, Cook wrote: "To make the result of our voyage entertaining to the generality of readers, as well as instructive to the sailor and scholar, Mr. Webber was pitched upon, and engaged to embark with me, for the express purpose of supplying the unavoidable imperfections of written accounts, by enabling us to preserve and send home, such drawings of the most memorable scenes of our transactions, as could be executed by a professed and skilful artist." Webber used watercolor with apparent meticulousness to record the Polynesian and Northwest Coast peoples encountered by the expedition—their rituals, domestic life, and landscapes.[42]

Fresh from his success with the landscapes of Captain Cook's voyages, William Hodges went to India in 1780, the first British professional landscape painter to do so. He immediately recorded his intention to view the new imperial landscape with a fresh eye: "The clear blue cloudless sky, the polished white buildings, the bright sandy beach, the dark green sea, present a combination totally new to the eye of an Englishman, just arrived from London, who, accustomed to the sight of rolling masses of clouds floating in a damp atmosphere, cannot but contemplate the difference with delight, and the eye thus gratified, the mind assumes a gay and tranquil habit, analogous to the pleasing objects with which it is surrounded."[43] Once Hodges moved from Madras to Calcutta, Warren Hastings became his patron and traveled with him on the artistic tours that gave authority to his *Select Views in India Drawn on the Spot in the Years 1780, 1781, 1782 and 1783* (1785–88). Hodges encouraged Zoffany to come to India, where he too enjoyed Hastings' patronage. Zoffany made a fortune painting portraits and conversation pieces of both British and Indian subjects, but he also developed an interest in Indian landscape and genre subjects. His success in turn encouraged the uncle and nephew team of Thomas and William Daniell to undertake their decade-long trip (1784–94) to India. They began by selling engravings of scenes in Calcutta, but used these sales to fund a series of artistic expeditions across the subcontinent's interiors, many of them far in advance of the company's agents and armies. The breathtaking six-volume *Oriental Scenery* resulted, with 144 folio-sized colored engravings.

Australia's aspect as a penal colony held little visual interest for British book and print buyers, but they showed keen interest in the continent's natural history and landscape. Representations by officers and convicts circulated widely, both originals and engravings that illustrated published accounts of the voyages to New South Wales. These early renderings, notably by the convict-artist Thomas Watling, often presented New South Wales as parklands populated by amenable Aborigines. The military government of New South Wales made it a nexus of artists representing the new British landscape. William Westall, for example, after serving as an artist on Captain Matthew Flinder's circumnavigation of Australia, then traveled to India, China, Jamaica, and Madeira before heading to Ceylon.[44]

By the 1780s dozens of landscape artists traveled the British world in search of appropriately imperial landscapes. Westall looked forward to Ceylon as "a Country where I could scarcely fail of success: for the rich picturesque appearance of that Island, every part affording infinite variety, must produce many subjects to a painter extremely valuable. And as no painter has yet been there what I should acquire would be perfectly new, and probably interesting from the island being one of the richest in India and lately acquired." George Isham Parkyns, having recently illustrated *Monastic Remains and Ancient Castles in England and Wales*, left England in 1795 for the United States, with plans to publish "striking and interesting prospects in the United States." When this project failed, he went to Halifax where he made sketches of its settlement, for publication in London as engravings. By the time Samuel Daniell (William's younger brother) published *A Picturesque Illustration of the Scenery, Animals and Native Inhabitants of the Island of Ceylon* in 1808, the term *picturesque* was a descriptive redundancy about the imperial landscape.[45]

The globalization of the British landscape extended to the old North American and West Indian settlement and plantation colonies as well to the new ones of conquest. Though the West Indies were the most important part of Britain's commercial empire, before the Seven Years' War neither colonists nor imperial agents had shown much topographic interest in its landscape. Topographic and genre art of the British Caribbean developed in response to the conquest of new islands and to the nascent anti-slavery movement of the 1770s. Agostino Brunias's celebrated paintings of African-Caribbeans were part of an increased interest in British West Indian topographic and genre art in the 1770s. William

Young, governor of Dominica and later Tobago, was a patron of Brunias and himself painted numerous watercolors of Tobago's landscape. Thomas Hearne, one of the most important eighteenth-century British topographic artists, began his career in Antigua in the 1770s, with a commission from the governor, Sir Ralph Payne, for a series of large watercolors depicting the island's public and military buildings in landscape settings.[46] Edward Long's virulently racist *History of Jamaica* (1774) contained illustrations of scenic features such as waterfalls and hot springs. As the case of Long suggests, picturesque representations of slave societies served a propagandistic function for their defenders by making them more resistant to abolitionist condemnation. On his way to his fourth North American station in 1786, Thomas Davies stopped at Grenada, St. Vincent, and St. Christopher, where he drew scenes of presumably enslaved African-West Indians walking peacefully through the lush vegetation and playing on the shore of a seaside village. British artists made the Caribbean a place that people back home could imaginatively visit with pleasure, as scenic beauty and genre curiosity displaced the abominations of slavery.[47] The process culminated in the efforts of William Beckford, a planter and author of *A Descriptive Account of the Island of Jamaica . . . Chiefly Considered from a Picturesque Point of View* (1790), who directed George Robertson to produce a series of engravings of Jamaica in Claudian style (Fig. 12.3).[48]

Although no longer a part of the British Empire, the early United States was incorporated into this global British landscape before Americans created their own nationalistic landscape. As with the West Indies, the old British North American colonies had not aroused much visual curiosity among Britons. The less Britain's visual culture differentiated the colonists, the happier they were. Generic townscapes predominated among subjects for landscape art in the British North American colonies before the Revolution. They showed colonial ports as respectable European commercial towns, with handsome public buildings and prosperous waterfronts. Colonists could do topographic landscape art; they just did not have much interest in it. Artistically ambitious colonists wanted to make names for themselves in the prestigious genre of history painting. As patrons, colonists overwhelmingly favored portraits. These sometimes had landscapes as backgrounds, but their idealized compositional elements came from European theory and models.[49]

Landscapes of the old British North American colonies that became the United States first appeared frequently as engraved illustrations in the national magazines that started in the late 1780s. The *Columbian Magazine,* the *New*

Fig. 12.3. James Mason after George Robertson, *A View in the Island of Jamaica of the Spring-Head of Roaring River on the Estate of William Beckford, Esquire* (London, 1778). Courtesy of the John Carter Brown Library at Brown University.

York Magazine, and the *Massachusetts Magazine* took the *Gentleman's Magazine* as their model. Because the London publication regularly carried engraved views of landscapes and landmarks, so did its American imitators. None of the American artists contributing to these magazines could specialize in landscape art for his livelihood, but the frequency of such images indicates a keener interest among Americans in their scenery. They looked to British advice for understanding it: the *New York Magazine* reprinted Gilpin's *Observations on the River Wye* in its December 1793 issue.[50]

British artists—notably George Beck, William Birch, William Groombridge, John James Barralet, George Isham Parkyns, and William Winstanley—picked up on this interest and went to the United States in the mid-1790s. Most of them had exhibited at the Royal Academy and/or the Society of Artists, and their artistic careers specialized in landscape. These artists showed Americans the aesthetic interest of their landscape. Most of them remained in the United States; some of them returned to metropolitan Britain. George Isham Parkyns, for example, engraved the only published view of Mount Vernon made during Washington's lifetime, but he returned to London after his work in Halifax and then capped his career as Draughtsman to Their Royal Highnesses. Whichever course their careers took, they succeeded in the United States by continuing to work in the style of the global British landscape.[51]

Of the British expatriate artists who remained in the United States, William Birch was the most successful. In 1800 he published a series of twenty-eight *Views of Philadelphia,* the richest body of landscape art produced thus far in the old British North American colonies or their successor United States. He apparently had this project in mind as soon as he arrived in Philadelphia from London six years earlier. Birch already had experience with such a project: in 1791 he had published *Délices de la Grande Bretagne,* a series of thirty-eight engravings of English towns and countryside. In his work on Philadelphia, he undertook to portray an "opulent city, famous for its trade and commerce, crouded in its port, with vessels of its own producing, and visited by others from all parts of the world." Birch's Philadelphia strengthened its inhabitants' civic identity as living in a lively, handsome urban space.[52]

The success of British artists in America showed how powerful British landscape sensibilities had become in Anglo-American culture. People in the United States initially learned to understand their landscape visually from the examples of styles and subject matters being redefined in the context of an empire they had forsaken. The most distinguished and successful landscape artists in the early United States were expatriate Britons who happened to make part of their careers in the United States. They represented American scenes in local terms that they knew to be consistent with the British global landscape.

Empires, like nations, are imagined communities, not natural entities. The British Empire had to be constructed for understanding back home, and first-hand observations had particular authority in this process. British landscape art helped Britons to identify with a global empire in response to military, political, and economic events in metropolitan Britain and overseas: conquests in North America, Asia, the West Indies, and Africa; the consolidation of aristocratic rule throughout the British Isles; and the expansion of British commerce on a global scale. In a reversal of centuries of aesthetic theory, topographic art gained prestige over idealized styles. To know a place required pictures as well as words: artists should have seen what they represented, and then have created landscapes that viewers could imagine seeing themselves. The topographic result showed that Britain had a picturesque empire, where beauty harmonized with power.

CHAPTER THIRTEEN

"Of the Old Stock"

Quakerism and Transatlantic Genealogies
in Colonial British America

Karin Wulf

In 1808 Deborah Norris Logan of Philadelphia penned an account of her lineage that situated generations of her family in the social and political contexts
she deemed most appropriate. In this genealogical diary, Logan documented
Norrises and Logans stretching back several centuries. A prefatory note
explained the logic of its composition:

> I have frequently thought that it would be both profitable and pleasant if some
> person in every family would make it their concern to keep a Book in which they
> would record such facts as came under their observation, together with their
> experience of various kinds, and such Recounts and notices of their families as
> they could either recount themselves or had received in tradition from their
> ancestors, for want of such a written record what a store of helpful and entertain-
> ing knowledge has been lost. This reflection has determined me to write from
> time to time what shall appear to me worthy of preservation; and if I should live
> some years . . . it may form a collection not unacceptable to those of my family
> who may survive me and to them it is affectionately offered.[1]

Logan's "collection" of "facts," "experiences," "notices," "traditions," and
"knowledge" included some records of birth, marriage, and death dates but was

mostly devoted to transcriptions of memoirs and prose anecdotes generated by her ancestors. Neither a family tree nor strictly a diary, the book defies genre conventions.

Logan's interests appear to presage the nineteenth-century enthusiasm for genealogy, which resulted in the founding of historical societies to house the papers of prominent families, the publication of formal genealogies, and the creation of heritage societies whose membership was based on the demonstration of specific, legitimate blood connections. Indeed, she eventually participated in all of these activities, most notably by contributing essential collections and serving as the first female member of the Historical Society of Pennsylvania.[2] More than a prescient foreshadowing of genealogical fervor, however, Logan's work was the result of generations of genealogical research and writing. Many of her ancestors had been devoted to the creation of a family history, which Logan then compiled, recounted, and recast through her organization of the material.[3] Like her ancestors before her and her descendants to follow, Logan aimed to position her family within a transatlantic tradition that valued British roots.[4]

For despite the extraordinary emphasis among both eighteenth-century contemporaries and later scholars on the individual and the nuclear family, kinship ties remained a crucial source of material and cultural support and a wellspring of identity.[5] From commercial kinship networks to marriage alliances within artisanal groups to religious dictates on endogamy to cultural retention among immigrant groups, kinship was the primary form of connection among early modern people. That did not change in the eighteenth century; indeed kinship connections may have become more significant. Although the rhetoric of individualism and the sentimental family was becoming prominent, the language and cultural currency of lineage was also thriving. Much political language decried hereditary claims to power, but lineage remained a recognizably valuable political commodity; as Thomas Jefferson wrote in a recommendation for Deborah Logan's husband, George, who went to France in 1798 on a diplomatic mission, he was descended "of one of the most ancient and respectable families."[6]

In material, literary, and legal form, genealogical representation was a crucial element of this trade in lineage.[7] Certainly property law depended at its very core on the knowledge and demonstration of genealogy, yet the popularity of heraldic devices on objects ranging from needlework to crypts vividly illustrates the grip of lineage imaginings.[8] On a daily basis many colonists recorded the basic information central to genealogical knowledge; they filled their interleaved almanacs with regular entries about their lives as well as

records of births, marriages, and deaths. Such genealogical efforts were important acts of cultural production and an overlooked class of evidence about how
the writers tried to understand themselves individually and collectively. Looking at Logan's sources of information about her family history as well as the
ultimate form of the genealogies—the diary in toto and the individual
entries—reveals the intersection of genealogy and broader patterns of cultural
identity. Logan and her kin scripted for themselves a transatlantic familial
identity, with an emphasis on British connections, and then, as the eighteenth
century progressed, a specifically American identity.

Quaker Family Ties

Deborah Norris Logan's genealogical diary provides a framework for
exploring the sources, forms, and cultural functions of colonial genealogy. It
encompasses a broad but emblematic range of materials—from anecdotes
attributed to oral traditions to truncated family trees to prose memoirs. Each
piece—as well as the diary as a whole—reflected its development in a particular moment. The pieces also were often linked to seventeenth- and eighteenth-
century materials beyond the diary itself, some of them private research notes
and some very public, even published, presentations of family history.

When Logan sat down to "write from time to time what shall appear to me
worthy of preservation," she drew upon the lineage musings of two of early
Pennsylvania's most powerful ancestries: the descendants of Thomas Lloyd and
of James Logan. Lloyd was one of the most influential of early Pennsylvania
Quakers and president of the provincial council in the late seventeenth century; his daughter Mary's marriage to Isaac Norris forged a prominent and
wealthy dynasty. Isaac Norris and his son Isaac Norris II, for example, served
as leaders in the Pennsylvania Assembly, the latter as speaker.[9] When Isaac Norris II died in 1766, his daughter, Mary, was reputed to be the wealthiest heiress
in the colonies.[10]

James Logan served as William Penn's secretary and as his agent in the
colony. He led the conservative Quaker party in the early years of the eighteenth century and thus was closely politically allied with the Norrises. A noted
scientist, intellectual, and bibliophile, his library formed the core of the
Library Company of Philadelphia. As a testament to his participation in a
transatlantic exchange of scientific ideas, principally botanical, the eminent
Swedish scientist Carl Linnaeus classified a family of trees and shrubs

"Loganaceae."[11] Both families built substantial estates outside of Philadelphia, the Norrises' "Fairhill," modeled on the ancient Lloyd estate of Dolobran in Wales, and "Stenton," the Logan's Georgian mansion.

In 1781, when Deborah Norris, granddaughter of Isaac Norris I and great-granddaughter of Thomas Lloyd, married George Logan, grandson of James Logan, she had every reason to feel secure in the knowledge that her family was preeminent, even among Friends. One of the marks of elite Quakers was their practice of intermarriage; Deborah Norris and George Logan were neither the first nor the last generation of their families to intermarry.[12] A distinguished lineage, however, could not guarantee the Logans' status either among Friends or in the new republic. A number of events over the eighteenth century unsettled the families' positions. During the mid eighteenth century, a reform movement within Quakerism emphasized a return to the original tenets of the religion, including an absolute ban on exogamy, and finally succeeded in abolishing slaveholding among its membership.[13] Important members of both the Logan and Norris families had married out of meeting, and ultimately some were disowned for marriage infractions.[14] The Norrises and their kin had been heavily involved in the slave trade as late as the 1730s, and both Norrises and Logans owned slaves well into the 1780s.[15]

Political complications beyond the Quaker meeting also challenged Deborah Logan's families. During the American Revolution, Quakers were officially loyalist, siding with the Crown and generally abhorring the violence of the war. In Philadelphia, alternately occupied by the British and the Americans, anti-Quaker violence reached a fever pitch with the exile of a group of Quaker leaders in 1778.[16] While some Quakers, including members of the Norris family, sided with the Patriots, the Quaker Yearly Meeting disowned those who took up arms on behalf of the nascent United States.

But even among Quakers who prudently declined to declare themselves for either side, political identity could be problematic. In particular, Deborah Logan's husband George, a curious figure, seemed to threaten the family's position at every turn. Despite his later participation in many high-level political activities and his dedication to scientific farming, his historical reputation is decidedly mixed. The Quaker biographer Frederic Tolles endorsed the assessments of Logan's contemporaries that he was "not a great man" and had "limited" perspectives on the world in which he lived.[17] Logan played no role in the American Revolution because his family packed him off to medical school in Edinburgh just a month after the first battles at Lexington and Concord. He

remained abroad until 1780, returning after other members of his family had suffered under patriot arrest for their loyalty to the Crown. Despite his alienation
from the Revolution, he, like other Quakers, greeted at least some aspects of the
government with favor, and he was elected to the Pennsylvania legislature in
1785, where he served until 1789, and again in the late 1790s. He served six years
in the U.S. Senate, from 1801 to 1807. In part he owed these elections to Pennsylvanians' memories of the extraordinary political service of other Logans, especially his grandfather. Yet renowned Quaker and pacifist George Logan was
disowned by the Society of Friends in 1790 for joining the militia. He allied himself with Thomas Jefferson and the Republicans when many of his class and religion were firm Federalists. His political service, in general, was marked by
blunders that earned him a reputation as a "busybody" and a "great fool."[18]

Deborah Norris Logan's efforts to rehabilitate her family's reputation may
have stemmed from her grief over these issues. Certainly George Logan's ban-
ishment from the Quaker meeting was a great blow. Deborah Norris was
known from girlhood as a very devout Quaker, and her influence on the less
devout George had been noted from the time of their marriage. She could not
save him from the determination of the meeting to punish his transgressions,
however, and he would not repent.[19] Among her other genealogical endeavors,
Logan also wrote an admiring biography of her husband, a *Memoir of Dr.
George Logan of Stenton.*[20]

By the time Deborah Norris Logan composed her genealogical diary in the
early years of the Republic, then, the Norris and Lloyd descendants were in a
peculiarly difficult position vis-à-vis both their nation and their religion. While
their ancestors had been both lauded political leaders and respected "weighty
Friends," many in Logan's family, post-Quaker reform and post-Revolution,
were neither particularly good Quakers nor particularly good Americans. Thus
Logan's resurrection of family history—recalling, recounting, and re-visioning
the past—seemed appropriate. And it was logical that Logan would turn to
family history, because so many of her ancestors had created the historical
materials she ultimately collected in her own unique presentation of the past.
Finding their footing as Quakers and as Americans had regularly required the
generation and maintenance of a collective family identity secured by public
knowledge of past kin.

For Deborah Norris Logan and her ancestors, family histories were imbed-
ded in the economic and cultural contexts of family fortunes. Three major
themes emerge from the collection Logan created: a strong investment in

transatlantic, particularly British, connections; the nagging question of racial slavery; and the creation of a nascent American identity. Throughout the long eighteenth century, and in conjunction with these other specific issues, genealogical materials focused more generally on delineating the foundations of American Quakerism and on the role of Quakers in founding Pennsylvania. Researching and writing within these contexts, Logan and her forbearers produced family accounts that would address each successive generation's challenges in meeting the standards of their era.

Transatlantic Families

The first major theme that appears in Logan's diary is transatlantic Quakerism, clearly important in her family history. Family history shored up connections, both in Britain and the West Indies, that were commercially and culturally valuable. Long exchanges of information about family births, marriages, and deaths kept family members abreast of their kin. Isaac Norris, for example, corresponded with both cousins Sampson Lloyd in London and Prudence Moore in Jamaica during the late 1740s. Both of these cousins were at different times part of the Norris and Lloyd network of commercial trade.[21] But when Isaac Norris wrote to each in this period, it was to exchange family information. To Sampson Lloyd he provided a brief account of a tumultuous period in his life. "Since I last wrote to thee I married and abt two years ago lost one of the best O[f] Women," he wrote, "I buryed two sons who both dyed young before their mother I have Two Daughters yet alive delightful Children."[22] To Prudence Moore, Norris provided a similarly brief account of his immediate family, adding some general information about the household composition of Norris town and country houses. He noted, for example that "My sister Betty lives with me in the country . . . my Brother Charles lives in town and My Sister Debby keeps his house." Norris acknowledged Moore's request for more exact information such as birth and death dates, but deferred to his sisters in supplying this data, noting that "the female branches of our family are the best genealogists."[23]

In many cases these relatives, separated by the Atlantic, never met in person, and yet they celebrated and mourned the arrival and passing of those they still considered close "family." In 1775, Sampson Lloyd wrote "From my Farm near Birmingham" to Elizabeth Norris.[24] His letter was full of the particulars of births and deaths, marriages and business partnerships among their mutual family and acquaintances. Despite never having met, Lloyd closed by passing along his "Dear Love to thy self & my other valued Relations tho' unknown." Similarly, when news of the death of Sampson Lloyd's daughter reached her American cousins they mourned her as if she had lived among them. Cousin Hannah Griffitts, a poet who regularly memorialized family, friends, and other significant Quakers, marked the passing of this distant cousin with a poem.[25]

This sense of connections among relatives who had not met or even lived on the same side of the Atlantic in two generations marks a particular interest among Quakers in securing their Old World ties. Quakerism was always a transatlantic religion; one of the remarkable features of colonial Quakerism is the extent to which meetings in America continued to be in regular and close contact with meetings abroad, particularly of course with meetings in England but also with those in Ireland and elsewhere. Receiving epistles from these meetings reasserted the relationship between the place of Quakerism's founding and the place of its colonial flowering. On a practical level, the information, advice, and spiritual counsel they provided also helped retain coherence in a religion that eschewed doctrine. These transatlantic connections were also strengthened by the regular visiting of Friends from England in America and vice versa. Thus, the sense of connection that Quaker families such as the Norrises and Lloyds felt with their distant relations paralleled the connections among Quaker meetings in Britain and America.

In his 1775 letter to Elizabeth Norris, Sampson Lloyd congratulated her on being "one of the Old Stock" and a fellow descendant of "that good man Thomas Lloyd." Thus, Lloyd celebrated their connection through a distinguished ancestor. But he also reaffirmed for Lloyd descendants one of their proudest connections. Over the course of the eighteenth century, the group became increasingly attentive to this particular ancestral tie. While they prized most aspects of their family history, it was the Lloyd connection that rose to paramount importance.[26] Elaborate family trees—they had to be elaborate, for there was significant marriage among cousins, thus making any clear depiction of relations quite difficult—were drawn, detailing the Lloyd lineage.[27] Throughout the eighteenth century family members requested research in Quaker records to verify birth, marriage, and death dates for Thomas Lloyd, his wife, and his children.[28] The significance of this root of the family tree lasted beyond the end of the century. Tellingly, when Rachel Moore died and was buried in 1796, she was described first as "the last surviving G[rand] Daughter of the respectable Tho[ma]s Lloyd."[29]

The Lloyd connection became increasingly significant as the meanings of a Quaker "birthright" shifted. Quakerism began as a seventeenth-century enthusiastic religion, but as the eighteenth century progressed several factors contributed to the perceived dilution of spiritual fervor. The birthright, which meant that all children of Quakers were assumed members of the meeting, as well as the increased material prosperity of New World Quakers, were cited as examples. The reform movement that began in the 1750s addressed some of these issues, as well as slavery and marriage discipline. As a consequence, old Quaker families who stood accused of many if not all of these transgressions may have become more sensitive to their changing place within the religion of their forbearers. Indeed the political consequences were already plain. Because of concerns about the spiritually corrosive effects of political participation, as well as the more immediate issue of supporting war activities, many prominent Quakers were forced to leave politics or relinquish their Meeting membership. Isaac Norris II, then speaker of the Pennsylvania assembly, was most prominent among those who felt the dissolving connection between Quaker founding families and political power in Pennsylvania. In this atmosphere, a reminder of the significance of their ancestors' place among the first Quakers, and among the first Quakers in Pennsylvania, was a useful salve.

This nexus of issues explains in part why the Lloyd ancestry was so attractive to eighteenth-century genealogists. In Deborah Logan's diary the Lloyd ancestry occupies a prominent place. She copied a prose description of the family in Wales and in Pennsylvania, as well as lists of vital dates for collateral kin. This twelve-page section of the diary is framed by the opening narrative, which situates Thomas Lloyd within two important groups: the British gentry and the earliest Quakers. "Thomas Lloyd, Son of Charles Lloyd of Dolobran," Logan wrote:

> was born at the seat of his family in North Wales, G: B: April 1640. married Mary Jones, daughter of Col. Jones Novr 9th 1665. was educated for the church, but being convinced of the blessed truth as held by the People called Quakers, He joined that society and came over with his family to Pennsylvania among the first settlers, he was greatly esteemed & trusted by W. Penn, who left the Province to his care and in many MSS letters which I have seen, expressed the highest sense of his abilities & worth. He died in Penn.a Sepr 10th 1694.[30]

In this passage Logan captured the multiple dimensions of Thomas Lloyd's enduring significance. She noted his early commitment to Quakerism, an enthusiastic conversion that paved the way for subsequent generations of "birthright" (as opposed to "convinced") Friends. She placed him in the first rank of Pennsylvanians by invoking the highest authority, William Penn. And she inserted herself into the process of historical validation by claiming the authenticity of the documentary evidence ("MSS letters which I have seen").

While Logan was among a group of Lloyd descendants celebrating that lineage, she also paid close attention to the Logan line of her husband's paternal ancestry. The Logan materials she included in her diary, some of which were transcriptions of memoirs, sounded similar themes about early Quakerism and early Pennsylvania. In fact the first item in the diary is a "Copy of a Paper in the hand writing of James Logan Senr. Grand Father of my Husband." By heading James Logan's memoir with this preface, Deborah Norris Logan was making a direct reference to her intimacy with the past through her unique access to important documents. One of her pet projects, begun in earnest several years after she began the genealogical diary, was the transcription and preservation of letters between James Logan and William Penn, now a celebrated collection at the Historical Society of Pennsylvania and Deborah Logan's chief gift to the society in its early years.

Here James Logan's authorial voice takes over, although Deborah Logan's role in placing the document is still significant. He, too, connected himself to a lineage of early Quakers and to the British gentry. James Logan chose to begin with the family's first Quaker: "My father was born in East Lothian in Scotland was educated for the Clergy and was a chaplain for some time but turning Quaker he was obliged to go to Ireland and to teach a Latin school there." He then told of his mother's connection to the Scottish gentry. Her father had managed the Earl of Murray's estate and had been owed a great deal of money by the earl. The debt was never paid. Her mother was a member of the Scottish aristocracy, daughter of a Laird, and "nearly related" to an earl.[31]

Subsequent portions of the Logan section of the genealogical diary emphasize the importance of understanding and valuing transatlantic roots and connections. Deborah Logan also copied an "old manuscript in my possession entitled 'An historical account of the Ancient & honorable family of Logan of Restalrig near to Edinburgh.'"[32] This piece traced the name of Logan from the time of William Wallace and also included an account of the Logan coat of arms. It was composed by George Logan, an Edinburgh minister, at the request of James Logan's brother, Dr. William Logan, who remained in Scotland. Its inclusion suggests that both genealogical knowledge and research were subjects of interest to generations that preceded Deborah Norris Logan and that it was not only of interest to American branches of the family.

Quaker Families and Atlantic Society

While proud of their Old World connections and their prominent place in the stories of early Quakerism and Pennsylvania, the family also struggled with one of the means they used to maintain their prominence and prosperity in eighteenth-century America: their complicity in the slave trade. Racial slavery posed particular problems for Logan and her genealogically inclined ancestors. While the Quaker reforms of the 1750s and 1760s had finally succeeded in requiring that Friends manumit their slaves, manumission could not erase the Norris family's complicity in the slave trade. Not only slaveowners, and slaveowners until the Meeting threatened their disownment, the Norris fortune had been acquired in no small measure through the slave importations conducted by Isaac Norris Senior in the early eighteenth century. The Logans were also slaveowners. As James Logan explained, his attachment to slave labor in 1757 was purely a practical matter: "I had been unsuccessful (as well as many others) in white Servants several having enlisted & prov'd bad & I found it difficult to hire Persons suitable to my Occasions & so determin'd to buy a Negro thinking he would answer my purpose better."[33]

Deborah Logan must have felt this keenly. During the 1770s the pressure to manumit slaves became intense, and finally the Philadelphia Yearly Meeting determined to disown slaveowners entirely. Logan's relations were among the last to comply.[34] Part of understanding her family history, then, entailed understanding their participation in an institution deemed morally wrong for Friends. Logan answered this challenge with the magazine publication in 1790 of a "Providential Anecdote," recounting events that occurred a century earlier in the West Indies.[35]

Deborah Logan's paternal ancestors, the Norrises, had come to Philadelphia by way of an earlier settlement in Jamaica, and her tale began there. In 1678 Thomas Norris of London traveled to Port Royal, Jamaica, and established a profitable trading enterprise with England and the American colonies. In March 1692 Norris's son Isaac was sent to Philadelphia, presumably to reinforce trading connections with the Quaker colony. Two critical things happened while Isaac Norris was in Philadelphia, both providential in the view of descendants. The first was that he met and became engaged to the daughter of

Thomas Lloyd, one of the most powerful men in Pennsylvania. The second was that during Isaac Norris's absence from Jamaica, a devastating earthquake struck Port Royal. Built opposite Kingston, everything in Port Royal was destroyed and swallowed into the bay on June 2, 1692. Thomas Norris and many members of his family were killed, along with two-thirds of the town's population. A few members of the Norris family survived the Port Royal earthquake, including Isaac Norris, who then permanently relocated to Philadelphia and married Mary Lloyd. [36]

The Port Royal earthquake remained in popular memory long after its occurrence.[37] The Philadelphia branches of the Norris and Lloyd descendants remembered the event with particular reverence. It is clear that the destruction of the island town was overwhelming. When the tremors stopped, survivors began to pick through the rubble, looking for other people and property. One Norris relation lost his wife and children but found "bonds and bills to the value of about £4000 . . . floating in the sea."[38] The loss of family and the loss of thousands of pounds in bonds and unpaid debts, as well as trade goods, seemed the work of "the just hand of the Lord."[39] Yet it was another event connected to the earthquake that continued to intrigue the descendants of the earthquake victims and that formed the core narrative of Deborah Logan's "Providential Anecdote."

As the story explains, an enslaved man belonging to Thomas Norris attempted to rescue his master. He rushed to the counting house where Norris was working when the quake struck, but both men perished in the ensuing floods. This heroic effort did not conclude the story. A baby's cradle was spotted floating in the bay. In the cradle the small daughter of the heroic slave was found, alive. Tucked into the cradle with her was a large silver dish. When Isaac Norris returned to Jamaica in late 1692 to view the ruins of Port Royal and his family, he retrieved the child and the silver dish and took both back to help establish his new family in Philadelphia. The girl was presented as a "little waiting maid" to the eldest daughter of Isaac and Mary Lloyd Norris. Then when this daughter, Mary Norris Griffitts, married and had her own family, she took the enslaved woman to serve them. The daughter eventually lived, according to the "Providential Anecdote" as "a free negro woman . . . in Philadelphia" and was cared for "by some of the family, to the last." She reportedly died in 1802, at age eighty-two. This extraordinary account of two families, one comprised of white Quakers with economic and political power, the other enslaved Africans, starkly illustrates the significance of race and slavery in the legitimating of

Quakers in the post-revolutionary era. Scholars have begun to explore the nuances of white Southerners' elision of their biological connections to Africans and African Americans, and they have also suggested that ideas about race were equally important to collective identities in the early American North.[40]

The "Providential Anecdote" demonstrates the subtle repositioning required of American Quakers. It combined many elements of Deborah Logan's efforts at situating her family, and of placing the family history in what she would see as the proper perspective. By describing their dependence upon the providential act of an enslaved man, Logan presented an inverted picture of her family's relationship to slavery. True, the man who tried to save Thomas Norris in 1692 had failed, but his daughter had survived to remind the family of his bravery and devotion. Surely no harsh master could compel such depth of loyalty. Thus, that man's actions demonstrated the benevolence of the enslavers. In addition, by emphasizing the family's continued gratitude to the rescued child rather than her continued enslavement to the family, the reality of Deborah Norris Logan's participation in slavery was elided. The eventual freedom of the black woman's daughter and her care "to the last" at the hands of the enslaving family is emphasized in the "Providential Anecdote," despite the fact that both mother and daughter probably served the family in exchange for little if any financial remuneration.[41] In an era in which Quakers' relationship to slavery had been fundamentally reconfigured, and in which Quakers continued to play a leading role in emancipation campaigns beyond their own denomination, representing the slaveownership of Deborah Norris Logan's family as grateful benevolence provided protective cultural cover.

In her genealogical diary, however, Logan treated the Port Royal episode somewhat differently. Recounting the history of the Lloyd and Norris connections, she noted that Isaac Norris had returned from Philadelphia to Jamaica in 1692 "to find that his father and most of his family had perished in the dreadful Earthquake that destroyed Port Royal, the vessel he was in sailing over the place where his father once had stood."[42] Rather than redemption in Port Royal, Norris's diary emphasized the work of providence once Norris returned to Philadelphia. There "it pleased divine Providence to bless him in an extraordinary manner for tho he had a very large family to provide for he grew rich." She reduced the role of the slave, both in form and substance, to a marginal note and supporting cast. Norris pointed to the famous silver dish, noting that her brother still had it, that it was engraved with "the arms of the family," and that after "that dreadful Earthquake it was taken up at Sea in the cradle of a little negro child belonging to the family & who was preserved alive."[43] Where was the brave slave, father of the child in the cradle? She omitted him. In a document meant for family and friends alone, Logan could afford to be more cavalier with the family's relationship to the harsh institution of slavery. In public, the "Providential Anecdote" served a much different audience and a much different purpose.

Quaker Families in Post-Revolutionary America

Extensive knowledge of kin abroad and of the precise relationships among a very large extended family in America pushed post-revolutionary Quakers to create a context for understanding their place in a changed environment. While their parents and aunts and uncles had collected family materials to document transatlantic connections, the post-revolutionary generation used family histories in a new way. Transatlantic origins remained important, but the significance of American roots and American connections intensified.

In Logan's diary, attention to an American identity took two forms: the repetition of an earlier stress on the founding of Pennsylvania and situating the family within the revolutionary generation. While in the genealogical texts generated by Logan's kin, connections to the origins of Quakerism had served both to bolster transatlantic ties as well as to burnish their image within American Quakerism; the family's connection to Pennsylvania's first settlers was equally important. That Thomas Lloyd and James Logan, for example, not only had impeccable credentials as early Quaker converts but that each had close ties to William Penn helped emphasize that the family's roots in the American soil were deep.

Because the Quaker community was as best tolerated, at worst reviled, by Patriots during the Revolution, Deborah Logan was at pains to establish her family's connection to revolutionary spirit. In her diary, Logan carefully documented her respect for and intimate knowledge of key figures of the American Revolution. "As I have lived," she wrote, "as it were, in the Heroic Age of my country, and as likewise during the short period of my existence the World has been agitated & convulsed by the most extraordinary events, I have thought it might be interesting to set down my own recollections."[44] In point of fact, neither Logan nor her husband was much in evidence during the Revolution. George Logan was abroad while his family was embroiled in the problems of loyalist Quakerism, and Deborah Logan was still quite young in the 1770s. She did remember clearly hearing the Declaration of Independence read out while standing in the garden of her family home on Chestnut Street, a story she told often.[45] But it was important to identify herself and her family as members of the revolutionary generation; by the time Norris was composing her diary, partisanship had grown fierce and only the Revolution itself remained a touchstone of common idealization.[46]

Thus Logan chose to emphasize her knowledge of figures who, by the early nineteenth century, were not politically controversial. The most significant among these was George Washington; she began with Washington, Logan wrote, "as he will stand Preeminent in the annals of his country." Logan's memories of Washington ranged from having heard him extolled during the pre-Revolutionary years, to a visit to Mount Vernon, and a return visit by Washington to the Logan home, Stenton. Logan related some modest anecdotes about their conversations, chiefly on domestic matters, but was clear that her admiration for him extended into the political realm. "I do not think it easy for one human being to respect and venerate another," she wrote, "more than I did this truly great man."[47]

Amid the partisan rancor of the early years of the nation, Washington was almost alone in maintaining his image as above the fray. Logan did not detail her husband's intimacy with Thomas Jefferson, for example.[48] Although the diary was begun in the years of Jefferson's second term, and her husband had been a Jeffersonian Republican, George Logan's complicated and contentious experience in partisan politics may have convinced his wife to stick to their credentials as supporters of the Revolution. Tellingly, one of the few anecdotes Logan included in the diary that was not directly related to either her family or to her own experiences was about the Empress Josephine and the bitterness of a husband's public downfall. Logan recounted the story of a neighbor, in which a fortuneteller predicted that Josephine would marry a man who would become king, "& she Empress of a great domain" but that afterward she would "be reduced and die in poverty." Logan wrote, too, that Josephine often "omitted the latter circumstances" of the prediction because "as the one part had been verified she probably dreaded the other would also."[49]

Logan did not directly challenge the political atmosphere that had poisoned her husband's reputation, but the narrative she created through her choice of genealogical anecdotes and memoirs stressed declension. The era of the Revolution, she posited, had given way to a period of indulgence and excess. In a piece devoted to a visit with John Randolph in 1815, Logan described how

Virginia had deteriorated since its heyday: "for many miles not a single family of eminence left." An affecting passage described the built landscape returned to nature. Logan laid the blame on "A decline in those habits of Regularity productive of civilization & refinement in society."[50]

Logan concluded her diary with a section that combined politically infused reflection with more conventional diary entries, commencing in June 1814. In it Logan reflected on what she called the revelation of Napoleon's character and on the age of democratic revolutions more generally. "The eventful Period in which we of the present Generation have lived," she wrote, "appears to have condensed into its short space, what one would think must have been the work of ages." [51]

Conclusion

Deborah Norris Logan's genealogical diary provides a record of how events altered, but did not extinguish, Americans' sense of being part of an Atlantic world. In an era of increased discursive volume eschewing lineage, arising both out of the contests over monarchical government and the role of aristocracy, as well as the developing emphasis on sensibility, genealogies that celebrated lineage connections may look to us to be out of place. In fact they perfectly fitted an era of uncertainty in which extensive kin connections retained their economic, political, and cultural importance. Despite the political language of democracy, many recognized the value of aristocratic and gentry connections, especially transatlantic ones; as one of Deborah Logan's relations wrote from England on the eve of the American Revolution, they were family "of the Old Stock."[52]

The genealogical work of Deborah Logan and her family bore some particular marks. It was largely literary rather than material. Unlike New Englanders, for example, Philadelphia Quakers rarely embroidered heraldry or family trees.[53] They also had a unique source base. Based in large measure upon the available trove of family information held by Quaker meetings, the family histories were remarkably accurate as to vital dates. Queries about such information could be directed to the clerks of monthly meetings. Accustomed to circulating materials that facilitated the transatlantic Quaker community, they were generally happy to respond.[54] The Quaker diaspora to the West Indies and to North America was reflected in the family connections that Logan and her ancestors documented. These genealogies were also particularly attuned to the complexities of Quaker prestige in a changing world. Once inhabitants of a world they made, over the eighteenth century elite Pennsylvania Quakers found that some aspects of their identity became burdensome, while others gained new distinction.

In a broader sense, Quaker genealogical practices reflected emerging tensions in transatlantic political culture. As scholars, including Jay Fliegelman and Lynn Hunt, have demonstrated, the political and cultural power of familial metaphor was both intense and complex in the age of the democratic revolutions. Family motifs informed political discourse, and literature was steeped in politicized representations of the family. Part of a movement from the vertical hierarchies, which marked the early modern world, toward the emphasis on horizontal connections, which characterized the modern era, a panoply of social, political, economic, cultural changes, and particularly religious changes encouraged the emerging notion of the "self"—of the individual. An intensive discourse of sentiment then came to focus on the nuclear, or "core" family, especially on children. The conflation of dynastic and monarchical power reached its zenith in the early modern period, and thus resistance to monarchy produced a similar critique of aristocratic family. The lineage family was disavowed for its association with hereditary rights and the dissonance with democratic rhetoric.[55]

In *Democracy in America,* Alexis de Tocqueville wrote that the "influence of democracy on the family" was profound. Not only did democracy encourage a more "natural" affection between fathers and their children than the artificial hierarchy of aristocracy but it created crucial bonds among brothers in particular. "It is not, then, by interest, but by common associations and by the free sympathy of opinion and of taste that democracy unites brothers to each other."[56] De Tocqueville's nineteenth-century characterization of the relationship of the American Revolution to the state of the family points to several themes in both contemporary and scholarly understandings of the changing family in eighteenth-century America. One is the opposition of interest and sympathy. By characterizing the aristocratic family in terms of interest, the democratic family in terms of sympathy, and by qualifying such sympathy as the "free sympathy of opinion and of taste," de Tocqueville contributed to one of the central projects of democratic political ideology: the construction of independent masculinity. Unencumbered by ties of interest or obligation, the democrat was free to create alliances, and to make decisions, based on natural sympathies and rational choice.

Writing of lineage in an era whose political discourse was mainly democratic produced its own tensions. Genealogists could describe their work as a
purely private matter, as did Richard Hill Morris, a second cousin to Deborah
Norris Logan. In 1822, he wrote to his aunt, Milcah Martha Moore, urging her
continued assistance in his genealogical work. "Tho' I see no positive use to
result from it, I should like to leave behind me, such a memorial of my mater-
nal ancestry as may operate at some future day, to continue in my children the
veneration I feel from the Stock from whence I am sprung."[57] Morris included
a list of details he needed to flesh out such a family history, such as "the time &
place of Grandfather Hill's marriage—the time and place of thy mothers
death—the date of the Birth of their children; & their marriages." Morris
requested a more complicated set of data than perhaps he recognized, involving a very intermarried and far-flung family, reaching the short distance from
Maryland to Pennsylvania and traversing the Atlantic by way of the Madeiras
to England. Nonetheless, Milcah Moore was easily able to comply with these
requests. Like many, she was intensely interested in family history and had
helped preserve the genealogical research of her ancestors.

There was no disguising, however, the connection between a hankering for
lineage and the political conflicts of the era. Real and metaphorical, discursive
and cultural, political and social, the notion that America was now the purview
of the accomplished and not just the well-born challenged those whose pride
in their "old families" was tinged with entitlement. At the height of George
Logan's political ignominy, a pamphlet called the "Quid Mirror" (after Logan's
rump faction of Republicans, the so-called Quid Tertium) appeared. While in
recommending Logan for a foreign mission some years earlier, Thomas Jefferson had comfortably pointed to Logan's family pedigree; in 1806 the Quids'
enemies stressed instead his family's financial resources as the illegitimate
source of his position. Logan, they claimed, "is a creature truly *sui generis*. By
his inheritance and marriage he became possessed of a large fortune, and to his
fortune may be ascribed whatever consideration he may possess in society."[58]
Under these circumstances, Deborah Norris Logan's genealogical reflections
are telling. She rejected the imputation that it was fortune alone that privileged
her family. Tracing her lineage to Pennsylvania's founding, as well as to early
British Quakerism, she attempted to traverse the opening chasm between
democracy and aristocracy, the New World and the Old.

Notes

INTRODUCTION

Epigraph. Jack P. Greene, "Beyond Power: Paradigm Subversion and Reformulation, and the Re-creation of the Early Modern Atlantic World," in *Interpreting Early America: Historiographical Essays* (Charlottesville, 1996), 40. Greene delivered this paper in 1995, almost a quarter of a century after founding, with colleagues at the Johns Hopkins University, the first Program in Atlantic History and Culture.

1. David Armitage, "Three Concepts of Atlantic History," in David Armitage and Michael J. Braddick, eds., *The British Atlantic World, 1500–1800* (Basingstoke, U.K., 2002), 13.

2. J. H. Elliott, "Afterword," in Armitage and Braddick, eds., *British Atlantic World,* 233–235; Fernand Braudel, *The Mediterranean and the Mediterranean World in the Age of Philip II,* 2 vols., trans. Sian Reynolds (New York, 1972); and Peter A. Coclanis, "Drang Nach Osten: Bernard Bailyn, the World-Island, and the Idea of Atlantic History," *Journal of World History* 13 (2002), 177–181.

3. J. H. Parry, *The Establishment of the European Hegemony, 1415–1715: Trade and Exploration in the Age of the Renaissance* (New York, 1961); Ralph Davis, *The Rise of the Atlantic Economies* (Ithaca, N.Y., 1973), xi. See more recently, David B. Abernethy, *The Dynamics of Global Dominance: European Overseas Empires, 1415–1980* (New Haven, Conn., 2000).

4. Bernard Bailyn and Philip D. Morgan, eds., *Strangers within the Realm: Cultural Margins of the First British Empire* (Chapel Hill, N.C., 1991), 31.

5. John K. Thornton, *Africa and Africans in the Making of the Atlantic World, 1400–1800,* 2nd ed. (Cambridge, U.K., 1998).

6. John Brooke, "Ecology," in Daniel Vickers, ed., *A Companion to Colonial America* (Malden, Mass., 2003), 44–75, is one example, and his essay contains references to the work of others in environmental and natural history. Two works have been written on what might be called the general history of the Atlantic: Paul Butel, *The Atlantic* (New York, 1999); and Barry Cunliffe, *Facing the Ocean: The Atlantic and Its Peoples, 8000 BC–AD 1500* (New York, 2001). Both are pioneering efforts but, as my colleague Peter Mancall has pointed out, both suffer from Eurocentrism.

7. Nicholas Canny, "Introduction," in Canny, ed., *The Oxford History of the British Empire,* Vol. 1, *The Origins of Empire: British Overseas Enterprise to the Close of the Seventeenth Century* (Oxford, 1997), 1.

8. See contributions by Anthony Pagden, John C. Appleby, and David Armitage in ibid.

9. David Armitage, *The Ideological Origins of the British Empire* (Cambridge, U.K., 2000).

10. Colin Kidd, *British Identities before Nationalism: Ethnicity and Nationhood in the Atlantic World, 1600–1800* (Cambridge, U.K., 1999). Interestingly, Armitage does not include Kidd in his bibliography, though they share a publisher. They appear to have been working in parallel but nonintersecting intellectual worlds.

11. Bruce Lenman, *England's Colonial Wars, 1550–1688: Conflicts, Empire, and National Identity* (Harlow, U.K., 2001), 284.

12. For essays on these themes see Philippa Levine, ed., *Gender and Empire* (Oxford, 2004).

13. This sense of the Atlantic world is in work on New England, the West Indies, New York City, and studies of slavery and seafaring men in the seventeenth and early eighteenth century. Examples include Virginia DeJohn Anderson, *New England's Generation: The Great Migration and the Formation of Society and Culture in the Seventeenth Century* (New York, 1991), and her "New England in the Seventeenth Century," in Canny, ed., *Origins of Empire*, 193–216; Edmund Morgan, *American Slavery, American Freedom: The Ordeal of Colonial Virginia* (New York, 1975); Ira Berlin, *Many Thousands Gone: The First Two Centuries of Slavery in North America* (Cambridge, Mass., 1998); Peter Linebaugh and Marcus Rediker, *The Many-Headed Hydra: Sailors, Slaves, Commoners, and the Hidden History of the Revolutionary Atlantic* (Boston, 2000).

14. Jacob M. Price, "Who Cared about the Colonies? The Impact of the Thirteen Colonies on British Society and Politics, circa 1714–1775," in Bailyn and Morgan, eds., *Strangers Within the Realm*, 395–436.

15. See Armitage and Braddick, eds., *British Atlantic World*, for the alternative view of expansion as the movement of peoples, goods, and ideas. Only one out of eleven chapters, Elizabeth Mancke's "Empire and State," 175–195, examines the politics of empire building.

16. Canny, ed., *The Origins of Empire*; and P. J. Marshall, ed., *The Oxford History of the British Empire*, Vol. 2, *The Eighteenth Century* (Oxford, 1998).

17. Elizabeth Mancke, "Early Modern Expansion and the Politicization of Oceanic Space," *The Geographic Review* 89 (1999), 225–236.

18. Abernethy, *Dynamics of Global Dominance*; Kenneth Pomeranz, *The Great Divergence: China, Europe, and the Making of the Modern World Economy* (Princeton, 2000); and Benjamin Schmidt, *Innocence Abroad: The Dutch Imagination and the New World, 1570–1670* (New York, 2001). Much of this paragraph and the next two are taken from my chapter, "The Origins of Transatlantic Colonization," in Vickers, ed., *A Companion to Colonial America*, 25–44.

19. T. K. Rabb, *Enterprise and Empire: Merchant and Gentry Investment in the Expansion of England, 1575–1630* (Cambridge, Mass., 1967); Carole Shammas, "English Commercial Development and American Colonization. 1560–1620," in K. R. Andrews, N. P. Canny, and P. E. H. Hair, eds., *The Westward Enterprise: English Activities in Ireland, the Atlantic, and America, 1480–1650* (Liverpool, 1979), 151–174; Kenneth R. Andrews, *Trade, Plunder, and Settlement: Maritime Enterprise and the Genesis of the British Empire, 1480–1630* (Cambridge, U.K., 1984).

20. David H. Sacks, *The Widening Gate: Bristol and the Atlantic Community, 1450–1700* (Berkeley, 1991); Robert Brenner, *Merchants and Revolution: Commercial Change, Political Conflict, and London's Overseas Merchants, 1550–1653* (Princeton, 1993); and Carla Gardina Pestana, "Compulsion to Remain Connected: The Ties that Bound the Early

Anglo-Atlantic Empire," paper delivered at the Fourth Biennial FEEGI conference, Huntington Library, February 2002.

21. Michael J. Braddick, "The English Government, War, Trade, and Settlement, 1625–1688," in Canny, ed., *The Origins of Empire*, 286–308; and Jonathan Israel, "The Emerging Empire: The Continental Perspective, 1650–1713," in ibid., 423–444.

22. *Transatlantic* is being used here differently from the way David Armitage defines transatlantic history in "Three Concepts of Atlantic History," 18–21. He conceptualizes it as comparative history, whereas in this volume the term *transatlantic experience* refers to the process of change accompanying the crossing of the Atlantic.

23. David Eltis, Stephen D. Behrendt, David Richardson, and Herbert S. Klein, eds., *The Trans-Atlantic Slave Trade: A Database on CD-ROM* (Cambridge, Mass., 1999) contains the data. For a recent update on findings, see the articles in the "New Perspectives on the Trans-Atlantic Slave Trade" issue of the *William and Mary Quarterly*, 3rd ser., 58 (2001).

24. The behavioral modification Indian peoples effected in the English and their descendents in New England are the themes in both Jill Lepore's *The Name of War: King Philip's War and the Origins of American Identity* (New York, 1998) and Mary Beth Norton's *Salem Witch Trials of 1692* (New York, 2002).

25. Thompson here modifies Kidd, *British Identities before Nationalism*, 288.

26. S. Sideri, *Trade and Power: Informal Colonialism in Anglo-Portuguese Relations* (Rotterdam, 1970), 4, 42; and H. E. S. Fisher, *The Portugal Trade: A Study of Anglo-Portuguese Commerce, 1700–1770* (London, 1971), 15.

27. J. H. Plumb, *England in the Eighteenth Century* (Harmondsworth, U.K., 1950), 60 and 64 on the crisis.

28. Pestana, "Compulsion to Remain Connected."

29. Ian K. Steele, *The English Atlantic, 1660–1740: An Exploration of Communication and Community,* (New York, 1986).

30. David Armitage, "The Cromwellian Protectorate and the Language of Empire," *Historical Journal* 35 (1992), 531–555; Stephen Saunders Webb, *The Governors-General: The English Army and the Definition of the Empire, 1569–1681* (Chapel Hill, N.C., 1979); and idem, *1676: The End of American Independence* (New York, 1984).

31. Namierite here refers to Lewis Namier, an influential mid-twentieth-century British historian. His characterization of British politics in the eighteenth century as being dominated by the Crown and aristocratic magnates kept in power not by elections over substantive issues but through the dispensing of patronage to kith and kin had a profound effect on British colonial historians' depiction of imperial politics. See Bernard Bailyn in *The Origins of American Politics* (New York, 1968) and the early work of his students Stanley N. Katz, *Newcastle's New York: Anglo-American Politics, 1732–1753* (Cambridge, Mass., 1968); James A. Henretta, "*Salutary Neglect*": *Colonial Administration under the Duke of Newcastle* (Princeton, 1972); and Michael G. Kammen, *A Rope of Sand: The Colonial Agents, British Politics, and the American Revolution* (Ithaca, N.Y., 1968), which stressed the problematic hold the metropolis had over colonial polities because of the British patronage system.

32. James D. Tracy, ed., *The Rise of Merchant Empires: Long-Distance Trade in the Early Modern World, 1350–1750* (Cambridge, U.K., 1990); idem, *The Political Economy of Merchant Empires* (Cambridge, U.K., 1991); Sidney Mintz, *Sweetness and Power: The*

Place of Sugar in Modern History (New York, 1985); T. H. Breen, "An Empire of Goods: The Anglicization of Colonial America, 1690–1776," *Journal of British Studies* 24 (1986), 467–499; Carole Shammas, *The Pre-industrial Consumer in England and America* (Oxford, 1990); John Brewer and Roy Porter, eds., *Consumption and the World of Goods* (London, 1993); Kenneth Pomeranz and Steven Topik, *The World That Trade Created: Society, Culture, and the World Economy, 1400-The Present* (London, 1999); and John J. McCusker and Kenneth Morgan, eds., *The Early Modern Atlantic Economy* (Cambridge, U.K., 2000). I discuss this literature in "The Revolutionary Impact of European Demand for tropical Goods," in ibid., 163–185.

33. Stephen Foster, *The Long Argument: English Puritanism and the Shaping of New England Culture, 1570–1700* (Chapel Hill, N.C., 1991), and Frederick B. Tolles, *Quakers and the Atlantic Culture* (New York, 1960).

34. Patricia U. Bonomi, *Under the Cope of Heaven: Religion, Society, and Politics in Colonial America* (New York, 1980); John M. Murrin, "Anglicizing an American Colony: The Transformation of Provincial Massachusetts" (Ph.D. diss., Yale University, 1966). Jack P. Greene discusses the growth of the Anglican Church in New England and also anglicization in *Pursuits of Happiness: The Social Development of Early Modern British Colonies and the Formation of American Culture* (Chapel Hill, N.C., 1988), 61 and 174–175.

35. Richard Drayton, *Nature's Government: Science, Imperial Britain, and the "Improvement" of the World* (New Haven, Conn., 2000).

O N E : Settlers and Slaves

1. For recent studies that consider European and African migration together, see David Eltis, *The Rise of African Slavery in the Americas* (Cambridge, U.K., 2000); idem, ed., *Coerced and Free Migration: Global Perspectives* (Stanford, 2002), esp. 1–74, 117–151; and Alison Games, "Migration," in David Armitage and Michael J. Braddick, eds., *The British Atlantic World, 1500–1800* (New York, 2002), 30–51, 254–257.

2. Henry A. Gemery, "Markets for Migrants: English Indentured Servitude and Emigration in the Seventeenth and Eighteenth Centuries," in P. C. Emmer, ed., *Colonialism and Migration: Indentured Labour before and after Slavery* (Dordrecht, 1986), 33–54; Russell R. Menard, "Toward African Slavery in Barbados: The Origins of the West Indian Plantation Regime," in *Lois Green Carr: The Chesapeake and Beyond: A Celebration* (Crownsville, Md., 1992), 26.

3. E. A. Wrigley and R. S. Schofield, *Population History of England, 1541–1871: A Reconstruction* (Cambridge, Mass., 1981), 208–209; Patrick Manning, *Slavery and African Life: Occidental, Oriental, and African Slave Trades* (New York, 1990), esp. 57–68, 82–84, 170–171. When comparing a small island, such as England, with a large continent, such as Africa, regional rates per 1,000 of population provide the most useful measure of migration rates.

4. For European migration, see Ida Altman and James Horn, eds., *"To Make America": European Emigration in the Early Modern Period* (Berkeley, 1991) and Nicholas Canny, ed., *Europeans on the Move: Studies on European Migration, 1500–1800* (Oxford, 1994). For African migration, see Manning, *Slavery and African Life*, esp. 9–12, 20–22, 73–81; Ralph A. Austen, "The Trans-Saharan Slave Trade: A Tentative Census," in Henry A. Gemery and Jan S. Hogendorn, eds., *The Uncommon Market: Essays in the Economic*

History of the Atlantic Slave Trade (New York, 1979), 39–41; idem, "The Mediterranean Islamic Slave Trade out of Africa: A Tentative Census," in Elizabeth Savage, ed., *The Human Commodity: Perspectives on the Trans-Saharan Slave Trade* (London, 1992), 227; William G. Clarence-Smith, ed., *The Economics of the Indian Ocean Slave Trade of the Nineteenth Century* (London, 1989).

5. Henry A. Gemery, "Emigration from the British Isles to the New World, 1630–1700: Inferences from Colonial Populations," *Research in Economic History* 5 (1980), 179–231; idem, "European Emigration to North America, 1700–1820: Numbers and Quasi-Numbers," *Perspectives in American History*, New Series, 1 (1984), 283–342; David Eltis, "Atlantic History in Global Perspective," *Itinerario: A Journal of European Overseas Expansion* 23 (1999), 141–161.

6. K. G. Davies, *The Royal African Company* (London, 1957); David W. Galenson, *Traders, Planters, and Slaves: Market Behavior in Early English America* (New York, 1986); Ann M. Carlos and Jamie Brown Kruse, "The Decline of the Royal African Company: Fringe Firms and the Role of the Charter," *Economic History Review* 49 (1996), 291–313.

7. On warfare and political prisoners, see Abbot Emerson Smith, *Colonists in Bondage: White Servitude and Convict Labor in America, 1607–1776* (Chapel Hill, N.C., 1947), chaps. 8–9; Ian Adams and Meredyth Somerville, *Cargoes of Despair and Hope: Scottish Emigration to North America, 1603–1803* (Edinburgh, 1993), chap. 2; Farley Grubb and Tony Stitt, "The Liverpool Emigrant Servant Trade and the Transition to Slave Labor in the Chesapeake, 1697–1707: Market Adjustments to War," *Explorations in Economic History* 31 (1994), 376–405; John Thornton, *Africa and Africans in the Making of the Atlantic World, 1400–1800* (New York, 1998), 98–125; idem, *Warfare in Atlantic Africa 1500–1800* (London, 1999), esp. 16–17, 127–147; Thomas Clarkson, *The History of the Rise, Progress and Accomplishment of the Abolition of the African Slave Trade*, 2 vols. (London, 1808), 1:374, cited in Keith P. Hertzog, "Naval Operations in West Africa and the Disruption of the Slave Trade during the American Revolution," *American Neptune* 55 (1995), 42.

8. T. C. Smout, N. C. Landsman, and T. M. Devine, "Scottish Emigration in the Seventeenth and Eighteenth Centuries," and Georg Fertig, "Transatlantic Migration from the German-Speaking Parts of Central Europe, 1600–1800: Proportions, Structures, and Explanations," in Canny, ed., *Europeans on the Move*, 76–112, 192–235; Manning, *Slavery and African Life*, 18.

9. Frederic Mauro, "French Indentured Servants for America, 1500–1800," 83–104; Ernst Van Den Boogaart, "The Servant Migration to New Netherland, 1624–1664," 55–81; and Gemery, "Markets for Migrants," 33–54, in Emmer, ed., *Colonialism and Migration;* Christian Huetz de Lemps, "Indentured Servants Bound for the French Antilles in the Seventeenth and Eighteenth Centuries," in Altman and Horn, eds., *"To Make America,"* 172–203; David Galenson, *White Servitude in Colonial America: An Economic Analysis* (Cambridge, U.K., 1981), 35, 40, 52, 57; Bernard Bailyn, *Voyagers to the West: A Passage in the Peopling of America on the Eve of the Revolution* (New York, 1986), 160; Farley Grubb, "The Transatlantic Market for British Convict Labor," *Journal of Economic History* 60 (2000), 94; A. Roger Ekirch, *Bound For America: The Transportation of British Convicts to the Colonies, 1718–1775* (Oxford, 1987), 52–55.

10. Alison Games, *Migration and the Origins of the English Atlantic World* (Cambridge, Mass., 1999), 19–25, 47–51; Roger Thompson, *Mobility and Migration: East*

Anglian Founders of New England, 1629–1640 (Amherst, Mass., 1994); Virginia DeJohn Anderson, New England's Generation: The Great Migration and the Formation of Society and Culture in the Seventeenth Century (Cambridge, U.K., 1991); Bailyn, Voyagers to the West, 91–93, 104–125, 128–175, 190–191, 201–225; David Dobson, Scottish Emigration to Colonial America, 1607–1785 (Athens, Ga., 1994); Marianne S. Wokeck, Trade in Strangers: The Beginnings of Mass Migration to North America (University Park, Pa., 1999), chap. 2; Mark Haberlein, "German Migrants in Colonial Pennsylvania: Resources, Opportunities, and Experience," WMQ, 3rd ser., 50 (1993), 555–574.

    11. Eltis, Rise of African Slavery, 97.

    12. David Eltis and Stanley L. Engerman, "Was the Slave Trade Dominated by Men?" Journal of Interdisciplinary History 23 (1993), 237–257; G. Ugo Nwokeji, "African Conceptions of Gender and the Slave Traffic," WMQ, 3rd ser., 58 (2001), 47–68.

    13. Thornton, Africa and Africans, 87–97, 99, 149, 306; Paul E. Lovejoy, Transformations in Slavery: A History of Slavery in Africa (Cambridge, U.K., 1983), 66–87. Cf. William D. Pierson, Black Legacy: America's Hidden Heritage (Amherst, Mass., 1993), 74–98.

    14. Raymond L. Cohn, "Maritime Mortality in the Eighteenth and Nineteenth Centuries: A Survey," International Journal of Maritime History 1 (1989), 159–191; Robin Haines, Ralph Shlomowitz, and Lance Brennan, "Maritime Mortality Revisited," ibid., 8 (1996), 133–172; Ralph Shlomowitz, Lance Brennan, and John McDonald, Mortality and Migration in the Modern World (Aldershot, U.K., 1996); Herbert S. Klein and Stanley L. Engerman, "Long-Term Trends in African Mortality in the Transatlantic Slave Trade," Slavery and Abolition 18, no. 1 (1997), 36–48; Stephen D. Behrendt, "Crew Mortality in the Transatlantic Slave Trade in the Eighteenth Century," ibid., 49–71; Wokeck, Trade in Strangers, 54, 79; Ekirch, Bound for America, 100; Marilyn C. Baseler, "Asylum for Mankind": America, 1607–1800 (Ithaca, N.Y., 1998), 93–99.

    15. Herbert S. Klein, Stanley L. Engerman, Robin Haines, and Ralph Shlomowitz, "Transoceanic Mortality: The Slave Trade in Comparative Perspective," WMQ, 3rd ser., 58 (2001), 93–117.

    16. Klein et al. "Transoceanic Mortality," 93–117; Robin Haines and Ralph Shlomowitz, "Explaining the Decline in Mortality in the Eighteenth-Century British Slave Trade," Economic History Review 53 (2000), 262–283 (quote on 264).

    17. Ekirch, Bound for America, 82, 90; Philip D. Curtin, Death by Migration: Europe's Encounter with the Tropical World in the Nineteenth Century (Cambridge, U.K., 1989); idem, "Migration in the Tropical World" in Virginia Yans-McLaughlin, ed., Immigration Reconsidered: History, Sociology, and Politics (New York, 1990), 21–36; Michael Duffy, Soldiers, Sugar, and Seapower: The British Expeditions to the West Indies and the War against Revolutionary France (Oxford, 1987), 134–135, 254–258, 326–334; Roger Norman Buckley, The British Army in the West Indies: Society and Military in the Revolutionary Age (Gainesville, Fla., 1998), 272–322; Philip R. P. Coelho and Robert A. McGuire, "African and European Bound Labor in the British New World: The Biological Consequences of Economic Choices," Journal of Economic History 57 (1997), 83–115.

    18. David Richardson, "Shipboard Revolts, African Authority, and the Atlantic Slave Trade," WMQ, 3rd ser., 58 (2001), 69–92; David Eltis, Stephen D. Behrendt, and David Richardson, "The Costs of Coercion: African Agency in Atlantic History," Economic History Review 54 (2001), 454–476.

19. Ekirch, *Bound for America*, 92, 99 (quote), 109–110 (1 in 37 convict voyages experienced a mutiny, based on about 450 convict shipments, Roger Ekirch personal communication); Farley Grubb, "The Transatlantic Market for British Convict Labor," *Journal of Economic History* 60 (2000), 104.

20. Bailyn, *Voyagers to the West*, 24–28; Mauro, "French Indentured Servants," 92–98; Huetz de Lemps, "Indentured Servants," 178–182, 194–198; Marianne Wokeck, "Harnessing the Lure of the 'Best Poor Man's Country': The Dynamics of German-Speaking Immigration to British North America, 1683–1783," in Altman and Horn, eds., *"To Make America,"* 206–210; Leslie Choquette, *Frenchmen into Peasants: Modernity and Tradition in the Peopling of French Canada* (Cambridge, Mass., 1997); Magnus Morner, "Spanish Migration to the New World to 1810: A Report on the State of Research," in Fredi Chiappelli, ed., *First Images of America: The Impact of the New World on the Old* (Berkeley, 1976), 732–782; Peter Boyd-Bowman, *Patterns of Spanish Emigration to the New World, 1493–1580* (Buffalo, N.Y., 1983); Ida Altman, *Emigrants and Society: Extremadura and Spanish America in the Sixteenth Century* (Berkeley, 1989); idem, *Transatlantic Ties in the Spanish Empire: Brihuega, Spain, and Puebla, Mexico, 1560–1620* (Stanford, 2000), 16–41; Nicolas Sanchez-Albornoz, "The First Transatlantic Transfer: Spanish Migration to the New World, 1483–1810," in Canny, ed., *Europeans on the Move*, 28–29, 34–36; Aaron Spencer Fogleman, *Hopeful Journeys: German Immigration, Settlement, and Political Culture in Colonial America, 1717–1775* (Philadelphia, 1996), 15–65; Wokeck, *Trade in Strangers*, 2–18.

21. James Horn, "British Diaspora: Emigration from Britain, 1680–1815," in P. J. Marshall, ed., *The Oxford History of the British Empire*, Vol. 2, *The Eighteenth Century* (Oxford, 1998), 31–49; Aaron S. Fogleman, "Migrations to the Thirteen British North American Colonies, 1700–1775: New Estimates," *Journal of Interdisciplinary History* 22 (1992), 691–709; Wokeck, *Trade in Strangers*, 37–47; Allan Kulikoff, *From British Peasants to Colonial American Farmers* (Chapel Hill, N.C., 2000), 39–71, 165–201.

22. Aaron S. Fogleman, "From Slaves, Convicts, and Servants to Free Passengers: The Transformation of Immigration in the Era of the American Revolution," *Journal of American History* 85 (1998), 70–76; Henry A. Gemery, "The White Population of the Colonial United States, 1607–1790," in Michael R. Haines and Richard H. Steckel, eds., *A Population History of North America* (New York, 2000), 166–174; idem, "European Emigration," 283–342; Kerby A. Miller, *Emigrants and Exiles: Ireland and the Irish Exodus to North America* (Oxford, 1985), 169; Maldwyn A. Jones, "Ulster Emigration, 1783–1815," in E. R. R. Green, ed., *Scotch-Irish History* (New York, 1969), 49; Smout et al., "Scottish Emigration," 97, 102; Eric Richards estimates a higher figure, about 20,000, for the period 1783–1803, *A History of the Highland Clearances*, Vol. 2, *Emigration, Protest, Reasons* (London, 1985), 195; J. M. Bumsted, *The Peoples of Canada: A Pre-Confederation History* (Oxford, 1992), 165–185.

23. David Eltis, "The Volume and Structure of the Transatlantic Slave Trade: A Reassessment," *WMQ*, 3rd ser., 58 (2001), 17–46.

24. David Richardson, "The British Empire and the Atlantic Slave Trade, 1660–1807," in Marshall, ed., *The Oxford History of the British Empire*, Vol. 2, *The Eighteenth Century*, 440–464.

25. Jan Lucassen, *Migrant Labour in Europe, 1600–1900: The Drift to the North Sea* (London, 1987), 133–171; Fertig, "Transatlantic Migration from the German-Speaking

Parts of Central Europe," 153–191, 203; Thomas Klingebiel, "Huguenot Settlements in Central Europe," in Hartmutt Lehmann, Hermann Wellenreuther, and Renate Wilson, eds., *In Search of Peace and Prosperity: New German Settlements in Eighteenth-Century Europe and America* (University Park, Pa., 2000), 40; Ida Altman, "Moving Around and Moving On: Spanish Emigration in the Sixteenth Century," in Jan Lucassen and Leo Lucassen, eds., *Migration, Migration History, History: Old Paradigms and New Perspectives* (Berne, 1997), 253–269; Joseph C. Miller, "The Significance of Drought, Disease, and Famine in the Agriculturally Marginal Zones of West-Central Africa," *Journal of Interdisciplinary History* 23 (1982), 17–61; J. Vansina, "Population Movements and Emergence of New Socio-Political Forms in Africa," in B. A. Ogot, ed., *General History of Africa*, Vol. 5, *Africa from the Sixteenth to the Eighteenth Century* (Berkeley, 1992), 46–73; Philip D. Curtin, *Why People Move: Migration in African History* (Waco, Tex., 1994); Igor Kopytoff, *The African Frontier: The Reproduction of Traditional African Societies* (Bloomington, Ind., 1987); Bailyn, *Voyagers to the West*, 271–285.

26. James Horn, "Servant Emigration to the Chesapeake in the Seventeenth Century," in Thad W. Tate and David L. Ammerman, eds., *The Chesapeake in the Seventeenth Century: Essays on Anglo-American Society* (Chapel Hill, N.C., 1979), 66–74, 87–94; John Wareing, "Migration to London and Transatlantic Emigration of Indentured Servants, 1683–1775," *Journal of Historical Geography* 7 (1981), 356–377; R. J. Dickson, *Ulster Emigration to Colonial America, 1718–1775* (London, 1966); Mauro, "French Indentured Servants," 98; Huetz de Lemps, "Indentured Servants," 178, 185–186; Bailyn, *Voyagers to the West*, 271–285; Manning, *Slavery and African Life*, 63–72.

27. Horn, "Servant Emigration," 66–74, 87–94; Wareing, "Migration to London"; Mauro, "French Indentured Servants," 98; Huetz de Lemps, "Indentured Servants," 178, 185–186; Choquette, *Frenchmen into Peasants*, 78–82, 86–87; Wokeck, *Trade in Strangers*, 60; David Eltis, Paul E. Lovejoy, and David Richardson, "Slave-Trading Ports: Towards an Atlantic Wide-Perspective, 1676–1832," in Robin Law and Silke Stickrodt, eds., *Ports of the Slave Trade (Bights of Benin and Biafra): Papers from a Conference of the Centre of Commonwealth Studies, University of Stirling, June 1998* (Stirling, U.K., 1999), 12–34.

28. Eltis, "Volume and Structure," 17–46; Stephen D. Behrendt, "Markets, Transaction Cycles, and Profits: Merchant Decision-Making in the British Slave Trade," *WMQ*, 3rd ser., 58 (2001), 171–204.

29. Wokeck, *Trade in Strangers*, 44, 167; Ekirch, *Bound for America*, 122–124; David Geggus, "The French Slave Trade: An Overview," *WMQ*, 3rd ser., 58 (2001), 126; Trevor Burnard and Kenneth Morgan, "The Dynamics of the Slave Market and Slave Purchasing Patterns in Jamaica, 1655–1788," *WMQ*, 3rd ser., 58 (2001), 209.

30. D. W. Meinig, *The Shaping of America. A Geographical Perspective on 500 Years of History*, Vol. 1, *Atlantic America, 1492–1800* (New Haven, Conn., 1986), part 3; Games, *Migration and the Origins of the English Atlantic World*, 132–162; Babette M. Levy, "Early Puritanism in the Southern and Island Colonies," *American Antiquarian Society, Proceedings* 70 (1960), 122–157; Fogleman, *Hopeful Journeys*, 69–153; Marianne Wokeck, "German Settlements in the British North American Colonies: A Patchwork of Cultural Assimilation and Persistence," in Lehmann et al., eds., *In Search of Peace and Prosperity*, 191–216; Patrick Griffin, *The People with No Name: Ireland's Ulster Scots, America's Scots Irish, and the Creation of a British Atlantic World, 1689–1764* (Princeton, 2001), 99–173, 202–221.

31. David Eltis, Stephen D. Behrendt, David Richardson, and Herbert S. Klein, eds., *The Trans-Atlantic Slave Trade: A Database on CD-ROM* (for Barbados) (Cambridge, U.K., 1999). Eltis, "Volume and Structure," 40, 46 (for Jamaica); Lorena S. Walsh, "The Chesapeake Slave Trade: Regional Patterns, African Origins, and Some Implications," *WMQ*, 3rd ser., 58 (2001), 139–170.

32. Horn, "Servant Emigration," 66–74; Wareing, "Migration to London," 356–377; Choquette, *Frenchmen into Peasants*, 37–45; Mauro, "French Indentured Servants," 92–95; Huetz de Lemps, "Indentured Servants," 178–182, 194–198; A. Gregg Roeber, *Palatines, Liberty, and Property: German Lutherans in Colonial America* (Baltimore, 1993); Fogleman, *Hopeful Journeys*, 15–65; Wokeck, "German Settlements," 191–216; Haberlein, "German Migrants," 555–574.

33. Meinig, *Atlantic America, 1492–1800*, 218.

34. David Northrup, "Igbo and Myth Igbo: Culture and Ethnicity in the Atlantic World, 1600–1850," *Slavery and Abolition* 21 (2000), 1–20. Cf. Douglas B. Chambers, "The Significance of Igbo in the Bight of Biafra Slave-Trade: A Rejoinder to Northrup's 'Myth Igbo,'" *Slavery and Abolition* 23 (2002), 101–120.

35. Karen Fog Olwig, "African Cultural Principles in Caribbean Slave Societies: A View from the Danish West Indies," in Stephan Palmie, ed., *Slave Cultures and the Culture of Slavery* (Knoxville, Tenn., 1995), 29; Northrup, "Igbo and Myth Igbo."

36. Ned C. Landsman, *Scotland and Its First American Colony, 1683–1765* (Princeton, 1985); Maldwyn A. Jones "The Scotch Irish in British America," in Bernard Bailyn and Philip D. Morgan, eds., *Strangers within the Realm: Cultural Margins of the First British Empire* (Chapel Hill, N.C., 1991), 184; Patrick Griffin, "The People with No Name: Ulster's Migrants and Identity Formation in Eighteenth-Century Pennsylvania," *WMQ*, 3rd ser., 58 (2001), 589–591; Wokeck, "German Settlements," 197.

37. Philip D. Morgan, "The Cultural Implications of the Atlantic Slave Trade: African Regional Origins, American Destinations, and New World Developments," *Slavery and Abolition* 18 (1997), 122–145; George Brandon, *Santeria from Africa to the New World: The Dead Sell Memories* (Bloomington, Ind., 1993), 55, 69.

38. See note 31 for sources.

T W O : Enslavement of Indians in Early America

1. Slowly, things change; the program for the Omohundro Institute of Early American History and Culture conference for 2003 (www.wm.edu/oieahc/conferences/9thannual/index.htm) included one panel that discussed Indian servitude and another that examined the Indian slave trade.

2. David Brion Davis, *The Problem of Slavery in Western Culture* (Ithaca, N.Y., 1966), 167–176; Robert A. Williams, Jr., *The American Indian in Western Legal Thought: The Discourses of Conquest* (New York, 1990), 82–83, 93–108; Anthony Pagden, *The Fall of Natural Man: The American Indian and the Origins of Comparative Ethnology*, rev. ed. (Cambridge, U.K., 1986); John Elliott, *Britain and Spain in America: Colonists and Colonized* (Reading, U.K., 1994), 17; Robin Blackburn, *The Making of New World Slavery: From the Baroque to the Modern, 1492–1800* (London, 1997), 133–137; Joyce E. Chaplin, "Race," in David Armitage and Michael J. Braddick, eds., *The British Atlantic World, 1500–1800* (New York, 2002), 161–163.

3. William S. Maltby, *The Black Legend in England: The Development of Anti-Spanish Sentiment, 1558–1660* (Durham, N.C., 1971); Edmund S. Morgan, *American Slavery, American Freedom: The Ordeal of Colonial Virginia* (New York, 1975), 6–24; Williams, *American Indian in Western Legal Thought*, 128.

4. Almon Wheeler Lauber, *Indian Slavery in Colonial Times within the Present Limits of the United States* (New York, 1913), 91, 106, 109–110, 112–117, 120–127, 172.

5. Lauber, *Indian Slavery*, 212, 218–219, 316; John M. Sainsbury, "Indian Labor in Early Rhode Island," *New England Quarterly* 48 (1975), 387–389.

6. Verner W. Crane, *The Southern Frontier, 1670–1732* (Ann Arbor, Mich., 1956); M. Eugene Sirmans, *Colonial South Carolina: A Political History, 1663–1763* (Chapel Hill, N.C., 1966), 22–23, 25, 33–34, 38, 40–43, 47, 53–54, 60; Jerome Handler, "The Amerindian Slave Population of Barbados in the Seventeenth and Early Eighteenth Centuries," *Caribbean Studies* 8 (1969), 38–64; Morgan, *American Slavery, American Freedom*, 99–100, 263–264, 328–330; Peter H. Wood, *Black Majority: Negroes in Colonial South Carolina from 1670 through the Stono Rebellion* (New York, 1974), 38–40, 155–156; J. Leitch Wright, Jr., *The Only Land They Knew: The Tragic Story of the American Indians in the Old South* (New York, 1981), 112–115, 125, 132–146; Alan Gallay, *The Indian Slave Trade: The Rise of the English Empire in the American South, 1670–1717* (New Haven, Conn., 2002), 299; Hilary McD. Beckles, *White Servitude and Black Slavery in Barbados, 1627–1715* (Knoxville, Tenn., 1989), 31; Eric Hinderaker, *Elusive Empires: Constructing Colonialism in the Ohio Valley, 1673–1800* (New York, 1997), 96; Barbara Olexer, *The Enslavement of the American Indian* (Monroe, N.Y., 1982); Peter H. Wood, "Indian Servitude in the Southeast," in Wilcomb E. Washburn, ed., *Handbook of North American Indians*, Vol. 4, *History of Indian-White Relations* (Washington, D.C., 1988); Yasuhide Kawashima, "Indian Servitude in the Northeast," ibid.; James H. Merrell, *The Indians' New World: Catawbas and their Neighbors from European Contact through the Era of Removal* (Chapel Hill, N.C., 1989), 36–37, 66, 100–101, 105; Helen Rountree, *Pocahontas's People: The Powhatan Indians of Virginia through Four Centuries* (Norman, Okla., 1990), 85–86; Daniel H. Usner, Jr., *Indians, Settlers, and Slaves in a Frontier Exchange Economy: The Lower Mississippi Valley before 1783* (Chapel Hill, N.C., 1992), 46–59.

7. Sherburne F. Cook, "Interracial Warfare and Population Decline among the New England Indians," *Ethnohistory* 20 (1973), 1–24; Sainsbury, "Indian Labor in Early Rhode Island"; Jill Lepore, *The Name of War: King Philip's War and the Origins of American Identity* (New York, 1998); April Lee Hatfield, *Atlantic Virginia: Intercolonial Relations in the Seventeenth Century* (Philadelphia, 2003); Russell M. Magnaghi, *Indian Slavery, Evangelization, and Captivity in the Americas: An Annotated Bibliography* (Lanham, Md., 1998).

8. David Beers Quinn et al., eds., *New American World: A Documentary History of North America*, 5 vols. (New York, 1996), 1:110; William C. Sturtevant and David B. Quinn, " 'This New Prey': Eskimos in Europe in 1567, 1576, and 1577," in Christian F. Feest, ed., *Indians and Europe: An Interdisciplinary Collection of Essays* (Aachen, Germany, 1987); Joyce E. Chaplin, *Subject Matter: Technology, the Body, and Science on the Anglo-American Frontier, 1500–1676* (Cambridge, Mass., 2001); A. Leon Higginbotham, *In the Matter of Color: Race and the American Legal Process: the Colonial Period* (New York, 1978), 160–162; Neal Salisbury, "Squanto: Last of the Patuxets," in David G. Sweet and Gary B. Nash, eds., *Struggle and Survival in Colonial America* (Berkeley, 1981),

232–235; idem, *Manitou and Providence: Indians, Europeans, and the Making of New England, 1500–1643* (New York, 1982), 96–101; James Axtell, *After Columbus: Essays in the Ethnohistory of Colonial North America* (New York, 1988), 171; Nicholas Canny, "England's New World and the Old, 1489s-1630s," in Nicholas Canny, ed., *The Oxford History of the British Empire*, Vol. 1, *The Origins of Empire: British Overseas Enterprise to the Close of the Seventeenth Century* (Oxford, 1997), 161–162; Alden T. Vaughan, "Trinculo's Indian: American Natives in Shakespeare's England," in Peter Hulme and William H. Sherman, eds., *The Tempest and Its Travels* (London, 2000).

9. Lauber, *Indian Slavery*, 25–34; Perdue, *Slavery and Creek Society*, chap. 1.

10. Higginbotham, *In the Matter of Color*, 66–70; Morgan, *American Slavery, American Freedom*, 74, 328–329; Ian K. Steele, "Surrendering Rites: Prisoners on Colonial North American Frontiers," in Stephen Taylor, Richard Connors, and Clyve Jones, eds., *Hanoverian Britain and Empire* (London, 1998).

11. [Tom Law], *The Rebels Reward: Or, English Courage Display'd . . .* (Boston, 1724), lines 193–196.

12. Rountree, *Pocahontas's People*, 54–55; Peter Hulme, *Colonial Encounters: Europe and the Native Caribbean, 1492–1797* (New York, 1992), chap. 4; Karen Ordahl Kupperman, *Facing Off in North America: Indians and English* (New York, 2000), chap. 6; Wright, *Only Land They Knew*, 237; Wolfgang Hochbruck and Beatrix Dudensing-Reichel, "'Honoratissimi benefactores': Native American Students and Two Seventeenth-Century Texts in the University Tradition," in Helen Jaskoski, ed., *Early Native American Writing: New Critical Essays* (New York, 1996), 1–14.

13. Gregory A. Waselkov, "Indian Maps of the Colonial Southeast," in Peter H. Wood, Gregory A. Waselkov, and M. Thomas Hatley, eds., *Powhatan's Mantle: Indians in the Colonial Southeast* (Lincoln, Neb., 1989), 313–320.

14. Martha W. McCartney, "Cockacoeske, Queen of Pamunkey: Diplomat and Suzeraine," in *Powhatan's Mantle*; Merrell, *Indians' New World*; Daniel K. Richter, "Native Peoples of North America and the Eighteenth-Century British Empire," in P. J. Marshall, ed., *The Oxford History of the British Empire*, Vol. 2, *The Eighteenth Century* (Oxford, 1998), 2:361–362; Harold W. Van Lonkhuyzen, "A Reappraisal of the Praying Indians: Acculturation, Conversion, and Identity at Natick, Massachusetts, 1646–1730," *New England Quarterly* 63 (1990), 396–428.

15. Alan Gallay, *The Formation of a Planter Elite: Jonathan Bryan and the Southern Colonial Frontier* (Athens, Ga., 1989), 5, 12, 16; John Demos, *The Unredeemed Captive: A Family Story from Early America* (New York, 1994).

16. Winthrop D. Jordan, *White over Black: American Attitudes toward the Negro, 1550–1812* (Chapel Hill, N.C., 1967), 89, 162–163, 239–240, 477–481; George M. Fredrickson, *White Supremacy: A Comparative Study in American and South African History* (New York, 1981), 37; Elliott, *Britain and Spain in America*, 17, 20; Peter Kolchin, *American Slavery, 1619–1877* (New York, 1993), 7–8; Blackburn, *Making of New World Slavery*, 133–137; Ira Berlin, *Many Thousands Gone: The First Two Centuries of Slavery in North America* (Cambridge, Mass., 1998), 144–145; David Eltis, *The Rise of African Slavery in the Americas* (Cambridge, U.K., 2000), 11, 24–25 (Spanish lack of Indian slavery), 27, 54 (Portuguese and English enslavement of Indians), 62–64 (multiple labor sources and counterfactual scenarios, meaning enslaved Europeans and indentured Africans); Betty Wood, *The Origins of American Slavery: Freedom and Bondage in the English Colonies* (New York, 1997), 29–39, 75, 95, 102–104.

17. Davis, *Problem of Slavery in Western Culture*, 176; Wood, *Black Majority*; Morgan, *American Slavery, American Freedom*; Usner, *Indians, Settlers, and Slaves*; Morgan, *Slave Counterpoint: Black Culture in the Eighteenth-Century Chesapeake and Lowcountry* (Chapel Hill, N.C., 1998).

18. Lauber, *Indian Slavery*, 283–292; Jordan, *White over Black*, 89–91; David Brion Davis, *Slavery and Human Progress* (New York, 1984), 65–66; Kolchin, *American Slavery*, 7–8; Fredrickson, *White Supremacy*, 56–58.

19. William Bartram, *Travels through North and South Carolina, Georgia, East and West Florida* . . . (1791), intro. by James Dickey (New York, 1988), 164, 183; Richard Ligon, *A True and Exact History of the Island of Barbados* (London, 1657), 54.

20. Chaplin, *Subject Matter*, chaps. 4, 6, 7; Thomas Jefferson, *Notes on the State of Virginia* (1787), ed. William Peden (Chapel Hill, N.C., 1954), 61.

21. Donald Grinde, Jr., "Native American Slavery in the Southern Colonies," *The Indian Historian* 10 (1977), 39–40; Douglas H. Ubelaker, "North American Indian Population Size: Changing Perspectives," in John W. Verano and Douglas Ubelaker, eds., *Disease and Demography in the Americas* (Washington, D.C., 1992), 172; Peter H. Wood, "The Changing Population of the Colonial South: An Overview by Race and Region, 1685–1790," *Powhatan's Mantle*, 78.

22. Alden T. Vaughan and Edward W. Clark, eds., *Puritans among the Indians: Accounts of Captivity and Redemption, 1676–1724* (Cambridge, Mass., 1981), 2–3; Richard Slotkin, *Regeneration through Violence: The Mythology of the American Frontier, 1600–1860* (Middletown, Conn., 1973).

23. Paul Baepler, "The Barbary Captivity Narrative in Early America," *Early American Literature* 30 (1995), 95–120; Joe Snader, "The Oriental Captivity Narrative and Early English Fiction," *Eighteenth-Century Fiction* 9 (1997), 267–298; Linda Colley, *Captives: Britain, Empire, and the World, 1600–1850* (New York, 2003).

24. Nancy Armstrong and Leonard Tennenhouse, "The American Origins of the English Novel," *American Literary History* 4 (1992), 386–410; Michelle Burnham, *Captivity and Sentiment: Cultural Exchange in American Literature, 1682–1861* (Hanover, N.H., 1997), 10–62.

25. Charles T. Davis and Henry Louis Gates, Jr., eds., *The Slave's Narrative* (New York, 1985); Rafia Zafir, "Capturing the Captivity: African Americans among the Puritans," *MELUS* 17 (1991/92); Eric J. Sundquist, *To Wake the Nations: Race in the Making of American Literature* (Cambridge, Mass., 1993), 2–24, 37–42, 83–93.

26. Hulme, *Colonial Encounters*, chap. 3; David Scott Kastan, "'The Duke of Milan / And His Brave Son': Dynastic Politics in the Tempest," in Virginia Mason Vaughan and Alden T. Vaughan, eds., *Critical Essays on Shakespeare's The Tempest* (New York, 1998).

27. Davis, *Problem of Slavery in Western Culture*, 11–13; Hulme, *Colonial Encounters*, esp. chaps. 5, 6; Joseph Roach, *Cities of the Dead: Circum-Atlantic Performance* (New York, 1996), chap. 4; Frank Felsenstein, ed., *English Trader, Indian Maid: Representing Gender, Race, and Slavery in the New World: An Inkle and Yarico Reader* (Baltimore, 1999), intro.

28. Peter C. Mancall, "Native Americans and Europeans in English America, 1500–1700," *Oxford History of the British Empire*, 1:345; Lepore, *Name of War*, chaps. 2, 5; David Waldstreicher, *In the Midst of Perpetual Fetes: The Making of American Nationalism, 1776–1820* (Chapel Hill, N.C., 1997), 271–274.

29. Lauber, *Indian Slavery*, 198 (Spotswood); Eleazar Wheelock, *A Plain and Faithful Narrative of . . . the Indian Charity School at Lebanon, in Connecticut* (Boston, 1763), 41; Samson Occom, *A Short Narrative of My Life*, in Paul Lauter, ed., *The Heath Anthology of American Literature*, 2 vols. (Lexington, Mass., 1990), 1:731.

30. Experience Mayhew, *Indian Converts: or, some Account of the Lives and Dying Speeches of . . . the Christianized Indians* (Boston, 1727), 295, 296; Lepore, *Name of War*, chap. 1.

31. David Murray, *Forked Tongues: Speech, Writing, and Representation in North American Indian Texts* (Bloomington, Ind., 1991), 49–64.

32. Bill Ashcroft, Gareth Griffiths, and Helen Tiffin, *The Empire Writes Back: Theory and Practice in Post-Colonial Literatures* (New York, 1989), 133–145; Arnold Krupat, *The Voice in the Margin: Native American Literature and the Canon* (Berkeley, 1989), chap. 1; Laura Murray, "'Pray Sir, consider a little': Rituals of Subordination and Strategies of Resistance of the Letters of Hezekiah Calvin and David Fowler to Eleazar Wheelock," in *Early Native American Writing*, 15–41; Dana D. Nelson, "'(I speak like a fool but I am constrained)': Samson Occom's Short Narrative and Economies of the Racial Self," in ibid., 42–62; Ives Goddard and Kathleen J. Bragdon, eds., *Native Writings in Massachusett* (Philadelphia, 1988), 1:373, 431.

33. Chaplin, *Subject Matter*, chap. 6.

34. Compare Gallay, *Indian Slave Trade*, which emphasizes Indian slavery as a frontier phenomenon, with James F. Brooks, *Captives and Cousins: Slavery, Kinship, and Community in the Southwest Borderlands* (Chapel Hill, N.C., 2002). On black-white relations, see Martha Hodes, *White Women, Black Men: Illicit Sex in the Nineteenth-Century South* (New Haven, Conn., 1997).

35. On mestizo populations in Southern colonies, see Berry Brewton, "America's Mestizos," in Noel P. Gist and Anthony Gary Dworkin, eds., *The Blending of Races: Marginality and Identity in World Perspective* (New York, 1972), 194–197; Wood, *Black Majority*, 98–99; Wright, *Only Land They Knew*, 234–237; Wood, "Changing Population of the Colonial South," 47; Gwendolyn Midlo Hall, *Africans in Colonial Louisiana: The Development of Afro-Creole Culture in the Eighteenth Century* (Baton Rouge, La., 1992), 15–16, 128–129, 239–243, 256–274; Usner, *Indians, Settlers, and Slaves*, 108; Colin G. Calloway, *The American Revolution in Indian Country: Crisis and Diversity in Native American Communities* (Cambridge, U.K., 1995), 17; Gary B. Nash, "The Hidden History of Mestizo America," *Journal of American History* 82 (1995), 941–962; Roach, *Cities of the Dead*, chap. 6; Morgan, *Slave Counterpoint*, 479–482. On métis in New France and later Canada, see Jennifer S. H. Brown, *Strangers in Blood: Fur Trade Company Families in Indian Country* (Vancouver, 1980); Sylvia Van Kirk, *"Many Tender Ties": Women in Fur-Trade Society, 1670–1870* (Winnipeg, 1980); Jacqueline Peterson and Jennifer S. H. Brown, eds., *The New Peoples: Being and Becoming Métis in North America* (Lincoln, Neb., 1985).

36. Peterson and Brown, *New Peoples*; Ruth Wallis Herndon and Ella Wilcox Sekatau, "The Right to a Name: The Narragansett People and Rhode Island Officials in the Revolutionary Era," *Ethnohistory* 44 (1997), 433–462.

37. Elaine G. Breslaw, *Tituba, Reluctant Witch of Salem: Devilish Indians and Puritan Fantasies* (New York, 1996); Sainsbury, "Indian Labor in Early Rhode Island," 379, 392–393; Lauber, *Indian Slavery*, 274.

38. Wilcomb E. Washburn, "The Moral and Legal Justification for Dispossessing the Indians," in James Morton Smith, ed., *Seventeenth-Century America: Essays in Colonial History* (Chapel Hill, N.C., 1959), 15–32.

39. Robert Boyle to the Commissioners of the United Colonies in New England, March 17, 1664, in Hazard, ed., *Historical Collections*, 2:491–492; John Eliot to Boyle, Dec. 17, 1675, in John W. Ford, ed., *Some Correspondence between . . . the New England Company in London and the Commissioners of the United Colonies in America* (London, 1897), 52–55; Eliot to Boyle, Oct. 23, 1677, in Thomas Birch, ed., *The Works of the Honourable Robert Boyle*, 5 vols. (London, 1744), 1:134–135.

40. James H. Tully, *An Approach to Political Philosophy: Locke in Contexts* (Cambridge, U.K., 1993), 137–176; Barbara Arneil, *John Locke and America: The Defence of English Colonialism* (Oxford, 1996); Commissioners of the United Colonies in New England to Robert Boyle, Sept. 13, 1665, Ford, ed., *Some Correspondence*, 11–15; Boyle to the Commissioners, June 4, 1668, ibid.; Commissioners to Boyle, Sept. 10, 1668, ibid., 18–21; John Locke, *A Letter Concerning Toleration*, ed. James H. Tully (Indianapolis, Ind., 1983), 43 (quotation).

41. Higginbotham, *In the Matter of Color*, 116 and note 4, above; Betty Wood, *Slavery in Colonial Georgia, 1730–1775* (Athens, Ga., 1984), chap. 1.

42. Lauber, *Indian Slavery*, 312–316, 319; Davis, *Problem of Slavery in Western Culture*, 177, 180–181.

43. Arthur Zilversmit, *The First Emancipation: The Abolition of Slavery in the North* (Chicago, 1967); Shane White, *Somewhat More Independent: The End of Slavery in New York City, 1770–1810* (Athens, Ga., 1991); Joanne Pope Melish, *Disowning Slavery: Gradual Emancipation and "Race" in New England, 1780–1860* (Ithaca, N.Y., 1998), which has some attention to Indians; Woody Holton, *Forced Founders: Indians, Debtors, Slaves, and the Making of the American Revolution in Virginia* (Chapel Hill, N.C., 1999).

44. James H. Kettner, *The Development of American Citizenship, 1608–1870* (Chapel Hill, N.C., 1978), chaps. 1–5.

45. Ralph Hamor, *A True Discourse of the Present Estate of Virginia* (London, 1615), 15; Robert Boyle to the Commissioners of the United Colonies, [1669?], in Ford, ed., *Some Correspondence*, 25–27; Daniel K. Richter, *The Ordeal of the Longhouse: The Peoples of the Iroquois League in the Era of European Colonization* (Chapel Hill, N.C., 1992), 155–156; Richard White, *The Middle Ground: Indians, Empires and Republics in the Great Lakes Region, 1650–1815* (New York, 1991), chaps. 7, 8, and pp. 463–468; Lauber, *Indian Slavery*, 174, 303–311 (Sharp on 306–307); Kettner, *American Citizenship*, 87.

46. Brian Slattery, "The Hidden Constitution: Aboriginal Rights in Canada," in Menno Boldt et al., eds., *The Quest for Justice: Aboriginal Peoples and Aboriginal Rights* (Toronto, 1985); White, *Middle Ground*, 256–268; Hinderaker, *Elusive Empires*, 134–170.

47. Christopher L. Brown, "Empire without Slaves: British Concepts of Emancipation in the Age of the American Revolution," *William and Mary Quarterly*, 3rd ser., 56 (1999), 273–306; Moira Ferguson, *Subject to Others: British Women Writers and Colonial Slavery, 1670–1834* (London, 1992), 85–90; idem, *Colonialism and Gender Relations from Mary Wollstonecraft to Jamaica Kincaid* (New York, 1993), 11, 27; Felsenstein, *English Trader, Indian Maid*, 13–18, 40–44.

48. A Citizen, *Cursory Remarks on Men and Measures in Georgia* (n. p., 1784), 18–21.

49. Jefferson, *Notes on the State of Virginia,* 61; Bartram, *Travels,* 69, 164, 183, 350, 351.

50. Calloway, *American Revolution in Indian Country;* Hinderaker, *Elusive Empires,* 260–270; Worthington C. Ford et al., eds., *Journals of the Continental Congress, 1774–1789,* 34 vols. (Washington, D.C., 1904–37), 9:919; Francis P. Prucha, *American Indian Policy in the Formative Years: The Indian Trade and Intercourse Acts, 1780–1834* (Cambridge, Mass., 1962); Reginald Horsman, "United States Indian Policies, 1776–1815," in *Handbook of North American Indians,* 4:29–39.

51. William Apess, *Indian Nullification of the Unconstitutional Laws of Massachusetts Relative to the Marshpee Tribe . . .* (1835), in Barry O'Connell, ed., *On Our Own Ground: The Complete Writings of William Apess, A Pequot* (Amherst, Mass., 1992), 188; Bernard W. Sheehan, *Seeds of Extinction: Jeffersonian Philanthropy and the American Indian Policy, 1783–1812* (Chapel Hill, N.C., 1973); Ronald N. Satz, *American Indian Policy in the Jacksonian Era* (Lincoln, Neb., 1975); Brian W. Dippie, *The Vanishing American: White Attitudes and United States Indian Policy* (Middletown, Conn., 1982), 1–138, 192; Kettner, *American Citizenship,* chap. 10.

THREE: "The Predicament of Ubi"

The author thanks the editors of this volume and the members of the Research Seminar in Early Modern Colonial British America at the Johns Hopkins University for their questions, comments, and suggestions regarding earlier drafts of this essay. The author also thanks Daniel Richter and the McNeil Center for Early American Studies for their support while he was preparing this essay.

1. According to Anthony Pagden, this "Roman Law argument . . . maintained that all 'empty things,' which included unoccupied lands, remained the common property of all mankind until they were put to some, generally, agricultural use. The first person to use the land in this way became its owner." He notes that "with very few exceptions this argument was employed by English colonists and their champions from the 1620s on." *Lords of All the World: Ideologies of Empire in Spain, Britain and France c. 1500–c.1800* (New Haven, Conn., 1995), 76–77.

2. Jack P. Greene, "Negotiated Authorities: The Problem of Governance in the Extended Polities of the Early Modern Atlantic World," and "The Colonial Origins of American Constitutionalism," in idem, *Negotiated Authorities: Essays in Colonial and Constitutional History* (Charlottesville, Va., 1994), 1–24, 25–42.

3. Early modern Europeans often thought of liberty, law, and allegiance as interrelated, but the colonial setting complicated those linkages. Colonial charters commonly guaranteed the extension of English law to settlers, but charters were products of the king's prerogative and thus frequently subject to alteration or revocation. Colonists nevertheless transformed allegiance into a guarantee of legal privileges by asserting a linkage between their status as subjects of the Crown and the extension of English liberties to colonial subjects. For colonists, subjection to the Crown signified membership in a political community—a kingdom—in which they held certain rights, liberties, and privileges. For the extension of English law to the colonies, see Jack P. Greene, *Peripheries and Center: Constitutional Development in the Extended Polities of the British Empire and the United States, 1607–1788* (Athens, Ga., 1986), chaps. 1 and 2. For the argument that liberty and common law were central elements of English national and imperial identity, see Greene, "Empire and Identity from the Glorious Revolution to the

American Revolution," in P. J. Marshall, ed., *The Oxford History of the British Empire*, Vol. 2, *The Eighteenth Century* (Oxford, 1998), 208–230. For the mid-seventeenth century, see Carla Pestana, *The English Atlantic in an Age of Revolution, 1640–1660* (Cambridge, Mass., 2004).

4. *Cobbett's Complete Collection of State Trials and Proceedings for High Treason, and Other Crimes and Misdemeanor from the Earliest Period to the Present Time*, 33 vols. (London, 1809–26), 2:436–437.

5. In *Lords of All the World*, Pagden defines *dominium* to encompass both concepts, but allows for different kinds of dominium (p. 51). By contrast, David Armitage, *The Ideological Origins of the British Empire* (Cambridge, U.K., 2000), distinguishes between ownership and sovereignty; *dominium* applies to the former and *imperium* to the latter (p. 63). English imperial apologists defined themselves in opposition to the Spanish by not insisting upon a claim to the bodies or labor of native American peoples.

6. Jurisdictional constructions shaped social practice by determining the kinds of roles and identities agents could perform or be expected to perform within a space, as Yong's writings demonstrate.

7. Harald Gustafsson, who deserves credit for being one of the most careful and sensitive historians of early modern political and ethnic identities, prefers not to refer to the "ethno-territorial political identities" he observes in sixteenth-century Scandinavia as "national identities." He notes that "'nations,' 'nationalism,' and so on, always convey to us associations with modern nationalist ideologies and sentiments, regardless of how often we remind ourselves and our readers of the opposite." When I use the term *national identity*, I trust that readers will be more capable of distinguishing the important differences between early modern and modern usages of *nation*. Gustafsson, "The Eighth Argument: Identity, Ethnicity and Political Culture in Sixteenth-Century Scandinavia," *Scandinavian Journal of History* 27 (2002), 112. In the mid and late seventeenth century, and especially in the eighteenth century, the ideological location of political authority shifted radically away from the Crown-centered visions promoted by the Stuarts and toward "the people." In this ideological shift toward popular sovereignty and the self-conscious elaboration of a territorially defined "people," we begin to see something that resembles the conventional view of the modern "nation."

8. Albert Cook Myers, ed., *Narratives of Early Pennsylvania, West New Jersey, and Delaware, 1630–1707* (New York, [1912] 1967), 33.

9. The greater body of evidence relating to Yong is in the correspondence pertaining to his voyage and in various royal records, including letters Yong wrote to royal officials and the king while in England, documents prepared by royal officials in response to his requests, letters Yong sent from America to royal officials or members of the royal court, third-party correspondence and records in Virginia that refer to Yong, and diverse texts from the 1640s that refer to Yong's expedition and the abortive, little-known mid-Atlantic colony of New Albion. Regarding Yong's connections to English Catholicism, we have evidence of his correspondence with the English Catholic Sir Tobie Matthew and his desire to aid Maryland's Catholic proprietor, Lord Baltimore. We also know that Yong's lieutenant for the mission, his nephew Robert Evelin, helped promote the colonial ambitions of Sir Edmund Plowden, another high-placed Catholic. Although Secretary Francis Windebanke, Yong's correspondent in the royal government, converted to Catholicism during his later exile in France, and many historians state that he was a Catholic when in royal service, evidence from the 1630s suggests

that he was more likely to be Arminian than actually Catholic; see Kevin Sharpe, *The Personal Rule of Charles I* (New Haven, 1992), 157–159. Other historians have assumed the "proceedings of Yong were apparently carried on in concert with those of Maryland," and that Yong was a Catholic involved in a larger effort to establish English Catholic colonies in America; see *Collections of the Massachusetts Historical Society* (hereafter, *CMHS*), Vol. 9, 4th ser., *Aspinwall Papers* (Boston, 1871), 83, 100.

10. G. D. Scull, ed., *The Evelyns in America, 1608–1805* (Oxford, 1881), 55–58. Scull's printed version, quoted here, differs slightly in punctuation and spelling from the original document (CO 1/8, 23–24), which I have consulted at the Public Record Office (PRO) at Kew.

11. Scull, ed., *The Evelyns in America*, 55.

12. In a subsequent letter to the king's secretary of state, dated April 1634, Yong asked that Sir Francis Windebanke speak to "my Lord Cheefe Justice Richardson about the freing of Mr. Baker, and for the delivery up off his surrties' bonds." Yong thus sought to mobilize the highest judicial authority to free his cosmographer; see ibid., 57–58. See also PRO, CO 1/8, 21–22.

13. On the early Stuart oaths of allegiance, see David M. Jones, *Conscience and Allegiance in Seventeenth Century England: The Political Significance of Oaths and Engagements* (Rochester, N.Y., 1999). The oath of allegiance was anathema to some English Catholics because it declared the king to be head of the church in England and explicitly disavowed papal authority in the kingdom. Russell Menard and Lois Green Carr note that "[v]essels carrying passengers from London were required to call at Gravesend at the mouth of the Thames so that those leaving the country could take the Oath of Allegiance to the crown as was now required (the stricter imposition of the Oath of Supremacy, which few Catholics would take, had been abandoned)"; see "The Lords of Baltimore and the Colonization of Maryland," in David B. Quinn, ed., *Early Maryland in a Wider World* (Detroit, 1982), 168.

14. The assembly passed three versions of the law on Feb. 21, 1632, Sept. 4, 1632, and Aug. 21, 1633. See William W. Hening, *Statutes at Large; Being a Collection of All the Laws of Virginia from the First Session of the Legislature in the Year 1619*, 18 vols. (Richmond, Va., 1809–23), 1:166, 191, 214. In 1629 Virginia's officials blocked Lord Baltimore from disembarking because he refused to swear the oath of supremacy. Afterwards, in a letter to the Privy Council, Virginia's governor and council explained that there was no blessing "whereby we have been made more happy than in the freedom of our religion which we have enjoyed, and that no papists have been suffered to settle their abodes among us." Quoted in Philip Alexander Bruce, *Institutional History of Virginia in the Seventeenth Century*, 2 vols. (New York, 1910), 1:264–265.

15. Scull, ed., *The Evelyns in America*, 58.

16. Letter from Yong to Windebanke, Oct. 20, 1634, in C. A. Weslager with A. R. Dunlap, *Dutch Explorers, Traders and Settlers in the Delaware Valley, 1609–1664* (Philadelphia, 1961), 303–305.

17. Thomas Rymer's *Foedera, conventiones, liter, et cujuscunque generis acta publica . . .*, 20 vols. (London, 1726–35), 19:472–474. According to the commission, the descendants of these colonists would have had the privilege of being considered natural-born subjects under English law.

18. Ibid., 472.

19. *CMHS*, 108–109.

20. On the civic mode of acting as counselor to the prince, see J. G. A. Pocock, *The Machiavellian Moment: Florentine Political Thought and the Atlantic Republican Tradition* (Princeton, 1975), 338–341, and Arthur B. Ferguson, *The Articulate Citizen and the English Renaissance,* (Durham, N.C., 1965).

21. *CMHS*, 114. Yong also requested that Matthew show the letter to Lord Baltimore, so that he might take appropriate action.

22. *CMHS*, 103, 107, 109, 110.

23. Harvey was thus an exemplary official in what Arthur B. Ferguson identifies as a medieval English tradition of counsel, though modified perhaps by echoes of a dormant republican patriotic tradition. In either case, his comments fit seamlessly into the early Stuarts' own vocal admonishments of wayward officials; see Ferguson, *The Articulate Citizen and the English Renaissance.* For republican patriotism, see Markku Peltonen, *Classical Humanism and Republicanism in English Political Thought, 1570–1640* (Cambridge, U.K., 1995) and Andrew Fitzmaurice, "The Civic Solution to the Crisis of English Colonization, 1609–1625," *The Historical Journal* 42, (1999), 25–51, for evidence of the survival of republican thinking in early-seventeenth-century English political thought.

24. *CMHS*, 109, 112, 107.

25. Ibid., 109. Yong does not mention his dispute with Mathews in his letters, but other correspondence from Virginia refers to a quarrel between Yong and Mathews. Governor Harvey, explaining to metropolitan officials Mathews's enmity toward himself, wrote that he "hath particular quarrells to mee, for that I have endeavoured to obey his Majesties command in assisting Captain Yonge, whom Mathewes opposed for no other cause then for that he came not to present his service to him and sought not his favour: And thereupon he tould mee, before divers persons that such condissions as Captaine Yonges would breed bad blood in Virginia," Warren M. Billings, ed., *The Old Dominion in the Seventeenth Century: A Documentary History of Virginia, 1606–1689* (Chapel Hill, N.C., 1975), 256. Another explanation for the dispute is that "Captain Matthews had disputed the Governor's construction of Yong's commission, and denied his authority to allow a planter's man, a shipwright to work in setting up Yong's shallop," *CMHS*, 146.

26. *CMHS*, 107–108, 110, 114.

27. Ibid., 106–107, 110.

28. Ibid., 114, 109.

29. Ibid., 114.

30. On perceptions of indigenous political organization, see Karen Ordahl Kupperman, *Settling with the Indians: The Meeting of English and Indian Cultures in America, 1580–1640* (Totowa, N.J., 1980), 46–55.

31. Myers, ed., *Narratives,* 37–38. Here Yong identified local Indians as a group linked to the river in territorial terms. These terms likely reflected the general lines of division among Indians in that region, although they also obscured the divisions among "like" peoples as well as the internal diversity and complexity of those peoples.

32. Myers, ed., *Narratives,* 38–39.

33. Ibid., 39. It is unclear whether Yong meant to imply that because these Indians were self-described Minquaos and one of them was "a king," that this individual was the king of the Minquaos. The English would later call these people Susquehannocks. They called the Delaware River's indigenous inhabitants "River Indians" or Delaware Indians.

34. "Answer to the Remonstrance of the Dutch Ambassadors, May 23, 1632," in E. B. O'Callaghan, ed., *Documents Relative to the Colonial History of the State of New York*, 15 vols. (Albany, 1856–1887), 1:58. The original document, written in French, is located in the Algemeen Rijksarchief in the Hague, Archief Staten-Generaal, "liassen Engelandt" (1.01.04, inventory number 5892). Significantly, Charles I made this assertion to counter Dutch claims to territory purchased from Indian peoples in North America.

35. Myers, ed., *Narratives*, 40.

36. Ibid., 41.

37. Ibid. On Spanish justifications for empire, see Pagden, *Lords of All the World*. For a comparative approach to practices of claiming the New World, see Patricia Seed's *Ceremonies of Possession in Europe's Conquest of the New World, 1492–1640* (New York, 1995). In a footnote she mistakenly refers to Yong as a Swedish explorer.

38. Rymer, *Foedera, conventiones*, 19:473.

39. Myers, ed., *Narratives*, 41–42.

40. Ibid., 43.

41. Ibid.

42. Kupperman writes that the Virginia Company "sternly objected to the use of the word *king* for Powhatan, saying Virginia knew no king but King James, and chided them for seeming to recognize the sovereignty of Opechancanough, Powhatan's successor." Colonists nevertheless "constantly used" the term, she writes. *Settling with the Indians*, 49.

43. Mark Thompson, "National Subjects in a Contested Colonial Space: Allegiance, Ethnicity, and Authority in the Seventeenth-Century Delaware Valley" (Ph.D. diss., The Johns Hopkins University, 2004).

44. Myers, ed., *Narratives*, 44.

45. Ibid., 44. It is unclear whether any colonists, as distinguished from the crew, were on the ship. It seems unlikely given that Yong never referred to passengers or settlers in his correspondence.

46. Ibid. 44–45.

47. See David Pietersz de Vries, *Korte Historiael ende Journaels Aenteykeninge van verscheyden voyagiens in de vier deelen des wereldts-ronde, als Europa, Africa, Asia, ende Amerika gedaen*, ed. H. T. Colenbrander ('s-Gravenhage, [1655] 1911), 169. For a partial English translation of de Vries's published journal, see de Vries, *Voyages from Holland to America, A.D. 1632 to 1644*, ed. and trans. Henry C. Murphy (New York, [1853] 1971), 50–51.

48. Myers, ed., *Narratives*, 45.

49. Ibid.

50. Ibid., 45–46.

51. Ibid., 46.

52. Ibid.

53. Ibid., 49.

54. Yong to Windebanke, Oct. 20, 1634, in Weslager, *Dutch Explorers*, 303–304. Yong may have been captured near Quebec in 1636 while continuing his search for a northwest passage. Evelin traveled to England to deliver Yong's reports from the Delaware, but returned to Virginia to be a planter.

55. It is not clear whether New Netherland's administrators forced the English settlers to leave the Delaware or whether they asked to be taken out. De Vries brought them

back to Virginia in 1635. See C. A. Weslager, *The English on the Delaware: 1610–1682* (New Brunswick, N.J., 1967), 49–52. On Yong's voyage and his writings in general, see 42–53.

56. Weslager, *The English on the Delaware*, 255.

57. Colin Kidd, *British Identities before Nationalism: Ethnicity and Nationhood in the Atlantic World, 1600–1800* (Cambridge, U.K., 1999), 288.

58. Yong to Windebanke, Oct. 20, 1634, in Weslager, *Dutch Explorers*, 304.

FOUR: "Subjects to the King of Portugal"

I would like to thank the editors of this volume, Carole Shammas and Elizabeth Mancke, for their helpful comments on drafts of this chapter and some assistance with sources. I would also like to thank Linda Rupert for her assistance.

1. Philip D. Curtin, "The Atlantic Slave Trade, 1600–1800," in J. F. A. Ajayi and Michael Crowder, eds., *History of West Africa*, 2 vols. (New York, 1972), 2:240–268; idem, *The Atlantic Slave Trade: A Census* (Madison, Wisc., 1969); idem, *The Rise and Fall of the Plantation Complex: Essays in Atlantic History* (Cambridge, U.K., 1990); idem, *Cross-Cultural Trade in World History* (Cambridge, U.K., 1984); Herbert S. Klein, *The Atlantic Slave Trade* (Cambridge, U.K., 1999); David Eltis, *The Rise of African Slavery in the Americas* (Cambridge, U.K., 2000); Jerry H. Bentley, "Sea and Ocean Basins as Frameworks of Historical Analysis," *The Geographical Review* 89 (1999), 215–224; Elizabeth Mancke, "Early Modern Expansion and the Politicization of Ocean Space," *The Geographical Review* 89 (1999), 225–236; Lauren Benton, "The Legal Regime of the South Atlantic World, 1400–1750: Jurisdictional Complexity as Institutional Order," *Journal of World History* 11 (2000), 27–56; Nicholas Canny, "Writing Atlantic History; or Reconfiguring the History of Colonial British America," *Journal of American History* 86 (1999), 1093–1114; Jack P. Greene, "Beyond Power: Paradigm Subversion and Reformulation and the Re-creation of the Early Modern Atlantic World," in Darlene Clark Hine and Jacqueline McLeod, eds., *Crossing Boundaries: Comparative History of Black People in Diaspora* (Bloomington, Ind., 1999), 319–342.

2. Robert Darnton, *The Great Cat Massacre and Other Episodes in French Cultural History* (New York, 1984), 6.

3. Hart to Board of Trade (hereafter BT), July 12, 1724, Colonial Office (hereafter CO) 152/14, R101; Dec. 24, 1724, CO 152/15, R121, Public Record Office, Surrey, U.K.

4. Copies of the detailed depositions can be found as enclosure no. 1 in Hart to BT, Dec. 24, 1724, CO 152/15, R121. The depositions were later entered in the minutes of the Antigua legislature: Minutes of Antigua Council in Assembly, Nov. 26, 1724, CO 9/5. In this same source, see all the minutes of Nov. 21, 1724.

5. "The Deposition of John Jones Mariner," Nov. 14, 1724, Minutes of Antigua Council in Assembly, Nov. 26, 1724, CO 9/5; Kenneth Morgan, *Bristol and the Atlantic Trade in the Eighteenth Century* (Cambridge, U.K., 1993).

6. Ralph Davis, *The Rise of the English Shipping Industry in the Seventeenth and Eighteenth Centuries* (London, 1962), 269; T. Bentley Duncan, *Atlantic Islands: Madeira, the Azores, and the Cape Verdes in Seventeenth-Century Commerce and Navigation* (Chicago, 1972), 25–79; A. D. Francis, *The Wine Trade* (London, 1972); David Hancock, "Commerce and Conversation in the Eighteenth-Century Atlantic: The Invention of Madeira Wine," *Journal of Interdisciplinary History* 29 (1998), 197–219.

7. Duncan, *Atlantic Islands,* 158–238.

8. Deposition of "William Snary Mariner," Nov. 15, 1724, Minutes of Antigua Council in Assembly, Nov. 26, 1724, CO 9/5.

9. Hart Report (1724), enclosed in Hart to BT, July 12, 1724, CO 152/14.

10. "The Deposition of Richard Condrick Mariner," Nov. 14, 1724, Minutes of Antigua Council in Assembly, Nov. 26, 1724, CO 9/5.

11. Deposition of "Mathew Peterson Mariner," Nov. 15, 1724, Minutes of Antigua Council in Assembly, Nov. 26, 1724, CO 9/5.

12. Deposition of "Francis Delgaudo a Christian Negro and a Subject of the King of Portugal," Nov. 15, 1724, Minutes of Antigua Council in Assembly, Nov. 26, 1724, CO 9/5.

13. Hart to BT, Dec. 24, 1724, CO 152/15, R121.

14. Richard S. Dunn, *Sugar and Slaves: The Rise of the Planter Class in the English West Indies, 1624–1713* (Chapel Hill, N.C., 1972), 185, 188, 276, 307–308; Richard Ligon, *A True & Exact History of the Island of Barbadoes* (London, [1673] 1976), 36–37, 118–119.

15. For Roure's Letter to Hart, see Minutes of Antigua Council in Assembly, Nov. 26, 1724, CO 9/5. See also Hart to BT, Dec. 24, 1724, CO 152/15, R121.

16. Hamilton to Popple, Feb. 16, 1720, in Cecil Headlam, ed., *Calendar of State Papers Colonial Series, America and West Indies* (hereafter CSP) (Jan. 1719–Feb. 1720), Vol. 31, n. 561 (London, 1933), 354–356; Hamilton to BT, March 28, Oct. 3, 1720, *CSP* (March 1720–Dec. 1721) Vol. 32, n. 28, 11, no. 251, 165–166. See also Marcus Rediker, "'Under the Banner of King Death': The Social World of Anglo-American Pirates, 1716 to 1726," *William and Mary Quarterly,* 3rd ser., 38 (1981), 203–227; Peter Linebaugh and Marcus Rediker, *The Many-Headed Hydra: Sailors, Slaves, Commoners, and the Hidden History of the Revolutionary Atlantic* (Boston, 2000), 143–173; J. S. Bromley, "Outlaws at Sea, 1660–1720: Liberty, Equality and Fraternity among the Caribbean Freebooters," in Frederick Krautz, ed., *History from Below: Studies in Popular Protest and Popular Ideology* (New York, 1988), 293–318; J. L. Anderson, "Piracy and World History: An Economic Perspective on Maritime Predation," *Journal of World History* 6 (1995), 175–199; Janice E. Thomson, *Mercenaries, Pirates, and Sovereigns: State-Building and Extraterritorial Violence in Early Modern Europe* (Princeton, 1994); Kris E. Lane, *Pillaging the Empire: Piracy in the Americas, 1500–1750* (New York, 1998).

17. Hart to BT, July 12, 1724, CO 152/14.

18. Hart to BT, Dec. 24, 1724, CO 152/15, R121; Minutes of Antigua Council in Assembly, Nov. 26, 1724, CO 9/5.

19. Hart to BT, Dec. 24, 1724, CO 152/15, R121; Minutes of Antigua Council in Assembly, Dec. 5, 1724, CO 9/5.

20. "The Petition of Peter Roure Master of the Sloop Two Brothers now at Anchor in the Road of Saint Johns," Minutes of Antigua Council in Assembly, Dec. 5, 1724, CO 9/5.

21. Hart to BT, Dec. 24, 1724, CO 152/15, R121; Minutes of Antigua Council in Assembly, Dec. 5, 1724, CO 9/5. Roure's certificate or character testimonial was signed by Thomas Stephens, Christopher Scandrett, Roger Adams, Robert Bryant, Caesar Rodeney, Edward Trant, Francis Delap, James Gamble, John Tomlinson, Thomas Coward, Simon Smith, Joseph Every, John Langelier, John Booth, Ambrose Lynch, John Delap, Samuel Langton, John Duncalf, Samuel Gillyatt, Peter Hasell, Marcus Browne, John Moore, John Mainwaring, Richard Oliver, Thomas Smith, and Edward Humphryes.

22. Hart to BT, Dec. 24, 1724, CO 152/15, R121; Minutes of Antigua Council in Assembly, Dec. 5, 1724, CO 9/5. Roure's pardon dated Dec. 8, 1724, is enclosure no. 2 in Hart's letter to BT as CO 152/15, R123.

23. Roure's Petition, Minutes of Antigua Council in Assembly, Dec. 5, 1724, CO 9/5.

24. See Hart's "Instrument of Writing" to the Portuguese authorities at the Cape Verde Islands, dated Dec. 26, 1724, in Hart to BT, Dec. 24, 1724, CO 152/15, R121, enclosure no. 3.

25. Hart to BT, Dec. 24, 1724, CO 152/15, R121.

26. Roure's Pardon, Hart to BT, Dec. 24, 1724, CO 152/15, R121, enclosure no. 2: CO 152/15, R123.

27. Hart's "Instrument of Writing," Hart to BT, Dec. 24, 1724, CO 152/15, R121, enclosure no. 3.

28. On "panyaring" see, for example, Daniel P. Mannix and Malcolm Cowley, *Black Cargoes: A History of the Atlantic Slave Trade 1518–1865* (New York, 1962), 27, 42–43, 92; Eltis, *The Rise of African Slavery in the Americas*, 155.

29. Larry Gragg, "The Troubled Voyage of the Rainbow," *History Today* 39 (1989), 36–41.

30. The documentation for the 1729 case can be found in Minutes of Antigua Council in Assembly, CO 9/6. See also David Barry Gaspar, "'Illegally and Forcibly Brought Away': Voyage of the Slave Ship 'Catherine,'" paper prepared for the conference Crossing Boundaries: The African Diaspora in the New Millennium, Sept. 20–23, 2000, New York University and the Schomburg Center for Research in Black Culture, New York.

31. "Minutes of the Council of War in the West Indies," March 24, 1693, *CSP* (1693–96), Vol. 14, n. 215, 64; Minutes of St. Christopher Council, June 15, 1722, CO 155/6.

32. David Barry Gaspar, *Bondmen and Rebels: A Study of Master-Slave Relations in Antigua* (Baltimore, 1985), 74–79; idem, "Slave Importation, Runaways, and Compensation in Antigua, 1720–1729," in Joseph E. Inikori and Stanley L. Engerman, eds., *The Atlantic Slave Trade: Effects on Economics, Societies, and Peoples in Africa, the Americas, and Europe* (Durham, N.C., 1992), 301–320.

33. Rev. William Smith, *A Natural History of Nevis, and the Rest of the English Leeward Charibee Islands in America* (Cambridge, U.K., 1745), letter 9, 226.

34. Governor Henry Worsley to Lord Carteret, Jan. 11, 1724, *CSP* (1724–25), Vol. 34, no. 8, 6–8.

35. Peter Mark, "The Evolution of 'Portuguese' Identity: Luso-Africans on the Upper Guinea Coast from the Sixteenth to the Early Nineteenth Century," *Journal of African History* 40 (1999), 173–191; idem, *"Portuguese" Style and Luso-African Identity: Precolonial Senegambia, Sixteenth-Nineteenth Centuries* (Bloomington, Ind., 2002); Eltis, *The Rise of African Slavery in the Americas*, 224–257; Walter Rodney, "African Slavery and Other Forms of Social Oppression on the Upper Guinea Coast in the Context of the Atlantic Slave Trade," *Journal of African History* 7 (1966), 431–443; idem, *A History of the Upper Guinea Coast 1545 to 1800* (New York, 1970); idem, "Portuguese Attempts at Monopoly on the Upper Guinea Coast, 1580–1650," *Journal of African History* 6 (1965), 307–322; Nicholas Canny and Anthony Pagden, eds., *Colonial Identity in the Atlantic World, 1500–1800* (Princeton, 1987); Emilio F. Moran, "The Evolution of Cape Verde Agriculture," *African Economic History* 11 (1982), 63–86.

36. Duncan, *Atlantic Islands*, 158–238; David Francis, *Portugal, 1715–1808: Joanine, Pombaline, and Rococo Portugal as seen by British diplomats and traders* (London, 1985),

1–65; Fernand Braudel, *The Wheels of Commerce* (New York, 1986), 211–212; Francis, *The Wine Trade*, 1–160; H. E. S. Fisher, *The Portugal Trade: A Study of Anglo-Portuguese Commerce, 1700–1770* (London, 1971); A. D. Francis, *The Methuens and Portugal, 1691–1708* (Cambridge, U.K., 1966).

37. Hart to BT, July 12, 1724, CO 152/14, R101.

F I V E :   From Catholicism to Moravian Pietism

1. John Thornton, *Africa and Africans in the Making of the Atlantic World, 1400–1800*, 2nd ed. (Cambridge, U.K., 1998). Marotta/Magdalena is not part of that Atlantic/comparative history about which Jack P. Greene writes so tellingly in "Beyond Power: Paradigm Subversion and Reformulation and the Re-creation of the Early Modern Atlantic World," in Darlene Clark Hine and Jacqueline McLeod, eds., *Crossing Boundaries: Comparative History of Black People in Diaspora* (Bloomington, Ind., 1999), 319–342. See also Paulin Hountondji, "Introduction: Recentering Africa" in Paulin Hountondji, ed., *Endogenous Knowledge: Research Trails* (Dakar, 1997), 1–39.

2. A. I. Aswaju and Robin Law, "From the Volta to the Niger, c. 1600–1800," in J. F. Ade Ajayi and Michael Crowder, eds., *History of West Africa*, 3rd ed., 2 vols. (Harlow, 1985), 1:412–464.

3. John Thornton, "Perspectives on African Christianity," in Vera Lawrence Hyatt and Rex Nettleford, eds., *Race, Discourse, and the Origin of the Americas: A New World View* (Washington, D.C., 1995), 183–187; idem, "On the Trail of Voodoo: African Christianity in Africa and the Americas," *The Americas* 44, 3 (1988), 263–267; Christian Degn, *Die Schimmelmanns im atlantischen Dreieckshandel. Gewinn und Gewissen* (Neumünster, 1974), 53. I wish to thank Professor Chris Ehret, Department of History, UCLA, for identifying the language of Marotta's 1739 petition.

4. For a 1682 description of Great Popo comprising three quarters or wards and a map of the town, see P. E. H. Hair, Adam Jones, and Robin Law, eds., *Barbot on Guinea: The Writings of Jean Barbot on West African 1678–1712*, 2 vols. (London, 1992), 2:619–621. Barbot does not give a population estimate. For an explanation of the different kinds of capital see Pierre Bourdieu, "The Forms of Capital," in John G. Richardson, ed., *Handbook of Theory and Research for the Sociology of Education* (New York, 1986), 241–258.

5. The annual average of slave exports from the ports of the Bight of Benin rose from around 1,200 in the 1640s to 5,500 in the 1680s, 10,000 in the 1690s, and a peak of 15,000 to 16,000 between 1700 and 1720. The ports included Jakin, Offra (or Little Ardra), Whydah (the largest of the ports), and Great Popo. Paul E. Lovejoy, *Transformations in Slavery: A History of Slavery in Africa*, 2nd ed. (Cambridge, U.K., 2000), 55–57; Robin Law, "The Slave Trade in Seventeenth-Century Allada: A Revision," *African Economic History* 22 (1994), 59–72; idem, "Warfare on the West African Slave Coast, 1650–1850," in R. Brian Ferguson and Neil L. Whitehead, eds., *War in the Tribal Zone: Expanding States and Indigenous Warfare* (Santa Fe, N.M., 1992); idem, "The Slave Trade in Seventeenth-Century Allada: A Revision," *African Economic History* 22 (1994); idem, *The Slave Coast of West Africa: The Impact of the Atlantic Slave Trade on an African Society* (Oxford, 1991), 156–157 and 132–133, 141–148.

6. For an overview of colonial plantations in the greater Caribbean, see Peter Hulme, *Colonial Encounters: Europe and the Native Caribbean, 1492–1797* (London, 1986), 3–5;

Anthony D. King, *Urbanism, Colonialism, and the World-Economy: Cultural and Spatial Foundations of the World Urban System* (London, 1990) 4, table 1.1; Sidney W. Mintz, *Sweetness and Power: The Place of Sugar in Modern History* (New York, 1985).

7. For the petition in Aja-Ayizo and Dutch Creole see "Der Aeltestin der Gemeine der Negros in St. Thomas Schreiben an die Königin von Dännemarck. An. 1739," *Büdingische Sammlung* 4 (1741), 485–486 (for an English translation see the appendix). The *Büdingische Sammlung* was an official publication of the Moravian Church. For historical and archaeological studies of Aja country see E. Adande, "Sièges et attributes royaux dans le Golfe du Bénin XVIIe-XIXes," in *Actes la Quinzaine de l'Archéologie du Togo* (Lomé, 1989), 79–91; F. de Medeiros, ed., *Peuples du Golfe du Bénin* (Paris, 1984).

8. David Wilkinson, "Spatio-Temporal Boundaries of African Civilizations Reconsidered: Part II," *Comparative Civilizations Review* 31 (1994), 66–74; Karin Barber, "*Oriki* and the Changing Perception of Greatness In Nineteenth-Century Yorubaland," in Toyin Falola, ed., *Yoruba Historiography* (Madison, Wisc., 1991), 31–41; A. L. Mabogunje and Paul Richards, "The Land and Peoples of West Africa," in Ajayi and Crowder, eds., *History of West Africa,* 1:5–47. In this study, civilization (or more properly, social formation) was both a structural and historical phenomenon. Cf. Eric Wolf, "Inventing Society," *American Ethnologist* 15, 4 (1989), 752–761.

9. Ideally, one would like to produce a "ritual history"/"ritual biography" of Marotta/Magdalena similar to J. Lorand Matori, *Sex and the Empire That Is No More: Gender and the Politics of Metaphor in Oyo Yoruba* (Minneapolis, 1994).

10. For studies of Ifa and Vodun see Suzanne Preston Blier, *African Vodun: Art, Psychology, and Power* (Chicago, 1995), chap. 1; Matori, *Sex and the Empire That is No More,* passim; Bassani, "The Ulm Ọpọn Ifá (1650): A Model for Later Iconography," in Rowland Abiodun, Henry J. Drewal, and John Pemberton III, eds., *The Yoruba Artist: New Theoretical Perspectives on African Art* (Washington, D.C., 1994), 80–84; Olaybiyi Babalola Yai, "In Praise of Metonymy: The Concepts of 'Tradition' and 'Creativity' in the Transmission of Yoruba Artistry over Time and Space," in ibid., 109–113; Henry Drewal, "Art and Divination among the Yoruba: Design and Myth," *Africana Journal* 14, 2/3 (1983), passim.

11. Unitätsarchiv, Herrnhut (hereafter UH). R.15.B.b.3.Diarium von St. Thomas 1742–49, "Von meinem Dario vom 1sten Sept. '44 [bis] Junius '45."

12. Generally, Ardra commoners ate fish, game, and dog; see Jourke S. Wigboldus, "Trade and Agriculture in Coastal Benin, c. 1470–1660: An Examination of Manning's Early-Growth Thesis," *AAG Bijdragen* 28 (1986), 354–353. He includes Popo in his account of Ardra's agricultural and livestock economy.

13. Hair et al., *Barbot on Guinea,* 2:620.

14. For sixteenth- and early-seventeenth-century Portuguese trade at Ardra and Popo, see Wigboldus, "Trade and Agriculture," 317–320. The seminary, which had a checkered career, was founded in 1571. Robin Law, "Religion, Trade, and Politics on the 'Slave Coast': Roman Catholic Missions in Allada and Whydah in the Seventeenth Century," *Religion in Africa* 21, 2 (1991), 43, 44.

15. "Carta de Colombino de Nantes a Peiresc (10–34)," in António Brásio, ed., *Monumenta Missionaria Africana,* 10 vols. (Lisboa, 1952–65), 8:279; Joseph Kenny, *The Catholic Church in Tropical Africa 1445–1850* (Ibadan, 1983), 34–35.

16. Thornton, *Africa and Africans,* 215. For evidence of contacts between Christian communities in the São Tomé diocese, see Hair et al., *Barbot on Guinea,* 2:433–434.

17. Thornton, *Africa and Africans*, 215; Adam Jones, ed., *West Africa in the Mid-Seventeenth Century. An Anonymous Dutch Manuscript* (Atlanta, Ga., 1995), 41, 46, 198–199.

18. "Journal du Voyage du Sr. D'Elbee, aux isles dans la Coste de Guinée" in Jean Clodoré, ed., *Relation de ce qui s'est passé dans les Isles et Terre-Ferme de l'Amerique*, 2 vols. (Paris, 1671), 2:405; Thornton, *Africa and Africans*, 215.

19. For a history of the diocese see Kenny, *The Catholic Church*, 34–60; Law, "Religion, Trade, and Politics," 45; idem, *The Slave Coast*, 153–155.

20. His successor, Tezifon (or De Zekpon, c. 1661–1682) sent an embassy to France in 1670 and, in response, a French mission was sent to Great Ardra in 1671. For these and other French missions to the Bight of Benin see Law, "Religion, Trade, and Politics," 49–57; Kenny, *The Catholic Church*, 38–39, 40–45; Raymond J. Loenertz, "Dominicans Français Missionnaires en Guinée au XVIIe Siècle," *Archivum Fratrum Praedicatorum* 24 (1954), 240–268.

21. Law, "The Slave Trade in Seventeenth-Century Allada," 71–72. For the suggestion concerning the dispatch of Spanish missionaries to Allada see Thornton, "On the Trail of Voodoo," 265–266.

22. The interpreter-catechist's name does not appear in the documents. Thornton suggests that he came from Ardra. Thornton, "On the Trail of Voodoo," 275.

23. For the documents pertaining to trade *(comercio)* and evangelizing *(prediquen el sagrado Evangelio)* see Buenaventura de Carrocera, "Misión Capuchina al Reino de Arda," *Missionalia Hispanica* 6 (1949), 523–533. One of the documents is a letter in Portuguese from Philip to the Ardra ("Arda") ruler *(noble y honrado Principe de Arda)*.

24. Thornton goes on to say that "the catechism, or at least a variant of it, seems to have eventually returned from Africa to America, for in 1708 a Portuguese Jesuit, Manuel de Lima, reported that he had produced a catechism in the language of Allada for use in Brazil, probably as a result of his experience in the mission of São Tomé in the late seventeenth century." Thornton, "On the Trail of Voodoo," 275; Law, "Religion, Trade, and Politics," 47–48; de Carrocera, "Misión Capuchina," 527–529, 535, 543–546; Henri Labouret and Paul Rivet, *Le Royaume d'Arda et son Évangélisation au XVIIe Siècle* (Paris, 1929), 20.

25. A missionary document describes him as a *cristiano de nación portugués*, "a Christian of the Portuguese nation." De Carrocera, "Misión Capuchina," 534. For "Captain Zupi" or Supÿn and other Allada officials, see Jones, *West Africa in the Mid-Seventeenth Century*, 40, 41, 46, 198.

26. De Carrocera, "Misión Capuchina," 535. For descriptions of the royal palace, see "Journal du Voyage du Sr. d'Elbee," 418; Olfert Dapper, *Naukeurige Beschrijvinge der Afrikaensche Gewesten van Egypten, Barbaryen, Lybyen, Biledulgerid, Negroslant, Guinea, Ethiopiën Abyssinie*, 2nd ed. (Amsterdam, 1676), 116.

27. Labouret and Rivet, *Le Royaume d'Arda*, 26–27.

28. Other difficulties included the deaths of five missionaries by May 1660 and the illnesses of the remaining seven. Law, "Religion, Trade, and Politics," 48–49; de Carrocera, "Misión Capuchina," 536–543; Labouret and Rivet, *Le Royaume d'Arda*, 25, 26, 29–30.

29. Thornton, "On the Trail of Voodoo," 275; Labouret and Rivet, *Le Royaume d'Ardra*, 17–18.

30. In this context "Portuguese" refers to Portuguese-speaking Africans, Afro-Europeans, and persons from Portugal. Thornton, "On the Trail of Voodoo," 266, 267. "Syncretic" is not a useful descriptive or analytical concept as it carries a presumed opposite

"purity." See Stephan Palmié, "Against Syncretism. 'Africanizing' and 'Cubanizing' Discourses in North American Òrìsà Worship," in Richard Fardon, ed., *Counterworks: Managing the Diversity of Knowledge* (London, 1995), 73–104.

31. Cf. Thornton, *Africa and Africans*, 235–262.

32. Ibid., 253; Labouret and Rivet, *Le Royaume d'Ardra*, 33–36.

33. UH. R.15.B.a.3. Acta Publica um der Mission im Thomas, Crux, und Jan betreffenden A 1733–1740. "Schreiben von 250 Negern an die König." For a discussion of the etymology and meanings of vodun see Blier, *Africa Vodun*, 37–41.

34. Ibid., 41–42, 186–188; Bernard Maupoil, *La Géomancie à l'Ancienne Côte des Esclaves* (Paris, 1981), 67–75.

35. For general histories of the Danish West Indies see Neville A. T. Hall, *Slave Society in the Danish West Indies: St. Thomas, St. John, and St. Croix*, ed. B. W. Higman (Baltimore, 1992); J. O. Bro-Jørgensen, ed., *Vore Gamle Tropekolonier*, 2 vols. (Copenhagen, 1966). The plantation owners were Danish, Dutch, English, and French. UH. R.15.B.a.2.a. Varia zu den Missionsfängen in St. Thomas. "Spangenbergs Nachricht von der Arbeit der Brüder unter den Heiden in St. Thomas u. St. Croix bis 1739"; C. G. A. Oldendorp, in Johann Jakob Bossard, ed., *History of the Mission of the Evangelical Brethren on the Caribbean Islands of St. Thomas, St. Croix, and St. John* (Ann Arbor, Mich., 1987), originally published in German in two volumes in 1770. See also L. Rømer, *Die Handlung verschiedener Völker auf der Küste von Guinea und in Westindien. Aus dem Dänischen übersetzt* (Kopenhagen, 1758), 107, 109–156.

36. Adam Jones, ed. and trans., *Brandenburg Sources for West African History, 1680–1700* (Stuttgart, 1985), 199–200, 202, 213, and note 1, 320; idem, "Brandenburg-Prussia and the Atlantic Slave Trade." Paper presented at the Colloque International sur la Traite des Noirs (Nantes, 1984), 1–14; Waldemar Westergaard, *The Danish West Indies Under Company Rule (1671–1754)* (New York, 1917), 151; Thorkild Hansen, *Slavernes Øer* (Haslev, 1970), 38–39. Also Ole Feldbæk, "The Danish Trading Companies of the Seventeenth and Eighteenth Centuries," *The Scandinavian Economic History Review* 34.3 (1986), 204–218.

37. Georg Nørregård, *Danish Settlements in West Africa 1658–1850* (Boston, 1966), 93. For a "list of slave cargoes arriving in Danish West Indies" between 1692 and 1715, see Westergaard, *The Danish West Indies*, 320–323. Also Peter Linebaugh, "All the Atlantic Mountains Shook," *Labour/Le Travailleur*, no. 10 (1982), 107–108; and King, *Urbanism, Colonialism, and the World-Economy*, 4.

38. Oldendorp, *History of the Mission*, 312.

39. "Oeffentliche Erklärung des Herrn Graf von Zinzendorf, auf die wider ihn edirte Holland. Geschrifften, dictirt zu Amsterdam nach seiner Zurückkomst aus West-Indien"; *Büdingische Sammlung* 3 (1741), 403–406; Jon F. Sensbach, *A Separate Canaan: The Making of an Afro-Moravian World in North Carolina, 1763–1840* (Chapel Hill, N.C., 1998), 19–24; Arnold R. Highfield, "Patterns of Accommodation and Resistance: The Moravian Witness to Slavery in the Danish West Indies," *Journal of Caribbean History* 28.2 (1994), 139, 140. For a general description of Pietism and its evangelism, see T. van der End, "Dutch Protestant Mission Activity: A Survey," *Itinerario* 7.1 (1983), 96–97; Sensbach, *A Separate Canaan*, 25–29, 36–37. See also Aaron Spencer Fogleman, " 'Jesus ist weiblich.' Die herrnhutische Herausforderung in den deutschen Gemeinden Nordamerikas in 18. Jahrhundert," *Historische Anthropologie. Kultur, Gesellschaft, Alltag* 9.2 (2001), 167–194; David Crantz, *Alte und neue Brüder-*

Historie oder kurzgefaste Geschichte der evangelische Brüder-Unität inden ältern Zeiten und insonderheit in dem gegenwärtigen Jahrhundert (Hildesheimand, [1772] 1973), 2; Johann Leonhart Dober, "Einfältiger Aufsass der Evangelisch Mährischen Kirche, wegen ihrer bisherigen und künstigen Arbeit unter den Wilden, Sclaven und andern Heyden," *Büdingische Sammlung* 1 (1742), 182–187; Hansen, *Slavernes Øer,* 40–42; Degn, *Die Schimmelmanns,* 43.

40. See, for example, UH. R.15.B.a.3. Acta Publica um der Mission im Thomas, Crux und Jan betreffenden A? 1733–1740. "Brief des schwarzen Anthon Ulerichs an der Hr. Graf [von Zinzendorf], Copenhagen, 6 October 1731," *Büdingische Sammlung* 3 (1741); "Aufsass wegen der Endes Verweigerung einiger Mährischen Brüder," in ibid., 401–406; Gottlieb Israel, "Diarium von der Gemeine der Negers in St. Thomas von dem 23. Sept. 1740 biss den 16 Decembr. Ejusd.," *Büdingische Sammlung* 5 (1741), 561–576; Friedrich Martin, "Ein anders Diarium aus St. Thomas von Posunberg den 11 Febr. 1741" in ibid., 588–599. For a wider context, see Colin A. Palmer, "Rethinking American Slavery," in Alusine Jalloh and Stephen E. Maizlish, eds., *The African Diaspora* (College Station, Tex., 1996), 73–99; Allison Blakely, *Blacks in the Dutch World: The Evolution of Racial Imagery in a Modern Society* (Bloomington, Ind., 1993), 214–223.

41. "Under the commercial trade name of 'negro' . . . the African mode of cultural reason was seen as a non-reason; and his internment in the plantation system as slave labor, as being carried out for the purpose of rationalizing him/her as an inferior mode of being in need of rational human baptism." Sylvia Wynter, "The Ceremony Must Be Found: After Humanism," *Boundary* 2 12 and 13 (1984), 35. Cf. Degn, *Die Schimmelmanns,* 53–54. See also Emmanuel Chukwudi Eze, ed., *Race and the Enlightenment: A Reader* (Cambridge, Mass., 1997).

42. Westergaard, *The Danish West Indies,* 159; and Highfield, "Patterns of Accommodation," 153–154. On the "great internments," see Wynter, "The Ceremony Must Be Found," 34, 35. The anti-rationalist nature of the Moravian knowledge/power formation needs to be seen in relation to modernity and the Enlightenment. James Schmidt, ed., *What is Enlightenment? Eighteenth-Century Answers and Twentieth-Century Questions* (Berkeley, 1996); Christopher Fox et al., eds., *Inventing Human Science: Eighteenth-Century Domains* (Berkeley, 1995); Peter Wagner, *A Sociology of Modernity: Liberty and Discipline* (London, 1994); and Paul Gilroy, *The Black Atlantic: Modernity and Double Consciousness* (Cambridge, U.K., 1993), chaps. 1 and 2.

43. Hans W. Debrunner, *Presence and Prestige, Africans in Europe: A History of Africans in Europe before 1918* (Basel, 1979), 106. Also Crantz, *Alte und neue Historie,* 188; Hansen, *Slavernes Øer,* 141; Degn, *Die Schimmelmanns,* 43. Ulrich spoke Dutch Creole and was literate in that language. He would have spoken Danish and German as well. German was the language of the Danish royal court. For Ulrich's letter to von Zinzendorf, see UH. R.15.B.a.3. Acta Publica von der Mission im Thomas, Crux, und Jan betreffenden A? 1733–1740. "Brief der schwarzen Anthon Ulerichs an der Hr. Graf [von Zinzendorf], Copenhagen, 6 October 1731." Von Zinzendorf was a relative of the Danish-Norwegian Queen Sophie Magdalene, a Princess of Brandenburgh-Kulmbach. For a brief account of the Count's ideas and his role in the development of the Moravian Church, see Sensbach, *A Separate Canaan,* 24–29.

44. Hansen, *Slavernes Øer,* 141–142; UH. R.15.B.a. 2.b. "Diarium von David Nitschmann [October] 1732-[July] 1733." Entry dated Oct. 8, 1732; and Sensbach, *A Separate Canaan,* 29–32.

45. Hansen, *Slavernes Øer,* 147; Degn, *Die Schimmelmanns,* 47. For the "Black Code," see Per Eilstrup and Nils Eric Boesgaard, *Fjernt fra Danmark. Billeder fra vore Tropekolonier, Slavehandel og Kinafart,* (Copenhagen, 1974), 59.

46. Debrunner, *Presence and Prestige,* 106; Crantz, *Alte und neue Historie,* 237–238; Degn, *Die Schimmelmanns,* 43–45; Hansen, *Slavernes Øer,* 142, 143, 144–145; Sensbach, *A Separate Canaan,* 32–33. For reasons that are not clear, Ulrich, on his return to St. Thomas, was completely alienated from the Moravians. His life on the island turned out badly (*hat ein elendes Ende genommen*). Crantz, *Alte und neue Historie,* 237–238n.

47. For a contemporary overview of Moravian missionary activity on the islands of St. Thomas and St. Croix in the 1730s, see UH. R.15.B.a.2.a. Varia zu den Missionsfangen in St. Thomas. "Spangenbergs Nachricht von der Arbeit der Brüder unter den Heiden in St. Thomas u. St. Croix bis 1739."

48. UH. R.15.B.a.3. Acta Publica um der Mission im Thomas, Crux und Jan betreffenden A? 1733–1740. "Pro Memoria des Ober-Kammerherrn von Plessen in Kopenhagen wegen Ansiedlung der Brüder auf St. Crux [1733]." For other important documents pertaining to the colonization of St. Croix see UH. R.15.B.a.3. Acta Publicum der Mission im Thomas, Crux und Jan betreffenden A? 1733–1740. "Copie eines Schreibens des Herrn Graff von Zinzendorf an H. P. Reuss nach Copenhagen dj: 28 May 1733," and "Vertrag der Brüder mit Ober-Kammerherrn von Plessen, ihre Dienst auf dessen Plantage auf St. Croix betr. 15 Oktober 1733." For Moravian attitudes toward slavery, see Sensbach, *A Separate Canaan,* 34–36; Highfield, "Patterns of Accommodation," 139–140.

49. Crantz, *Alte und neue Historie,* 238–240; Hansen, *Slavernes Øer,* 145–146; Degn, *Die Schimmelmanns,* 44, 52–53. For the missionary-settlers' instructions, see UH. R.15.B.a.3. Acta Publica um der Mission im Thomas, Crux und Jan betreffenden A? 1733–1740. "Instruktion für die dänischen-westindischen Mission," n.d.

50. Eilstrup and Boesgaard, *Fjernt fra Danmark,* 110–111; Degn, *Die Schimmelmanns,* 47, 52–54.

51. "Herrn Johnn Lorenta Carsten, Herrns von Sundrop, Directoris der Dänischen West-Indischen Compagnie auf der Insul St. Thomas, Declaration vor die Mährischen Brüder, die sich auf dieser Insul befinden," *Büdingische Sammlung* 8 (1742), 199; UH. R.15.B.a.3. Acta Publica um der Mission im Thomas, Crux, und Jan betreffenden A? 1733–1740. "J. L. Carstens Kaufbrief für Domine Decknadel bei Verkauf seiner Plantage an die Bruder, Amsterdam, 29 July 1739"; Hansen, *Slavernes Øer,* 146–148. For Carstens's personal views about his slaves see Eilstrup and Boesgaard, *Fjernt fra Danmark,* 104–106.

52. Sensbach, *A Separate Canaan,* 32–34; Hansen, *Slavernes Øer,* 147; Degn, *Die Schimmelmanns,* 48–51; Oldendorp, *History of the Mission,* 332–333.

53. Crantz, *Alte und neue Historie,* 309–310. UH. R.15.B.a.2.b. "Diarium von Friedrich Martin 1736–37"; "Diarium von Friedrich Martin 1738"; UH. R.15.B.a.2.a.3. "Zinzendorfs Reisedarium 1738/39"; Oldendorp, *History of the Mission,* 352, 354–356, 363–364; Hansen, *Slavernes Øer,* 147; Degn, *Die Schimmelmanns,* 46–47, 52.

54. Christianus R., "An den Præsidem und Directorn der West-Indisch-und Guineischen Compagnie," *Büdingische Sammlung* 1 (1742), 177–178; UH. R.15.B.a.3. "Conditionen op welke manier men denn dat de Moravische Broeders konde toe gestan hier te woonen en leeren tot nadere Aprobatie of order van J: Koniglicke Majestet," Gouv. Moth to von Zinzendorf, Feb. 6, 1739.

55. N. A. T. Hall, "Establishing a Public Elementary School System for Slaves in the Danish Virgin Islands, 1732–1846," *Caribbean Journal of Education* 6 (1979), 2–4.

56. "Des Hrn. Grafen von Zinzendorff Abschied-Schreiben an die Negers in St. Thomas, in Cariolischer Sprache," St. Thomas, den 15 Febr. 1739. *Büdingische Sammlung* 7 (1742), 453–457. On resistance to the Moravian missionary project see Highfield, "Patterns of Accommodation," 154, 155–157; N. A. T. Hall, "Maritime Maroons: *Grand Marronage* from the Danish West Indies" in Hilary Beckles and Verene Shepherd, eds., *Caribbean Slave Society and Economy: A Student Reader* (New York, 1991), 387–400.

57. Hansen, *Slavernes Øer,* 153, 154; A. von Dewitz, *In Dänisch-Vestindien. Hundert und Fünfzig Jahre der Brüdermission in St. Thomas, St. Croix und St. Jan,* 2 vols. (Nieslin, 1882), 1:1.

58. See the converts' correspondence in UH. R.Ba.15. "Briefe von Neger-Geschwistern 1737–65; 1768."

59. Highfield, "Patterns of Accommodation," 152.

60. For examples of the converts' *Lebensläufe,* see Hansen, *Slavernes Øer,* 183–185; Oldendorp, *History of the Mission,* 330, 411–413.

61. Oldendorp, *History of the Mission,* 312–313.

62. Ibid., 332, 361, 419, emphasis in the original. For a description of the baptism ceremony see "Hr. M. Steinhofers Relation von der ersten Neger-Tauffe in unsern Gemeinen," *Büdingische Sammlung* 6 (1742), 782–787.

63. Oldendorp, *History of the Mission,* 333. Also Highfield, "Patterns of Appropriation," 143–144.

64. Oldendorp, *History of the Mission,* 360–361; Highfield, "Patterns of Appropriation," 142–144.

65. For the first petition, see "Der erweckten Negros in St. Thomas Schreiben an Ihro Majest. Den König in Dännemarck. An. 1739," *Büdingische Sammlung* 4 (1741), 483–485. At the end of her 1739 petition Magdalena wrote: "In the name of 250 Black women who love Lord Jesus, written by Marotta now Madlena of Popo in Africa (*Op naam van over twee hondert en vyftig Negersken vrouuwen die Heere Jesus beminnen, geschreven door Marotta nu Madlena van Poppo uyt Africa*)." "Der Aeltestin der Gemeine der Negros in St. Thomas Schreiben an die Königin von Dännemarck. An. 1739," ibid., 485–487.

66. See, for example, "Einige Brieffe der in St. Thomas zu Jesum Christum bekehrten Negers an die Mährische Brüder-Gemeine in Europa, in Cariolischer Sprache geschrieben, und von Wort zu Wort ins Deutsche übersetzt," *Büdingische Sammlung* 5 (1741), 600–621.

67. The letters were written in Dutch and Dutch Creole. UH. R.15.B.a.3. Acta Publica um der Mission in Thomas, Crux, und Jan betreffenden A? 1733–1740. "Erklärung Fr. Martin und seiner Mitarbeiders, St. Thomas, 14 February 1739."

68. Cf. Zinzendorf's speech (in Dutch Creole) of Feb. 1739 to the 300 slaves on J. L. Carstens's plantation. "Des Hrn Grafen von Zinzendorff Abscheid-Schreiben an die Negers in St. Thomas, in Cariolischer Sprache," *Büdingische Sammlung* 7 (1742), 453–457.

69. That is, reading the church-building experience of the Moravian congregation in the context of Hegel's narrative of the master-slave relationship. For an extended discussion see Gilroy, *The Black Atlantic,* 48–58.

70. For a 1747 painting and a 1757 etching (with text) of baptized Moravian Pietists in the Danish Caribbean see Hugh Honour, ed., *The Image of the Black in Western Art,* Vol. 4, Part 1, (Cambridge, Mass., 1989), 58–59.

71. The Aja-Ayizo text and the Dutch Creole translation are to be found in "Der Aeltesin der Gemeine der Negros in St. Thomas Schreiben an die Königin von Dännemarck. An. 1739," *Büdingische Sammlung* 4 (1741), 485–487. Degn, *Die Schimmelmanns,* 52, gives both the original in Dutch Creole and the Aja-Ayizo versions of Magdalena's petition. For the English translation, see Oldendorp, *History of the Mission,* 365.

CHAPTER SIX: Mariners, Merchants, and Colonists in Seventeenth-Century English America

1. August 31, 1643, in Susie M. Ames, ed., *County Court Records of Accomack-Northampton, Virginia, 1640–1645* (Charlottesville, Va., 1973), 301–306. For Ingle's rebellion in Maryland two years later, see Russell R. Menard, "Maryland's 'Time of Troubles': Sources of Political Disorder in Early St. Mary's," *Maryland Historical Magazine* 76 (1981), 124–140; Lois Green Carr, "Sources of Political Stability and Upheaval in Seventeenth-Century Maryland," *Maryland Historical Magazine* 79 (1984), 54–56; and J. Frederick Fausz, "Merging and Emerging Worlds: Anglo-Indian Interest Groups and the Development of the Seventeenth-Century Chesapeake," in Lois Green Carr, Philip D. Morgan, and Jean B. Russo, eds., *Colonial Chesapeake Society* (Chapel Hill, N.C., 1988), 78–80.

2. Ames, ed., *Accomack-Northampton, 1640–1645,* 304–305.

3. Jesse Lemisch, "Jack Tar in the Streets: Merchant Seamen in the Politics of Revolutionary America," *William and Mary Quarterly,* 3rd ser., 25 (1968), 371–407; Gary B. Nash, *Urban Crucible: Social Change, Political Consciousness, and the Origins of the American Revolution* (Cambridge, Mass., 1979); Marcus Rediker, *Between the Devil and the Deep Blue Sea: Merchant Seamen, Pirates, and the Anglo-American Maritime World, 1700–1750* (New York, 1987); Margaret S. Creighton and Lisa Norling, eds., *Iron Men, Wooden Women: Gender and Seafaring in the Atlantic World, 1700–1920* (Baltimore, 1996); Colin Howell and Richard J. Twomey, eds., *Jack Tar in History: Essays in the History of Maritime Life and Labour* (Fredericton, NB, 1991); Julius Sherrard Scott III, "The Common Wind: Currents of Afro-American Communication in the Era of the Haitian Revolution" (Ph.D. diss., Duke University, 1986); and W. Jeffrey Bolster, *Black Jacks: African American Seamen in the Age of Sail* (Cambridge, Mass., 1997). See also Daniel Vickers, *Farmers and Fishermen: Two Centuries of Work in Essex County, Massachusetts, 1630–1850* (Chapel Hill, N.C., 1994); idem, "Beyond Jack Tar," *William and Mary Quarterly,* 3rd ser., 50 (1993), 418–424; Christine Leigh Heyrman, *Commerce and Culture: The Maritime Communities of Colonial Massachusetts, 1690–1750* (New York, 1984); Bernard Bailyn, *The New England Merchants in the Seventeenth Century* (Cambridge, Mass., 1955); and Frederick B. Tolles, *Quakers and the Atlantic Culture* (New York, [1947] 1960).

4. For an introduction to admiralty law and its application in American colonies, see David R. Owen and Michael C. Tolley, *Courts of Admiralty in Colonial America: The Maryland Experience, 1634–1776* (Durham, N.C., 1995), esp. 1–19.

5. John D. Cushing, comp., *The Laws and Liberties of Massachusetts 1641–1691,* 3 vols., (Wilmington, Del., 1976), 1:41, 2:433, 2:284–285, 1:199–204.

6. Northampton County, Virginia, Order Books, 1654–1661, Virginia Historical Society Mss. 3N8125a, typescripts by Susie M. Ames, fol. 2, 29.

7. C. A. Drew, ed., *Suffolk Deeds,* Vol. 12 (Boston, 1902), 204–206.

8. Two courts in New Netherland handled maritime cases; the Supreme Court of New Netherland (consisting of the governor and his council) heard all maritime cases until 1653. After the city government of New Amsterdam was established in that year, the Court of Burgomasters and Shepens of New Amsterdam heard almost all maritime cases. Morton Wagman, "Liberty in New Amsterdam: A Sailor's Life in Early New York," *New York History* 64 (1983), 105–106, 111.

9. Ibid.

10. Ibid.

11. Norfolk County, Wills and Deeds C, 1651–1656 (Library of Virginia, microfilm), 158a-159. The Norfolk County records also state that the Antigua court oversaw two arbitrations dealing with repairs done in Holland. Ibid., 159–159a.

12. Norfolk County, Wills and Deeds C, 1651–1656, 159a-162.

13. Seaman John Gelney, mate Aldred Follett, seaman Robert Viccary, seaman Thomas Lambert, and boatswain Richard Bott testified in the case; Norfolk County, Wills and Deeds C, 1651–1656, 162a-163.

14. W. B. Trask, ed., *Suffolk Deeds*, Vol. 4 (Boston, 1888), 295.

15. Charles J. Hoadly, ed., *Records of the Colony or Jurisdiction of New Haven, from May 1653 to the Union, together with the New Haven Code of 1656* (Hartford, Conn., 1858), 425.

16. Ian K. Steele, *The English Atlantic, 1675–1740: An Exploration of Communication and Community* (New York, 1986), 213–228; Rediker, *Between the Devil and the Deep Blue Sea*, 20, 74–75.

17. David Peterson [Pietersz] De Vries, *Voyages from Holland to America, AD 1632–1644*, trans. and ed., Henry C. Murphy. (New York, 1853), 64. Barnaby Brian's ability to recruit mariners in Boston, discussed below, also reflects such flexibility.

18. Hoadly, *Records of the Colony or Jurisdiction of New Haven*, 227. On June 3, 1632, the Massachusetts Bay Court of Assistants fined Mr. James Parker and Mr. Samuel Dudley forty shillings each for drunkenness committed aboard a Virginia ship; John Noble, ed., *Records of the Court of Assistants of the Colony of the Massachusetts Bay 1630–1692*, Vol. 2, *1630–1644* (Boston, 1904), 25.

19. Norfolk County, Wills and Deeds C, 1651–1656, 141.

20. Henry Fleet, "A Brief Journal of a Voyage Made in the Bark 'Warwick,' to Virginia and Other Parts of the Continent of America," in Edward D. Neill, *The Founders of Maryland as Portrayed in Manuscripts, Provincial Records and Early Documents* (Albany, N.Y., 1876), 21.

21. Nov. 28, 1642, Ames, ed., *Accomack-Northampton 1640–1645*, 168, 221, 237.

22. For an example in which four Virginians and three Dutch crew members (a cook, carpenter, and boatswain) all participated in shipboard trading of cloth for tobacco, see Aug. 31, 1643, Ames, ed., *Accomack-Northampton, 1640–1645*, 300–301.

23. At least early in the seventeenth century, the term mariner did not carry status connotations and referred to any one involved in the sailing of ships. Masters and ship captains were often of high status and served in various political offices. The term merchant referred to anyone involved in trade. Not all merchants were mariners, though many merchants traveled at least periodically with their cargoes to trade their merchandise directly and reinforce their economic and social contacts.

24. Cheryl Fury, "Elizabethan Seamen: Their Lives Ashore," *International Journal of Maritime History* 10 (1998), 33. According to Fury, "in Stepney almost all parish officials

were shipmasters or prominent shipwrights," and the vestry book for Stepney "reads like a 'who's who' of London's maritime elite" between 1579 and 1662.

25. De Vries, *Voyages from Holland*, 183–184, passim.

26. W. Noel Sainsbury, ed., *Calendar of State Papers, Colonial Series, 1574–1660* (thereafter *CSPC*), 390, #68.

27. Larry D. Gragg, "Shipmasters in Early Barbados," *The Mariner's Mirror* 77 (1991), 105.

28. Gragg, "Shipmasters in Early Barbados," 109. In at least one case Gragg underestimates colonial landownership by a ship captain, listing Thomas Willoughby as a landowner in Barbados, but not in Virginia.

29. For a particularly compelling exploration of the potential implications of such exchanges, see Marcus Rediker and Peter Linebaugh, *The Many-Headed Hydra: Sailors, Slaves, Commoners, and the Hidden History of the Revolutionary Atlantic* (Boston, 2000).

30. *CSPC, 1669–1674*, 71, #203. For similar examples, see *CSPC, 1669–1674*, 85, #245; 88, #250.

31. William Frederick Poole, ed., "The Mather Papers," *Massachusetts Historical Society Collections*, 4th ser., Vol. 8 (Boston, 1868), 199–200. The discontent may have been a response to strengthened Navigation Acts of the Restoration, or this may have referred to the opposition to delayed payments for navy seamen described in Pepys's diary. Henry B. Wheatley, ed., *The Diary of Samuel Pepys (1659–1669)*, transcribed by Mynors Bright (New York, 1893), 1:200, 427.

32. De Vries, *Voyages from Holland*, 187–189.

33. Steele, *The English Atlantic*, 45–47, 216.

34. Mariners were in particularly high demand in the Caribbean. Because free labor was scarce and mortality high, seamen could desert their ships and drive wages up. Rediker, *Between the Devil and the Deep Blue Sea*, 60, 104–105.

35. Scott, "The Common Wind."

36. Richard Hall, ed., *Acts Passed in the Island of Barbados from 1643 to 1762* (London, 1764), 19.

37. Hall, *Acts Passed in the Island of Barbados*, 63–64. David Conroy, *In Public Houses: Drink and the Revolution of Authority in Colonial Massachusetts* (Chapel Hill, N.C., 1995), 6, 12–56, argues that such recognition of public houses as necessary and legitimate places of business and socializing pervaded English society until it faced Puritan challenges in England and New England during the seventeenth century.

38. John Clayton, *The Reverend John Clayton: A Parson with a Scientific Mind*, ed. Edmund Berkeley and Dorothy Smith Berkeley (Charlottesville, Va., 1965), 53. For additional discussion of Chesapeake geography and settlement, see Kevin P. Kelly, " 'In dispers'd Country Plantations': Settlement Patterns in Seventeenth-Century Surry County, Virginia," in Thad W. Tate and David L. Ammerman, eds., *The Chesapeake in the Seventeenth Century: Essays on Anglo-American Society and Politics* (New York, 1979), 183–205; D. W. Meinig, *The Shaping of America: A Geographical Perspective on 500 Years of History*, Vol. 1, *Atlantic America, 1492–1800* (New Haven, 1986), 144–160. For a different perspective, see James O'Mara, *An Historical Geography of Urban System Development: Tidewater Virginia in the 18th Century*, Geographical Monographs, 13 (Downsview, ON, 1983).

39. The harvesting, processing, and transportation requirements of tobacco did little to encourage urban development. See Carville Earle and Ronald Hoffman, "Staple Crops and Urban Development in the Eighteenth-Century South," *Perspectives in American History* 10 (1976), 5–78. In Carolina, where a similar network of navigable waterways could have allowed similarly dispersed settlement and trade, the port town of Charlestown quickly developed instead, reflecting differences in marketing and transporting rice. See S. Max Edelson, "Planting the Lowcountry: Agricultural Enterprise and Economic Experience in the Lower South, 1695–1785" (Ph.D. diss., Johns Hopkins University, 1998).

40. Steele, *The English Atlantic*, 42.

41. Ames, *Studies*, 69, cites a 1678 court case in Accomack County, Wills and Deeds, 1676–1690, 139; see also Steele, *The English Atlantic*, 4, 42, 216; and De Vries, *Voyages from Holland*, 112–113.

42. Steele, *The English Atlantic*, 59; cites Isaac Norris to William Righton, July 11, seventh month 1699, Historical Society of Pennsylvania, Isaac Norris Letterbook, 1699–1702, 72, 123.

43. For examples, see Sainsbury, ed., *CSPC, 1574–1660*, 287–288, #5 and Norfolk County, Wills & Deeds C, 1651–1656, 161.

44. Francis Mackemie, "A Plain and Friendly Perswasive to the Inhabitants of Virginia and Maryland for Promoting Towns and Cohabitation," *Virginia Magazine of History and Biography* 4 (1897), 255–271.

45. Lois Green Carr, "Diversification in the Colonial Chesapeake: Somerset County, Maryland, in Comparative Perspective," in Carr et al., eds., *Colonial Chesapeake Society*, 344; James Horn, *Adapting to a New World: English Society in the Seventeenth-Century Chesapeake* (Chapel Hill, N.C., 1994), 144–146. For estates consisting primarily of intercolonial goods, see Norfolk County, Wills and Deeds C, 1651–1656, 83a; Ames, *Studies*, 206; Accomack Order Book, 1666–1670, 432, 451; Norfolk County, Wills and Deeds C, 1651–1656, 89a; and Edmund Morgan, *American Slavery, American Freedom: The Ordeal of Colonial Virginia* (New York, 1975), 138 (citing Norfolk and Northampton records).

46. Carl Bridenbaugh, *Cities in the Wilderness: The First Century of Urban Life in America, 1625–1742* (New York, [1938] 1964), 143. Earlier in century, however, a greater percentage of the population lived in these port towns and therefore had more direct access to interaction with seamen and merchants.

47. Wagman, "Liberty in New Amsterdam," 102–103.

48. By midcentury seamen could trade goods worth two months' pay, ibid., 104–106, 111.

49. Ibid., 105–107, 111.

50. De Vries, *Voyages from Holland*, 148.

51. Wagman notes that there were really twelve taverns (it is unclear what year), which equaled about an eighth of the houses in the city. "Liberty in New Amsterdam," 109.

52. De Vries, *Voyages from Holland*, passim; Jasper Danckaerts, *Journal of Jasper Danckaerts, 1679–1680*, ed. Bartlett Burleigh James and J. Franklin Jameson (New York, 1913).

53. Wagman, "Liberty in New Amsterdam," 114.

54. Ibid., 118. Wagman says that instances of mariners settling in New Amsterdam to marry residents were common, though he does not offer other examples.

55. Massachusetts General Court, February 7 and March 31, 1683, in Cushing, comp., *Laws and Liberties of Massachusetts*, 3:588.

56. Ibid., 1:140. The General Court restated its concerns in its 1682 Act "For the Prevention of great Trouble and Inconvence that often befals Masters and Commanders of Ships and other Vessels by reason of their Men running themselves into Debt . . . to the great hindrance and prejudice of the Commanders and Owners of such Ship or Vessel." Ibid., 3:579.

57. The Book of the General Laws, 1660, in ibid., 1:114.

58. Ibid., 1:114–116.

59. Conroy, *In Public Houses*, 33, 44–46. As Conroy argues, the court did attempt to regulate the social behavior of residents, but the laws discussed above suggest that officials wanted to do so without prejudicing commercial activity. For similar conclusions, see Stephen Innes, *Creating the Commonwealth: The Economic Culture of Puritan New England* (New York, 1995).

60. Conroy, *In Public Houses*, 53–56.

61. "Laws and Ordinances of Warre," 1675, in Cushing, comp., *Laws and Liberties of Massachusetts*, 2:472.

62. The Massachusetts General Court, September 10, 1684, in ibid., 3:605.

63. Book of the General Laws, 1660 (law originally from 1647), in ibid., 1:87.

64. Ibid., 1:204 (1668). The court was also concerned with runaways using ships, as were courts in other colonies. Ibid., 3:561.

65. Rediker, *Between the Devil and the Deep Blue Sea*, 65.

66. Cushing, comp., *Laws and Liberties of Massachusetts*, 1:201 (1668).

67. Ames, ed., *Accomack-Northampton 1640–1645*, 378–379.

68. Northampton County Court, ibid., 149–152.

69. Steele, *The English Atlantic*, chap. 11.

70. Rediker noted that "sailors circulated from ship to ship" through legal means and desertion, and that it is difficult to tell whether they specialized in particular routes. However, the greater efficiency of trade in the eighteenth century and regularization of routes meant mariners' travels probably became more predictable and their knowledge of the Atlantic world more specialized after the seventeenth century. Rediker, *Between the Devil and the Deep Blue Sea*, 83, 86–87.

SEVEN: The Atlantic Rules

Epigraph. Jack P. Greene, "Empire and Identity from the Glorious Revolution to the American Revolution," in P. J. Marshall, ed., *The Oxford History of the British Empire*, Vol. 2, *The Eighteenth Century* (Oxford, 1998), 221–222.

1. Jack P. Greene, "Social and Cultural Capital in Colonial British America: A Case Study," *Journal of Interdisciplinary History* 29 (1999), 491.

2. Mark DeWolfe Howe, "The Sources and Nature of Law in Colonial Massachusetts," in George Billias, ed., *Law and Authority in Colonial America* (Barre, Mass., 1965), 1–3.

3. My understanding of the legal imagination as the essential part of legal culture is drawn from Paul Kahn, *The Cultural Study of Law: Reconstructing Legal Scholarship* (Chicago, 1999), esp. 66–73, 91–92. This internal conception of the impact of social capital also reflects the influence of Richard Ross's notion of legal culture and memory

jurisprudence; Richard Ross, "The Legal Past of Early New England: Notes for the Study of Law, Legal Culture, and Intellectual History," *William and Mary Quarterly*, 3rd ser., 50 (1993), 31–39.

4. Mary Sarah Bilder, "The Lost Lawyers: Early American Legal Literates and Transatlantic Legal Culture," *Yale Journal of Law and the Humanities* 11 (1999), 47–177.

5. Howe, "Sources and Nature of Law in Colonial Massachusetts," 2–3; David Thomas Konig, *Law and Society in Puritan Massachusetts: Essex County, 1629–1692* (Chapel Hill, N.C., 1979), 6.

6. Daniel Coquillette, "Legal Ideology and Incorporation II: Sir Thomas Ridley, Charles Molloy, and the Literary Battle for the Law Merchant, 1607–1676," *Boston University Law Review* 61 (1981), 315–371; idem, "Ideology and Incorporation III: Reason Regulated—the Post-Restoration English Civilians, 1653–1735," *Boston University Law Review* 67 (1987), 289–361; Donald Veall, *The Popular Movement for Law Reform, 1640–1660* (Oxford, 1970); Nancy Mathews, *William Sheppard, Cromwell's Law Reformer* (Cambridge, U.K., 1984).

7. Richard Ross, "The Memorial Culture of Early Modern English Lawyers: Memory as Keyword, Shelter, and Identity, 1560–1640," *Yale Journal of Law and the Humanities* 10 (1998), 232–234, 237, 239, 255 (quote), 277–279, 296.

8. Coquillette, "Legal Ideology and Incorporation II," 316, 322–328, 338, 341–343.

9. Barbara Shapiro, "Law Reform in Seventeenth Century England," *American Journal of Legal History* 19 (1975), 286–287; G. B. Warden, "Law Reform in England and New England, 1620 to 1660," *William and Mary Quarterly*, 3rd ser., 35 (1978), 670–671; Veall, *Popular Movement for Law Reform*; Kahn, *Cultural Study of Law*, 91–92, 105.

10. David Sugarman, *In the Spirit of Weber: Law, Modernity and "The Peculiarities of the English"* (Madison, Wisc., 1987), quote on 21; C. W. Brooks, *Pettyfoggers and Vipers of the Commonwealth: The "Lower Branch" of the Legal Profession in Early Modern England* (Cambridge, U.K., 1986), 26–28; Wilfred Prest, "The English Bar, 1550–1700," in Prest, ed., *Lawyers in Early Modern Europe and America* (New York, 1981), quote on 65; Brian P. Levack, "The English Civilians, 1500–1750," in ibid., 108.

11. Zechariah Chafee, Jr., "Colonial Courts and the Common Law," in David Flaherty, ed., *Essays in the History of Early American Law* (Chapel Hill, N.C., 1969), quotes on 57; Joseph H. Smith and Thomas Barnes, *The English Legal System: Carryover to the Colonies* (Los Angeles, 1975), 7; Charles Edward Smith, "Massachusetts Law and Liberties and the Revolutionary Idea that Law Should Serve the Public Good" (Ph.D. diss., University of Chicago, 1998), 238; Julius Goebel, "'Law Enforcement in Colonial New York: An Introduction," in Flaherty, ed., *Essays in the History of Early American Law*, 372; John Hart, "Colonial Land Use Law and Its Significance for Modern Takings Doctrine," *Harvard Law Review* 109 (1996), 1284–1285; Staughton George, Benjamin Mead, and Thomas McCamant, eds., *Charter to William Penn, and Laws of the Province of Pennsylvania: passed between the Years 1682 and 1700* (Harrisburg, Pa., 1879), 84.

12. Bilder, "The Lost Lawyers," 55–103, quotes on 51 and 83.

13. David Konig, "'Dale's Laws' and the Non-Common Law Origins of Criminal Justice in Virginia," *American Journal of Legal History* 26 (1982), 354, 363–367; Warren Billings, "English Legal Literature as a Source of Law and Legal Practice for Seventeenth-Century Virginia," *Virginia Magazine of History and Biography* 87 (1979), 413–415; idem, "Justices, Books, Laws, and Courts in Seventeenth-Century Virginia," *Law Library Journal* 85 (1993), 283–288; idem, "The Transfer of English Law to Virginia

1606–50," in K. R. Andrews, N. P. Canny, and P. E. H. Hair, *The Westward Enterprise: English Activities in Ireland, the Atlantic, and America, 1480–1650* (Liverpool, 1978), 215–244.

14. A. G. Roeber, *Faithful Magistrates and Republican Lawyers: Creators of Virginia Legal Culture, 1680–1710* (Chapel Hill, N.C., 1981), 42–58.

15. Lois Green Carr, *County Government in Maryland, 1689–1709* (New York, 1987), 82–192; John Douglass, "Between Pettifoggers and Professionals: Pleaders and Practitioners and the Beginnings of the Legal Profession in Colonial Maryland 1634–1731," *American Journal of Legal History* 39 (1995), 363–367.

16. Julius Goebel, "Kings Law and Local Custom in Seventeenth-Century New England," *Columbia Law Review* 31 (1931), 417, 423–425, 430, 433–435; David Grayson Allen, *In English Ways: The Movement of Societies and the Transferal of English Local Law and Custom to Massachusetts Bay in the Seventeenth Century* (Chapel Hill, N.C., 1982), 5, 205–223; John Frederick Martin, *Profits in the Wilderness: Entrepreneurship and the Founding of New England Towns in the Seventeenth Century* (Chapel Hill, N.C., 1991), 131–139, 257–280.

17. Thomas Barnes, "Thomas Lechford and the Earliest Lawyering in Massachusetts, 1638–1641," in Daniel Coquillette, ed., *Law in Colonial Massachusetts 1630–1800* (Boston, 1984), 3–4, 21; George Haskins, "Lay Judges: Magistrates and Judges in Early Massachusetts," in ibid., 42–43, 48–51; Neil Allen, Jr., "Law and Authority to the Eastward: Maine Courts, Magistrates, and Lawyers, 1690–1730," in ibid., 238–240.

18. Smith, "Massachusetts Law and Liberties," 238, 247, 253, 268–269, 291, 359–374; Warden, "Law Reform in England and New England," 676–685; George Haskins, "Law and Colonial Society," in Flaherty, ed., *Essays in the History of Early American Law*, 46–48.

19. Mary Bilder, "The Origin of the Appeal in America," *Hastings Law Journal* 48 (1997), 913–967, quote on 967.

20. Konig, *Law and Society in Puritan Massachusetts*, 58, 92, 108, 188–191.

21. Karen Kupperman, "The Beehive as a Model for Colonial Design," in Kupperman, ed., *America in European Consciousness, 1493–1750* (Chapel Hill, N.C., 1995), 282; Bilder, "The Origin of the Appeal," 946–947.

22. Warden, "Law Reform in England and New England," 676; George Haskins, "The Influence of New England Law on the Middle Colonies," *Law and History Review* 1 (1983), 239–250; George Haskins and Samuel Ewing, "The Spread of Massachusetts Law in the Seventeenth Century," in Flaherty, ed., *Essays in the History of Early American Law*, 186–191.

23. Bradley Nicholson, "Legal Borrowing and the Origins of Slave Law in the British Colonies," *American Journal of Legal History* 38 (1994), 49–53.

24. David Cressy, *Coming Over: Migration and Communication between England and New England in the Seventeenth Century* (Cambridge, U.K., 1987), 178–190.

25. Craig Horle, *The Quakers and the English Legal System, 1660–1688* (Philadelphia, 1988).

26. Caroline Robbins, "Laws and Governments Proposed for West New Jersey and Pennsylvania, 1676–1683," *Pennsylvania Magazine of History and Biography* 105 (1981), 373–392; Veall, *Popular Movement for Law Reform*, xvii; William Offutt, Jr., *Of "Good Laws" and "Good Men": Law and Society in the Delaware Valley, 1680–1710* (Champagne, Ill., 1995), 15–21.

27. Offutt, *Of "Good Laws" and "Good Men,"* 45, 119–120; Roy Lokken, *David Lloyd, Colonial Lawmaker* (Seattle, 1959); Alfred Brophy, "'For the Preservation of the King's Peace and Justice': Community and English Law in Sussex County, Pennsylvania, 1682–1696," *American Journal of Legal History* 40 (1996), 191–203.

28. Brophy, "Community and English Law in Sussex County," 198–202; Edwin Wolf, II, "The Library of a Philadelphia Judge, 1708," *Pennsylvania Magazine of History and Biography* 83 (1959), 182–191; Alfred Brophy, "'Ingenium est Fateri per quos profeceris:' Francis Daniel Pastorius' *Young Country Clerk's Collection* and Anglo-American Legal Literature, 1682–1716," *The University of Chicago Law School Roundtable* 3 (1996), 668–669, 683–686.

29. Cornelia Dayton, *Women Before the Bar: Gender, Law, and Society in Connecticut, 1639–1789* (Chapel Hill, N.C., 1995), 31.

30. Jane Kamensky, *Governing the Tongue: The Politics of Speech in Early New England* (New York, 1997), 71–98, 128.

31. Kathleen Brown, *Good Wives, Nasty Wenches and Anxious Patriarchs: Gender, Race and Power in Colonial Virginia* (Chapel Hill, N.C., 1996), 96–99, 145–147, 188–191; Mary Beth Norton, *Founding Mothers and Fathers: Gendered Power and the Forming of American Society* (New York, 1996), 258–260; Helena Wall, *Fierce Communion: Family and Community in Early America* (Cambridge, Mass., 1990), 46–47; James Horn, *Adapting to a New World: English Society in the Seventeenth-Century Chesapeake* (Chapel Hill, N.C., 1994), 367. Norton does not share Brown's opinion regarding the lessening of the sexual double standard in the Chesapeake.

32. Konig, *Law and Society in Puritan Massachusetts,* 57–88.

33. Offutt, *Of "Good Laws" and "Good Men,"* 25–60; William Offutt, "The Limits of Authority: Courts, Ethnicity, and Gender in the Middle Colonies, 1670–1710," in Christopher L. Tomlins and Bruce H. Mann, eds., *The Many Legalities of Early America* (Chapel Hill, N.C., 2001), 357–387.

34. Horn, *Adapting to a New World,* 337, 351, 367–368; Philip Schwartz, "Forging the Shackles: The Development of Virginia's Criminal Code for Slaves," in James Ely and David Bodenhamer, eds., *Ambivalent Legacy: A Legal History of the South* (Jackson, Miss., 1984), 130–131.

35. Brophy, "Community and English Law in Sussex County," 171; George Haskins, "The Legal Heritage of Plymouth Colony," in Flaherty, ed., *Essays in the History of Early American Law,* 123–124; Kamensky, *Governing the Tongue,* 95–96; Smith, "Massachusetts Laws and Liberties," 6–9.

36. Brown, *Good Wives, Nasty Wenches,* 190–191, 420n; Coquillette, "Legal Ideology and Incorporation II," 319–320; Daniel Coquillette, "Legal Ideology and Incorporation IV: The Nature of Civilian Influence on Modern Anglo-American Commercial Law," *Boston University Law Review* 67 (1987), 877; J. H. Baker, "The Law Merchant and the Common Law Before 1700," in J. H. Baker, *The Legal Profession and the Common Law: Historical Essays* (London, 1986), 350, 367; Veall, *Popular Movement for Law Reform,* 225–240, quote on 228.

37. Roeber, *Faithful Magistrates and Republican Lawyers,* 57–60.

38. Eben Moglen, "Settling the Law: Legal Development in New York, 1664–1776" (Ph.D. diss., Yale University, 1993), 27, 48–49, 58–61; Donna Merwick, *Death of a Notary: Conquest and Change in Colonial New York* (Ithaca, N.Y., 1999), 180–182; John Murrin, "English Rights as Ethnic Aggression: The English Conquest, the Charter of Liberties

of 1683, and Leisler's Rebellion in New York," in William Pencak and Conrad Wright, eds., *Authority and Resistance in Early New York* (New York, 1988), 57–60, 72–73; Julius Goebel, Jr., "The Courts and the Law in Colonial New York," in Flaherty, ed., *Essays in the History of Early American Law,* 268–272: Herbert Johnson, "The Advent of Common Law in Colonial New York," in Billias, ed., *Law and Authority in Colonial America,* 74; Randall Balmer, *A Perfect Babel of Confusion: Dutch Religion and English Culture in the Middle Colonies* (New York, 1989), 29–30.

39. Martin, *Profits in the Wilderness,* 262–266; Konig, *Law and Society in Puritan Massachusetts,* 159–164; Kamensky, *Governing the Tongue,* 183–184; Russell Osgood, "John Clark, Esq., Justice of the Peace, 1667–1728," in Coquillette, ed., *Law in Colonial Massachusetts, 1630–1800,* 113, 144.

40. Bruce Mann, "Rationality, Legal Change, and Community in Connecticut, 1690–1760," *Law and Society Review* 14 (1980), 212; idem, *Neighbors and Strangers: Law and Community in Early Connecticut* (Chapel Hill, N.C., 1987), 90–93; Dayton, *Women Before the Bar,* 301, 45–48, 196–197, 234, 246.

41. James Mitchell and Henry Flanders, eds., *The Statutes at Large of Pennsylvania from 1682 to 1801,* 26 vols. (Harrisburg, 1896–1919), 2:149; Offutt, *Of "Good Laws" and "Good Men,"* 65, 85–92; Lokken, *David Lloyd,* 105–106, 166, 190.

42. Joseph Smith, "Administrative Control of the Courts of the American Plantations," in Flaherty, ed., *Essays in the History of Early American Law,* quotes on 282, 310.

43. Ibid., 281–335; Richard Morris, *Studies in the History of American Law: With Special Reference to the Seventeenth and Eighteenth Centuries* (New York, 1974), 62–63.

44. Ian Steele, *The English Atlantic, 1675–1740: An Exploration of Communication and Community* (New York, 1986), 224–231; Roeber, *Faithful Magistrates,* 26, 101.

45. William Bryson, *Census of Law Books in Colonial Virginia* (Charlottesville, Va., 1978), xi–xxii; Herbert Johnson, *Imported Eighteenth-Century Law Treatises in American Libraries, 1700–1799* (Knoxville, Tenn., 1978), xi–xxvi, 59–64; John Conley, "Doing it by the Book: Justice of the Peace Manuals and English Law in Eighteenth Century America," *Journal of Legal History* 6 (1985), 262–270.

46. Alan Day, "Lawyers in Colonial Maryland, 1660–1715," *American Journal of Legal History* 17 (1973), 146; John Douglass, "Between Pettifoggers and Professionals," 368–369, 375; John Murrin, "The Legal Transformation: The Bench and Bar of Eighteenth-Century Massachusetts," in Stanley Katz, ed., *Colonial America: Essays in Politics and Social Development* (Boston, 1971), 418–424; Anton-Hermann Chroust, *The Rise of the Legal Profession in America,* Vol. 1, *The Colonial Experience* (Norman, Okla.,1965), 198–199, 212–214; John Douglass, "Power of Attorneys: Formation of Colonial South Carolina's Attorney System, 1700–1731," *American Journal of Legal History* 37 (1993), 5–7; Milton Klein, "From Community to Status: The Development of the Legal Profession in Colonial New York," *New York History* (1979), 140, 144.

47. Douglass, "Power of Attorneys," 2, 6, 12–14; Day, "Lawyers in Colonial America," 149–150; Murrin, "Transformation of Bench and Bar," 420–421; David Flaherty, "Criminal Practice in Provincial Massachusetts," in Coquillette, ed., *Law in Colonial Massachusetts,* 194, 210–211; Allen, "Maine Courts, Magistrates, and Lawyers," 283–284.

48. Steele, *The English Atlantic,* 221–223, quote on 222; Mary Schweitzer, *Custom and Contract: Household, Government, and the Economy in Colonial Pennsylvania* (New York, 1987), 118–119, 131; Cathy Matson, *Merchants and Empire: Trading in Colonial New York* (Baltimore, 1998), 69–70, 90, 112, 143–144, 147, 184–185, 201, 328–329, 356n.

49. Nuala Zahedieh, "Overseas Expansion and Trade in the Seventeenth Century," in Nicholas Canny, ed., *The Oxford History of the British Empire*, Vol. 1, *The Origins of Empire: British Overseas Enterprise to the Close of the Seventeenth Century* (Oxford, 1998), 419; James Rogers, *The Early History of the Law of Bills and Notes: A Study of the Origins of Anglo-American Commercial Law* (Cambridge, U.K., 1995); Coquillette, "Ideology and Incorporation III," 322, 338; Coquillette, "Legal Ideology and Incorporation IV," 886–920; Eben Moglen, "Commercial Arbitration in the Eighteenth Century: Searching for the Transformation of American Law," *Yale Law Journal* 93 (1983), 137; Deborah Rosen, *Courts and Commerce: Gender, Law, and the Market Economy in Colonial New York* (Columbus, Ohio., 1997), 38–40.

50. Peter Hoffer, *Law and People in Colonial America* (Baltimore, 1992), 50–52; Mann, *Neighbors and Strangers*, 27–30, 34–37, 171; Dayton, *Women Before the Bar*, 85–90; Rosen, *Courts and Commerce*, 36, 40, 60–65, 76, 79, 83–92.

51. Dayton, *Women Before the Bar*, 88.

52. Ibid., 58, 72, 84–85, 89–92.

53. Linda Biemer, *Women and Property in Colonial New York: The Transition from Dutch to English Law 1643–1727* (Ann Arbor, Mich., 1983), 1–7; David Narrett, *Inheritance and Family Life in Colonial New York City* (Ithaca, N.Y., 1992), 42–49, 83; Rosen, *Courts and Commerce*, 96–97.

54. Brown, *Good Wives, Nasty Wenches*, 287–289.

55. Flaherty, "Criminal Practice in Massachusetts," 210; Brown, *Good Wives, Nasty Wenches*, 186–193; Dayton, *Women Before the Bar*, 186, 196, 206–207, 232–234, 286–287, 301–303.

56. Hart, "Colonial Land Use Law," 1257–1285, 1298; John Hart, "Takings and Compensation in Early America: The Colonial Highways Acts in Social Context," *American Journal of Legal History* 40 (1996), 254–256.

57. Daniel Hulsebosch, "*Imperia in Imperio:* The Multiple Constitutions of Empire in New York, 1750–1777," *Law and History Review* 16 (1998), 319–379.

58. Jack Greene, *Pursuits of Happiness: The Social Development of Early Modern British Colonies and the Formation of American Culture* (Chapel Hill, N.C., 1998) informs this entire concluding section.

59. Jack Greene, *Peripheries and Center: Constitutional Development in the Extended Polities of the British Empire and the United States 1607–1788* (Athens, Ga., 1986); idem, "From the Perspective of Law: Context and Legitimacy in the Origins of the American Revolution," *South Atlantic Quarterly* 75 (1986), 56–77; Greene, "Empire and Identity," 227.

E I G H T : Jonathan Edwards, the Enlightenment, and the Formation of Protestant Tradition in America

1. See, for example, Timothy H. Breen, "An Empire of Goods: The Anglicization of Colonial American, 1690–1776," *Journal of British Studies* 25 (1986), 467–499, and David G. Allen, *In English Ways: The Movement of Societies and the Transferal of English Local Law and Custom to Massachusetts Bay in the Seventeenth Century* (Chapel Hill, N.C., 1981). Also Neil McKendrick, John Brewer, and J. H. Plum, eds., *The Birth of a Consumer Society: The Commercialization of Eighteenth-Century England* (Bloomington, Ind.,

1982); Frank Lambert, *"Pedlar in Divinity": George Whitefield and the Transatlantic Revivals, 1737–1770* (Princeton, 1994); and Harry S. Stout, *The Divine Dramatist: George Whitefield and the Rise of Modern Evangelicalism* (Grand Rapids, Mich., 1991).

2. For an analysis of Edwards's response to the scientific revolution, see Avihu Zakai, "The Conversion of Jonathan Edwards," *Journal of Presbyterian History* 76, no. 1 (Summer, 1998), 1–12; idem, "Jonathan Edwards," *American National Biography* (New York, 1999); and idem, "Jonathan Edwards and the Language of Nature: The Re-Enchantment of the World in the Age of Scientific Reasoning," *Journal of Religious History* 26 (2002), 15–41.

3. W. R. Ward, *The Protestant Evangelical Awakening* (Cambridge, U.K., 1992), 91, 168, 275, 322.

4. An analysis the Enlightenment "new science" of morals and history can be found in Ernst Cassirer, *The Philosophy of the Enlightenment* (Boston, 1951); Peter Gay, *The Enlightenment: An Interpretation: The Rise of Modern Paganism* (New York, 1966); idem, *The Enlightenment: An Interpretation: The Science of Freedom* (New York, 1969); Isaac Kramnick, ed., *The Portable Enlightenment Reader* (New York, 1995); and more recently, J. G. A. Pocock, *Barbarism and Religion*, Vol. 1, *The Enlightenments of Edward Gibbon, 1737–1764*, and Vol. 2, *Narratives of Civil Government* (Cambridge, U.K., 1999); Roy Porter, *Enlightenment: Britain and the Creation of the Modern World* (London, 2000); Jonathan Israel, *Radical Enlightenment: Philosophy and the Making of Modernity, 1650–1750* (Oxford, 2001); Ann Taves, *Fits, Trances, and Visions: Experiencing Religion and Explaining Experience from Wesley to James* (Princeton, 1999); and two studies by Isabel Rivers, *Reason, Grace, and Sentiment: A Study of the Language of Religion and Ethics in England, 1660–1780*, Vol. 1: *Whichcote to Wesley*, and Vol. 2, *Shaftesbury to Hume* (Cambridge, U.K., 1991 and 2000).

5. Edwards's various works on Natural Philosophy appear in Wallace E. Anderson, ed., *Works of Jonathan Edwards* (hereafter *WJE*), Vol. 6, *Scientific and Philosophical Writings*, (New Haven, Conn., 1980).

6. Edwards's works on ethics and morals appeared in Paul Ramsey, ed., *WJE*, Vol. 8, *Ethical Writings* (New Haven, Conn., 1989).

7. Wallace E. Anderson, "Introduction," *WJE*, Vol. 6, *Scientific and Philosophical Writings*, 15; Elizabeth Flower and Murray G. Murphey, *A History of Philosophy in America*, 2 vols. (New York, 1977), 1:81–83.

8. Edwin A. Burtt, *The Metaphysical Foundations of Modern Physical Science: A Historical and Critical Essay*, 2nd ed. (London, [1932] 1967), 294.

9. See Ward, *The Protestant Evangelical Awakening*; Michael J. Crawford, *Seasons of Grace: Colonial New England's Revival Tradition in Its British Context* (New York, 1991); and Mark A. Noll et al., eds., *Evangelicalism: Comparative Studies of Popular Protestantism in North America, the British Isles, and Beyond, 1700–1900* (New York, 1994). An important discussion of the theological origins of the Great Awakening in New England can be found in Alan Heimert and Perry Miller, eds., "Introduction," *The Great Awakening: Documents Illustrating the Crisis and Its Consequences* (Indianapolis, 1967), xiii–lxv. An excellent bibliography of the body of secondary literature on eighteenth century religion and society appears in Stout, *The Divine Dramatist*, 288–296.

10. Jaroslav Pelikan, *The Christian Tradition: A History of the Development of Doctine*, Vol. 5, *Christian Doctrine and Modern Culture (since 1700)* (Chicago, 1989), 119–121.

11. Taves, *Fits, Trances, and Visions*, 47.

12. Roland H. Bainton, *Christianity* (Boston, 1964), 338.

13. John Pudney, *John Wesley and His World* (New York, 1978), 57.

14. John E. Smith, ed., "Introduction," in *WJE*, Vol. 2, *Religious Affections* (New Haven, Conn., 1959), 9–42.

15. Robert W. Jensen, *America's Theologian: A Recommendation of Jonathan Edwards* (New York, 1988), 66–69.

16. Taves, *Fits, Trances, and Visions*, 38.

17. Conard Cherry, *The Theology of Jonathan Edwards: A Reappraisal* (Bloomington, Ind., 1990), 57.

18. Crawford, *Seasons of Grace*, 227, 99, 104, 161, 149.

19. Albert C. Outler, ed., *John Wesley* (New York, 1964), 15–16, as cited in Crawford, *Seasons of Grace*, 290 n25. For the relationship between Edwards and Wesley's interpretation of religious experience, see Taves, *Fits, Trances, and Visions*, 50. The publications of Edwards's revival writings in England and Scotland, such as *Faithful Narrative, Distinguishing Marks, and Some Thoughts Concerning the Revival*, are discussed in C. C. Goen, ed., "Introduction," in *WJE*, Vol. 4, *The Great Awakening* (New Haven, Conn., 1972), 1–90.

20. Rivers, *Reason, Grace, and Sentiment*, 2:194.

21. Ward, *The Protestant Evangelical Awakening*, 90–91, 275.

22. Crawford, *Seasons of Grace*, 138. See also Joseph A. Conforti, *Jonathan Edwards, Religious Tradition, and American Culture* (Chapel Hill, N.C., 1995), 47–49.

23. Edwards, "To a Correspondent in Scotland," Nov. 1745, in George C. Claghorn, ed., *WJE*, Vol. 16, *Letters and Personal Writings*, (New Haven, Conn., 1998), 180.

24. Perry Miller, *Errand Into the Wilderness* (Cambridge, Mass., 1956), vii.

25. Edwards as cited in Perry Miller, "Jonathan Edwards's Sociology of the Great Awakening," *New England Quarterly* 21 (1948), 54–55.

26. Edwards, *A History of the Work of Redemption*, in John F. Wilson, ed., *WJE*, Vol. 9, *A History of the Work of Redemption* (New Haven, Conn., 1989), 438.

27. Edwards, "Letter to the Trustees of the College of New Jersey," 1757, in Claghorn, ed., *WJE*, Vol. 16, *Letters and Personal Writings*, 727.

28. Henry F. May, *The Enlightenment in America* (New York, 1976), xii, 49.

29. William Breitenbach, "The Consistent Calvinism of the New Divinity Movement," *William and Mary Quarterly*, 3rd ser., 41 (1984), 257.

30. William K. B. Stoever, "The Calvinist Theological Tradition," in C. H. Lippy and Peter W. Williams, eds., *Encyclopedia of the American Religious Experience: Studies of Traditions and Movements*, 3 vols. (New York, 1988), 2:1047–1048; James D. German, "The Social Utility of Wicked Self-Love: Calvinism, Capitalism, and Public Policy in Revolutionary New England," *Journal of American History* 82 (1995), 965–998.

31. William Breitenbach, "Piety and Moralism: Edwards and the New Divinity," in Nathan O. Hatch and Harry S. Stout, eds., *Jonathan Edwards and the American Experience* (New York, 1988), 177–204.

32. Bruce Kuklick, "Jonathan Edwards and American Philosophy," in Hatch and Stout, eds., *Jonathan Edwards and the American Experience*, 257.

33. John F. Wilson, "Introduction," in *WJE*, Vol. 9, Wilson, ed., *A History of the Work of Redemption*, 92–93. See also Ruth Bloch, *Visionary Republic: Millennial Themes in American Thought, 1756–1800* (New York, 1985); and Donald Weber, *Rhetoric and History in Revolutionary New England* (New York, 1988).

34. Conforti, *Jonathan Edwards, Religious Tradition, and American Culture,* 47–49.

35. Henry F. May divided the Enlightenment in Europe into four categories, the first of which is the Moderate, or Rational, Enlightenment which preached "balance, order and religious compromise, and was dominant in England from the time of Newton and Locke until about the middle of the eighteenth century." May, *The Enlightenment in America,* xvi. The theory of moral sense was developed by people who belonged to the Moderate, or Rational, Enlightenment.

36. Edwards read many works by British moral philosophers, including Hutcheson and Hume. See "Jonathan Edwards' Reading 'Catalogue' with Notes and Index," ed. L. Brian Sullivan, "Works of Jonathan Edwards," unpublished manuscript, Yale Divinity School Office, New Haven, Conn.; Norman Fiering, *Jonathan Edwards's Moral Thought and Its British Context* (Chapel Hill, N.C., 1981); and Paul Ramsey, ed., "Appendix II: Jonathan Edwards on Moral Sense, and the Sentimentalists," in *WJE,* Vol. 8, *Ethical Writings,* 689–705.

37. See Francis Hutcheson, *An Inquiry Concerning Beauty, Order, Harmony, Design,* ed. Peter Kivy (The Hague, 1973); R. S. Donwie, ed., *Francis Hutcheson: Philosophical Writings* (London, 1994); and Thomas Mautner, ed., *Francis Hutcheson: On Human Nature* (Cambridge, U.K., 1993).

38. Jonathan Edwards, *Concerning the End for which God Created the World,* in Ramsey, ed., *WJE,* Vol. 8, *Ethical Writings,* 550.

39. Jonathan Edwards, *The Nature of True Virtue,* in ibid., 548.

40. Shaftesbury [Anthony Ashley Cooper], *An Inquiry Concerning Virtue or Merit* (1699) in L. A. Selby-Bigge, ed., *British Moralists: Being Selections from Writers Principally of the Eighteenth Century,* 2 vols. (Oxford, 1897), 1:23, 33.

41. Rivers, *Reason, Grace, and Sentiment,* 2:154.

42. Norman Fiering, *Moral Philosophy at Seventeenth-Century Harvard* (Chapel Hill, N.C., 1981), 180.

43. Rivers, *Reason, Grace, and Sentiment,* 2:159.

44. Hutcheson, *An Inquiry Concerning the Original of Our Ideas of Virtue or Moral Good,* 2nd ed. (1726) in Selby-Bigge, ed. *British Moralists,* 1:87.

45. Ibid., 1:99, 118.

46. Ibid., 1:83.

47. Hutcheson, *Essay on the Passions,* rev. ed., (1742), in Paul McReynolds, ed., *Four Early Works on Motivation* (Gainesville, Fla., 1969), 4–5.

48. Hume, *Philosophical Essays Concerning Human Understanding* (1748), 14, as quoted in Mautner, ed., *Francis Hutcheson: On Human Nature,* 152.

49. Rivers, *Reason, Grace, and Sentiment,* 2:282.

50. Ibid., 2:288.

51. Knud Haakonssen, *Natural Law and Moral Philosophy: From Grotius to the Scottish Enlightenment* (Cambridge, U.K., 1996), 66.

52. Rivers, *Reason, Grace, and Sentiment,* 2:298.

53. Gerhard Ebeling, "Theology and the Evidentness of the Ethical," *Journal for Theology and the Church* 2 (1972), 102, as quoted by Fiering, *Moral Philosophy at Seventeenth-Century Harvard,* 301.

54. Fiering, *Jonathan Edwards's Moral Thought,* 136–138.

55. Edwards, *The Nature of True Virtue,* in Ramsey, ed., *WJE,* Vol. 8, *Ethical Writings,* 622.

56. Edwards, *Concerning the End for which God Created the World,* in ibid., 424.

57. Fiering, *Moral Philosophy at Seventeenth-Century Harvard,* 301.

58. Edwards's scientific writings are in Anderson, ed., *WJE,* Vol. 6, *Scientific and Philosophical Writings.*

59. Edwards, Miscellany # 704; Edwards, *Freedom of the Will,* in Ramsey, ed., *WJE,* Vol. 1, *Freedom of the Will,* 177.

60. Edwards, *Charity and Its Fruits* (1738), in Ramsey, ed., *WJE,* Vol. 8, *Ethical Writings,* 63, 137, 142.

61. Edwards, *The Nature of True Virtue,* in ibid., 560.

62. Paul Ramsey, "Jonathan Edwards on Moral Sense, and the Sentimentalists," in ibid., 703.

63. Paul Ramsey, "Introduction," in ibid., 2.

64. Edwards, *Charity and Its Fruits,* in ibid., 137, 142.

65. Edwards, *Freedom of the Will,* in Ramsey, ed., *WJE,* Vol. 1, *Freedom of the Will* 163, 431–433.

66. Edwards, *Original Sin,* in Clyde A. Holbrook, ed., *WJE,* Vol 3, *Original Sin,* (New Haven, Conn., 1970), 102, 395, 403.

67. Edwards, *The Nature of True Virtue,* in Ramsey, ed., *WJE,* Vol. 8, *Ethical Writings,* 539–551.

68. Rivers, *Reason, Grace, and Sentiment,* 2:194.

69. Edwards, *The Nature of True Virtue,* in Ramsey, ed., *WJE,* Vol. 8, *Ethical Writings,* 552–560.

70. Fiering, *Jonathan Edwards's Moral Thought,* 148.

71. Henry F. May, "Jonathan Edwards and America," in Hatch and Stout, eds., *Jonathan Edwards and the American Experience,* 21–22.

72. William Breitenbach, "The Consistent Calvinism of the New Divinity Movement," 257.

73. Mark Valeri, *Law and Providence in Joseph Bellamy's New England: The Origins of the New Divinity in Revolutionary America* (New York, 1994), 48–49.

74. Ibid., 4.

75. See Mark A. Noll, "Jonathan Edwards and Nineteenth Century Theology," in Hatch and Stout, eds., *Jonathan Edwards and the American Experience,* 260–288.

76. James D. German, "The Social Utility of Wicked Self-Love: Calvinism, Capitalism, and Public Policy in Revolutionary New England," *Journal of American History* 82 (1995), 970–971.

77. Hans W. Frei, "H. Richard Niebuhr," in George Hunsinger and William C. Placher, eds., *Theology and Narrative: Selected Essays,* (New York, 1993), 221.

78. H. Richard Niebuhr, "The Anachronism of Jonathan Edwards," *Christian Century* 20 (1996), 481–482. Niebuhr originally delivered this address in Northampton, Mass., on March 9, 1958, to commemorate the bicentennial of the death of Jonathan Edwards.

79. H. Richard Niebuhr, *The Kingdom of God in America* (New York, [1937] 1959), 137–138.

80. The development of the various Enlightenment narratives of history is discussed, among others, in Karen O'Brien, *Narratives of Enlightenment: Cosmopolitan History from Voltaire to Gibbon* (Cambridge, U.K., 1997); Pocock, *Barbarism and Religion: The Enlightenments of Edward Gibbon, 1737–1764;* idem, *Barbarism and Religion:*

Narratives of Civil Government; Cassirer, *The Philosophy of the Enlightenment;* Gay, *The Enlightenment: The Rise of Modern Paganism;* idem, *The Enlightenment: The Science of Freedom* (New York, 1997); Carl L. Baker, *The Heavenly City of the Eighteenth-Century Philosophers* (New Haven, Conn., [1932] 1959); Philip Hicks, *Neoclassical History and English Culture: From Clarendon to Hume* (London, 1996); and Donald R. Kelley, ed. *Versions of History from Antiquity to the Enlightenment* (New Haven, Conn., 1991).

81. Paul Tillich, *A History of Christian Thought: From Its Judaic and Hellenistic Origins to Existentialism,* ed. Carl E. Braaten (New York, 1968), 323. Cf., Immanuel Kant, "What is Enlightenment?" (1784), in Kramnick, ed., *The Portable Enlightenment Reader,* 1: "Enlightenment is man's release from his self-incurred tutelage. Tutelage is man's inability to make use of his understanding without direction from another."

82. Cassirer, *The Philosophy of the Enlightenment,* 199.

83. J. G. A. Pocock, "Modes of Action and their Pasts in Tudor and Stuart England," in Orest Ranum, ed., *National Consciousness, History, and Political Culture in Early Modern Europe* (Baltimore, 1975), 98–117; idem, *The Machiavellian Moment: Florentine Political Thought and the Atlantic Republican Tradition* (Princeton, 1975).

84. Reinhart Koselleck, "Modernity and the Planes of Historicity," in *Futures Past: On the Semantics of Historical Time* (Cambridge, Mass., 1985), 5.

85. Gay, *The Enlightenment: The Science of Freedom,* 372–373.

86. Eric Voegelin, *From Enlightenment to Revolution,* ed. John H. Hallowell (Durham, N.C., 1975), 21.

87. G. Barraclough, "Universal History," 1962, as quoted in Sidney Pollard, *The Idea of Progress: History and Society* (Harmondsworth, U.K., 1971), 33. Cf., Condorcet, "The Future Progress of Human Mind" (1794), in Kramnick, ed., *The Portable Enlightenment Reader,* 26–38.

88. Koselleck, "Modernity and the Planes of Historicity," 10.

89. Peter Harrison, *"Religion" and the Religions in the English Enlightenment* (Cambridge, U.K., 1990), 5.

90. Keith Ward, *Religion and Revelation: A Theology of Revelation in the World's Religions* (Oxford, 1994), 284.

91. See "Jonathan Edwards' Reading 'Catalogue,'" in Sullivan, ed., *Works of Jonathan Edwards.*

92. Pocock, *Barbarism and Religion: Narratives of Civil Government,* 2–8.

93. O'Brien, *Narratives of Enlightenment,* 10, 1.

94. Cassirer, *The Philosophy of the Enlightenment,* 207–208.

95. Pierre Bayle, "David," in *Historical and Critical Dictionary* (Indianapolis, 1965), 62–63.

96. Samuel Pufendorf, *An Introduction to the History of the Principal Kingdoms and States of Europe* (1702), in Kelley, ed. *Versions of History,* 435–438.

97. David Hume, *Essays, Moral, Political, and Literary,* ed. T. H. Green, 2 vols. (London, 1882), 2:388–391.

98. Hume, "History as Guide," in Kramnick, ed., *The Portable Enlightenment Reader,* 359.

99. Lord Bolingbroke, "Remarks on the History of England," in Isaac Kramnick, ed., *Historical Writings [of] Lord Bolingbroke* (Chicago, 1972), 177.

100. Ephraim Chambers, *Cyclopaedia; or an Universal Dictionary of Arts and Sciences* (1728), in Kelley, ed., *Versions of History,* 441.

101. David Hume, "Of Parties in General" (1741), in Hume, *Essays Moral, Political and Literary*, ed. Eugene F. Miller (Indianapolis, 1985), 62–63.

102. Bolingbroke, "Letters on the Study and Use of History," in Kramnick, ed., *Historical Writings*, 35–36, 51, 53–55.

103. Edwards, *History of the Work of Redemption*, in Wilson, ed., *WJE*, Vol. 9, *A History of the Work of Redemption*, 291.

104. Ibid., 511, 143.

105. Tillich, *A History of Christian Thought*, 1.

106. Compare Tillich's distinction with the more secular approach of Walter Benjamin: "History is the subject of a structure whose site is not homogenous, empty time, but time filled by the presence of the now." Benjamin, "Theses on the Philosophy of History," in Hannah Arendt, ed., *Illuminations* (New York, 1969), 261. In Edwards's case, historical events acquired their meaning and significance from a meta-historical structure.

107. Edwards, *History of the Work of Redemption*, in Wilson, ed., *WJE*, Vol. 9, *A History of the Work of Redemption*, 285.

108. Ibid., 511, 143.

109. Edwards, Miscellanies (hereafter Mis.) 547 (ca. 1731), Yale University Archives, New Haven, Conn.

110. Edwards, "To the Trustees of the College of New Jersey," 728; Edwards, *God Glorified in the Work of Redemption*, July 8, 1731, in Wilson H. Kimnach et al., eds., *The Sermons of Jonathan Edwards: A Reader* (New Haven, Conn., 1999), 78.

111. Edwards, *Notes on Scriptures* (1739), in Stephen J. Stein, ed., *WJE*, Vol. 15, *Notes on Scriptures* (New Haven, Conn., 1998), 373, 389.

112. Edwards, "To the Rev. Joseph Bellamy," Jan. 21, 1741–42, in Claghorn, ed., *WJE*, Vol. 16, *Letters and Personal Writings*, 99.

113. Edwards, Mis. 547 (ca. 1731).

114. Edwards, Mis. 702 (ca. 1736).

115. Ibid.

116. Stephen Stein, "Introduction," in Stein, ed., *WJE*, Vol. 5, *Apocalyptic Writings*, (New Haven, Conn., 1977), 22.

117. Edwards, *History of the Work of Redemption*, Wilson, ed., *WJE*, Vol. 9, *A History of the Work of Redemption*, 285.

118. Ibid., 511, 143.

119. Ibid., 143.

120. Crawford, *Seasons of Grace*, 132.

121. Jonathan Edwards, *The Distinguishing Marks of a Work of the Spirit of God*, in Goen, ed., *WJE*, Vol. 4, *The Great Awakening*, 230.

122. Jonathan Edwards, *Some Thoughts Concerning the Present Revival of Religion in New England* (1742) in ibid., 353.

123. James H. Moorhead, *World without End: Mainstream American Protestant Visions of the Last Things, 1880–1925* (Bloomington, Ind., 1999), 5–6.

124. Valeri, *Law and Providence*, 48–49.

125. Conforti, *Jonathan Edwards, Religious Tradition, and American Culture*, 48–49.

126. Niebuhr, *The Kingdom of God in America*, 138.

127. Ibid., 135–138.

128. John F. Wilson, "Introduction," in Wilson, ed., *WJE*, Vol. 9, *A History of the Work of Redemption*, 95.

129. Ibid., 94.

130. Jon Butler, *Becoming America: The Revolution Before 1776* (Cambridge, Mass., 2000).

NINE: Order, Ordination, Subordination

1. Heinrich Nilber et al. to Ziegenhagen, Oct. 15, 1739, *Halle Reports. New Edition, with extensive historical, critical and literary annotations, and numerous documents, copied from the manuscripts in the archives of the Francke Institutions at Halle* (hereafter *HR*), ed. William J. Mann, Beale M. Schmucker, and Wilhelm Germann, trans. C. W. Schaeffer (Reading, Pa., 1882), 102. Text in German: [*Hallesche] Nachrichten von den vereinigten Deutschen Evangelisch-Lutherischen Gemeinen in Nord-America, absonderlich in Pen[n]sylvanien* (hereafter *HN*), 2 vols. (1: Allentown, Pa., 1886; 2: Philadelphia, 1895), 1:67–68. References to the German text quoted verbatim from works in English translation are set in square brackets.

2. On Mühlenberg's attitude toward blacks, see Wolfgang Splitter, "'Neger,' 'Miterlöste,' 'Nebenmenschen': Heinrich Melchior Mühlenberg über die afro-amerikanische Ethnie und die Sklaverei," *Amerikastudien/American Studies* 45, no. 3 (2000), 293–323.

3. From 1742 to 1786, the Francke Foundations sent fourteen missionaries to Pennsylvania. For biographical details, see Charles Henry Glatfelter, *Pastors and People: German Lutheran and Reformed Churches in the Pennsylvania Field, 1717–1793,* 2 vols. (Breinigsville, Pa., 1980–81), 1: passim.

4. See Mühlenberg to Francke and Ziegenhagen, December 3, 1742, *The Correspondence of Heinrich Melchior Mühlenberg* (hereafter: *CM*), trans. and ed. John W. Kleiner and Helmut T. Lehmann, 2 vols. (1740–52) to date (Camden, Maine, 1993), 1:47–48. The German original of this edition is Kurt Aland et al., eds., *Die Korrespondenz Heinrich Melchior Mühlenbergs: Aus den Anfängen des deutschen Luthertums in Nordamerika* (hereafter *KM*) 5 vols. (Berlin, 1986–2003), 1:40.

5. Theodore G. Tappert and John W. Doberstein, trans. and eds., *The Journals of Henry Melchior Muhlenberg* (hereafter *MJ*), 3 vols. (Philadelphia, 1942–58), 1:65 (Nov. 25, 1742); William Germann, ed., *Heinrich Melchior Mühlenberg, Patriarch der Lutherischen Kirche Nordamerika's. Selbstbiographie, 1711–1743* (hereafter *Selbstbiographie)* (Allentown, Pa., 1881), 122; and Mühlenberg to Francke and Ziegenhagen, Dec. 3, 1742, *CM* 1:47 [*KM* 1:40].

6. *MJ* 1:66 (Nov. 25, 1742) [*Selbstbiographie,* 122].

7. Mühlenberg to Francke and Ziegenhagen, Dec. 3, 1742, *CM* 1:48 [*KM* 1:41]; *MJ* 1:77; *Selbstbiographie,* 143–144; *CM* 1:47, 50, 68; *KM* 1:40, 42, 60.

8. *Selbstbiographie,* 144; Mühlenberg to Francke and Ziegenhagen, March 12, 1743, *CM* 1:64 [*KM* 1:56]; *MJ* 1:71.

9. Mühlenberg to Francke and Ziegenhagen, March 17, 1743, *CM* 1:70 [*KM* 1:61].

10. *MJ* 1:67, 74–75; *Selbstbiographie,* 124–126, 137–138; *CM* 1:24–30, 73, 169; *KM* 1:24–29, 64, 145.

11. *MJ* 1:69 (Dec. 6, 1742).

12. Ibid., 1:67 (Nov. 28, 1742) [*Selbstbiographie,* 126].

13. *MJ* 1:71 (Dec. 14, 1742) [*Selbstbiographie,* 133].

14. Mühlenberg to Francke and Ziegenhagen, March 17, 1743, *CM* 1:69 [*KM* 1:60]; *MJ* 1:69; *Selbstbiographie,* 128.

15. Mühlenberg to Joachim Oporin, Aug. 12, 1743, *CM* 1:116 [*KM* 1:101]. On Pennsylvania rules for arbitrations in religious matters, see Thomas Müller, *Kirche zwischen zwei Welten: Die Obrigkeitsproblematik bei Heinrich Melchior Mühlenberg und die Kirchengründung der deutschen Lutheraner in Pennsylvania* (Stuttgart, 1994), 55–56.

16. Sydney Ahlstrom, *A Religious History of the American People* (New Haven, Conn., 1972), 100–101.

17. Arthur Cross, *The Anglican Episcopate and the American Colonies* (Cambridge, Mass., 1902), 57–58.

18. Mühlenberg et al. to the Hamburg Ministerium, Nov./Dec. 1745, *CM* 1:204 [*KM* 1:169].

19. *MJ* 1:73–74 (Dec. 25, 1742); *Selbstbiographie*, 136; *KM* 1:58n10. See also *CM* 1:72; *KM* 1:64.

20. Glatfelter, *Pastors and People*, 1:211.

21. *MJ* 1:74–75 (Dec. 27, 1742) [*Selbstbiographie*, 137–138].

22. Mühlenberg to Francke and Ziegenhagen, March 17, 1743, *CM* 1:73 [*KM* 1:65].

23. *MJ* 1:74 (Dec. 25, 1742).

24. Mühlenberg to Ziegenhagen and Francke, Feb. 18, 1752, *CM* 2:208 [*KM* 1:480].

25. *Pen[n]sylvanische Berichte*, 1. Feb. 1750 (trans. Wolfgang Splitter [hereafter *WS*]).

26. *MJ* 1:75; *Selbstbiographie*, 138.

27. Mühlenberg to Ziegenhagen and Francke, Feb. 18, 1752, *CM* 2:212 [*KM* 1:483].

28. Mühlenberg to Francke and Ziegenhagen, Sept. 22, 1743, *CM* 1:124, 127 [*KM* 1:106, 109].

29. Francke to Mühlenberg, June 16, 1745, *CM* 1:194 [*KM* 1:163].

30. Mühlenberg to Stöver, Nov. 4, 1747, *CM* 1:355 [*KM* 1:304]. The two notions *conference* and *synod* reappeared in Mühlenberg's report on the first conference in 1748 (see *MJ* 1:202; *HN* 1:393). The divines at the meeting were Pastors P. Brunnholz, J. F. Handschuh, H. M. Mühlenberg, and Johann Christoph Hartwig, Catechist J. N. Kurz, and Swedish Provost John Sandin. Delegates came from Germantown, Earltown, Lancaster, New Hanover, Northkill, Philadelphia, Providence, Saucon, Tulpehocken, and Upper Milford. York sent no delegate.

31. *Documentary History of the Evangelical Lutheran Ministerium of Pennsylvania and Adjacent States . . .* , ed. Board of Publication of the General Council of the Evangelical Lutheran Church in North America (Philadelphia, 1898), 9 [*HN* 1:209].

32. The pastoral college was also called College of Pastors, Evangelical Lutheran Ministerium, [United] Ministerium of Pennsylvania, Ministerium of the Swedish and German Nations, Pennsylvania Ministerium, United Evangelical Ministerium, United Preachers, or United Swedish and German Ministerium. The association of parishes was also called United Evangelical Congregations or United German Congregations. The annual meeting was also called conference, synod, or synodical meeting.

33. People in Germany joined a church by birth, whereas colonists did so voluntarily. German pastors could enforce church statutes, but Pennsylvania clerics had no means to bind anyone to any rule. Germans were liable to church taxes, while colonials were free to pay or to refuse. The "Constitution of the Ministerium of the Evangelical Lutheran Church of North America" went into effect in 1781. See *Documentary History*, 165–176. On the Lutheran institutions in Germany and Pennsylvania, see Müller, *Kirche zwischen zwei Welten*, 253–256.

34. For biographical sketches of Andreä and Streiter, see Glatfelter, *Pastors and People*, 1:16–18, 147–148.

35. *Documentary History*, 11 [*HN* 1:210].

36. Jakob Friedrich Schertlin (1696–1768?). For a biographical sketch, see Glatfelter, *Pastors and People*, 1:116–117.

37. *Documentary History*, 11 [*HN* 1:210]. The conflict over the liturgy partly originated from different religious, historical, and political experiences of people in various parts of Germany. Whereas most Hallensians came from Central, North, and Northeast Germany, Stöver, Wagner, and other pastors came from the western and southwestern regions of the country. See *MJ* 1:193 and Winters, "John Caspar Stoever," 129–130.

38. *Documentary History*, 11 [*HN* 1:210].

39. Lucas Raus (1723–88) attended the 1750 convention; Johann Albert Weygand (1722–70) 1750; Ludolph Henry Schrenck (b. 1716?) 1753; Jakob Friedrich Schertlin (b. 1715) 1754; Paul Daniel Bryzelius (1713–73) 1760; Johann Andreas Friderichs (b. 1712?) 1760; Johann Samuel Schwerdtfeger (1734–1803) 1762; Johann Georg Bager (1725–91) 1763; Nikolaus Hornell (no dates available) 1763; Johann Friedrich Ries (d. 1791) 1763; Johann Joseph Roth (d. 1764) 1763; Johann Caspar Stöver, Jr. (1707–79) 1763; Johann Schwarbach (1719–1800) 1766; Karl Friedrich Wildbahn (1733–1804) 1769. Glatfelter, *Pastors and People*, 1:passim.

40. *Documentary History*, 5, 6; *HN* 1:173. In Germany, *conferences* (conventions) provided a forum for clergy and laity to discuss church affairs, while *synods* exclusively united church and state officials who exercised executive and supervisory powers. See Müller, *Kirche zwischen zwei Welten*, 253–254.

41. See Splitter, *Pastors, People, Politics: German Lutherans in Pennsylvania, 1740–1790* (Trier, 1998), 32, 259.

42. Mühlenberg to Francke and Ziegenhagen, Dec. 12, 1745, *CM* 1:235 [*KM* 1:198]. See also *MJ* 1:99.

43. On Germantown congregants' dissatisfaction with signing this call, see Mühlenberg to Francke and Ziegenhagen, Dec. 12, 1745, *CM* 1:236. See also *MJ* 1:99 [*KM* 1:198].

44. Mühlenberg et al. to Ziegenhagen and Francke, Sept. 29, 1753, *KM* 2:100–101 (trans.WS). See also Mühlenberg et al. to Ziegenhagen and Francke, Sept. 29, 1753, *KM* 2:104–108.

45. Müller, *Kirche zwischen zwei Welten*, 241, 265.

46. Mühlenberg to Ziegenhagen and Francke, July 5, 1754, *KM* 2:161–163.

47. Glatfelter, *Pastors and People*, 2:308–326; Splitter, *Pastors, People, Politics*, 95–108.

48. Mühlenberg to Ziegenhagen and Francke, July 5, 1754, *KM* 2:163; Francke to Mühlenberg, June 24, 1756, ibid., 291 (trans. WS).

49. Mühlenberg et al. to R. H. Morris, Oct./Nov. 1754 (version B), *KM* 2:223–224.

50. Splitter, *Pastors, People, Politics*, 88–94, 103–104.

51. Francke to Mühlenberg, June 24, 1756, *KM* 2:292 (trans. WS).

52. Müller, *Kirche zwischen zwei Welten*, 267.

53. *MJ* 2:55 (March 29, 1764), 56 (March 31, 1764), 102 (July 25, 1764). On Mühlenberg's political activities, see Splitter, *Pastors, People, Politics*, 155–170.

54. *MJ* 2:102, 107, 111.

55. Ibid., 122 (Sept. 28–29, 1764); Mühlenberg to Francke and Ziegenhagen, Oct. 9, 1760, *KM* 2:401 (trans. WS).

56. *MJ* 2:122 (Sept. 30, 1764), 192 (Feb. 15, 1765), and 122 (Oct. 1, 1764).

57. Penn to Smith, March 8, 1765, quoted in Dietmar Rothermund, *The Layman's Progress: Religious and Political Experience in Colonial Pennsylvania, 1740–1770* (Philadelphia, 1961), 104.

58. Mühlenberg to Friedrich Wilhelm Pasche, Oct. 14, 1765, *KM* 3:332 (trans. WS); *HN* 2:617; *KM* 3:325–329; and *HN* 2:629–632.

59. Quote in Theodore G. Thayer, *Pennsylvania Politics and the Growth of Democracy, 1740–1776* (Harrisburg, Pa., 1953), 120; Gary B. Nash, *The Urban Crucible: Social Change, Political Consciousness, and the Origins of the American Revolution* (Cambridge, Mass., 1979), 306.

60. *MJ* 3:250 (June 12, 1779); *KM* 3:193 (June 16, 1764) (trans. WS). Mühlenberg to Pasche, Oct. 14, 1765, *KM* 3:332 (trans. WS). For Smith's and Peters' roles in obtaining the charter, see *MJ* 2:88 and 3:250. For Mühlenberg's description of the state of the Pennsylvania Lutherans, see Mühlenberg to Peters, May 4, 1764, *KM* 3:180–185.

61. *MJ* 2:88 (June 12, 1764).

62. Müller, *Kirche zwischen zwei Welten,* 267 (trans. WS).

63. Mühlenberg to Pasche, Oct. 14, 1765, *KM* 3:331 (trans. WS).

64. Cf. Mühlenberg to Pasche, Oct. 14, 1765, to Francke, Nov. 23, 1765, and to Ziegenhagen, Dec. 12, 1765, *KM* 3:331–332, 336–339, 346–348.

65. See *HN* 2:617–619, 629–632.

66. Henry E. Jacobs, *A History of the Evangelical Lutheran Church in the United States* (New York, 1893), 245.

67. Cf. *Documentary History,* 56, and *HN* 2:372.

68. *Documentary History,* 21.

69. Mühlenberg to Richard Peters, May 4, 1764, *KM* 3:184.

70. By 1763 Mühlenberg had grown so exhausted by overwork that he pondered returning to Germany; Mühlenberg to Ziegenhagen and to Count Heinrich Ernst of Stolberg-Wernigerode, Nov. 15, 1763, *KM* 3:125–133.

71. J. A. Weygand (admitted in 1750), L. Raus (1752), L. H. Schrenck (1752/53), J. A. Friderichs (1760), J. W. Kurz (1761), J. S. Schwerdtfeger (1762), J. J. Roth (1763), J. C. Stöver (1763), J. Schwarbach (1766), and K. F. Wildbahn (1769) had not completed academic studies of Lutheran theology. L. H. Schrenck, J. Schwarbach, K. F. Wildbahn. J. A. Friderichs and J. J. Roth may never have studied theology. Glatfelter, *Pastors and People* 1: 41, 77, 107, 111, 122, 129, 130, 142, 162, 165.

72. J. A. Weygand (ordained in 1750), L. Raus (1752), L. H. Schrenck (1752), J. Schwarbach (1766), K. F. Wildbahn (1778?). J. J. Roth may have been ordained by the ministerium in 1763 or 1764. Glatfelter, *Pastors and People,* 1:107, 111, 122, 129, 162, 165.

73. *Documentary History,* 71; Glatfelter, *Pastors and People,* 1:24, 66, 130; *MJ* 1:450 (Oct. 19, 1760).

74. Francke to Ziegenhagen (and Mühlenberg?), April 1, 1764; Francke to Mühlenberg, Jan. 14, 1764, *KM* 3:146, 174 (trans. WS).

75. Calculated from data on German-born Hallensians whose ages at ordination could be established: J. F. Handschuh (30), J. D. M. Heinzelmann (25), J. H. C. Helmuth (23), J. A. Krug (31), J. C. Kunze (25), H. M. Mühlenberg (27), J. F. Schmidt (22), C. E. Schultze (24), J. L. Voigt (32). American-born preachers: J. v. Buskirk (24), J. Göring (21), F. A. C. Mühlenberg (20), G. H. E. Mühlenberg (16), C. Streit (21). For data, see Glatfelter, *Pastors and People,* 1:25, 45, 50, 55, 57, 73–74, 93–95, 119–120, 125, 146, 152.

76. Knapp to Mühlenberg, May 14, 1770, *KM* 4:155 (trans. WS).

77. *Documentary History,* 126–127.

78. Calculated from data in Glatfelter, *Pastors and People* and the protocols of the conventions in *Docmentary History.*

79. Glatfelter, *Pastors and People,* 1: 41.

80. Regular German Lutheran pastors serving in Pennsylvania in 1748: P. Brunnholz, J. F. Handschuh, J. C. Hartwig, J. N. Kurz, H. M. Mühlenberg. Serving in 1776: J. G. Bager, J. C. Hartwig, J. H. C. Helmuth, J. A. Krug, J. C. Kunze, J. N. Kurz, F. A. C. Mühlenberg, G. H. E. Mühlenberg, H. M. Mühlenberg, J. H. Schaum, J. F. Schmidt, C. E. Schultze, J. L. Voigt. Ratios calculated from data ibid., 1:17, 23, 50, 52, 57, 73–74, 76, 93–95, 115, 119, 125, 152; 2:39, 145. Halle missionaries arriving in Pennsylvania in the 1760s to 1780s: J. A. Krug (1764), J. L. Voigt (1764), C. E. Schultze (1765), J. F. Schmidt (1769), J. H. C. Helmuth (1769), J. C. Kunze (1770), J. F. Weinland (1786). Ibid., 2:190, 433.

81. J. v. Buskirk, J. A. Friderichs, J. G. Jung, L. Raus, J. J. Roth, L. H. Schrenck, J. Schwarbach, J. S. Schwerdtfeger, J. A. Weygand, and K. F. Wildbahn were apprentice pastors. See ibid., 1:25, 41, 107, 111, 122, 129, 130, 162, 169; 2:202–203.

82. Mühlenberg to Francke and Ziegenhagen, June 6, 1766, *KM* 3:377 (trans. WS).

83. *MJ* 2:295 (Dec. 16, 1765).

84. Francke to Mühlenberg, Aug. 12, 1766, *KM* 3:433–434 (trans. WS); Mühlenberg to Francke and Ziegenhagen of June 6, 1766, *KM* 3:378–379, and Splitter, *Pastors, People, Politics,* 179–180.

85. *MJ* 1:138 (Jan. 1747). Mühlenberg to Francke and Ziegenhagen, Dec. 12, 1745, *CM* 1:238. See also *MJ* 1:101 [*KM* 1:200].

86. Mühlenberg to Ziegenhagen, Francke, and Johann August Majer, Dec. 20, 1749, *CM* 2:39 [*KM* 1:341]; *HN* 1:521.

87. *MJ* 1:133 (Jan. 1747).

88. Mühlenberg to Leonhard Heinrich Niemeyer, Nov. 23, 1765, quoted in William Germann, "The Crisis in the Early Life of General Peter Mühlenberg," *Pennsylvania Magazine of History and Biography* 37 (1913), 305 [*KM* 3:341].

89. *HN* 2:712–713; Splitter, *Pastors, People, Politics,* 181–186.

90. *MJ* 2:200 (Feb. 24, 1765).

91. See Article 14 of the Augsburg Confession, *Die Bekenntnisschriften der evangelisch-lutherischen Kirche,* ed. Deutscher Evangelischer Kirchenausschuß (Göttingen, 1930), 296; Müller, *Kirche zwischen zwei Welten,* 221–222.

92. Mühlenberg to the Evangelical-Lutheran Congregations in Providence and New Hanover, January 30?, 1743, *CM* 1:55 [*KM* 1:49].

93. *MJ* 1:239 (early March 1750).

94. Mühlenberg to Schaum, April 2, 1747, *CM* 1:328, 330; *KM* 1:281, 283.

95. Mühlenberg to Francke, Ziegenhagen, and Majer, Oct. 30, 1746, *CM* 1:295 [*KM* 1:248; *HN* 1:256].

96. Debra D. Smith and Frederick S. Weiser, trans. and eds., *Trinity Lutheran Church Records, Lancaster, Pennsylvania,* 3 vols. (Apollo, Pa., 1988–98), 1:362, 363 (entries of Aug. 1750).

97. Mühlenberg to Francke, Ziegenhagen et al., Oct. 30, 1746, *CM* 1:296 [*KM* 1:248–249; *HN* 1:256].

98. *HN* 1:541 (trans. WS).

99. Ibid., 2:436 (§ 2) (trans. WS).

100. *Documentary History,* 51.

101. Helmuth to Ziegenhagen, Oct. 28, 1772, *HN* 2:689, 690 (trans. WS).

102. *MJ* 1:136 (Jan. 1747) [*HN* 1:337]. *HN* 1:256 (trans. WS).

103. *MJ* 1:317–318 (Feb. 1752).

104. Ibid., 2:241 (June 5, 1765), and 2:89–90 (June 17, 1764).

105. Helmuth to Ziegenhagen, Oct. 28, 1772, *HN* 2:690 (trans. WS).

106. Mühlenberg to Francke and Ziegenhagen, Aug. 24, 1753, *KM* 2:41 (trans. WS).

107. Mühlenberg to Francke and Ziegenhagen, March 6, 1745, *CM* 1:174. See also *MJ* 1:97 [*KM* 1:151].

108. *MJ* 1:265 (Jan. 1751).

109. Helmuth to Freylinghausen, June 5, 1785, *HN* 2:792 (trans. WS).

110. *MJ* 1:260 (Nov. 1750). Mühlenberg to Francke and Ziegenhagen, December 3, 1742, *CM* 1:49 [*KM* 1:41].

111. Mühlenberg to Ziegenhagen and Francke, Feb. 18, 1752, *CM* 2:212 [*KM* 1:483].

112. Mühlenberg to Francke and Ziegenhagen, Aug. 24, 1753, *KM* 2:36–38 (trans. WS); Müller, *Kirche zwischen zwei Welten*, 129–149; Splitter, *Pastors, People, Politics,* 68–70.

113. Quoted in Müller, *Kirche zwischen zwei Welten,* 138n228 (trans. WS).

114. *Pen[n]sylvanische Berichte,* Aug. 16, Sept. 16, and Nov. 16, 1752.

115. Mühlenberg to Francke and Ziegenhagen, Aug. 24, 1753, *KM* 2:35 (trans. WS).

116. Mühlenberg to Francke and Ziegenhagen, Sept. 1, 1753, ibid., 57 (trans. WS).

117. Mühlenberg to Francke and Ziegenhagen, Oct. 9, 1760, ibid., 401 (trans. WS).

118. Splitter, *Pastors, People, Politics,* 73–86.

119. *Documentary History,* 118.

120. Jacob Fry, *The History of Trinity Lutheran Church, Reading, Pa., 1751–1894* (Reading, Pa., 1894), 47.

121. Mühlenberg to the ministerium's party in Reading, Feb. 25, 1771, *KM* 4:268, 269 (trans. WS).

122. Quoted in Fry, *The History of Trinity Lutheran Church,* 69 (§ 3).

123. *HN* 2:440 (§ 1), 441 (§ 3).

124. Quoted in Fry, *The History of Trinity Lutheran Church,* 69 (§§ 2, 3), 70–71 (§§ 9, 10).

125. Mühlenberg to Schultze, March 7, 1776, quoted in Paul A. W. Wallace, "The Muhlenbergs and the Revolutionary Underground," *Proceedings of the American Philosophical Society* 93 (1949), 120. J. L. Voigt seems to have been the only Hallensian with loyalist leanings. On Halle clergy's posture toward the Revolution, see Glatfelter, *Pastors and People* 2:377–416, and Splitter, *Pastors, People, Politics,* 187–203.

126. Wallace, "The Muhlenbergs and the Revolutionary Underground," 120. In 1782, Friedrich Mühlenberg gave his father another treatise by Paine (see *MJ* 3:504). *MJ* 3:28 (April 3, 1777).

127. Ibid., 56 (July 1, 1777) (italics added).

128. Mühlenberg to Schaum, April 2, 1747, *CM* 1:330; *KM* 1:283 (italics added). Minutes of the ministerium's 1760 convention, *Documentary History,* 47 [*HN* 2:368]. For the dates of Halle clergy taking the oath of allegiance to Pennsylvania, see Glatfelter, *Pastors and People,* 2:408–409. H. M. Mühlenberg and J. D. M. Heinzelmann married daughters of Conrad Weiser, provincial Indian agent. J. F. Handschuh, J. H. C. Helmuth, F. A. C. Mühlenberg, G. H. E. Mühlenberg, J. P. G. Mühlenberg, and J. H. Schaum married daughters of church councilors, two of them politicians. J. C. Kunze and C. E. Schultze married daughters of H. M. Mühlenberg. J. F. Schmidt's father-in-law exhibited

such pronounced interest in American victory that the British jailed him in 1777. *MJ* 1:239; 2:301, 466, 763; 3:128; *MK* 4:379; Glatfelter, *Pastors and People* 1:55, 57, 74, 95, 116, 125; Splitter, *Pastors, People, Politics*, 344, 353.

129. *MJ* 2:412 (June 27, 1769).

130. *The Pennsylvania Chronicle, and Universal Advertiser*, Sept. 18–25, 1769.

131. Mühlenberg to Wrangel, Oct. 25, 1784, quoted in *MJ* 3:625, 626.

132. *MJ* 2:181 (Feb. 4, 1765).

133. Mühlenberg to Wrangel, Oct. 25, 1784, ibid., 3:625.

134. Esp. Friedrich Kuhl, Lorenz Seckle, and John Steinmetz. Splitter, *Pastors and People*.

135. "Protest and Remonstrance of divers Members of the German Luth[eran] Congregation against the proceeding of several Members of the former Corporation read the 6th Januar[y], 1780," in *MJ* 3:289.

136. Ibid., 112 (Dec. 11, 1777).

137. Ibid., 225 (March 24, 1779).

138. On the Philadelphia dispute, see ibid., 225–296; and Splitter, *Pastors and People*, 237–241.

139. Mark A. Noll, "Revolution and the Rise of Evangelical Social Influence in North Atlantic Societies," in Mark A. Noll, David W. Bebbington, and George A. Rawlyk, eds., *Evangelicalism: Comparative Studies of Popular Protestantism in North America, the British Isles, and Beyond, 1700–1900* (New York, 1994), 118–119.

140. *The Pennsylvania Packet and General Advertiser*, June 29, 1784.

141. Splitter, *Pastors, People, Politics*, 277.

142. Jack P. Greene, *The Intellectual Construction of America: Exceptionalism and Identity from 1492 to 1800* (Chapel Hill, N.C., 1993), 114 (italics added), 113.

143. Splitter, *Pastors, People, Politics*, 179–186.

144. Anthony G. Roeber, "J. H. C. Helmuth, Evangelical Charity, and the Public Sphere in Pennsylvania, 1793–1800," *Pennsylvania Magazine of History and Biography* 121 (1997), 82–84. See also Kunze to Freylinghausen, June 13, 1780 and March 13, 1782, *HN* 2:738–740.

145. Helmuth to Freylinghausen[?], Dec. 28, 1781, quoted in Anthony G. Roeber, "The von Mosheim Society and the Preservation of German Education and Culture in the New Republic, 1789–1813," Henry Geitz, Jürgen Heideking, and Jurgen Herbst, eds., *German Influences on Education in the United States to 1917* (Cambridge, U.K. 1995), 161.

146. Roeber, "J. H. C. Helmuth," 84.

147. Kunze to the German Society of Pennsylvania, Sept. 20, 1782, quoted in Oswald Seidensticker, *Geschichte der Deutschen Gesellschaft von Pennsylvanien von der Gründung im Jahre 1764 bis zur Jubelfeier der Republik 1876* (Philadelphia, 1917), 188 (trans. WS).

148. Roeber, "J. H. C. Helmuth," 85.

149. Ibid., 86.

150. Conspicuously, the ministerium did not ordain any candidates at all between 1792 and 1800. See ibid., 92.

151. Helmuth to the 37th synodical convention at Lancaster, June 4, 1784, "Archives of the Ev[angelical] Luth[eran] Ministerium of P[ennsylvani]a and adjac[ent] States . . . ," ed. Wilhelm Germann (ms., Philadelphia, 1892; microfilm version deposited at LAC), 2703–2705 (trans. WS).

152. See *MJ* 3:669.

153. *Documentary History,* 168 (§ 5).

154. Ibid., 195–196.

155. Kunze to the Pennsylvania synod in 1804, quoted in Helen E. Pfatteicher, *The Ministerium of Pennsylvania: Oldest Lutheran Synod in America Founded in Colony Days* (Philadelphia, 1938), 41.

156. Helmuth and Schmidt to Halle, Oct. 8, 1789, quoted in Roeber, "The von Mosheim Society," 165.

157. Helmuth in his diary for Aug. 28, 1789, quoted ibid., 166.

158. Helmuth published *Betrachtung der Evangelischen Lehre von der Heiligen Schrift und Taufe . . .* (Germantown, Pa., 1793), his only major theological tract.

159. Anthony G. Roeber deserves much credit for elucidating the various stakes underlying the language question.

160. Roeber, "The von Mosheim Society," 165.

161. Ibid., 170.

162. Helmuth in his diary for April 17, 1784, *HN* 2:748 (trans. WS).

163. Helmuth to Göring, March 18, 1789, LAC: ms. PH 48 D1.

164. Roeber, "J. H. C. Helmuth," 92.; idem, "The von Mosheim Society," 175; [Justus Heinrich Christian Helmuth], *Geliebte Mitbrüder und Glaubens Genossen in Northampton County* (Philadelphia, 1799); [idem], *Klagen über den Tod des General Waschingtons am 22sten Februar 1800 in dem Deutsch Evangelisch Lutherischen Zion, zu Philadelphia* (Philadelphia, 1800).

165. Roeber, "J. H. C. Helmuth," 93.

166. The United Congregations' new name was adopted in 1792; Splitter, *Pastors, People, Politics,* 259.

167. Roeber, "The von Mosheim Society," 173.

T E N : Chartered Enterprises and the Evolution of the British Atlantic World

An earlier version of this essay was presented at an Atlantic seminar hosted by Bernard Bailyn at Harvard University. Comments by seminar participants, especially David Armitage, Michael Braddick, Eliga Gould, and Andrew O'Shaughnessy, were extremely helpful. The comments of my coeditor, Carole Shammas, enhanced the final version.

1. Thomas Jefferson, "A Summary View of the Rights of British-America," in Jack P. Greene, ed., *Colonies to Nation 1763–1789: A Documentary History of the American Revolution* (New York, 1975), 227, 228; and Michael Kammen, "The Meaning of Colonization in American Revolutionary Thought," *Journal of the History of Ideas* 31 (1970), 337–358.

2. Jack P. Greene, *Peripheries and Center: Constitutional Development in the Extended Polities of the British Empire and the United States, 1607–1788* (Athens, Ga., 1986), 12, 84–85, 99–100. In the mid nineteenth century, people interested in political liberalization in British colonies analyzed the charters of the former thirteen colonies; see Samuel Lucas, *Charters of the Old English Colonies in America with an Introduction and Notes* (London, 1850), vii–xx.

3. See for example, Vincent T. Harlow, *The Founding of the Second British Empire, 1763–1793,* 2 vols. (London, 1952–64). For earlier assessments of this interpretive problem

see Elizabeth Mancke, "Another British America: A Canadian Model for the Early Modern British Empire," *Journal of Imperial and Commonwealth History* 25 (1997), 1–36; and idem, "Negotiating an Empire: Britain and its Overseas Peripheries, c. 1550–1780," in Christine Daniels and Michael V. Kennedy, eds., *Negotiated Empires: Centers and Peripheries in the New World, 1500–1820* (New York, 2002), 235–265.

4. William R. Scott, *The Constitution and Finance of English, Scottish and Irish Joint-Stock Companies to 1720,* Vol. 2, *Companies for Foreign Trade, Colonization, Fishing and Mining,* (Cambridge, 1912); Niel Steensgaard, "The Companies as a Specific Institution in the History of European Expansion," in Leonard Blussé and Femme Gaastra, eds., *Companies and Trade: Essays on Overseas Trading Companies during the Ancien Régime* (Leiden, 1981), 245–264; Eveline C. Martin, *The British West African Settlements 1750–1821: A Study in Local Administration* (New York, [1927] 1970), 9–14; Wesley Frank Craven, *The Dissolution of the Virginia Company: The Failure of a Colonial Experiment* (Gloucester, Mass., [1932] 1964); Philip S. Haffenden, "The Crown and the Colonial Charters, 1675–1688," *William and Mary Quarterly,* 3rd ser., 15 (1958), 297–311, 452–466; Gillian T. Cell, *English Enterprise in Newfoundland 1577–1660* (Toronto, 1969); Joyce Lorimer, "The Failure of the English Guiana Ventures, 1595–1667 and James I's Foreign Policy," *Journal of Imperial and Commonwealth History* 21, no. 1 (1993), 1–30; and Karen Ordahl Kupperman, *Providence Island, 1630–1641: The Other Puritan Colony* (Cambridge, U.K., 1993). The French followed the same pattern in the late sixteenth and early seventeenth centuries; see Elizabeth Mancke and John G. Reid, "Elites, States, and the Imperial Contest for Acadia," in Reid et al., *The "Conquest" of Acadia, 1710: Imperial, Colonial, and Aboriginal Constructions* (Toronto, 2003), 25–47.

5. Lucas, *Charters of the Old English Colonies,* 7, 44; Lorimer, "The Failure of the English Guiana Ventures," 1–5, 12–18, 22–23.

6. Christopher Tomlins, "Law's empire: chartering English colonies on the American mainland in the seventeenth century," *Law, History, Colonialism: The Reach of Empire* (Manchester, U.K., 2001), 26–45.

7. Armand Budington DuBois, *The English Business Company after the Bubble Act, 1720–1800* (New York, [1938] 1971), 1–41; and Mancke, "Negotiating an Empire," 257.

8. For the international politics of expansion, see Elizabeth Mancke, "Empire and State," in David Armitage and Michael J. Braddick, eds., *The British Atlantic World, 1500–1800* (Basingstoke, U.K., 2002), 175–182.

9. Cell, *English Enterprise in Newfoundland,* 65; Lucas, *Charters of the Old English Colonies,* 1.

10. Lucas, *Charters of the Old English Colonies,* 1, 32, 36, 89; E. E. Rich, ed., *Minutes of the Hudson's Bay Company, 1671–1674* (London, 1942), 132.

11. Lucas, *Charters of the Old English Colonies,* 1; Cecil T. Carr, ed., *Select Charters of Trading Companies* A.D. *1530–1707* (London, 1913), 53. There was a one degree gap between 45° and 46° north latitude.

12. John G. Reid, *Acadia, Maine, and New Scotland: Marginal Colonies in the Seventeenth Century* (Toronto, 1981), 23–24; Rich, ed., *Minutes of the Hudson's Bay Company,* 131–132; Mancke, "Spaces of Power in the Early Modern Northeast," in Stephen J. Hornsby and John G. Reid, eds., *New England and the Maritime Provinces: Connections and Comparisons* (Kingston and Montréal, 2005).

13. For examples see Lucas, *Charters of the Old English Colonies,* 12, 33. On the territorial conflicts in the United States, see Peter S. Onuf, *The Origins of the Federal Republic: Jurisdictional Controversies in the United States, 1775–1787* (Philadelphia, 1983).

14. Lucas, *Charters of the Old English Colonies*, 32, 54, 89, 101; Carr, ed., *Select Charters*, 54; and Rich, ed., *Minutes of the Hudson's Bay Company*, 139. For a discussion of these feudal terms and their efficacy, see Charles M. Andrews, *The Colonial Period of American History*, 4 vols. (New Haven, Conn., 1934–38), 2:201–204.

15. Carr, ed., *Selected Charters*, 177; Rich, ed., *Minutes of the Hudson's Bay Company*, 139; and H. V. Bowen, *Revenue and Reform: The Indian Problem in British Politics, 1757–1773* (Cambridge, U.K., 1991), 54–66.

16. Wesley Frank Craven, *Dissolution of the Virginia Company: The Failure of a Colonial Experiment* (New York, [1932] 1964), 316.

17. Andrews, *The Colonial Period of American History*, 2:279–282. George Calvert died before the grant was issued; his son Cecilius became Lord Baltimore and the proprietor of Maryland.

18. David S. Lovejoy, *The Glorious Revolution in America* (New York, 1972), 36–52; Edmund S. Morgan, *American Slavery, American Freedom: The Ordeal of Colonial Virginia* (New York, 1975), 244–245.

19. Andrews, *The Colonial Period in American History*, 3:182–183; and J. M. Sosin, *English America and the Restoration Monarchy of Charles II: Transatlantic Politics, Commerce, and Kingship* (Lincoln, Neb., 1980), 98–104, 125–149.

20. John Frederick Martin, *Profits in the Wilderness: Entrepreneurship and the Founding of New England Towns in the Seventeenth Century* (Chapel Hill, N.C., 1991), 257–259; and Roy Aidemichi Akagi, *The Town Proprietors of the New England Colonies: A Study of Their Development, Organization, Activities and Controversies, 1620–1720* (Gloucester, Mass., [1924] 1963), 2–3, 5–8, 47.

21. Martin, *Profits in the Wilderness*, 260–270; Akagi, *The Town Proprietors of the New England Colonies*, 55.

22. Joseph J. Malone, *Pine Trees and Politics: The Naval Stores and Forest Policy in Colonial New England* (Seattle, 1964), 10–27; and Robert Greenhalgh Albion, *Forests and Sea Power: The Timber Problem of the Royal Navy, 1652–1862* (Hamden, Conn., [1926] 1965), 238–255.

23. Albion, *Forests and Sea Power*, 231–280; Malone, *Pine Trees and Politics*; David E. Van Deventer, *The Emergence of Provincial New Hampshire, 1623–1741* (Baltimore, 1976), 101–102, 132–149; Elizabeth Mancke, "Corporate Structure and Private Interest: The Mid-Eighteenth Century Expansion of New England," in Margaret Conrad, ed., *They Planted Well: New England Planters in Maritime Canada* (Fredericton, NB, 1988), 161–177.

24. Thomas Perkins Abernethy, *Western Lands and the American Revolution* (New York, 1959), 5–13.

25. Jack M. Sosin, *Whitehall and the Wilderness: The Middle West in British Colonial Policy, 1760–1775* (Lincoln, Neb., 1961), 165–180, 239–255; Eric Hinderaker, *Elusive Empires: Constructing Colonialism in the Ohio Valley, 1673–1800* (Cambridge, U.K., 1997), 167–170.

26. Bowen, *Revenue and Reform*, 15, 53–66, quotes on 15 and 53.

27. Jean Barman, *A History of British Columbia*, rev. ed. (Toronto, 1996), 53–71, 81–82, 91–98; Gerald Friesen, *The Canadian Prairies: A History* (Toronto, 1987), 129–161; and Chester Martin, *Dominion Lands Policy* (Toronto, 1938).

28. Craven, *Dissolution of the Virginia Company*, 251–336. For a detailed description of the human suffering, see Morgan, *American Slavery, American Freedom*, 92–107. Virginia was the only case in which the welfare of subjects was a primary reason to revoke a charter.

29. Craven, *Dissolution of the Virginia Company*, 330–333, quote on 330.

30. Robert M. Bliss, *Revolution and empire: English politics and the American colonies in the seventeenth century* (Manchester, U.K., 1990), 11–20; and Craven, *The Dissolution of the Virginia Company*, 47–80.

31. Andrews, *The Colonial Period of American History*, 1:365–372.

32. Charles M. Andrews, *British Committees, Commissions, and Councils of Trade and Plantations, 1622–1675* (New York, [1908] 1970), 61–114; Joseph H. Smith, *Appeals to the Privy Council from the American Plantations* (New York, 1950), 3–5, 71–77; Haffenden, "The Crown and the Colonial Charters, 1675–1688," 297–311, 452–466.

33. Lovejoy, *The Glorious Revolution in America*, 126–150, quote on 149.

34. Lucas, *Charters of the Old English Colonies*, 101–108, quotes on 103 and 105; Haffenden, "The Crown and the Colonial Charters," 306–308.

35. Van Deventer, *The Emergence of Provincial New Hampshire*, 42–46.

36. Jeff A. Webb, "Leaving the State of Nature: A Locke-Inspired Political Community in St. John's, Newfoundland, 1723," *Acadiensis* 21, 1 (1991), 156–165; Christopher English, "The Development of the Newfoundland Legal System to 1815," *Acadiensis* 20, 1 (1990), 89–119; Jerry Bannister, *The Rule of the Admirals: Law, Custom, and Naval Government in Newfoundland, 1699–1832* (Toronto, 2003).

37. Bowen, *Revenue and Reform*, 93–94, 99–101, 164–165, 179–180. The full name for 10 Geo. III, c. 47 was "A Bill for the Better Regulation of the Affairs of the East India Company and of Their Servants in India, and for the Due Administration of Justice in Bengal."

38. Clause XIV, "North's Regulating Act, 1773," in P. J. Marshall, *Problems of Empire: Britain and India, 1757–1813* (London, 1968), 152–153.

39. Sosin, *Whitehall and Wilderness*, 242–246; Gerald M. Craig, *Upper Canada: The Formative Years, 1784–1841* (Toronto, 1963), 9–19.

40. "An Act for extending the Jurisdiction of the Courts of Justice in the Provinces of Upper Canada and Lower Canada, to the Trial and Punishments of Crimes, and Offences within certain parts of North America adjoining the Provinces," 43 George III, c. 138 (1803); and Friesen, *The Canadian Prairies*, 72–84.

41. 1 & 2 George IV, c. 66 (1821); Hamar Foster, "Long-Distance Justice: The Criminal Jurisdiction of the Canadian Courts West of the Canadas," *American Journal of Legal History* 43 (1990), 1–48; and Tina Loo, *Making Law, Order, and Authority in British Columbia, 1821–1871* (Toronto, 1994), 18–33.

42. Charles Morse, "Provincial and Local Government," in Adam Shortt and Arthur G. Doughty, eds., *Canada and Its Provinces: A History of the Canadian People and their Institutions*, Vol. 14, *Atlantic Provinces* (Toronto, 1914), 14:479–480; Adam Shortt, "Municipal History, 1791–1867," in ibid., Vol. 18, *Province of Ontario*, 18:405–452.

43. Haffenden, "The Crown and the Colonial Charters," 309–311, quote on 309; Michael Craton and Gail Saunders, *Islanders in the Stream: A History of the Bahamian People*, Vol. 1, *From Aboriginal Times to the End of Slavery* (Athens, Ga., 1992), 97.

44. Lorimer, "The Failure of the English Guiana Ventures," 5.

45. The expansion of the Crown's role in foreign policy can also be seen in Europe. In the late seventeenth century, English companies chartered for trade within Europe, such as the Eastland Company, the Spanish Company, and the Muscovy Company, ceased operations, in part because the English government had assumed responsibility

for negotiating the commercial rights of English subjects in foreign countries, previously one of the reasons for these companies to exist. The government, however, tended not to negotiate commercial privileges with non-Christian powers. The Levant Company continued to do business in the Ottoman Empire into the nineteenth century, and the British ambassador to the Ottoman court operated under company auspices. Michael J. Braddick, "The English Government, War, Trade, and Settlements, 1625–1688," in Nicholas P. Canny, ed., *The Oxford History of the British Empire*, Vol. 1, *The Origins of Empire: British Overseas Enterprise to the Close of the Seventeenth Century* (Oxford, 1998), 292–296.

46. Lucas, *Charters of the Old English Colonies*, 2–3, 5, 7, 15, 16, 17, 40, 53, 62; Carr, ed., *Selected Charters*, 177, 180, 181; and Rich, ed., *Minutes of the Hudson's Bay Company*, 146.

47. Rich, ed., *Minutes of the Hudson's Bay Company*, 146; Carr, ed., *Select Charters*, 191; Lucas, *Charters of the Old English Colonies*, 106.

48. Max Savelle, *The Origins of American Diplomacy: The International History of Angloamerica, 1492–1763* (New York, 1967), 46–50; Frances Gardiner Davenport, *European Treaties Bearing on the History of the United States and Its Dependencies*, 4 vols. (Washington, D.C., 1917–37), 2:329–346; and Mancke, "Empire and State," 175–195.

49. W. J. Eccles, *France in America*, rev. ed., (Markham, ON, 1990), 98–99; Emerson Baker and John G. Reid, *The New England Knight: Sir William Phips, 1651–1695* (Toronto, 1998), 86–109; Robert Ritchie, *Captain Kidd and the War against the Pirates* (Cambridge, Mass., 1986), 170–178.

50. Fred Anderson, *A People's Army: Massachusetts Soldiers and Society in the Seven Years' War* (Chapel Hill, N.C., 1984).

51. Hilda Neatby, *The Quebec Act: Protest and Policy* (Scarborough, ON, 1972); Andrew O'Shaughnessy, *An Empire Divided: The American Revolution and the British Caribbean* (Philadelphia, 2000), 124.

52. Brian Slattery, "The Hidden Constitution: Aboriginal Rights in Canada," in Menno Boldt et al., eds., *The Quest for Justice: Aboriginal Peoples and Aboriginal Rights* (Toronto, 1985), 114–138.

53. Richard White, *The Middle Ground: Indians, Empires, and Republics in the Great Lakes Region, 1650–1815* (Cambridge, U.K., 1991), 269–314.

54. Hilda Neatby, *Quebec: The Revolutionary Age, 1760–1791* (Toronto, 1966), 37; P. J. Marshall, "Parliament and property rights in the late eighteenth-century British Empire," in John Brewer and Susan Staves, eds., *Early Modern Conceptions of Property* (London, 1996), 530–544; Andrew Porter, "Trusteeship, Anti-Slavery, and Humanitarianism," in Porter, ed., *The Oxford History of the British Empire*, Vol. 3, *The Nineteenth Century* (Oxford, 1999), 198–221.

55. Glyndwr Williams, "The Hudson's Bay Company and its Critics in the Eighteenth Century," *Transactions of the Royal Historical Society*, 5th ser., 20 (1970), 149–171; and Bowen, *Revenue and Reform*.

56. Lucas, *Charters of the Old English Colonies*, 56.

57. Elizabeth Mancke, "Imperial Transitions," in Reid et al., *The "Conquest" of Acadia*, 178–202.

58. Sudipta Sen, *Distant Sovereignty: National Imperialism and the Origins of British India* (New York, 2002); H. V. Bowen, "British India, 1765–1813: The Metropolitan Context," in P. J. Marshall, *The Oxford History of the British Empire*, Vol. 2, *The Eighteenth Century* (Oxford, 1998), 2:531–534.

59. David Richardson, "The British Empire and the Atlantic Slave Trade, 1660–1807," in ibid., 2:444–445; James W. St. G. Walker, *The Black Loyalists: The Search for a Promised Land in Nova Scotia and Sierra Leone, 1783–1870* (New York, 1976), 94–114.

E L E V E N : Seeds of Empire

1. James Grant to Henry Bouquet, Aug. 15, 1765, James Grant Letterbook, MacPherson-Grant Papers, Ballindalloch Castle, Scotland [hereafter JGL, MGP]. I wish to thank Mr. Oliver Russell for allowing me to consult these manuscripts.

2. James Grant to Lord Bute, Dec. 24, 1765, JGL, MGP.

3. James Grant to Edward Mason, Oct. 10, 1765, JGL, MGP.

4. Report of Lieutenant Colonel Robertson to General Gage, March 10, 1764, Public Record Office, London, CO/5 540, 36–53.

5. Charles Loch Mowat, *East Florida as a British Province, 1763–1784* (Berkeley, 1943), 8–9, 14.

6. A shift toward a more bilateral (or multilateral) focus is apparent in John J. McCusker and Kenneth Morgan, eds., *The Early Modern Atlantic Economy* (Cambridge, U.K., 2000).

7. Richard Drayton, *Nature's Government: Science, Imperial Britain, and the "Improvement" of the World* (New Haven, Conn., 2000), xi, passim.

8. Charles M. Andrews, *The Colonial Background of the American Revolution* (New Haven, Conn., 1924), 122–124.

9. H. V. Bowen, "British India, 1765–1813: The Metropolitan Context," in P. J. Marshall, ed., *The Oxford History of the British Empire,* Vol. 2, *The Eighteenth Century* (Oxford, 1998), 530–551; Lawrence Henry Gipson, *The British Empire Before the American Revolution,* 15 vols. (New York, 1936–1970), 9:345.

10. Lewis Namier, *The Structure of Politics at the Accession of George III* (London, 1928); John Brewer, *Party Ideology and Popular Politics at the Accession of George III* (Cambridge, U.K., 1976).

11. On this point see J. G. A. Pocock, "1776: The Revolution against Parliament," in *Virture, Commerce, and History: Essays on Political Thought and History, Chiefly in the Eighteenth Century* (Cambridge, U.K., 1985), 73–88.

12. On state formation, see John Brewer, *The Sinews of Power: War, Money, and the English State, 1688–1783* (New York, 1988). On nationalism, see Benedict Anderson, *Imagined Communities: Reflections on the Origin and Spread of Nationalism* (London, 1983); and Linda Colley, *Britons: Forging the Nation, 1707–1837* (New Haven, Conn., 1992).

13. H. V. Bowen, *Elites, Enterprise and the Making of the British Overseas Empire, 1688–1775* (Basingstoke, U.K., 1996), 5–10.

14. Drayton, *Nature's Government,* xiii.

15. P. J. Marshall, "The Eighteenth-Century Empire," in Jeremy Black, ed., *British Politics and Society from Walpole to Pitt, 1742–1789* (Basingstoke, U.K., 1990); Colley, *Britons,* 101–145; Eliga H. Gould, *The Persistence of Empire: British Political Culture in the Age of the American Revolution* (Chapel Hill, N.C., 2000).

16. P. J. Marshall, "Introduction," in Marshall, ed., *The Oxford History of the British Empire,* 2:7. On this point see Gould, *The Persistence of Empire,* 35–71.

17. Kathleen Wilson, *The Sense of the People: Politics, Culture and Imperialism in England, 1715–1815* (Cambridge, U.K., 1995), 23–24.

18. Lord Hardwicke to the Duke of Newcastle, Oct. 29, 1760, quoted in Frank O'Gorman, "The Myth of Bute's Secret Influence," in Karl W. Schweizer, ed., *Lord Bute: Essays in Re-Interpretation* (Leicester, U.K., 1988), 58; this and the following paragraph are based closely on Brewer, *Party Ideology and Popular Politics.*

19. The disruption of the usual networks of patronage was one of the factors that allowed James Grant, an untitled lieutenant colonel, to be appointed governor of East Florida.

20. David Elliston Allen, *The Naturalist in Britain: A Social History* (London, 1976), 43.

21. Thomas Whately, *The Regulations Lately Made, Concerning the Colonies and the Taxes Imposed Upon Them, Considered* (London, 1765); and idem, *Observations on Modern Gardening* (London, 1771).

22. Lisbet Koerner, *Linnaeus: Nature and Nation* (Cambridge, Mass., 1999), 43–55.

23. Allen, *The Naturalist in Britain,* 42–43.

24. Drayton, *Nature's Government,* 41. See also Michel Foucault, *The Order of Things: An Archaeology of the Human Sciences* (New York, 1970), 125–165.

25. Allen, *The Naturalist in Britain,* 45.

26. David P. Miller, "'My Favourite Studdys': Lord Bute as Naturalist," in Schweizer, ed., *Lord Bute,* 218; John Hill, *The Vegetable System; or, the Internal Structure and Life of Plants; Their Parts, and Nourishment Explained; Their Classes, Orders, Genera, and Species Ascertained, and Described; in a Method Altogether New; Comprehending an Artificial Index, and a Natural System. With Figures of All the Plants Designed and Engraved by the Author. The Whole From Nature Only,* 26 vols. (London, 1761–75).

27. *The Royal Botanic Gardens Kew. Souvenir Guide* (London, 1979), 5.

28. J. C. D. Clark, *English Society, 1688–1832: Ideology, Social Structure, and Political Practice during the Ancien Regime* (Cambridge, U.K., 1985), 179–184.

29. James Lee McKelvey, *George III and Lord Bute: the Leicester House Years* (Durham, N.C., 1973), 34.

30. Although it was not until the death of his mother in 1772 (and his inheritance of Kew) that George III had the wall dividing the two parks removed, they actually were merged long before. The royal family regarded them as combined and was as likely to walk the grounds of Kew as Richmond.

31. John Hill, *An Idea of a Botanical Garden in England* (London, 1758). After studying the harmful effects of snuff taking and examining the pharmaecology of the tobacco plant, Hill was the first person to posit a link between tobacco and cancer. See G. S. Rousseau, ed., *The Letters and Papers of Sir John Hill, 1714–1775* (New York, 1982). On the other hand, Hill had a knack for making enemies. In 1753, Christopher Smart published a satire entitled *The Hilliad,* in which he described Hill as "Pimp, Poet, Puffer, 'Pothecary, Player," 20.

32. Lord Bute to James Wright (Governor of Georgia), Sept. 21, 1767, quoted in Ray Desmond, *Kew: The History of the Royal Botanic Gardens* (London, 1995), 40.

33. William Chambers, *Designs of Chinese Buildings, Furniture, Dresses, Machines, and Utensils* (London, 1757), v.

34. William Chambers, *Plans, Elevations, Sections, and Perspective Views of the Gardens and Buildings at Kew in Surry* (London, 1763), 2.

35. Quotes from *A Description of the Gardens and Buildings at Kew, in Surrey* (London, 1768), reprinted in John Dixon Hunt, ed., *The English Landscape Garden: Examples of the Important Literature of the English Landscape Garden Movement Together with Some Earlier Garden Books* (New York, 1982).

36. George C. Rogers, "The East Florida Society of London, 1766–1767," *Florida Historical Society Quarterly* 56 (1976), 479–96.

37. Anon., *An Account of the Spanish Settlements in America* (Edinburgh, 1762), 62.

38. William Stork, *An Account of East-Florida, with Remarks on its Future Importance to Trade and Commerce* (London, 1766), xv.

39. "Dr. Campbell's Account of Florida," a manuscript in the papers of Charles Jenkinson, an M.P. and secretary to Bute, Liverpool Papers, British Library, Add. Mss. 38336/155.

40. Ibid.

41. Quoted in George Nobbe, *The North Briton: A Study in Political Propaganda* (New York, 1939), 164.

42. Ibid., 161–168.

43. Desmond, *Kew*, 40.

44. Archibald Menzies, *Proposal for Peopling His Majesty's Southern Colonies on the Continent of America* (Perthshire, 1763), n.p. For Menzies's background, see A. G. Morton, *John Hope, 1725–1786: Scottish Botanist* (Edinburgh, 1986), 26.

45. Richard Oswald to James Grant, March 6, 1766, MGP 34/295.

46. Bernard Bailyn, *Voyagers to the West: A Passage in the Peopling of America on the Eve of the Revolution* (New York, 1986), 433. For Stork's background and later career, see Philip Hamer et al., eds., *The Papers of Henry Laurens* (Columbia, S.C., 1968–) 6:73n–74n.

47. Stork, *An Account of East-Florida*, 26n.

48. Adam Gordon to James Grant, May 15, 1766, MGP 50/474.

49. Richard Oswald to James Grant, June 9, 1766, MGP 34/295.

50. William Stork to James Grant, July 8, 1766, MGP 29/243.

51. Mowat, *East Florida as a British Province*, 58–59.

52. John Bartram to Peter Collinson, March 4, 1764, in Edmund Berkeley and Dorothy Smith Berkeley, eds., *The Correspondence of John Bartram, 1734–1777* (Gainesville, Fla., 1992), 622.

53. Peter Collinson to John Bartram, April 9, 1765, in ibid., 644–645.

54. Ibid.

55. James Grant to William Knox, Dec. 21, 1765, JGL, MGP.

56. The second edition was titled *A Description of East-Florida, with a Journal Kept by John Bartram of Philadelphia, Botanist to His Majesty for the Florida: upon a Journey from St. Augustine up the River St. John's, as Far as the Lakes* (London, 1766).

57. Peter Collinson to John Bartram, Aug. 21, 1766, in *Correspondence of John Bartram*, 673–674.

58. John Bartram to John Fothergill, Nov. 28, 1769, in ibid, 726–727.

59. William Knox to James Grant, Sept. 29, 1768, MGP 36/313.

60. P. J. Toynbee, ed., *Horace Walpole's Journals of Visits to Country Seats, &c* (Oxford, 1928), 38.

61. Richard Oswald to James Grant, 9 June 1766, MGP 34/295. Even Bartram's journal of his expedition up the St. John's River, which was appended to the second edition

of Stork's book, did not escape ridicule. One anonymous reviewer reported that it would "afford entertainment only to a botanist, and to a botanist not much." *Gentleman's Magazine* 62 (October 1766), 486–487.

62. David Armitage, *The Ideological Origins of the British Empire* (Cambridge, U.K., 2000), 11.

63. Anthony Pagden, *Lords of All the World: Ideologies of Empire in Spain, Britain, and France, c. 1500–1800* (New Haven, Conn., 1995), 106.

64. Colley, *Britons*, 102.

65. *A Plan for the Abolition of Slavery in the West Indies*, (London, 1772), quotes on 2, 9, 26, and 27.

66. Marshall, "Introduction," in Marshall, ed., *Oxford History of the British Empire*, 2:8.

67. John Almon, ed. *The New Foundling Hospital for Wit, Being a Collection of Fugitive Pieces, in Prose and Verse, Not in any Other Collection, with Several Pieces Never Before Published*, 6 vols. (London, 1784), 2:22.

68. Quoted in Colley, *Britons*, 102–103.

69. E. P. Panagopoulos, *New Smyrna: An Eighteenth Century Greek Odyssey* (Gainesville, Fla., 1966).

70. Bernard Romans, *Concise Natural History of East and West Florida* (New York, 1775), 179.

71. *The New Foundling Hospital for Wit*, 2:11–16.

72. See, for example, "Scotch Amusements," *Oxford Magazine* 1 (1768).

73. John Horne Tooke, *Petition of an Englishman* (London, 1765), 16, 19.

74. John Almon, ed., *Political Register* 1 (London, 1767).

75. This jibe may have been inspired by a recent work by Bute's client, John Hill, *Centuary, the Great Stomachic: Its Preference to All Other Bitters with an Account of the Plant and a Few Rules for Such as Have Weak Stomachs* (London, 1765).

76. Geoffrey Ashe, *The Hell Fire Clubs: A History of Anti-Morality* (Stroud, U.K., 2000), 161.

TWELVE: A Visual Empire

A fellowship from the Yale Center for British Art and research grants from the Social Sciences and Humanities Research Council of Canada (410-00-153) and the Faculty of Graduate Studies at Dalhousie University supported research for this essay. Marian Binkley provided helpful criticism.

1. Townscapes were an important exception, to be discussed below.

2. Gerald S. Graham, *The Concise History of the British Empire* (New York, 1971); Stephen W. Sears, ed., *The Horizon History of the British Empire* (New York, 1973); P. J. Marshall, ed., *The Cambridge Illustrated History of the British Empire* (Cambridge, U.K., 1996).

3. On the geographic broadening of British visual experience, see Ronald Russell, *Guide to British Topographical Prints* (London, 1979), 23–54; Barbaria Maria Stafford, "Toward Romantic Landscape Perception: Illustrated Travels and the Rise of 'Singularity' as an Aesthetic Category," in Harry C. Payne, ed., *Studies in Eighteenth-Century Culture* (Madison, Wisc., 1981), 17–75; P. J. Marshall and Glyndwr Williams, *The Great Map of Mankind: Perceptions of New Worlds in the Age of Enlightenment* (Cambridge, Mass.,

1982); Barbara Maria Stafford, *Voyage into Substance: Art, Science, Nature, and the Illustrated Travel Account, 1760–1840* (Cambridge, Mass., 1984).

4. J. G. A. Pocock, "British History: A Plea for a New Subject," *Journal of Modern History* 47 (1975), 601–628; idem, "The Limits and Divisions of British History: In Search of the Unknown Subject," *American Historical Review* 87 (1982), 311–336.

5. For example, see Claude Lorrain, *The Judgment of Paris* (1645–46), as reproduced in Robert C. Cafritz, Lawrence Gowing, and David Rosand, *Places of Delight: The Pastoral Landscape* (Washington, D.C., 1988), fig. 99.

6. John Locke, "Some Thoughts Concerning Education," 5th ed. (1705), in James L. Axtell, ed., *The Educational Writings of John Locke* (Cambridge, U.K., 1968), 264–265.

7. Seymour Slive, *Dutch Painting, 1600–1800* (New Haven, Conn., 1995), 177–224, 320–327; Eddy de Jongh and Ger Luijten, *Mirror of Everyday Life: Genreprints in the Netherlands, 1550–1700* (Amsterdam, 1997), 149–151, 272–275, 307–310, 344–347. Landscapes in Venetian art's pastoral tradition were even less likely to be topographic than Roman landscapes because their subjects and settings were deliberately imaginary; Cafritz, Rosand, and Gowing, *Places of Delight;* and Timothy Clayton, *The English Print, 1688–1802* (New Haven, Conn., 1997), 35–37, 75–76, 154–168. The best discussion of topography in early modern European landscape art is Bernard Smith, "Art in the Service of Science and Travel," *Imagining the Pacific: In the Wake of the Cook Voyages* (Melbourne, 1992), 1–40. Stafford, *Voyage into Substance,* concentrates on scientific empiricism, but is invaluable on landscapes as well.

8. For example, see John Kip after Leonard Knyff, *Wimple in the County of Cambridge* (London, 1701), as reproduced in Clayton, *English Print,* fig. 60.

9. For example, see Arthur Devis, *Edward Rookes-Leeds and Family* (1760), as reproduced in Michael Rosenthal, *British Landscape Painting* (Ithaca, N.Y., 1982), fig. 32.

10. Michael Rosenthal, "Landscape as High Art," in Katharine Baetjer, ed., *Glorious Nature: British Landscape Art, 1750–1850* (New York, 1993), 13–30; idem, *British Landscape Painting,* 10–71; Clayton, *English Print,* 157–161; John Harris, *The Artist and the Country House: A History of Country House and Garden View Painting in Britain, 1540–1870* (London, 1979); Colin Campbell, *Vitruvius Britannicus or the British Architect,* 3 vols. (London, 1715–25); J. Badeslade and J. Rocque, *Vitruvius Britannicus, Being a Collection of Plans, Elevations, and Perspective Views, of the Royal Palaces, Noblemen, and Gentlemen's Seats, in Great Britain,* 2 vols. (London, 1739); John Woolf and James Gandon, *Vitruvius Britannicus,* 2 vols. (London, 1767, 1771).

11. Joshua Reynolds, *Discourses on Art* (1771), Robert R. Wark, ed. (New Haven, Conn., 1975), 57, 63.

12. For example, see William Gilpin, "River Landscape," in *Observations on the River Wye, and Several Parts of South Wales, etc. Relative Chiefly to Picturesque Beauty; Made in the Summer of 1770* (London, 1783), as reproduced in *Glorious Nature,* fig. 1.

13. William Gilpin, *Observations on the River Wye,* 1–2, as quoted in Rosenthal, "Landscape as High Art," 29; Kim Sloan, "Drawing—A 'Polite Recreation' in Eighteenth-Century England," *Studies in Eighteenth Century Culture* 11 (1982), 217–240; Malcolm Andrews, *The Search for the Picturesque: Landscape Aesthetics and Tourism in Britain, 1760–1800* (London, 1989); William Vaughan, "The Englishness of British Art," *Oxford Art Journal* 13 (1990), 11–23; Timothy J. Standring, "Watercolor Landscape Sketching during the Popular Picturesque Era in Britain," in *Glorious Nature,* 73–84; Luke Herrmann, *British Landscape Painting of the Eighteenth Century* (London, 1973);

Stephen Daniels, "Re-visioning Britain: Mapping and Landscape Painting, 1750–1820," in *Glorious Nature*, 61–72; Ann Bermingham, *Learning to Draw: Studies in the Cultural History of a Polite and Useful Art* (New Haven, Conn., 2000), 76–181.

14. *ESTC on CD-ROM English Short Title Catalogue, 1473–1800* (London, 1998).

15. Jack P. Greene, "Colonial Political Culture," and George Dargo, "England and its Colonies," in Jacob Ernest Cooke, ed., *Encyclopedia of the North American Colonies*, 3 vols. (New York, 1993), 265–285, 302–312; Ian K. Steele, "Metropolitan Administration of the Colonies, 1696–1775," and Alison G. Olson, "The Changing Socio-Economic and Strategic Importance of the Colonies to the Empire," in Jack P. Greene and J. R. Pole, eds., *The Blackwell Encyclopedia of the American Revolution* (Oxford, 1991), 9–16, 17–28; Richard Koebner, *Empire* (New York, 1965), 61–104; Anthony Pagden, *Lords of All the World: Ideologies of Empire in Spain, Britain and France c.1500–c.1800* (New Haven, Conn., 1995), 126–155; Jack P. Greene, *Peripheries and Center: Constitutional Development in the Extended Polities of the British Empire and the United States* (Athens, Ga., 1986), 43–76; Arthur Herbert Basye, *The Lords Commissioners of Trade and Plantations Commonly Known as the Board of Trade, 1748–1782* (New Haven, Conn., 1925), 1–104. For a qualification of these generalizations see Elizabeth Mancke, "Another British America: A Canadian Model for the Early Modern British Empire," *Journal of Imperial and Commonwealth History* 25 (1997), 1–36, which demonstrates state intervention of an imperial character in Britain's marginal and newly acquired territories from the period of Anglo-French wars (1689–1713) onward.

16. For example, see Frans Post, *Panorama in Brazil* (1652), as reproduced in Hugh Honour, *The New Golden Land: European Images of America from the Discoveries to the Present Time* (New York, 1975), fig. x.

17. Hugh Honour, *The European Vision of America* (Cleveland, 1975); Ladislaw Bugner et al., eds., *The Image of the Black in Western Art*, Vol. 3, *From Europe to America: Sixteenth to the Twentieth Century* (New York, 1979); Susan Danforth, *Encountering the New World, 1493 to 1800* (Providence, 1991). For most of the early modern period European artists had more interest in the flora and fauna of the Americas than in their human landscapes; Victoria Dickenson, *Drawn from Life: Science and Art in the Portrayal of the New World* (Toronto, 1998).

18. Vincent T. Harlow, *The Founding of the Second British Empire, 1763–1793*, 2 vols. (London, 1952, 1964), 1:62; P. J. Marshall, "Britain Without America—A Second Empire?" in P. J. Marshall, ed., *The Oxford History of the British Empire*, Vol. 2, *The Eighteenth Century* (Oxford, 1998), 576–595.

19. William Robertson, *Historical Disquisition Concerning the Knowledge Which the Ancients had of India; and of the Progress of Trade with that Country Prior to the Discovery of the Passage to it by the Cape of Good Hope*, 2nd ed. (London, 1794), 331–333.

20. J. C. Beaglehole, *The Life of Captain James Cook* (London, 1974); I. S. MacLaren, "Samuel Hearne and the Landscapes of Discovery," *Canadian Literature* 103 (1984), 27–40, esp. 36.

21. Franklin and Mary Wickwire, *Cornwallis: The Imperial Years* (Chapel Hill, N.C., 1980); Marshall, "Britain Without America," 384.

22. Peter Roebuck, ed., *Macartney of Lisanoure, 1737–1806* (Belfast, 1983).

23. For Bligh's instructions regarding breadfruit, see William Bligh, "A Voyage to the South Sea," in George Mackaness, ed., *A Book of the "Bounty"* (New York, 1981), 6–8.

24. Alan Frost, *Convicts and Empire: A Naval Question, 1776–1811* (Melbourne, 1980); Barry M. Gough, *The Northwest Coast: British Navigation, Trade, and Discoveries to 1812* (Vancouver, 1992), 104–115.

25. James Kirker, *Adventure to China: Americans in the Southern Ocean 1792–1812* (New York,1970), 6.

26. Stephen E. Ambrose, *Undaunted Courage: Meriwether Lewis, Thomas Jefferson, and the Opening of the American West* (New York, 1996), 70–77, quote on 70; Gough, *Northwest Coast,* 180–187.

27. William Ferguson, "James Ferguson and 'The Invention of Ossian,'" *The Identity of the Scottish Nation* (Edinburgh, 1998), 227–249.

28. Blackstone, *Commentaries on the Laws of England* (1765–69), quoted in Dargo, "England and its Colonies," 303.

29. P. J. Marshall, "Empire and Authority in the Later Eighteenth Century," *Journal of Imperial and Commonwealth History* 15 (1987), 105–122; C. A. Bayly, "The First Age of Global Imperialism, c. 1760–1830," *Journal of Imperial and Commonwealth History* 26 (1998), 28–47.

30. Linda Colley, *Britons: Forging the Nation 1707–1837* (London, 1994), 132–145; Kathleen Wilson, *The Sense of the People: Politics, Culture and Imperialism in England, 1715–1785* (Cambridge, U.K., 1995); P. J. Marshall, "'Cornwallis Triumphant': War in India and the British Public in the Late Eighteenth Century," in Lawrence Freedman et al., eds., *War, Strategy, and International Politics: Essays in Honour of Sir Michael Howard* (Oxford, 1992), 65–66.

31. P. J. Marshall, "A Nation Defined by Empire, 1755–1776," in Lawrence Stone, ed., *An Imperial State at War: Britain from 1689 to 1815* (London, 1994), 208–222; Mancke, "Another British America," 3–5; Philip Lawson, *The Imperial Challenge: Quebec and Britain in the Age of the American Revolution* (Montréal and Kingston, 1989), 126–146; Jack M. Sosin, *Whitehall and the Wilderness: The Middle West in British Colonial Policy, 1760–1775* (Lincoln, Neb., 1961); Christopher L. Brown, "Empire without Slaves: British Concepts of Emancipation in the Age of the American Revolution," *William and Mary Quarterly* 3rd ser., 56 (1999), 276, 282–286, 305–306; Eliga H. Gould, "American Independence and Counter-Revolution," *Past and Present* 154 (1997), 123–125, 137–138, 140; idem, *The Persistence of Empire: British Political Culture in the Age of the American Revolution* (Chapel Hill, N.C., 2000).

32. Michael Jacobs, *The Painted Voyage: Art, Travel, and Exploration 1564–1875* (London, 1995), 38.

33. Patrick Eyres, "Neoclassicism on Active Service: Commemoration of the Seven Years' War in the English Landscape Garden," *New Arcadian Journal* 35/36 (1993), 62–126; Bruce Robertson, "Venit, Vidit, Depinxit: The Military Artist in America," in Edward Nygren et al., eds., *Views and Visions: American Landscape before 1830* (Washington, D.C., 1986), 83–103.

34. For example, see Paul Sandby, *Scottish Beggars Resting near a Well* (1750), as reproduced in Bruce Robertson, *The Art of Paul Sandby* (New Haven, Conn., 1985), fig. 31.

35. Luke Herrmann, "Paul Sandby in Scotland," *Burlington Magazine* 106 (1964), 339–343.

36. Julian Halsby, *Scottish Watercolors, 1740–1940* (London, 1986), 15–32, quote on 29–30.

37. Thomas Pennant, *A Tour in Scotland MDCCLXIX* (Chester, 1771); idem, *A Tour in Scotland, and Voyage to the Hebrides; MDCCLXXII* (Chester, 1774); James Boswell, *Journal of a Tour to the Hebrides* (Sept. 17, 1773), as quoted in *Dictionary of National Biography,* "Pennant, Thomas."

38. Richard Short, *Twelve Views of the Principal Buildings in Quebec, from Drawings, Taken on the Spot, at the Command of Vice-Admiral Saunders* (London, 1761); Paul A. Hachey, *The New Brunswick Landscape Print, 1760–1860* (Fredericton, NB, 1980), 14–15; Kathleen M. Fenwick and C. P. Stacey, "Thomas Davies—Soldier and Painter of Eighteenth-Century Canada," *Canadian Art* 13 (1956), 270–276, 300; R. H. Hubbard, *Thomas Davies, c. 1737–1812. Thomas Davies vers 1737–1812* (Ottawa, 1972); Mary Allodi, *Printmaking in Canada: The Earliest Views and Portraits* (1980); F. St. George Spendlove, *The Face of Early Canada: Pictures of Canada Which Have Helped to Make History* (Toronto, 1958), esp. 36–39 for early views of Niagara Falls; Elizabeth McKinsey, *Niagara Falls: Icon of the American Sublime* (Cambridge, U.K., 1985); Jeremy Elwell Adamson, "Nature's Grandest Scene in Art," and Elizabeth McKinsey, "An American Icon," in *Niagara: Two Centuries of Changing Attitudes, 1697–1901* (Washington, D.C., 1985), 11–82, 83–101.

39. Mary Sparling, *Great Expectations: The European Vision in Nova Scotia, 1749–1848* (Halifax, 1980); Mary Allodi, *Canadian Watercolours and Drawings in the Royal Ontario Museum* (Toronto, 1974); Northrop Frye, "The Canadian Scene: Explorers and Observers," in R. H. Hubbard, ed., *Canadian Landscape Painting, 1670–1930* (Toronto, 1973); Hachey, *New Brunswick Landscape Print,* 16–24; *The Diary of Mrs. John Graves Simcoe* (Toronto, 1911). On other early landscape artists in Canada, nearly all of them military, see *Image of Canada: Documentary Watercolours and Drawings from the Permanent Collection of the Public Archives of Canada. Visage du Canada: Aquarelles et dessins historiques tirés de la collection permanente des Archives publiques du Canada* (Ottawa, 1972).

40. Bernard Smith, *European Vision and the South Pacific,* 2nd ed. (New Haven, Conn., 1985), 1–157.

41. For example, see William Hodges, *View of Part of the Island of Ulietea* (1773), as reproduced in Smith, *European Vision and the South Pacific,* fig. 7.

42. Jacobs, *Painted Voyage,* 82–84, quote on 90.

43. Ibid., 63.

44. Bernard Smith and Alwyne Wheeler, eds., *The Art of the First Fleet and Other Early Australian Drawings,* (New Haven, Conn., 1988); Smith, *European Vision,* 159–188; Elizabeth Johns et al., *New Worlds from Old: Nineteenth-Century Australian and American Landscapes* (Canberra, 1998).

45. Mildred Archer, *Early Views of India: The Picturesque Journeys of Thomas and William Daniell, 1786–1794* (London, 1980); G. H. R. Tillotson, "The Indian Picturesque: Images of India in British Landscape Painting, 1780–1880," in C. A. Bayly, ed., *The Raj: India and the British, 1600–1947* (London, 1990).

46. For example, see Thomas Hearne, *Parham Hill House and Sugar Plantation, Antigua* (1779), as reproduced in David Morris, *Thomas Hearne and His Landscape* (London, 1989), fig. 9.

47. John E. Crowley, "Picturing the Caribbean in the Global British Landscape," *Studies in Eighteenth-Century Culture* 32 (2003), 323–346; Susanne Seymour, Stephen Daniels, and Charles Watkins, "Estate and Empire: Sir George Cornewall's Management of Moccas, Herefordshire and La Taste, Grenada, 1771–1819," *Journal of Historical Geography* 24 (1998), 313–351.

48. Beth Fowkes Tobin, *Picturing Imperial Power: Colonial Subjects in Eighteenth-Century British Painting* (Durham, N.C., 1999), 139–173; David Morris, *Thomas Hearne and His Landscape* (London, 1989), 9–23; Elizabeth A. Bohls, "The Gentleman Planter and the Metropole: Long's *History of Jamaica* (1774)," in Gerald MacLean et al., eds., *The City and the Country Revisited: England and the Politics of Culture, 1550–1850* (Cambridge, U.K., 1999), 180–196; Hubbard, *Thomas Davies*, fig. 42–46. On contemporaneous British verbal appreciations of Caribbean landscapes, see Jack P. Greene, "Changing Identity in the British Caribbean: Barbados as a Case Study," in Nicholas Canny and Anthony Pagden, eds., *Colonial Identity in the Atlantic World, 1500–1800* (Princeton, 1987), 256–257.

49. Frank Weitenkampf, "Early American Landscape Prints," *Art Quarterly* 8 (1945), 40–67; Martin P. Snyder, *City of Independence: Views of Philadelphia before 1800* (New York, 1975); Gloria Dilda Deak, *Picturing America: Prints, Maps, and Drawings Bearing on the New World Discoveries and on the Development of the Territory That is Now the United States* (Princeton, 1988); Jack P. Greene, *The Intellectual Construction of America: Exceptionalism and Identity from 1492 to 1800* (Chapel Hill, N.C., 1993), illustrations between 82–127.

50. Karol Ann Peard Lawson, "An Inexhaustible Abundance: The National Landscape Depicted in American Magazines, 1780–1820," *Journal of the Early Republic* 12 (1992), 303–330; Bruce Robertson, "The Picturesque Traveler in America," in Nygren et al., eds., *Views and Visions*, 189.

51. J. Hall Pleasants, "Four Late Eighteenth-Century Anglo-American Landscape Painters," *Proceedings of the American Antiquarian Society* 52 (1943), 187–324.

52. For example, see William Birch, "Second Street North from Market St. wth. Christ Church," in *The City of Philadelphia* (1800), as reproduced in Danforth, *Encountering the New World*, fig. 75; Martin P. Snyder, "William Birch: His Philadelphia Views," *Pennsylvania Magazine of History and Biography* 73 (1949), 271–315.

THIRTEEN: "Of the Old Stock"

1. Diary of Deborah Norris Logan, began "Stenton August 1st: 1808," Library Company of Philadelphia (hereafter LCP). I am grateful to Jim Green for pointing me to this extraordinary—and storied—source.

2. Perhaps Logan's most famous achievement is her transcription and annotation of the letters of James Logan and William Penn, a task she began in 1814. Logan also provided material to early nineteenth-century historians of colonial Philadelphia, including John Fanning Watson. Terri Premo's analysis of Deborah Logan's old age and her interest in the past is compelling; see *Winter Friends: Women Growing Old in the New Republic, 1785–1835* (Urbana, Ill., 1990), esp. 139–142, 142n.

3. The organization of copied manuscript materials as a cultural artifact is addressed in Catherine Blecki and Karin Wulf, *Milcah Martha Moore's Book: A Commonplace Book from Revolutionary America* (University Park, Pa., 1997).

4. On the related phenomenon of colonial revivalism, Karal Ann Marling, *George Washington Slept Here: Colonial Revivals and American Culture, 1876–1986* (Cambridge, Mass., 1988).

5. A substantial literature on family structure and meanings locates important changes in the eighteenth century. See, for example, Lawrence Stone, *The Family, Sex,*

and Marriage in England, 1500–1800 (New York, 1977); Jay Fliegelman, *Prodigals and Pilgrims: The American Revolution against Patriarchal Authority, 1750–1800* (Cambridge, U.K., 1982); and Jan Lewis, *The Pursuit of Happiness: Family and Values in Jefferson's Virginia* (Cambridge, 1983).

6. As quoted in Frederick B. Tolles, *George Logan of Philadelphia* (New York, 1953), back cover. Logan's mission was highly controversial and his efforts earned him much enmity and scant respect.

7. This essay is part of a larger project on genealogical representation in British America, 1680–1820.

8. See, for example, the chapters on inheritance and genealogy in William Blackstone, *Commentaries on the Laws of England* (Oxford, 1765–69). On New England heraldry in needlework, see Betty Ring, *Girlhood Embroidery: American Samplers and Pictorial Needlework, 1650–1850*, 2 vols. (New York, 1993) 1:60–75.

9. For accounts of the Norrises in Pennsylvania politics, see Gary B. Nash, *Quakers and Politics: Pennsylvania, 1681–1726* (Princeton, 1968).

10. For Mary Norris Dickinson's administration of her father's estate, see Wulf, "A Marginal Independence: Unmarried Women in Colonial Philadelphia" (Ph.D. diss., Johns Hopkins University, 1993), 306–320.

11. Frederick B. Tolles, *Meeting House and Counting House: The Quaker Merchants of Colonial Philadelphia, 1682–1763* (New York, 1948), 235.

12. For example, Deborah's uncle, Isaac Norris, married George's aunt, Sarah Logan. An attempted match between Deborah's father, Charles, and George's mother, Hannah, was not approved and thus they married others, producing children who would marry one another. George and Deborah's son Albanus married Deborah's niece Maria Dickinson, daughter of Mary Norris Dickinson and John Dickinson. Tolles, *George Logan of Philadelphia*, 48–50, 282.

13. Jean Soderlund, *Quakers and Slavery: A Divided Spirit* (Princeton, 1985) describes and analyzes the slow movement toward abolition and the conflicts within the Quaker meeting about the issues of the slave trade and slaveholding.

14. Most notably Mary Norris, daughter of Isaac and his sole heir, married Anglican John Dickinson. Other family members were disowned for marrying "contrary to discipline." Milcah Martha Hill Moore and Charles Moore were disowned for marrying; they were first cousins. This marked a change, for when their sister and brother, respectively, had married in the 1740s, their offense was pardoned. The Moores, however, married in the late 1760s, by which time the reform movement within Quakerism was intent on disciplining these kinds of lapses. Jack Marietta, *The Reformation of American Quakerism, 1748–1783* (Philadelphia, 1983), explores in depth the parameters and consequences of this movement, particularly regarding marriage.

15. Darold D. Wax, "The Negro Slave Trade in Colonial Pennsylvania" (Ph.D. diss., University of Washington, 1962), 372–373. For an example of slave ownership late in the period, see manumissions by Elizabeth Norris dated 1776 and taking effect 1776–94, in the bound "Original Papers of Manumission recorded by the Several Monthly Meetings Composing the Quarterly Meeting of Philadelphia," Quaker Collection, Haverford College (hereafter QC), 228–235.

16. Thomas Gilpin, *Exiles in Virginia: With Observations on the Conduct of the Society of Friends During the Revolutionary War* (Philadelphia, 1848), 3.

17. Tolles, *George Logan*, ix.

18. Tolles, *George Logan,* viii, 17, 43, 59, 107. The Society of Friends charged Logan with carrying on "in a military way." The meaning of this phrase is unclear, but Friends' reports suggest he wore a sword during the 1780s, and he joined the militia as an active soldier.

19. Tolles, *George Logan,* 48–50, 106–107, details the efforts of Quaker elders to entreat Logan to give up this behavior, but he was in this, as in many other things, very stubborn.

20. This memoir was edited and published by a descendant, Frances Logan, in 1899, but I believe was available in mss. at the Historical Society long before that date.

21. On the commercial history of the Lloyd and Hanbury connections, see Jacob Price, "The Great Quaker Business Families of Eighteenth-Century London: The Rise and Fall of a Sectarian Patriciate," in Richard S. Dunn and Mary Maples Dunn, eds., *The World of William Penn* (Philadelphia, 1986), 363–399, esp. 377–381.

22. Isaac Norris to Sampson Lloyd, Fairhill, Dec. 27, 1746, Isaac Norris "Wallpaper" Letterbook, Logan Papers, Historical Society of Pennsylvania (hereafter HSP).

23. Isaac Norris to Prudence Moore by Captain Lloyd, Fairhill, Nov. 21, 1747, in Wall-paper book, HSP.

24. Sampson Lloyd to Elizabeth Norris, near Birmingham, June 15, 1775, Logan Papers, HSP. Others of Sampson Lloyd's correspondence with the Philadelphia family can be found in this collection.

25. Hannah Griffitts, "On the Death of Mary Hanbury-Daughter to Sampson Lloyd the elder of Dolobron in Wales," LCP MSS, HSP.

26. See, for example, the many genealogical notes of Thomas Lloyd's great-grand-daughter, Milcah Martha Hill Moore. Many notes detail the Lloyd connections while few explore the Hill side of her family. Of particular interest is the set of notes on Samp-son Lloyd's children collected by Sarah Hill Dillwyn on a visit to England in 1787. Edward Wanton Smith Collection, Haverford College (hereafter EWS, HC).

27. On the intermarriage among cousins see, for example, the genealogical chart of two Lloyd-descended families, the Moores and the Hills, in Blecki and Wulf, *Milcah Martha Moore's Book.* An elaborate family tree, probably drawn by Isaac or Elizabeth Norris in the mid-1760s, is in the Pemberton Family Papers, QC.

28. See notes of Richard Jones, dated 1765, in EWS, HC. See also the letter of Tacy Endon, to "Loving Frds& Cousins" [1799], EWS, HC.

29. See genealogical notes of Milcah Martha Moore, dated July 20, 1796, EWS, HC.

30. Logan Genealogical Diary, LCP, 27.

31. Ibid., 2.

32. Ibid., 18.

33. Philadelphia Monthly Meeting Minutes, Aug. 26, 1757 as quoted in Jean Soder-lund, *Quakers and Slavery,* 169.

34. For the records of Elizabeth Norris's manumissions, see "The Original Papers of Manumission Recorded by the Several Monthly Meetings Composing the Quarterly Meeting of Philadelphia," 228–235, QC.

35. A transcription in Deborah Norris Logan's hand describes this piece as published in *American Magazine* Aug. 1790. Norris Family Notebooks, Norris MSS, HSP.

36. H. J. Cadbury, "Quakers and the Earthquake at Port Royal, 1692," *Jamaican Historical Review* 8 (1971), 20.

37. See for example, the earthquake's inclusion in the historical chronologies in *An Almanack* (Philadelphia, 1728) and the *Universal American Almanack* for 1764 (Philadelphia, 1763).

38. Isaac Norris to John and Hannah Delavall, Linguanee, Oct. 19, 1692, reprinted in Cadbury, "Quakers and the Earthquake," 27.

39. Joseph Norris to Isaac Norris, Jamaica, [Sept. 1692], reprinted in Cadbury, "Quakers and the Earthquake," 24.

40. Jan Ellen Lewis, "The White Jeffersons," in Jan Ellen Lewis and Peter Onuf, eds., *Sally Hemings and Thomas Jefferson: History, Memory, and Civic Culture* (Charlottesville, Va., 1999), 127–160; Joanne Pope Melish, *Disowning Slavery: Gradual Emancipation and "Race" in New England, 1780–1860* (Ithaca, N.Y., 1998).

41. I believe the woman's daughter is the "Betty" of Hannah Griffitts's family correspondence. Griffitts would have "inherited" Betty and perhaps Betty's mother from her mother, Isaac Norris Senior's daughter Mary Norris Griffitts, who was gifted with the baby of the cradle.

42. Logan Genealogical Diary, LCP 29.

43. Ibid., 33.

44. Ibid., 81.

45. Premo, *Winter Friends*, 115.

46. On the shifting political currency of revolutionary experience during the early republic, see Alfred Young, *The Shoemaker and the Tea Party: Memory and the American Revolution* (Boston, 1999).

47. Logan also wrote about a visit with Washington's mother at her home in Fredericksburg, Virginia; Logan Genealogical Diary, LCP, 84–85.

48. The other figure about whom Logan wrote at length was her cousin by marriage, John Dickinson. Conservative during the Revolution, Dickinson's moderation meshed well with George Logan's less intellectual brand of republicanism. In writing about Dickinson's virtues, Logan also addressed complex interfamily conflicts over Dickinson's religious identity as a sometime-Quaker; Logan Genealogical Diary, LCP, 87–91.

49. Logan Genealogical Diary, LCP, 80.

50. Ibid.

51. Ibid., 99.

52. Sampson Lloyd to Elizabeth Norris, Birmingham, July 15, 1775, Logan Papers, HSP.

53. Betty Ring, *Girlhood Embroidery*.

54. See, for example, the following notation on a list of the children of Thomas and Mary Jones Lloyd: "Taken out of ye Registry belonging to Hevrford Monthly Meeting by Richard Jones," 1765, EWS, QC.

55. A huge literature includes Gordon Wood, *Radicalism of the American Revolution* (New York, 1992); and Joyce Appleby's recent *Inheriting the Revolution: The First Generation of Americans* (Cambridge, Mass., 2000).

56. Alexis de Tocqueville, *Democracy in America*, 2 vols. (New York, [1834] 1954), 2:207.

57. Richard Hill Morris to Milcah Martha Moore, Philadelphia, Aug. 22, 1822, EWS, HC.

58. "The Quid Mirror," (Philadelphia, 1806), 12–13. Logan's friend Joseph McKean was similarly described as dependent on his familial connections for his successes—and failures.

Contributors

Joyce E. Chaplin (Ph.D., The Johns Hopkins University, 1986) is Professor of History at Harvard University. She is the author, most recently, of *Subject Matter: Technology, the Body, and Science on the Anglo-American Frontier, 1500–1676,* and is currently writing a book about Benjamin Franklin's science.

John E. Crowley (Ph.D., The Johns Hopkins University, 1970) is George Munro Professor of History at Dalhousie University. His most recent book is *The Invention of Comfort: Sensibilities and Design in Early Modern Britain and Early America.* He is writing a new book tentatively titled *The Counterfeit of Empire: The Development of a Global Landscape in British Visual Culture, ca. 1750–1820.*

David Barry Gaspar (Ph.D., The Johns Hopkins University, 1974) is Professor of History at Duke University, where he specializes in the study of European expansion, slavery, the slave trade, slave society, emancipation, and revolution in Atlantic history and culture. He is the author of *Bondmen and Rebels: A Study of Master-Slave Relations in Antigua* and coeditor with Darlene Clark Hine of *More than Chattel: Black Women and Slavery in the Americas.*

April Lee Hatfield (Ph.D., The Johns Hopkins University, 1997) is Associate Professor of History at Texas A&M University. She is the author of the recently published *Atlantic Virginia: Intercolonial Relations in the Seventeenth Century* and is currently working on Spanish-English relations in the early modern Atlantic world.

James Horn (Ph.D., University of Sussex, 1982) is Abby and George O'Neill Director of the John D. Rockefeller, Jr., Library at the Colonial Williamsburg Foundation. He has written *Adapting to a New World: English Society in the Seventeenth-Century Chesapeake* and numerous articles on early American immigration history.

Ray A. Kea (Ph.D., School of Oriental and African Studies, University of London, 1974) is Professor of African History at the University of California–Riverside. He is the author of *Settlement, Trade, and Polities in the Seventeenth-Century Gold Coast* and is currently working on a book that examines the social and cultural history of the eighteenth- and nineteenth-century Gold Coast within the context of the Atlantic world.

Elizabeth Mancke (Ph.D., The Johns Hopkins University, 1990) is Associate Professor of History at the University of Akron. She is the author of *The Fault Lines of Empire: Political Differentiation in Massachusetts and Nova Scotia, ca. 1760–1830*, as well as numerous essays on the relationship between the British Empire and state.

Philip D. Morgan (Ph.D., University College London, 1977) is Harry C. Black Professor of History at the Johns Hopkins University. Among other works, he authored *Slave Counterpoint: Black Culture in the Eighteenth-Century Chesapeake and Lowcountry* and coedited *Strangers within the Realm: Cultural Margins of the First British Empire*. He is presently studying the early Caribbean.

William M. Offutt, Jr. (Ph.D., The Johns Hopkins University, 1987) currently serves as Director of the Pforzheimer Honors College and Associate Professor of History at the Pace University. He authored *Of "Good Laws" and "Good Men": Law and Society in the Delaware Valley, 1680–1710*, and specializes in colonial American legal history with a focus on the middle colonies.

Robert Olwell (Ph.D., The Johns Hopkins University, 1991) is Associate Professor of History at the University of Texas, Austin. He is the author of *Masters, Slaves, and Subjects: The Culture of Power in the South Carolina Low Country, 1740–1790*, and is currently at work on a study of British colonial enterprise and imperial imagination in Florida, 1763–1783.

Carole Shammas (Ph.D., The Johns Hopkins University, 1971) holds the John R. Hubbard Chair in History at the University of Southern California. She specializes in the socio-economic history of early modern Great Britain and British America. Her most recent book is *A History of Household Government in America*.

Wolfgang Splitter (Ph.D., The Johns Hopkins University, 1993) specializes in the history of the German-Lutheran presence in British North America and nineteenth-century emigration from the Rhineland to the United States. He is the author of *Pastors, People, Politics: German Lutherans in Pennsylvania, 1740–1790,* and "Divide et Impera: Some Critical Remarks on Halle Missionaries' Formation of a Lutheran Church in Pennsylvania," in *Halle Pietism, British North America, and the Young United States,* edited by Hans-Jürgen Grabbe.

Mark L. Thompson (Ph.D., The Johns Hopkins University, 2004) is Assistant Professor of History at Louisiana State University. His research explores how ethnic and national affiliations shaped English, Dutch, and Swedish efforts to colonize the seventeenth-century Delaware Valley.

Karin Wulf (Ph.D., The Johns Hopkins University, 1993) is Associate Professor of History at American University, Visiting Associate Professor of History at the College of William and Mary, and Book Review Editor of *The William and Mary Quarterly.* She is the author of *Not All Wives: Women of Colonial Philadelphia* (2000) and coeditor of *Milcah Martha Moore's Book: A Commonplace Book from Revolutionary America.* Her current book project is a cultural history of genealogical representation and conceptions of lineage in British America from 1680 to 1820.

Avihu Zakai (Ph.D., The Johns Hopkins University, 1982) is Professor of Early Modern and Early American History at the Hebrew University of Jerusalem. His books include *Exile and Kingdom: History and Apocalypse in the Puritan Migration to America* and *Jonathan Edwards's Philosophy of History: The Re-Enchantment of the World in the Age of Enlightenment.*

Index

Africa, West (Bight of Benin, Greater Ardra): Catholicism in, 118, 119–23; cosmology of, 117, 121–23, 135; history of, 116–19 (*see also* Marotta)

African migration: to the Americas, 7, 21–35 passim; ethnicity in, 40–42; within sub-Saharan Africa, 35 (*see also* slave trade)

allegiance, to Crown: conferring imperial authority, 72–73; German ethnicity and, 217; guarantees of liberties and, 335n3

American literature, captivity narratives and, 58–59

American national identity: revealed in family history, 306, 309, 316–18; the Revolution and, 316–17. *See also* national identity

American Protestant culture: European Enlightenment and, 207, 208; formation of, 182, 188; influence of Jonathan Edwards on, 189, 196, 206

American Revolution: imperial evolution and, 237–38, 262; Indian enslavement and, 66; legalistic turn and, 181; motifs of family and, 305, 318, 319–20; Quaker loyalties in, 307–8, 316–17; religious convictions and, 189, 224–27; as touchstone of national identity, 316–17

Andrews, Charles, imperial history and, 265–66, 267, 282

anglicization: of colonial legal culture, 16, 160, 176, 180–81; Lutherans and, 16, 216, 230–31; resistance to, 182 (*see also* Edwards, Jonathan); as transatlantic connection, 12

Anglo-American culture: British landscape sensibilities in, 303; formed in rejection of British traditions, 187, 207. *See also* American Protestant culture

Anglo-Portuguese relations: in Atlantic basin, 102, 104, 113–15; impact on repatriation of Cape Verdeans, 9–10, 106–7, 111–12, 114. *See also* Cape Verdeans

Antigua, 94, 102–3, 106, 109. *See also* Anglo-Portuguese relations; Hart, John

Atlantic
—history: concept of, 1, 15–16; goals of, 4–5; imperial history and, 2, 15–16; perspective, 94, 107, 141, 238, 264, 267, 284; population movements and, 19
—rules, definition of, 168
—world: in broader imperial context, 14, 15; integration of, through maritime law, 141; role of chartered enterprises in, 237. *See also* transatlantic

Barbados, 155, 167, 288

Bartram, John, 275, 380–81n61

Bartram, William, 69, 275

Black Legend, Indian slavery and, 48, 55

Board of Trade (Lords Commissioners of Trade and Plantations): assuming function of monarch in empire, 248; colonial administration and, 287; enforcing common law standards, 174

British Empire: as colonial or commercial, 238; compared with other empires, 11, 277–78; as cultural production, 282; debate over emergence of, 13–14, 262, 265–66, 289–90, 293; fears of, among British, 277, 282, 293–94; globalization of, 289–93; ideology of, 3–4; institutional developments in, 240, 246, 248, 250–51, 257–59, 261–62 (*see also* chartered enterprises). *See also* Anglo-Portuguese relations; imperial ideology

British landscape art: history of, seventeenth and early eighteenth centuries, 284–89; as illustrated by military officers, 15, 295; public interest in, 289, 298, 301–2; visualizing a benign empire, 283–84, 289, 295–97, 299–301, 303. *See also* landscape: art

Bute, Third Earl of (John Stuart): as botanical enthusiast, 269, 270, 271; opposition to, 280–81

Canada, 296–97. *See also* Hudson's Bay Company

Cape Verdeans: kidnapping of, 94–95; as Portuguese subjects, 94, 111–12; repatriated, 103–6, 108; suit of, in Atlantic context, 107, 111, 114; testimony concerning, 96–101, 108

man, and migration, 40; German-American, 229, 230–31; Scottish, as "foreign" influence in British political culture, 268, 279–80
Evangelical Moravian Brotherhood: doctrines of, 124–25, 347n42; mission on St. Thomas, 116, 124–36; opposition to, on St. Thomas, 128–29, 132–33, 136; in Pennsylvania, 209–12, 232; relationship to Lutheran Church, 124; slavery and, 124–29. *See also* von Zinzendorf, Count Nikolaus Ludwig
evangelical movements, transatlantic, 183, 185–87, 206

Florida: botanical collection from, 263–64, 282; colonization schemes for, 274, 277–79; promotion of, 272–73, 274–75; role in British imperial imagination, 264, 277–78, 282; Spanish evacuation of, 264
Francke Foundations: decline of, 232–33; distrust of religious freedom, 220; reluctance to organize mission into church, 215, 218; sponsoring missionaries in Pennsylvania, 209–10, 366n3; transitions in, 225, 230

genealogy: cultural function of, 304, 306, 315, 317; kinship and, 305, 318; post-revolutionary politics and, 317–18; public and private versions of, 15, 315–16; as transatlantic connection, 309–13, 320. *See also* Logan, Deborah Norris
German Lutheran missionaries (Halle Pietists)
—in colonial Pennsylvania: anglican alliance and, 13, 216–17; challenged by American circumstances, 210, 211–12, 213, 219–22, 233–34; in conflict with other Lutherans, 210–12, 220, 223–24, 233, 368n37; in conflict with patrons, 215, 218, 219; confronting anti-authoritarianism of laity, 211–12, 215, 219, 221–25, 233–34; efforts of, to form colonial Lutheran Church, 213–15, 218, 222, 367n30, 367n32; Revolutionary loyalties of, 226–27, 371n125, 371–72n128; standards for clergy and, 218–21. *See also* Mühlenberg, Heinrich Melchior
—in new nation: decline of, 231, 232; defining "authentic" Lutheranism, 229–30, 234; politics of, 231–32; public role of, 227–29, 231
Grant's seeds, 263–64, 267–70, 282
Great Awakening, 187, 205–6
Greene, Jack P.: Atlantic world history and, 1; cited on comparative history, 343n1; on

law and national identity, 160, 335–36n3; synthesis of, refined, 179–80

Halle clergy/missionaries. *See* German Lutheran missionaries
Hanoverian court: botanical enthusiasts in, 268–69; at Kew Palace, 270–71; Lutheran chaplain at, 209, 218, 225
Hart, John (governor of British Leeward Islands), resolving repatriation case, 94–96, 99, 102–7, 111, 112, 113, 114
Hudson's Bay Company: as commercial chartered enterprise, 238, 251; governing non-British peoples, 259–60, 261–62; governmental oversight of, 247–48; merger with North West Company, 253; military action of, against French, 257; as territorial power, 260–61
hybridity, 62–64

identity: "African," 41; Christian (*see* Logan, Deborah Norris; Marotta; Mühlenberg, Heinrich Melchior); "Indian," 46, 61; persistence of British, after the Revolution, 15, 305
imperial history: compared with Atlantic history, 1–7; "new," 266–67; reimagined, 13–16, 282. *See also* Andrews, Charles
imperial ideology: accompanying institutional developments, 254; common law and, 180–81 (*see* legalistic turn); Crown sovereignty and, 254; embodied in the design of Kew gardens, 265, 270, 272, 280, 282; fears about empire and, 294; imagined in British culture, 266–67, 284, 287, 303; reflected in British landscape art, 15, 283–303 passim; science and, 273; in spatial contexts, 87, 90, 91–92; triggered by encounters with non-British peoples, 71–72, 261–62
imperial landscapes. *See* British landscape art
indentured servants, 27, 147
Indian political authority: English perception of, 82–83; and "kingship" as colonizing discourse, 81, 83, 85, 86
Indians: British imperial governance of, 257–58; and colonial legal status, 47, 66–68; in Delaware Valley, 82–83, 84–85; as intermediaries between Europeans, 87; legal status of, in Early Republic, 47, 69; slaveholding and, 51 (*see also* Indian slavery: scholarship on)
Indian slavery: in colonial culture, 62–64; compared with African slavery, 49, 51, 55–56; connection of, to African slavery, 47, 68, 69–70; destructive impact of, 58; economic significance of, 46, 53–54, 64;

Indian slavery *(cont.)*
historical significance of, 8; mestizoism
and, 63; motives for, 50–52; opposition
to, 64–66; regional comparisons of, 50,
54, 56–57, 63, 65–66; scholarship on,
45–46, 49–50, 54–56, 62, 329n1; in Spanish empire, 48; statistics on, 49, 50,
57–58; as unlawful in Leeward Islands,
109–10
information exchange: awareness of Atlantic
world and, 107, 114, 150; between
Quaker meetings, 310, 318; role of
mariners in, 140, 144–46, 159

Jamaica, 301, 302, 314

Kew gardens: as focus of debate over empire,
272, 280, 282; origin and design of, 265,
267, 271–72, 379n30

land claims, in Americas: of "empty" lands, 71,
335n1; held as feudal grants, 242; jurisdictional disputes over, 245–46, 258; role
of chartered enterprises in, 240–41
landscape: art, in British North American
colonies, 288–89, 301–3, 383n17 (*see also*
British landscape art); art, history of,
284–86, 382n7; artists, 295–303; defined,
289; land claims and, 241
law, colonial, 162–81 passim; commercial needs
and, 142, 143, 144, 174, 176; maritime,
functions of, 153–54, 155–57, 354n59
(*see also* mariners)
legal:
—capital: defined, 160, 166; intercolonial
exchange of, 167–68; transatlantic
transfer of, 161, 166–67
—culture: early inclusivity of, 168–70; "legal
literates" in, 158, 164–65, 166,
169–70; women and, 178
—history, colonial, 179–80
—imagination: defamation suits and, 173;
defined, 161, 354–55n3; overtaken by
common law legalism, 162, 171, 172–
75, 177–81 (*see also* legalistic turn)
legalistic turn: defined, 162; dominating colonies
after 1680, 170–79; impact of, 162, 175,
178, 179; providing legal infrastructure
for trade, 180–81; significance of, to
American Revolution, 181
Linnaeus, Carl, 269, 306–7
Locke, John, 65, 190–91, 252
Logan, Deborah Norris: genealogical diary of,
304, 308, 315, 317–18; historical contributions of, 305, 312, 386n2; political
views of, 317–18, 320; and "Providential
Anecdote" concerning slave ownership,

313–16; scripting a transatlantic familial
identity, 306, 308–9, 316–18, 389n48
Logan, George: life of, 307–8, 317, 320, 387n6,
388nn18–19
Lutheran Church: Danish, on St. Thomas, 124;
Swedish, in Pennsylvania, 212. *See also*
Evangelical Moravian Brotherhood; German Lutheran missionaries
Lutheranism: "authentic," and German ethnicity,
230–34; transatlantic differences in,
209–10, 213–14, 219–22, 229–30,
367n33, 368n40

Magdalena. *See* Marotta
mariners: compared, seventeenth and eighteenth
centuries, 140–41, 159, 354n70; defined,
351n23; demand for, in Caribbean,
352n34; desertion of, 150, 157; elite, 147,
148, 152; giving testimony, 96–99, 144–45;
interaction with settlers, 141–42, 146–49,
150–51, 156, 158; lives of, 145–47, 151,
153–54, 156, 353n48; in local economies,
141, 146, 152, 153, 351n22; role of, in
transatlantic information exchange, 11,
140, 158–59; using ships as social centers,
140, 141, 147
maritime networks, regional variations in,
152–53
Marotta: becomes Magdalena, 131; on Christian
faith, 130–31; as elder in Moravian
Church, 131–32; life of, 115–16, 124–35;
petitions of, 116, 122, 132–33, 349n65;
religious worlds of, 118, 121
Maryland: colonial legal system of, 175; land
patent granted, 243, 375n17; in sixteenth
century, 78, 80. *See also* Chesapeake;
Yong, Thomas
Massachusetts: colonial law in, 165, 166–67,
169–70, 175, 178; colony charter, 249–50;
maritime law in, 142–43, 155–57
migrants, to the Americas: background of European, 27–28; destinations for, 37–38; destinations for, in eighteenth century, 38;
diversity among African, 40–42; ethnic
origins of European, 32–34, 39–40; European, and cultural identity, 38–39, 40, 42;
regional origins of African, 34–35, 39,
42–43. *See also* migration
migration: centrality of coerced over voluntary, 7,
27; character of forced African, 28, 29;
comparing conditions of, 30–32; from
east to west, 7, 35; factors behind, 25–27;
intercolonial, eighteenth century, 43; mortality rates in, 30–31; regional variations
in African, 28–29; regional variations in
European, 32–35, 42–43; statistical comparisons of, European and African, 19,

21–24; within sub-Saharan Africa, 35. *See also* migrants

Moravians. *See* Evangelical Moravian Brotherhood

Mühlenberg, Heinrich Melchior: breach with patrons, 215–16, 217–18; comments on religion in colonies, 213, 220, 222, 223; innovations of, 211–12, 217; as Lutheran missionary in Pennsylvania, 209–18, 369n70; organizational efforts of, 213–14; political activity of, 216–17; Revolution and, 226–27

national identity: British versus English, 281; as a cultural construction, 284, 336n7; English common law and, 72; ethnic diversity and, 41–42; in spatial contexts, 74, 92. *See also* American national identity

national subjecthood, 9, 74, 92, 94, 135–36; contested, 111–12, 114; defined, 87. *See also* national identity

New Divinity School, 188–89

New Imperial History. *See* imperial history

New York: colonial legal system in, 143, 172, 177, 178; interaction in, between mariners and settlers, 153–54, 155, 353n54

Northwest Passage, 76, 291

Penn, William, 167–68, 312, 316

Pennsylvania: colonial charter of, 251; colonial legal system of, 174; and early Quakers, 306–7, 309, 311, 316; Lutheran missionaries in, 209–34 passim; political conflict in, eighteenth century, 216–17

pietism: appropriated as "community of imagination," 134–36; as colonizing discourse, 125, 134; conservative, 233–34; described, 124, 129–30. *See also* Evangelical Moravian Brotherhood; German Lutheran missionaries

piracy: in Atlantic basin, 9, 101–2, 255; Crown use of, 256–57; implied in kidnapping of Cape Verdeans, 99–100; legal definition of, 103; pardons for, 103. *See also* Anglo-Portuguese relations

Popo Kingdom. *See* Africa, West

port towns: African and European, as departure points, 36–37; in British landscape art, 288; differential development of, 353n39, 353n46; integrating the Atlantic world, 152–53; lack of, in Virginia, 151; as New England entrepots, 155

Proclamation of 1763, 245–46, 258, 265–66

Protestant culture, American. *See* American Protestant culture

Protestant revivals, colonial, 184, 185–86, 187, 189. *See also* Edwards, Jonathan

public houses. *See* taverns

Quakerism: eighteenth-century reforms in, 307, 311, 313, 387n14; in post-revolutionary America, 308, 316–318; transatlantic, 12, 309–13. *See also* Logan, Deborah Norris

Quakers: distinctive legal needs of, 167–68; in founding narrative of Pennsylvania, 309; intermarriage among, 307, 387n12, 387n14; as loyalists, 307–8, 316–17; material prosperity of, 311, 313; political conflicts among, 216–17; slave ownership and, 307, 309, 311, 313, 314–15. *See also* Logan, Deborah Norris; Logan, George

Quebec Act, 252–53, 258, 294

regionalism: in Indian slavery, 50, 54, 56–57, 63, 65–66; in mariner-settler interaction, 149–58; in migration to Americas, 28–29, 32–38, 39, 42–43; in relations between colonies, 146

religion. *See* Africa, West: cosmology of; Catholicism; Christianity; Edwards, Jonathan; Evangelical Moravian Brotherhood; German Lutheran missionaries; Lutheranism; pietism; Quakerism

religious persecution: as factor in migration, 26, 35, 39; of Indian converts, 65; of slave converts, 128, 132–33

religious "syncretism": as contending hermeneutical traditions, 122–23, 135–36; in the life of Marotta/Magdalena, 131; misleading presumptions of, 345–46n30; in West Africa, 121–23

repatriation: of Cape Verdeans, 104–7, 111; cases of, in British slave trade, 108–12; international ramifications of, 9–10, 113–14. *See also* Anglo-Portuguese relations

Restoration: and law reform, 163; repercussions of, for chartered enterprises, 243–44, 250, 256–57, 260

Roure, Captain Peter, charged with kidnapping of Cape Verdeans, 94–108, 112–14 passim

science: botanical, and imperial ideology, 285; Enlightenment, and Jonathan Edwards, 183; Enlightenment, and Protestant evangelical movements, 184–86; serving imperial politics, 269–70, 273–75, 279, 281

scientific exploration: government-sponsored, in Florida, 275; role of artists in, 298–99

seamen. *See* mariners

Second Great Awakening, 189, 206

Seven Years' War: imperial expansion and, 14, 238, 289–90, 293; Indian status after, 67

slavery: depicted as benign in landscape art, 301; impact on free status, 111, 114; Quaker identity and, 313–16; skin color and, 112

Printed in the United States
65744LVS00002B/53

Elizabeth Mancke
is an associate professor in the Department
of History at the University of Akron.

Carole Shammas
is a professor in the Department
of History at the University of
Southern California, Los Angeles.

Anglo-America in the Transatlantic World
Jack P. Greene, General Editor